C0-ARS-372

SOCIAL SERVICE ORGANIZATIONS

The Greenwood Encyclopedia of American Institutions

Each work in the *Encyclopedia* is designed to provide concise histories of major voluntary groups and nonprofit organizations that have played significant roles in American civic, cultural, political, and economic life from the colonial era to the present. Previously published:

1. *Labor Unions*
Gary M Fink, Editor-in-Chief

The Greenwood Encyclopedia of American Institutions

Social Service Organizations

editor-in-chief PETER ROMANOFSKY

advisory editor CLARKE A. CHAMBERS

Volume 1

GREENWOOD PRESS
Westport, Connecticut • London, England

Library of Congress Cataloging in Publication Data
Main entry under title:

Social service organizations.

    (The Greenwood encyclopedia of American institutions; no. 2)
    Bibliography: p.
    Includes index.
    1. Charitable societies—History. 2. Charities,
Medical—United States—History. 3. Social service—
Societies, etc.—History. 4. Charitable societies—
Directories. 5. Charities, Medical—United States—
Directories. 6. Social service—Societies, etc.—Direc-
tories. I. Romanofsky, Peter. II. Chambers, Clarke A.
III. Series.
HV88.S59   361.7'0973   77–84754
ISBN 0–8371–9829–1 (set)

Copyright © 1978 by Peter Romanofsky

All rights reserved. No portion of this book may
be reproduced, by any process or technique, without
the express written consent of the publisher.

Library of Congress Catalog Card Number: 77–84754
ISBN: 0–8371–9829–1 (set)
      0–8371–9902–6 (vol. 1)
      0–8371–9903–4 (vol. 2)

First published in 1978

Greenwood Press, Inc.
51 Riverside Avenue, Westport, Connecticut 06880

Printed in the United States of America

10 9 8 7 6 5 4 3 2

813429

LIBRARY
ALMA COLLEGE
ALMA, MICHIGAN

FOR MY PARENTS, FRED AND HELEN ROMANOFSKY

LIBRARY
N.W. COLLEGE
MICHIGAN

Contents

B _____

D _____

E _____

F

G

H

I

J

L

Contributors

Paul Gerard Anderson, a former Ford Fellow at the University of Chicago, is preparing a doctoral dissertation on the history of the Juvenile Protective Association of Chicago*

Louis L. Athey, associate professor of history, Franklin and Marshall College, wrote his doctoral dissertation at the University of Delaware on the history of the National Consumers' League.* He also serves as the editor of the Social Welfare History Group *Newsletter*

Joseph Brandes, professor of history, William Paterson College of New Jersey, has authored several studies in American history, including *Immigrants to Freedom: Jewish Communities in Rural New Jersey since 1882* (1971)

Judi Breault, managing editor of *Friends Journal,* received a doctorate in American studies from the University of Pennsylvania; she has written *The World of Emily Howland: The Odyssey of a Humanitarian* (1976)

Ellen Chesler, doctoral candidate at Columbia University, is a fellow of the Ford and Rockefeller foundations' Joint Program in Population Policy Research

Robert L. Daniel, professor of history, Ohio University, has written *American Philanthropy in the Near East, 1820–1960* (1970)

Philip De Vencentes, graduate student at the University of Chicago, served as an editor for *Notable American Women* and has taught at Western Illinois University and Jersey City State College

Marilyn Domer, professor of history, George Williams College, has written about fund raising and urban affairs

Estelle B. Freedman, assistant professor of history, Stanford University, has published articles about women's history, specializing in the history of female corrections in America, the subject of her doctoral dissertation at Columbia University, which she completed in 1976

Andrea Hinding, curator, Social Welfare History Archives Center, University of Minnesota, Minneapolis, has written about social workers

Milton J. Huber, professor of urban affairs, University of Wisconsin, Milwaukee, wrote his doctoral dissertation at Boston University about the history of the Methodist Federation for Social Service*

Robert Jennings, Department of Education, Suffolk University

William McGuire King, acting assistant professor of religious studies, University of Virginia

David John Klaassen, assistant curator of the Social Welfare History Archives Center, University of Minnesota, Minneapolis, has edited, with Paul Murphy and Kermit Hall, *The Passaic Textile Strike* (1973)

Henry B. Leonard, assistant professor of history, Kent State University, has written about the Immigrants' Protective League of Chicago,* and he is studying ethnicity and religion in the Catholic diocese of Cleveland, a subject on which he has authored an article in the *Catholic Historical Review*

Frank Levstik, Archivist, Ohio Historical Society, is working on a doctoral thesis in social welfare history at Ohio State University

Doris Lunden, Social Welfare History Archives Center, University of Minnesota, Minneapolis

John J. McLoughlin, research associate, Center for Policy Research Inc., helped to prepare a study of the history of tenant associations in New York City from 1890 to 1970

Raymond A. Mohl, professor of history, Florida Atlantic University, and editor of *The Journal of Urban History,* authored *Poverty in New York, 1783–1825* (1971) and edited *Urban America in Historical Perspective* (1970) and *The Urban Experience: Themes in American History* (1973). His most recent book is *Progressive Education and Social Order: The Gary Plan and Urban Schooling, 1900–1940* (1976)

Ann W. Nichols, associate professor, School of Social Work, Arizona State University, also serves on the National Board of the Young Women's Christian Association of the U.S.A.*

Mary Ostling, Social Welfare History Archives Center, University of Minnesota, Minneapolis, served as project coordinator for the Minnesota Welfare Records Project

Marvin A. Palecek, professor of history, Winona State University, wrote *Battle of the Bureaucracies: The United Defense Fund* (1972)

David Rosner, graduate student, Department of the History of Science, Harvard University, is preparing a doctoral thesis on medical services in Brooklyn, New York, during the Progressive era

Gary Rubin, adjunct instructor of American Jewish history, Bernard Revel Graduate School of Yeshiva University

Lynn Ann Schweitzer, Immigration Research Center, University of Minnesota, Minneapolis, has written descriptions of some of the center's holdings

Robert Segal, program director for social work, Institute for the Study of Mental Retardation, and Associate Professor, School of Social Work, University of Michigan

Robert Sullivan, assistant professor of government, John Jay College, City University of New York, has written widely about international affairs; his doctoral dissertation at the Johns Hopkins University dealt with agencies' overseas relief efforts

Eugene M. Tobin, assistant professor of history, Miami University of Ohio, has written several essays on progressivism appearing in *New Jersey History, American Journal of Economics and Sociology,* and *The Historian*

William R. VanEssendelft, program director in the Department of Extension Classes, Continuing Education and Extension, University of Minnesota, Minneapolis, is preparing his doctoral thesis on the history of the Association for Voluntary Sterilization*

Narayan Viswanathan, professor of social work, Adelphi University, served as a consultant for numerous agencies and programs, has authored several articles in the field of social work, and wrote his doctoral dissertation at Columbia University on the history of the American Public Welfare Association*

William Wallach, Social Welfare History Archives Center, University of Minnesota, Minneapolis

Nancy Weiss, associate professor of history, Princeton University, has written widely about the history of blacks. She also wrote *Charles Francis Murphy, 1858-1924: Respectability and Responsibility in Tammany Politics* (1968) and *The National Urban League, 1910-1940* (1974)

Herbert A. Wisbey, Jr., professor of history, Elmira College, has published histories of both the Volunteers of America* and the Salvation Army,* the subject of his doctoral dissertation at Columbia University (1951)

*An asterisk (*) after a title indicates that there is a sketch of the organization in this work.

FOREWORD

This work makes a contribution of enormous importance to the relatively new field of social welfare history. It will be consulted as a reliable reference tool by historians and other scholars seeking to unravel the bewildering complexities of social and health services provided by a multitude of agencies in the voluntary welfare sector. By that criterion alone, the volume is justified. But its significance runs wider and deeper. The entries provide not routine chronologies and chronicles but critical and analytical agency and associational biographies. The accounts are neither official nor admiring; they offer balanced and insightful narratives and summaries that enrich our understanding of the diverse roles of voluntarism in American social life. They offer abundant evidence of the histories of these associations and never get bogged down in a recitation of bureaucratic or institutional detail.

The variety of issues addressed by these groups and the multitude of clientele served is truly staggering. Here one finds concern for the handicapped, the crippled, the blind, the mentally retarded, the mentally ill, the alcoholic, neglected, dependent, and delinquent children, for those whom society has defined as criminally deviant, for those who are dependent for whatever cause—insecure employment, poor health or old age. Here also one discovers societies devoted to the protection and advancement of minority groups in American life. The impact of welfare associations is demonstrated in services provided in a number of different settings and through a variety of means. Their influence is also evidenced in the evolution of public policies in such diverse fields as employment, social insurance, public assistance, housing, public health, civil rights, and recreation (to cite but a few).

A final benefit to both scholars and practitioners relates to the bibliographic notes that accompany each entry. Mr. Romanofsky and the contributors have provided annotated guides to secondary historical accounts, to the printed records of each association, and to the primary manuscript sources. This volume is bound to stimulate the research of scholars drawn from a number of academic disciplines and inform the programs of persons active in voluntary associations.

CLARKE A. CHAMBERS
Professor of History, and Director,
Social Welfare History Archives Center, University of Minnesota

PREFACE

In his survey, "The State of Social Welfare History," in Herbert J. Bass, editor, *The State of American History* (1970), social welfare historian Professor Robert Bremner mentioned the need to study further the histories of social welfare agencies. This *Social Service Organization* volume of the multivolume Greenwood Encyclopedia of American Institutions series contains historical sketches of nearly two hundred national and local voluntary social service agencies that have been part of American social work. These are not the kinds of histories I think Professor Bremner had in mind, but I hope this volume, with its obviously limited structure, will help to explain the particular histories of agencies of interest to students and that it will promote further and deeper studies. The bibliographies that appear at the conclusion of each entry were prepared with this thought in mind. Except for the thirty-odd entries clearly identified as being prepared by a contributor, I have written the entry of each of these groups.

The nature and clientele of these organizations differ widely. Some service clients directly, others are advocacy agencies, and still others are professional agencies that helped shape welfare policies in particular fields. Many agencies have been successful. Some have influenced public policy, others have assisted people in need. Critics would be correct to argue that, collectively, they have failed to bring about a fully just society with full employment and little or no poverty. But the overwhelmingly majority of these organizations did not really have such goals, despite the lofty prases of their statements, annual reports, and the like. It is fashionable to criticize philanthropists, social workers, and charitable agencies as regulators of the poor. As I hope these sketches suggest, the charitable impulses of the various organizations have generally been greater then their desires to control their clients. The motives of people who through the Save the Children Fund* arranged to send clothes and food to hungry and ill-clothed striking miners' children in Harlan County, Kentucky, during the Great Depression, of those who work through the American Cancer Society, Inc.* (ACS), to counsel and rehabilitate patients, of those clergymen who founded the American

*An asterisk (*) after a title indicates that there is a sketch of the organization in this work.

Christian Committee for Refugees, Inc.,* to assist refugees from the terror of nazism in Germany, and of the women who sewed and otherwise repaired and purchased clothes for the needy through the Needlework Guild of America, Inc.,* seem far more benevolent than power driven. I will not quarrel with the argument that public housing projects, for which social agencies fought for so long, have become slums, that playgrounds, the ideal of many urban social justice Progressives, have become dangerous turfs, and that even day care centers, for which reformers and others worked for nearly a hundred years, provide lucrative profits for big landlords who are friends of city officials. There is little evidence, however, to suggest that the designers and promoters of these and other projects could foresee that their plans would yield such deleterious effects.

The importance of these agencies varies considerably. Some have helped to shape and to implement federal social services and antipoverty programs. The details in the various entries provide such evidence. A few have had very little impact on either the development and/or implementation of federal services and/or the national social work community, but they serve as important examples of one or another type of social service organization.

The emphases in these entries are historical. The contributors and I have attempted to prepare each entry in a basically chronological format, supplying details of its founding, leaders, structure, major structural changes, mergers, absorptions, and highlights of activities. Except in a few cases, chiefly with the national health agencies, fund-raising efforts have been consciously neglected, and there has been little attempt to recount the statistics of cases and individuals served. Rather, the emphasis has been on social service programs with occasional assessments of the size of the social problems with which the agency was dealing. The length of an entry is generally a guide to its importance, but there are some exceptions.

One of the most difficult, but nevertheless stimulating, aspects of the project was to develop a list of agencies to be included in the volume. The standards for inclusion were not always clear-cut or hard and fast. As in the case of a companion volume on labor organizations by Gary M Fink, some loose and rather subjective criteria were applied. Initial considerations included historical significance, longevity, size, influence, what I perceived to be popularly viewed as a "charity," and whether an agency had nationally prominent individuals in the social service community active in the organization. I also made an effort to include representative organizations in the major fields of social service, such as child welfare, child health, the blind, physical rehabilitation, youth serving, prison, family service, alcoholism, foreign aid, mental health, migrants and immigrants, and so forth. A list of agencies according to these functional categories appears in appendix 3. To help distinguish between social service agencies and closely allied civic, political, and fraternal organizations, I referred frequently to the lists of voluntary agencies that appeared toward the end of most issues of the *Encyclopedia of Social Work,* formerly the *Social Work Year Book.*

Another list I used was the membership of the National Assembly of National Voluntary Health and Social Welfare Organizations, Inc.* (NANVHSWO), the major planning and coordinating agency in the social service field. I have, however, excluded three of its member agencies—the Association of Junior Leagues, the National Council of Jewish Women (NCJW), and the National Council of Negro Women. I felt that each is more appropriately part of a companion volume in this series, *Fraternal Organizations.* I am aware generally of the social service activities of each of these three agencies, especially those of the NCJW, which is mentioned often in this book. But with one or two exceptions, the leaders of these three agencies were not prominent in the social service community, another criterion I used to determine an agency's inclusion or exclusion. I am quite aware of the social service activities of other fraternal organizations, for example, the work with crippled children of the Benevolent and Protective Order of Elks and of the Masonic Order, Nobles of the Mystic Shrine, of the efforts for the mentally ill by the Scottish Rites Masons, and of the child welfare and prison-related projects of the General Federation of Women's Clubs (see *Fraternal Organizations* for each of these groups). I have even written previously about the child welfare projects of one fraternal organization, the B'nai B'rith (see *Fraternal Organizations*). But these social services are not the major function of the organization. Each has therefore been excluded from this volume but will appear in *Fraternal Organizations.* Readers will note, however, the inclusion here of the National Children and Youth Division (NCYD) of the American Legion (AL). The AL is clearly a fraternal organization. Its NCYD, however, seemed a definite part of the national social work community at many points in its history, and its first and long-time executive, Emma Puschner, was well known in child welfare circles.

The number of church-related social service agencies is staggering. I have tried to include the most important of them. Unlike the National Conference of Catholic Charities,* Catholic Charities is not a national organization. Rather, it is a diocesan, and thus a fairly local, agency. This volume contains an entry for the Catholic Charities of the Archdiocese of New York,* one of the oldest and most important of its type. The National Council of the Young Men's Christian Associations of the United States of America* (YMCA) and the National Board of the Young Women's Christian Association of the U.S.A.* (YWCA), both members of the NANVHSWO, are included in this volume, but the Young Men's Hebrew Association (YMHA), which is not a NANVHSWO member, is excluded. The YMHAs do not have a national structure similar to that of the YWCA and the YMCA. In addition, the YMHAs are dealt with in the entry for The National Jewish Welfare Board,* with which many local YMHAs are affiliated. A list of religiously oriented social service agencies according to the three major sectarian groups—Catholic, Jewish, and Protestant—appears in appendix 1.

Generally a strictly local agency was included only if it gained prominence in the national social service community. Few historians would argue against including Jane Addams's Hull-House,* the Juvenile Protective Association of Chicago, and The Immigrants' Service League,* also of Chicago. Each developed programs that were widely known, and each had prominent figures in the national social work community affiliated with them. Readers might observe the large number of local New York agencies, such as The Charity Organization Society of the City of New York* (COS), the New York Association for Improving the Condition of the Poor,* (AICP), The Children's Aid Society* (CAS) of New York, the Jewish Family Service* (JFS), the State Communities Aid Association* (SCAA) of New York, The Fresh Air Fund* (FAF), and The New York Society for the Prevention of Cruelty to Children* (NYSPCC). Each of these organizations was either the pioneering, the largest, the most influential, and/or the most well known of its type. Leaders from these agencies, specifically Josephine Shaw Lowell and Edward Devine from the COS, Robert Hartley and John Kingsbury of the AICP, Charles Loring Brace and Owen Lovejoy of the CAS, Lee K. Frankel of the JFS, Louisa Lee Schuyler and Homer Folks from the SCAA, and Elbridge Gerry from the NYSPCC, constitute a who's who of prominent social service figures. Other local New York–based agencies were pioneers or leaders in their respective fields, as their entries indicate. This category includes the Jewish Board of Guardians,* the Speedwell Services for Children, Inc.,* the Girls and Boys Service League of America,* the Maternity Center Association,* and the Henry Street Settlement Urban Life Center.*

Some students might wonder why I have included The American Humane Association* (AHA) but not the American Society for the Prevention of Cruelty to Animals (ASPCA). I drew the line at providing services for people, not animals. While the AHA did strive to protect animals, its well-known and important children's protective services qualified it for inclusion.

Students of social welfare might be surprised by the number of so-called health agencies, such as the ACS, The National Easter Seal Society for Crippled Children and Adults,* and the Muscular Dystrophy Association, Inc.* Each of this type of agency is listed in the *Social Work Year Book* and the *Encyclopedia of Social Work,* many are perceived widely as "charities," many provide or supervise medical social services, and a number of them had and still have clear-cut ties to the social work community.

Advisory Editor Professor Clarke Chambers, the chairman of the Department of History at the University of Minnesota and the director of the Social Welfare History Archives Center at the University of Minnesota, in Minneapolis, advised—and convinced—me to include particular agencies. He also discussed with me, in considerable detail, the overall list of agencies. As with the entire volume, however, I, of course, bear full and sole responsibility for the inclusion and exclusion of particular agencies and for the content.

It is disappointing to admit that the quality of these sketches varies. In the cases of the entries I prepared, the overwhelming factor influencing the length and content of an agency's entry was the availability of its records. I relied either on the great and rich libraries in the New York metropolitan area and/or upon the headquarter files of the agencies studied, many of which are located in the New York area. Most agencies I visited during the course of this project were extremely cooperative. Some gave me full and unfettered access to their inevitably uncataloged files, others were much more selective in which materials they gave me, and some did not allow me to see their records. It is inappropriate to mention specific agencies here because the bibliographies convey clearly the availability of records still in agencies' possession. I generally turned to agencies for materials I could not find in libraries in the New York area. My research in literally dozens of agency headquarters convinced me further of the importance of the work that archives such as the Social Welfare History Archives at the University of Minnesota, Minneapolis, and the Temple University Archives in Philadelphia, Pennsylvania, are doing to preserve the primary source materials of social service agencies. I am only afraid that more precious documents will be destroyed before archivists can rescue and preserve them. When the various sources suggested different and conflicting dates, names, and such, I relied generally on *The New York Times,* the newspaper of record, to resolve the issue. Accordingly, many bibliographies acknowledge this important source.

Appendix 4, "Genealogies," contains detailed information about name changes and appropriate dates, mergers, and dissolutions of each agency included in this volume. When primary sources, such as manuscript collections, letterheads, published annual reports, and newsletters and journals, did not provide this information clearly, I relied on the information about national voluntary agencies in most issues of the *Social Work Year Books* and its successor, the *Encyclopedia of Social Work,* on reports in *The New York Times,* and on entries in the volumes of the *Directory of Social and Health Agencies of New York.* Except for *The New York Times* accounts, I am not convinced that these sources were always accurate, but in the absence of other data, I have had to rely on them.

Whatever the strengths of this reference volume are, they are due partly to the rich library collections in the New York area. Chief among these are the beleaguered New York Public Library (NYPL) and the Whitney M. Young, Jr., Memorial Library of the School of Social Work at Columbia University, a veritable storehouse of rare newsletters, annual reports, publications, and other ephemeral publications. The latter library received part of the apparently rich library of the Russell Sage Foundation,* parts of which also went to the Cohen Library at the City College of New York. To study several organizations— especially the health agencies but also some of the social work organizations—I used the library of the New York Academy of Medicine. In the New York area there are numerous specialized libraries in the field of social work, and virtually each one of them I approached allowed me access to its materials. These libraries are mentioned in the appropriate bibliographies following each entry.

In many ways, I owe special thanks to the libraries and agencies that helped me. My first thanks go to Ruth Arnold, Epp Turk, and Nick Senopolous of the reference department of the Forrest Irwin Library at Jersey City State College. Especially in the project's early stages but also throughout, they patiently checked details, names, addresses, dates, and such, virtually each of which found its way into this volume. I am grateful to the trustees of Columbia University for allowing me library privileges there through my membership in a University Seminar. Words, especially at this point, are an inappropriate way to thank the NYPL, which facilitated my research by granting me special privileges to the Wertheim Study Room. It is sad that I cannot name here each of the many librarians, archivists, agency executives, and social workers who spent hours talking with me and who often supplied a pleasant relief from the dusty confines of old annual reports or of files neglected too long. It is not that I do not know their names but that the list is too unwieldy to include. Undoubtedly, some of these people will have forgotten me and my name, but I recall excitedly the hours I spent in their libraries and archives. Of all these people, none was more helpful to me in this project than Harriet Hoptner of the Whitney M. Young, Jr., Memorial Library of the School of Social Work at Columbia University. Formerly on the staff of some major national agencies, Mrs. Hoptner guided me to an incredible array of newsletters and other ephermeral publications, and her knowledge of agency histories is reflected in some of these pages. She and her colleague, Celestine Tutt, often pulled materials from the downstairs "cage"— the collection's great storeroom—held materials for me, and generally assisted me in so many ways, and I am grateful to them.

Several people have assisted me in a variety of ways during this nearly three-year project, which involved so many different places, agencies, and sources. To those contributors who cooperated by responding to my often detailed questions and who have lightened my load, I owe a great deal of thanks. In this regard, I am especially indebted to both Mary Ostling and David Klaassen of the Social Welfare History Archives Center at the University of Minnesota, Minneapolis, who, well beyond the call of duty, stepped in at the last minute to prepare entries that were needed. Steve Siegel of the Research Foundation for Jewish Immigration, Inc., shared some of his notes with me and thus helped me to strengthen some of the bibliographies, and Gary Rubin answered several questions in his field of specialization, recent Jewish and Catholic social work. Under intense, last-minute pressure, Judith Goldstein and Barbara Schwartz of New York typed this manuscript efficiently and quickly. Professor Clarke Chambers has been an ideal advisory editor, offering advice but not being too insistent. At Jersey City State College, the Research Council and the college administration, headed by President William Maxwell, himself a social welfare historian, granted me released time for research for one semester. Jim Sabin of Greenwood Press conceived of this project and assisted me throughout, particularly in the last, hectic days. Members of my family, Sandy Pulliam, Grace, and especially Helen Romanofsky helped me in many ways. Fred Romanofsky took time from his own busy schedule to assist me at the library, checking citations and performing other chores that lightened my load in the final, hectic months. This book is dedicated to Helen and Fred Romanofsky, who, perhaps unwittingly, got me interested in the world of agencies in the first place.

PETER ROMANOFSKY
New York, New York   March 1977

SOCIAL SERVICE
ORGANIZATIONS

AFL-CIO DEPARTMENT OF COMMUNITY SERVICES (AFL-CIO-DCS). Organized labor can claim a long tradition of concern for social conditions in the nation and the local community; but until World War II, the direct involvement of unions in community activities was limited. The American Federation of Labor (AFL) (see *Labor Organizations*), the dominant organization in the late nineteenth and early twentieth centuries, eschewed social and political activism and concentrated on the collective bargaining process to achieve higher wages, shorter hours, and improved working conditions.

Its contacts with social agencies increased somewhat during the depression of the 1930s when thousands of unemployed workers found it necessary to accept the agencies' services. At the same time, legislative recognition of the right of labor to organize and to bargain collectively freed unions—including those affiliated with both the AFL and the newly formed Congress of Industrial Organizations (CIO) (see *Labor Organizations*)—to turn to out-of-plant concerns, which had long been subordinated.

Fund raising and the exigencies of war stimulated the trend in organized labor that culminated in a comprehensive community service program. In 1938, the AFL formed the Labor League for Human Rights (LLHR), a committee dedicated to aiding refugees from nazism. The league raised money for foreign relief, particularly to aid free trade union movements in warring countries, and for domestic defense-related programs such as the United Service Organizations for National Defense* (USD). AFL Vice-President Matthew Woll was associated with the league from its inception, serving first as chairman and later as president. At its 1941 convention in Detroit, the CIO followed the urging of its president, Philip Murray, and authorized formation of a similar organ, the National CIO Committee for American and Allied War Relief, to respond to the specific problems and needs growing out of the defense effort. In 1943, the agency's name was shortened to the National CIO War Relief Committee.

The shift from war relief to a broader range of social services came easily. Both labor committees desired to eliminate the multiple solicitations of workers at their plants. They found a natural ally in the federated fund movement. Community chest organizers, eager to mobilize labor support as a means of encouraging larger employee contributions, had made overtures that were rejected in the late 1930s, but the increased urgency of wartime needs made labor leaders more receptive. In August 1942, the two labor committees reached a working agreement with the Community Chests and Councils (CCC). The unions abandoned plans for independent fund drives and promised to cooperate in a single joint appeal wherever local arrangements could be agreed upon. In return, chest officials agreed to include labor representatives on policy-making boards and committees and to acknowledge publicly that the contributions came from the unions, not simply employees. This relationship brought representatives of labor into contact with the many social agencies who received their funding from community chests.

The amount of labor's contribution was affected markedly by another development. Beginning July 1, 1943, employers were required to withhold federal income tax and social security payments from paychecks. This led to the establishment of the accounting apparatus that made it possible to handle workers' contributions to fund drives on a payroll deduction basis, thus spreading the impact of the contribution over several installments. The dramatic increase in contributions strengthened labor's hand in seeking a voice in community affairs.

The newly formed National War Fund negotiated an agreement in 1943 similar to that of the CCC. As cooperating agencies, the AFL and CIO relief committees were permitted to sponsor certain projects with an intrinsic appeal for workers, but all contributions were made to local campaigns to the appropriate program. Special labor staff, paid out of the fund's administrative budget, were employed at the national and regional headquarters.

The ardor for cooperative ventures cooled somewhat with the end of the war. Significant opposition had to be overcome before the CCC opened a department of labor-employee participation in 1947 with a promise to maintain parity between AFL and CIO personnel. Full-time staff members, employed by CCC but nominated by the unions, spoke for the interests of labor and promoted increased labor activity in fund drives. The pattern was duplicated in other organizations, most notably the American National Red Cross.* The development solidified the unions' commitment to cooperation with existing programs rather than develop parallel services for union members.

This postwar tendency of labor to integrate itself with the larger community reflected both an appreciation of the opportunity to improve its image in the public mind and a conviction that workers could bring a valuable new perspective to the planning and administration of social services. Toward this end, the labor committees campaigned vigorously to increase the number of labor representatives on boards and committees of agencies and chests at both the local and national levels. By 1948, they claimed to have brought more than ten thousand union members into social agency board and committee service.

Another aspect of the same general trend was the effort to increase union members' use of social agency services. To do this it was necessary to overcome a tendency among workers to equate all social services with charity. The CIO Community Services Committee (CIO-CSC), which grew out of the War Relief Committee in 1945, established a union counseling program to meet this need.

Local community service committees were urged to set up courses to train union members who would act as referral agents for workers with out-of-plant problems. By 1946, three thousand union counselors in forty-eight cities had been trained.

The AFL counterpart to union counselor training was the labor institute, which brought together within a community representatives of labor, management, and social agencies for one-day workshops. The institutes were often supplemented by "come-and-see tours" designed to give union members a firsthand look at social service agencies. The initiative for these AFL community service activities after the war shifted from the LLHR to the AFL staff members in the CCC labor participation department. This was the situation until the 1953 convention created a standing Committee of Community Relations.

The CIO-CSC developed its worker education function in a number of areas of special concern. It collaborated with the National Association for Mental Health* and the National Committee on Alcoholism* to produce and distribute pamphlets aimed specifically at workers. It worked with the ANRC to stimulate and coordinate labor involvement in disaster relief, civil defense, and blood programs. The union counseling network was utilized to spread information to workers approaching retirement, as well as those in need of unemployment or strike relief.

To publicize its involvement with community concerns, the CIO-CSC established the Philip Murray Award given to individuals and organizations in the fields of health and welfare who have made outstanding achievements. General Omar Bradley received the first award in 1947 for his continuous efforts to improve the conditions of veterans. Other recipients of the award, known since the 1955 merger as the Murray-Green Award, have included Eleanor Roosevelt in 1955 for a "lifetime of service in behalf of many people," Governor Luis Muñoz Marín in 1962 for his contributions to health and welfare in Puerto Rico, and Henry J. Kaiser in 1965 for his development of a prepaid group health insurance program.

The merger of the AFL and the CIO was approved by the AFL-CIO convention in New York City in December 1955. The new constitution's provision for a standing committee on community services to "stimulate active participation by members of affiliated unions in the affairs of their communities and the development of sound relationships with social agencies in such communities" simply restated a philosophy that had been elaborated by the two predecessor programs.

Choosing from the presidents and secretary-treasurers of member international unions, AFL-CIO President George Meany named thirteen members to the new AFL-CIO Community Services Committee (AFL-CIO-CSC). The chairman was Joseph Beirne, president of the Communications Workers of America, who had headed the CIO-CSC. Named to guide day-to-day operations as national director was Leo Perlis, a former labor organizer and journalist, who had held the same position with CIO-CSC since 1944. He has been the only director in the history of the department.

As the program expanded, it became cumbersome to refer to both the governing board and the overall program as Community Services Committee; thus the name AFL-CIO Community Service Activities emerged as the designation for the overall program, and the term Department of Community Services (DCS) denotes the national staff and program. Several other AFL-CIO national departments, particularly civil rights, education, and social security, have responsibilities that occasionally overlap those of community services.

Under Perlis's direction, AFL-CIO-DCS maintained the union counseling program and the existing cooperative relationships, most notably with the United Community Funds and Councils of America, Inc.* (UCFCA) and the Red Cross. The former relationship was culminated in 1966 by the selection of Joseph Beirne as president of UCFCA, the first time a labor official had been so honored. The AFL-CIO-DCS's headquarters remained in New York near most of the voluntary social service and health organizations until 1964 when it joined the other AFL-CIO departments in Washington.

Unemployment and strike relief predictably remained the areas where union members most consistently needed help from public or voluntary service agencies. Here, as in all other areas, AFL-CIO-DCS worked as a facilitator rather than a direct provider. It used local affiliates to alert members to available services and monitored situations to ensure that strikers were not denied the benefits of programs for which they qualified.

In addition to the ongoing activities, the department responded to specific events and needs. The Hungarian revolution in 1956 produced an influx of refugees into the United States. Acting in cooperation with the President's Committee for Hungarian Refugee Relief, AFL-CIO-DCS sent a staff member to the Joyce Kilmer Reception Center in New Jersey to provide vocational counseling for refugees planning to relocate. In 1961, a representative went to the Refugee Emergency Center in Miami to assist Cuban refugees facing union-related problems. Victims of floods, earthquakes, hurricanes, tornadoes, and other natural disasters, such as the Alaskan earthquake in 1964 and Hurricane Camille on the Gulf Coast in 1969, benefited from the numerous union members participating in Red Cross cleanup operations, their efforts coordinated by AFL-CIO-DCS. A series of regional workshops provided preparatory training for selected union members.

Fearing that wage improvements won at the bargaining table might be absorbed by inflated prices, AFL-CIO-DCS designated consumer counseling as one of its priority items in 1959. It developed a course outline designed to teach union members and their spouses how to budget their money in various areas, including groceries, health care, legal services, insurance, and installment buying. Later it provided instructions for offering a similar course tailored to the specific needs of low-income families.

The availability of a polio preventive, first the Salk vaccine in 1956 and then the Sabin oral vaccine in 1960, led to an extensive campaign to increase distribution. AFL-CIO-DCS lobbied for a federal allocation system to alleviate local shortages of the vaccine, worked to overcome apathy regarding the vaccine's importance, and sought cooperation with local medical societies to provide mass inoculation programs at low cost in accessible locations.

The anticipation of a shorter work week stimulated a series of projects designed to help workers make constructive use of their leisure time. The annual conference for community service representatives and committee members in 1963 was devoted entirely to the subject, stressing the value of educational, recreational, cultural, and service opportunities of which workers had seldom availed themselves. As one aspect of this emphasis, the agencies encouraged greater union involvement in scouting. This led in 1965 to the naming of an AFL-CIO-DCS staff representative to the Boy Scouts of America.* The representative worked to stimulate union sponsorship of scout troops and trained union members to become scout leaders. Work with other youth-serving agencies, including the Girl Scouts of the United States of America,* Camp Fire Girls,* and Boys' Clubs of America,* continued as well.

In 1968, the department sponsored a demonstration arts project in Minneapolis, Louisville, Buffalo, and New York City. The National Endowment for the Arts assisted by assigning one of its staff to the project. Its purpose was, in the words of Director Perlis, ''to present the labor movement with a smorgasbord of cultural tidbits'' by sponsoring special labor nights at concerts, theater productions, and the opera and by scheduling special performances in working class neighborhoods.

Public assistance was another area that received special attention in the 1960s. In 1961, Joseph Mitchell, the city manager of Newburgh, New York, precipitated considerable controversy with his vigorous efforts to reduce the city's welfare rolls. The DCS staff, aware that a crackdown on ''welfare chiselers'' might attract considerable sympathy from union ranks, responded by helping to organize an ad hoc national citizens' committee in defense of public welfare. The department also responded to the emergence of the numerous War on Poverty programs during Lyndon Johnson's presidency by convening a special conference in Washington, D.C., in 1967 to introduce community services representatives to new federal programs and projects.

Priorities shifted in the 1970s, again reflecting social changes that affected labor. With the establishment of wage and price controls in 1971, the AFL-CIO-DCS expanded its consumer activities by taking the lead in an AFL-CIO price monitoring system. Local community services representatives were mobilized to report any violations of price control regulations. In a related field, the department helped to form and finance the National Center for Legal Services in 1972 to offer prepaid legal services for citizens in the $5,000 to $15,000 annual income range.

Noting the increasing problem of alcoholism and drug abuse in industry, the department cooperated with the National Council on Alcoholism* and the National Institute on Alcohol Abuse and Alcoholism in an educational venture to impress upon union and management officials the magnitude of the problem. By 1973, both organizations had full-time labor representatives on their staffs. During the same year, the department joined the National Council on Crime and Delinquency* in a Federal Law Enforcement Assistance Administration–funded project to acquaint union leaders with the criminal justice system and to enlist volunteers to aid in the employment of ex-offenders, parolees, and individuals on probation.

In 1976, there were five staff members in the Department of Community Services. Supplementing their efforts were more than two hundred full-time labor representatives on local United Way staffs and another thirty serving with seven national agencies.

The inactive files of the AFL-CIO-DCS have been placed in the Social Welfare History Archives Center, University of Minnesota, Minneapolis. They include published reports and pamphlets, along with correspondence and reference files and committee minutes. More widely available are the biennial reports of the department director, included in the *Proceedings of the AFL-CIO Constitutional Conventions*. The *Proceedings* of the conventions of the AFL and the CIO have no similar reports, but they do record resolutions and actions related to community services. The department publishes a mimeographed newsletter, *Community*, which is most likely to be found in the files of a labor representative in a local United Way headquarters. Arthur J. Katz, "A Study of Conflict and Voluntary Social Welfare in America, 1905–1955" (Ph.D. dissertation, New York University, 1968), offers a somewhat garbled account of premerger developments. There is no published history.

David Klaassen

ALCOHOLICS ANONYMOUS (AA). In New York City in 1934, Bill Wilson was hospitalized at the Charles B. Towns Hospital for his alcoholic condition. That summer Dr. William D. Silkworth, Wilson's physician and a pioneer in alcohol studies, described to him the hopelessness of his disease. Dr. Silkworth subsequently became a revered figure in Alcoholics Anonymous (AA). At the hospital in December 1934, Wilson apparently had a religious experience, a vision of helping others like himself to overcome alcoholism. After his release from the hospital, Wilson attended meetings of the local Oxford Group (OG), which conducted a spiritual program for all kinds of people, including alcoholics. The OG held meetings in New York City at the Calvary Church, where mostly respectable people met. The church's mission, located some distance from the church itself, was where alcoholics, homeless men, and other deviants, including Wilson, came for sustenance and lectures on spiritualism. Wilson worked with alcoholics at the mission and at the Towns Hospital. In early 1935, one of the drunks came to live with Wilson and his wife, Lois, in their home in Brooklyn, New York. In the spring of 1935, Wilson and some of his business colleagues traveled to Akron, Ohio, to work out plans to gain control of a little machine tool company. The business venture failed, and the rest of the group returned to New York, but Wilson remained in Akron. Feeling the temptation to drink, Wilson called a member of the local OG, Henrietta Siberling, of the wealthy rubber manufacturing family in Akron. Seiberling gave Wilson the name of another alcoholic to contact, Dr. Robert Smith, a local surgeon who had lost his position on the staff of the Akron City Hospital. In late May 1935, Wilson and Smith talked together from the late afternoon well into the night. At this meeting in Akron, the idea for establishing a fellowship of alcoholics was crystallized in Wilson's mind. He returned to New York and continued to work through the OG and the Towns Hospital, gradually gathering a small group of alcoholics. By the fall of 1935, he and his wife were holding weekly meetings with alcoholics at their home in Brooklyn. The group in New York, led by Wilson, split from the OG in mid-1937 because they felt the time had come when they should be on their own. The group felt they should not remain with a movement whose practices did not represent their own needs or aims, or their vision of what they wanted to do. Wilson's group also broke from the OG because it used names, and Wilson thought that alcoholics wanted to remain anonymous. Wilson's group called themselves "a nameless bunch of alcoholics," using the name Alcoholics Anonymous as a working title. With the publication of a book in 1939, *Alcoholics Anonymous,* the name stuck with the movement, which developed as a well-known important, international fellowship devoted to the recovery of the alcoholic.

The group in New York grew gradually after breaking from the OG. Through Bill's brother-in-law, Dr. Leonard V. Strong, Jr., who knew the head of the Rockefeller personal charities, Willard Richardson, an important meeting occurred in December 1937, in the Rockefeller board room of the Rockefeller enterprises. The meeting was attended by Albert Scott, chairman of the board of trustees of the Riverside Church in New York; Frank Amos, an advertising executive; A. LeRoy Chipman, who was treasurer of Rockefeller's personal charities division; Dr. Strong; and Richardson. These men helped to establish, in May 1938, the Alcoholic Foundation (AF) to accept contributions and funds and to be the AA service agent. Some of these prominent men agreed to be trustees of the AF, which would also include alcoholics as board members. The first board of trustees had five members: Richardson, Amos, John Wood, a prominent lawyer who had set up the structure of the AF, and alcoholics Dr. Bob, a cofounder of AA, and another New York AA member. The nonalcoholics on the board would always, the group agreed, have at least a majority of one. In January 1939, an alcoholic, Harry B. of the New York group and Dr. Strong, who became secretary of the AF, joined the foundation. In January 1939, the size of the board was enlarged to seven members.

Other events helped to develop the AA movement. An article, "Alcoholics and God," in the issue of September 1939, of *The Liberty Magazine* gave the group some national publicity and recognition. The magazine's editor, Fulton

Oursler, later became a trustee of AA. Another event that helped the early AA was a dinner of about seventy-five Rockefeller associates, hosted by Nelson Rockefeller, in the absence of his father in February 1940 at the Union Club in New York City. In 1939, following the idea of Bill and Henry P., a former executive of Standard Oil of New Jersey, AA established, under the board of trustees of the AF, its own Works Publishing, which published *Alcoholics Anonymous* (1939), as well as other later AA publications. In 1940, Works Publishing was incorporated and moved with the AF from offices in Newark, New Jersey, to New York City. In 1940, the AF office began to publish the national *Newsletter* describing AA activities and beliefs. The first nationwide coverage of AA appeared in an article in *The Saturday Evening Post* issue of March 1, 1941. This helped to publicize AA and to increase the membership significantly.

The membership and local groups of AA grew rapidly in the early 1940s. In 1940, the first AA clubhouse for AA members in New York and a rest farm in Connecticut were established. Both projects were developed and supported by local AAs in these areas. By the end of 1941, eight thousand alcoholics belonged to the AA, and in 1944, the office moved to larger headquarters at 415 Lexington Avenue in New York near Grand Central Railroad Station. This move placed the office closer to the numerous out-of-town visitors arriving in New York. In 1941, the AA published a directory of groups, and in 1944, a local magazine, *The Grapevine,* developed into an international journal. By 1957, it had a circulation of about forty thousand. In 1944, cofounder Bill read a paper at the annual meeting of the Medical Society of the State of New York, increasing interest in the movement and gaining new members and support.

After 1944, AA increasingly carried its message to alcoholics in all parts of the world. An important development occurred in 1946, when the *Twelve Traditions,* guidelines for AA unity, were initially formulated and published. The importance and uniqueness of these traditions are the emphases on self-support and self-help. Tradition number seven, for instance, stipulates, "Every AA group ought to be fully self supporting, declining outside contributions." The ninth tradition warned against formal organization but did approve of establishing service boards or committees directly responsible to the people they would serve. This tradition has resulted in a conscious attempt to minimize organization structure and details, and AA still does not refer to itself as an organization. In 1949, Bill read a paper on AA fellowship at the annual meeting of the American Psychiatric Association. In 1951, AA received the prestigious Lasker Award from the American Public Health Association* (APHA) for its pioneer work in the field of alcoholism recovery. Initially the award was to be presented to cofounder Bill, but, consistent with his wishes to remain anonymous and to shun publicity, the APHA agreed to give it instead to the entire AA society.

As AA grew in stature, it also continued to strengthen its structure. In the fall of 1950, before he died, cofounder Dr. Bob had agreed, at Bill's urging, to a five-year experiment with a central service conference replacing the founders. The founders had been providing the link between the headquarters and the local groups. The conference selected the alcoholic trustees for the AF. At the first session of the conference in April 1951, it authorized the renaming of the AF. In 1954, the AF became the General Service Board of AA, but it continued to act as the service center of the movement. This and subsequent organizational activities, however, generally adhered to the ninth tradition disapproving of organization. A further indication of the passing of the movement from the pioneer founders to the newer generation occurred in July 1955 at the twentieth anniversary and international convention in St. Louis, when Bill, as the surviving cofounder gave the leadership to the Conference, both in fact and symbolically by turning over the "Three Legacies of Recovery, Unity, and Service." In 1958, AA helped to develop a full-length television production, "The Days of Wine and Roses," which became a motion picture in 1963, partly with AA cooperation. In the late 1950s, AA members around the country began to record their feelings and experiences on tape, urging others to follow this kind of oral history through the pages of the variously named *Bulletin,* published by the headquarters staff in New York since 1940. Ending this decade characterized by expansion in the United States, in 1959, the AA Publishing became the AA World Services, Inc., a change heralding greater activities abroad.

Some internal structural changes of the General Service Board and expansion of the AA movement abroad characterized the period of the 1960s. In 1963, the first regional AA trustees were elected to the General Service Board, replacing the so-called area trustees, who, despite the designation, were elected from a single state. The new procedures adopted in 1963 also divided the United States into six regions for organizational purposes. In 1965, the group produced a color film documentary on the early history of AA, narrated by Lois and Bill. An important structural development occurred in 1966, when it was agreed that alcoholics would have a two-thirds majority of the trustees of the General Service Board. Consistent with AA beliefs, this action symbolized the recognition that AA members could, despite their pasts, handle the affairs of their movement. With this important change, the number of regional AA trustees was raised to eight, six from the United States and two from Canada. Such prominent individuals as Austin MacCormick, noted prison reformer and head of The Osborne Association,* and Fulton Oursler, editor and author, have served as trustees. Concluding this successful decade, in October 1969, with delegates from fourteen countries, AA held the first world service meeting in New York City.

In 1970, cofounder Bill appeared briefly for the last time at the thirty-fifth anniversary convention in Miami Beach, Florida; he died on January 24, 1971, at the age of seventy-five. Only after his death did AA leaders reveal his last name. On February 14, 1971, AA groups throughout the world held memorial services for Bill. To help alcoholics further, AA published *Living Sober* (1975), detailing some techniques that AA members have used to resist the desire to drink alcohol.

The primary sources for studying the history of the AA fellowship are diverse. The most recent edition of *AA Comes of Age* (1975), itself a helpful history of the movement, contains a list of key events. Other sources of information are the variously named but difficult to locate *Bulletin*, published from 1940 to the present. Press releases, mimeographed bulletins, and other materials from the national headquarters, in addition to the coverage in *The New York Times*, also describe AA activities. Articles on AA have appeared in magazines and professional journals. The files of the AA, including Bill's correspondence, reports from local and state groups and from individuals, and oral histories and tapes from members throughout the country are in the archives at the New York City headquarters. The archives are not available to students or researchers except through permission from the archives committee of the board of trustees of the General Service Board of AA.

There is apparently no scholarly history of AA.

AMERICAN ASSOCIATION FOR COMMUNITY ORGANIZATION: see UNITED WAY OF AMERICA.

AMERICAN ASSOCIATION FOR HYGIENE AND BATHS, THE (AAHB). During the late nineteenth century, social reformers, sanitarians, public health physicians, and social workers were concerned about the poor hygienic conditions in the teeming, congested, tenement-ridden slums of major American cities. One public health measure that developed to deal with these health problems was the idea of public baths for tenement dwellers whose substandard housing lacked proper water and bathing facilities. European cities generally pioneered in promoting public baths, and by the 1890s, the movement was active in American cities. In New York, the first baths were established by a leading and pioneering social work agency, the New York Association for Improving the Condition of the Poor* (AICP). Dr. Simon Baruch of New York City was the recognized leader in the field. People from around the country supporting public baths communicated with each other. At the suggestion of Reverend Thomas M. Beadenkoff, a group of reformers met at the City Hall of New York in May 1912 and established the American Association for Hygiene and Baths (AAHB) as the American Association for Promoting Hygiene and Baths (AAPHB). This activity institutionalized an aspect of the urban-oriented social justice Progressive movement. The group of largely public health officials and physicians who met in New York City in May 1912 read some professional papers, drew up a constitution, and elected officers. Reverend Beadenkoff declined the presidency, deferring to the widely recognized leader in the field, Dr. Baruch. Other initial offices included a vice-president, a secretary, a corresponding secretary, and a treasurer. The new organization had an eight-member board of directors, and President Baruch appointed committes as the organization expanded. In 1916, for instance, he appointed two: publicity, consisting of three members, and the four-member committee on the revision of the constitution. At a meeting on May 9, 1917, the organization agreed to have three vice-presidents instead of one.

As its name suggested, the organization existed primarily to promote the development and improvement of public baths, but its concerns related to the broader public health movement of the Progressive era. Members and other medical and social welfare leaders agreed that such services were important urban reform measures. At the second annual meeting, at which prominent public health leader, Dr. William Welch, endorsed the work of the AAPHB, the organization supported the concept of school baths and worked to establish them. In 1915, the AAPHB promulgated swimming pool standards, which served as the basis for regulation and supervision in most states. The widespread adoption of its standards, stressing refiltration and disinfection, promoted the popularity of indoor as well as outdoor public swimming pools throughout the country. On October 29, 1917, New York City opened the Dr. Simon Baruch Public Bath in the crowded Lower East Side ghetto. Socially committed but constantly abreast of technological developments that improved public sanitation and health, the organization appointed a three-member committee on shower bath standards in 1922. Although public health and social welfare activitists had formed and led the organization in its early period, commercial interests began to dominate the AAHB in the late 1920s. As the organization itself argued in 1930, an outstanding event was the establishment of a commercial division, the National Pool and Beach Association (see *Business Associations*), headed and led by manufacturers and representatives of commercial enterprises as filter companies. The AAHB continued to issue its journal in the early 1930s. The organization seems to have disbanded, however, in the mid-1930s.

The primary sources for studying the AAHB's history include published *Proceedings* and the *Journal,* which are not widely available. Studies in the history of public health, such as John Duffy, *A History of Public Health in New York City* (1968 and 1974), neglect the organization, but Marilyn Williams, "The Municipal Bath Movement in the United States, 1890–1915" (Ph.D. dissertation, New York University, 1972), discusses its role in the movement for public baths.

AMERICAN ASSOCIATION FOR LABOR LEGISLATION (AALL). In 1900, a group of reformers established the International Association for Labor Legislation in Paris. American social scientists and reformers, particularly Dr. Adna F. Weber, the chief statistician of the New York State Department of Labor, wanted to establish a similar American organization. At the meeting in December 1905 of the American Economic Association in Baltimore, Maryland, a group interested in such an organization met and appointed a five-member organizing committee, composed of Professors Henry W. Farnam of Yale University, Henry Seager of Columbia University, Richard T. Ely of the University of Wisconsin, and Clinton Rogers Woodruff, an expert on municipal government. Dr. Weber chaired the committee, which drew up a constitution and bylaws. The committee then called a meeting in New York City on February 15, 1906, at which the AALL elected Ely as president and chose the other traditional officers, including as secretary, Dr. Weber, who established headquarters in Albany, New York. When Weber resigned in October 1907, a temporary secretary served until the first annual meeting in December 1907. Meeting again with the AEA, the AALL elected as its secretary Professor John R. Commons, who in March 1908 established headquarters in a section of his office at the Wisconsin State Historical Society in Madison. A student of his, Irene Osgood, became the assistant secretary, and in December 1908, the AALL hired John R. Andrews, another Commons student who had won his Ph.D. in economics from the University of Wisconsin in 1908, as executive secretary.

Even before the AALL constitutional amendment of 1910 urging it to study labor conditions "with a view to promoting desirable labor legislation," the organization had established its basic pattern of operation, chiefly through Executive Secretary Andrews. As early as 1910, for example, Andrews initiated the first of many studies of occupational disease, a study of phosphorous poisoning, or "phossy jaw," among match workers. It was published in 1910 in *Bulletin #86* of the United States Bureau of Labor. Based on this and other studies, in late 1910, the AALL began to lobby for federal regulation, working closely through the sponsor of the bill, Congressman John Esch. An agreement with the Diamond Match Company reducing hazards and the enactment of a federal law in 1912 suggested the enormously successful activities of the AALL. In the field of occupational disease, a constant AALL focus, the organization held the first national conference on industrial disease in Chicago in June 1910 and another in 1912, a joint session with the American Medical Association.

In this pre–World War I era, the AALL developed some further organizational details and continued in the vanguard of Progressive era reforms, such as promoting, with the Women's Trade Union League and the National Consumers' League,* the campaign in states for minimum wages for women. In early 1910, the AALL office moved from the University of Wisconsin to New York City, where it remained until the AALL's demise in 1945. In 1911, the organization began to publish its journal, *The American Labor Legislation Review,* which developed as an important reform voice in the Progressive and later eras. In March 1910, the AALL helped to initiate in New York State the successful campaign for workmen's compensation, an essential Progressive era reform measure. In 1912, the AALL established a committee to press for one day of rest for workers. An important campaign dealing with unemployment attracted considerable AALL efforts. In 1914, the AALL made a brief but careful analysis of the problems of the economic slump in over a hundred American cities and studied measures to revive the economy. It recommended that permanent central labor exchanges be established, and it urged local governments to plan public works projects in times of unemployment. In February 1914, the AALL sponsored the first national conference on unemployment; its resolutions called for public employment agencies and labor reforms that heralded those of the New Deal. A second conference, held in Philadelphia in December 1914, presented "A Practical Program for the Prevention of Unemployment in America," featuring unemployment insurance plans, another major Progressive measure. In 1914, the organization drafted and worked for the first of many measures for employees in Washington, D.C., a workmen's compensation plan. In 1915, its social insurance committee issued "Standards in Workmen's Compensation Laws," which remained the best guide for decades in the field nationally. In 1916, the AALL developed its national health insurance program, with its "health first" slogan. Throughout much of the history of the AALL, Professor Joseph Chamberlain of Columbia University wrote many of its legislative proposals, but the most important figure was John Andrews, one of those few leaders in the field of social welfare whose career singularly influenced his organization.

World War I and its aftermath did not, as in the histories of other Progressive era social agencies, significantly dissipate the energies of the AALL; rather, the AALL seemed to use the war to promote Progressive measures. For instance, in late 1917, it urged Senator Joseph Robinson to push his bill for federal public employment offices as a war emergency measure. In early 1917, Andrews began to publish a series of special bulletins, *Labor Laws in Wartime;* and a trip to Europe in the summer of 1919 for the War Department gave him an opportunity to influence postwar federal labor developments, for he was able to advise the federally appointed organizing committee planning an international legislation conference for October 1919. In the immediate postwar period, the AALL campaigned vigorously for important federal labor legislation, particularly in 1920, when it pushed successfully for the Fess-Kenyon Act to promote vocational rehabilitation services for industrial cripples. The AALL's program in the next few years included such reforms as maternal health protection, coal mine and other types of industrial safety, and the unsuccessful child labor amendment. Other early and mid-1920s AALL efforts typified other Progressive era concerns: old age pensions, industrial disease and accident prevention measures, and unemployment insurance. The enactment in 1927 of the federal longshoremen's workmen's compensation program culminated nearly ten years of AALL efforts. Such activities helped to merit Professor Clarke Chambers's interpretation in *Seedtime for Reform* (1963) that the AALL helped to keep the reform impulse alive in the interim between progressivism and the New Deal.

Some important organizational developments occurred in the late 1920s. By early 1927, the effect on the AALL of the splinter group of members who established and led the American Association for Old Age Security* (AAOAS) became evident. Many AAOAS officers, including its leader, Abraham Epstein, were or had been AALL members. In 1927, Paul Douglas, Rabbi Stephen Wise, and others began unsuccessfully to try to unite the two organizations, and in early

1928, disturbed by the AALL position, important social reformer Florence Kelley charged that the AALL lacked depth. In late 1926, Thomas Chadbourne, a wealthy Wall Street financier and the AALL president between 1920 and 1926, pledged to donate $10,000 per year for the next three if the AALL raised $15,000, a proposal that failed to work out fully. Concerned with both the financial problems and the organizational strife, the AALL nevertheless continued in the late 1920s to promote such measures as the 1928 federal law providing workmen's compensation for private employees in the District of Columbia and the workmen's compensation campaigns in some regressive southern states.

In the depression years of the 1930s, the AALL was concerned with the problems of unemployment and economic security in America. The year 1931, dominated by unemployment problems, opened for the organization with the resignation in early February of Vice-President William Doak, the United States secretary of labor, who disagreed with AALL's advocacy of Senator Robert Wagner's unemployment bills. In early 1932, Edwin Witte, a leader in the Wisconsin unemployment insurance movement, credited the AALL with the passage of an unemployment insurance bill in his state. Some active AALL members worked with the President's Committee on Economic Security (see *Government Agencies*), a cabinet-level research organization of which Witte became the executive director. In 1935, the AALL helped to pressure Congress to enact what became the Social Security Act of that year.

The depression also brought hard times for the AALL and its staff. In the mid-1930s, Chadbourne declined to renew his annual $10,000 gift. The budget in 1930 was about $72,000, compared to $37,000 with a $1,000 deficit in 1933. Pressed for funds and office space, Andrews even offered to sell the AALL's collection of early literature on workmen's compensation. By mid-1936, the financial state was so bad that neither Andrews or Assistant Secretary Irene Osgood Andrews, his wife, received a salary for six months. In 1938, the budget reached a new low of $25,000.

The financial problems of the organization, the death of Executive Secretary Andrews in January 1943, and the achievement of some important labor legislation during the New Deal combined to effect the decline of the AALL in the late 1930s and early 1940s. Renewed interest in industrial disease occupied AALL activities in 1936 but, except for some studies of the administration of labor laws in the 1930s, AALL activities diminished. In 1942, the AALL published the last issue of its journal, and because of World War II, the organization canceled its annual meeting in the same year. The AALL searched unsuccessfully for a replacement for Andrew and finally disbanded in 1945.

There are full primary sources for studying not only the organizational history of the AALL but also its many activities. The well-inventoried AALL Papers at Cornell University have been microfilmed by the Microfilm Corporation of America. Because the AALL was such a central factor in reform movements and for reformers, materials relating to its history can be found in many other collections, such as the Paul Kellogg Papers at the Social Welfare History Archives at the University of Minnesota and the Samuel McCune Lindsay Papers and the Abraham Epstein Papers at Columbia University. *The American Labor Legislation Review* contains not only organizational developments but also materials reflecting AALL activities.

The AALL is one of the most widely studied social welfare organizations. The best study of its history is Lloyd F. Pierce, "The Activities of the AALL in Behalf of Social Security, and Protective Labor Legislation" (Ph.D. dissertation, University of Wisconsin, 1953). Others, such as Richard Martin Lyon, "The AALL and the Fight for Workmen's Compensation Laws, 1906–1942" (Master's thesis, Cornell University, 1952), describe some of its activities. The AALL figures importantly in Daniel S. Hirschfield, *The Lost Reform: The Campaign for Compulsory Health Insurance in the United States from 1932 to 1943* (1970) and less so in Clarke Chambers, *Seedtime for Reform: American Social Service and Social Action, 1918–1933* (1963). Historians seem to embroil the AALL in their debates about the very nature of progressivism. David Eakins, "The Class Consciousness of Some Social Justice Progressives, 1903–1921" (unpublished paper, Organization of American Historians Meeting, 1973), interprets the AALL members as fundamentally conservative reformers, but Irwin Yellowitz, *Labor and the Progressive Movement in New York State, 1897–1916* (1965), sees it as part of the social justice movement, as does Robert Wesser, "Conflict and Compassion: The Workmen's Compensation Movement in New York, 1890s–1913," *Labor History*, 12 (Summer 1971): 345–372.

AMERICAN ASSOCIATION FOR OLD AGE SECURITY: see AMERICAN ASSOCIATION FOR SOCIAL SECURITY, INC.

AMERICAN ASSOCIATION FOR ORGANIZING SOCIAL WORK: see FAMILY SERVICE ASSOCIATION OF AMERICA.

AMERICAN ASSOCIATION FOR SOCIAL SECURITY, INC. (AASS).
In the early twentieth century, social workers, economists, and reformers became aware of the need for some type of old age security. One of the most important figures in this struggle was Abraham Epstein. Since 1918, Epstein had served as research director and executive secretary of the Pennsylvania Commission on Old Age Pensions. During the 1920s, he studied the need for old age insurance, and he published articles and books on the subject. Reform organizations, especially those dominated by socially conscientious economists, had been advocating for many years all forms of social insurance, including not only old age pensions but also unemployment insurance and workmen's compensation. The American Association for Labor Legislation* (AALL) in particular had advocated old age pensions, but by the mid-1920s, it had lost interest in this

issue. Epstein, an important AALL member, however, maintained his interest and enthusiasm and began to discuss the establishment of a new organization to promote this interest. John Andrews, the long-time AALL executive secretary, grew annoyed with the talk of separation, and, to prevent a split in the AALL, asked Epstein to head an old age pension department in the AALL. Relations between the two men deteriorated, and Epstein persisted in his insistence on establishing a new organization. In the spring of 1927, Andrews concluded that Epstein—a difficult man who alienated even his closest colleagues—was more of a liability than an asset for the AALL and decided to let him break with the group.

In 1926, Epstein began soliciting nationwide support for the group he envisioned. In January 1927, he organized and incorporated in the state of Ohio the National Old Age Pension League. Supporters of the league included prominent social worker Florence Kelley, the first woman factory inspector in Illinois and a founder and leader of the National Consumers' League* (NCL), Mary Simkhovitch of Greenwich House, a social settlement in New York City, and Philip Ziegler, the editor of *The Railway Clerk's Magazine*. On February 4, 1927, in New York City, the American Association for Social Security (AASS) was established as the American Association for Old Age Security (AAOAS) when a number of people interested in old age pensions gathered at a meeting convened by Epstein, who was the most important founder and the most important figure in the history of the organization. Among the other founders were Professor Joseph Chamberlain of Columbia University, who was active in the AALL, Florence Kelley, and William H. Mathews, a prominent local social worker from the New York Association for Improving the Conditions of the Poor* (AICP).

The group elected Epstein chairman of the meeting. After Epstein spoke on the problems of old age, the conference decided to constitute itself as an organizing committee. Kelley prepared a constitution, which was adopted with some amendments. The group then established a five-member nominating committee, including Kelley and Dr. Leo Wollman, an economics professor and head of the research department of the Amalgamated Clothing Workers of America (see *Labor Unions*). Epstein was elected temporary executive secretary. The constitution provided for a president, eleven vice-presidents, a treasurer, and an executive secretary. The initial thirteen-member executive committee included the vice-presidents, the president, and the executive secretary. The executive committee determined the duties and compensation of the executive secretary, but throughout much of the history of the organization, Epstein himself determined policies, and he even spent his own money on the organization's activities. The constitution also called for an advisory council of a hundred members. The first president of the AAOAS was Bishop Ethelbert Talbot of the Episcopal diocese of Pennsylvania. In December 1927, Talbot retired, and Bishop Francis J. McConnell, a liberal who was president of the Methodist Federation for Social Service,* became president. Other early supporters of the AAOAS included Isaac M.

Rubinow, Paul Douglas, and others, all important figures, and mostly economists, in the AALL.

In the early years of the AAOAS, the organization solidified its structure and support, maintained its conflict with the AALL, and developed a solid campaign for old age pensions in the United States. The structure in 1920 included fourteen vice-presidents, such as Jane Addams of Hull-House* in Chicago, Mary Simkhovitch, and John Ryan, head of the Social Action Department of the National Catholic Welfare Conference* (SAD). The structure also included a ninety-seven-member advisory council, which had a host of important social reformers and social workers. The AAOAS opened an office in New York City, and Executive Secretary Epstein dominated the organization, as he did throughout its short history. Attempts by Paul Douglas and Rabbi Stephen Wise, an important twentieth-century social reformer, failed to unite the AAOAS and the AALL. Relations between the two leaders, Andrews and Epstein, deteriorated further. In 1928, when Epstein and the AAOAS presented an old age pension bill to the New York State legislature and the AALL countered with a proposal to establish an investigating commission first, the rivalry between the two men and their organizations became more heated than before. In 1928, the AAOAS helped to develop a united movement, sponsoring in New York City in April a conference of about a hundred organizations concerned with old age security. This conference developed into an annual forum for the discussion of the ramifications of this important social issue.

An important shift in the ideology of social security occurred in 1929, when Epstein, impressed with and influenced by European methods, began to argue for old age benefits as social insurance, a basic right, rather than as a pension. Social security would thus benefit only those who had worked and who had contributed to pension plans. Senator Clarence C. Dill of Washington introduced a bill written by the AAOAS for a federal plan, and the AAOAS model bill of a pension system for the District of Columbia was introduced in the House of Representatives. When the pioneering old age pension system went into effect in early 1931, the information bureau of the AAOAS—a local New York City agency—provided an important social service by helping six thousand people to enroll. Beginning around late 1931, when opponents of state-sponsored social insurance generally attacked existing state old age pension plans, the AAOAS, with other reform groups, led the successful fight to preserve their hard-won victories. Closing out the first phase of the history of the AAOAS, the depression began to affect the budget of the organization, a foretaste of financial problems that continued to plague it through the 1930s.

The election of Franklin D. Roosevelt as president in November 1932 seemed to usher in a new phase for the AAOAS. In February 1933, it changed its name to the AASS, broadening its focus and igniting the national movement once again. It continued to emphasize old age but dealt increasingly with health and unemployment insurance, vital factors in the concept of social security generally. For instance, in April 1934, AASS representatives, chiefly Epstein, testified in sup-port of an unemployment compensation bill in New York State. Although drafted by the New York State Federation of Labor, the AASS, which disagreed with some of the bill's provisions, nevertheless supported it "for the sake of unity." The AASS also contributed to the drafting of the Wagner-Lewis unemployment bill in the Congress. The AASS suffered its first deficit apparently in 1934, forcing the organization to curtail its field service. It did, however, increase the number of its field representatives in Congress and expand its publication, ini-tially called *The Old Age Herald,* but now called *Social Security.* The organiza-tion continued to help individuals in New York City through its information bureau. In 1933, the AASS published Epstein's *Insecurity—a Challenge to America,* a widely read book that made an effective impact on the public. The AASS continued to help state pension campaigns; it played an especially impor-tant role in the Missouri legislature in the mid-1930s by distributing about twelve thousand copies of its health insurance bill. The enactment of the Social Security Act of 1935, which Epstein denounced consistently, helped to initiate another phase of the AASS's history.

The achievement of a federal social security program, however limited and rudimentary, lessened financial support for the AASS, forcing it to curtail some legislative services. The AASS bill to provide federal funds to state health insurance plans was introduced beginning in 1934, but it never became law. Within a few years, some groups and individuals began looking to the AASS for leadership in changing some of the injustices and abuses in the social security system, a four-year movement culminating with the revisions in August 1939. Chiefly through Epstein, the AASS continually emphasized that the existing unemployment insurance plans could not deal effectively with this difficult social problem. The AASS bills for national health insurance remained unwelcomed and rejected by Congress. Organization funds continued to dwindle, and the agency did little more than sponsor the annual conferences, which addressed themselves consistently to timely social issues. In early May 1942, Epstein died at the age of fifty, depriving the organization of its crucial figure.

Epstein's colleagues tried desperately, but unsuccessfully, to carry on with his work. A series of meetings of the board of directors, alone and with friends and supporters of the AASS, culminated in the appointment in June 1942 of an administrative committee of five members. In late May 1942, the board of directors appointed Adele Bloom as acting executive secretary; she had been a close Epstein associate who had headed the information bureau on legislation and administrative conditions since 1930 and had served as assistant editor of *Social Security* since 1935. The AASS issued a policy statement of its aims in the June 1942 issue of *Social Security,* which proved to be the last. With its guiding spirit Epstein gone and with the federal social security system established and ever changing, the AASS maintained itself feebly. In mid-1944, it was officially disbanded.

The primary sources for styding the AASS's history are diverse. The Abraham Epstein Papers at Columbia University contain many materials about the AASS, and the AALL Papers, at Cornell University and on microfilm, have references to its work. The published *Proceedings* of the annual meetings and *Social Security,* the organization's journal, yield relevant information. Other collections, such as the Stephen Wise Papers at the American Jewish Historical Society at Waltham, Massachusetts, contain AASS materials.

Standard works in the field, such as Roy Lubove, *The Struggle for Social Security* (1968), offer information about the AASS, but there does not appear to be a scholarly history of this organization.

AMERICAN ASSOCIATION FOR THE STUDY AND PREVENTION OF INFANT MORTALITY: see AMERICAN CHILD HEALTH ASSOCIATION.

AMERICAN ASSOCIATION OF HOSPITAL SOCIAL WORKERS: see AMERICAN ASSOCIATION OF MEDICAL SOCIAL WORKERS, INC.

AMERICAN ASSOCIATION OF MEDICAL SOCIAL WORKERS, INC., THE (AAMSW). Among the changes in American society that accompanied nineteenth-century urbanization and industrialization and altered the structure of its institutions were those in the organization and practice of medicine. Increasingly in the early twentieth century, the treatment of sick persons took place in hospitals or in outpatient departments and clinics where patients who were ambulatory received care. As medicine entered a more scientific and holistic era, physicians gradually became aware of the impact of social and emotional factors in medical problems. Motivated by this awareness, some hospitals, primarily in cities in the eastern United States, organized social service departments and hired social workers to practice in a medical setting.

One of the first departments was established in 1905 by Dr. Richard Clarke Cabot at Massachusetts General Hospital in Boston. Through his staff work there, Cabot had realized that human burdens of poverty, chronic ill health, and inadequate housing frequently made the task of prescribing medicine for a particular illness difficult and even futile; it was comparable, he said, to "giving medicine to a tired horse dragging uphill a weight too great for him. What was needed was to unload the wagon or rest the horse." To devise methods for helping individuals with their burdens, he employed a social worker whose understanding of social problems and the resources for solving them would assist him in diagnosing and treating his patients more effectively.

Between 1905 and 1917, more than a hundred hospitals in thirty-five cities hired hospital social workers whose backgrounds were most often in nursing, education, and social work. By 1915, some workers had begun to discuss a national organization; in 1917, as World War I began and the pressure to find qualified hospital social workers increased, a group met at the National Conference of Charities and Correction (NCCC)* in Pittsburgh to propose a national organization to maintain standards and promote communication among hospital social workers. On May 18, 1918, at the recently renamed National Conference of Social Work* (NCSW) in Kansas City, thirty women signed a constitution to create the American Association of Hospital Social Workers (AAHSW).

The purpose of the association, as stated in its constitution, was "to serve as an organ of intercommunication among hospital social workers, to maintain and improve standards of social work in hospitals and dispensaries, and to stimulate its [hospital social work's] intensive and extensive development." In 1926, the association was incorporated in Massachusetts, and in 1934, it became the American Association of Medical Social Workers (AAMSW), a name it retained until 1955, when it merged with six other professional social work membership organizations to become the National Association of Social Workers* (NASW). From 1918, the association had included among its members those practicing psychiatric social work, and in 1920, it formally recognized the group as the Psychiatric Social Work Section. In 1925, the psychiatric social workers voted to disband the section, and, in 1926, they formed a separate professional organization, the American Association of Psychiatric Social Workers.

The AAHSW's work was conducted by its officers—a president, three vice-presidents, a secretary, and a treasurer—its standing committees, and paid staff members—an executive secretary, a titled executive director after 1953, and consultants on education and practice. In 1920, the AAHSW provided for the organization of individual members within districts, of which there were sixteen in 1955; districts were formed when a group of medical social workers demonstrated it had a sufficient number of professional workers, leadership and financial stability, and established geographic limits (for example, Michigan, California, the Pacific Northwest).

Executive directors of the association have been M. Antoinette Cannon, 1918–1920; Ruth Emerson, 1920–1922; Lena R. Waters, 1922–1926; Helen Beckley, 1927–1935; Mary M. Maxwell, 1935–1941; Marian E. Russell, 1942–1946; Margaret Lumpkin, 1946–1947; Mary Blanche Moss, 1947–1952; Lelia I. Dickinson (acting), 1953; and Mary L. Hemmy, 1953–1955.

Active membership in the AAHSW was open initially to anyone, regardless of training, who had been employed for at least one full year as a paid hospital social worker; later, the association amended its constitution to provide for associate, junior, student, corporate, and honorary membership classes. Over time, as social work established standards for training and moved toward accreditation of schools and certification of individuals, requirements for active membership came to be based on completion of a full course (two-year) in an accredited school of social work combined with either a medical social work sequence or some combination of other professional education and supervised experience. Throughout its history, the association was funded primarily by dues from its members, supplemented by contributions from individuals, association districts, and foundations.

Although the association engaged in a variety of activities, the greatest part of its efforts for nearly forty years was concentrated on educating medical social workers and improving medical social work practice. By December 1925, the association had appointed a part-time education secretary, Kate McMahon, also a professor of social work at Simmons College, who held the position for thirty years. Together the secretary and the association's education committee worked to articulate standards for preparation for medical social work and to devise a curriculum for integration in professional social work education. The education consultant and the committee advised schools of social work that were establishing medical social work sequences and assisted them in incorporating new theories and changes in practice into the curriculum. They also advised universities about integrating social factors of medical care into training for nursing, medical, and hospital administration students.

A concern for practice also dated from the first years, when the AAHSW, fearing that hospital social work would be confined to administrative work such as admitting patients and investigating their financial status, created a committee on functions in 1922 to consider the content of medical social work and the conditions under which it should be practiced. Because of their close association with other professions, especially medicine and psychiatry, medical social workers worked unusually hard and persistently to define what their appropriate functions in a medical setting ought to be; they also studied the operation of social service departments to ascertain actual practice. The functions committee and various other association committees concerned with practice stressed that casework, research, and education, rather than administrative responsibilities, were primary components of medical social work. When the association was reorganized in 1942, the medical social practice committee was formed by merger of the functions committee and the practice committees; it devoted its attention to contributions by and relations with other members of the professional health and medical team, the definition of a "medical social work position," the collection and analysis of case records, and the processes of administering a social service department.

In the first decade of AAHSW work, when medicine was practiced largely in hospitals, the AAHSW focused on the use of medical social casework in institutional care of the ill. With advances in the health sciences, the impact of the Great Depression, and the coming of World War II, however, the patterns of organization and distribution of medical care began another dramatic shift. As health sciences discovered significant increases in life expectancy and chronic illness, new services were devised accordingly, and public health expanded its field beyond the control of communicable diseases to include preventive medicine as well. For the first time, federal and state governments began to assume some responsibility, primarily through social security legislation, for the funding and distribution of medical care. As the association struggled with the training and staffing implications of these new trends, World War II brought renewed demands for additional personnel and still more programs, especially in rehabilitation. Although many medical social workers continued to practice casework in hospitals, as they had in 1918, others found themselves with new responsibilities in community planning and medical care. In order to reflect these changed circumstances and new areas of responsibility, the association voted in 1944 to amend its original purpose to state, "to promote the quality and effectiveness of social work in relation to health and medical care."

The association continued its work until February 1955, when AAMSW representatives voted to dissolve the organization and merge with six other associations to form a single social work membership organization, the NASW. The final meeting to vote on disbanding AAMSW was convened at Massachusetts General Hospital, where medical social work began. In attendance at the meeting were some of the association's founders, including Antoinette Cannon, the first executive secretary, and Ida M. Cannon, who had directed the Massachusetts General social service department from 1906 to 1946.

Mary A. Stites's *History of the American Association of Medical Social Workers* (1954) contains a bibliography listing major association publications and other studies of the association. Especially useful in understanding the origins of medical social work are Richard C. Cabot's *Essays on the Meeting Ground of Doctor and Social Worker* (1919) and Ida M. Cannon's *On The Social Frontier of Medicine* (1952). Harriett M. Bartlett, *50 Years of Social Work in the Medical Setting: Past Significance, Future Outlook* (1957), is a brief but superb study of the evolution of medical social work. The records of the NASW, including extensive records of AAMSW, are held by the Social Welfare History Archives, University of Minnesota Libraries, Minneapolis, which also has some papers of Harriett Bartlett.

Andrea Hinding

AMERICAN ASSOCIATION OF SOCIAL WORKERS (AASW). In early 1911, in New York City, a group of alumnae from the largest and most famous eastern women's colleges established the Intercollegiate Bureau of Occupations (IBO) to provide information about jobs and careers for young women. The IBO was incorporated officially on May 1, 1911, and on October 1, 1911, it opened its office and began its work. The IBO was one of several such organizations created in several American cities during the Progressive era. Because of the heavy volume of inquiries about the emerging field of social work, the IBO created a department for social workers in 1913. The department had its own eight-member executive committee that included some of the most well-known social workers in New York City and the nation. Mary Vida Clark, a child care specialist from the State Charities Aid Association* (SCAA) of New York, chaired the executive committee, and Margaret Byington of the Russell Sage Foundation* (RSF), Edward Devine, the executive secretary of The Charity Organization Society of the City of New York* (COS), John M. Glenn, one of the principal founders of the RSF, and Mary Van Kleeck of the RSF, served on the executive committee. Presaging the later day AASW's prestige in the profession, the department's eighteen-member advisory committee included such social work luminaries as Homer Folks, the executive secretary of the SCAA, Owen Lovejoy, "The Children's Statesman," of the National Child Labor Committee,* Francis McLean, the founder in 1911 of the National Association of Societies for Organizing Charities,* Mary Richmond of the RSF, and Lillian Wald, the founder and head resident of the Henry Street Settlement.* The department had an annual budget of $4,500, to which the RSF and the New York School of Philanthropy (NYSP) each contributed $1,000. The department opened formally on March 1, 1913, with assistant manager Sigrid V. Wynbladh in charge of the office. She had headed the employment work of the NYSP. As expected, the department received assistance from the several private agencies in New York City whose staff members were active in the department. Anticipating the later work of the AASW and even of the National Association of Social Workers, Inc.* (NASW), the department served as a clearinghouse for information about positions in social service, and it emphasized the need for better standards generally for charity workers.

The IBO's department for social workers quickly became an integral part of the New York and even national social service community. In 1914 and 1915, it developed closer relations with several RSF departments. Most of the women using its services came from the NYSP, and they were placed in social work positions in New York City and throughout the country. During this period, the department and the NYSP conducted a study of opportunities in organized social work in New York City; the study was financed by the NYSP. In 1915, the department established its committee on volunteer service to promote this aspect of social work. In 1916, Emelyn Peck, who later prepared an important United States Children's Bureau publication, became the department's manager. Further reflecting the department's significance, the RSF asked it to move its offices to the RSF Building, the famous building that also housed several other national social service organizations. By 1917, the department leaders decided to establish an independent agency. Discussions and activities in New York subsequently led to the establishment in 1917 of the AASW as the National Social Workers' Exchange (NSWE).

The NSWE's announced purpose was "to develop a better adjustment between workers and positions in the social field, to discover new opportunities, to encourage adequate preparation and professional training, to facilitate the choice of competent candidates for positions, and to secure equitable standards of employment." In August 1917, the NSWE opened its offices in the RSF Building. A committee on organization, primarily members of the former executive committee of the IBO's department for social workers, handled the transition. The early NSWE structure included a chairman, a secretary, and a treasurer. At its first meeting, at the National Conference of Social Work* in Kansas City in May 1918, the NSWE elected a twenty-five-member board of directors. New York social workers continued their activities in the NSWE, but the board included more social workers from other parts of the United States, such as Robert A. Woods of Boston and Sophonisba Breckenridge of the University of Chicago. The structure also now included the four traditional officers, and Edith Shatto King became the manager.

At the NSWE's annual meeting in 1920, the group passed a resolution to incorporate according to the laws of New York State. Also in 1920, the board of directors established a central council, which, in turn, appointed committees that reflected the NSWE's earliest concerns: jobs and standards. These included committees on placement, job analysis, training, and publicity and education. In late 1920, at a meeting attended by about two hundred members, some constitutional changes were made. For instance, the placement department was disbanded, and its activities became part of the following new activities: recruiting service, job analysis, and information service. Suggesting its development as a professional organization, in December 1920, the NSWE first published *The Compass,* the agency's official journal. At a meeting on February 8, 1921, the members discussed an appropriate name change, and in June, the group proposed becoming the American Social Workers. To centralize work and make operations more efficient, the NSWE established a nine-member executive committee. An important development occurred in early 1921, when settlement house pioneer Graham R. Taylor, the famous founder of Chicago Commons, became the national director, the chief executive officer. The NSWE continued to operate as a nonprofit employment agency, but it became clear that social work needed a professional organization similar to the recently founded American Association of Hospital Social Workers.*

Discussions in *The Compass* helped to promote the creation of the AASW in 1921. The first president of the AASW was Owen Lovejoy, and the structure included three vice-presidents, a secretary, and a treasurer. Reflecting its continuing concern and interest, the organization held a conference on social work personnel in December 1921. In June 1922, the central council became the national council. Further solidifying the organizational structure, in October 1922, the AASW adopted requirements for establishing chapters; a new group needed at least ten charter members. Also in 1922, a report by a special committee, headed by Harry Hopkins, led to the so-called Providence resolution to have only members' dues and contributions support AASW activities after January 1, 1923; foundations and other outside support, however, continued to assist the agency, as the deadline for implementing the Providence resolution was eventually extended to January 1927. Meanwhile, in 1926, the vocational bureau, an early agency activity, separated from the AASW. In 1928, thirty-two hundred of the four thousand AASW members responded to a questionnaire; the organization used the data to publish a useful directory of its members. In 1929, prompted by social workers' endorsements of political candidates in New York, the executive committee discussed and then agreed that social workers were free to publicly support politicians, and *The Compass* carried discussions and opinions about this controversial issue. In the 1920s, the AASW was concerned with improving salaries and the status of social workers, job placement, establishing standards for accredited professional schools and the certification of trained personnel, recruiting capable people to social work, and initiating schools and brief courses for social workers. AASW activities in the 1920s seemed to confirm the point in Roy Lubove's *The Professional Altruist: The Emergence of Social Work as a Career, 1880–1930* (1965)—that in the 1920s social workers emphasized professionalization.

In the 1920s and early 1930s, the AASW had several different organizational structures. The national council became so unwieldy by 1926 that the executive committee assumed the administrative duties full time. By the early 1930s, however, administrative details overburdened the executive committee. This situation prompted a decentralization plan, through divisions. The division names reflected the primary and traditional AASW interests: personnel standards, employment practices and personnel practices, for instance. One division on government and social work had a complex history that was not atypical of agency development in American social service. In June 1931, amid the devastating signs of economic depression, the AASW established a commission on unemployment that sought to obtain information about local unemployment through AASW chapters. This data would allow the commission to study and then report on proposed government programs to deal with unemployment. Like the famous study on unemployment that Helen Hall supervised for the National Federation of Settlements,* *Case Studies of Unemployment* (1931), the AASW effort planned to study the social and economic effects of unemployment. The first chairman of this commission was, appropriately, Mary Van Kleeck, who had previously conducted studies of industrial workers. Also in the early 1930s, executives of several national social service agencies urged the Social Work Conference on Federal Action to discuss plans for influencing federal relief programs, and the steering committee of this conference became the AASW's committee on federal relief, which was under the auspices of the commission on unemployment. Discontent with this name led to the committee's being called the federal action on unemployment committee, but lack of funds led to its dissolution in April 1933. The division on government and social work, however, absorbed several of the committee's functions and became an important AASW division. With few exceptions, in the early 1930s, the AASW seemed interested only in its members' welfare.

The AASW conference in February 1934 signaled the organization's concern with public policy. Calling for federal programs to deal with the Great Depression, the conference was "a landmark in our professional history," observed *The Social Service Review,* the leading professional social work journal. The focus on welfare programs through the federal government prompted discussions that the AASW establish an office in Washington, D.C. Still constantly concerned for its members' welfare, the AASW protected against exempting social agencies' workers from the payroll tax in the proposed Social Security bill in 1935. By early 1935, there were sixty-eight chapters. At the mid-winter delegate meeting in Washington, D.C., in February 1935, the AASW was divided over the effectiveness of the federal welfare programs, but the conference did end with unanimity. A discussion of the federal work relief program concluded that this was just another form of relief and that it was administered most effectively by casework principles. There was, however, a sharp difference of opinion over AASW membership for the ineligible welfare workers who were performing important jobs in the expanding social service system. The executive committee proposed two controversial changes: to abolish the junior membership category and to raise the dues by 50 percent. One faction charged that these efforts were exclusionary, and a roll call vote defeated the proposals. To the third International Conference of Social Work in London in July 1936, the AASW reported on *Unemployment and Its Treatment in the United States,* and in 1937 the AASW published the report. A basically professional and nonradical group, the AASW did not seem enthusiastic about the Rank and File Movement of the 1930s.

In 1938, Florence Taylor, the wife of Graham Taylor, resigned as assistant executive secretary, pointing out that the executive committee and its divisions left too much decision-making to the executive secretary. Her criticism fueled the existing dissatisfaction with the divisional structure. Her further complaints were that the committees were organized too loosely, that the national office, which was still in New York City, was overburdened with administration, and that there were differences of opinion on basic policies and programs. Consequently, in 1939, to change this situation, the AASW created a new governing body, the national board of directors, that chose the executive committee from its ranks; the divisional structure ended gradually, and regionalized national committees replaced it. In early 1941, the leading committees were executive, national membership, personnel practices, government and social work, chapter, personnel practices for national staff, and nominating. This basic structure remained until the AASW was dissolved in 1955.

In the 1940s, the AASW still suffered from some internal debates and differences, but it continued its traditional activities of promoting social work and social workers' welfare. Internal dissension in the early 1940s led to the resignation, in 1942, of Executive Secretary Walter West, who had held the position since 1927. The AASW had an acting executive secretary, and then Joseph P. Anderson became the permanent agency head. Financial problems and the preoccupation of social workers with defense-related activities caused the cancellation of the 1943 and 1945 national conferences. There was some growth in the postwar period, however. In 1947, the AASW established a committee to work on appeal procedures for personnel practice violations. The agency continued to conduct research and to issue reports on developments in the field. For example, in 1948, it reported an increase in male enrollments in social work schools.

Reflecting further professional growth, in 1948, *The Compass* was renamed *The Social Work Journal*. Discussions of merging with other professional social work organizations, such as the American Association of Psychiatric Social Workers (AAPSW), led to the creation of the Temporary Inter-Association Council of Social Work Membership Organizations in which the AASW had a leading role. In 1953, the AASW issued a set of guidelines on considering complaints of members' unethical conduct, and the Delegate Conference was renamed the Delegate Assembly. After several years of discussion, the AASW merged with the Association for the Study of Community Organization, the American Association of Group Workers, The American Association of Medical Social Workers, Inc.,* the National Association of School Social Workers, the Social Work Research Group, and the AAPSW, to form the new NASW, providing the single, unified professional organization the AASW had wanted.

The primary sources for studying the AASW's history include the agency's papers on file at the Social Welfare History Archives at the University of Minnesota, Minneapolis. *The Compass* and the IBO's published annual reports contained information about the early years of AASW. *The Social Work Journal, The Social Service Review,* and *The Survey,* each contained materials about the AASW, as did the files of *The New York Times*.

Mary Jane Fout, "American Association of Social Workers," in *Descriptive Inventories of Collections in the Social Welfare History Archives Center* (1970), 208–214, is a helpful brief history, but there does not appear to be any full-length, scholarly history of the AASW.

AMERICAN ASSOCIATION OF SOCIETIES FOR ORGANIZING CHARITIES: see FAMILY SERVICE ASSOCIATION OF AMERICA.

AMERICAN ASSOCIATION OF WORKERS FOR THE BLIND (AAWB). In the nineteenth century, one of the major social services for the blind was providing educational services for such people. Schools to teach the blind, both public and private, sprung up around the country. In 1895, a group of people concerned with educating the blind met in St. Louis, Missouri, and established the American Association of Workers for the Blind (AAWB) as the American Blind Peoples Higher Education and General Improvement Fund (ABPHEGIF). The most important figure in the group of founders was Ambrose T. Shotwell of Lansing, Michigan, who had taught at the Arkansas School for the Blind and who then served as librarian at the Michigan School for the Blind. Shotwell became an early president and leader of the ABPHEGIF and the AAWB. As its initial name implied, the organization developed an early and persistent interest in the education of the blind. It began to expand its concerns in the late 1890s, when it showed interest in pensions and retreats, especially for older blind persons. The improvement of conditions of the blind at existing colleges and in special colleges for the blind, however, remained the focus of the early organization, which became the AAWB in 1905. The AAWB essentially conducted its activities at its biennial meetings and thus developed as a professional conference in the field of social service.

In the first decades of the twentieth century, the newly named AAWB developed further organizational structures and initiated new concerns and movements to improve the condition of the blind. In 1907, for instance, the biennial convention established four committees that indicated the AAWB's interests in higher education, federal pensions for the blind, a uniform system of embossed type, and prevention of blindness. At the 1907 conference, the delegates also discussed such issues as nurseries for blind babies and the occupations of the blind in the United States. In the Progressive era, the AAWB demonstrated further concern for the welfare of the blind; in 1909 it called for a national bureau of information on the blind and blindness, a census of the blind, and, true to the Progressive faith in public education as a key element in dealing with a problem, improved publicity about the condition of the blind in America. In the pre–World War I years, the AAWB pressed closer to a national uniform printing method, establishing in 1917 the Revised Braille Grade 1–1½. In the following year, two national organizations in the field of services to the blind, the American Association of Instructors for the Blind (AAIB) and the American Printing House for the Blind,* endorsed this standard. In 1917, the newly established legislative committee of the AAWB drafted a bill to provide noninstitutional relief for the blind.

In the 1920s, the AAWB continued to conduct its activities to protect the interests of the blind at its biennial conventions. In 1921, it played a key role in establishing the American Foundation for the Blind* (AFB) as a central organization. It developed cordial ties with the AFB, which helped the older organization to pursue some of its concerns, such as in 1927, when the AFB worked to protect broom shops for the blind against the advances in this field by prison industries. Other issues concerning the AAWB in the 1920s included the social adjustment of the blind in schools and beyond, the vocational adjustment of the blind, and housing problems. In 1927, the AAWB appealed to federal officials, including the federal Tariff Commission (see *Government Agencies*), to increase the duties on imported rag rugs, which were competing with workshops for the blind for the American market.

In the years before World War II, the AAWB continued to work to improve conditions for the blind. In 1931 it established its committee on ethics to develop and implement standards for workers in institutions serving the blind. The AAWB participated little in the legislative advances for the blind in the 1930s, but it maintained its concern for the welfare of the blind. In 1939, for example, it urged local agencies to develop friendly visitor services for the lonely adult blind, and it recommended that railroads charge only one fare for a blind person and the accompanying traveling guide. Late in the decade, the AAWB tried again, unsuccessfully, to unite with the AAIB. In 1941, both to improve services and to promote professionalization in the field, the AAWB established a board of professional standards to certify home teachers of the adult blind.

Like other national organizations dealing with the handicapped, the AAWB participated in the post–World War II rehabilitation movement. It also worked to strengthen its organizational structure. The AAWB cooperated with the federal Veterans Administration (VA) (see *Government Agencies*) in caring for blinded veterans. In 1947, the AAWB changed its administrative structure by establishing eight new interest groups within the organization, such as rehabilitation specialists and librarians from libraries for the blind. The new structure provided for each of the eight groups to elect one of its members to serve on the board of directors, which the organization reduced from sixteen to thirteen members. The other members of the board continued to be the five officers: the president, two vice-presidents, a secretary general, and a treasurer, each serving two-year terms. In 1949 the AAWB added the position of past president to the board. To streamline the organization further, in 1947 the AAWB dissolved some ineffective committees, such as the one on vocational guidance and the joint advisory committee on research. In 1950, the AAWB established its ninth interest group, business enterprises counselors and vending stand specialists, which then elected the fifteenth member of the board of directors. In 1951, the AAWB strongly condemned the VA for its declining activities in helping war-blinded veterans, and in 1953, the convention highlighted the need for improved rehabilitation of the rural blind. Most importantly, in July 1953, the AAWB adopted its code of ethics, which became the basis for awarding the seal of good practice to local agencies and organizations. A permanent committee on ethics, established in 1952, considered applicants for this seal. In 1955, at the AAWB convention in Quebec, Canada, a long-range planning committee recommended administrative and structural changes, but the AAWB generally ignored them.

Despite the lack of interest in the Quebec recommendations of 1955, the AAWB implemented further organizational changes in the 1960s. Responding to recommendations from the special committee on structure and fiscal control, in 1961 the AAWB established a home teachers' certification committee as a regular component of the agency, and it realigned the interest groups to number six. The AAWB also changed its officers to a president, a president-elect, a corporate secretary, and a treasurer. It also hired an executive secretary, responsible to the board of directors and its executive committee of seven. Under the first executive secretary, Dr. Gordon B. Connor, the AAWB began to develop research projects in the national office. Grants from the Vocational Rehabilitation Administration (see *Government Agencies*) helped the AAWB to compile a bibliography and to develop teaching demonstration programs and an annual publication in the field of blindness. The proposal in 1963 to regionalize the structure of the AAWB, featuring regional workshops, was implemented successfully in the mid- and late 1960s. In 1964, with a grant from the Department of Health, Education, and Welfare (DHEW) AAWB began to issue its annual *Blindness*. In the late 1960s, AAWB developed plans to expand the organization, and by 1970, there were twenty-eight chapters, covering forty-one states and the District of Columbia. During this period, the AAWB joined with other agencies to reverse the secretary of DHEW's decision to abolish the federal Division for the Blind and Visually Handicapped.

The loss of executive officers proved to be a continuing problem for the AAWB. Another crisis occurred in 1973, when, still without an executive director, the agency's federal grants were expiring. The board of directors decided in 1973 to increase individual dues. This new funding helped the AAWB to continue publication of its *Blindness* and its *Contemporary Papers*. Also in 1973, the AAWB inaugurated its job exchange. In 1975, there were thirty-one chapters covering nearly every state and several Canadian provinces.

The sources for studying the AAWB's history include the reports from AAWB officers in the published *Proceedings*. There is information about the AAWB in such journals as *Outlook for the Blind*.

Frances A. Koestler, *The Unseen Majority: A Social History of Blindness in America* (1976), discusses the AAWB, and Norman Yoder, "AAWB, 1895–1964," in *AAWB Annual, 1964*, 151–175, is a helpful account.

AMERICAN ASSOCIATION ON MENTAL DEFICIENCY (AAMD).
During the nineteenth century, institutions for the feebleminded and for idiots were established in the United States. Physicians affiliated with these institutions began to discuss common issues and concerns informally. In 1876, representatives from the Pennsylvania Training School took the initiative in organizing a formal group. Responding to the call to establish an organization were Dr. Edward Seguin of New York City, an international authority on the education of the mentally retarded, Dr. Harvey B. Wilbur of Syracuse, New York, Dr. Gustavus A. Doren of Columbus, Ohio, Dr. Charles T. Wilbur of Jacksonville, Illinois, and Dr. H. M. Knight of Barre, Massachusetts. Each was a physician by training and administered either a state-supported or private institution for the mentally retarded. Consequently, on June 6, 1876, in Media, Pennsylvania, the American Association on Mental Deficiency (AAMD) was established as the Association of Medical Officers of American Institutions for Idiotic and Feeble-Minded Persons (AMOAIIFMP). Created to discuss all questions relating to the causes, conditions, and statistics of idiocy and to the management, training, and education of idiots and the feebleminded, the AMOAIIFMP was the first national organization to concern itself with the general welfare of the mentally retarded. The organization further attempted to influence the establishment and fostering of institutions for idiots and the feebleminded.

Seguin was elected AMOAIIFMP's first president, and dues were set at five dollars annually. At its organizational meeting in June 1876, *The Chicago Journal of Mental Science* was suggested as the official organ of the association. The organization established no permanent headquarters, although the secretary-treasurer provided continuity for his duties by checking membership, receiving dues, billing for memberships, keeping the books on expenses, paying expenses, and acting as the editor of early publications. The original constitution, adopted in 1876, provided for a president, vice-president, secretary, treasurer, and an executive committee of three. In 1920 provision was made for a council to handle the association affairs. During the first decade after its creation, the AMOAIIFMP met annually. Meetings centered on the delivery of technical papers on the subject of mental retardation. Some attempt was made to standardize the collection of scientific data for the various institutions throughout the nation. Membership remained small and was largely composed of superintendents of institutions for the mentally retarded. The association's publications consisted of the minutes of the annual business meetings and papers delivered at the meeting.

By 1886, the association was focusing its attention on institutional operations, as facilities for the mentally retarded became larger, more numerous, and of a residential nature. Technical papers presented at the annual meeting dealt with the surgical aspects of helping the mentally retarded. Association membership during the second decade still consisted largely of medical personnel. Interest in the epileptic also surfaced during the late 1880s, although it never became a major concern of the organization.

At the opening of the third decade of AMOAIIFMP's existence in the mid-1890s, the organization still remained relatively small, boasting only sixty-two members. In September 1896, the association launched the *Journal of Psycho-Asthenics;* it was the only periodical in the English language of general circulation devoted exclusively to the interests of the feebleminded and epileptic. The establishment of a publication program reflected the increasing professionalization of the AMOAIIFMP. Journal articles focused on case studies and placed special emphasis on eugenics and hereditary influences of mental retardation. Eugenics, which Charles B. Davenport has defined as "the science of the improvement of the human race by better breeding," dealt with the study of human heredity and its application to human propagation.

At the turn of the century, AMOAIIFMP membership came to be more broad-based, drawing from educators, administrators, and medical personnel alike. Professor Naomi Noseworthy of Columbia University, Charlotte Hoskins, a New Jersey teacher, and Dr. William Healy of Chicago, a psychologist, were among those reporting on special classes in public schools. Social service professionals remained largely outside the organization, although such national figures as William P. Letchworth, New York reformer and philanthropist, and Joseph P. Byers, secretary of Ohio's State Board of Charities, brought attention to the plight of the mentally retarded. Increased attention was given to the place of special classes for the mentally retarded in the public-school system. The mentally retarded were viewed as a threat to the community, and professionals such as Henry H. Goddard of the Training School at Vineland, New Jersey, Alexander Johnson, former superintendent of the Indiana School for the Feeble-Minded, and Dr. Walter E. Fernald of Massachusetts advocated the segregation of the retarded from society into institutions and farm colonies. In 1906 the organization was renamed the American Association for the Study of the Feeble-Minded (AASFM), and in 1910, the AASFM formally recognized the nature of mental deficiency with its classification of the various grades of mental retardation into moron, idiot, and imbecile. Annual meetings emphasized testing, the defective delinquent, and sterilization. As a result, the AASFM stood in the front ranks of the eugenics movement in the United States. The emphasis on science placed the AASFM in close relation to the general trends of the Progressive era reform movements. The discussion of eugenics and defective delinquents paralleled the dominant themes of National Conference of Charities and Correction* (NCCC) meetings. In 1917, the AASFM reversed itself on the menace of the feeble-minded, publicly recanting its old superstitions. The reversal was due in large measure to the results of army tests and to the publication of follow-up studies of the feebleminded. Because of American entry into World War I and strained financial conditions, the AASFM curtailed the publication of the *Journal of Psycho-Asthenics* in 1918.

Opening its fiftieth year of service in 1926, the AASFM numbered nearly 230 members. The interdisciplinary nature of the organization brought it into contact with other associations dealing with the condition of the mentally ill. It worked closely with the National Committee for Mental Hygiene* in developing a uniform statistical system for residential facilities for the mentally retarded. It sent delegates to the International Congress on Mental Hygiene in 1924 and planned annual meetings to be held a week apart from those of the American Psychiatric Association (APA). In 1926, members rejected an attempt at amalgamation with the APA because of a concern for the loss of organizational identity. Moving into its second half-century, the AASFM sought to return the mentally retarded to the community from the institution rather than to segregate them from society.

At the annual convention held at Boston in 1933, the organization underwent a third name change to the AAMD. Five years later, on March 11, 1938, in Delaware County, Pennsylvania, the AAMD incorporated for the first time. By 1940, with 645 members, the publication program was revived with the issuance of the *American Journal of Mental Deficiency*. Editorial comments in the first issue noted that the journal looked beyond custodianship and would investigate arrests in human development. In recognition of the varied aspects of mental retardation, the journal would include sections on genetics, neurology, psychology, psychiatry, education, and sociology.

During the 1940s and 1950s, AAMD grew rapidly in size and impact. Its growth came as it acknowledged that the study of human deficiency went beyond one professional group to include psychologists, psychiatrists, teachers, social workers, prison officials, and physicians. With nearly six thousand members in 1959, the AAMD began to develop a greater advocacy role than before. It actively lobbied Congress and federal agencies on legislation affecting the mentally retarded. It commissioned Herschel V. Nisonger of the Bureau of Special and Adult Education at Ohio State University to undertake "A Study of the Central Office and Executive Leadership Function of the American Association on Mental Deficiency in Relation to Future Needs and Resources." One of the recommendations of the study was the creation of the position of executive director. By 1960, the AAMD hired its first executive director. Prior to the creation of the post, executive leadership was voluntary. The administrative details of the association were handled by the council, publications by the editor, and inquiries by the secretary. During the 1960s the AAMD reflected upon the changing roles of institutions, accepted new challenges, and sought out community alternatives to institutions.

From the beginning the AAMD had taken an active interest in research leading to the prevention or mitigation of mental deficiency, but nearly a century passed before it actively engaged in research itself. In September 1955, the AAMD undertook a special project on technical planning with a grant from the federal National Institute of Mental Health (see *Government Agencies*). The impact of that project has stimulated research, aided the proper classification of the institutionalized mentally retarded, and promoted cooperative relationships between college and institutional personnel working with the retarded.

Increasing interest by educators and mental health professionals in the general welfare of the mentally subnormal and deficient person brought a new thrust in the 1970s. Autism, hyperactivity, speech, and language were the new catchwords and concerns of the 9,500-member association in the mid-1970s.

No comprehensive history of the AAMD has been written. Glenn E. Milligan, "History of the American Association on Mental Deficiency," *American Journal of Mental Deficiency* 66 (November 1961): 357–269, is a brief chronology of highlights in the organization's history. Elwyn Institute, Elwyn, Pennsylvania, is the AAMD depository for the history of mental retardation and maintains AAMD's archives. Peter L. Tyor, "Segregation or Surgery: The Mentally Retarded in America, 1850–1920" (Ph.D. dissertation, Northwestern University, 1972), places the AAMD into the historical context of the mental health movement. Mark H. Haller, *Eugenics: Hereditarian Attitudes in American Thought* (1963), documents the viewpoints of the AAMD membership and gives an extremely brief notation of formal association positions. The most valuable source for the study of the AAMD are the *Proceedings of the Association of Medical Officers of American Institutions for Idiotic and Feeble-Minded Persons*, the *Journal of Psycho-Asthenics, Proceedings of the American Association for the Study of the Feeble-Minded,* and the *American Journal of Mental Deficiency,* all of which contain information on annual business meetings and scholarly papers on mental retardation.

Frank R. Levstik

AMERICAN CANCER SOCIETY, INC. (ACS). In the early twentieth century, despite the widespread reluctance to speak publicly about cancer due to its association with death, medical organizations initiated discussions of the subject. At the 1905 meeting of the American Medical Association, the organization's president pointed out the need for a group to help reduce cancer deaths. Later in 1905, the gynecological section of the International Congress of Arts and Science appointed a committee of three members to study such an organization and to report to the AMA. These plans faded, but at a symposium of the American Gynecological Society in Baltimore in May 1912, a three-member committee again emerged to develop plans for such an organization. In March 1913, this group influenced Dr. Clement Cleveland, a prominent New York surgeon, to appoint a larger group, which included Dr. Livingston Farrand, an important public health activist, and James Speyer, a prominent New York banker who was active in many charities and civic organizations, such as the Charity Organization Society of the City of New York* (COS). This committee continued to meet in the spring of 1913. Valentine Everett Macy, a banker, philanthropist, and commissioner of charities and corrections in Westchester County, suggested that the American Gynecological Society discuss the organizing work publicly and that the New York group stay in the background. Subsequently, in May 1913, when the society and the Congress of American Physicians and Surgeons met jointly in Washington, D.C., the negotiations matured. Dr. Frederick L. Hoffman, a statistician who was active in the American Association for Labor Legislation,* proposed the new organization, and the three-member committee presented its report, which urged further meetings. On May 22, 1913, at the Harvard Club in New York City, a group of ten physicians and five laymen met and established a new organization. Elsie Mead, Dr. Cleveland's daughter, brought the group of physicians and laymen together after years of discussions. Dr. Cleveland convened the group, which resolved to establish a national organization and then elected as president George C. Clark, a roentgenologist, and as secretary, Thomas M. Debevoise, a successful New York attorney and the partner of Mead's husband. The same group of fifteen people met again on June 4, 1913, and named the organization the American Society for the Control of Cancer (ASCC).

The ASCC structure developed gradually. The agency elected traditional officers and established both a board of directors and an executive committee, which met monthly and which developed subcommittees. The most important and active committees in the early period were those on organization, statistics, publicity, and ways and means, which Mrs. Mead chaired. The ASCC hired as executive secretary Curtis Lakeman, the former secretary to the New York City commissioner of health. Apparently inspired by the establishment of the ASCC, similar local groups began around the country. In 1914, the executive committee decided to work to affiliate these local organizations with the ASCC and to develop other affiliates by working through prominent doctors in particular areas. Mead developed the ASCC's financial basis, which had been generally unstable; because the organization was unincorporated, it could not receive bequests. In

October 1915, each board and executive committee member pledged responsibility for raising $100 each. In late 1915, Mead initiated a guarantee fund of $15,000, and in one month alone, she obtained fifteen pledges of $1,000 each. In 1916, the ASCC moved from its original headquarters in the Charities Building in New York to new quarters in uptown Manhattan, a symbol of slow but steady organizational growth.

The early ASCC activities also developed gradually. Committed to educating the public about cancer, which was still considered an improper subject for public discussion, ASCC members, particularly Dr. Frederick Hoffman, lectured in cities throughout the country in the first year of the new organization. ASCC members also conducted "parlor discussions," chiefly through local affiliates of the General Federation of Women's Clubs (GFWC). The ASCC developed its own printing service, and in January 1918, it began to publish its monthly *Campaign Notes,* the first official bulletin. The organization influenced the study on cancer deaths in the United States published by the United States Bureau of the Census in the fall of 1917. No significant organizational changes occurred until Spring 1917 when the ASCC established its national council, consisting of the medical men from the board of directors, to develop medical policies.

The postwar years brought the ASCC increased public attention, but, despite some major organizational developments, it still was not an effective national agency. In the war era, the executive committee focused on organizing affiliates, building them around state medical societies, and, in some states, using congressional districts or, as in New Jersey, Colorado, and West Virginia, local communities. Efforts by the ASCC's national council of physicians led in 1921 to a grant from the Commonwealth Fund* to sponsor a field director, the first of whom resigned suddenly in July 1923. His replacement did not begin until June 1924. Despite field activities, by 1928, the state divisions remained ineffective organizations. In February 1923, the ASCC established the position of managing director to supervise staff work. Dr. George A. Soper, a consulting engineer in public health, filled the post. In late 1923, Soper's "Statement of Principles and Policies," modified slightly by the executive committee, became the basis for activities through the 1930s: to develop the ASCC as a source of information; to insist on accurate statements about cancer but to use fear as the force to motivate people to action; to develop an endowment fund; and to establish cancer clinics and institutions. Sectional animosities, especially against New York, pervaded the ASCC in the 1920s. Partly to reduce these tensions, the organization worked to obtain a national charter from the United States Senate. The Senate's Judiciary Committee, however, did not cooperate, and on May 15, 1922, so not to lose bequests, the ASCC was incorporated in New York State. Mead worked constantly to raise funds. Between 1919 and 1923, for example, she successfully brought in two thousand new members. In this four-year period, the ASCC budget grew from $10,000 to $60,000. Responding partly to Soper's "Statement" in 1923 and also to the delay of an anticipated sizable grant, the ASCC hired professional fund raisers to develop the successful drive to raise a million dollar endowment fund.

ASCC activities in the late 1920s were more successful than its organizational efforts. Late in 1921, the ASCC sponsored the successful first national cancer week. A publication in 1922, *What We Know About Cancer,* was distributed widely in the country and in England. In the early 1920s, similar messages appeared in such journals as the popular *The Delineator* and *The Survey,* the leading social work journal. Aided significantly by an $8,000 grant from the Laura Spelman Rockefeller Memorial (see *Foundations and Research Associations*), Mead's idea led to the development in 1921 of the ASCC's first film, "The Reward of Courage." In September 1926, the ASCC sponsored an international cancer symposium at Lake Mohawk, New York. Following internal debate, the organization agreed in 1927 to referee a New York City businessman's offer of $100,000 for the person developing the cancer cure. Abounding with quackery, the incident helped to give the ASCC some unwanted notoriety. In October 1928, the executive committee forced Dr. Soper's resignation, ending the first phase of the history of the ASCC.

In its next phase, the ACSS focused on organizational developments. In 1928, the board of directors was expanded from five to thirty members. Only three board members came from west of the Allegheny Mountains, demonstrating that the ASCC was still a regional rather than a national agency. Also in 1928, Dr. Clarence Little, former president of the universities of Maine and Michigan and a highly regarded administrator, became the managing director. He quickly emphasized educating the medical profession, exhibits, literature, and speakers. In the early 1930s, retrenchments occurred; in January 1932, staff pay was cut 10 percent, and in April 1932, the ASCC abolished the position of executive secretary and halted many publications.

An important split developed between the ASCC and its New York affiliate. Conflicts over sales of Christmas booklets and over dues occurred in the early 1930s. In 1932, the ASCC executive committee voted to return to local affiliates 80 percent of locally collected dues. Partly because New Yorkers contributed heavily to the ASCC, a result apparently of Mead's efforts, the New York group incorporated itself independently in 1936 so it could collect bequests in its own, not in the ASCC's, name. Only in 1939, following heated discussions, did the New York committee agree to honor national ASCC practices, but personality conflicts sustained the dissension through the 1940s. In the late 1930s and 1940s, New York City did not participate, for instance, in the important Women's Field Army (WFA); thus small towns often attracted more ASCC members than did the New York area.

The WFA proved to be an important development. Managing Director Little initiated contacts with the GFWC, leading ultimately to the establishment of the WAF in 1936. His presentation to the GFWC advisory council in May 1933, focusing on deaths from breast and uterine cancer, influenced the GFWC in 1933 to endorse cancer education as a major activity. The GFWC's successful work led to Little's proposal in 1936 of a WFA, which began to enlist members in the spring of 1937. The WFA had its own organizational structure, held conventions, and, by the end of 1938, cooperated well with ASCC affiliates in some forty-five states. Its importance became clear in 1939 when its $40,000 in contributions represented about 60 percent of the ASCC budget. The WFA established clinics, campaigned successfully for state funds for cancer control, donated hospital beds, and the like. During World War II, the WFA conducted two national training schools designed to give women the knowledge to deal better with medical committees in their localities. In the late 1940s, the ACSS overshadowed and neglected the WFA, which lost its identity and dissolved in 1951.

Beginning in 1943, the efforts of philanthropist Mrs. Albert Lasker changed the history and direction of the organization. Upset by the recent death of a friend from cancer and astonished that the ASCC did not have a strong research program, Mrs. Lasker acted. She offered funds to publish a study of research in the field. Negotiations between Mrs. Lasker and Managing Director Little led eventually to the work of the advertising agency of Emerson Foote, a brilliant young business associate of Mrs. Lasker's husband. Foote urged the group to call itself the American Cancer Society (ACS), a name it adopted in 1944, and to call the corps of volunteers the Field Army to show that both sexes actively supported the organization's work. Foote stressed the importance of publicity and fund drives. Through Mrs. Lasker, the president of the United States Chamber of Commerce and one of the most popular business personalities at the time, Eric Johnston, agreed to head the drive in 1945. Foote's and Johnston's advice led to the establishment of a governing board, which quickly became the executive council, a lay group composed of such business leaders as airline president Thomas Braniff, Albert Lasker, and Elmer H. Bobst, president of Hoffman-LaRoche, the pharmaceutical company. In early 1945, Mrs. Lasker retained the John Price Jones Corporation to help the Field Army and the ACS raise new funds. In 1944, the organization established the Cancer Research Foundation (see *Foundations and Research Associations*), and Mrs. Lasker solicited the initial contributions.

The involvement of lay leaders, such as Mrs. Lasker and Elmer Bobst, prompted other significant changes. A joint meeting in May 1945 of the executive committee, chaired by physicians, and the lay executive council led quickly to a change in the bylaws minimizing the role of physicians. A sixty-member board of directors had thirty-six lay people, and the executive committee became all lay people. The board appointed a nine-member professional executive committee to supervise the professional program, but lay dominance became evident. The executive committee appointed an executive business director as well as the medical and scientific director. Torn between the two factions, Dr. Little resigned in 1946. Annoyed at their apparent ouster, the physicians precipitated further changes in early 1946 when the board of directors was reduced to fifty-six members, half of whom represented the physician-scientist group. Further compromise called for a physician-scientist president and a lay chairman of the board. The new plan created four major standing committees: medical and scientific, research, finance, and field organizations, broken into seven regions, providing the structure for a national program. The generally autonomous affiliates retained 60 percent of funds raised regionally for research, administration, publicity, and other activities. During the reorganization, the ACS ended the WFA, but women nevertheless continued to help to popularize cancer's seven danger signals. In the late 1940s, women volunteers also popularized the Pap test for detecting uterine cancer, which Dr. George Papanicolaou had developed in 1926. At the beginning of 1947, there were around twenty-five hundred units of the ACS, with over a half million volunteers. Guarding its own fund-raising campaign, in early 1946, the ACS decided that local affiliates should not join community chests or other local fund-raising federations.

The reorganization also promoted, as Mrs. Lasker had hoped, an increased research and professional program. In 1945, the ACS decided to focus research through a fellowship program; it had sixty-seven fellows in its first five years. The ACS also developed a grants-in-aid program. In September 1947, it began making grants to scientific and medical institutions, which by 1950, attracted nearly half of all the ACS research funds. In 1951, the ACS established a six-member institutional grants policy advisory committee, which broadened eligible institutions to include those not associated with medical schools and their affiliated research hospitals. With the National Cancer Institute (see *Government Agencies*), the ACS sponsored the first national cancer conference in 1949 and another in 1952. In 1947, the ACS had begun publishing *Cancer Current Literature,* a monthly bibliography. In 1950, it initiated *CA-A Bulletin of Cancer Progress,* another professional publication.

Continuing and expanding research in the 1950s brought the ACS closer to the medical community. In 1952, the organization began a long-range study to determine the relationship between smoking and lung cancer, and it sponsored the first lung cancer conference. In 1954, the first findings of the study which showed a direct association between smoking and lung cancer, appeared in *The Journal of the American Medical Association.* With other agencies and the pharmaceutical industry, the ACS helped to establish a cancer chemotherapy national service center to be conducted by the federal National Cancer Institute. Following other national health agencies, the ACS began its lifetime research professorships in 1957. In 1959, it inaugurated its six-year nationwide cancer prevention study to determine environmental factors and conditions that might cause cancer. Fund raising continued successfully, and in 1956, the ACS adopted "fight cancer with a checkup and a check" as its crusade slogan. Highlights of patient services in the 1950s included a pilot project, with other agencies, to establish patterns for mass examinations of women for early uterine cancer by a cytologic technique in 1955. Two years later, based on this project, the ACS initiated a ten point uterine cytology project in Toledo, Ohio. Continuing a long-time agency concern, in

1954, the ACS established its committee on new or unproved methods of treatment as the central agency to combat cancer quackery.

The 1960s brought an all-out crusade against cancer. In October 1963, further developments established the present-day organization of the ACS. The reorganization hoped to reinstitute the lay-medical balance, to discontinue regional meetings, to increase division participation in policy decisions, to provide proportional representation according to population, and to reduce the size of the board of directors. In 1965, the ACS established long-term goals by focusing on six specific cancer sites as targets. During this period, the ACS increased its efforts against lung cancer. In 1966, the expanded film program included television network spots on the hazards of cigarette smoking. In 1967, the ACS helped to organize the world conference on smoking and health, attended by over five hundred delegates from thirty-four countries. The agency also adopted a policy of using the voluntary end to all cigarette advertising in the media. By the late 1960s, the anticigarette smoking campaign was contributing to the decline of cigarette sales. In the middle of the decade, the ACS emphasized developing new affiliates, especially in and around cities. In the late 1960s, it widened its range of educational information available in Spanish, and it conducted more intensive efforts to develop programs among low-income and hard-to-reach groups. Based partly on a research evaluation in the mid-1960s, professional research expanded consistently. In 1967, for instance, over $18 million was spent on research; in 1969, the figure reached more than $21.6 million. The appointment of a council for analysis and projection sharpened the focus of ACS's research programs. In 1969, the agency began its new clinical investigation program to support clinicians and scientists in the field. In 1969, the organization sponsored a world conference on cancer of the uterus. With the United States Public Health Service (USPHS) (see *Government Agencies*), the ACS cosponsored a national conference on breast cancer in 1969, when the Reach to Recovery program became an integral part of ACS's expanded rehabilitation program for women who have had breast surgery. This activity was begun in 1952 by Terese J. K. Lasser of New York City, who after her own surgery developed a counseling service for new patients by volunteers who had had surgery. In the late 1960s, the ACS developed an employee education program in such states as Illinois and Florida. The fund-raising campaign continued to set yearly records.

ACS-sponsored research and public education continued and increased in the 1970s as the agency developed new services for patients. Beginning in about 1970, the ACS instituted a concentrated drive to get all women to have the Pap test by 1976. The ACS designated the year 1972 as the Year of the Patient. During this period, with the federal government, the ACS helped to establish about twenty-five breast cancer detection centers throughout the country. In 1972, a national conference on human values in cancer focused on patient services. The ACS participated in the famous studies of occupational hazards and cancer by Dr. Irving J. Selikoff of Mount Sinai Hospital in New York City.

Other major patient services in the mid-1970s included the ACS-sponsored International Association of Laryngectomees, and for patients with surgery of the bowel and bladder, the United Ostomy Association, two self-help organizations. The ACS also supported the training of enterostomal therapists, a new type of allied medical specialist who counsels and otherwise assists patients with ostomies. The ACS also promoted intensified screening for breast cancer by the new technique of mammography.

The primary sources for studying the ACS's history include the published *Annual Reports*. *The New York Times* reports the ACS's major activities. The files of the organization are located in its headquarters in New York City. These records are available only to qualified scholars.

Donald Francis Shaughnessy used the ACS's files for his "The Story of the American Cancer Society" (Ph.D. dissertation, Columbia University, 1957), a detailed organizational history. Richard Carter, *The Gentle Legions* (1961), contains a brief history of the ACS. There are several agency publications indicating organizational highlights and programs.

AMERICAN CHILD HEALTH ASSOCIATION (ACHA). In the late nineteenth and early twentieth centuries, one of the most difficult and disturbing social problems in American cities was the high rate of infant mortality. A host of social service agencies and reform-minded pediatricians had developed various plans to reduce infant mortality in cities, but even in the first decade of the twentieth century, babies continued to die at high rates. In 1907, Dr. Helen C. Putnam, a physician from Providence, Rhode Island, who was active in social causes, attended a child health conference in England, where there was also considerable interest in preventing infant mortality. Influenced by British developments, Dr. Putnam proposed in June 1908 that the American Academy of Medicine (AAM) appoint a special five-member committee with authority to organize and to conduct a conference on preventing infant mortality. Her efforts resulted in a two-day conference on infant mortality and child health held at Yale University in New Haven, Connecticut, in November 1909. Immediately after the conference, on November 13, 1909, the American Child Health Association (ACHA) was established as the American Association for the Study and Prevention of Infant Mortality (AASPIM). Dr. Putnam was the most important figure in the establishment of the AASPIM. The five-member AAM committee, which included Dr. Putnam, in turn appointed an advisory committee of thirteen members, including such prominent social reformers and social workers as Jane Addams of Hull-House* in Chicago and Samuel McCune Lindsay of the National Child Labor Committee* (NCLC). The organizing meeting adopted a constitution and elected a forty-eight-member board of directors, which then designated six of its members as the executive committee. The AASPIM also chose as its first president, Dr. John H. Knox, Jr., of Baltimore, a pediatrician active in social movements. As one student suggested later, the AASPIM seemed patterned after the National Association for the Study and Prevention of Tuberculosis* (NASPT) in name, organization, and principles.

The early AASPIM activities, except the annual meeting, were conducted largely by committees, such as the committees of birth registration, nursing, and social work, which cooperated actively with the National Organization for Public Health Nursing* (NOPHN), and medical prevention, which conducted studies of infant deaths in institutions. For over ten years, the AASPIM developed and used a traveling exhibit on infant mortality, and the agency helped to stimulate and to develop birth registration areas and local child health organizations. Its first headquarters was a small office at the Medico-Chirurgical Faculty Buildings of the Johns Hopkins University School of Medicine, where Dr. Knox taught. In early 1910, the Maryland Association for the Study and Prevention of Infant Mortality became the first affiliated organization of the AASPIM. By its first annual meeting in November 1910, 503 paid members, including thirty-three affiliate societies, belonging to the AASPIM. The entire staff consisted of a general executive, Gertrude B. Knipp, and one assistant.

World War I and the era of postwar domestic reconstruction brought expansion to the AASPIM. Influenced by the tragedies of war affecting childhood, such as starvation and dependency, the organization planned to deal with a broader range of child welfare activities. Consistent with its broadened visions, the agency changed its name to the American Child Hygiene Association (ACHA) in January 1919. Later that year, in her presidential address, Dr. S. Josephine Baker, the head of the pioneering Bureau of Child Hygiene of New York City, called on the ACHA to lead movements to expand government services to children. During this period, however, financial problems plagued the ACHA. In 1920, Dr. Philip Van Ingen, once labeled its "diplomatic secretary," began to approach Herbert Hoover about using funds from the American Relief Administration,* a private organization begun by the federal government, to help American children. Van Ingen's efforts succeeded, and in 1921, Hoover was elected president of the ACHA. This inaugurated Hoover's long-time interest in the ACHA, and more funds subsequently became available to the organization. It received $20,000 from the American National Red Cross,* for example, which it used to add to its staff several clerical assistants, a director of field services, and a research editor, Ellen C. Babbitt, formerly with the famous Child-Helping Department of the Russell Sage Foundation.* In 1920, the ACHA began publishing *Mother and Child*. This journal was succeeded by *The Child Health Magazine* in 1923, which was renamed *The Child Health Bulletin* in 1925. According to Carl Christian Carstens, the head of the Child Welfare League of America* and a widely respected child welfare authority, these publications were the best specialized child welfare magazines in national social work in the early to mid-1920s. Suggesting further its national leadership in the spring of 1922, the ACHA moved its offices from Baltimore to Washington, D.C., but without Knipp, who had been a very important figure in the early organization. In 1924, the organization moved its headquarters to New York City, where it remained.

The ACHA broadened its activities further when it absorbed the work of the Child Health Organization of America* (CHOA) in early 1923. As soon as he became president of the ACHA in 1921, Herbert Hoover worked to combine with the CHOA, which had been established in 1918 primarily to promote school health campaigns. With the merger, Dr. Emmett Holt, a famous pediatrician who presided over the CHOA, became the first of three vice-presidents of the new American Child Health Association (ACHA) in January 1923, when the amalgamation occurred. The ACHA was quickly incorporated on February 14, 1923, according to the laws of the state of West Virginia. The expanded ACHA changed its structure by organizing itself through divisions, such as medical service, public health relations, health education, and research. In 1923, Courtenay Dinwiddie, an important leader in child welfare work who later headed the NCLC, became the general executive in charge of administrative affairs of the ACHA.

From the early 1920s until it disbanded in 1935, the ACHA was the leading national organization in child health work. Beginning in 1920, the division of research published the yearly *Statistical Report of Infant Mortality,* a valuable source for social and health workers. In 1923, the agency initiated its nearly ten-year Better Milk campaign. In 1924, the ACHA began to develop a program of health education in American Indian schools in the Southwest and the Midwest. The ACHA's *A Health Survey of 86 Cities* (1925) stimulated local health activities and also led the ACHA to develop, with the American Public Health Association,* appraisal forms to help rate the efficiency of local health departments. In the early 1920s, in cooperation with the Commonwealth Fund* (CF), the ACHA developed child health demonstration projects in selected communities. These demonstrations and other ACHA campaigns led especially to the growth of nutrition clinics for children. At the request of local school and health officials, the ACHA conducted a study of nearly 180,000 children in 156 cities and rural localities in forty-two states. The division of public health's investigation of Negro midwives in the South led to certain reforms. Throughout the 1920s and early 1930s, the organization sponsored annually May Day, a well-publicized reminder of the importance of child hygiene. In 1928, President Calvin Coolidge proclaimed it as Child Health Day, a tradition that later American presidents continued. May Day, ACHA studies of local child health conditions, and publicity campaigns all promoted child hygiene work in communities throughout the country.

In late 1925, Dinwiddie resigned as general executive to head the ACHA demonstrations programs. The former Kansas state health commissioner, Dr. Samuel J. Crumbine, replaced him. In 1926, when the ACHA terminated its child health demonstrations, Dinwiddie left the organization to head demonstrations for the Commonwealth Fund. Prominent, reform-oriented physicians, such as Dr. Livingston Farrand, a renowned public health activitist, and Dr.

Thomas Wood of Columbia University, served the ACHA. Reflecting on the nature of the ACHA, in May 1927, General Executive Crumbine hoped that public consciousness of hygiene and of expanded governmental medical programs would make the ACHA unnecessary someday.

The ACHA continued its basic activities in the early 1930s. In 1931, for example, the Metropolitan Life Insurance Company asked the organization to study health activities in the New York City schools. The resulting research document, *Physical Defects—The Pathway to Correction* (1934), characteristically developed new ideas for local action in the emerging field of physical rehabilitation. But the increasingly duplicate activities of both federal agencies and other national voluntary organizations and a significant downward trend in infant mortality led the ACHA leaders to discuss dissolution. At a special meeting of the executive committee on August 13, 1935, with Dr. Crumbine's vision of 1927 a reality, the ACHA came to an end.

The primary sources for studying the ACHA's history are the variously named journals of the organization, its published *Transactions* of its annual meetings, and some of its own publications, particularly Philip Van Ingen, *The Story of the American Child Health Association* (1935), which is reprinted in *The Child Health Bulletin* (September–November 1935). The Papers of Dr. Samuel J. Crumbine at the University of Kansas Medical Library contain annual reports of the general executive and other unpublished materials, including correspondence relating to his work with the ACHA in the 1920s and 1930s. A more extensive manuscript collection relating to the ACHA in the 1920s and 1930s can be found in the Herbert Hoover Presidential Library, West Branch, Iowa. A detailed container list to the collection facilitates research in specific issues relating to the organization. Box 48 of the Dr. Arnold Gesell Papers at the Library of Congress in Washington, D.C., contains less extensive items relating to the ACHA, including minutes of various committee meetings in the 1920s and 1930s.

Walter Trattner, *Homer Folks* (1968), describes briefly Folks's role in the early AASPIM, but there are no scholarly accounts of the ACHA. Some of the interpretative statements in the text stem from Peter Romanofsky's previous research in the field of child welfare history.

AMERICAN CHILD HYGIENE ASSOCIATION: see AMERICAN CHILD HEALTH ASSOCIATION.

AMERICAN CHRISTIAN COMMITTEE FOR REFUGEES, INC. (ACCR). Amid the rise of Adolf Hitler in Germany in the mid-1930s, Protestants were fleeing Nazi Germany in increasing numbers. The League of Nations high commissioner for German refugees, James G. McDonald, suggested that a group in the United States assist these refugees. Two Protestant clergymen, Dr. Henry Smith Leiper, a secretary of the Universal Church Council, and Dr. Samuel McCrea Cavert, general secretary of the Federal Council of the Churches of

Christ in America (FCC), convened a series of luncheon meetings between Protestant church leaders and representatives from Jewish relief agencies. Following these meetings, in May 1934, in New York City the ACCR was organized as the American Committee for Christian German Refugees (ACCGR). The announcement of its establishment was made on May 21, 1934, by the first chairman, Reverend Dr. S. Parkes Cadman, the former president of the FCC. The ACCGR chose Dr. Cadman as its first chairman and Dr. Leiper as its secretary. Dr. Robert A. Ashworth became the first executive director. Other members included some of the most prominent clergymen in America, such as Dr. Henry Sloane Coffin, the president of Union Theological Seminary in New York, John Haynes Holmes, the respected minister of the Community Church in New York City, and Reverend Dr. R. A. MacGowan of the National Catholic Welfare Conference. Catholic leaders participated in the discussions, but they decided to form their own organization, so the ACCGR dealt essentially with Protestants in its early years.

Despite some problems in the very early years, the ACCGR began its work earnestly. Its purpose—to help refugees fleeing from oppression in Germany—tested the sincerity of Protestant ministers in the United States, particularly German ones, some of whom did not believe that serious problems existed in Germany. Also, some members of the National Coordinating Committee for Aid to Refugees and Emigrants Coming from Germany* (NCC), essentially a Jewish relief agency, were critical of groups they felt did not understand the full scope of the problems. Despite these frustrations, the ACCGR, whose leaders did understand the German situation, went ahead with its plans, initiating in late 1935 a campaign to raise $400,000 to aid German refugees. Executive Secretary Frank Ritchie, a former secretary of the National Council of the Young Men's Christian Association of the United States of America,* affiliated himself with people from the executive committee, who sent him to Europe to study the problem. Abroad, he strengthened ties with the International Committee for Christian German Refugees, headquartered in London. He also contacted representatives of the American Friends Service Committee* (AFSC) in Vienna, Paris, Prague, and other cities. In this period, the ACCGR began to cooperate in a plan to resettle German refugees in South America.

Influenced by the refusal of some people to believe the seriousness of events in Germany, the ACCGR felt initially that it had little work in America. But it became increasingly clear that a major immigrant relief service was needed in New York City, and ACCGR leaders contacted the National Coordinating Committee to determine which services it could provide. The ACCGR then established in New York its personal service department, helping German refugee intellectuals, for example, to file citizenship papers and locate friends from abroad in the United States. The staff of the personal service department grew quickly from one to nine workers.

By 1940, when the agency was renamed the American Committee for Christian Refugees, Inc. (ACCR), it had a new executive director, K. Brent Woodruff, who had served as field secretary of the agency. In September 1940, he replaced the late Frank Ritchie. At that point, the ACCR was working on nearly nineteen hundred cases, involving over four thousand people representing twenty-one nationalities. In 1943, with the International Rescue and Relief Committee* and the Unitarian Service Committee,* the ACCR founded the Refugee Relief Trustees to coordinate the relief work. The ACCR established its own advisory groups in fourteen cities throughout the country, such as Los Angeles, Cleveland, and Detroit, and in Toronto, Canada. Beginning in 1943, the ACCR received the bulk of its funds from the National War Fund, founded in 1943. About one-fifth of its funds, however, continued to come from church groups. In February 1944, following a visit by the ACCR's service supervisor to Cuba, Haiti, and the Dominican Republic, where conditions for refugees were especially poor, the agency established a relief office in Ciudad Trujillo. In October 1944, to emphasize its close relation with the churches in America, the agency changed its name to the American Christian Committee for Refugees, Inc. (ACCR).

Throughout its brief history, the ACCR cooperated with other agencies. In 1943–1944, it participated with three other groups in the Refugee Scholar Fund, and in early 1945, it represented the Refugee Relief Trustees in joining the National Refugee Service* (NRS), a Jewish agency, to establish the American Committee for Refugee Scholars, Writers, and Artists. The ACCR cosponsored with other agencies, such as the AFSC, the International Migration Service,* and the American Jewish Joint Distribution Committee,* the Central Locator Index, which helped to locate members of refugee families. The ACCR also cooperated with governmental agencies, lending six staff members to the United Nations Relief and Rehabilitation Administration (UNRRA) in the 1940s.

Its cooperation with the UNRRA suggested the ACCR's activities in postwar rehabilitation work. Even before the official end of the war, in 1945, the agency shifted its focus more fully to Europe, preparing to open offices in France and in Switzerland. The ACCR helped to develop a special labor aid project for activists in the European labor movement. The agency also assisted other groups, such as the AFSC, involved in vocational guidance and training and in relief abroad. It also continued its own services of vocational guidance and resettlement, working through active local groups throughout the United States. Its junior consultative service specialized in work with younger clients, although by 1945 the service dealt generally with refugees of all ages. The ACCR helped some prominent refugees, such as the French writer André Breton. During this period, the ACCR cooperated with four other relief groups to study recent immigrants from Europe, a study that resulted in Maurice R. Davie's *Refugees in America* (1947). With the field full of similar relief and rehabilitation organizations, in May 1947, the board of directors authorized the organization to liquidate itself and to transfer its work, funds, and records to a reconstituted committee on displaced persons of the Church World Service* and to other appropriate welfare agencies in the United States. Consequently, in early June 1947, having served about seventeen thousand refugees representing forty-two nationalities, mostly Protestant, Eastern Orthodox, and others not served by Catholic, Jewish, or child welfare agencies, the ACCR announced its dissolution as a corporate entity.

Primary sources for studying the ACCR's history are the files of *The New York Times,* an agency publication, *Toward a New Life: 10 Years of Stewardship: The American Christian Committee for Refugees* (1945), and the agency's *Newscast.*

The recent scholarly histories of World War II refugees and relief efforts, such as Henry Feingold, *The Politics of Rescue: The Roosevelt Administration and the Holocaust, 1938–1945* (1970), and David S. Wyman, *Paper Walls: America and the Refugee Crisis, 1938–1941* (1968), either neglect the ACCR or mention it very briefly, and there is no scholarly history of the ACCR.

AMERICAN COMMUNITY CHESTS AND COUNCILS, INC.: see UNITED WAY OF AMERICA.

AMERICAN CORRECTIONAL ASSOCIATION (ACA), THE. Some of the earliest reform and charitable agencies in the United States dealt with prisons and prisoners. One was the Philadelphia Prison Society, established in 1787. Similar agencies were founded in Boston in 1826 and in New York City in 1844. In 1862, a New England clergyman and educator, Enoch C. Wines, became the corresponding secretary of the Prison Association of New York (PANY). In 1865, Wines toured North American penal institutions along with Columbia law professor Theodore Dwight. Their *Report on the Prisons and Reformations of the United States and Canada* (1867) highlighted the problems facing American corrections in the mid-nineteenth century. Penitentiaries and juvenile institutions, which had once promised reformation of the criminal, had become, at best, merely custodial and, more often, degrading. Seeking new penal methods, Wines corresponded with European reformers and penologists, from whom he learned of the English and Irish systems of prisoner classification, indeterminate sentencing, and gradual reentry into society. Wines also heard of plans for an international congress on penal reform and, in 1869, along with other members of the New York and Philadelphia societies, issued a resolution calling for a preliminary national prison reform conference. Consequently, on October 18, 1870, at the National Congress of Penitentiary and Reformatory Discipline in Cincinnati, Ohio, the American Correctional Association (ACA) was established as the National Prison Association (NPA). This meeting signaled a revival of interest in prison reform correspondent with other late nineteenth-century efforts to reorganize charitable and correctional institutions. While older reformers, such as Francis Lieber, and members of the Philadelphia and Boston societies helped to form the NPA, its driving force was Enoch Wines.

The founding meeting opened in Cincinnati in October 1870, presided over by

Ohio governor and later United States president Rutherford B. Hayes, and attended by over two hundred representatives from twenty-three states, Canada, and South America. In addition to local prison reformers such as Theodore Dwight of the PANY, Indiana Quaker Charles Coffin, Zebulon Brockway of the Detroit House of Correction, and Franklin Sanborn of the Massachusetts Board of Charities, a number of judges and penal administrators were present. Approximately half of the delegates worked in prisons or juvenile institutions, and half were philanthropists or directors of state institutions or charity boards. The papers featured at the congress concerned criminal law reform, the penitentiary system, and preventive or reformatory institutions. Brockway's "The Ideal of a True Prison System for a State" introduced several future tenets of American prison reform, including the indeterminate sentence, industrial and intellectual training, and separate reformatories for women and misdemeanants. These were incorporated into a thirty-seven article declaration of principles. To further these ideals the congress resolved to form the NPA and appointed a committee that formally incorporated the organization in New York in 1871. Enoch Wines became its secretary; he also served as United States commissioner to the International Prison Congress in London in 1872. Wines organized four NPA congresses in the 1870s at which delegates exchanged ideas and materials on penal reform. Committees of prison wardens, reformatory superintendents, prison society officers, and public board members formed in 1876, providing the foundation for the association's later committee structure, as well as for later conflicts.

With the death of Wines in 1879 the NPA faltered seriously until after 1883, when Brockway, then superintendent of the Elmira Reformatory for Men, Sanborn, and W. M. F. Round of the PANY revived the NPA and attempted to mend divisions between reformers and prison wardens, who had begun to meet separately in 1884. The association stabilized its organization and expanded its membership over the next two decades under the leadership of its president, Rutherford B. Hayes (1883–1892), Secretary Frederick H. Wines, the founder's son (1887–1890), and Secretary J. L. Milligan (1891–1905). Since 1885, it has met annually for up to six days of paper presentations and committee meetings. Wardens continued to meet as a subgroup, as did prison chaplains and, later, prison physicians. After 1897, an agreement to alternate the presidency annually between institutional administrators and noninstitutional reformers partially settled the conflicts between the two groups.

From the late nineteenth century through the 1920s, the NPA served chiefly as a forum for discussion and debate of published proceedings. During this period, the association pointed out problems in American corrections and suggested responses, sometimes innovative ones. One major weakness of the prison system, according to those who spoke at the annual congresses, was the indiscriminate mixing of prisoners—male and female, young and old, misdemeant and felon, unconvicted and convicted—particularly in the county jails and houses of corrections. By the turn of the century, the NPA supported the separation of those awaiting trial, first and minor offenders, and women. After much debate, the NPA adopted the views of Indiana Quaker Rhoda Coffin, New York charities leader Josephine Shaw Lowell, and Massachusetts social service worker Ellen Cheney Johnson that separate prisons for female offenders should be managed and staffed by women. Methods of "prison discipline"—meaning both control and rehabilitation of inmates—were another NPA concern. Brockway's reformatory plan of indeterminate sentencing (by which a prisoner's progress toward reformation determined the date of release), combined with industrial training, physical exercise, and moral uplift, gradually replaced the traditional penitentiary model of isolation and the silent system. By 1906, over a dozen states had adopted the indeterminate sentence and had incorporated reformatory methods for young, first, and female offenders. The South lagged noticeably behind in these innovations. In the controversy over convict labor, the NPA favored prison industries for their economic and reformative values and claimed that prison-made goods would not undermine free labor. The association also called for better state and federal statistics of crime and imprisonment and improved methods of criminal identification. To aid the latter, it helped introduce the Bertillion system of measurements, which was an early system for classifying prisoners.

According to historian Blake McKelvey, the association, which became the American Prison Association (APA) in 1908, did not attain a truly national character until the first decade of the twentieth century. Between 1890 and 1910, the work of Samuel June Barrows, United States commissioner to the International Prison Commission, fostered the association's interest in national issues. Barrows chaired the committee that framed an indeterminate sentence and parole law for federal prisoners and that successfully testified on its behalf before Congress. He also laid the foundation for the International Penitentiary Congress of 1910 held in Washington, D.C. By that time, the APA had over five hundred representatives from forty states.

During the Progressive era, the APA declared its support for most elements of the "new penology"—probation, parole, the indeterminate sentence, reformatory methods, and inmate classification. But the association had neither the official mandate nor the means of effecting change within state or federal institutions. As NPA President Roland Brinkerhoff explained in 1905, "The National Prison Congress does not meet to formulate penological dogmas, but to exchange experiences and consider remedies." Thus it is not surprising that in 1920, when the APA took stock of changes in the correctional system since its founding, the record was disappointing. The county jails, Hastings H. Hart of the Russell Sage Foundation* lamented, although the subject of numerous papers and special reports by the APA, remained as disgraceful as fifty years earlier. Only "small progress" had been made in juvenile reformatories. "On the whole," another member found, "the progress made in the condition of convict labor has not met the anticipation of the founders of the Association." New "criminological laboratories'' had begun to diagnose the needs of individual inmates through the influence of court psychiatrist William Healy and New York women's reformatory superintendent Katherine Bement Davis. Nevertheless, Davis concluded, prisons were still weak in educational and industrial opportunities for their inmates. Other speakers lauded reforms that had been implemented, yet it was evident that enforcement of the new laws was lax and their effect minimal in most of the nation's prisons.

The ineffectiveness of the APA can be explained in part by the conflicting interests of its members and by its fragmented structure. Despite resolutions favoring the innovations of the new penology, the APA could not take any action that would alienate its constituency of wardens and prison officials, many of whom came from conservative and southern states that relied on traditional penal methods. At the same time, the committee structure of the 1880s had expanded into dozens of separate interest groups, most notably the auxiliaries, which fostered the professionalization of corrections between 1900 and 1920. In addition to separate wardens', chaplains', and physicians' associations, sections of governing boards, women, clinical criminologists, boys' schools, and parole boards had formed by 1915. Members seemed to devote much of their energy to professional advancement for their field.

The direction and scope of APA activity altered during the 1920s and 1930s in response to both new leadership and increased national concern over crime. While the association's management was stable under General Secretary Edward R. Cass, who served between 1922 and 1962, its membership was transformed by the addition of new young reformers, as well as criminologists, psychologists, and social workers. These groups adhered to the new penology and rejected older emphases on religious uplift and strict discipline, and they favored affirmative programs of reforms rather than mere discussion. The result of their involvement in the APA was a decline in warden domination of annual congresses and the introduction of new services provided by the association.

Indicative of this trend was the publication of the APA *Directory of Juvenile and Adult Correctional Institutions and Agencies,* since 1922 a valuable reference and a spur to prison reform. While surveying correctional facilities during the 1920s, the APA exposed and criticized prison conditions in the South and elsewhere. At the same time, APA committees produced reports that urged public action to reform aspects of the criminal justice system. Through the efforts of Hastings Hart some of these reports were published by the Russell Sage Foundation, including the *Report of the Committee on the Treatment of Persons Awaiting Court Action and Misdemeanant Prisoners* (1922) and *United States Prisoners in County Jails* (1926). Similarly, surveys of prison libraries and educational facilities made by APA member Austin MacCormick, later head of the Osborne Association,* led to the formation of the APA committee on education in 1930. It sponsored *The Prison Library Handbook* in 1932 in conjunction with the American Library Association. In the late 1930s, the APA published a journal, *Correctional Education,* as well as a yearbook. Through these and other publications the APA not only offered a more critical approach to corrections but also provided useful guidelines for upgrading prison standards.

By the 1930s the APA had begun to expand its activities beyond the annual meetings. According to long-time member Howard Gill, after 1935 the association "began to develop a philosophy of corrections which was something more than a custodial warehousing philosophy." Leaders such as Austin MacCormick, Massachusetts Corrections Commissioner Sanford Bates, who in 1936 became executive director of the Boys' Clubs of America,* and Dr. Walter Thayer, New York state commissioner of corrections, Gill recalled, provided a "wholly new professional point of view of corrections." A major impetus to this shift was the creation of the Federal Bureau of Prisons (see *Government Agencies*) in 1929 and the concomitant increase in the role of the national government in corrections. The bureau, first headed by former APA President Sanford Bates, directed the federal prisons and reformatories that had been built in the preceding decades, planned and constructed new facilities, and established standards for personnel training, health care, and educational services. Federal interest in state institutions expanded under President Franklin D. Roosevelt's New Deal, and the Federal Bureau of Prisons was able to influence policies in state prison systems through the power of federal financial aid.

One of the major issues discussed by the APA during the 1930s was prison labor. Concern over this long controversial topic peaked after the passage in 1929 of the Hawes-Cooper Act, which barred prison-made goods from interstate commerce after 1934. While massive unemployment during the depression heightened public antipathy to prison labor, the APA continued to argue that the effect of prison industries on the economy was minimal but that its importance in preventing idleness and providing training for inmates was great. Although the decline in prison industries after 1935 dismayed many APA members, it may also have fostered new educational and recreational programs in correctional institutions.

The other widely discussed issue in the 1930s was prisoner classification, an outgrowth of the new penology's emphasis on studying the backgrounds of individual criminals and treating them accordingly. The influx of social workers and psychiatrists into corrections furthered the importance of classification. In 1934, the APA published its first *Handbook of Casework and Classification Methods for Offenders,* which was employed by Sanford Bates in the Federal Bureau of Prisons and by state correctional systems.

During the 1930s the APA's journal began publication. In 1938, Richard McGee and Austin MacCormick started the *Jail Journal* as the publication of the National Jail Association, an auxiliary of the APA. The magazine was renamed *Prison World* in 1940 and, in 1954, *The American Journal of Corrections,* which remains the organization's official publication.

During and after World War II, the APA continued to take a more active part in implementing correctional policies, often in cooperation with the federal government. A plan to parole prisoners for military service gained the release of a hundred thousand men during the war; prison-made goods were utilized for the war effort; and APA members influenced the management of military prisons. In 1942, an association committee, chaired by Harvard University criminologist Sheldon Glueck, issued a report on crime prevention in wartime and the postwar period. The federal War Production Board prompted one of the APA's most important projects, the *Manual of Suggested Standards for a State Correctional System,* first issued in 1946 and authored chiefly by Austin MacCormick and Roberts Wright. Similar handbooks for correctional work were published by the association during the next decade, including those on prerelease (1950), on inmate relations with those outside prison (1953), and on college curricula for preparing correctional workers (1954).

Prison riots in the early 1950s and late 1960s, renewed attention to problems of crime and poverty in the 1960s, the availability of federal money, and the proliferation of new agencies concerned with delinquency all provided the background for the organization's activities in the postwar decades. In response to the first wave of prison riots, an APA position paper directed by Richard McGee cited idleness, overcrowding, the failure to implement educational programs, and the lack of effective personnel as the root of disturbances. The document was not widely circulated, however; its findings reached the public only after the next series of riots in the 1960s. Then, with funds from the federal Law Enforcement Assistance Administration, a revised report was published by the association, which discussed both causes of riots and methods of controlling them. Meanwhile, in cooperation with other agencies, new handbooks were issued, including one on correctional services (1966), cosponsored by the National Council on Crime and Delinquency,* and, with the American Bar Association, one on the legal responsibilities and authority of correctional officers (1974).

The first in a series of organizational changes occurred in 1954, when the title American Correctional Association (ACA) was adopted. The change reflected both a rejection of mere "prison discipline" for more educational goals, as well as stirrings of change within the organization which, since 1922, had been under the "penurious management" of General Secretary Edward R. Cass. Until 1962, the ACA was housed at the PANY and staffed solely by Cass, who headed both organizations, and an assistant. The availability of federal and foundation grants in the 1960s permitted staff expansion and, after Cass retired in 1962, the ACA separated from the PANY. In 1976, its headquarters were in College Park, Maryland. The membership in 1976 included approximately ten thousand individuals and over thirty affiliated organizations. In 1970, a revised constitution and bylaws ensured representation on the board of directors of black, native American, and Spanish-speaking minorities, as well as for ex-offenders. The major new project of the 1970s was accreditation of correctional institutions, a continuation of the evaluation of prisons that began in the 1920s. In addition, the topics of work and home furloughs, treatment of drug abuse, and the balance between prison security and prisoner rights and rehabilitation are discussed at annual congresses and in *The American Journal of Corrections*. While the association has retained its original function as a forum for exchanging information and ideas, it has added the tasks of establishing professional status for correctional workers, influencing national and state policy, and setting standards for prison personnel, treatment of offenders, and prevention of crime through its directories, handbooks, guidelines, and special reports.

The major sources for studying the ACA, besides the records at the association's offices, are its publications. The *Proceedings* of the annual congresses include delegate names and affiliations, committee structure and membership, papers, comments, and some business meetings. Most of the volumes are covered by the three indexes of the *Proceedings*. The most useful years for a historical overview are 1870, 1876, 1886, 1920, 1940, and 1970. Published committee reports, handbooks, and directories indicate the concerns and policies of the ACA in the twentieth century, as does *The American Journal of Corrections*, which is indexed for 1938–1950. Two articles in the *Journal* are particularly useful: memorials to Edward R. Cass in the March–April 1976 issue and transcripts of interviews with several long-time association members, including Sanford Bates, Howard Gill, and James Bennet in the September–October 1970 issue. Austin MacCormick kindly granted an interview for this article. Peter C. Buffum's paper, "The Origins of the National Congress on Penitentiary and Reformatory Discipline, Cincinnati, 1870" (mimeographed, Pennsylvania Prison Society), presents much original material. Blake McKelvey's *American Prisons: A Study in American Social History prior to 1915* (1936) provides both an overview of corrections in the early period and a description of the association's origins. David Rothman's *The Discovery of the Asylum: Social Order and Disorder in the New Republic* (1971) discusses penology in the period before the founding of the ACA. On the debate in the APA over women's prisons, see Estelle B. Freedman, "Their Sisters' Keepers: The Origins of Female Corrections in America" (Ph.D. dissertation, Columbia University, 1976). Isabel Barrows, *A Sunny Life* (1913), a biography of Samuel June Barrows, and Zebulon Brockway's autobiography, *Fifty Years of Prison Service* (1912), discuss their subjects' roles in the association.

Estelle B. Freedman

AMERICAN COUNCIL FOR NATIONALITIES SERVICE (ACNS). In 1958, preparations began for a merger between the Common Council for American Unity* (CCAU) and the American Federation of International Institutes* (AFII). This was a logical step because the programs of the CCAU, emphasizing various nationwide services for immigrants, and those of the AFII, representing some forty local agencies working with newcomers, complemented each other. The two organizations effected a merger on January 1, 1959, in New York City, and the new agency took the name American Council for Nationalities Service (ACNS). It would be strengthened and enriched by local experience. The affiliates, being social service agencies, could gain from the stimulus and assistance of a stronger and better equipped national headquarters, able to bring their local experience to bear in shaping its national policy. As a result, expanded services were carried into more and more communities. The member organizations of the ACNS, many of which are known as International Institutes, were autonomous nonsectarian agencies, situated in cities with a high percentage of foreign born. They are supported chiefly by the local community chests or united funds. As centers of service and fellowship for all nationalities, the member organizations provide technical assistance on immigration and citizenship matters, counseling and assistance in job placement, vocational training, learning English, second generation difficulties, and other personal problems. They work with the local press and radio and organize exhibits, folk festivals, conferences, and other community projects. Multilingual caseworkers, group workers, and community organization specialists provide the services of these agencies. The ACNS advises and assists its member agencies through fieldwork, personal conferences, technical information, an annual convention, and other services.

The ACNS constitution provided for a board of directors, an assembly of delegates, a president, chairman of the board, one or more vice-chairmen, a treasurer, an executive director, and "such officers as the Board may elect." The organization holds an annual convention. Since the early days of its predecessor organizations, the council's financial status has depended on grants and contributions from a variety of foundations, corporations, and individuals. The assistant director acts as liaison with the National Conference on Social Welfare,* helping to plan their general sessions, as well as those conducted or cosponsored by ACNS. The director is also the national office's official representative on committees of the National Social Welfare Assembly of National Voluntary Health and Social Welfare Organizations* concerned with individualized services, group work techniques, theories, and such. The ACNS has considered its active membership in the American Immigration and Citizenship Conference* (AICC) of primary importance. Regular and special material in the field was obtained from the AICC for distribution to ACNS member agencies. Persons from the ACNS national office played intimate parts in AICC's executive board, committees, and legislative activities, promoting a humanitarian, nondiscriminatory immigration policy for the United States. Close relationships have been maintained with other major national agencies whose programs paralleled and were tangential to those of the ACNS. Among these have been Church World Service,* Catholic Relief Services,* International Social Service,* Tolstoy Foundation, and American Council for Emigrés in the Professions.

In the early 1960s, when hospitality programs began, many ACNS member agencies became the centers for such community activities. The various types of individuals, ranging from United States Department of State visitors sponsored by private organizations to tourists, exchange students, and foreign seamen, needed different services. These varied from assistance in finding lodging to solving visa problems. In 1964, the ACNS established the annual Golden Door Award, given to Americans of foreign birth who had made distinguished con⌐ tributions to American life and culture. Recipients of this award have included Samuel Goldwyn, Sol Hurok, and David Dubinsky, leader of the International Ladies' Garment Workers' Union.

The ACNS carries on most of the projects and activities of its predecessor organizations, including its close work with the foreign-language press and radio, nationality groups, and the United States government. Many of the council's previous publications have been reprinted several times. It still continues to furnish hundreds of social agencies, libraries, and government officials with its weekly *Interpreter Releases,* giving the latest technical information needed in working with immigrants and the foreign born. In 1959 the ACNS published *Americans Abroad—Spokesmen for the United States.* Both the United States Department of Defense and the United States Information Agency purchased over three hundred thousand copies. This booklet, which suggests answers to some forty questions most frequently asked in other countries about the United States and its policies, has appeared in several different editions since then.

In 1962, the ACNS became active in the Cuban refugee resettlement program. Although it did not maintain a representative at the Cuban Refugee Center in Miami, its consultant kept in contact with agencies that did, especially the Church World Service.* Several "freedom flights" were sponsored by some of the ACNS affiliates. These agencies also found jobs and sponsors for Cuban families, counseled them, organized community resettlement committees, and stimulated public interest and response to their plight. The ACNS received a grant from the Rockefeller Brothers Fund in 1963 to develop increased community receptivity to the resettlement of Cuban refugees and to improve facilities and procedures for resettlement throughout the country. Since 1975, ACNS has directed its efforts toward the resettlement of Vietnamese refugees. Its activities include translating drivers' training books into Vietnamese, setting up special English classes, and sponsoring clothing drives.

In 1962 the ACNS and the General Federation of Women's Clubs (see *Fraternal Organizations*) joined in a nationalities division to encourage its member clubs to form nationalities committees. These committees contacted immigrants and refugees in their communities, acquainted them with local service resources, and drew them into community activities. The ACNS prepared booklets and other literature for the member clubs.

The humanitarian premise upon which the ACNS and its affiliated agencies operate is that immigration is one of the great forces making American an open society. It believes that the mere admission of these immigrants and refugees is not enough; they must be helped to become an integral part of the American community and encouraged to play a constructive role in the main currents of American life.

Sources on the ACNS include the Papers of the ACNS, deposited in the archives of the Immigration History Research Center (IHRC) at the University of Minnesota, Minneapolis. These papers consist of 175 linear feet of correspondence, minutes, reports, and publications of the ACNS as well as its predecessor organizations. In addition see ACNS, *Building American Unity,* (1963).

Lynn Ann Schweitzer

AMERICAN COUNCIL OF VOLUNTARY AGENCIES FOR FOREIGN SERVICE, INC. (ACVAFS). In late 1943, the ACVAFS was established in New York City to develop and coordinate American relief efforts in the liberated areas of Europe. The most important figures in the creation of this clearinghouse organization were Professor Joseph Chamberlain of the International Migration Service* (IMS), a professor at Columbia University who had been active since the early 1930s in relief efforts for refugees; Clarence Pickett, the long-time and eminently respected head of the American Friends Service Committee* (AFSC); and C. E. Miller of the Near East Foundation. Representatives from twelve other voluntary relief and rehabilitation agencies also participated in the establishment of the ACVAFS. The initial officers of the organization were: as chairman, Professor Chamberlain, and as the two vice-chairmen, Monsignor Patrick A. O'Boyle, the executive director of the War Relief Services of the National Catholic Welfare Conference,* and Joseph C. Hyman, executive secretary of the American Jewish Joint Distribution Committee.* Suggesting its early ties to the social work community, the ACVAFS acquired as its first executive secretary Clarence King from the faculty of the New York School of Social Work. When he surrendered the position in 1944, another trained social worker, Charlotte Owen, headed the ACVAFS staff.

Under Owen's long-time leadership, the ACVAFS quickly developed its structure and began to participate in the field of overseas relief and rehabilitation. In 1944, it helped to develop the personnel standards for the United Nations Relief and Rehabilitation Administration (UNRRA). The basic feature of the ACVAFS's structure was the system of committees on particular topics and countries, composed of representatives from member agencies. By 1945 and 1946, area committees for each country abroad were organized and functioning. The child welfare committee, established in January 1946 with about forty members, was an important early group. It held an all-day conference in 1946 on the problems of child welfare in the chaotic world situation and also began to concentrate on the development of the United Nations International Children's Fund. During this period the displaced persons committee had two major subcommittees: one on immigration and the project subcommittee. Representatives from each member agency with any kind of material aid program comprised the committee on material aid. Typical of the early and continuing ACVAFS cooperation with international and intergovernmental agencies, in 1945 and 1946, a staff member became a liaison personnel with the allocations committee of the UNRRA's clothing collection drive, and in the spring of 1946, the ACVAFS cooperated with the UNRRA's emergency food campaign. The ACVAFS's shipping and purchasing committee worked with the Credit Commodities Corporation on its special offer of food for relief. This committee also became the chief liaison between the federal President's War Relief Control Board (see *Government Agencies*) and the voluntary relief agencies. An ACVAFS practice called for member agencies to reach a consensus on each issue. This situation led to some failure to act aggressively, as some critics have charged, but on the whole, the agency continued to be effective. In the fall of 1945, the ACVAFS's committee on cooperatives organized the Cooperative for American Remittances to Europe* (CARE). In December 1945, the ACVAFS established its joint procurement mission for Europe, composed of twenty-eight agencies interested in buying United States Army surplus supplies—from machinery and blankets to entire hospitals—located overseas. Another group, the Pacific Procurement Mission was established by fifteen agencies providing relief in the Far East. More importantly, the ACVAFS's committee on Germany approved a new organization, the Council of Relief Agencies Licensed to Operate in Germany (CRALOG), and in March 1945, the ACVAFS created the Licensed Agencies for Relief in Asia (LARA). Because of the chaotic situation of displaced persons, the ACVAFS decided to conduct a study to try to clarify each voluntary agency's responsibility and thus to eliminate duplication. Issued in June 1946, the report provided information about the field. During this period, the nine-member, full-time staff was especially dedicated, and temporary workers were hired for special projects, such as the survey of displaced persons. Throughout the late 1940s, the ACVAFS continued its cooperation with the UNRRA and the Intergovernmental Committee for European Migration (ICEM). The displaced persons committee and its subcommittees were the most active, meeting more times in 1949 than any other ACVAFS committee.

In the early 1950s, the ACVAFS began to broaden its activities. The agency continued to coordinate CRALOG, whose files and office were housed at the ACVAFS's headquarters in New York City. In 1950, involving itself in the increasingly emphasized field of technical assistance, as opposed to relief, the ACVAFS established its committee on technical assistance and projects, which quickly gathered and tabulated information on these subjects from various agencies. In the early 1950s, the ACVAFS developed a way for it to operate without a deficit by generally getting the member agencies to increase their contributions. During this period, the newly named committee on migration and refugee problems focused on the need to change the restrictive aspects of the McCarran-Walters Nationality Act of 1952. The highlight of this period, however, was the ACVAFS's role in securing Public Law 480 in 1954, the culmination of efforts to give the voluntary agencies access to American surplus commodities since as early as 1950, when the entire executive committee traveled to Washington, D.C., to speak with legislators. Part of the ACVAFS's testimony in favor of the legislation before the House Committee on Agriculture was "The Moral Challenge of Abundance,'' expressing the basic humanitarian attitude that permeated the ACVAFS.

The enactment of Public Law 480 in 1954 helped to make the ACVAFS's surplus commodities policy committee one of the most active in the organization. Comprised of five major agencies in the field, the committee displayed unity in the years through 1959. In December 1955, it influenced the government's adding wheat and corn to the list of surplus commodities available to the voluntary agencies. In November 1956, its recommendations to increase the available commodities, presented as "The Continued Challenge of American Abundance,'' was well received by the federal Advisory Committee on Voluntary Foreign Aid. During this period, many of the committee's concerns involved the ACVAFS's shipping and purchasing committee; the two committees often held joint meetings. In 1959, the organization completed a manual on surplus commodities, distributing it to member agencies for their overseas representatives.

Other highlights of the ACVAFS's activities in the 1950s include the establishment in 1956 of an ad hoc committee on Hungary to coordinate material relief efforts for Hungarians in Austria and in nearby nations and for relief in Hungary itself. In 1955, the ACVAFS established its Technical Assistance Information Clearing House (TAICH) under the auspices of the technical assistance and projects committee. TAICH also operated under contract with the federal Foreign Operations Administration, which later became the Agency for International Development (AID). TAICH quickly developed as a major ACVAFS service, publishing the *Technical Assistance Quarterly Bulletin,* and holding a conference in 1956 on technical assistance in Africa. Early in its existence, TAICH established itself as a significant medium for keeping member agencies informed of such things as ACVAFS committee activities and international developments. In 1958, the ACVAFS reestablished its committee on Poland after a ten-year lapse. Also in 1958, the ACVAFS prepared a statement, "The Philosophy of Voluntarism,'' for its members. The organization helped the chairman of the Council of National Organizations of the White House Conference on Children and Youth, famous social worker Robert E. Bondy, to ensure the adequate representation at the conference in 1960 of all nationality and ethnic groups.

The diverse committee structure and activities of the ACVAFS adapted to and even anticipated the trends and events of the 1960s. In 1961, for instance, the organization established its committee on the Peace Corps, and, consistently concerned with preserving and strengthening voluntarism, in February 1961, the executive committee held two days of discussion on the effect of government subsidies on the nature of voluntarism. In the early 1960s, an ACVAFS committee assumed responsibility for reuniting parents with unaccompanied Cuban children who had been in the United States previously. The personnel committee conducted an extensive search for an executive director to replace Charlotte Owen, and in 1964, Eugene Shenefield, a former administrator with the American National Red Cross,* assumed the position. During this period, the ACVAFS began briefing member agencies' personnel before they went overseas. The agency also helped indigenous representatives, such as nine Brazilians in 1964, who participated in member agency programs, in this case Food for Peace, cosponsored by the Catholic Relief Services,* the Church World Service,* and the Lutheran World Relief.* In the mid-1960s, the important officers of the ACVAFS chaired the Southeast Asia committee because of American military involvement there and the war-related relief problems. Influenced by reports from the food resources policy committee, in the mid-1960s, the executive committee showed greater concern for the situation of dwindling supplies and the uncertainty of Food for Peace legislation. Characteristically serving as the link between the government and the voluntary agencies, the ACVAFS arranged for representatives from member agencies to meet with a representative of the United States AID/Vietnam Voluntary Agency Liaison. Collectively and individually, members of the migration and refugee problem committee petitioned and appeared before Senator Edward Kennedy's committee in 1966 to have the United States Department of Labor ease the process of immigration of the unskilled. In 1966, the ACVAFS cosponsored a successful information exhibit, gaining greater recognition of its work, at the International Conference of Social Work in Washington, D.C. In 1966, it approved the lease for new headquarters at 200 Park Avenue South in New York City. Important organizational changes occurred in the late 1960s, when three primary groups—food, materials, and disaster; migration and refugee problems; and technical assistance—replaced the old committee structure. Because of the situations in particular areas, however, the following area committees were continued on an ad hoc basis: Latin America, Southeast Asia, and Near and Middle East. Responding to new situations and needs in the late 1960s, the ACVAFS formed a Nigeria/Biafra coordinating committee, which obtained considerable information about conditions there.

Enormously diverse activities, reflecting the interests and needs of its fifty-odd constituent members, characterized the ACVAFS in the 1970s. In 1971, the ACVAFS published an impressive directory of agencies engaged in services abroad. This publication is updated continually with profile reports. During the Peruvian earthquake relief efforts, the staff coordinated the work of member agencies with the Disaster Coordination Office of AID, and TIACH issued a directory of agencies active in Peru for the interested public. The ACVAFS also participated in White House–level activities to aid survivors of the Peruvian earthquake. Responding to the continuing difficulties, the ACVAFS reactivated its committee on the Near and Middle East in September 1970. In 1971, the agency hosted the International Council of Voluntary Agencies conference in New York City in June and July. Responding to President Richard Nixon's message on foreign aid, the ACVAFS prepared "Restructuring Foreign Assistance Programs of the United States." At the suggestion of the migration and refugee affairs committee, the agency joined as amici curiae in a successful suit before the United States Supreme Court to prevent states from denying public welfare to people solely because they are aliens. That committee was also concerned with the problems of children in Vietnam, and it began in the early 1970s to plan future social services in South Vietnam, such as provisions for the aged, the war wounded, and the like. After a lengthy search, in December 1971, Leon O. Marion, an administrator in the field of international service, replaced Shenefield as executive director. The ACVAFS organized a committee on the Tax Reform Act of 1969 and its effects on the voluntary agencies. The ACVAFS met with the highest-level officials in the United States Department of State and other government agencies to try to clarify American policy on refugees. At the suggestion of the ACVAFS's children's subcommittee, a conference on child welfare in Vietnam was held in New York City in December 1974. In a common effort with federal agencies to implement the Foreign Assistance Act of 1973, the ACVAFS characteristically emphasized the reliance on American voluntary agencies. During the early 1970s, it spearheaded activities in nutrition, influencing AID's Office of Nutrition to sponsor conferences, for which the ACVAFS was invited to select the participants. To facilitate the exchange of information about programs of member agencies and nonmembers such as AID, the UN, and the United Nations International Children's Emergency Fund (UNICEF), the ACVAFS established its ad hoc committee on the Sahel, where drought conditions and starvation were extensive. At a conference on foreign disaster in late October 1974, the ACVAFS circulated a disaster preparedness memorandum giving the twenty-four-hour telephone numbers of the professional staff, who, in turn, were prepared to reach agency, UN, and other personnel when necessary.

The chief sources for the history of the ACVAFS are the mimeographed annual reports and minutes of meetings, which I found only at the agency's headquarters in New York City. At the headquarters also are the files of the organization, which were used in Robert Sullivan, "The Politics of Altruism" (Ph.D. dissertation, the Johns Hopkins University, 1968). Sullivan's study focuses on the surplus commodity program of the United States and the voluntary agencies. Merle Curti, *American Philanthropy Abroad* (1963), briefly mentions the ACVAFS, but there is apparently no scholarly history of this leading agency.

AMERICAN FEDERATION OF INTERNATIONAL INSTITUTES (AFII). In 1910, the National Board of the Young Women's Christian Associations of the United States of America* (YWCA) began an experiment to provide social services for immigrants in large industrial cities. Directed by former settlement house worker Edith Terry Bremer, this program was known as International Institutes. Within five years, Bremer's work in New York City was imitated by local YWCAs in other cities; additional institutes had sprouted in Trenton, Los Angeles, Pittsburgh, and Lawrence, Massachusetts. The institute movement proliferated at the end of World War I when the YWCA's war work council transformed itself into a department of immigration and foreign communities, with the initial objective of assisting immigrant women and girls in the

United States. The National Board of the YWCA urged the formation of local institutes in industrial cities with heavy ethnic populations. By the mid-1920s, fifty-five had been established in such cities as Buffalo, Boston, Detroit, San Francisco, Philadelphia, St. Paul, St. Louis, Milwaukee, Duluth, Toledo, Akron, and Gary. To coordinate this work of the International Institutes on December 13, 1933, again under Bremer's leadership, the American Federation of International Institutes (AFII) was founded as the National Institute of Immigrant Welfare (NIIW). The NIIW planned to work for "tolerance, fair play, better justice and better treatment and understanding generally for foreign-born peoples."

As founder of the first institute and executive director of the national organization until 1954, Bremer became the national spokesman for the International Institutes and for immigrant welfare generally. Prior to beginning YWCA work in 1910, she had been a resident at the University of Chicago Settlement and the Union Settlement in New York, a field investigator for the Chicago Juvenile Court, a researcher for the Chicago Women's Trade Union League, and a special agent for the United States Immigration Commission. Her writings established the philosophy and the goals of the International Institute movement. Rather than urging assimilation or Americanization, Bremer promoted an early form of cultural pluralism. "We believe," she wrote in an important statement of purpose in 1923, "there is no richer material for cultural growth than that which can be saved for the foreigner out of his own inheritance."

Each International Institute engaged in traditional settlement house work, handled citizenship and naturalization problems, and sent caseworkers into the immigrant neighborhoods. Following Bremer's lead, each institute found its most important task in assisting various ethnic groups to maintain cultural identity. Often immigrants themselves, institute social workers (called "nationality workers") with multiple language skills sought to build consciousness and pride in the immigrant heritage, fostered interethnic cooperation and understanding, and emphasized ethnic contributions to American life. They urged newcomers to retain their languages and customs while simultaneously learning American ways. At the same time, they worked among native-born Americans to develop understanding of immigrant traditions. These were important, almost unique, objectives during the nativist years of the 1920s and the depression period of the 1930s.

The work of the International Institutes generally conformed to the principles of cultural pluralism articulated by Bremer in her many memos and directives to local institute workers. The International Institute of Gary, Indiana, provides a case in point. Founded in 1919 by local YWCA people, the Gary Institute began with four professionally trained nationality workers—one each for the Polish, Czech, Bulgarian, and Italian communities of the city; Greek, Serbian, and Mexican caseworkers were added by the mid-1920s. These workers spent much of their time doing individual and family casework in the immigrant communities. They were especially helpful in handling the legal and technical problems most immigrants faced in connection with naturalization. Nationality workers also engaged in reform politics and in some of the more traditional kinds of settlement house tasks—visiting hospitals, serving as employment agents, interceding with government agencies, translating letters, locating relatives, teaching English classes, and so on. Moreover, the Gary International Institute, like all the others, considered group work, community organization, and the sponsorship of cultural programs as exceedingly important in promoting the ideal of cultural pluralism. Building ethnic consciousness through group activities became one of the organization's most significant tasks. The Gary Institute worked closely with local affiliates of such groups as the Polish National Alliance, the Serb National Federation, and the Croatian Catholic Union, and nationality workers went into the community to help organize a host of local ethnic associations: mutual aid societies, women's and children's clubs, and dramatic, musical, athletic, and political groups. The institute threw open its facilities to these groups, serving as a central gathering place for organized ethnic activities. In addition, the Gary Institute held innumerable ethnic concerts, dances, festivals, pageants, plays, and exhibits. The agency sponsored lectures on the art, literature, and history of native countries, as well as foreign-language classes for the American-born children of immigrants. Through such programs, the institute sought to preserve immigrant traditions, foster a sense of ethnic pride and self-identity, and build cultural pluralism. These were important goals and purposes at a time when immigrants were denigrated and when demands for assimilation and conformity were strong.

The program of the Gary International Institute was typical of the movement in general. Although each institute was essentially independent, the ideals Bremer had set forth had a shaping influence on the movement. During the period of institute affiliation with the YWCA (1910–1933), Bremer headed the YWCA's department of immigration and foreign communities, changed in March 1932 to the bureau of immigration and foreign-born. From this position, she provided a central direction for the institutes. She made field visits to the institutes to advise on programs, sponsored annual meetings of institute workers, and generally sought to coordinate institute activities through a continuous series of policy memos from the national office. These policy statements in immigration law, urged sensitive and humane dealings with the ethnic communities, and adhered to the ideals of cultural pluralism.

During the 1920s, institute people began discussing possible separation from the YWCA. The reasons seemed logical and compelling. The YWCA had designed its program for women, but the International Institutes dealt with families. The YWCA engaged in group activities, but institutes did casework as well. Moreover, the YWCA had a distinctly Protestant orientation, and the clientele of the institutes was almost entirely non-Protestant. Finally, Bremer and other institute spokesmen argued that the immigrant cause was too important to be submerged as a partial concern of a women's agency. An independent organization could consolidate pro-immigrant forces on the national level, lobby for favorable congressional legislation, serve as an information clearinghouse, and perhaps secure foundation support for institute work. These arguments eventually won out, and in December 1933, Bremer and her supporters founded the National Institute of Immigrant Welfare (NIIW).

Essentially the NIIW built upon the immigrant social service work Bremer had initiated under YWCA supervision. The national organization sponsored conferences and established a case consultation service to aid local agencies on the technical aspects of immigration. The NIIW maintained contacts at immigrant arrival stations such as Ellis Island and sought to do follow-up welfare work with the new arrivals in local communities. Moreover, the agency conducted research programs on immigrant social conditions and the treatment of aliens, promoted legislation for "humanizing the immigration law," and fostered the organization of folk festivals, folk art exhibits, and adult education programs for immigrants. The purposes of the new national agency, in short, remained much what they had been under the YWCA: "to develop permanent work in local communities for the protection, education, social adjustment, and civic advancement of foreign-born men and women." Most of the local International Institutes separated from the YWCA during the 1930s and joined with the NIIW. Efforts to promote cultural pluralism remained at the heart of the NIIW activities; the famous annual International Folk Festival sponsored by the St. Paul International Institute typified this side of the program. But increasingly, naturalization activities consumed a greater share of local institute work, a pattern evident through the 1930s and reinforced by the passage of the Alien Registration Act in 1940. In 1943, the NIIW officially changed its name to the American Federation of International Institutes (AFII).

Like the NIIW, the AFII supervised the casework and group work of the local International Institutes and offered technical advice on immigration and naturalization problems. During World War II, the agency sought to secure fair treatment for immigrant aliens (immigrants who had not yet become citizens were discriminated against in employment, for instance) and to eliminate internationality conflicts among the foreign born. In the period immediately following World War II, the AFII sent workers overseas and, in cooperation with agencies of the United Nations (first the United Nations Relief and Rehabilitation Agency and then the International Refugee Organization), aided in the resettlement of thousands of European displaced persons in the United States. The AFII also helped in the adjustment of war brides and in the resettlement of Japanese-Americans who had been incarcerated during the war. Later, special assistance programs were established by local International Institutes to aid Hungarian refugees in the 1950s and Cuban refugees in the 1960s. During this period, the AFII continued to represent local institutes before federal immigration authorities and lobby in Congress for more liberal and more humane immigration legislation. However, by the mid-1950s, both the AFII and the individual institutes experienced budget problems. About the same time, AFII personnel initiated merger talks with the Common Council for American Unity,* an organization with similar purposes but no local affiliates. In 1958, the two agencies joined to create the American Council for Nationalities Service* (ACNS).

In all of its work, the AFII upheld the immigrant cause. Rather than undermining the immigrant heritage, the institutes fostered ethnic consciousness and pride. Rather than urging immediate assimilation of rigorous Americanization, the institutes promoted the ideals of service and pluralism. As Bremer wrote, "in the very diversity of our origins and mores lies the unified strength of America." Under the leadership of Bremer and her successor, the professional sociologist and immigration expert William S. Barnard (executive director, 1954–1958), the AFII maintained a consistent stand for the protection and service of immigrants and affirmed the values of a democratic society. Thus, the AFII and its numerous local affiliates were unique social service agencies for newcomers in twentieth-century America.

Sources for studying the AFII include the papers of the AFII, deposited with the papers of the ACNS. These are located in the Immigration History Research Center at the University of Minnesota, Minneapolis. This article is also based on an examination of the papers of three International Institutes: Gary, Boston, and St. Paul. Published primary materials include the writings of Edith Terry Bremer: "Foreign Community and Immigration Work of the National Young Women's Christian Association," *Immigrants in America Review* 1 (January 1916): 73–82; "The Foreign Language Worker in the Fusion Process: An Indispensable Asset to Social Work in America," National Conference on Social Work, *Proceedings* (1919), 740–746; *The International Institutes in Foreign Community Work: Their Program and Philosophy* (1923); "Immigration: A Look Ahead," *The Survey* 52 (May 15, 1924): 207–210; "Immigrants and Foreign Communities," *Social Work Yearbook,* 1929 (1930), 214–221; "Development of Private Social Work with the Foreign-Born," American Academy of Political and Social Science, *Annals* 262 (March 1949): 139–147. Also important is Alice L. Sickels, *Around the World in St. Paul* (1945). Secondary studies include Raymond A. Mohl and Neil Betten, "Ethnic Adjustment in the Industrial City: The International Institute of Gary, 1919–1940," *International Migration Review* 6 (Winter 1972): 361–376, and Raymond A. Mohl and Neil Betten, "Paternalism and Pluralism: Immigrants and Social Welfare in Gary, Indiana, 1906–1940," *American Studies* 15 (Spring 1974): 5–30.

Raymond Mohl

AMERICAN FOUNDATION FOR OVERSEAS BLIND, INC. (AFOB). When the *Lusitania* was sunk in early May 1915, one of the survivors was George A. Kessler, a wealthy American businessman. In his personal battle to survive, Kessler clung for hours to an oar, vowing to help unfortunate people if he survived the ordeal. He did, and while recuperating in London, he became aware of the rehabilitation work being done for the British war blinded at St. Dunstan's, a venture begun and led by Arthur Pearson. After his recuperation, Kessler traveled to Paris, where he saw the pathetic condition of the war blinded. These episodes prompted him and his wife, Cora Parsons Kessler, to found what became the American Foundation for Overseas Blind (AFOB) as the British, French, Belgian Permanent Blind Relief War Fund (BFBPRWF) on November 11, 1915. Kessler chose his former secretary, Georges Raverat, to assist his project. With his characteristic flair for the episodic and the dramatic, Kessler enlisted support for his organization from government and civic leaders in the United States and Europe. The American committee included August Belmont, a banker, civic leader, and philanthropist, Nicholas Murray Butler, the president of Columbia University and a national celebrity, Elihu Root, the former secretary of state and of war, and William K. Vanderbilt, a wealthy New Yorker.

With the organization established, the Kesslers began a campaign to raise funds on both sides of the Atlantic Ocean. When he returned to the United States to lead this campaign, Kessler met Helen Keller. This began her lifelong relation with and work for the organization. The fund-raising drive in the United States featured a nationwide speaking tour by a war-blinded veteran from England, Sergeant Major Robert Middlemiss. By early 1917, these efforts had helped to raise about $400,000 for the organization, which became the American, British, French, Belgian Permanent Blind Relief War Fund (ABFBPBRWF) after the United States entered World War I in April 1917. During the war, the organization worked through local agencies in France, Belgium, and England to establish schools and workshops for the blind. The ABFBPBRWF also helped to fund St. Dunstan's in England. When a crisis developed because workshops in France could not obtain supplies resulting from shortages caused by the war, Kessler gave the organization his home in Paris to be used as a warehouse. Even though it stressed education and self-help, the ABFBPBRWF occasionally provided pensions to clients needing money. The organization also helped to fund the work at Evergreen, a pioneering institution for the war blinded in Baltimore, Maryland, conducted by the American National Red Cross* and by the United States Blind Veterans of the World War I. After the armistice in November 1918 ending the war, on October 21, 1919, the agency was incorporated according to the laws of the state of New York and it changed its name to the Permanent Blind Relief War Fund for Soldiers and Sailors of the Allies, Inc. (PBRWFSSA). At this time, the board of directors included William Nelson Cromwell of New York, a prominent attorney and public figure who had conducted negotiations with Panama for a canal built by the United States, Helen Keller, a deaf-blind woman who was gaining a nationwide reputation as a humanitarian, and, of course, the Kesslers. In 1920, John Foster Dulles, Cromwell's law partner, joined the board of directors, and in 1927, he became the vice-president, a position he held until 1953 when he was named United States secretary of state.

The death of George Kessler on September 13, 1920, ended the first phase of the history of the AFOB.

The presidency shifted to Cromwell in late 1920, and he shaped a program for the organization that became one of its long-standing activities. In late 1921, he argued that the PBRWFSSA should concentrate on printing and on furnishing literature and music in braille. Many welfare workers in the field opposed this program because they believed the war blinded had little desire to learn braille. Cromwell, however, held to his goal, and by January 1923, the organization had acquired a building in Paris, renovated it, and installed equipment to print in braille. It employed at this office forty-five staff members, about thirty of whom were blind. The first page printed in braille at the Paris building appeared the very next month; later the printing of other magazines developed. Cromwell influenced another important shift in 1925 when the organization expanded its sphere to include efforts for the civilian blind as well as for the war blind. Consequently, in July 1925, the organization amended its certificate of incorporation to include its new objective, at the same time changing its name to the American Braille Press for War and Civilian Blind, Inc., commonly known as the American Braille Press (ABP).

The ABP expanded the printing program and laid the foundation for improved methods of assisting the blind throughout the world. One of its major concerns in the 1920s, to establish a worldwide braille music code, was arranged through an international conference that the ABP convened at its Paris printing house in April 1929. After the conference, the ABP began to publish the monthly *Musical Review for the Blind*. Two years later, the ABP, the American Foundation for the Blind* (AFB), and the American Association of Instructors for the Blind cosponsored a world conference on work for the blind, the first such meeting in the United States. The success of that conference prompted the ABP to change its focus again, resolving to deemphasize its own publishing and to establish braille presses in other countries. Announced in December 1931, this program set the foundation for later self-help projects. The implementation of this plan began immediately, and by the spring of 1935, the ABP had founded and/or equipped two printing plants in France, two in Belgium, and one each in Poland, Portugal, Yugoslavia, Colombia, and Brazil. In 1937, the ABP introduced the first talking book program in Europe.

In the era of World War II, the ABP expanded its services and improved its mechanical instruments. By April 1940, for instance, the ABP developed a new apparatus for teaching blind soldiers to read quickly. Near the end of the war, the organization initiated the rehabilitation work that prompted activities throughout the world. During this period, John Foster Dulles represented his aging colleague, William Nelson Cromwell, in negotiations reorganizing the ABP for global services. As a result of these discussions, the ABP became affiliated with the AFB in November 1945. M. C. Migel, the AFB's benefactor and leader, became the president of the ABP, and Robert Irwin, the AFB's executive director, began to serve in the same post for the ABP. Also, at this time, Helen Keller became the counselor for international relations of the ABP. In February 1946, the ABP changed its name to the American Foundation for Overseas Blind, Inc. (AFOB). The AFOB not only sent abroad all types of braille-related equipment but it also provided clothing to the blind in France, Belgium, Holland, and Norway to meet basic needs. In the late 1940s, the AFOB also sent a group of malnourished blind schoolchildren in France to a school for the blind in England. In France, where institutions for the blind had been damaged and destroyed during the war, the AFOB helped to establish a central purchasing and sales agency for several workshops for the blind. An important conference was the international conference of workers for the blind at Oxford University in England chaired by Executive Director Irwin and cosponsored by the AFOB and the Royal National Institute for the Blind of England. This meeting prompted the establishment in 1951 of the World Council for the Welfare of the Blind, in which the AFOB continued to play a role. In 1946, International Relations Counselor Helen Keller made the first of many trips in the 1940s and 1950s to investigate the condition of the blind all over the world.

A new era of the AFOB began in 1949 when M. Robert Barnett replaced the retiring Irwin as executive director of both agencies. Self-help projects and educational programs became the characteristic activities of the AFOB, which was a member of the American Council of Voluntary Agencies for Foreign Service.* In 1950, for instance, the AFOB began providing experienced teachers of the blind to India and Rhodesia to help modernize instruction for the blind there. The AFOB helped to rebuild the war-damaged Lighthouse for the Blind in Seoul, Korea, and in 1954, it sent a team of experts in education, vocational training, handicrafts, administration, and legislation to Korea. On Taiwan, the AFOB supported a campaign to eliminate trachoma, supplied hospitals, opened three clinics designed to prevent blindness, and sponsored two mobile units for rural areas. Activities in the Far East stimulated the opening of an AFOB regional office in Manila, the Philippines, in 1957. Self-help projects in Europe continued. In Greece, for example, the AFOB began teaching deaf-blind children and provided a residential workshop for blind women. In the Middle East, the AFOB cooperated in a demonstration project with the United Nations in Cairo to train leaders in work for the blind from eight Arab countries. The AFOB established vocational training centers in Jordan and Iran, supported schools for the blind in four Arab countries, and in 1956 helped to open the first rehabilitation center for social and psychological readjustment, vocational training, and employment of the blind in Israel. These and other activities led the AFOB to open a regional office in Beirut, Lebanon, in 1962. In Latin America in June 1954, the AFOB helped to sponsor the first Pan-American conference on the welfare of the blind and the prevention of blindness, a conference that stimulated work in the area. The AFOB also stimulated the establishment of indigenous national organizations for the blind, and it provided them with equipment. In 1955, in cooperation with the University of Chile, the AFOB initiated the first training for teachers in Latin America, and two years later, it opened a regional office in Santiago, Chile. In 1955, with the United Nations and other international agencies, the AFOB began training the blind for resettlement in rural communities in Uganda, a project serving as an international demonstration. Similar agricultural training and training centers were conducted in Taiwan, India, and Syria. In 1958, the AFOB initiated, with the American Israeli Lighthouse, a pioneering program integrating blind with normal-signted children in school classes. An important organizational event occurred in May 1959 when a group of prominent Americans, in a special ceremony at the United Nations, initiated the Helen Keller World Crusade for the Blind, establishing a committee, chaired by actress Katherine Cornell, a friend of Keller.

The Helen Keller World Crusade of the AFOB funded, developed, and continued basic and innovative services in the 1960s and 1970s. In 1961, for instance, the AFOB held the inter-American conference in Guatemala. In late 1963, delegates from eight African countries participated in a seminar in Tunis to prepare for educational work with blind children and adults in their home communities, and a Middle East seminar in Lebanon in July 1965 gave intensive instruction to teachers of the blind from ten Arab countries. In 1968, the AFOB clarified another leading objective: to promote the prevention of blindness in areas with the highest incidence of blindness—Africa, Asia, and Latin America. Other activities included giving braille duplicating facilities to Ethiopia, sponsoring a mobile eye unit in a vast, remote area of Kenya, and in 1970, helping the Bolivian government to establish the first rehabilitation center for the blind in that country. The AFOB assisted local governments in administering large quantities of vitamin A to afflicted areas. In 1972, to guide this venture, the AFOB established an advisory committee of specialists in eye care, pediatrics, nutrition, and public health. An important organizational development occurred in 1974 when Executive Director M. Robert Barnett, who had held the position for twenty-five years, retired. A widely experienced administrator in work for the blind, Harold G. Roberts, the former AFOB associate director, became the new executive director in 1974. Activities in the mid-1970s included completing a vitamin A project in El Salvador and initiating new vitamin A projects in the Philippines and Haiti, where the AFOB tried to develop a model system for delivering vitamin A. In 1974, the AFOB issued its first publication on the subject, *Vitamin A Deficiency and Blindness Prevention,* and, characteristically, it helped to establish a national center for the blind in Ecuador, in Quito.

The primary sources for studying the AFOB's history include the published *Annual Reports.* The papers of the AFOB are located in its headquarters in New York City. The Helen Keller Papers at the AFB archives also contain materials relating to the AFOB's history.

There are some helpful secondary studies of the AFOB. Bernard Lacy, comp., *An International Adventure: A Brief History of the American Foundation for*

Overseas Blind, 1915–1965 (1965), is more informative about the AFOB than Frances A. Koestler, *The Unseen Majority: A Social History of Blindness in America* (1976).

AMERICAN FOUNDATION FOR THE BLIND (AFB). In 1902, Mary Fowler, a leading worker with the blind, envisioned a national organization. Charles Campbell, an AFB founder in 1921, had similarly envisioned a national organization in 1906, and in 1907, he established and edited an important journal, *Outlook for the Blind*. Support for the establishment of a national organization came some ten years later from officials at both the American National Red Cross's* institution, Evergreen, in Baltimore, Maryland, which developed in 1918 to train blind sailors and soldiers, and at the Perkins Institution in Watertown, Massachusetts, an important and pioneering school for the blind. Following the address by L. W. Wallace, the director of Evergreen, delegates to the convention of the American Association of Workers for the Blind* (AAWB) in 1921 adopted a resolution supporting the idea of a national agency. At the same time, Robert B. Irwin, who supervised classes for the blind in Ohio, solicited the feelings of other prominent workers, particularly the president of the AAWB, H. Randolph Latimer, who introduced the resolution at the ninth biennial convention of the AAWB in Vinton, Iowa. The leaders who drafted the resolution of June 28, 1921, which called for the establishment of a committee to develop plans, were Edward M. Van Cleve, the principal of the New York Institute for the Education of the Blind and the first managing director of the National Committee for the Prevention of Blindness,* Edward Allen, the director of the Perkins Institution, Charles Campbell, the assistant director of Evergreen, Irwin, and Olin H. Burritt. This group worked to implement the resolution, and on September 23, 1921, the AFB was incorporated according to the laws of the state of Delaware.

Pending financial support from philanthropist Major M. C. Migel, who was then in Europe, the organizing committee elected Burritt as president of the temporary organization. Latimer agreed to serve as the secretary-general pending his employment as a full-time executive of the agency. Major Migel returned home in May 1922 enthused about the organization, and he agreed to finance it for three years at $10,000 per year. Migel also influenced some friends to donate $30,000 per year to the organization. Well financed, the AFB opened its national headquarters in New York City on February 1, 1923, with Dr. Joseph C. Nate, the former assistant secretary of the board of education of the Methodist Episcopal Church, as director general. Three bureaus were established to conduct the activities: the bureau of research, headed by Robert Irwin; the bureau of information and publicity, headed by Charles B. Hayes, the former director of the Massachusetts Commission for the Blind who also became editor of *Outlook for the Blind;* and the bureau of education, which the staff itself directed initially. Major Migel became the president, a position he held until his retirement in November 1945, when he became chairman of the board of trustees.

The AFB developed as the most important national agency among many in the field. In the 1920s, through the field service of the bureau of information, the AFB helped to draft legislation in many states and conducted surveys of the condition of the blind in many localities. For example, in 1924, at the request of the Iowa governor's committee on the blind, the AFB prepared legislation to create a state commission for the blind. The most famous of the AFB leaders, Helen Keller, herself deaf and blind, appeared before a joint session of the Iowa house and senate. In 1925, at the request of local citizens, the AFB helped to organize a committee for the blind in Omaha, Nebraska, and then, at its invitation, conducted a survey of the blind there. These activities were done only at the request of local officials, organizations, or individuals. Helen Keller and her party traveled throughout the United States, and in the early 1920s, AFB's director of information worked full time to develop the Helen Keller Endowment Fund. In the mid-1920s, with funds from the Carnegie Corporation and through the cooperation of the American Library Association, the AFB began to study two-sided braille printing. In 1927, with the help of United States Senators James Wolcott Wadsworth, Jr., of New York and David T. Schall of Minnesota and Congressman Walter Hughes Newton of Minnesota, the AFB in March 1927 influenced an amendment to the Interstate Commerce Act allowing railroads to offer reduced fares for blind travelers and their guides. It was a while, however, before the railroads, particularly in the East, implemented the plan. In 1928, the AFB began a five-year project with the Perkins Institution to determine the best ways to teach blind schoolchildren. The AFB issued many publications, including the helpful Laws Governing State Commissions for the Blind (1927). In 1926, the AFB established its library of reference sources on the blind, and in 1929, a trained professional librarian reorganized the collection. In 1929, Robert Irwin, himself blind, became the AFB's executive director.

Under Irwin's leadership, the AFB continued its basic services and, more importantly, branched out into new areas, pioneering in some. In April 1931, with the AAWB and another organization, the AFB cosponsored the world conference on work with the blind in New York City, and in 1932, the AFB helped to influence the adoption of a uniform braille code in the English-speaking world. Recognition of the AFB's leadership was reflected in the appointment of Irwin as the chairman of the subcommittee of the visually handicapped of the White House Conference of Child Health and Protection. Irwin quickly began a nationwide survey of the education of blind children.

Throughout the 1930s and despite the Great Depression, the AFB gave blind individuals gifts such as radios, clocks, and smoking pipes. In 1932, the AFB completed the development of a stereotyping machine able to print in braille on both sides of a page. Continuing development and perfection of devices serving the blind remained a major activity of the AFB. In the mid-1930s, the organization influenced the Congress to insert Title X in the Social Security Act of 1935, which authorized federal and state relief to the needy blind. The AFB helped to shape the Stand Concession Law, allowing blind individuals to operate news and candy stands in the lobbies of federal buildings. The AFB also influenced the enactment of a federal bill authorizing funds to supply embossed books to the blind through circulating braille libraries. The most important legislation the AFB influnced was that relating to the so-called talking books, basically recordings of literature and such. The AFB cooperated with the Library of Congress in Washington, D.C., to get federal funds so workers from the Works Project Administration (see *Government Agencies*) could make about seventeen thousand talking book reading machines. In 1935, AFB efforts resulted in an appropriation of $75,000 per year to the library for a talking book library. Also in late 1935, the AFB moved into new headquarters in its own building on West Sixteenth Street in New York City. Funds from an AFB benefactor enabled it to install a studio to produce talking books in the new building. In the late 1930s, the AFB influenced the federal regulation requiring government departments to purchase brooms and such from workshops for the blind, and, at the request of the government, the AFB organized and nurtured the National Industries for the Blind* (NIB). During this period, the AFB conducted a study of the total program for the blind in Rhode Island. To improve the education of the Negro blind in the South, the AFB gave a course for teachers and welfare workers in the summer of 1939 at West Virginia State College. In 1939, the AFB began to prepare an annotated bibligraphy of work for the blind, aided by a grant from the Carnegie Corporation.

In the 1940s, established activities and interests, such as talking books, gifts, and the education of blind children, continued, but the AFB branched out into new areas. It especially pioneered in providing services for the war-blinded veterans. In the early 1940s, with funds from the Rockefeller Foundation, the AFB promoted dramatics in schools for blind children to improve their elocution, posture, self-confidence, and such. During this period, the AFB provided talking book machines for blind veterans in hospitals, and when it learned the name and hospital of a war-blinded veteran, the AFB quickly sent him a braille watch with his name embossed on it. The AFB developed thinner and lighter records for talking books, and beginning in 1942, through a contract with the Library of Congress, it repaired all federally owned talking book machines. By 1945, the AFB had three full-time staff workers serving the war blinded in hospitals. Representing the AFB, Helen Keller spent most of 1945 visiting the blind in such hospitals. In the early 1940s, with a grant from the W. K. Kellogg Foundation, the AFB conducted its talking book education project. In 1943, the AFB was given Rest Haven in Monroe, New York, a vacation home for blind women from New York, New Jersey, Pennsylvania, and Connecticut. In 1945, the organization established its technical research department and opened a model shop to develop more special appliances for the blind. Also in 1945, at the request of John Foster Dulles, the future United States secretary of state, the AFB took over the American Foundation for Overseas Blind* (AFOB). In 1945, M. C. Migel retired as president. The AFB inaugurated important new activities in 1946 when it established its department of services for the deaf-blind.

Improving the education of blind schoolchildren and providing services to blind individuals and to the field generally were the major functions of the 1950s. For instance, the AFB appointed a consultant on education, who spent most of the time developing programs to guide parents and educators of preschool blind children. During the summer of 1950, the consultant supervised training courses for teachers of the young blind at the University of Wisconsin, for Negro teachers of the Negro blind at the Hampton Institute in Virginia, and for workers with the adult blind at the University of Michigan. In 1952, the AFB helped to establish what became the National Study Committee on Education of Deaf-Blind Children, and in August 1953, it launched a national work session on the education of the blind with sighted children at Pinebrook, New York. In March 1954, the AFB held the first institute for houseparents of residential schools, cosponsored with the Tennessee School for the Blind. Throughout the period, the AFB staff provided consultation services for preschool blind children and their parents. The late 1950s featured a study with Syracuse University on services for blind children in New York State and conducting a Northwest regional conference for teachers of blind children in Portland, Oregon. The AFB's research department developed an important device allowing a normal person to communicate with deaf-blind persons in 1950. This deaf-blind communicator was a typewriter-like device, which the deaf-blind person touched to receive braille letters. In 1954, the organization added to its staff a special consultant to conduct a nationwide search for deaf-blind persons under twenty years of age and to catalog their needs. In February 1951, it helped to bring together adjustment personnel from all over the country to coordinate ideas about ways of restoring functions to the newly blinded. In 1954, with the NIB and the federal Office of Vocational Rehabilitation (OVR) (see *Government Agencies*), the AFB held the first national workshop on industrial homework. The AFB developed close ties with the Blinded Veterans Association, helping to fund its *BVA Bulletin,* providing it with two full-time staff members as advisers, and cooperating with it on a two-year study to reevaluate vocational rehabilitation programs for blind veterans. A major project began in May 1954 to publish in two years a manual codifying the principles and standards of services for the blind. In the mid-1950s, the AFB also began studies to help people with low vision disabilities. In the mid-1950s, the AFB sponsored a four-day national workshop on vocational training and employment of deaf-blind adults, and it conducted a four-year Industrial Homework Pilot Project in Vermont in cooperation with the NIB and the OVR. In the late 1950s, it worked with the New York School of Social Work to develop principles and standards of social casework in services for the blind. The AFB established its new division of research and statistics to stimulate social and applied research and to act as a clearinghouse for programs for the blind and the deaf-blind.

During the 1960s, when general social services expanded creatively, the AFB was in the vanguard in its field, developing similarly new and innovative programs. The agency continued to conduct citywide and statewide surveys of existing programs and services but only at the request of local governmental or voluntary organizations. In 1960, the AFB established its division of research and statistics to stimulate social and applied research and to act as a nationwide clearinghouse for projects dealing with the blind and the deaf-blind. To fulfill its efforts in behalf of the deaf-blind, a general agency commitment influenced by Helen Keller, the AFB maintained a national register of deaf-blind persons and sponsored numerous institutes, conferences, and seminars, such as the comprehensive workshop for teachers of the deaf-blind held in Jacksonville, Illinois, in the spring of 1962. By the mid-1960s, these concerns influenced a broader effort to help multiple-handicapped children, including the mentally ill. The AFB recruited experts in education, blindness, and mental retardation to implement programs. A film produced by the AFB explained modern methods, including the Tellatouch machine developed by the AFB. The AFB also arranged for deaf-blind children and their parents to attend the diagnostic center at Syracuse University in New York for intensive, interdisciplinary evaluations.

The AFB continued to demonstrate leadership in the field of services for the blind and for persons with low vision. In the early 1960s, for instance, the AFB organized the first International Congress on Technology and Blindness, which confirmed the AFB as a major world clearinghouse for information on blindness. Throughout the decade, the AFB's full-time representative in its office in Washington, D.C., participated in legislation and studies affecting the blind and the deaf-blind. The representative, for example, provided information in the mid-1960s on Books for the Blind programs and on the extension of the Library Services and Construction Act of 1966 to include services and facilities for the physically handicapped. He also documented needed services for the blind for a congressional study. During this period, AFB leadership was demonstrated in its appointing the first commission on standards and accreditation in the history of organized services for the blind. In the fall of 1965, the commission held a national conference for leaders in the field, who discussed and helped to revise the standards. At its meeting in April 1966, the commission authorized the establishment of a new independent organization to administer accreditation, the National Accreditation Council for Agencies Serving the Blind and Visually Handicapped. This activity, like the AFB's role in the creation of the NIB in the late 1930s, indicated its continuing leadership in the field.

Creativity in developing new programs characterized the AFB activities in the 1970s. The AFB developed a national task force to design new programs to improve services for older blind persons. In the early 1970s, the AFB conducted and partly funded a pilot project to integrate older blind persons with their sighted peers, done in conjunction with Retired Senior Volunteer Program (RSVP) in New York City and in the Serve and Enrich Retirement by Volunteer Experience (SERVE) on Staten Island in New York City. Both of these were projects of the Community Service Society* (CSS) of New York. At the twenty-fifth anniversary meeting of the National Council on the Aging* (NCOA), the AFB held a session on innovative services for older blind persons, and the AFB planned to participate in an outreach demonstration project as part of its involvement in

Operation Independence, a three-year nationwide project of the NCOA to develop in-home services for the elderly through coalitions of local voluntary and public agencies. An interesting and innovative activity in the early 1970s was the series of regional symposia on attitudes toward blindness, where sighted persons, by wearing blindfolds and the like, experienced the feeling of blindness. So successful were the AFB sessions that many state and local groups began to sponsor similar conferences on attitudes. Constantly working to improve the quality of blind and deaf-blind peoples' lives, the AFB continued to develop and to perfect mechanical devices, held workshops to integrate blind and sighted youngsters in youth-serving programs and agencies, such as local Young Men's Christian Associations and Girl Scout troops, and in the early 1970s conducted pilot projects in Minnesota and New Hampshire to study the delivery of comprehensive care systems for the visually impaired preschool children and their families in both rural and urban areas.

The mid-1970s were characterized by self-evaluation and a reorganization to provide better and more efficient services. In 1973, as the result of a two-year study by an outside marketing consultant, the AFB expanded its role in developing devices, initiating its new sensory aids development program. In early 1974, the Greenleigh Associates, a management consultant specializing in social welfare agencies, evaluated the AFB's programs and operations and recommended changes. The board of directors, however, decided to delay implementing the recommendations until it hired a new executive director to replace twenty-five-year AFB veteran, M. Robert Barnett, who retired. In January 1975, Loyal E. Apple, himself blind—like his predecessors Irwin and Barnett—became the executive director. The AFB redesigned its publication, *New Outlook for the Blind,* appointed two new task forces, hired a new director of low vision services, and developed a new consolidated research and technological department.

There are many primary sources for studying the AFB's history. The often detailed *Annual Reports* are helpful. One of the AFB's journals, *Outlook for the Blind,* and its *New Outlook for the Blind,* contain items about the organization. A host of other publications, such as Robert B. Irwin's autobiography, *As I Saw It* (1955), mention the AFB. The archives of the AFB contain the records of the organization, as well as the personal papers of leaders such as Helen Keller and Robert Irwin. The AFB restricts the use of the archives, however.

An AFB publication, *AFB* (1952), is a helpful, short history, and Frances Koestler, *The Unseen Majority: A Social History of Blindness in America* (1976) is, as its subtitle suggests, more a history of blindness than of the AFB, which nevertheless does figure prominently in the book. There does not appear to be a full-scale, scholarly history of this important agency, which has been neglected by social welfare historians.

AMERICAN FREEDOM FROM HUNGER FOUNDATION (AFFHF). When he became president, John F. Kennedy was concerned about the plight of the hungry and malnourished in the world. Consequently, at the president's urging, the American Freedom from Hunger Foundation (AFFHF) was founded in November 1961 "to eliminate hunger and malnutrition from the earth." President Kennedy announced its establishment in Washington, D.C., on November 22, 1961, and he called for American citizens to support the AFFHF, which planned to work in cooperation with the Food and Agricultural Organization of the United Nations (FAO). Organizing ceremonies at the White House were held, featuring singer and AFFHF founder Marion Anderson. A group of thirty-two prominent Americans helped to organize the AFFHF, among them former President Harry Truman, Arthur H. Sulzberger, David Sarnoff, chairman of the board of the Radio Corporation of America, Mary Lasker, who was active in a host of philanthropies, Walter P. Reuther, the president of the United Auto Workers of America, Mrs. E. Lee Ozburn, president of the General Federation of Women's Clubs, Reverend Edward E. Swanstrom, executive director of the Catholic Relief Services-National Catholic Welfare Conference* (CRS-NCWC), and George McGovern, chairman of the White House Office of Food for Peace, a government program. The AFFHF planned to work in the worldwide freedom from hunger campaign.

In its brief history, the AFFHF served as a catalyst in the field of hunger and malnutrition. In 1963, for instance, it helped to sponsor the first World Food Congress in Washington, D.C. In 1964, the organization gained national attention when Lady Bird Johnson, the wife of President Lyndon Johnson, dedicated its mobile kitchen in Central and South America. The AFFHF is perhaps best known for its Walk for Development program, which began in 1968 when about three thousand people, mostly young, walked a thirty-three mile route near Fargo, North Dakota, and Morehead, Minnesota to publicize and to raise funds for the organization. These thirty-odd mile walks, eventually made by about two million people, helped the AFFHF to raise about $12 million between 1968 and 1975. The organization was justly proud that about 85 percent of its funds went directly to food projects, making the AFFHF one of the least expensive agencies to administer in the field of hunger and malnutrition. During the 1960s and 1970s, the AFFHF aided emergency relief efforts in such needy areas as Biafra, Bangladesh, Nicaragua, and the Sahel, in Africa.

Highlights of the 1970s included efforts in 1970 to coordinate the participation of voluntary agencies at the Second World Food Congress at the Hague, Netherlands, and to organize the United States steering committee to facilitate the participation of nongovernmental agencies at the World Food Conference in Rome, Italy, in 1974. Also in 1974, the AFFHF established the World Hunger Action Coalition to mobilize the private sector's support for the Rome conference. The AFFHF staffed the coalition, which held a series of meetings all over the United States. In 1975, the AFFHF received a grant for an eighteen-month project to hold a series of regional conferences overseas on rural development. The first such conference was held for governmental and voluntary agencies in Nairobi, Kenya, in January 1976. Annual programs include the national Week of Concern each September and summer seminars about food and hunger-related issues for a hundred congressional interns. In 1975, the AFFHF began to publish a monthly *Bulletin,* it issued the *Hunger Action Handbook,* and in the mid-1970s, it produced a film, *The Right to Eat.*

The primary sources for studying the history of the AFFHF consist largely of the files of *The New York Times.* The Agency has the records of its activities in its offices in Washington, D.C. Some agency publications, such as the short "History and Activities," prepared in 1976, were also helpful.

AMERICAN FRIENDS SERVICE COMMITTEE (AFSC). "The alternative to war is not inactivity and cowardice. It is the irresistible and constructive power of good will." Part of an advertisement in leading American newspapers and magazines, these words reflected the spirit and intention of the Religious Society of Friends (Quakers) (see *Religious Institutions*) as the United States entered World War I on April 6, 1917. Many Quakers felt that they could not engage in military service but wanted to work constructively under civilian control to operate against war itself as an alternative to military service. The American Friends Service Committee (AFSC) was founded on April 30, 1917, by members of the Religious Society of Friends in the United States at a meeting of twelve representatives from various American Quaker groups. Held at the Young Friends Building in Philadelphia, this meeting arose out of American Friends' concern to find immediate practical expression for their pacifism. In subsequent meetings a committee was organized, officers were selected, and various service projects were considered to provide young Quakers and other conscientious objectors to war with an opportunity to perform "a service of love in wartime." Among the founders were Rufus Jones, philosopher, teacher, and historian who became the first chairman of the board of AFSC, and Henry Cadbury, a biblical scholar and humanitarian.

Since its inception, AFSC has attempted to serve as a channel for Quaker concern growing out of the basic Quaker belief that "there is that of God in every person" and the basic Quaker faith that the power of love can "take away the occasion for all wars." Since that time, the AFSC has sought to reduce the causes and effects of violence and to create a wider and deeper community among people. AFSC has perhaps been best known for its work of relief and rehabilitation for war victims. In 1917, it sent young men and women to France, where they worked in cooperation with British Friends, feeding and caring for refugee children, founding a maternity hospital, repairing and rebuilding homes, and providing returning refugees with the necessities with which to start life once more.

With the cessation of hostilities in 1918, the work of the AFSC spread into other war-ravaged lands: into Russia where workers helped to fight famine and disease; into Poland and Serbia where they established an orphanage and helped in agricultural rehabilitation; into Germany and Austria where they fed hungry children.

Eventually the Quaker service teams completed these tasks and went home, leaving behind them small Quaker centers to supervise the turnover of projects and to support the small groups of nationals who had become interested in Quakerism during the time of war relief. This was an early example of community self-help, an important contemporary principle in the social services.

During the first ten years of its existence, the AFSC worked in ten nations abroad, as well as in projects within the United States. Besides the extensive relief and reconstruction work in France, Germany, Austria, Russia, and Poland, there were shorter-term projects in Albania, China, Syria, Bulgaria, and Serbia.

The home service program of the AFSC also originated during this time to handle large-scale domestic problems as well as individual assignments. By 1925, the AFSC was assigning as many as thirty volunteers each year to work in settlement houses, reform schools, and schools for blacks, native Americans, and isolated mountain children. Programs to feed undernourished children in depressed mining areas in West Virginia and western Pennsylvania began during the 1920s and expanded during the 1930s with funds supplied by the American Relief Administration* and private matching funds from the AFSC with the expression of support from such groups as the Federal Council of the Churches of Christ in America (see *Religious Institutions*).

Under the AFSC's direction, a furniture cooperative was established. It later became the Mountaineer Craftsmen Cooperative Association in Morgantown, West Virginia. Health clinics, summer educational camps for girls, adult educational programs, and work camps to establish government subsistence homesteads similarly flourished in the mining area with AFSC's assistance.

In 1937, the AFSC purchased two hundred acres in Fayette County, Pennsylvania, with funds contributed by the United States Steel Corporation and other large firms for the creation of a model homestead community, Penn-Craft. Each family built its own home and operated a large communal garden. Through the AFSC's help, a sweater knitting mill was brought into the community. A consumer's cooperative store was established as well as a community center. Taking the experience they had gained at Penn-Craft, in the late 1930s, AFSC workers helped to encourage self-help cooperative housing projects near Flanners Run, Indianapolis, among auto workers in Lorain, Ohio, in a slum neighborhood in Philadelphia, and among migrant farm workers in California.

Scarcely had the problems of World War I and the 1920s been met at home and abroad when those of the 1930s called forth fresh efforts. Quaker workers were soon engaged in helping refugees escape from Adolf Hitler's Germany, in providing relief for children on both sides of the Spanish civil war, with feeding refugees in occupied France, and later in helping victims of the 1941 London blitz.

In the United States, aiding refugees from Europe, working with southern sharecroppers, and continuing the relief and self-help projects with the miners were the main thrust of AFSC's efforts. Peace caravans, work camps, and institutes of international relations were other areas for AFSC's energies. Early work in the field of peace education included a news service, oratorial peace contests for young people, and work with college students. Institutes were held for special groups, such as labor leaders, farm leaders, editors of religious newspapers, and the general public. A discussion of the spiritual and ethical basis of international problems was developed in the course of each institute.

In 1941, as the entrance of the United States into World War II and the passage of the draft act both became imminent, the AFSC once again faced the situation that originally called the organization into being: the need to provide alternative service for conscientious objectors (COs). The Civilian Public Service (CPS) program was established under federal government auspices in which COs worked in reforestation, conservation and the improvement of national parks. Three historic peace churches—the Friends, the Church of the Brethren (see *Religious Institutions*), and the Mennonites—agreed to set up camps for the men in buildings provided by the government and to provide them with maintenance. Under this arrangement, the AFSC, acting for the Friends, administered some twenty camps and thirty small units in which over thirty-four hundred men participated. Only 25 percent were Quakers, for the three peace churches had agreed to take care of all declared COs regardless of their church affiliations.

The COs worked in soil conservation, as helpers on farms and as smoke jumpers, and in training schools and mental hospitals. Still others served as experimental subjects, exposed to starvation diets, sleeplessness, extremes of heat and cold, and a variety of diseases to advance medical science. When women asked AFSC to find them work of national significance during World War II, it organized a voluntary women's service in mental hospitals in 1943, beginning with a unit of eight young women in the Philadelphia State Hospital. Thus was born the AFSC's program of institutional service units, which assigned young high school and college students for eight weeks each summer to serve as volunteers at state institutions. This program operated for over thirty years before being terminated.

On March 2, 1946, six months after the conclusion of hostilities with Japan, the AFSC ended its administration of CPS, feeling that it was wrong to continue to operate the draft in peacetime. As the war ended, a few COs who had become deeply engrossed in the problems of mental illness helped to found the National Mental Health Foundation,* which continues to this day as the National Association for Mental Health* to increase public awareness of the problems of the mentally ill.

During World War II, the AFSC helped refugees from nazism in Europe and Japanese-Americans interned in relocation camps. Following the war, the AFSC sponsored relief and rehabilitation programs in France, Germany, Italy, and Japan. In 1947, in conjunction with the Friends Service Council of Great Britain, the AFSC was awarded the Nobel Prize for peace, the only American organization ever to have received that honor. In that same year, the AFSC helped to resettle refugees who had lost their homes as a result of communal rioting upon the partition of India. In 1948, Quaker workers undertook a program of relief for Arab refugees on the Gaza Strip. The Korean War, the Hungarian revolution, and the Algerian war all produced new areas for Quaker service through the AFSC. During this time, Henry Cadbury was chairman of the board of directors with Clarence Pickett continuing to serve as executive secretary, a position he had held since 1929.

In 1966, the AFSC undertook programs of child care and prosthetics with war-injured Vietnamese civilian refugees and their children, and shortly after this, extended their aid to civilians in North Vietnam and in the areas held by the National Liberation Front through gifts of medical supplies. During the Nigerian-Biafran war there were AFSC workers on both sides of the battle, and after the cessation of hostilities the workers stayed on to conduct rehabilitation programs. To meet the severe food shortage in Laos, the AFSC sent $50,000 in 1975 to the nation's government for the purchase of 270 tons of rice. An additional $30,000 was sent later that year to feed fifty-four hundred persons trying to reestablish themselves in the war-devastated plain of Jars. The AFSC also donated a tractor with plow, rototillers, mine detectors, and medical kits to the returning refugees in accordance with its self-help philosophy.

While it continues to minister to the victims of people's inhumanity to one another around the world, the AFSC has turned its attention more and more to programs designed to relieve the tensions that lead to war. Since the disparity between rich and poor nations is one cause of such tensions, the AFSC has concentrated since World War II on establishing programs of social and technical assistance in developing nations—Pakistan, India, Zambia, Peru, Mexico, Algeria, and Mali among others. Work in the area of family planning has been conducted in Hong Kong, India, Africa, and elsewhere, usually in conjunction with other ongoing AFSC projects.

In a related effort to get at potential sources of tensions, the AFSC has sought, since the early 1950s, to bring together midcareer diplomats from many nations in informal conferences where they may come to know each other as individuals, free of the armature of office. Beginning in Europe, this program has been extended to Africa, the Middle East, and all parts of Asia and has expanded to include young leaders and professionals as well as diplomats. In Japan, in Southeast Asia, in Africa, and at the United Nations headquarters both in Geneva and New York, Quaker workers seek to bring together women and men who may be in a position to help prevent conflicts from developing between their nations. In 1975, the AFSC also launched a major nationwide Middle East peace education program in the United States.

Recognizing that most conflicts have their roots in injustice, the AFSC has been long concerned with eliminating such injustice at home. This has led to a long history of their involvement with native Americans, Mexican-Americans, migrant workers, prisoners, blacks, and the poor. The AFSC's approach is to help these people find the tools with which to organize themselves for community action and thus to work for better schools, housing, and working conditions.

Throughout the United States, the AFSC works continually to create an informed public opinion on the issues of war and peace. By the means of speaking tours, by the publication of peace literature, through its own vigils, and by participation in other demonstrations and protests, the AFSC works to arouse Americans against the dangers of increasing militarism and the growing hold of the military-industrial complex upon this nation. In 1975, the AFSC began a program in research, education, and action on government surveillance and citizens' rights as well as a program of public education of Senate bill 1, a 753-page bill originally intended to revise and reform the United States Criminal Code. Since 1974, the nationwide women's program, the Third World coalition, and the National Action Research on the Military-Industrial Complex programs have been added to the AFSC roster to identify, challenge, and change sexist, racist, and militaristic practices and attitudes. In 1976, over four hundred AFSC staff members worked through twenty regional and area offices in the United States and through permanent offices located in Europe, Africa, Asia, and Latin America. These staff members are currently operating over sixty different projects with hundreds of volunteers.

The AFSC is a nonprofit organization entirely dependent on voluntary contributions and gifts and does not attempt to advance any particular political theory. It is under the guidance of an executive secretary and a board of directors who are members of the Religious Society of Friends (Quakers). Many of its employees belong to the Religious Society of Friends also. Its work is conducted through three divisions: international division, community relations, and peace education. The national headquarters are located in the Friends Center Building, Fifteenth and Cherry Streets, Philadelphia, Pennsylvania 19102.

The primary sources for studying the AFSC consist largely of its own publications, including *Annual Reports,* and mimeographed materials, available to all students upon request from the information services department at AFSC's national headquarters in Philadelphia. The well-organized archives at the national headquarters also provide a comprehensive view of AFSC since 1917.

Helpful secondary studies of the AFSC include Gerald Jones, *On Doing Good: The Quaker Experiment* (1971), and Marvin R. Weisbrod, *Some Form of Peace: True Stories of the AFSC* (1968). Clarence Pickett's *For More Than Bread* (1953) is an autobiographical account of his twenty-two years' work with the AFSC. See also Elizabeth Gray Vining, *A Friend of Life: The Biography of Rufus M. Jones* (1958), for information about the AFSC's founding and early years.

Judi Breault

AMERICAN FUNDS FOR THE RELIEF OF JEWISH WAR SUFFERERS: see AMERICAN JEWISH JOINT DISTRIBUTION COMMITTEE, INC.

AMERICAN HEART ASSOCIATION (AHA).   In the second decade of the twentieth century, physicians and social workers began experimenting with the rehabilitation of cardiac victims. In Boston, for instance, two physicians at the

Children's Hospital clinic conducted a cardiac clinic. The most important work in this field was done in and around New York City. One experimental program was conducted at the Trade School for Cardiac Convalescents, known also as the Sharon Shop, in Sharon, Connecticut, and with an office in New York City under Dr. Lewis A. Conner. Some ten years later Conner helped to organize what became the American Heart Association (AHA) and became its first president. Another experiment more directly related to the establishment of the AHA in 1932—and one that reflects its social work origins—was the clinics for cardiacs being held by social workers and physicians, especially Dr. Herbert Guile from Bellevue Hospital. This program apparently began in 1911. Social workers visited the cardiacs' homes and paid close attention to the patients' adjustments and progress. During this period, a separate study showed that about twenty thousand schoolchildren in New York City had some type of heart disease. This report and the social workers' project at Bellevue prompted interest among doctors, social workers, and others in New York City. Discussions about the work culminated in the establishment, in 1915 and 1916, of the Association for the Prevention and Relief of Heart Disease (APRHD). Its main purpose was to found cardiac clinics, and within a few months, twenty such clinics were established.

During American participation in World War I, the APRHD was suspended, but the clinics continued to function. In February 1917, these clinics established the Association of Cardiac Clinics (ACC) to standardize methods, classification, and nomenclature. The ACC continued as a separate organization until February 1923, when it became a committee to the APRHD, which had resumed activities in 1919. These efforts were discussed and publicized at the meetings of the American Medical Association (AMA) in the early 1920s. The interest displayed there prompted the New York group to send invitations to about a hundred doctors to meet at the Hotel Claridge in St. Louis, Missouri, on May 24, 1922, during the annual AMA meeting. About forty-five physicians met and established the AHA. At this meeting, an organizing committee was appointed. It met often during the next two years, and it drew up a certificate of incorporation. Dr. Conner and Dr. Paul Dudley White, the famous heart doctor, were among the six physicians who signed the document that made the AHA a legal entity on March 20, 1924. On June 10, 1924, the group completed organizational formalities and elected its first slate of officers: a president, a vice-president, a secretary-treasurer, and the first executive committee.

The AHA developed slowly as an organization. In the early 1920s, the organizational structure included an advisory council of no more than sixty members, from which a fifteen-member board of directors was chosen. There were also a seven-member executive committee and many standing and special committees appointed to carry out the agency's work. The AHA had only a one-room office in the New York City headquarters of the National Tuberculosis Association* (NTA). It also had a half-time secretary donated by the NTA, and Dr. H. M.

Marvin, a cardiologist from New Haven, Connecticut, came to the office weekly and worked as a volunteer. The early AHA concerned itself primarily with establishing cardiac clinics, classifying heart diseases accurately, and promoting better training in the field and proper standards in heart-related medicine. The first issue of its bimonthly professional publication, *The American Heart Journal,* appeared in October 1925. In 1936, the journal became a monthly publication, and since January 1950, it has been published as *Circulation—The Journal of the AHA.* Throughout the late 1930s and early 1940s, the AHA contributed to research, for example, by drafting standards for both electrocardiograms and blood pressure. The Section for the Study of Peripheral Circulation joined the AHA in 1936, thus helping to solidify the notion that "circulation" was part of "heart" research.

By 1940 the AHA had already made many scientific and technical contributions. Even so, many members urged expansion. A distinguished committee drafted reorganizational plans, which the board of directors approved in 1941. With American entry into World War II, however, and many AHA members participating in war-related medical work, implementation of the plans was delayed. Immediately after the war, expansion activity resumed. Because of the large number of rheumatic fever cases in the armed forces, the AHA urged that a meeting be convened to discuss this problem, and in January 1944, a two-day conference was held. At this meeting, ten health agencies founded the Council on Rheumatic Fever, which quickly became affiliated with the AHA. It eventually became the AHA's council on rheumatic fever and congenital heart disease. In 1946, the American Legion gave the AHA grants of $25,000 for research and $25,000 for community rheumatic fever programs and allowed part of these funds to be used to hire a full-time medical director. David B. Rutstein filled the position, beginning immediately to prepare for the AHA's becoming a national voluntary health organization. The annual meeting in 1946 approved the change, which was implemented in 1947.

The AHA began as a national voluntary health agency with considerable success. Determined not to have volunteer lay people take over the AHA as they had the American Cancer Society* (ACS), AHA medical leaders stipulated that the lay group would have no voice in scientific policies and that physicians would have the final vote on nonmedical policies. Mrs. Albert Lasker, a well-known philanthropist from New York, offered $50,000 to help the new AHA if it would accept the promotional services of Emerson Foote, who had been publicizing the ACS. The AHA leaders rejected the offer because they did not want to risk the eventuality of lay control. Shortly after the reorganization in 1946, Fred Arkus began to direct the AHA's public education campaigns, which proved successful almost from the beginning. In 1947, the AHA established its assembly, which admitted lay members. In June 1949, the former general secretary of the American Bible Society, Rome A. Betts, became the AHA's executive director. In its first decade the AHA experienced tremendous growth. In 1946, for instance, there were no local chapters. By 1949, there were seven, and by 1956, 240. Similarly, there were five affiliates in 1946, and ten years later, there were fifty-five. In 1949, the fund-raising campaign yielded about $2.65 million, and in 1956, it earned almost $30 million. The organization conducted the first National Heart Week in January 1947. In 1948, it was named recipient of the proceeds of a nationally famous contest, the "walking man" identification on Ralph Edward's radio show, "Truth or Consequences." In 1949, the now well-recognized AHA conducted the first national heart fund campaign and established its own fund-raising machinery.

The proceeds from the highly successful fund-raising campaigns largely supported the AHA's broad research programs. One-fourth of all funds collected by the affiliates went to the national headquarters in New York; 60 percent is allocated for research. The AHA was the first agency to establish the concept of career investigators, researchers who receive financial support for their entire professional lives. Affiliates spend about 30 percent of their funds for research, helping to make the AHA the organization devoting the highest percentage of its funds to research. AHA-supported research covers all areas of heart-related conditions and has contributed to AHA statements, beginning in 1956, on smoking and heart disease and, in 1957, on dietary fat and arteriosclerosis.

To complement its research programs and to support its positions on public health issues, the AHA has conducted and sponsored important scientific programs. In 1945, it established the American Foundation for High Blood Pressure, which merged with the AHA five years later, becoming its council for high blood pressure. In 1950, the AHA and the National Heart Institute (see *Government Agencies*) jointly sponsored the first national conference on cardiovascular disease. AHA's scientific sessions have been held annually since 1925.

Much of the activity in specialized areas was and is conducted by councils, which before 1957 were known as sections. There are councils on basic science, community service, and rheumatic fever and congenital heart disease. In 1957, the AHA streamlined its structure: all the councils became part of the new central committee for medicine and community health programs. Other new councils and committees are created periodically to meet special needs; for example, the Commitee on Ethics, established in 1967, helps develop guidelines for heart transplants, and in 1959, the American Society for the Study of Arteriosclerosis affiliated with the AHA as its committee on arteriosclerosis. In addition to the voluntary officers, the AHA had a large paid staff and maintained a library of heart-related publications in the national headquarters in New York City. In the late 1950s, the AHA took a major step, beginning to work in politics to influence the establishment of a federal heart institute. In 1959, there was a spirited internal debate over a resolution that would have urged children not to smoke. The resolution was referred back to a committee, but in 1960, the AHA reported that tobacco was possibly harmful.

In the late 1960s and 1970s, the AHA developed a number of heart disease programs and approaches. In 1964, it launched a nationwide stroke program. AHA respresentatives testified before congressional committees dealing with medical research. In 1965, President Lyndon B. Johnson filmed a personal heart fund appeal, one of the few such statements by an American president in behalf of a national voluntary health organization. In 1963, the AHA began an active campaign against smoking and a whole series of activities, including the publication in about 1973 of the *AHA Cookbook,* which educated the public about diet and the leading cause of death in the United States: heart disease. AHA research has continued to advance, developing ever improving artificial pacemakers and more sophisticated drugs. In the early 1970s, the AHA adopted a clear-cut set of priorities, headed by detecting high blood pressure. A national conference on partnership in productivity, held in Boston in 1973, concluded that low-income and minority people were especially susceptible to cardiovascular problems. To deal with this problem, the AHA added a specialist in minority affairs to its national staff, and the national office initiated a nationwide educational campaign about high blood pressure. Research continued to be the single largest allocation, but local heart chapters and affiliates began to offer diet counseling by paid full-time as well as volunteer part-time nutritionists. Local groups also conducted clinics and provided low-cost rapid screening for high blood pressure. In 1973, the year the AHA claimed for its twenty-fifth anniversary, the agency realigned its national headquarters staff to stress consultant and other services for chapters and affiliates. The AHA also reorganized its board of directors and executive committee and restructured its organization to create a greater role for volunteer leaders. In 1973, over 2 million volunteers, led by Kemmons Wilson, the chairman of the board of Holiday Inns, helped to raise a record high of almost $5.5 million in voluntary contributions. In 1975, the AHA moved from its long-time headquarters in New York City to new facilities in Dallas, Texas.

The best primary source for studying the AHA's history is the published *Annual Reports.* Public, university, and even medical libraries might not have complete files of them, but the AHA's library does. In 1975, the library moved to Dallas, Texas.

The AHA library has two organizational histories: the detailed "A History of the AHA," an unpublished typescript, and Dr. H. H. Marvin, *1924–1964, The Forty Year War on Heart Disease* (n.d., [1964]), based on a report that he, as the AHA historian, delivered at the 1964 AHA convention. Other secondary sources, such as the popular Richard Carter, *The Gentle Legions* (1961), deal briefly with the AHA's history. There does not appear to be a scholarly history of the AHA.

AMERICAN HUMANE ASSOCIATION, THE (AHA). In the mid-nineteenth century, Henry Bergh was the secretary of the United States legation at St. Petersburgh, Russia. During his tenure there, Bergh often spoke out publicly against cruelty to animals. In 1865, on his way back to the United States,

Bergh stopped in London and met John Colam, the secretary of the Royal Society for the Prevention of Cruelty to Animals. Established in 1824, this society was followed by others developed throughout Europe. Bergh became interested in these organizations, and on February 8, 1866, he gave a public lecture in New York City on cruelty to animals. Many people, as well as the press, rallied to support Bergh. An aroused public opinion led quickly to the establishment of the American Society for the Prevention of Cruelty to Animals in April 1866. At about the same time, a society in Boston was being established. George T. Angell of Boston was interested in protecting animals. In February 1868, Angell was aroused by the deaths of two horses during a horse race. Angell promptly placed an advertisement in a local newspaper calling for action. Mrs. William Appleton of Boston appeared at this meeting. Mrs. Appleton reported that she had met with Bergh and she and some of her influential friends agreed to support the new Massachusetts Society for the Prevention of Cruelty to Animals, organized in March 1868 and modeled after Bergh's society in New York. Prominent people soon organized a similar society in Pennsylvania, and others began to appear in the late 1860s and 1870s. These humane societies dealt primarily with preventing cruelty to animals. Discussions about forming a national organization of humane societies persisted for a few years, until John G. Shortall, the president of the Illinois Humane Society, convened a meeting in Cleveland, Ohio, at the fashionable Kennard House. At this meeting on October 9, 1877, twenty-two representatives from nine existing humane societies established The American Humane Association (AHA) as the International Humane Society (IHS). The IHS elected Edwin Lee Brown, who had been the president of the Illinois Humane Society, as its first president. The gathering in Cleveland adopted a resolution calling for a federal law against the ill treatment of animals in transit. The group—which in the next year changed its name to the American Humane Association (AHA)—antagonized railroad interests and their allies but maintained their battle until they achieved their goal in the late 1950s.

The AHA's early activities focused on organizational details and on obtaining laws protecting animals. At the second convention in Baltimore in 1878, for instance, the AHA appointed a committee to work to obtain a federal charter for the organization. The AHA also rejected an amendment to the bylaws that it deal with the protection of children; not until 1885 did this activity begin. Meanwhile, in 1879, the organization established a fund of $5,000 for a prize to the individual who designed the most humane cattle railroad car. In 1880, the AHA published the first of many pamphlets, *Cruelty to Animals on the Railroads*. In 1882, the AHA began its long battle for a federal humane slaughtering bill, which was enacted finally in 1958. In 1884, an organizational crisis— particularly that the national organization dominated the local societies—nearly forced the demise of the AHA, but the convention rallied to unite and elected founder Shortall of Illinois as president for a year. Between 1893 and 1898, Shortall again served as president. Major activities continued to focus on the conditions of cattle killings and of slaughtering and on the organization of new local societies. Beginning in 1879, George T. Angell, a leader in the allied movement promoting humane education, became the first of many field agents promoting new societies.

The national charter incorporating the AHA, granted in Washington, D.C., in November 1903, ushered in a new era of the organization. When AHA President Dr. Albert Leffingwell resigned in 1904 to become United States consul to Russia, the board of directors asked one of its members, Dr. William O. Stillman, to become president, a position to which the convention in 1905 elected him. Trained as a physician, active in his native Albany, New York, area humane society, Stillman more than any other AHA leader influenced the expansion of the organization. Stillman transformed the sputtering agency, which had no office or staff, into a truly national society. From his own funds, he established headquarters in Albany and hired a secretarial staff. Under Stillman, the AHA also employed the first salaried field director, established new local societies and reactivated old ones, and, most importantly, founded in 1913 the journal of the AHA, *The National Humane Review*. During World War I, Dr. Stillman organized the American Red Star Animal Relief to care for wounded animals much like the American National Red Cross* cared for human war victims. The AHA also sponsored Be Kind to Animals Week. The death of AHA leader Stillman on March 15, 1924, ended an era in the organization's history. In May 1924, the board of directors named Sidney Coleman general director of the AHA. Coleman had written for *The National Humane Review* and had published *Human Society Leaders in America* in 1924.

Although in its first fifty years, the AHA focused on protecting animals, child welfare developed as its other major focus. Local societies for the protection of children, like the ones in New York and Boston, were affiliated with the AHA. Local humane societies, such as the ones in Cleveland and Illinois, dealt with the protection of children, and in 1924, two affiliated humane societies maintained homes for unmarried women and their illegitimate children. In 1920, particularly in the pages of the *National Humane Review,* the AHA allied with the national campaign advocating "a square deal for children born out of wedlock." The AHA was concerned both with the quality of American childhood in the 1920s, especially with children's apparently increased use of drugs and with the evils of child labor. In April 1929, at a board of directors meeting, the AHA created its committee on child protection, headed by Colonel Ernest K. Coulter, a leader in the movement to protect children and a founder of the Big Brother movement.

During the 1930s and 1940s, although it developed some new programs, the AHA essentially continued its traditional activities in child and animal protection. In 1932, noting the depression but careful not to blame it for an apparent increase in juvenile crimes, AHA President Sidney Coleman called for a special department of child protective work. In the early 1930s, the board of directors finally developed a pension plan for the staffs of member agencies. The humane trapping activities became part of the new wildlife department, and in the early 1930s, the AHA attempted to stop bullfights in the United States. In 1938, the AHA moved to new national headquarters in Albany, New York. In the late 1930s, it worked to establish new affiliates, sending a representative to travel to unorganized communities in the United States. Claiming that marijuana was dangerous to American children, in 1940, the AHA urged Governor Culbert Olson of California to stop the illicit drug importation from Mexico. In 1939, the AHA established an office in Hollywood, California, to help protect animals that appeared in motion pictures, and in December 1940, partly because of the AHA's influence, the Motion Picture Producers Association agreed to abolish practices endangering animals and to accept an AHA representative as an industry arbiter on such matters. In the early 1940s, the board of directors established a committee on child protection, which held a meeting in New York City in 1942 and chose Judge William A. Ekwall of the United States Customs Court in New York as chairman. The committee expressed the desire to have a field secretary for children's work. Like other national social service agencies, the AHA provided a field service, which also conducted studies of community needs, such as the one in the mid-1940s of Union and Morris counties in New Jersey. Also in the mid-1940s, the AHA hired a representative to oversee legislation in Washington, D.C.

World War II and its aftermath affected the AHA. During the war, both the wildlife and the children's departments were suspended, reopening only in 1947. An AHA affiliate, the American Red Star Animal Relief, cared for the animals stranded in transit during the railroad strikes in 1946.

In the 1950s and 1960s, traditional activities continued. The AHA's division of children became increasingly important in the national social service community. In the early 1950s, Horace Sodt of the AHA's field service conducted an investigation to determine if the Seeing Eye, Inc.,* mistreated seeing-eye dogs. In the late 1950s, the AHA began its nationwide inspection program (NIP) to prevent cruelty to and abuse of animals in traveling shows, and in 1959, it helped to incorporate the International Society for the Protection of Animals. In the 1950s, it strengthened its children's department, developing a program to interpret and to promote standards for agencies conducting child protection work. It created a consultation service for member agencies and finally established training facilities for the staffs of children's protective agencies. In the 1950s, the children's division sponsored workshops on child protection to discuss cooperative efforts, model legislation, and the like with representatives of such national agencies as the Child Welfare League of America,* the National Probation and Parole Association,* the United Community Funds and Councils of America,* and the United States Children's Bureau (see *Government Agencies*). In the mid-1950s, the children's division published two important studies, both by Director Vincent De Francis: *The Fundamentals of Child Protection* (1955) and *Child Protective Societies in the United States,* which showed that most cities had no effective protective services. This prompted a campaign by the AHA to develop such services. The effectiveness of the children's division became clear in the early 1960s, when, for example, the Ohio Welfare Association and other similar organizations asked it to conduct institutes of child protection at state and other welfare conferences. To strengthen both the central organization and affiliates, the AHA began regional service councils in the early 1960s. These councils helped to develop new societies and distributed materials formerly available only from the national headquarters, which moved from Albany, New York, to Denver, Colorado, in 1954. In 1967, there were over seven hundred affiliates of the AHA.

The children's division still headed by Dr. De Francis provided the AHA's closest ties to the national social work community in the 1970s. In 1971, for example, with other groups, the AHA held the first annual symposium dealing with child neglect and abuse. In 1973, with funds from the Children's Bureau of the Office of Child Development of the United States Department of Health, Education, and Welfare, the AHA opened its national clearinghouse on child abuse and neglect. Throughout the period, Dr. De Francis and the staff conducted training sessions, institutes, and conferences for social workers and educators. In 1971, the division began a research study to obtain information about the jurisdiction of family and juvenile courts in the field of child neglect and dependency. In 1973, the AHA conducted a study of juvenile courts as they related to abused children. In 1974, states began sending data to the national clearinghouse on neglect and child abuse. Other AHA activities included the completion of two studies of laws protecting animals in 1972, and in the mid-1970s, a campaign against pet overpopulation. Traditional activities in the field of humane legislation for animals and in the humane treatment of animals in motion pictures continued in the 1970s.

The basic source for studying the AHA's history and interests is *The National Humane Review;* the January–February 1962 issue is especially helpful. The published *Proceedings of the Annual Meetings* and some other organization publications also contain information about the agency. The AHA has its files at its national headquarters in Denver, Colorado.

There is a little information about the AHA's history in Roswell C. McCrea, *The Humane Movement* (1910), but historians have generally neglected the AHA. There does not appear to be a scholarly history of this veteran agency.

AMERICAN IMMIGRATION AND CITIZENSHIP CONFERENCE (AICC). The large number of voluntary agencies and organizations devoted to meeting the special needs of recently arrived immigrants and other resident aliens in the United States gave rise to two umbrella organizations in the field. The National Council on Naturalization and Citizenship* (NCNC) was founded in 1930 to share information and to coordinate the activities of organizations and individuals who were concerned with improving naturalization laws and procedures. A similar desire to achieve a more humane, nondiscriminatory immigration policy led to the formation of the American Immigration Conference* (AIC) in 1954.

Because the goals of the two organizations were so closely related, many agencies were members of both. The AIC and NCNC also shared office space in New York, and both enjoyed the services of Ruth Z. Murphy as their executive officer. They formed a joint committee on the integration of the foreign born into the community and cosponsored numerous meetings and luncheons. Cooperation led ultimately to the creation of the American Immigration and Citizenship Conference (AICC) on March 18, 1960.

According to its constitution (an amended version of the AIC constitution), AICC exists to "bring together nonprofit, nonpolitical American agencies which believe in humanitarian, non-discriminatory immigration, naturalization and citizenship policies in keeping with the best traditions of the United States"; at least part of its permanent programs are aimed at achieving such policies. Sixty-seven national and local religious, social service, nationality, labor, educational, and civic agencies became members in 1960. Among them were the Amalgamated Clothing Workers of America, the American Council for Nationalities Services,* the American Friends Service Committee,* the Community Council of Greater New York, the International Institute of Philadelphia, the Japanese American Citizens League, the National Council of Women (see *Fraternal Organizations*), the National Travelers Aid Association,* and the United HIAS Service.* A comparable number of organizations and individuals who could not meet the active membership requirements affiliated as cooperating (nonvoting) members.

The annual meeting in 1960 elected Angier Biddle Duke, former United States ambassador to El Salvador, president of AICC. He served until 1965, when he was succeeded by Senator Kenneth B. Keating. Immigration attorney Edward J. Ennis continued to serve as chairman of the board of directors, as he had with the AIC. Ruth Murphy remained as executive vice-president.

AICC functioned as a clearinghouse for the exchange of information and as a facilitator of joint action when members desired it. It developed and circulated proposed statements on issues, collected members' signatures, and presented the statements to appropriate officials. Policy statements were issued over the names of only those members who approved; thus no member was bound by the collective will of the conference. Standing committees responsible for the areas of legislation, administration, public information, education for citizenship, research, integration of the immigrant into the community, and international affairs carried out most conference programs.

The federal government's national origins quota system attracted most of AICC's early efforts. Believing the system to be discriminatory in its implication that some nationalities are less desirable than others and unworkable in view of the fact that a majority of immigrants actually had to be accommodated by legislation for refugees and other special groups, the AICC drew up a series of recommendations for an alternative system. It promoted its cause through numerous local and regional conferences and through frequent contacts with government officials. United States Senator Philip Hart's immigration bill, first introduced in 1962, closely followed the AICC recommendations and drew attention to the issue; President John F. Kennedy forwarded a somewhat similar proposal the following year. It required an additional two years of intensive campaigning before President Lyndon Johnson signed the Immigration and Naturalization Act of 1965. The law substantially altered the quota system and made permanent provision for the admission of refugees. Senator Hiram Fong of Hawaii, one of the bill's chief supporters, paid tribute to the significant contribution made by AICC. *Congressional Quarterly* identified AICC as "a major force . . . not by lobbying as such [but as] a clearinghouse and coordinator of immigration and nationality problems."

AICC concern was not limited to the reform of immigration policy. In 1962, its education for citizenship committee conducted a survey of teachers and concluded that the federal textbooks on citizenship—the primary resource for aliens preparing for citizenship tests—were in need of revision. Thus alerted, the Immigration and Naturalization Service (see *Government Agencies*) contracted with three AICC members to carry out the revision. Similarly, another committee studied the treatment of immigration and ethnic groups by secondary school textbooks and offered to consult with publishers to help correct misconceptions.

Continued interest in the experience of immigrants after their arrival was a primary responsibility of the integration committee. The committee paid particularly close attention to the reception accorded to Cubans and Mexicans. This issue was of special concern not only because of the large numbers of immigrants involved but also because, in the minds of AICC members, the 1965 law failed to deal adequately with the problem of immigrants from nations in the Western Hemisphere.

In the 1970s, the AICC provided an impressive array of services. It maintained a legislative reporting service and issued studies on the administration of immigration laws, ethnic relations, and immigrant-related governmental and nongovernmental activities. It also prepared educational materials, including guides to research on immigration, and it assisted communities in developing meetings and regional conferences that focused on immigrant-related issues. In 1975, the AICC committees suggested the breadth of its activities: research and statistics, information and education, integration of the foreign-born, international, legislation, and, sustaining a long-standing activity in work with immigrants, education for citizenship.

The primary sources for studying the AICC's history include some of the agency's, as well as some of its predecessors', materials at the Social Welfare History Archives Center, University of Minnesota, Minneapolis. The AICC issues its bimonthly *News,* which is not available widely in libraries. There does not appear to be a scholarly history of the AICC.

AMERICAN IMMIGRATION CONFERENCE (AIC). The unsettled political conditions in many parts of the world after World War II produced a new wave of immigration to the United States, largely by people who had been virtually forced out of their home countries. Those who sought entry to the United States faced a quota system based on national origins that was most restrictive for the very countries from which the majority of refugees were fleeing. The need for a less discriminatory policy and for assistance to individual immigrants attracted the efforts of a sizable number of voluntary agencies.

Recognizing the duplication and overlapping of these efforts, representatives of the several immigration-related organizations made a number of attempts to coordinate their efforts through groups such as the Immigration Policy Committee, the Joint Conference on Alien Legislation, and the Immigration Luncheon Group. But all of these were essentially ad hoc responses to particular problems and failed to provide a continuous direction and coordination. It was this perceived need that inspired individuals such as Ruth Larned, International Social Service,* Roland Elliott, Church World Service,* Read Lewis, Common Council for American Unity,* and Jules Cohen, National Community Relations Council to convene a series of meetings in 1954 to discuss the formation of a new, broadly representative association that would bring together agencies with an interest in immigration policy. On October 1, 1954, representatives of thirty-one organizations, meeting at the Willkie Memorial Building in New York City, formed the American Immigration Conference (AIC).

Active membership as defined by the AIC constitution was limited to nonprofit, nonpolitical agencies, at least part of whose permanent operating programs were devoted to the achievement of a humanitarian, nondiscriminatory immigration policy. Active members included long-established agencies like the Common Council for American Unity, sectarian agencies like the United HIAS Service,* nationality organizations like the Polish Immigration Committee, local societies like the Michigan Committee on Immigration, and other organizations such as the American Civil Liberties Union (see *Political and Civic Organizations*) and the United Auto Workers (see *Labor Organizations*), whose broader programs included an active concern for immigration policy. Individuals and organizations who did not meet the requirements for active membership could become cooperating (nonvoting) members, but in practice few did. Active membership increased from the original thirty-one to more than seventy in 1960. Members' dues and additional contributions constituted the sole source of financial support for the conference.

Because the member organizations were so diverse, there was no inclination to create in the AIC any binding authority over members' actions; the conference could take no official stand on immigration policy matters except when authorized to do so by the unanimous approval of its members. Its primary function was to act as a clearinghouse of information to enable member organizations to carry out their programs more effectively, not to provide the services itself. It monitored current developments—both governmental and nongovernmental—in the immigration field, provided a forum for members to share opinions and experiences, and generated educational materials for use either as internal study documents or in public education programs.

The conference enjoyed stable leadership. Earl Harrison, the first president, died in 1955 and was replaced by George Schuster, president of Hunter College. But Board Chairman Edward Ennis, an immigration attorney, served throughout the conference's six-year history as did two-thirds of the original forty-member board. Ruth Z. Murphy, executive officer of the National Council on Naturalization and Citizenship* (NCNC), served as secretary and unpaid executive of the AIC as well.

The principle that the AIC would not take an official policy stance without the unanimous support of its members faced a stern test before the conference was a year old. The controversy developed when Secretary of State John Foster Dulles dismissed Edward Corsi as his special adviser on refugee and migration problems. Corsi, who was also president of the American Federation of International Institutes* (AFII) and a vice-president of the AIC, subsequently engaged in an often-bitter exchange with State Department official Scott McLeod over administration of the Refugee Relief Act of 1953, for which McLeod was responsible. Before the Corsi affair erupted, the AIC had invited McLeod to speak at a meeting it was sponsoring at the annual forum in 1955 of the National Conference of Social Work* (NCSW). AIC members—particularly the AFII—protested that his appearance would place the AIC in a position of appearing to endorse a refugee relief policy of which many members were critical. Faced with AFII's threat to withdraw from membership, AIC asked McLeod to find himself suddenly unable to appear at the San Francisco meeting.

Most AIC work was carried out by a series of committees that were organized soon after the conference formed. The legislative committee immediately began a careful analysis of the provisions of the 1952 McCarran-Walter Act. In 1956, they released a series of forty recommendations for amending certain provisions. The committee called for an end to the national origins quota system but, recognizing that this was not likely to happen soon, also recommended reforms in the existing system, such as the pooling of unused portions of national quotas to accommodate persons from countries with waiting lists. In 1959, they issued a revised set of recommendations known as the 34 Points. In both cases submission of the recommendations to Congress was left to the discretion of member organizations.

The administrative committee developed recommendations for a sound administration of the Immigration and Nationality (McCarran-Walter) Act and reported procedural changes in the federal Immigration and Naturalization Service and the State Department. The information and education committee compiled the *AIC News,* a bimonthly newsletter that reported on conference activities and other developments in the immigration field. In 1957, it sought to refute the notion emanating from the House Committee on Un-American Activities that all agitation for change in immigration policy was coming from communist sympathizers by preparing a pamphlet containing statements on immigration by a wide variety of respected public figures. It also sponsored production of an animated film, *The Golden Door,* which was released in 1959. The international committee worked closely with the American Council of Voluntary Agencies for Foreign Service* and the American section of the United Nations–sponsored International Conference of Nongovernmental Organizations Interested in Migration while considering the international impact of American immigration policy.

AIC activities always were substantially interrelated with those of the National Council on Naturalization and Citizenship* (NCNC) if for no other reason than that they shared the same office and executive officer. They sponsored joint luncheon and dinner meetings at NCNC and NCSW conferences and, after 1956, a joint committee on integration, which was concerned with the way in which American communities received newcomers and the way in which they were affected by them. It produced three issues of *Integration Digest,* a summary of books and articles on the subject. The committee surveyed agencies in the twenty cities having the largest number of Hungarian refugees in 1957–1958 to analyze the Hungarians' resettlement experience. Also concerned about the Mexican immigrants, it planned but did not complete a similar study of their situation.

NCNC, always the junior partner in terms of budget and scope of activity, began to consider the possibility of merger as early as 1956, but not until late 1959 did it formally decided to approach the AIC with such a proposal. The formation of the American Immigration and Citizenship Conference* was accomplished within the context of the AIC constitutional structure by means of a constitutional amendment that added naturalization and citizenship to the scope of conference activities. The merger became official on March 18, 1960.

Committee and board minutes, finance and membership records, correspondence files, and copies of publications of the AIC are included in the American Immigration and Citizenship Conference records held by the Social Welfare History Archives, University of Minnesota. There is no secondary literature that focuses on the AIC.

David Klaassen

AMERICAN JEWISH JOINT DISTRIBUTION COMMITTEE, INC. (JDC). In October 1914, the United States ambassador to Turkey, Henry Morgenthau, Sr., wired an urgent plea to American Jews to provide $50,000 for the approximately sixty thousand Jews in Palestine who were threatened by the hostilities that became World War I. In response to this message, the Union of Orthodox Congregations (see *Religious Organizations*) organized the Central Committee for the Relief of Jews (CCRJ) in early October 1914. Also in October 1914, the American Jewish Committee (AJC) (see *Political and Civic Organiza-*

tions), the major Jewish organization in America at the time, began to contribute funds to aid Jewish war victims. Later in the month, to coordinate the work and to avoid duplication, the head of the AJC and an acknowledged American Jewish community leader, Louis Marshall, convened a conference of representatives from forty different agencies. To develop a new organization, the American Jewish Relief Committee (AJRC), the conference chose a committee of five members representing the spectrum of interests in the American Jewish community. The Reform-oriented AJC faction, however, dominated the AJRC. Marshall became the president, and David Bressler, who had experience in immigrant and refugee work as general manager of the Industrial Removal Office* (IRO), became a leader. Felix M. Warburg, a prominent New York City banker, became treasurer of the AJRC, which received a $100,000 grant from the AJC. To coordinate the relief work further, on November 27, 1914, in New York City, the AJRC joined the CCRJ to establish the American Jewish Joint Distribution Committee (JDC) as the Joint Distribution Committee of American Funds for the Relief of Jewish War Sufferers (JDCAFRJWS).

The early history of the JDCAFRJWS reflected the diversity of interests within the American Jewish community, but, as in other areas, the Reform-oriented AJC faction assumed early leadership. Warburg, for example, became the chairman. The CCJR, however, maintained its independence, conducting a separate campaign in its synagogues and community organizations. Prodded by relief efforts of the other groups, in the summer of 1915, Jewish socialists and Zionists, representing generally the Jewish labor movement, established the People's Relief Committee (PRC). Meyer London, a socialist and a United States congressman between 1914 and 1922, chaired the PRC. The PRC joined the JDCAFRJWS in the fall of 1915. Influenced by these factional orientations, the JDCAFRJWS remained timid in its first year, but it nevertheless raised about $1.5 million by December 1915. Organized to aid war sufferers, the JDCAFRJWS helped Polish Jews and sent about nine hundred tons of food to Jews in Turkish-controlled Palestine in 1915.

In the next few years, the fledgling organization crystallized and expanded its activities. Fund-raising chairman Nathan Straus, a philanthropist especially interested in public health and better milk campaigns, boldly set the goal of $5 million for the 1916 campaign, which shifted to the use of mass appeals. United States President Woodrow Wilson proclaimed January 27, 1916, as Jewish War Sufferers Relief Day, the American National Red Cross* agreed to help in the collection of the funds, and the campaign raised $4.75 million, a fantastic increase from the previous year. In 1917, the JDCAFRJWS developed a more systematic campaign, which Jacob Billikopf headed. The executive director of the Federation of Jewish Charities in Kansas City and leader in Jewish social service, Billikopf gave the campaign professional guidance. To implement its chief function of organizing the channeling of funds to local European Jewish community agencies, the JDCAFRJWS sent abroad Boris Bogen, another national figure in Jewish social work, and Max Senior, a Cincinnati businessman and philanthropist active in Jewish charities. United States entry into the war curtailed the assistance program, but the Department of State permitted the JDCAFRJWS to establish an agency in neutral Holland.

Conceived as a temporary agency to relieve suffering during the war, the JDCAFRJWS developed more fully and complexly in the period of postwar reconstruction. During the war years, valuable volunteers, such as Dr. Julius Goldman, the field director, had served the organization, and in the postwar years, a professional staff developed gradually. In January 1919, Dr. Bogen went abroad again to arrange for sending units of trained American workers in specialized fields such as sanitation, child care, and economics. To guide American rehabilitation of war-torn Europe, Congress established in 1919 an official relief agency headed by Herbert Hoover, the American Relief Administration* (ARA). Hoover wanted to treat all Europeans equally, but Warburg convinced him that this policy was unfair to Jews. JDCAFRJWS grants totaling $3.3 million allowed some special programs for European Jews. In 1920, however, the JDCAFRJWS began reluctantly to administer funds directly; agency leaders, secure in America, did not want to interfere in European internal affairs. This ideology also prompted the leaders not to regard migration to Palestine as a special, emotional issue.

The postwar activities influenced a shift in emphasis from temporary relief to reconstruction and self-help projects. This shift was evident by late 1920. The JDCAFRJWS aided local agencies, striving to make them independent and self-sustaining. It also developed certain programs, such as sending a group of medical workers to Poland in January 1921. Agreements worked out between the American and Russian governments allowed the JDCAFRJWS to operate in Russia under the auspices of the ARA. The effort, developed finally by mid-1922, focused on the work of Dr. Joseph A. Rosen, an agronomist who obtained agency funds for agricultural development, such as tractors and other implements. Rosen's experiments proved so successful that in July 1924, the Russian government and the JDCAFRJWS established the American Jewish Joint Agricultural Corporation to promote self-sustaining Jewish agricultural communities there. The JDCAFRJWS developed KASSAS, loan cooperatives that implemented the agency goal of postwar reconstruction through self-help efforts. To conduct the loan cooperative program, the JDCAFRJWS joined with the wealthy, prestigious, businesslike Jewish Colonization Association (JCA)—a Paris-based agency that aided emigrating Jews throughout the world—to form the American Joint Reconstruction Foundation (AJRF). The AJRF wanted to develop independent local cooperative banks as the mechanism for reconstruction, but the JDCAFRJWS retained its relief-giving heritage. Despite its cooperation with the JCA on this venture, the JDCAFRJWS was criticized widely for failing to participate with world Jewry, for instance, in the 1920 conference of the Committee of Jewish Delegations, and for its neutrality, if not outright opposition, to Zionism. Some American-born social workers of the Reform-dominated JDCAFRJWS simply did not understand or appreciate the national aspirations, movements, and customs of East European Jewry.

In the summer of 1922, the JDCAFRJWS sent a group of experts to observe the work abroad. This group was led by Lee K. Frankel, another important Jewish social worker who had had a diverse career. The group returned with a major reorganization plan that established five functional committees, each headed by an expert in the particular field. For example, a committee on refugees was led by David Bressler from the IRO; one on orphans was led by Solomon Lowenstein, a specialist in Jewish child care work; and, most important, one on economic reconstruction was headed by Herbert Lehman, a banker and future national political statesman. The quality of the committee leaders, which also included Dr. Cyrus Adler, a prominent scholar and communal worker (cultural and religious affairs) and Bernard Flexner (medical and sanitary aid), meant that the work of the JDCAFRJWS became more sophisticated and entrenched.

Beginning in the 1920s, when the leaders still hoped to dissolve the agency, the JDCAFRJWS both developed programs of lasting importance and crystallized a group of professional and lay leaders whose services continued for another generation. In 1925, a professional administrator who had been Lehman's administrative assistant on the reconstruction committee since 1922, Joseph C. Hyman, became the secretary of the agency. The JDCAFRJWS began to cooperate in developing vocational training with the JCA, and, more importantly, with the Organization on Rehabilitation through Training (ORT). Gradually abandoning hope of dissolution, the agency in 1926 began to revitalize loan societies (*gemelath chesed*) in European Jewish communities. In 1928, to continue the Russian agricultural activities, the JDCAFRJWS established the American Society for Jewish Farm Settlements in Russia, headed by James Rosenberg of New York City, a lawyer, artist, and philanthropist.

As news of Adolf Hitler's atrocities against Jews spread in the 1930s, the JDCAFRJWS became a much-needed and permanent agency. In 1931, the organization changed its name to the American Jewish Joint Distribution Committee (JDC). Throughout the 1930s, the JDC aided European Jews. Its Paris office became the relief center for Jews fleeing Nazi oppression. It contributed to the operating budget of the High Commission for Refugees, which the League of Nations established in December 1933, and it supported HICEM, a cooperative venture of the ICA, Emig-Direkt, and the Hebrew Sheltering and Immigrant Aid Society* (HIAS). In the 1930s, the American German Jewish leaders who generally opposed the establishment of a Jewish national state in Palestine still dominated the JDC. Tensions between Zionist and JDC leaders developed in the 1930s, but the JDC agreed nevertheless with the Jewish Agency for Palestine in 1934 to raise funds jointly through the United Jewish Appeal (UJA) (see *Foundations and Research Associations*).

By the late 1930s, when the European problem became more evident, the solid and professional structure of the JDC allowed it to conduct important war-related work. The twenty-five-member executive committee met monthly to determine policy and to supervise the agency generally, and the administrative committee met weekly, conducting the agency operations. During a reorganization in 1940, Hyman became the executive director. Replacing him as secretary was Jacob Leavitt, a trained engineer who in 1923 had begun to serve the Jewish Social Service Association of New York,* then shifted to the JDCAFRJWS in 1929, and became secretary of the Palestine Economic Corporation, a Zionist organization, in 1933. Beginning annually in 1939, except for 1941, the JDC cooperated with the Zionists in the UJA, and in the face of the oppression of Jews during the war, the JDC shifted its position, supporting more fully than before the concept of a Jewish state in Palestine. In the early 1940s, the JDC appropriated $1 million to help take German-Jewish children out of Vichy, France, but the Allied invasion of northern Africa in November 1942 stymied the plan, since Allied troops and supplies were focused on that area. Nevertheless, with other relief agencies, the JDC continued to rescue children through the underground. JDC's contacts with around two thousand Jewish organizations throughout the United States helped the agency to finance war-related work, such as establishing soup kitchens and training schools, and to provide similar social services in Jewish ghettos in Poland. In June 1940, the JDC established its transmigration bureau, a clearinghouse for Americans who supported refugee families. Within one year, this bureau's staff numbered seventy. In 1943 and 1944, the JDC dramatically parachuted funds and supplies to the Jewish underground in Poland. In a sensational episode, a JDC representative in Switzerland, Saly Mayer, singlehandedly negotiated with and outmaneuvered a group of Nazis, rescuing two trainloads of nearly seventeen hundred Jews headed for concentration camps. Beginning in January 1944, the official United States War Refugee Board centralized all war-related efforts. The JDC, as it had the ARA after World War I, financed the board heavily.

The peak of JDC work came in the postwar reconstruction years, when it developed even closer relations with UJA and with the American and world Jewish communities. A national council of over five thousand members met yearly and elected a 210-member board of directors, which in 1947, was increased to 350 members. In 1947, Leavitt replaced the retiring Hyman as executive secretary, and Louis H. Sobel became the secretary. In the mid-1940s, when about 20 percent of its budget went to health activities, the JDC opened the Merano Sanitarium for tuberculars, and it began its dental care program abroad. Beginning in 1947, and renewed annually since, the JDC contributed between $1 million and $2 million to the ORT for vocational training programs. In the late 1940s, the JDC coordinated social services for the approximately forty thousand homeless refugees in British-seized detention camps in Cyprus. Particularly after 1947, when the less effective International Refugee Organization succeeded the resourceful United Nations Relief and Rehabilitation Agency (UNRRA) as the chief international machinery, the JDC increasingly helped Jews to leave Europe. Still ideologically cool to a Jewish state in Palestine, the JDC inevitably promoted migration to Palestine as a practical issue. The establishment of the state of Israel in 1948 resolved the matter for the JDC, which conducted some dramatic efforts to get oppressed Jews to Israel. In 1949–1950, for instance, through Operation Magic Carpet, a large group of Yemenite Jews in Aden flew to Israel. Zionist organizations resented JDC emigration activities, and by 1952, a clear division of activities had developed; the JDC would conduct specific activities in Israel, leaving emigration to the Zionists.

A new and important phase of the work began in 1949 when the JDC cooperated with the Israeli government and with the Jewish Agency for Palestine to establish Malben, an organization in Israel that aided sick, handicapped, and aged immigrants. In early 1951, the JDC alone assumed full responsibility for Malben, which developed health care facilities in the temporary buildings the British had left behind. The opening of a five-hundred-bed tuberculosis hospital in 1953, the establishment of sheltered workshops, and the provision of loans to the handicapped to help them open small shops and retail services typified the early Malben program in Israel. In 1958, Malben established a special projects division, which, for example, in June 1961, developed a program for adults with cerebral palsy. As Israel developed its own public services for these people, Malben, in the early 1960s, began to shifts its focus from individual clients to both voluntary and governmental social service agencies. The founding in 1969 of the JDC's Association for the Planning and Development of Services for the Aged, which helped local communities plan, develop, and implement these services, typified the Malben thrust. For its innovations and achievements with the Malben, in 1969, the JDC received the coveted Shroder Award at the general assembly of the Council of Jewish Federations and Welfare Funds.*

In addition to its concern for and activities in Israel, the JDC developed similar projects for oppressed and needy Jews throughout the world. In Europe, the JDC provided relief, health services and, with the ORT, vocational training in communist countries, such as Poland (it terminated its activities there in 1967 at the request of the Polish government). It also provided relief services to nearly four thousand Libyan Jews who had migrated to shabby districts in Italian cities in the 1960s. But, most importantly in Europe, JDC aided the increasingly overburdened French Jewish community, helping them to provide services and to absorb Jewish refugees from Algeria. Tunisia, and Morocco. For instance, in 1961, the JDC established in France the North African Housing Fund, and ten years later, it contributed more than one-fourth of the budget of the Fonds Social Juif Unifie, the major French Jewish social service agency. Continuing its efforts to aid oppressed Jews, in the 1970s, the JDC helped Jews especially aged and infirm ones, in hostile countries in the Middle East, in North Africa, and in Eastern Europe.

The sources for studying JDC's history are extensive. The primary sources include voluminous manuscripts at the agency's archives in New York City. These records are available to qualified students. The YIVO Institute for Jewish Social Research in New York City has two thick catalogs of JDC materials through 1932. Also at YIVO are ninety-seven rolls of microfilm of the transmigration bureau, 1946–1954, relating to individual cases. YIVO has over five hundred folders of newspaper clippings relating to JDC activities, 1950–1969. It also has the papers of Dr. Joseph A. Rosen, which cover JDC work in Russia in the 1920s and 1930s. Published *Annual Reports* since the 1930s describe the agency's activities, and *The New York Times,* which is indexed, covered the agency.

A number of secondary sources, including Oscar Handlin, *A Continuing Task: The American Jewish Joint Distribution Committee, 1914–1964* (1964), describe the agency. Merle Curti, *American Philanthropy Abroad* (1963), also discusses the JDC. Yehuda Bauer, *My Brother's Keeper: A History of the American Jewish Joint Distribution Committee, 1929–1939* (1974), is a scholarly study.

AMERICAN LEGION (AL), NATIONAL CHILDREN AND YOUTH DIVISION (NCYD) OF THE. In the early 1920s, members of the American Legion (AL) (see *Fraternal Organizations*) began to discuss the possibility of establishing a national home for dependent children as a memorial for the four Legionnaires killed by members of the International Workers of the World at Centralia, Washington, on Armistice Day, November 11, 1919. Also in the early 1920s, there were reports that disabled veterans refused to go to hospitals for proper care because they feared their children and families would suffer in their absence. Work in child welfare developed naturally in local AL posts and by AL state groups, called departments. George Withers of Kansas and Mark T. McKee of Michigan, for instance, developed child welfare projects in their respective departments, or states. Also in the early 1920s, Mrs. Donald Macrae, Jr., of Iowa, began to discuss the need for formal child welfare activities within the AL Auxiliary, a women's group. These developments prompted proposals at the AL's annual convention in New Orleans in 1922 to involve the organization formally in child welfare activities. Consequently, in October 1922, to consider such child welfare work, the AL founded its National Children and Youth Division (NCYD) as the National Child Welfare Committee (NCWC), chaired initially by Withers.

With the appointment of the NCWC, the group moved to develop a program. Child welfare workers throughout the country conferred with local Legionnaires, following the advice of respected leader Carl Christian Carstens, the executive director of the recently established Child Welfare League of America* (CWLA). The program that the NCWC developed was both progressive and regressive. It endorsed the ideals of the White House Conference on the Care of Dependent Children in 1909 to strive to preserve family homes. Financial aid to troubled veterans' families would implement this ideal. If efforts to preserve the home failed, however, the NCWC planned to place children in AL-sponsored institutions (which it called billets), despite the advice of professional child care agents, who urged them not to institutionalize children. In 1923, the Kansas Department raised $100,000 for a home in Legionville, Kansas. The early NCWC plan called for this Kansas institution to become a facility of the national agency, which would develop at least five other such institutions in different regions of the country. Michigan established a similar billet in 1921, and in the mid-1920s, the AL established a third at Clarksboro, New Jersey. In 1924, the agency became an official program of the AL, which moved the NCWC away from the regressive practice of promoting the institutionalization of dependent and even temporarily dependent children.

Making the program an official agency in 1924 helped to strengthen it significantly and to bring it more into line with modern trends in child welfare work. The new national commander in 1924, James A. Drain, elevated the agency to become the Children's Welfare Department (CWD), and he began to raise a fund to finance its work. Mark McKee of Michigan became chairman, and he worked to establish headquarters at Indianapolis, Indiana, the site of national AL headquarters. The agency hired a Michigan Legion worker, Robert Byers, who, together with Drain, searched for and found a director for the agency, now called the National Child Welfare Division (NCWD). A fortunate choice, Emma Puschner was a trained social worker and lawyer who had directed the St. Louis Board of Children's Guardians, a public agency. She had also worked for private child welfare agencies in St. Louis. Puschner, who remained head of the NCWD until 1950, had also been active in the AL Auxiliary. The first major activity of the NCWD was a survey, under the direction of George Withers, to compile state laws relating to child care, such as mothers' aid and the interstate placement of children. The agency began also to build a library of materials relating to child welfare, an effort helped by Grace Abbott and the United States Children's Bureau (USCB) (see *Government Agencies*), which she headed. On January 6, 1925, the national commander asked all state commanders to have each post appoint a local child welfare chairman, and by August 15, 1925, there were 715 Legion and 665 Auxiliary posts with functioning child welfare groups. On May 1, 1925, Puschner became the national field secretary, and on July 1, 1925, she became the director of the agency. She began, especially at the National Conference of Social Work* (NCSW), to develop relations with other agencies. During the early history of the NCWD, the CWLA particularly helped it. In 1926, the first year of its operation under Puschner, the agency provided supplemental financial aid to parents to preserve their families, and it continued to operate the billets, an activity that the agency began to deemphasize. The financial aid plan predated the federal Aid to Dependent Children program of the Social Security Act of 1935. Signaling the reception of the NCWD in the professional social work community, in 1926, the agency joined the CWLA and received an important place at the NCWS meeting in Cleveland. By 1926, it became clear that the problems of appointing state chairmen, some of whom were honorary and temporary, hindered the work nationwide. But the gradual development of a regional field service, through three officers by 1926, began to improve the national structure. In the 1920s, the agency initiated its area conferences, which discussed common problems and drafted important resolutions. In 1927, the executive committee of area chairman was established, and the field staff increasingly helped locals. By 1928, these efforts to improve the national structure had proven successful: the stability of area chairmen and the enthusiasm of the Auxiliary became important assets. Also, in the late 1920s, Forty and Eight, an organization within the AL, began to raise funds, do volunteer work with children, and promote the NCWD. In 1927, the NCWD sent to every state department data on legislation in its particular state, launching the agency into the field of legislation for better child care. In 1928, the NCWD provided grants to departments for special welfare projects. Ended in 1946 by the national executive committee of the AL, the program anticipated the system of federal grants to states. In 1930, in his position of national leadership in the child care field as executive director of the CWLA, Carl C. Carstens testified that the NCWD had "been a very useful organization because of [its] backing . . . progressive child welfare legislation . . . in the various states."

The NCWD adjusted well to the depression period of the 1930s, when it initiated some new activities. In 1930, for instance, the agency participated in the White House Conference on Child Health and Protection. More importantly, beginning in 1931, the group became concerned about juvenile delinquency. At a meeting of the executive committee in November 1931, the group discussed the section on juvenile offenders in the federal system of the report of the National Commission on Law Observance and Enforcement, the so-called Wickersham commission. This section was written by a famous social worker, Dr. Miriam Van Waters. At its November meeting, the NCWD also appointed a subcommittee, which studied the issue further in late 1931 and early 1932. It conferred with federal officials from the USCB and the Bureau of Prisons, as well as with Dr. Van Waters, who seemed interested in the planned activities of the NCWD in juvenile delinquency work. At the NCSW in May 1932, a group from the NCWD conferred with representatives of both the United States Department of Justice and the USCB about their respective programs relating to juvenile delinquency, helping the NCWD to develop a program. A resolution at the AL national convention in 1934, pledging the organization to work to improve conditions in juvenile detention facilities, prompted further activities in the field of juvenile delinquency. By the mid-1930s, the NCWD had broadened its efforts to include not only veterans' children in federal facilities but also those in local correctional institutions. In May 1937, with representatives from other AL groups, the Law and Order and the Americanism commissions, the NCWD began to develop a comprehensive plan on and to prepare a handbook on juvenile delinquency, an activity that developed into a nationwide campaign in the 1940s.

In the 1930s, other activities for child welfare included a survey in the early 1930s of nurseries and clinics for children maintained by the AL at hospitals of the Veterans' Administration. Beginning in 1935, the NCWD used Mothers' Day to alert the country to the importance of maternal and child care. Pamphlets, especially from the Maternity Center Association of New York,* contributed to this activity. Later in the decade, materials from the USCB and articles in *The American Legion Magazine* helped to stimulate this continuing activity. Also in the mid-1930s, the agency surveyed the conditions of the women and children of veterans. In some states, funds from the Federal Emergency Relief Administration (FERA) helped these surveys. Although the Social Security Act of 1935, particularly with its aid to children, had implemented the chief goals of the NCWD, the agency nevertheless continued to provide emergency relief to individual families. The NCWD also continued its legislative efforts, and it endorsed the proposed child labor amendment to the Constitution throughout the 1930s.

During World War II, the NCWD lost some of its staff to war-related programs of the AL, but the children's agency nevertheless continued its basic activities. The NCWD designated April 1942 as the first so-called child welfare month, and in the early 1940s, especially through the efforts of Dr. Edward Clay Mitchell of Memphis, Tennessee, the NCWD began cooperating with the American Academy of Pediatrics to publish child welfare guides and articles on maternal and child health in AL publications. It also developed a nationwide program to prevent juvenile delinquency, cooperating with local community councils and publishing a booklet on juvenile delinquency, which thirty state training schools adopted. In the early 1940s, the NCWD began the campaign for what became the federal Aid and Services to Needy Families with Children, known popularly as AFDC, of the Social Security Act Amendments of 1962.

In the immediate postwar period, the NCWD called attention to the growing number of children of veterans, and it developed a series of radio spots, as well as a twenty-minute film on child welfare and the agency's work. The NCWD intensified its efforts to provide social security benefits to widows and orphans of men participating in World War II. Congress enacted this legislation in 1950. In 1947, under a general reorganization of the AL structure, the National Child Welfare Committee, which supervised the NCWD, became the National Child Welfare Commission (NCWC). In 1947, the formerly independent committee on education of war orphans became part of the NCWC. In 1961, education and scholarship activities were transferred to the Americanism Commission of the AL. After his election as national commander in October 1949, George N. Craig developed an ambitious child welfare program that included working for legislation making parental desertion across state lines a federal crime, alerting the public about the impact of the high birth rate on the schools, developing greater spiritual training for America's children, and developing a mental health program to detect individual children's personality defects and abnormal behavior. In the early 1960s, working through departments, the NCWD achieved state legislation in most states providing for newborn babies being tested for phonylketonuria, a metabolic disorder of the newborn, which, if undetected, causes brain damage in a short time period.

The NCWD began to implement this program in the early 1950s, initiating a week in April 1950 to focus on spiritual training to reverse the increasing disruptions and dislocations in American society. This activity received favorable publicity. To implement the NCWD's goals further, in May 1950, the executive committee agreed to support federal antidesertion legislation. An important organizational event occurred on April 30, 1950, when Emma Puschner, who had shaped the first twenty-five years of the NCWD's history, retired as director. Her replacement was Randel Shake, the former assistant director since January 1946, who had wide experience in child welfare work. Moving more into the mental health aspects of juvenile delinquency the agency also initiated an antinarcotics program in the early 1950s. In 1951, the NCWD completed a study of the problem of children's use of narcotics, and in June, the agency sponsored a clinic in New York City, which attracted nationwide attention. The NCWD continued its concern for maternal and infant care services, testifying before Congress on the need to reestablish such services for servicemen's wives. Earlier AL concern for research and prevention had led to the establishment in 1954 of the American Legion Child Welfare Foundation to provide grants to agencies and programs. In 1955, for example, the foundation provided funds to the National Association for Retarded Children* for an educational consultant. Other representative grants included underwriting the cost of police officers attending the delinquency control institute at the University of Southern California and funds to the National Hospital for Speech Disorders. In late 1958, the now-named Child Welfare Commission issued pamphlets on the problem of school dropouts and on child welfare in the community to promote programs and services for all children, not just those of veterans. In January 1959, an area conference resolved against restrictive residence requirements in welfare laws, indicating another progressive concern of this agency.

In the 1960s and 1970s, the agency continued its programs to help children. In the early 1960s, for instance, it studied the extent of child abuse and then developed model state legislation to curb this problem. Local affiliates then supported anti–child abuse legislation in the states. In 1968, the staff at agency headquarters in Indianapolis numbered six. In October 1970, the National Child Welfare Division was renamed the National Children and Youth Division (NCYD), but its aims and policies remained the same.

The primary sources for studying the history of the NCYD include the archives of the agency at the national headquarters of the AL in Indianapolis, Indiana. The *Reports to the Annual Convention* of the AL contain detailed accounts of the work of the NCYD. In the papers of the United States Children's Bureau, Record Group 102, in the National Archives in Washington, D.C., there is correspondence between National Director Puschner and the USCB. There is also a folder of Puschner's correspondence in the Miriam Van Waters Collection at the Schlesinger Library on the History of Women in America in Cambridge, Massachusetts. In the 1920s, the *Bulletin* of the CWLA contained information about the agency.

The NCWD wrote a twenty-eight-page unpublished history of itself. Richard Seelye Jones, *A History of the American Legion* (1946), pp. 255–264, contains a helpful but biased history of the children's agency. Other histories of the AL mention the child welfare agency, but there is no scholarly history of the NCYD of the AL, nor is it mentioned in the standard histories of social welfare.

AMERICAN LUNG ASSOCIATION (ALA).   In the era of industrialization and urbanization in the late nineteenth and early twentieth centuries, public health physicians and workers and social workers became concerned about people afflicted with tuberculosis. Dr. Herman Biggs, the distinguished director of the New York City Department of Health laboratories, and Dr. Lawrence F. Flick of the Phipps Institute in Philadelphia were important figures in the antituberculosis movement in the late nineteenth century. This movement had led in 1892 to the establishment of the Pennsylvania Society for the Prevention of Tuberculosis and to another state group in Ohio in 1901. Other medical groups, such as the American Congress on Tuberculosis in December 1902, organized brief and unsuccessful national organizations. In the early twentieth century, another group proved more successful. Led by a prominent public health physician from Baltimore, Dr. William Welch, a group of doctors and reformers met on January 28, 1904, at The Johns Hopkins University in Baltimore to establish an antituberculosis organization. This group chose Dr. Welch as its chairman, who then appointed a fifteen-member committee to prepare the formalities of organization. At another meeting on March 3, 1904, at the College of Physicians in Philadelphia, the American Lung Association (ALA) was established as the United States Society for the Study of Tuberculosis (USSST). A committee of five representatives was chosen to prepare the constitution and bylaws, which the organization then adopted on April 22, 1904.

The constitution and bylaws provided for a thirty-member board of directors, which chose its executive committee. The founders agreed to become life members, paying dues of $200 each. The group of founders included such prominent physicians as Dr. S. Adolphus Knopf, a New York City physician, and Dr. William Osler of Baltimore. It also included Edward T. Devine, the general secretary of the Charity Organization Society of the City of New York* (COS). The combination of lay and medical men as founders, patterned after the pioneering Pennsylvania organization in 1892, ensured a broad range of interests and activities and suggested the agency's development as an important social service organization. On April 22, 1904, the USSST changed its name to the National Association for the Study and Prevention of Tuberculosis (NASPT). Meeting again on June 4, 1904, at the convention of the American Medical Association, the NASPT elected traditional officers, including two vice-presidents, and formed its executive committee of seven, which included Devine. The executive committee met frequently in late 1904 and early 1905. It realized quickly the need for funds, and it therefore appointed a subcommittee on membership, which successfully approached such philanthropists as John D. Rockefeller and Jacob Schiff in the summer of 1904. The executive committee met initially in the Charities Building in New York City, where Devine hired a secretary who worked in offices loaned by the National Consumers' League.* The need for a professional executive secretary became apparent, and on Devine's recommendation, the organization hired Dr. Livingston Farrand of Columbia University. Dr. Farrand began his work as the NASPT began to function in the winter of 1905.

As with other national organizations, the NASPT spent its early years developing activities and determining its structure. In 1905, the board of directors established an advisory council of representatives from both state and local societies. Beginning in 1906, when delegates from institutions and sanitariums joined the advisory council, it became significantly less representative of the affiliates, which had developed considerable autonomy. By May 1908, there were 140 such affiliates; there had been only fifteen in 1904. The NASPT also developed its first sections, later called divisions, such as the sociology one whose members were Devine and Dr. Knopf, Homer Folks, the general secretary of the State Charities Aid Association* of New York. Lilian Brandt of the COS staff, and Frederick L. Hoffmann, a New Jersey statistician active in social reform who was also active in the American Association for Labor Legislation* (AALL). These particular individuals, as well as its early activities, reflected clearly the close NASPT association with the urban social justice movement of the Progressive era.

The NASPT helped to produce the important pioneering *A Directory of Institutions and Societies Dealing with Tuberculosis in the United States and Canada,* prepared by the COS, with which the NASPT also cooperated in an early tuberculosis exhibit. In this so-called era of exhibits from 1906 to 1912, the NASPT experimented with other publicity activities, pioneering in establishing in 1908 its publicity bureau, sponsoring initially in 1910 an annual Tuberculosis Sunday, and beginning as early as May 1906 to work successfully to hold the International Congress on Tuberculosis in Washington, D.C., in 1908. President Theodore Roosevelt, a friend of urban Progressives, remained an honorary vice-president of the organization for about fifteen years. Beginning in 1916, at the institute for tuberculosis workers at the New York School of Philanthropy, the NASPT conducted a three-week training course for lay workers.

An important organizational development occurred in the summer of 1910 when the American National Red Cross* (ANRC) suggested that the NASPT become a partner with it in the sales of tuberculosis seals. This idea of seals originated in Denmark, and a woman from the Delaware Red Cross used it successfully to raise funds for an open air cottage in Wilmington. The Christmas seals had been an instant success, raising about $250,000 for the ANRC in 1909.

The sales continued to raise money for the NASPT after 1910; and in 1920, the ANRC turned the enterprise entirely over to the NASPT. The NASPT registered the seal as a trademark in 1920, and a federal court upheld it in 1954. The machinery of affiliates selling the seals locally established the structure for the nationwide coordination of the larger work of the NASPT. In 1908, the NASPT began to circulate as a house organ its *Confidential Bulletin,* which in October 1914 became the printed *Bulletin of the National Association for the Study and Prevention of Tuberculosis.* The first journal, however, to represent the NASPT was *The Outdoor Life,* which, as the renamed *Journal of the Outdoor Life,* became the official publication in 1906. It ceased publication in 1935. The organization also inaugurated in March 1917 *The American Review of Tuberculosis,* which developed as a leading professional and scientific journal.

Another important organizational event occurred in 1914 when Dr. Charles J. Hatfield, an associate of pioneer Dr. Flick in Philadelphia and his successor as the director of the Phipps Institute, replaced Dr. Farrand as the managing director. Farrand had shaped the unknown organization into a prestigious national agency, and under Hatfield, the organization crystallized its structure and developed more businesslike procedures. In 1918, it shortened its name to the National Tuberculosis Association (NTA), and it incorporated in the state of Maine. In 1918, the agency moved its headquarters from the Charities Building to larger headquarters. The headquarters changed locations in New York frequently until 1940, when it moved with the National Health Council* to the famous health building in New York at 1790 Broadway. The professional staff numbered fifteen in 1919, and it increased to twenty-six in 1921.

The NTA also developed a series of important and influential programs and activities. In 1915, the Modern Health Crusade for children developed. The project, which taught schoolchildren basic personal hygiene, spread quickly; over three million children were enrolled by April 1919. In 1921, the National Education Association recommended that all schools adopt the crusade, and the United States Bureau of Education sponsored a series of lectures on the relation of education to health by the founder of the movement, Charles M. de Forrest of the NTA staff. In 1925, the NTA eliminated the crusade, but established a child health education service, which functioned through the 1940s, when it combined with a similar service to form the health education service of the NTA. Beginning in 1916, the NASPT initiated its Framingham, Massachusetts, demonstration, the first medical survey of an entire population. The program developed various clinics and services, reduced significantly the infant mortality rate of the community, and elicited cooperation from local voluntary and federal government agencies. Concerned with the plight of migrants—a constant source of concern for the Progressive social work community—the NASPT supported a bill in 1916 that would have provided funds for poor, nonresident tuberculosis patients. The NASPT proposed that the United States Public Health Service (USPHS) administer this program, which was begun finally in 1944.

During the World War I period, the NTA screened army inductees, implemented preventative programs in military camps, and advised the United States Veterans' Bureau on the establishment of tuberculosis hospitals. In 1920, the executive committee broadened NTA activities, defining antituberculosis work to include all forms of child hygiene. This opened the way for affiliates to participate in diverse public health movements, such as the child hygiene movement in Missouri, where the state association played a major role. Also, during the war era, the administrative structure coalesced into services: medical, nursing, publicity, field, statistics, and campaign.

More important activities followed after 1922, when Dr. Linsly R. Williams became the managing director. By the mid-1920s, the prewar training institutes had become regionalized, such as the five held in the spring of 1926. There were other organizational changes. In 1922, the research services divided into further specialized functions, such as a statistics service. The number of committees increased in the 1920s. Implementing Managing Director Williams's attitude of having the NTA and its associations cooperate with all health movements, the agency developed standing committees, for example, to cooperate with the American Child Health Association.* In January 1925, the NTA inaugurated its annual Trudeau Medal to honor the person contributing most to the antituberculosis movement. In the 1920s, the new committee on medical research supported fifteen basic studies. The amount of grants increased from about $4,500 in 1921 to $27,000 in 1928. Also in the 1920s, NTA leaders determined that Christmas seal sales remain independent of local community chest drives, a policy adhered to even through the many joint communitywide fund-raising campaigns of the World War II years. In October 1928, Dr. Kendall Emerson, an important figure in public health, began his tenure as managing director.

The expansion of NTA activities declined during the depression years of the 1930s under Dr. Emerson. There were no new studies except the one of tuberculosis in Negroes, done with the Rosenwald Fund (see *Foundations and Research Associations*). In 1931, the NTA established a special committee on tuberculosis among Negroes, which began this five-year study in 1932. In 1934 and 1935, conflict developed with the International Society for Crippled Children* (ISCC) whose state branches sold Easter seals similar to those of the NTA. Despite this episode, the NTA maintained very cordial relations with other national social service agencies, particularly with the ANRC and the American Heart Association* (AHA), which the NTA helped to found and to foster. The NTA continued activities in the NHC, and in 1935, Dr. Emerson served part time as acting executive secretary for the American Public Health Association* (APHA), a major organization, which the NTA thus helped to survive. The NTA continued this cooperation, establishing standing committees on cooperation with both the American Social Hygiene Association* (ASHA) and the American Society for the Control of Cancer.* Soon after the United States entered World War II, the NTA established its war emergency committee, which influenced developments in federal centers concerned with controlling tuberculosis.

Postwar developments brought a significant reduction in deaths from tuberculosis. NTA sponsorship of major research and further organizational crystallization were all signs of NTA leadership in the national voluntary social service agency field. Following the famous Gunn-Platt report analyzing national health agencies, the NTA in October 1945 began a study of its organization, conducted by the Barrington Associates, a New York management consultant firm. Its recommendations prompted, in the late 1940s and early 1950s, some organizational changes, particularly the designation of the American Trudeau Society (ATS) as the medical section of the NTA, with offices and facilities at the Phipps Institute in Philadelphia. This development, in effect, gave the NTA its own research facilities, but the organization nevertheless established in 1948 its research fellowship program for scientists affiliated with other institutions. NTA-sponsored research helped to develop new and effective drugs and vaccines in the tuberculosis field. Most importantly, activities begun in the late 1940s culminated in a proposal on June 12, 1950, to involve the NTA in such broader issues as general infection prevention, smoke control, industrial air pollutants, and control over colds, influenza, pneumonia, and asthma. The board of directors, however, reduced this ambitious proposal to authorizing limited immunization of children. But in the mid-1950s, when the board rejected a proposed and apt name change to the National Tuberculosis and Health Association, the organization had liberalized. It broadened its programs to include respiratory diseases other than tuberculosis, which it still continued to fight.

Commitments to eradicate tuberculosis and to expand its activities to cover all respiratory diseases occupied the NTA in the late 1950s and 1960s. The board of directors' recommendation in 1956 that NTA and its affiliates deal with other respiratory diseases became effective. In 1959, for instance, the scientific and professional journal of the NTA changed its name to *The American Review of Respiratory Diseases,* suggesting the new emphasis. In the spring of 1963, the NTA sponsored the first nationwide respiratory disease campaign, urging the public to consult physicians for chronic coughs, shortness of breath, and other similar symptoms. With its affiliates, the NTA helped also to establish local committees to promote action for clean air. To resolve the gains made in the long fight against tuberculosis, with the USPHS, the NTA sponsored an important conference at Arden House in Harriman, New York, in late 1959. The group of experts resolved to eradicate tuberculosis, and the NTA implemented the conference's establishing in 1960 its committee for the guidance of the tuberculosis program. The conference also drafted the tuberculosis educational program, which the board of directors adopted and which a United States surgeon general's advisory committee on tuberculosis approved. The NTA began in 1959 and 1960 to help other agencies in their campaigns against tuberculosis. A conference in early 1965 led to the development of a major activity, known as the clinic project, to improve out-patient clinics. The NTA hired a prominent behavioral scientist to guide programs concerned with the psychosocial aspects of tuberculars' lives. In 1967, the NTA and many of its affiliates adopted the promotion of chemoprophylaxis, using drugs to help eradicate tuberculosis. Also, partly hoping to influence general hospitals rather than special sanitariums, which isolated tubercular patients, the NTA issued an important statement pointing out that the disease is almost entirely airborne, not transmitted generally by direct contact. A conference in October 1966, similar in its influence to the Arden House Conference in 1959, launched more formally the respiratory disease programs. In 1966, the NTA established its national air conservation commission (NACC), and the NTA became a charter member of the National Interagency Council on Smoking and Health, which approved a NTA twenty-minute film, *Point of View*. This film was nominated for an Oscar award. In 1967, the NACC held a conference to involve NTA affiliates in their local clean air campaigns. In 1968, the NTA changed its name appropriately to the National Tuberculosis and Respiratory Disease Association (NTRDA). Partly because of NTA activities and partly because of the surgeon general's report in 1964 on the dangers of air pollution, the American public had become more aware of respiratory disease by the late 1960s.

During this period of developing new program concerns and activities, the NTA also effected some important organizational changes. To develop staff services to meet its expanding role in respiratory diseases, in 1959, the medical, research, and medical education directors all became full-time positions, and the NTA established a committee to evaluate the effectiveness of the local associations. Another change implemented in 1959 combined three former units into the new education and public relations division. In the late 1950s, the board adopted a policy to phase out smaller, inefficient associations and to promote the consolidation of existing societies. In 1950, for example, there were over three thousand such tuberculosis associations, but by 1964, there were only 1,913, and the reorganizing and consolidating efforts of the associations were continuing. In 1970, however, the board decided finally and firmly to eliminate these smaller units, establishing a standard of population and of Christmas seal sales for each type—state, local, and branch—of association. The board also envisioned more regional associations to deal with such nonspecific area problems as air pollution. In the long-established tradition of allowing affiliates considerable autonomy and independence, the board in 1970 did not make consolidation mandatory but asked affiliates to submit their organizing plans to the new reorganization committee within two years. The board itself implemented changes in its own structure in 1970, reducing the number of its standing committees. The board also adopted proportional representation and, for the first time, the policy of rotating board memberships. It decided to have biennial gatherings rather than the annual meetings. Consistent with its concern for regional approaches to problems and to organization, the board decided to continue the present regional conferences.

In the late 1960s and early 1970s, the NTRDA developed important services for its affiliates and supervised further structural changes. In 1965, for instance, it developed and published a performance index, which affiliates used increasingly. To help fill affiliates staff positions, the NTRDA established a career development program in 1968 to recruit and train more specialists in the field. More importantly, to improve the quality of its field services, beginning in 1971, the NTRDA increased by 1 percent per year through 1976 its percentage of Christmas seal sales. In the early 1970s, the NTRDA contracted with the federal Environmental Protection Agency to provide funds for affiliates' workshops to strengthen their roles in developing local standards for clean air. The NTRDA helped associations deal with inner city and minority activities, providing guidelines, field services, staff personnel, publications, and other such services. Through its electronic data processing system, the organization also helped about half of the associations by 1974 to improve their seal sales and to modernize their financial record keeping.

An important metting of the board of directors in 1970 solidified and expanded the concern of the agency for the plight of inner city residents, especially ethnic and racial minorities. Born amid the urban slums at the turn of the century, the NTRDA reaffirmed its commitment to social justice. Although the board action in 1970 was dramatic, the organization had been urging its affiliates to deal with the issue of poverty to help eradicate tuberculosis and other respiratory diseases in the 1960s. In 1968, the board itself had established a committee on metropolitan problems, which reported in February 1970. It recommended, and the board approved, an annual conference on city health affairs. The NTRDA added to its staff a specialist in big city health problems, and the career development program, established in 1968, began to recruit and train blacks and other minorities for positions in the field. In February 1970, the board also implemented a series of recommendations dealing with cities. In the early 1970s, the NTRDA, as well as many of its associations, provided funds and other services to train inner city workers. In 1972, the NTRDA began to work on Spanish-oriented materials, resulting, for instance, in a comic book and a film on the tuberculosis experiences of baseball player Rico Carty. The organization worked with National Urban League,* the black National Medical Association, and other organizations to develop better services for minorities.

In the 1970s, the organization continued to lead the campaigns against all respiratory disease, emphasizing especially the problems of air pollution and cigarette smoking. It also continued to emphasize its initial goal, fighting tuberculosis. The NTRDA opened the 1970s with the publication of *Standards for Tuberculosis Treatment in the Field,* which detailed measures to improve the care of patients. In the field of air pollution, the agency provided evidence for a number of federal agencies and cosponsored with the Air Pollution Control Association Cleaner Air Week in 1972. Keeping ahead of socioeconomic factors affecting respiratory diseases, the NTRDA sponsored a conference on clean air and the energy crisis. Active similarly in the frustrating drive against cigarette smoking, the NTRDA and, after 1973, the American Lung Association (ALA), produced many pamphlets, media spot announcements, and other sources of information, and staged a Kick the Habit Week in June 1970. The agency led the nonsmokers' rights campaign, signing the nonsmoking bill of rights in Philadelphia in 1973, thereby dramatizing the theme of its national education week on smoking. The ALA provided educational materials for professionals in the field as well, for instance, providing a film, "The Modern Management of Tuberculosis," and developing cassettes and new publications to convey important current information, a tradition the organization established when it originated during the Progressive era.

The best place to begin a study of the ALA's history is *The National Tuberculosis Association* (1957) by a distinguished medical historian, Richard Harrison Shryock. It is one of the few scholarly histories of a national social service agency, although its lack of citations throughout will inevitably distress some specialists. Shryock's research is based on the archives of the ALA, an important source. These archival materials are located in the New York national headquarters and are open to scholars under certain conditions. The published and extremely detailed *Annual Reports* provide a convenient and important primary source, as do the wide-ranging publications, both serialized and specialized, of the ALA.

AMERICAN NATIONAL RED CROSS (ANRC). During the Crimean War in the 1850s and the American Civil War in the early 1860s, relief efforts for those touched by the war proved beneficial. To institutionalize humanitarian relief during wars, representatives from European nations met in 1863 and organized the International Committee of the Red Cross (ICRC). In 1864, eleven European nations agreed to the Treaty of Geneva, providing for humanitarian relief during wars. Meanwhile, during the American Civil War, the United States Sanitary Commission* (USSC) demonstrated the effectiveness of organized relief. During this war, Clara Barton had gained a nationwide reputation for helping the sick and wounded. During the Franco-German War in 1870, Barton worked for the German Red Cross. All of these developments had influenced her to campaign, since the late 1870s, for an American group to affiliate with the ICRC. On May 12, 1881, Barton finally assembled a group of people in Washington, D.C., interested in such an organization.

On May 21, the ANRC was established as the American Association of the Red Cross (AARC). At this meeting, the AARC adopted the Treaty of Geneva, but added the so-called American amendment, providing for additional relief in pestilence, famine, and other natural calamities. The group adopted a constitution, establishing in addition to the officers an executive board and a board of consultation, which included the president of the United States and other high-ranking military and medical federal officials. The group hoped to have Mrs. James Garfield, the wife of the president of the United States, become its president, but when she declined, the organizers elected Clara Barton. Important founders of the AARC included Senator Omar Conger of Michigan, newspaper editor Richard J. Hinton, Barton's nephew Stephen E. Barton, and Adolphus S. Solomons, a Washington businessman who became important in the early organization. Barton, who came to personify the organization, directed its energies toward obtaining a federal charter. The original articles of incorporation were revised in 1893 when the AARC became the American National Red Cross (ANRC). On June 6, 1900, President William McKinley signed a congressional bill granting the ANRC a federal charter. The charter enlarged the organization, established a board of control and an executive committee, required that annual financial statements be given to Congress, and, significantly, allowed the organization to work to prevent as well as to relieve sufferings caused by war and disasters. This last provision served as the basis for ANRC activities in the best tradition of American social service: relief and prevention. The federal charter gave the group the official stature Clara Barton and her associates wanted.

The ANRC conducted its work with dedication, largely by Barton's personal efforts and influence. The ANRC rehabilitated victims of Michigan forest fires in 1881 and of Ohio Valley floods in 1882 and 1884, aided victims of the disastrous Johnstown flood of 1889, and aided Cuban victims of the Spanish-American War. These activities helped to establish the national reputation of the group and its leader. Barton did not want rival local societies to develop. Nevertheless, local affiliated relief agencies recognized by the ANRC developed particularly in cities. Other agencies, like the eleven auxiliaries of the Minnesota Red Cross, were totally unconnected with the national organization. Only the reorganization in 1904 made the ANRC a truly national agency with functioning and organizationally valid affiliate societies, which became known as chapters.

The movement to reform the organization and to remove Barton as leader stemmed both from charges that she did not delegate authority and from a bitter rivalry between two strong-willed women—Barton and the socially prominent Mabel T. Boardman, a family friend of United States President William Howard Taft. Signs of internal discontent, evident during the Spanish-American War, related also to charges of laxity in handling funds. Boardman represented partly the Progressive era concern for greater efficiency in welfare agencies. In 1904, her supporters ousted Barton, established a new board of trustees chosen jointly by the two factions, and elected new officers. On January 5, 1905, President Theodore Roosevelt signed the act reincorporating the organization, bringing it in closer relation with the government as a quasi-official agency and establishing a new central committee, which delegated much of its authority to an executive committee. In 1908, the central committee numbered eighteen members. Through 1915, Boardman, however, really led the group, solidifying its structure of local affiliates and establishing the work of three administrative boards: war relief, international relief, and national relief, which she chaired. In 1908, the ANRC appointed as its national director Ernest Bicknell, who had served as secretary of the Indiana State Board of Charities and as general superintendent of the Chicago Bureau of Charities. Bicknell's appointment demonstrated Boardman's concern for elevating relief work and for developing more professional standards. After years of frequent moves, national headquarters were established permanently in Washington, D.C., in February 1917 in a building especially constructed for the ANRC, known as the Marble Palace.

Although the various membership drives were not as successful as the leaders had hoped, the ANRC established important social services in the Progressive era. The San Francisco earthquake in 1906, floods on the Ohio River in 1913, a mining disaster killing 256 men in Cherry, Illinois, in 1909, and the Triangle Waist Company fire in New York City in 1911, killing 145 women, developed ANRC disaster relief techniques. The nursing service grew and was ready to serve in World War I. ANRC concern for industrial accidents resulted in first aid programs in safety campaigns, such as the nationwide one for railroad safety between 1909 and 1912. Public health work, chiefly rural nursing, developed beginning in 1907. This activity was suggested initially by Lillian Wald of the Henry Street Settlement* in New York City and financed partly by philanthropist Jacob Schiff. This service contributed importantly to local child and general rural hygiene movements in the Progressive era and the 1920s. Formalized in 1912 and entitled town and country nursing in 1913, it became the bureau of public health nursing in May 1918. The complex name changes of this activity were typical of similar name changes for other ANRC services and activities. World War I prompted the development of what became home service, which aided families of men in the armed forces, plunged the ANRC into casework techniques, and helped to develop programs in medical social service. Providing preventive services, the sanitation service conducted programs to vaccinate people, developed malarial prevention projects in rural areas, and recruited public health nurses to help the United States Public Health Service (USPHS) in its preventive programs. In New York City in 1917 the ANRC established the Institute for the Crippled and Disabled, which became the most important facility in the rehabilitation field. To involve young people in the national health movement, the Junior Red Cross was inaugurated in September 1917.

World War I also prompted the well-known ANRC services abroad. The canteen services, which cared for both American and Allied troops, developed as one of the most popular programs. It also donated blankets and provided recreation and personal articles. Civilian aid developed to combat problems of malnutrition and poor milk, and so on in war-torn Europe. In the spring of 1921, the ANRC initiated a project establishing nearly five hundred health centers in Central and Eastern Europe. In the period of general isolationism of the 1920s and 1930s, the ANRC did not participate actively abroad but did have limited programs—for instance, during the Spanish Civil War. It also developed an experimental work relief program to deal with the famine in China in the early 1920s.

The ANRC adjusted well to the developments of the depression of the late 1920s and the New Deal. In the 1920s, as unemployment increased frighteningly in some areas, the organization debated whether its charter granting it authority to relieve distress caused by national calamities included economic depression. A policy statement issued during the brief depression of 1921 had declared that unemployment was a community problem and not properly an ANRC activity. But local chapters, particularly in their home service work, inevitably aided victims of hard economic times by helping transients and providing school lunches. Like President Herbert Hoover, the ANRC national leaders believed firmly that massive governmental aid to combat the economic depression would weaken private initiative, reduce private donations, and ultimately destroy the ANRC. In the winter of 1930–1931, when it was clear throughout the country that private relief could not deal with the effects of the enormous depression, the central committee rejected a federal government offer of $25 million to aid people. But, responding to President Hoover's request, the ANRC distributed surplus wheat and cotton to help relieve the unemployed.

The generally conservative national leadership, particularly in the central committee, did not initially endorse the New Deal social and economic programs. Charges of racial discrimination in relief work surfaced, particularly by blacks in the aftermath of flood relief in the Mississippi delta in the late 1920s. The national organization nevertheless refused to take a strong stand against racism. Moreover, the conservative ANRC alienated organized labor, refusing in 1928 to relieve strikers' families. In 1932, the ANRC did not aid the so-called bonus marchers, veterans who had marched to Washington, D.C., to seek early payment of pensions. The ANRC may have even tried to undermine the march, offering to transport stranded women and children back to their home towns. While other, more liberal agencies, like the American Friends Service Committee,* the Conference of Southern Mountain Workers,* and the new Save the Children Fund,* responded in humanitarian ways to the particular problems of Harlan County, Kentucky—a kind of symbol for liberals in the 1930s—officials of the local Red Cross threatened unanimously to resign if the organization aided strikers' families. No real spokesman for industrial labor was on the central committee, and for years the Congress of Industrial Organizations refused to endorse the annual roll call of the ANRC. The variously named volunteer special services, led by Mabel Boardman until 1946, appealed primarily to socially elite women. Throughout the country, local Red Cross chapter officials continued to be the socially and financially prominent in their communities.

The history of the ANRC, however, showed how noblesse oblige in American social welfare history has been transformed to aid the less fortunate. Disaster relief in flood areas in 1936 and 1937 demonstrated what Harry Hopkins called, in the fall of 1937, "the symbol of hope and mercy." While many chapters, particularly in smaller towns, were generally inactive most of the time, disaster relief elicited their best compassions. Despite criticisms that stemmed inevitably from the tribulations of war, during World War II, the ANRC aided the armed forces in countless ways: communicating urgent messages to the men and their families, counseling couples and preventing some divorces, and cheering the wounded. It helped to develop the blood transfusion and plasma programs during the war, saving countless lives that would have been lost under World War I conditions. As *The New York Times* argued in 1945, the ANRC was "one of the few bright spots in this ruthless war."

In the postwar period, the ANRC assumed its traditional role of pioneering in social welfare and participated in the major developments in the field. Some administrative streamlining occurred to make the organization more effective: a new separate division, services to veterans, developed to aid in all rehabilitation and former home service work; the office of social welfare combined the welfare, health, and safety activities; and international activities supervised all work abroad, which the ANRC left generally to the newly created United Nations Relief and Rehabilitation Administration. Beginning in May 1945, the ANRC initiated the nationwide blood program, a major development. More chapters founded relief committees, and although governmental agencies increasingly aided the needy, the ANRC responded beneficently.

In 1947, amid another internal controversy involving liberal and conservative factions, the ANRC undertook major administrative and structural changes. Conservatives charged the administration of Basil O'Connor, whom President Franklin D. Roosevelt had appointed as general director in 1944, as being too liberal, particularly because of wartime agreements with labor. Liberals had prompted the movement to democratize the organization. In 1947, a new fifty-member board of governors—with thirty people elected by the chapters, ensuring geographical and size-related representation—replaced both the former board of incorporators and the central committee. Formal ties to the government were maintained: the president of the United States, who became honorary ANRC chairman, appointed eight board members in addition to the principal executive officer, now called president. To create more chapter representation, the area managers also became vice-presidents. The ANRC abolished a special classification of membership for large donors, stipulating equality of membership at one dollar. On October 1, 1949, Basil O'Connor resigned. The widely respected former secretary of state, General George Marshall, succeeded him.

From the 1950s through the early 1960s, the ANRC developed the blood program as an important organizational and national activity, continued its basic programs of social services to the armed forces and disaster relief, and developed a few new programs. In August 1951, helped by a nationwide appeal by the United States Department of Defense (USDD), the ANRC began its blood collection program. By 1954, it operated forty-five regional and over a hundred local blood programs, which also supplied the armed forces with blood. In 1957, to improve the blood program in smaller chapters, the organization established a new blood program aide corps of volunteers trained to help specialists on "donor days," which became increasingly popular throughout the country. In 1960, the board of governors authorized new regional blood centers in areas where chapters were willing to support them. Research in the blood program continued, and in the early 1960s, the ANRC developed an important technique of using plastic containers to collect and to distribute blood. The agency conducted regular laboratory training courses at research centers in both Los Angeles and Washington, D.C. In the early 1960s, the ANRC provided gamma globulin to protect all Peace Corps workers against hepatitis. Under a contract with the Defense Supply Agency of the USDD, the ANRC was the coordinating agency for blood in a national emergency.

Well prepared to deal with disasters, the ANRC responded to the most calamitous events of the 1950s and 1960s. In July 1951, the agency spent nearly $14.1 million to relieve the tragedy of midwestern floods, a series of disasters unmatched since 1937. The tornados in the spring of 1952 provided initial work for many personnel who had been trained at the agency's disaster relief institute in Atlanta. In the summer of 1951, the ANRC assigned nearly seven hundred nurses to work with the National Foundation for Infantile Paralysis* in the polio epidemic at scattered points throughout the country. Helping nearly 150,000 people after floods in the Northwest in 1955, the ANRC appealed for $10 million. President Dwight Eisenhower endorsed the campaign, helping to net $16 million. In the mid-1950s, the agency developed a joint course in emergency mass feeding with the federal Civil Defense Administration. Throughout the period, working chiefly through the International League of Red Cross Societies, the ANRC helped abroad, lending the personnel in the early 1960s to assist Algeria in repatriating some 200,000 refugees. Traditional ANRC services to the armed forces continued through direct programs, such as recreational facilities abroad, and through home service, a wide-ranging program for the men's families. Activities in hospitals conducted by the Veterans Administration (VA) (see *Government Agencies*) increased as men were wounded during the Korean War in the 1950s. The agency maintained staff at the administration headquarters in Washington, D.C., to represent veterans and their families in obtaining services, an especially valuable activity when the VA cut back services in the 1960s. In the late 1950s, the nursing service as well as chapter nursing programs began to deal with the chronically ill, the aged, the mentally ill, and the handicapped. In 1962, with the Office of Civil Defense of the Department of Defense and the USPHS, the instructional course in nursing developed ten thirty-minute teaching films, *The Home Nursing Story,* and a publication, *The Badge of Distinction,* helped to draw nurses to ANRC programs. Throughout the post–World War II era, the ANRC conducted a little-known inquiry service to help locate family members separated by the war; its activities increased after the Hungarian revolt of 1956. The establishment in August 1959 of an ANRC office of educational relations led to a greater emphasis on youth programs in the organization.

Beginning with a reorganization of its structure in the mid-1960s, the ANRC changed gradually to become a more activist social service agency, although it still retained its traditional ties to the military. The consolidation of smaller chapters into combined service areas was one organizational change; a more important one was the ANRC's modernization of its volunteer structure. The agency abandoned the generally inflexible compartmentalization of former volunteer categories, such as gray lady and social welfare aide, and developed a single course for all, now known as "Red Cross volunteers," who all wore the same uniform. Bringing the chapters closer together allowed the ANRC to develop better services, such as disaster action teams and immediately identifiable emergency action in disaster relief. The change of direction became evident in the publication of a Spanish-language edition of *Home Nursing Service* in the mid-1960s, the beginning in June 1966 of youth service demonstration projects in both urban and rural low-income areas, such as an Appalachian community and an Indian reservation, and the increased activities of home nursing to serve the blind, the poor, American Indians, and migrant workers. Responding to the urban riots of the late 1960s, actions by the board of governors and endorsed at the national conference in May 1968 defined new community-centered activities in poverty-stricken areas. Many chapters had already begun to provide social services in inner cities, such as prenatal care for unwed teenagers and school health programs. In the late 1960s and early 1970s, chapters participated in a program helping veterans, sponsored by the National Urban League.* In communities without league affiliates, ANRC chapters conducted a variety of services for veterans. With the federal Head Start program, the ANRC began a pilot nutrition program for Head Start mothers and children. The blood and disaster relief programs became increasingly sophisticated, and the ANRC became more active in prevention work, such as training chapters in the late 1960s to use the new natural disaster warning system of the federal Environmental Science Service Administration.

Despite these activities, reminiscent of the social activism of the 1960s, the ANRC consistently showed its alliance with the administration's war efforts. It followed orders by the Department of Defense to increase its recreational centers, clubmobile units, and the like in South Vietnam. It recruited nurses for South Vietnamese hospitals for the United States Agency for International Development (USAID). In 1966, the ANRC completed plans with the USAID to operate a refugee center and to settle displaced persons in "normal village environments," probably to bolster the countryside against the National Liberation Front, the insurgent group in South Vietnam. In the fall of 1969, the ANRC began its Write Hanoi campaign to aid and comfort American prisoners of war in North Vietnam, an extensive nationwide activity.

As American participation in the war diminished, the ANRC became a more socially active agency in the 1970s, fulfilling an agency goal. The organization, still a voluntary one despite its close ties with the federal government, adjusted well to the expanded government role in disaster relief through the federal Office of Emergency Preparedness (see *Government Agencies*). An important statement by the board of governors in the early 1970s urged public as well as national voluntary agencies to join the ANRC in establishing a nationwide blood service. In the early 1970s, the ANRC initiated a pilot project in rural areas showing how individuals, community groups, and the state could improve social services. In the area where the ANRC was criticized by blacks for racist activities in 1927, the ANRC developed and expanded its quad-state project, an emergency response program developed in cooperation with the National Medical Association to train Mississippi delta rural volunteers to operate in disasters and to improve long-range health and welfare conditions there. The ANRC also translated its multimedia standard first aid course into Spanish, developed a pilot project to teach first aid techniques to illiterates, and conducted drug abuse courses. Supporting further federal activities to help in disaster relief, such as the federal Disaster Relief Act of 1974, the ANRC began, in the mid-1970s, to develop, with a consortium of mental health agencies, crisis counseling for disaster victims with disaster-related emotional problems. With other agencies, the ANRC sponsored conferences and seminars as well as pilot projects in areas such as child abuse, unwed motherhood, and problems of aging, drug abuse, high blood pressure, and, in the tradition of Progressive social workers in the early twentieth century, in venereal disease. In 1974, the ANRC provided volunteers for Project SSI-Alert, in which the federal government sought out the elderly and the handicapped eligible for supplemental security income, a federal program. In the 1970s, the ANRC also promoted the revival of the use of volunteers in social service. For instance, in 1974, the ANRC began its annual Be Somebody Week to stimulate youth to help others, a continuing emphasis of this major national social service agency.

The most important source for the ANRC's history is the detailed and comprehensive Foster Rhea Dulles, *The American Red Cross: A History* (1950), one of the few scholarly histories of a national social service agency. This study, which unfortunately does not have footnotes, was based on the ANRC's extensive archives at its headquarters in Washington, D.C. Dulles's bibliography discusses numerous other accounts dealing with the ANRC. The detailed published *Annual Reports* are extremely helpful.

Some of the standard histories, especially Merle Curti, *American Philanthropy Abroad* (1963), and Robert Bremner, *American Philanthropy* (1960), mention the ANRC, but many of the standards in social welfare history, such as Clarke A. Chambers, *Seedtime for Reform* (1963), and Walter I. Trattner, *From Poor Law to Welfare State* (1974), either briefly mention or neglect it altogether. There seems to be plenty of room and need for further studies of the multifarious ANRC activities.

AMERICAN ORGANIZATION FOR REHABILITATION THROUGH TRAINING FEDERATION (AORTF). In 1880, the Jewish community in Petrograd, Russia, developed the Organization for Rehabilitation through Training (ORT) to promote vocational training. It established trade schools, mutual credit societies, artisan cooperatives, and the like. Its programs became very popular with the Jewish masses, especially in Eastern Europe, and these types of organizations developed in other European Jewish communities. As early as 1913, the Russian leaders decided to send delegates around the world to expand and to unify the ORT, but World War I, beginning in 1914, delayed these efforts. The anti-Semitism during the Russian Revolution also weakened Jews generally and the ORT specifically. Consequently, after 1918, the Russian ORT was financed chiefly by the Joint Distribution Committee of American Funds for the Relief of Jewish War Sufferers* (JDCAFRJWS), an American organization created during World War I to help Jews abroad. In August 1921, representatives from European nations established the World ORT Union (WORTU). By the early 1920s, about fifty-five ORT societies in Europe were united in the WORTU. The WORTU, however, lacked an affiliate in the United States, an obviously important source of support.

In Petrograd, the WORTU leaders decided to send two representatives to solicit American assistance for this self-help organization. On April 16, 1922, Dr. Leon Bramson and Dr. Aaron Syngalowski arrived in New York and established themselves at a local hotel. The next day, Dr. Bramson wrote to Herbert Lehman, the chairman of the important reconstruction committee of the JDCAFRJWS. On April 20, 1922, the two representatives presented their appeals for American support to the leaders of the JDAFRJWS, hoping to arouse Jewish communal, labor, and other agencies. The natural allies of supporters in America were the Jewish labor groups, represented by the Workmen's Circle (WC) (see *Fraternal Organizations*). At the WC convention in early May 1922, Dr. Syngalowski developed further support: on May 15, the Ukranian Jewish Federation pledged to raise $100,000 for the ORT, and other groups, such as the International Ladies Garment Workers Union, the Amalgamated Workers Union, and the B'nai B'rith, each affiliated with the People's Relief Committee of the JDCAFJWS, also supported the Russian envoys. Further efforts by Syngalowski and Bramson led representatives from 125 labor, Zionist, so-called landsmaschaft, and WC organizations to meet on June 22, 1922, at the Hebrew Sheltering and Immigrant Aid Society* Building in New York. At this meeting the American ORT Federation (AORTF) was established as the American ORT Society (AORTS).

The new AORTS elected as its president Judge Jacob Panekn of the New York City Municipal Court. Other initial officers included Louis B. Boudin, a lawyer and a scholar, the Yiddish poet Samuel Niger, and Jacob Baskin, the general secretary of the WC. In September 1922, the Russian delegates left America, satisfied with the establishment of an American group. The AORTS, however, floundered and dissolved in March 1924. New York Jewish communal leaders sponsored a convention in June 1924 to revive the organization; representatives from 130 organizations participated. On November 5, 1924, the AORTS was incorporated according to the laws of New York State. The news that the

JDCAFRJWS was going to dissolve prompted further efforts to strengthen the AORTS to promote rehabilitating Jewish communities abroad. In November 1924, the leaders developed the ORT reconstruction fund. Ludwig Lewisohn became the national chairman; joining him in this fund-raising effort were Paul Baerwald, a banker who served the JDCAFRJWS, David Sarnoff, president of the Radio Corporation of America, who led the New York drive, and Judge Joseph Proskauer of New York. In 1924, the organization launched its ORT reconstruction fund campaign, headed by Paul Felix Warburg from the JDCAFRJWS. The contributions of these individuals, important figures in the older, established Jewish community, showed the diversity of the AORTS, which was identified in the popular mind more with the Jewish labor organizations. A campaign, or gezeig, to raise money and obtain tools began in 1924, was led by journalist and civic leader Baruch Carney Vladeck, and culminated in 1929 with a dinner addressed by Eleanor Roosevelt and Herbert Lehman. This and other campaigns in the early period helped the AORTS to grow.

The development of the Women's American ORT (WAORT) in the 1920s proved especially important. Established in Brooklyn at the home of Louis Boudin on October 12, 1927, the WAORT elected Dr. Anna P. Boudin, a dentist, as its first president. The WAORT became primarily a fund-raising organization; in Jewish communities abroad, it supported adult training, scholarships for teachers, equipment for vocational education, and the construction of schools. The Aron Syngalowski Center in Tel Aviv, Israel, sponsored by the WAORT, remains the showcase of the ORT system in that country. By the 1970s, now a membership organization like other groups in the American ORTF, the WAORT was the fastest growing Jewish women's organization in the United States with around 90,000 members in 700 chapters throughout the country.

Between the late 1920s and the end of World War II, there were few significant developments in the AORTS, which remained essentially a fund-raising organization supporting the World ORT Union, which, in turn, sponsored vocational activities in Jewish communities abroad. In 1936, the American organization was renamed the AORTF. An important event occurred in 1940 when the AORTF established in New York City the New York ORT Trade School to provide vocational training for Jewish refugees in America. In 1942, the AORTF established another vocational school in New York City to teach refugees the needle trades, the traditional Jewish skill in New York and America. Initially called the Leon Bramson School, it became the Leon and Vera Bramson School in the early 1950s, when Vera Bramson died. The first school closed in February 1957, but the Bramson School still exists. The two schools trained around 22,000 refugees, chiefly from Eastern and Central Europe, in vocational skills, providing new jobs and livelihoods for thousands of refugees.

The most important period of the AORTF occurred in the years after World War II. In 1947, the AORTF reached an agreement that affected profoundly the

structure of the AORTF: the American Jewish Joint Distribution Committee*
(JDC) agreed to give a fixed sum of money from the annual United Jewish
Appeal (UJA) (see *Foundations and Research Associations*) to the AORTF,
which in turn agreed to stop its own fund-raising drives, a major organizational
activity. The AORTF and the JDC have renewed this agreement annually since
1947. In light of this agreement, a convention of the AORTF reorganized the
agency to be based on membership rather than fund raising. In the early 1950s,
Professor William Haber, an economist and university administrator, became the
president of the AORTF.

President Haber, who remained in office until 1974, supervised the enormous
growth and organizational development of the AORTF. Direct services and
activities supporting the overseas program, not part of the AORTF earlier, became regular functions. In the early 1960s, for instance, under a contract from
the United States Agency for International Development, the AORTF conducted
vocational training programs in Africa. At home in New York, the curriculum of
the Bramson ORT Trade School changed constantly to keep up with shifting
demands and technological changes. Strengthening its services and technical
assistance programs, the AORTF established a purchasing department in the
1960s, when it directly assisted vocational educators abroad for the first time.
The central focus of the AORTF under Dr. Haber was the new state of Israel,
where the Syngalowski Center, sponsored by the American women's group,
capped the vocational education program. This special concern for Israel was
evidenced in June 1967; following a visit to study the effects of the Arab-Israeli
Six-Day War, the AORTF began a drive to raise $100,000 through its member-
ship. Also in 1967, in an agreement with the Israeli Ministry of Education, the
AORTF pledged to double the vocational school facilities there by 1972.

The reliance on membership rather than on mass appeals for funds became the
central factor in the organizational structure after 1949. The great increase in
membership paralleled the important American contributions after World War II.
The most dramatic membership growth occurred in the women's group. In 1960,
fifty thousand members in 350 chapters raised about $836,000; by the twentieth
biennial meeting in 1969, nearly ninety thousand members in seven hundred
chapters, double the 1960 figure, raised $1.7 million, more than twice the
amount in 1960.

The national organizational structure grew slowly, but the first national workshop, held in January 1967, established a more definite structure. A national
workshop committee developed a five-year program to organize ten new chapters
and attract twenty thousand new members. The establishment of a scholarship
program proved popular, attracting new supporters, as did the "divisions," such
as in the garment industry and among rabbis. An important organizational development occurred in 1968 when Samuel Jaffee became the legacy consultant;
for fifteen years the overseas public relations director for the JDC, Jaffee was an
important figure in Jewish fund raising. The visit to nearly all the chapters in

1969 by the director of the World ORT Union, Dr. Vladimir Halperin, as well as some important local dinners and other programs, also increased support for the AORTF. The growth since 1967 of men's ORT organizations, while not as dramatic as that of the women's groups, helped to shift gradually the public view that the AORTF was simply a women's organization.

In the 1970s, the AORTF continued to support programs abroad, especially in Israel, but also in the changing Jewish communities in Africa, Europe, and the Middle East. In January 1975, when the AORTF membership of 130,000 made it the largest component of the World ORT Union, the communal leader and banker Harold Freedman of New York replaced Dean Haber as president, ending a chapter in the history of the AORTF.

The sources relating to the AORTF's history are diverse. Agency publications and documents, such as Adam Penn, "The Beginnings of American ORT," *ORT Bulletin* 25 (Winter 1971), and "Membership and Organizational Developments" (unpublished manuscript, January 25, 1970), are helpful. Another primary source is Dr. Frank F. Rosenblatt, "The ORT," *Jewish Social Service Quarterly* 2 (February 1924): 23–50. AORTF's files are in the archives of YIVO Institute for Jewish Research in New York City and in its headquarters in New York.

Jack Rader, *By the Skill of Their Hands: The Story of ORT* (1970), is a helpful history. There is no published scholarly history of the AORTF, but a study of the international ORT being prepared by Professor Leon Shapiro will include the AORTF.

AMERICAN ORTHOPSYCHIATRIC ASSOCIATION, THE (AOA). On January 13, 1924, in Chicago the AOA was established as the Association of American Orthopsychiatrists (AAO). Six practitioners and a few members of the staff of the Institute for Juvenile Research in Chicago, where the meeting convened, founded the AAO, but the origins of the group related to the frequent discussions between Dr. Karl A. Menninger of the Menninger Foundation of Kansas and Dr. Herman M. Adler, a Chicago psychiatrist and the former state criminologist of Illinois, to establish an organization of psychiatrists working in the fields of delinquency and criminology. At the annual meeting of the Central Neuropsychiatric Association in Chicago in 1923, Adler and Menninger discussed this idea with some of their colleagues. These talks prompted the men to send letters to twenty-three psychiatrists throughout the United States, inviting them to attend the conference held in January 1924. The organizing meeting chose officers, including as temporary chairman, V. V. Anderson, and as temporary secretary, Karl Menninger. Three others, including Lawson G. Lowrey, who became one of the most important figures in the early history of the organization, were chosen as temporary officers. The group planned to meet again at the annual meeting of the American Medical Association (AMA) in Chicago. On June 10, 1924, at the Institute for Juvenile Research, the AAO adopted a constitution and elected officers. The first president was William Healy of Boston, a pioneer in psychiatric studies of juvenile delinquency, and Menninger was elected secretary-treasurer. There was also a vice-president and a counsellor and editor.

In the 1920s, sponsoring annual meetings was the major activity, but some organizational developments did occur. The five-member executive committee of the AAO included the three officers in addition to the editor-in-chief and the retired president. In this early period, there were three classes of membership, including the active, or fellow, which was limited to those in the field. As early as January 1925, the executive committee rigorously discussed including non-medical people as AAO members, and it invited social workers, psychologists, educators, and sociologists to join. At the annual meeting in 1925, held at the Russell Sage Foundation* Building in New York City, the AAO discussed several substitutes for "orthopsychiatry" but decided to keep it in the organization's name. In 1926, the organization, now called the AOA, received funds from the disbanded American Association of Clinical Criminologists. At the business meeting in 1926, the AOA amended its bylaws to include social workers and other professionals. Also in 1926, the AOA elected its first honorary member, Ellen Sturges Dummer of Chicago, a philanthropist interested in the mental health aspects of juvenile delinquency. Treatment became a significant aspect of the annual program in 1926, and it continued as a major organizational concern. In the late 1920s, there was an active effort to establish permanent functional committees, and in the fall of 1929, the first issue of the *President's Bulletin* appeared. In October 1930, the AOA began to publish its *Journal of Orthopsychiatry,* a continuing and important publication in the field.

In the 1930s, cooperating with other organizations, the AOA became more involved than before in national issues. Committees handled most of the agency's activities. There was a tighter organizational structure than before, reflected in a greater concern for professional standards and requiring that new members have not only specific professional training but also experience with an interdisciplinary team in a clinical setting. In 1934, to develop a pamphlet on mental hygiene in the school classroom, the committee on education cooperated with the journal committee on health problems of the National Education Association (NEA) and the AMA. The AOA established a committee to cooperate with the division on community clinics of the National Committee for Mental Hygiene* (NCMH), and with the National Probation Association* (NPA), the AOA created a committee to evaluate practices, standards, personnel, and goals of juvenile courts for the purpose of developing a manual for juvenile courts and clinics. In September 1937, the AOA was incorporated according to the laws of the state of New York. In 1938, with the NEA and the National Progressive Education Association, the AOA cosponsored a resolution calling for better schools and for greater attention than before being paid to the many mental health problems in education.

In the period after World War II, the agency grew. Collaborative efforts continued in the 1940s. In 1944, for instance, the AOA participated in developing plans for the postwar period with such agencies as the NCMH and the American Association on Mental Deficiency.* An important organizational event occurred in 1953 when Dr. Marion Langer joined the staff and began to shape year-round activities in the national office, located in New York City, in offices leased from the National Health Council* (NHC). In October 1954, the AOA began to issue a *Newsletter,* an idea of Jessie Edna Crampton, the secretary of the organization. By the mid-1950s, the central office was developing as the "hub of the Association's activities," establishing a closer integration of committee and board activities, for instance. Beginning in 1954, an employment service functioned at the annual meeting. In 1955, the AOA began a three-year experiment in joint board-committee meetings. In 1956, the organization resolved in favor of racially integrated schools, and it appointed a desegregation committee to implement the ruling of the Supreme Court of the United States in *Brown* vs. *Board of Education of Topeka* (1954). Recognition of its leadership in the field came, for example, from an invitation in 1957 to serve as a sponsor of a conference on the training of child psychiatrists. At the annual meetings, workshops were increasingly held. In 1952, three hundred participants registered for ten workshops; by 1961, there were thirty-nine workshops enrolling about two thousand delegates. Two important developments in the late 1950s were establishing a policy and planning committee and holding an annual meeting on the West Coast to show that the AOA was a nationwide organization. Also, for the first time, in the late 1950s, the AOA published a digest of papers from the annual meeting. Representatives from the AOA participated in such conferences as the White House Conference on the Aging in 1960.

In the early 1960s, the AOA began to focus on a particular theme at the annual meeting. Discussions also focused on the issue of clinical versus social action programs, and in 1962, the AOA voted that it indeed had a responsibility to translate clinical knowledge into social action. In 1964, an ad hoc committee of the board began preliminary work to develop a structure for social action. In 1962, editorial and publication operations were shifted to the central office in New York. The executive committee took on added importance in the mid-1960s. During this period, the social issues committee was working to develop an explanation for the problems of blacks preparing for and entering into graduate programs in mental health. Ties to public health and social welfare were reflected in 1968, when the AOA called a meeting of over sixty organizations to discuss government reductions in human services and the problem of creating adequate human services.

In the 1970s, the AOA strove to maintain a balance between clinical knowledge and social action. At the annual meetings in the early 1970s, the AOA began to hold special institutes emphasizing treatment skills. Committees worked as task forces or study groups within the structure of four committees: administration, children and youth, clinical services and research, and social issues. With a contract from the federal Department of Health, Education and Welfare, the AOA participated in a project to develop guidelines to screen children in the federal Medicaid program. In the 1970s, the AOA joined lawsuits, for example, in an Alabama case dealing with the adequacy of services and the civil rights of mental patients and in a case in Texas involving adjudged delinquents. With the American Civil Liberties Union and the Council on Law and Social Policy, the AOA sponsored the mental health law project to win civil rights for patients. In 1973, at the annual meeting, the AOA, the National Association of Social Workers,* and other organizations, held an emergency session on dealing with reductions in governmental social services. In 1976, major AOA activities included the annual meeting, which is held alternately in New York, Washington, San Francisco, and Chicago, the publishing of a scientific journal, and the ongoing development of a continuing education program on a multidisciplinary basis. The AOA remains essentially problem centered rather than discipline centered. In 1976, its membership of about forty-six hundred included anthropologists, educators, lawyers, nurses, pediatricians, psychiatrists, psychologists, social workers, and sociologists.

The sources for studying the history of the AOA include mimeographed annual reports, minutes of meetings, and *Newsletters* on file at the agency's headquarters in New York City. The records of executive committee meetings, 1923–1963, are on microfilm at the Social Welfare History Archives Center at the University of Minnesota, Minneapolis. *The New York Times* covered primarily the sessions at the annual meetings. Some essays in Lawson G. Lowrey and Victoria Sloane, eds., *Orthopsychiatry, 1923–1948: Retrospect and Prospect* (1948), provide historical materials, as did an essay, "Fifty Years of AOA," which appeared in the AOA's *50th Anniversary Meeting* (1973). There is no scholarly history of the AOA, and few historians have written about it.

AMERICAN PRINTING HOUSE FOR THE BLIND, INC. (APHB). In the 1840s and 1850s, a group of philanthropists had been publishing special books for the blind in the basement of the Kentucky School for the Blind (KSB), in Louisville. The school was established in 1842. Beginning in the late 1850s, the publishing work had progressed sufficiently to the point where a group decided to develop this activity as an independent organization. In 1858, the founding group decided to press for state funds to support this work. The group included James Gutherie, a former United States senator from Kentucky who also served as secretary of the treasury under President Franklin Pierce; William B. Bullock, a lawyer, judge, and professor of law at the University of Louisville, where he taught, and who headed the Kentucky branch of the United States Sanitary Commission,* the leading national social service agency of the Civil War era; and Bryce M. Patten, the first superintendent of the KSB. On January 23, 1858, the APHB was established officially in Louisville by an act of the general assembly of the commonwealth of Kentucky. The group chose Bryce Patten, the KSB's superintendent, as its first superintendent.

Events moved slowly for this struggling organization. The leaders and friends of the APHB convinced the Kentucky legislature in June 1865 to authorize a payment of five dollars per year to the organization for each blind person in Kentucky counted by the United States Census. In May 1871, the National Association of Publishing Literary and Musical Works for the Blind joined the APHB, giving it thousands of dollars worth of printed materials. During its first twenty years, the APHB's average yearly budget was about $10,000, and the organization had about six to eight employees. A federal act of March 3, 1879, "To Promote the Education of the Blind," significantly increased the fortunes of the organization. The act provided for funding for operations, administration, and construction, helping the APHB to complete its first building in 1883. The act also stipulated that the superintendents of all the schools for the blind in the country be ex officio members of the board of trustees. In 1880, the APHB's charter from Kentucky was amended to incorporate this structural change.

The APHB continued to supply books for educating blind children, but not until about the 1920s did any substantial changes occur. By the 1920s, the annual budget was about $38,000 and the APHB had about twenty staff personnel. Aware of the increased number of children attending classes for the blind and perhaps sensitized by the well-publicized tragedies affecting children in war-torn Europe, the United States Congress raised its annual appropriation to the APHB from $10,000 to $40,000 in 1919. In 1922, the Kentucky legislature appropriated $25,000 for an addition to the main building. Five years later, the United States Congress increased its annual appropriation to $75,000. Because of the vision and insight of Superintendent Dr. E. E. Bramletee, beginning in September 1928, the APHB began to publish an edition for the blind of *Reader's Digest*. This activity gained the support of *Reader's Digest* owners, Mr. and Mrs. DeWitt Wallace, who supported other charities and organizations, such as the Girls Clubs of America.* The resolution in the 1920s of the long-time "type fight" in the field of work for the blind, establishing the use of revised braille grade 1½, also helped to increase the APHB's activities.

Real expansion occurred after 1930. In November 1930, the chief clerk of the United States Treasury examined the methods, bookkeeping, and such of the APHB, and he praised its operations. The Pratt-Smoot Act of 1930, which provided federal funds for literature for the adult blind, revolutionized the field. This act provided for the Library of Congress to participate in and to administer library services for the blind, a stipulation that especially helped to expand the use of so-called talking books. The APHB expanded its services further in 1939 when it began to publish talking book editions of *Reader's Digest*. A three-member publication committee of the board of trustees selected the books to be published. An advisory committee of four trustees assisted this committee and recommended books, as did the superintendent. A three-member music committee determined publications in that field. In the 1930s, the organizational structure included the board of trustees, comprised of seven Louisville area residents and all the superintendents of schools for the blind as ex officio members. The agency's bylaws called for an executive committee of the board of trustees. The president came from the Louisville area, and the vice-president was chosen by the superintendents of schools for the blind. The APHB's superintendent, elected biennially by the board of trustees, was responsible to the executive committee.

In 1953, the APHB established its department of educational research to evaluate the methods of educating blind children. In the fall of 1954, the organization began its Recorded Educational Aids to Learning (REAL) program, initially using tapes from the University of Minnesota and then from Kent State University. By the late 1950s, the annual budget had grown to $1 million and the staff included 210 full-time and thirty-five part-time personnel. In 1957, the organization was publishing sixty magazines in braille, including eight weeklies, and seven talking book magazines. Its Talking Book program, however, was not as large as the one conducted by the American Foundation for the Blind,* the leading service agency in the field.

The published annual *Reports of the Trustees* is the most important convenient primary source for studying the APHB's history. An agency publication, *American Printing House for the Blind* (1930), is helpful. More informative are descriptions by others associated with the organization, specifically, F. E. Davis, "99 Years of Service to Blind Children," *New Outlook for the Blind* 51 (March 1957): 109–116, and William C. Dabney, "American Printing House for the Blind.," *Filson Club Historical Quarterly* 36 (January 1962): 5–17. Frances A. Koestler, *The Unseen Majority* (1976), mentions the APHB, but there does not appear to be a scholarly history of this old organization.

AMERICAN PRISON ASSOCIATION: see AMERICAN CORRECTIONAL ASSOCIATION, THE.

AMERICAN PUBLIC HEALTH ASSOCIATION (APHA). The urban public health movement in the United States emerged in the mid-nineteenth century. In the 1840s, Dr. Elisha Harris of New York City conducted pioneering studies of the health conditions in his increasingly crowded city. In 1866, New York City created its metropolitan board of health, a realization that public health was a full-time activity rather than a short-term response to deal with epidemics and other temporary disasters. Other cities and states followed suit, and boards of health sprang up around the country. To promote this movement, a group of public health physicians and sanitarians concerned with improving sanitary measures for the control of epidemic disease met in New York City on April 18, 1872, and organized the American Public Health Association (APHA). The key figures in the establishment were Dr. Stephen Smith, a physician, sanitarian, and a major figure in the New York City Board of Health, Edward M. Snow of Rhode Island, J. Ordonoux of Roslyn, New York, Elisha Harris, Moreau Morris, Carl Pfieffer, and E. H. Jones of New York, C. C. Cox of the District of Columbia, and Heber Smith of the federal Marine Hospital Service. The founding members were primarily physicians and sanitarians, but some had ties with other aspects of social welfare. Elisha Harris, for instance, had participated in a multifaceted housing evaluation and social reform program in New York. A larger meeting was called for September 12, 1872, to develop the organization further.

Sanitarians and physicians from New York, Pennsylvania, the District of Columbia, Louisiana, Rhode Island, Connecticut, Ohio, and Illinois attended the convention in September. A constitution was adopted that defined the purpose of the new organization. Its major objective according to its constitution was to promote progress in sanitary science and to promote the application of sanitary knowledge to solve the prevalent public health problems. The founders envisioned the APHA as a voluntary organization that would use public opinion and political power to push for effective sanitary measures; the control of environmental hazards and epidemic disease were of transcending importance. Accordingly the first volume of the APHA official publication, *Public Health Papers and Reports* (1879), was largely devoted to the problems of current epidemics of cholera and yellow fever in the West and South. During the early years of the association, most public health problems were approached as technological issues to be solved by experts in specialized fields.

The original founders of the APHA saw state and local government as the vehicle through which these general technological reforms would be accomplished. The state would be responsible for controlling epidemics, disposing of sewage and garbage, providing pure water, and promoting other general health measures. "The time is near when neither the State nor national authority . . . will be justifiably withheld from local and general inquiries and from advising [methods for the improvement] of life and health," wrote Dr. Elisha Smith, secretary of the new organization, in the first editorial column of *Public Health Papers and Reports*. Although the APHA emphasized the future role of the state in promoting public health, it also feared close association with government because its leaders perceived government to be under the control of corrupt officials. The proper role for the APHA was to provide objective, scientific, and rational goals and direction upon which government policy could be based when and if reform-minded persons gained political power.

It is not surprising that the organization's official publication was at first almost solely devoted to technical investigations of special environmental health problems. Technical papers delivered at the annual convention made up the bulk of material printed in *Public Health Papers and Reports*. Topics relating to epidemic diseases such as diphtheria, typhoid, yellow fever, malaria, and tuberculosis were numerous, and articles on the means of disease transmission were also of tremendous concern. By the time of the 1875 convention, however, reports on other areas of environmental control appeared, and the APHA broadened its interests. Topics on infant mortality, perils to health in public places, sanitation in schools, safety in railways and steam vessels, park planting, and health in the marketplace were added to epidemiologic surveys of disease transmission, sewerage, and provision of pure water. Environmental control was an early focus of concern for the APHA. Although formal links with social welfare groups interested in related areas were not made until late in the Progressive era, these early papers indicate the broadening areas of APHA concern at the end of the nineteenth century.

The original membership of the AHPA was drawn primarily from physicians associated with state and local boards of public health. But as the issues of water supply, sewage disposal, and disease identification increased in scope and complexity, bacteriologists, engineers, social workers, and other professionals and nonprofessionals alike began to play a larger role in the organization. Outbreaks of typhoid in Pennsylvania in 1885 and in Massachusetts in 1890 spurred APHA interest in the problems of bacteriological identification. The association's committee on pollution of water supplies organized a subcommittee to standardize procedures for disease identification. In 1895, this subcommittee organized a convention of bacteriologists, thereby formalizing the growing importance of bacteriology in public health practice. In 1899, at the convention of the association in Minneapolis, the section on bacteriology and chemistry was organized, and, under the guidance of William Sedgwick, Charles V. Chapin, and C.-E.A. Winslow, leading bacteriologists and spokesmen in the public health movement, the first of a series of "Standard Methods" publications was produced. This first publication dealt with the standardization of bacteriological and laboratory procedures in disease identification.

The growing importance of specialist and nonmedical expertise was further indicated in 1908 when two more sections—one on vital statistics and one on public health administration—were incorporated into the APHA. In 1913, Rudolph Hering, an engineer, was the first person without a medical degree to serve as president of the APHA. In the next few years, the organization added sections on sociology, sanitary engineering, industrial hygiene, and food and drugs. These changes indicated a growing and broadening interest in both the scientific and social definitions of health and disease.

In the first decades of the twentieth century, the growing diversification and increasing specialization of the organization led to major moves for reform within the APHA. Rather than compete with other national and local specialist organizations for limited membership, the APHA sought ways to incorporate smaller organizations into the APHA structure. Organizations with narrow though related interests were encouraged to meet jointly with the APHA at its annual convention. If both the APHA and the smaller organization agreed, the smaller organization would be incorporated as a section or an affiliated independent body.

In addition to incorporating smaller professional bodies, the APHA expanded its membership by setting up and incorporating state and local branches of the larger association. In 1916, an active drive was opened to increase membership as well as to decentralize the APHA's decision-making process. These factors all tended to increase the organization's ability to adapt to its changing professional makeup as well as to increase in size. Although the organization had an almost stagnant membership of about seven hundred in the early years of the twentieth century, the second and third decades showed strong membership growth: by 1916, there were over sixteen hundred members, and by 1921 there were over three thousand. Responding to the generalized Progressive era ethos of "organize or perish," professionals were recruited by and joined the APHA.

The diversification of the APHA membership led to clear changes in its publications. When the *Journal of the American Public Health Association* commenced publication in 1911, the editor acknowledged that its articles would be decidedly less technical than were the articles in the *Public Health Papers and Reports,* which had ceased publishing some years before. Most members were no longer urban sanitarian physicians, the editor conceded. What was needed was journal to interest the "ninety percent" of the health officers who had neither training nor interest in the technical articles that had appeared previously. The APHA's membership now included a wide range of health workers—from the poorly trained, rural political appointee in need of practical knowledge to the urbane, highly educated specialist physician.

At the same time that the membership increased, the success of the APHA-led sanitary campaigns was evident throughout the country as the morbidity and mortality rates from specific communicable diseases dropped. New areas of concern were then seen to be within the purview of the association. In 1920, a gift of $5,000 from the Metropolitan Life Insurance Company for the investigation of health departments in eighty-three cities began a process of transformation and redefinition for the organization. C.-E.A. Winslow and Charles Chapin joined with Wade Frost, a pioneering epidemiologist, and Louis Dublin, a well-known public health statistician, to form the leadership of the committee on municipal health department practice. In 1925, this committee was reorganized and its name changed to the committee on administrative practice. Although organized to investigate health department practices and administration, committee members soon became involved in the debate over the public health official's role in providing medical care services.

C.-E.A. Winslow, in his famous presidential address in 1926, said that public health was at a "crossroads" and had to decide on new directions. Winslow advocated the involvement of public health professionals in organizing health services for their constituency but was strongly opposed by others within the profession, including Haven Emerson, a Columbia University professor and spokesman for the public health movement. Emerson and others rejected the idea that public health officers and professionals had any role in providing personal health services. Those opposed to the profession's involvement in such areas as health planning and medical care organization generally looked to the past for the model by which the profession had gained and would maintain eminence. Public health, it was asserted, should be concerned only with the prevention of disease through sanitary and environmental science and should not become involved in treatment, which should be left in the hands of private practitioners and the medical profession. C.-E.A. Winslow and others in favor of public health involvement in medical care pointed out that there was no longer a clear demarcation between disease prevention and treatment. Communicable disease treatment, chronic diseases, and child health problems were now issues with which the health professional had to become involved. The health official's responsibility was to maintain the health of the community, and, now that communicable disease was no longer the sole threat to health, the health officer had a responsibility to involve himself in the newer issues, which included the provision of adequate medical as well as social services for the entire population. Advocates for involvement in issues of the provision of medical care were spurred on by surveys indicating that both the high cost and unavailability of medical services had seriously undermined the health of the American population. With the advent of the depression in the 1930s, these studies took on added significance. It was not until 1948, however, that enough APHA members agreed with advocates for such involvement to form the section on medical care, which is today one of the largest within the APHA. This fight illustrates a basic schism between the older members of the association who define public health narrowly and the younger members who accept a broader definition of the role of public health.

In the 1950s, there were still serious rifts between health officers in favor and those opposed to the broadened definition of public health responsibility. Some doctors organized a short-lived group, the American Association of Public Health Physicians, to counteract the growing diversity of the professional makeup of the organization as the APHA became involved in health planning, medical care, social work, and even city planning. The old idea of public health as sanitary science seemed to be on the wane, and this change was objectionable to older members and physicians within the organization. During the mid-1950s, crises over this expanding and changing definition of the sphere of public health led to serious threats to the APHA's stability. One annual meeting was, in fact, devoted to the future goals, direction, and even viability of the APHA.

The APHA emerged from the 1950s with a much more activist orientation. Spurred by the social activism of the 1960s, by a larger and more diversified membership and by governmental policies such as the War on Poverty, the renewal of Hill-Burton funds for the construction of new hospital facilities, and various mental health and retardation programs, the APHA developed into a strong voice for social action programs. Comprehensive health planning, poverty, and welfare issues, and other health-related issues became prime areas of concern for many of its members. The older issues of sanitary science and epidemic disease, while still important, appeared to be eclipsed by newer, less clearly defined areas of interest. By the end of the 1960s, the APHA had clearly transformed itself from a small body of public health officers and physicians concerned with sanitary science to a broad coalition of professionals and community spokesmen interested in a wide range of social and political issues. New publications emanating from the APHA reflect this broadened concern with health care. Such publications as a new journal, entitled *Medical Care,* indicate the current interests of many APHA members. In 1969, the APHA policy statement, "Social Policy and Medical Care," formalized the association's new direction. From a small group of elite professional sanitarians and physicians in 1872, the APHA has developed into a broad-based movement of health professionals and nonprofessionals interested in improving the quality of life in America.

The National offices of the APHA are located in Washington, D.C., and much archival material is available there. Arthur Visaltear at Yale University is the archivist for the medical care section. The early history of the APHA is found in its own publications—*Public Health Papers and Reports, Journal of the Massachusetts Association of Public Health,* the *American Journal of Public Health,* the *Journal of the American Public Health Association,* and the *American Journal of Public Hygiene. A Half Century of Public Health,* edited by Mazyck Ravenel, was published in 1921 in celebration of the association's fiftieth anniversary and is useful. Although no academic study of the entire history of the APHA is available, there is a useful and extremely interesting short history. This study, *The First One Hundred Years: Essays on the History of the American Public Health Association* (1972) by Nancy Bernstein was published by the APHA in commemoration of its hundredth anniversary. George Rosen had published a number of interesting articles on the association's history, many of which appear in recent issues of the *American Journal of Public Health.* Arthur Visaltear has published an important essay, "Emergence of the Medical Care Section of the American Public Health Association, 1926–1948," *American Journal of Public Health* 63 (November 1973): 986–1007. The numerous special reports and publications of the association are widely available in medical and public health libraries.

David Rosner

AMERICAN PUBLIC WELFARE ASSOCIATION (APWA). During the late nineteenth and early twentieth centuries, public social services became increasingly important and visible. An intensification of this trend in the 1920s resulted in a significant expansion of the scope and scale of public social services. Public agencies became progressively more involved in social welfare and needed the professional recognition and representation that would enable them to contribute effectively to the shaping of public social policies. True to Alexis de Tocqueville's observation of the "American genius" for creating new organizations to cope with new needs and contingencies, the idea of an organization to represent the rapidly growing constituency in public social services began to take shape. At a national meeting of the National Conference of Social Work*

(NCSW) in San Francisco in 1929, the delegation representing public social services voted to undertake the establishment of a voluntary membership organization, with representation from all levels of government and from geographical areas throughout the country. The idea was timely. One year later, on June 12, 1930, about forty persons from twenty different states gathered in Boston to found the new organization. Nearly half were state welfare administrators. The convenor of the group was Richard K. Conant, commissioner of the Massachusetts Department of Public Welfare. Grace Abbott, chief of the United State Children's Bureau, and her deputy, Katharine Lenroot, spoke of the help that the proposed association would be to federal agencies. The assembled group lost no time in reaching a quick consensus that the time was ripe to inaugurate the new association to reflect their interests. It was christened the American Association of Public Welfare Officials (AAPWO); its scope and mission was "to coordinate and improve the activities of public welfare organizations throughout the country, through the education of public opinion to the importance of public welfare, and through the development and maintenance of high standards."

The birth of the AAPWO came closely after the onset of the Great Depression. As the depression persisted and its severity increased, there was great pressure to mobilize national resources to meet critical human needs. It was during such troubled times that the AAPWO was launched. Even in its formative years, the association began to break new grounds. Its first project in 1931 was to assist President Herbert Hoover's Emergency Committee for Employment (later renamed the President's Organization for Unemployment Relief) in gathering information on the need for emergency relief and in organizing national resources to meet that need. A grant for the project funded by the Spelman Fund of the Rockefeller Foundation enabled the AAPWO to employ its first full-time staff and to open an office in Washington, D.C., on September 16, 1931. Frank Bane, commissioner of the Virginia State Department of Public Welfare, was appointed the first executive director. The Children's Bureau, which actively sponsored the AAPWO in its early days, loaned Dr. Marietta Stevenson to provide staff services. The field staff of the AAPWO prepared several research studies to document the conditions of unemployment, the resulting needs for relief, and detailed descriptions of the desperate relief situations in the forty-eight states of the country. These studies were used skillfully by Frank Bane in his testimonies before congressional committees. This was probably the first time in the history of the United States that social workers who had firsthand knowledge of the needs and deprivations of the underprivileged were invited to make public statements before the legislative branches of the United States Congress and to participate in the formulation of national legislation and public social policies.

In addition to its research and advocacy roles during the depression years, the AAPWO also contributed to the evolving conception of a federal-state-local partnership in the design and delivery of public social services. Throughout the depression there was a continuous development of public social services, at first uneven and entirely local; later it became more orderly as one state after another went into the business of unemployment relief; and still later, it became stronger, as the federal government created new legislation and programs of far-reaching significance. AAPWO was an active participant, catalyst, and, at times, even instigator in this process of change and development.

In February 1932, the Spelman Fund responded once again; it granted $25,000 annually for a period of five years for the association to carry on its work and to implement a plan to create a more permanent secretariat. The office of the AAPWO was moved from Washington, D.C., to a building in Chicago, known familiarly as "850," which also housed several other national organizations, including the American Legislators Association, the American Municipal Association, and several others that shared the overall mission of improving the quality and distribution of public social services. The new office was near the University of Chicago, where Edith Abbott, Sophonisba Breckinridge, and other loyal association friends were teaching and training graduate students. They were among the most nationally prominent proponents of public social policy during this period.

Over the next two years, the AAPWO expanded its staff activities in response to increasing requests for assistance from congressional committees, federal agencies, state officials, and local bodies. It worked actively for federal financial participation in state and local programs and helped to implement the Federal Emergency Relief Act in May 1933.

The formative years of the AAPWO were the most critical and innovative period in its history. Its membership and financial backing gained momentum. In a span of two years from its birth, the association's membership grew from an initial 151 persons to nearly a thousand. With a view to broaden its base of membership support, the association's board of directors, on May 18, 1932, voted to change its name from the American Association of Public Welfare Officials to the American Public Welfare Association (APWA).

The New Deal era ushered in an exciting period in American social welfare history. The enactment of both the Emergency Relief Appropriation Act and the Social Security Act in 1935 marked the beginning of a paradigm shift from emergency relief to a federal work program and to federal provision on a permanent basis for social security in the form of social insurance and special public assistance. After working assiduously for passage of the social security legislation and aiding in its implementation, APWA assumed the function of liaison between federal agencies and the states.

A new frontier was opened up in the formulation and development of public social policies, and the result was a rapid succession of new agencies and programs. Illustrative were the Public Works Administration, the Works Progress Administration, the Federal Security Administration, and the like. There was a continuous process of social program experimentation, and their successful design and implementation required a great deal of administrative and organizational innovation. APWA provided leadership at the grass-roots level. It helped in establishing communication linkages, in strengthening intergovernmental relationships, in training staff, and in mobilizing human resources and talents.

APWA's growing membership highlighted the need for more planned organizational responses to the focal concerns and needs of its members. This resulted in new and more strategies of membership participation. Two component groups were formed within the APWA in 1939 and 1940—the National Council of State Public Welfare Administrators and the National Council of Local Public Welfare Administrators—to provide a forum for the interchange of experience about needs and problems peculiar to their respective regions. These two councils supplemented and buttressed the roles played by APWA's staff. In this way, APWA's involvement as a catalyst and advocate of public social policy gave it national visibility and recognition among relevant constituencies in public welfare and public social services. A decade of uninterrupted progress toward better public social services was the historical backdrop to the commemoration of the tenth anniversary of the APWA in 1940.

After the attack on Pearl Harbor in December 1941, APWA shifted its priorities and moved toward new fields of action to aid the nation's people during the war effort and to ensure continuity and coordination of public social services. It became involved in work with the National Defense Council and later with the Office of Civilian Defense and the Office of Defense Health and Welfare Services within the President's Office for Emergency Management. The APWA's newly appointed committee on defense activities, later known as the committee on war services, under the chairmanship of David C. Adie, commissioner of the New York State Department of Social Welfare, was of invaluable help to the federal offices. The committee had the staff services of Elizabeth Wickendon, who helped in preparing a number of memoranda on defense services. Through this same staff the APWA committee had also developed documentation related to postdefense planning and fiscal policies of defense and nondefense expenditures. The APWA also collaborated intensively with the American National Red Cross,* (ANRC), which resulted in the development of policy statements governing the relationship of ANRC and public welfare agencies with regard to their services to the armed forces. Cooperative agreements were also drawn up with the Family Welfare Association of America* to make special facilities available to families of servicemen. The APWA was also involved in planning services for discharged servicemen and a continuance of nationwide efforts to integrate newly established services and programs. The Children's Bureau was still another federal agency to invite APWA's participation in the formulation and development of policies pertaining to child welfare services. In December 1940, APWA established the children's committee, later known as the committee on child welfare, to provide a major new thrust in public social policy. From its inception, APWA's children's committee was instrumental in shaping legislation and national social policies, in influencing the steady buildup of child welfare services and programs throughout the country, and in broadening the concept of child welfare.

The administrative integration of public welfare agencies, which was held in abeyance during the war years, was resumed in the postwar period with greater awareness of the need for such integration. APWA was a principal advocate of unification of public social services and programs. Also, when the first major amendments to the Social Security Act of 1935 were proposed, in 1946, APWA served as a forum for clearance of information, discussion of ideas, and clarification of goals. During the postwar years, the APWA began to transfer financial reliance from foundation grants to membership. The APWA had five thousand individual members and nine hundred agency members as the decade closed.

The 1950s marked a more extensive development of social security than had occurred previously. The Social Security Amendments of 1956 were another significant step in the evolutionary development of social security legislation, as were the 1958 and 1960 amendments. The APWA, under the able and dynamic leadership of its executive director, Loula Dunn, was especially active in supplying information and the viewpoint of public welfare personnel on a number of proposals to the congressional committees considering legislation. "The Federal Legislative Objectives" was an important document series that the APWA pioneered. The principles and guidelines utilized in these documents were often helpful in formulating national legislation and public social policies.

Another major and long-standing program innovation launched by the APWA during this time was its project on aging. The relative increase in the number of old people in the population and the whole composite of changes in social attitudes and conditions were among the factors that influenced the growing public concern over the needs of the aged. The interest of the APWA in exploring this field culminated in the presentation of a special request to the Doris Duke Foundation for funds that were to be applied toward financing the cost of short-term projects. The foundation authorized a grant to the APWA of $10,000 for 1952 and renewed it for 1953. One of the first steps to be taken after the project funds became available was the formation of the APWA committee on aging. This committee continued to move ahead by issuing statements of policy, presenting testimonies before the Senate and House committees, and establishing cooperative relationships with the United States Department of Health, Education, and Welfare. The progress of APWA's committee on aging was necessarily slow at first because of a lack of adequate funds to embark on any major effort. The turning point came in 1958 when the Ford Foundation announced a grant of $380,000 to enable the APWA "to help state and local welfare agencies to establish and operate or expand and improve programs designed to meet the social, economic, and health needs of aging people." This grant paved the way for APWA's major and long-term project on aging. Leadership to this project was provided by J. L. Roney, who had previously served the Bureau of Public Assistance. This project greatly strengthened the APWA in its training and research activities and enabled it to take an active part in the development of national policy on services to senior citizens. In April 1962, APWA's project on aging gained even further momentum when the Ford Foundation appropriated a grant of $800,000 for a six-year period to extend APWA's policy and program thrust in services for the aged.

In the wake of broadened national legislation and a concomitant rise in the scope, volume, and importance of human services in the public sector in the 1960s, the APWA became involved in a broad spectrum of activities. There was also a more pronounced diversification of its organizational structure, staff, and activities. More internal differentiations intensified the processes of organizational complexity. A self-study of the organization was launched in 1964 to appraise APWA's goals and structure in light of changing needs. It laid the groundwork for implementation of major structural changes in the association in 1966. Aided by a three-year foundation grant, APWA reorganized along lines that would give its membership a greater voice and representation in the development of policy and program.

The first in a series of executive development seminars was launched in 1966. These seminars were developed by APWA in collaboration with several leading educational centers—Columbia University Graduate School of Business, University of Wisconsin Center for Advanced Study, University of California Institute of Industrial Relations and Social Welfare, and the Menninger Foundation. Sessions held throughout the country presented local and state welfare administrators with an opportunity to develop new management skills and attitudes and to update their technical knowledge. More than six hundred administrators took part in the program over a four-year period.

Another significant, long-term undertaking of the association was the technical assistance project, which began in 1966 with funding provided by the Office of Economic Opportunity. Over a two-year period, project staff worked with state and local administrators, as well as with OEO, Community Action, Model Cities, and other related programs, to open doors to new methods and attitudes about public welfare administration. The contributions of this project were multifold. It involved, at the outset, the identification of problems in the organization and delivery of public welfare services. This provided the needed data base for APWA's staff to give more timely and relevant technical assistance to state and local public welfare agencies in such areas as youth services, day care, interstate placement of children, liaison with states in the organization of supplemental security insurance programs, and the like.

The mission and objectives of APWA again came under scrutiny in 1970. A study conducted by the board of directors in 1970 and 1971 provided the future orientation. The board's imperatives were that APWA begin to focus primary attention on national policy issues and on federal-state relationships and that the association move its headquarters to Washington, D.C. Upon completion of a subsequent organization and management study by an outside consulting firm in

1973, preparations were made for the change. APWA headquarters were relocated in the nation's capital in January 1974.

The APWA marked its forty-sixth anniversary in 1976. It had more than eighteen hundred agency members and over sixty-five hundred individual members. Throughout its history, the APWA has made significant contributions to public social policy. Indeed, it has become inextricably linked to the growth and development of public social policy and the resultant public welfare and public social services.

APWA has provided a forum for the presentation of ideas, opinions, and research on public social services. Its annual (later biennial) round table conferences, first held in December 1936, the first year of the social security program, made an important contribution to public policy development. These conferences brought together national leaders, researchers, educators, practitioners, and interested individuals and groups to discuss vital issues in public social policy. Regional conferences, held annually in the varying states and localities throughout the country, helped members in the outlying areas to know about the APWA and to benefit from its services. These conferences, both national and regional, in conjunction with numerous workshops and training sessions have provided both a national and grass-roots forum, as well as opportunities for professional development. APWA's monthly *Newsletter,* now known as the *Washington Report,* and its quarterly journal, *Public Welfare,* which first appeared in the spring of 1933, at the beginning of the Federal Emergency Relief Administration, have constituted an invaluable running record of important conceptual, legislative, and organizational developments in public social services since that time.

In 1947, in *The Division of Labor in Society,* the French sociologist Emile Durkheim depicted associations and other secondary groups in society as "forces near enough to individuals to attract them strongly in their own sphere of action and drag them, in this way, into the general torrent of social life." Certainly the process of "attracting"—as experienced by APWA—often involved a literal "dragging" or "drawing out" of public support in behalf of needed social policy and social action. APWA's national constituency of membership enabled it to address a broader range of public needs and became a cutting edge for national social policy formulations. This process also led it to develop an understanding and participation in the legislative process in public policy development. Furthermore, the association fulfilled many crucial, instrumental roles. It called for the mobilization of resources and talents to upgrade the quality and distribution of human services in the public sector. It also entailed the creation of opportunities to foster and nurture the growing sense of community and professional identity among staff in such services. In spite of its explicit commitment to public social policy and public welfare, APWA often sought and succeeded in finding pluralistic solutions to the question of the public-voluntary role in human services. Toward this end, APWA was willing to compromise and coalesce with other human service organizations and to foster imaginative collaboration between the public and voluntary sectors. The devotion of APWA's executive directors and staff, and their versatile skills, craftsmanship, and professional talents, were noteworthy features of APWA's role in influencing public policy and public social services. The vitality of the association can be attributed to the political, organizational, and professional skills that its directors and staff have displayed over the years. Internal adaptations have also facilitated its self-renewal and regenerative capabilities.

Primary sources for studying the APWA's history consist largely of its own publications and in-house documents, which are available at its Washington, D.C., headquarters. Most helpful are the published *Annual Reports,* self-study reports, autobiographical statements, historical highlights, and the like, which contain a wealth of data and information. The Papers of the APWA have also been deposited at the Social Welfare History Archives Center at the University of Minnesota, Minneapolis.

The early history of the APWA, spanning three decades of the association's growth and development, has been chronicled and more fully elaborated in Narayan Viswanathan, "The Role of the American Public Welfare Policies in the United States: 1930–1960" (Ph.D. dissertation, Columbia University School of Social Work, 1961).

Narayan Viswanathan

AMERICAN REHABILITATION COMMITTEE (ARC). During and after World War I, physicians, social workers, and others began to think seriously about the problems of wounded soldiers and the development of physical rehabilitation. One such physician was Dr. Fred H. Albee, who at a conference of surgeons in Rome, New York, at the end of World War I promoted the adoption of vocational and physical rehabilitation as a medical responsibility and dedicated himself to this work in his native state, New Jersey. Dr. Albee helped to establish rehabilitation facilities at the United States General Hospital #3 in Colonia, New Jersey, where he directed soldiers' therapy. At the same time, Frederic G. Elton, head of the Division of Vocational Rehabilitation of the New York State Department of Education, became interested in the medical rehabilitation of the wounded and crippled. The two men's interests and training complemented one another. Dr. Albee and Elton wanted to establish a medical school stressing physical medicine and rehabilitation. Instead, in 1922, with a few others, including Dr. Leo Mayer, they founded the ARC to promote the establishment of a curative workshop in New York City. The major aim of the ARC was to apply the technique of work therapy in rehabilitating soldiers, especially those wounded and disabled during World War I.

The new organization had a very limited structure and staff, but it sponsored important and new work and services in the field of rehabilitation. Elton realized that New York State was not providing proper rehabilitation services for industrially injured workers, so after conferring with Dr. Albee, the new organization hired a vocational expert, Edward Chester, who surveyed conditions and needs in New York City. Based on his findings, the ARC then began to sponsor, beginning in January 1924, a curative workshop for the disabled at 325 West Forty-first Street in New York City, the first reconditioning center in the city. Between 1933 and 1946, this facility—which applied the work therapy technique of having the injured produce various objects—was called the Rehabilitation Clinic for the Disabled. Consistent with the founders' early ideas to establish a medical school, the clinic served as a teaching facility for the New York Post Graduate Hospital. Beginning in 1946, the ARC began to cooperate with the New York City Bureau for Children with Retarded Mental Development, making its workshop available to these subnormal children.

Although the workshop became a primary activity of the ARC, the organization conducted other activities in the rehabilitation field. Between 1927 and 1938, the ARC published *The Rehabilitation Review*. Elton contributed his own services to *The Review,* and an advisory editorial staff, composed of some leaders in the field, assisted in producing it. The printing department of the ARC's workshop published the monthly journal. In the spring of 1927, spurred by the instant success of the journal, the printing department began to do commercial work. In the 1920s, the ARC established an information service for patients, in which it cooperated with the J. C. Penney Foundation and the American Medical Association. In the late 1920s, the staff consisted of an unpaid director, an unpaid treasurer, a salaried executive secretary, supervisors in various departments of the workshop, and secretaries. Dr. Albee was the president of the ARC from its inception until his death on February 15, 1945, when his wife, Lovell Albee, succeeded him in the position.

As the activities of its workshop suggested, the ARC made important contributions to the developing field of rehabilitation. The methods of the organization so impressed Jerry Wadsworth, chairman of a joint New York State legislative committee on reemployment, that he incorporated these principles and methods in a bill to provide rehabilitation services, which he sponsored unsuccessfully in 1939. The federal Public Law 113—the Federal Rehabilitation Law of 1943— however, recognized the ARC's concept of work therapy, a development that made the organization rightfully proud.

The federal law of 1943 promoted the entire field of rehabilitation, and the ARC benefited from it, expanding its services and developing new ones. Soon after its enactment, ARC leaders conferred with New York State rehabilitation officials and established cooperative weekly medical-vocational work clinics for patients and state supervisors. In the early 1940s, federal officials from the United States Department of Labor discounted the suggestion that the ARC clinic merely duplicated the work of another important facility, the Institute for the Crippled and Disabled (ICD). ARC methods relied more heavily than did the institute's on prior skills and on instilling competitiveness in rehabilitating patients. Executive Secretary Elton anticipated the need for neuropsychiatric services, and in 1944, he developed an ARC committee to promote this area. This psychiatric advisory committee was composed of representatives from industry, mental hygiene, and vocational rehabilitation. The efforts of the committee led to the establishment in the mid-1940s of Dr. John A. P. Millet's psychiatric consultation service. The ARC's chief of medical service also appointed a volunteer panel of consultants, which included some of the most prominent workers in the rehabilitation field. The eleven-member board of directors voted to change the name of its primary operating unit from the Curative Workshop for the Disabled to the Rehabilitation Center for the Disabled as of October 1946.

In the mid-1940s, as the work began to expand, the ARC organizational structure was composed of a volunteer professional staff, which included Dr. Madge C. L. McGuiness, the physical medical consultant who won an award in 1952 from the New York State Women's Medical Society. She served also as the secretary-treasurer. Other important officers included the president, vice-president, chairman of the eleven-member board of directors. Katherine Ecob, executive secretary since 1931 of the New York State Committee on Mental Hygiene of the State Charities Aid Association* (SCAA) of New York, served on the psychiatric advisory committee in the 1940s, and in 1952, she was elected president. At the annual meeting in 1952, founder Elton was also appointed director of the ARC. The ARC continued to serve the handicapped in New York with a variety of social services. When Elton died in the early 1970s, the ARC was running out of funds. Consequently, in 1975, the ARC amalgamated with the Federation Employment and Guidance Service, a service of the Federation of Jewish Philanthropies of New York.

The best sources for studying the ARC's history include the ARC's variously named *Rehabilitation Review* and *Bulletin,* which is, unfortunately, not widely available, a few published *Annual Reports,* the National Council on Rehabilitation *Newsletter,* also difficult to locate, and contemporary publications in the field, such as Frederic G. Elton, *Work Therapy* (1948). These publications can be found at the New York Academy of Medicine, in the Russell Sage collection at the Library of the City College of New York, and at the Library of the ICD in New York City, which also has a helpful folder of miscellaneous materials relating to the ARC.

Standard histories in the field of social services completely neglect the ARC, and even such specialized studies as Nathan Nelson, *Workshops for the Handicapped in the United States* (1971), mentions the ARC only briefly.

AMERICAN RELIEF ADMINISTRATION EUROPEAN CHILDREN'S FUND (ARAECF). During World War I, the United States aided people in war-torn Europe, especially through the Commission for Relief in Belgium, headed by Herbert Hoover. In the final months of the war, the American government wanted to continue its relief efforts. Because of his earlier successes as a humanitarian engineer who fed the starving Belgians, Herbert Hoover was asked by President Woodrow Wilson to head continued American relief efforts. At Hoover's prompting, in late January 1919, President Wilson asked the United States Congress for an appropriation of $100 million for European relief. The Congress approved these funds on January 24, 1919, and on the next day, Hoover urged President Wilson to establish an agency to implement the program. A month later, on February 24, 1919, through an executive order written in fact by Hoover, President Wilson created the American Relief Administration (ARA), with Hoover as its director-general.

With such a huge initial funding and with the prestigious leadership of Herbert Hoover, the new agency grew quickly. The ARA was given extensive powers to distribute food, clothing, and other supplies, and it was granted the cooperation of the federal Food Administration, the United States Navy, and the United States-owned Grain Corporation, which Hoover also headed. An amendment by Senator Henry Cabot Lodge of Massachusetts prevented the ARA from aiding the enemy, so Germany initially was not assisted by the relief agency. The ARA quickly assembled a staff, and because of its ties to the government, attracted many volunteers. United States Army officers on leave to serve the ARA, followers of Herbert Hoover, and social workers joined the enterprise, which had about four thousand volunteers working for it.

The ARA sent supplies abroad to feed devastated and starving children in Hungary. The program there ended in 1919 when Bela Kun set up a pro-communist government and ousted the ARA. As he later suggested, the former ARA director in Hungary in November 1919, T. C. C. Gregory, possibly used ARA resources to overthrow Bela Kun later in 1919. Relief efforts resumed in Hungary in November 1919, some months after a nonbolshevik government came to power. During the spread of typhus in Eastern Europe in the spring and summer of 1919, the ARA cooperated with a number of voluntary agencies, such as the American National Red Cross* (ANRC) and the United States Army, which provided clothing, soap, portable baths, and medical equipment. According to a massive study of American relief abroad by historian Merle Curti, this was a "life-saving program of impressive magnitude." The ARA organized a food contribution system through which Americans could send gift packages to friends and relatives abroad. This activity served as the model for the creation of Cooperative for American Remittance to Europe* (CARE) in the reconstruction period after World War II. In March 1919, when the ANRC determined that it could not provide a special feeding program in enemy and liberated areas, the ARA established its children's relief bureau. This subagency used about $12 million. It distributed funds and supplies through local communities. Often in cooperation with national governments, these local committees, for instance, provided transportation for food and supplies and established orphanages.

During this period, the American Friends Service Committee* (AFSC) asked Hoover for a useful assignment, and he asked them to serve as a representative of the children's feeding program in Germany. This effort—which deftly circumvented the Lodge amendment because the AFSC was a voluntary organization—provided about $5 million in aid for German children. Meanwhile, plans were approved by President Wilson to convert the ARA from a government agency to a private relief organization. Consequently, in July 1919, it became a private agency called the American Relief Administration European Children's Fund (ARAECF). The organization kept the original first three words to show continued American interest in European welfare and relief, but it soon became popularly known as the ARA. In 1919, Edgar Rickard, who directed earlier famine relief activities, became the director-general, and Hoover became the chairman. With its headquarters in New York City, the ARA was incorporated as a private agency in 1921 according to the laws of the state of New York. As a private agency, the ARA could and did conduct humanitarian work on a scale much larger than other voluntary agencies, and it allowed Chairman Hoover a freer hand in his use of relief as a diplomatic and political instrument. Indeed, Hoover's international relief efforts—including his tenure as the ARA's leader—shaped his popular image as the selfless humanitarian. But Hoover also was clear about using food relief as a way of bringing about Western-style democracy in Europe.

By the winter of 1919–1920, as the congressional appropriation was running out, it became clear that the ARA was inadequately equipped to conduct all the child feeding programs. This situation prompted Chairman Hoover to suggest an appeal for funds from the American people. Consequently the European Relief Council was established. The council's constituent agencies included such important national organizations as the AFSC, the Joint Distribution Committee of American Funds for the Relief of Jewish War Sufferers* (JDC), the Federal Council of the Churches of Christ in America (FCC), and, of course, the ARA.

The ARA conducted humanitarian child feeding programs in Czechoslovakia, Hungary, Poland, and other countries, but nowhere were Hoover's diverse motives revealed more clearly than in ARA activities in Russia. Beginning in 1919, Hoover held dreams of aiding Russia and of thereby establishing a program that would dictate the Russian economy. A determined foe of communism, Hoover saw relief as aiding the White Russians and as contributing to the demise of the Bolsheviks. In the early 1920s, Hoover also used food relief abroad to aid American farmers suffering from the effects of surplus markets. During the summer and fall of 1919, for instance, Hoover found a way to aid the White Russians, supplying them with gasoline, food, and clothing to sustain their offensive against Petrograd. By the summer of 1920, the ARA was feeding over a million children in Poland and in territory occupied by the Polish army in Soviet Russia. This provided a launching site for the ARA's first attempt to negotiate with the Soviets. With a Polish delegation, in August 1920, two ARA representatives crossed the Soviet border and went to Minsk. One of these representatives was Maurice Pate, the emissary of the ARA's European director.

(Pate's experiences with the ARA during World War I undoubtedly influenced him to establish the United Nations International Children's Emergency Fund in 1946.) Pate and the other representative, an ARA medical officer, were detained by Soviet authorities in Minsk, but after many conferences with communist leaders, a deal to establish ARA programs in Russia was worked out. Hoover seemed only interested in areas in Poland under the Soviet army, so he apparently failed to continue these negotiations in the summer of 1920. Still determined, in late January 1921, Hoover offered the AFSC $100,000 worth of food for the Soviets, with the conditions that the Russians release American prisoners they had detained. The AFSC, however, felt that some imprisoned Americans were guilty of anticommunist activities and, for other reasons as well, decided not to become involved in political negotiations. The AFSC's position angered Hoover, but he nevertheless reimbursed the AFSC for providing food and supplies to Russia.

Hoover's best opportunity to influence Russian politics came in the summer of 1921 just when the ARA was winding up its activities in Europe. The Soviets were suffering crop failures and starvation, and Maxim Gorky, a Soviet leader, appealed for relief on July 13. On August 20, the Soviets and the ARA signed an agreement at Riga, Russia. This agreement called for the communists to release Americans held as prisoners and to provide for the free and uncontrolled administration of the relief program and for the storage and transportation of ARA materials. One week later, on August 27, the ARA relief activities in Soviet Russia officially began. The ARA initiated its massive transatlantic efforts in transportation and distribution. Colonel William N. Haskell, the former ARA administrator in Southeastern Europe and Armenia, headed the Russian enterprise. Chairman Hoover called together the other social service agencies operating in Russia and instructed them to coordinate their efforts through the ARA. These agencies included the AFSC, the FCC, the JDC, the National Catholic Welfare Conference, the Mennonite Central Committee* (MCC), and the International Committee of the Young Men's Christian Association.*

The ARA moved quickly to ship and distribute food, supplies, and medicine and to establish kitchens to help sick and starving Russian children. In 1922, at the height of the program, 10.5 million people were being fed at eighteen thousand feeding stations. Hundreds of ARA workers and volunteers struggled against heavy obstacles to provide relief. Inadequate transportation and distribution, pilfering of supplies, and the sheer magnitude of the enterprise frustrated many. The Soviets also stymied ARA activities by delaying transportation, censoring mail, and the like. By June 1923, when the ARA relief in Russia ended, the agency had fed about 16.5 million people and distributed over seven hundred thousand tons of food, flour, milk, corn, and seeds. The ARA's efforts to clean up conditions helped to control and to prevent typhus and cholera. All totaled, the ARA activities in Russia saved the lives of 10 million to 11 million people.

Indeed, despite the Soviets' criticisms of the ARA, there was strong evidence of their appreciation. An official banquet on the eve of its departure in 1924 honored the ARA, its workers, and Chairman Hoover.

The ARA's reputation at home was not as uniformly enthusiastic. In 1921, for instance, evidence surfaced of the ARA's being a counterrevolutionary force rather than a strictly humanitarian relief agency. In 1921, in *The World's Work,* T. C. C. Gregory, the former ARA director in Hungary, wrote that he had used ARA resources to overthrow the communist leader Bela Kun in 1919. Because of these revelations, American liberals decided to work through the AFSC and other relief agencies instead of the ARA. Now secretary of commerce, Hoover, however, insisted on the ARA supervision and coordination of all relief efforts in Russia, and he ordered the United States Department of State to issue no passports for Quaker relief workers without the permission of the ARA. The leading magazine in the social service field, *The Survey,* criticized the ARA's unwillingness to fight the Russian famine with full vigor, and there were charges by liberals that Hoover misquoted Colonel Haskell's field reports to make the ARA appear more successful in its famine relief efforts than it really was. Nevertheless, contemporaries and historians generally viewed the ARA as an expression and fulfillment of some of the basic principles of American humanitarianism.

The ARA had headquarters in New York City and an office in Washington, D.C. The assistant director was Christian A. Herter, who became the American secretary of state in the late 1950s. The ARA ceased operations in late 1923 and for the next three years liquidated its resources. In 1926, apparently, the ARA officially ceased to exist.

There are numerous sources for studying the ARA's history. The published *Annual Reports of the Executive Committee* and the ARA's *Bulletin* provide extraordinary details. *The New York Times* reported on the major ARA activities. The ARA had an official historian and staff, so there are many contemporary publications describing activities in particular countries. Frank M. Surface and Raymond L. Bland, *American Food in the World War and Reconstruction Period* (1931), and Suda L. Bane and Ralph H. Lutz, eds., *Organization of American Relief in Europe, 1918–1919* (1943), are two of the massive volumes that contain documents and descriptions. Hoover's files dealing with the ARA are deposited at the Archives of the Herbert Hoover Institution on War, Revolution, and Peace in Stanford, California, but there are some materials relating to the ARA in the Herbert Hoover Presidential Library in West Branch, Iowa.

Merle Curti, *American Philanthropy Abroad* (1963), discusses the ARA, but his generally favorable account contains some error. For instance, he does not recognize the transition of the ARA from a governmental to a private organization. Peter G. Filene, *America and the Soviet Experiment, 1919–1933* (1967), and Joan Hoff Wilson, *Herbert Hoover: Forgotten Progressive* (1975), focusing on the Russian programs, present more balanced views of the ARA as a humanitarian and political enterprise. Indeed, historians have concentrated on the ARA activities in Russia. A recent example is Benjamin M. Weissman, *Herbert Hoover and Famine Relief to Soviet Russia, 1921–1923* (1974).

AMERICAN SCHOOL HYGIENE ASSOCIATION (ASHA). During the Progressive era, reform-minded public health officials, physicians, educators, and child care workers became concerned about hygiene and sanitary conditions especially in urban schools in America. Throughout the late nineteenth century, especially in the major cities, reform coalitions, including socially concerned physicians, campaigned for better sanitary conditions, sunlight, ventilation, heating, and the like in schools, many of which were especially unhealthful. Despite these concerns in the nineteenth century, the origins of the ASHA relate directly to a letter from Sir Lauder Brunton, an important British physician, to Dr. Arthur Tracy Cabot, a pediatrician at the Massachusetts General Hospital and the Boston Children's Hospital. Dr. Brunton wanted to establish an American committee for the International Congress on School Hygiene (ICSH) meeting in London in August 1907. Dr. Cabot contacted a group of reformers, doctors, and educators to form a committee on organization. Cabot chaired the group. Another important founder was Dr. Luther Halsey Gulick, the director of physical training in the New York City public schools, who had helped to organize in the spring of 1906 and then became the first president of the Playground Association of America.* Dr. Gulick later headed the division of child hygiene of the Russell Sage Foundation.* The committee on organization convened a meeting at the New York Academy of Medicine in New York City on March 3, 1907, where the ASHA was founded.

The ASHA began its activities immediately. The group of founders drafted a tentative constitution, which they presented at the first congress of the ASHA in Washington, D. C., in May 1907. The new organization established a program committee and instructed the secretary of ASHA, Dr. Gulick, to obtain suitable stationery to issue the call for the Washington conference, the major event of the first year. The ASHA elected as honorary president, United States President Theodore Roosevelt, who had been interested in school hygiene movements in the 1890s in New York City, where he had served as police commissioner. The new group adopted the constitution, which provided for a council of thirty members and a five-member executive committee of the country. The officers of the council became, according to the constitution, the traditional officers of the ASHA: a president, a vice-president, and a secretary-treasurer. The association elected as its first president, Dr. Henry P. Walcott, a public health activist in Massachusetts who had served in 1900 and 1905 as acting president of Harvard University. The council elected Dr. Gulick as a member of the executive committee. Other early members of the ASHA included Dr. Livingston Farrand, already developing as a major public health activist, Dr. S. A. Knopf, who had been involved in many public health campaigns and organizations, and Dr. Thomas

Wood of Columbia University, an important student of child health conditions in America.

Despite the interest of many reformers and activitists, the ASHA remained a conference organization rather than an agency delivering social services. Nevertheless, the ASHA promoted interest in school hygiene, an issue affecting virtually all children. By 1910, when many American schools showed little concern for child health and hygiene, the organization had a committee on the status of the medical inspection of school children. Throughout the United States, and within a few years, it organized committees on increasingly specialized subjects, such as the committee on variable temperature and the one on heating and ventilating, three issues that had concerned reformers since the nineteenth century. By 1916, the ASHA had organized its special activities and concerns into sections, each headed by a chairman active in that particular area. M. Adelaide Nutting, a leader in nursing education and in the National League of Nursing Education, appropriately chaired the school nursing section.

The ASHA represented the Progressive era's spirit and ideals of combining social consciousness and expertise to deal with social problems. During the twentieth century the organization discussed at its annual conference issues of importance to public health and social reformers. At the first conference in 1907, papers focused on medical inspection in the schools. In the next year, Joseph Lee of Boston spoke about his specialty, legislation for playgrounds, and in 1909, papers dealt with the place of crippled children in the schools, another concern of social justice Progressives.

World War I affected the ASHA negatively, forcing cancellation of its annual meeting of 1918. By then the ASHA leadership included such important child hygiene activists as Dr. S. Josephine Baker, the head of the pioneering New York City Bureau of Child Hygiene and the president of the American Child Hygiene Association* (ACHA), Ella P. Crandall, the executive secretary of the National Organization for Public Health Nursing* (NOPHN), and Sally Lucas Jean, the director of the Child Health Organization of America* (CHOA). The CHOA, organized in 1918 to promote child hygiene campaigns, particularly in the schools, was one of the many groups dealing with child hygiene and health issues in the period of World War I. The ACHA, the National Child Health Council, created in 1920, and especially the CHOA, seemed to make the ASHA unnecessary. Moreover, a nationwide child hygiene campaign in the early 1920s, involving local chapters of the American National Red Cross,* the National Tuberculosis Association,* women's clubs, the federal United States Public Health Service, the United States Children's Bureau, and others contributed to the demise of the ASHA. Subsequently, in about the mid-1920s, the ASHA, which had stimulated local reform movements, disbanded.

The primary source for studying the ASHA's history is its published *Proceedings* of its annual congresses. Some of the interpretive statements in the text stem from research and an unpublished manuscript about the child hygiene movement by Peter Romanofsky.

AMERICAN SEAMEN'S FRIEND SOCIETY (ASFS). On May 19, 1811, during a fire at the Brick Street Presbyterian Church on Beekman Street in Lower Manhattan, in New York City, a sailor climbed up the church's lightning rod and put out the fire. The sailor never claimed his reward, and his actions inspired the church's minister, Dr. Gardiner Spring, to establish a society for the protection and welfare of seamen. By 1816, Reverend Spring, a central figure in the early development of New York's city missions, was holding outdoor prayers on Water Street in Lower Manhattan, and many sailors attended. Members of the Brick Street Presbyterian Church began to pay special attention to sailors' needs. Meanwhile, in Boston, the Society for the Religious and Moral Improvement of Seamen had been formed. Another New York minister, Reverend Ward Stafford, began to interest a number of businessmen in a church for mariners, and on March 14, 1817, he organized the Marine Bible Society of New York. At a meeting on April 16, 1818, in the home of a prominent New York businessman, Stafford's group organized what became the Society for Promoting the Gospel Among Seamen in the Port of New York, which was incorporated in April 1819. From January 1822 to April 1825, Reverend John Truair was the minister at the Mariners' Church. He edited *The Mariner's Magazine,* and in an editorial in the April 23, 1825 issue, he advocated the establishment of a national welfare agency for seamen like the one in England. In September 1825, the magazine published a petition from 114 seamen asking for such a national society. These events prompted a public meeting in New York City on October 25, 1825. Smith Thompson, the former United States secretary of the navy and a justice of the United States Supreme Court, chaired the meeting. This meeting resolved to establish a national organization, and a committee of eighteen leading citizens was appointed to prepare a constitution and to create the agency. On January 11, 1826, the constitution was adopted and the group elected officers. Reverend Truair was employed as the organization's first agent.

The new organization initially attracted interest and support, but, as its fortunes soon began to wane, it apparently disbanded. Then, on May 5, 1828—the date the ASFS considers as its founding—the organization was revived. The organization elected Smith Thompson as president and had a recording secretary, a corresponding secretary, and a treasurer. The first general agent of ASFS was Reverend Joshua Leavitt, a temperance lecturer for the American Temperance Society and a revivalist who was an antislavery leader and a charter member of the Liberty Party in 1840. The majority of the initial trustees on the board were not from New York but rather, from such port cities as Boston, Philadelphia, Charleston, and Savannah, and the United States Navy.

The ASFS began to shape its program in the late 1820s. The first action by the executive committee, on July 24, 1828, was establishing a journal, *The Sailors' Magazine and Naval Journal,* which began publication in September 1828. Leavitt was its first editor, a position he held until December 1831, when he resigned. Subsequently, each succeeding executive leader, now called general secretary, generally became the editor. The ASFS also began to establish local

affiliates, urging societies for seamen's welfare in other cities to become auxiliaries of it. Groups in Newport, Rhode Island, and Galveston, Texas, for
instance, affiliated with the ASFS in the mid-nineteenth century. The ASFS
published worship manuals for the sailors, and the organization began to develop
the idea of sailors' homes, an important facility to deter them from seamy and
degrading boarding homes. Plans finally matured on October 10, 1837, when the
ASFS opened a small home in Lower Manhattan. By 1840, there were three such
seamen's homes, including one exclusively for Negroes. The cornerstone for the
first full-fledged sailors' home in the United States maintained by a welfare
society was laid on October 14, 1841. This facility opened in May 1842 and
served generations of sailors until June 1, 1903, when New York City took over
the property to build the Manhattan Bridge. Like other nineteenth-century charity
organizations that established provident loan societies and banks, on May 11,
1829, the ASFS began to sponsor the Seamen's Bank for Savings, in New York
City. The most long-term service of the ASFS, however, began in 1837, when
the organization established libraries on ships. Religious books dominated this
increasingly large activity. During the mid-nineteenth century, the ASFS also
sent sailor missionaries all over the world—including to China, Sweden, and
Japan. The organization continued to publish its journal, which became *The
Sailors' Magazine* in 1837 and *The Sailors' Magazine and Seamen's Friend* in
1858. ASFS leaders in the nineteenth century included President Anson G.
Phelps, a wealthy merchant and revivalist, and the long-time secretary, Samuel
H. Hall, D.D., who served between 1865 and 1888.

In the early twentieth and mid-twentieth century, the ASFS expanded its
facilities and moved closer to the mainstream of American social services. In
1907, Reverend Charles A. Stoddard, a well-known Presbyterian minister and
author, became president. In the next year, the ASFS opened its Sailors' Home
and Institute in New York City. This facility was financed largely by $150,000 in
donations from Mrs. Russell Sage, a well-known philanthropist in the social
work field and a relative of President Stoddard. Dedicated officially on October
7, 1908, the Sailors' Home and Institute provided social and recreational opportunities for the men. During the early twentieth century, the ASFS held the first
International Conference for Welfare Workers for Seamen attended by delegates
from such nations as England, Sweden, and Denmark. In October 1914, George
Webster, who had served as pastor of the Presbyterian Covenant in New York
City, became the secretary. Reverend Webster also served as superintendent of
the Sailors' Home and Institute. Beginning in 1915, the ASFS participated in the
joint conference of seventeen seamen's organizations in New York City. The
ASFS maintained its ties to the United States Navy. Each year, the ASFS, under
the auspices of the Naval Academy's Christian Association, presented the Scrip-
tures to each cadet with his name inscribed. In October 1924, the ASFS began
presenting copies of the Bible to cadet graduates of the New York State Merchant
Marine Academy.

Highlights of the 1930s included the opening in November 1931 of the Seamen's House at Eleventh Avenue and Twentieth Street in New York City. An agreement with the local Young Men's Christian Association, exchanging certain properties, for instance, and the help of the Seamen's Christian Association, aided this effort. In the early 1930s, the Seamen's House was the finest building of its type. Five trustees from the ASFS served on the house's board of management, preserving a close relation between the agency and the facility. During this period, the ASFS sponsored annual Sailors' Day services in churches in New York City and Brooklyn. With the cooperation of the New York Bible Society, the agency continued to give Bibles to sailors, and the library loan program expanded. A ship visitor employed by the ASFS supervised the library program. Affiliates in the mid-1930s included the Fishermen's Institute in Gloucester, Massachusetts, the Seamen's Bethel in New Orleans, and similar facilities in Galveston, Texas, Genoa, Italy, Antwerp, Belgium, and Rio de Janeiro, Brazil. Late in the decade, the ASFS transferred its Bible program at the Merchant Marine Academy to the New York Bible Society. In response to changing conditions in the New York shipping industry, the ASFS moved its headquarters from 72 Wall Street to West Twentieth Street and the Hudson River. The agency continued to assist destitute and unemployed seamen, and in November 1939 it published *Who's Who in Seamen's Welfare Agencies.* The assistant secretary, Mary G. Jackson, was elected to the executive committee of the National Group of Seamen's Agencies, and she attended the conference of seamen's agencies at the National Conference of Social Work* in Buffalo, New York, in June 1939. In November 1939, the ASFS opened a library service at the Seamen's House.

In the early 1940s, overcrowding at the Seamen's House prompted the ASFS to move its executive offices to 175 Fifth Avenue, but it kept the library at the sailors' facility. In the early 1940s, the agency opened a library in Brooklyn. In the summer of 1942, the ASFS established a free telephone information service to help men find housing, doctors, laundries, and the like. The organization also began working with hospitals in aftercare work for seamen, and in June 1943, opened its dental service at the Seamen's House. The American Women's Hospitals Reserve Corps donated supplies for this activity. In the mid-1940s, the ASFS helped to organize a branch of Alcoholics Anonymous,* called the Alcoholic Seamen's Club, at its Seamen's House.

Since the late 1940s, when other private and governmental agencies conducted social services for seamen, the ASFS has concentrated on its library program and on assisting individual seamen. In 1959, for instance, it supplied 100,000 books and 400,000 magazines to over 3,500 ships. In the mid-1970s, the ASFS closed its headquarters in New York City and gave its materials to the library of the Marine Historical Association in Mystic, Connecticut.

The primary sources for reconstructing the ASFS's history included the published *Annual Reports,* which apparently ceased publication in the 1950s, and some agency publications, especially George Sidney Webster, *The Seamen's*

Friend (1932). *The New York Times* occasionally covered the agency. The files of the ASFS have been transferred to the library of the Marine Historical Association in Mystic, Connecticut. There does not appear to be a scholarly history of this veteran agency.

AMERICAN SOCIAL HEALTH ASSOCIATION (ASHA). In the late nineteenth century, reformers, religious leaders, physicians, and sanitarians became concerned with vice in American cities. Early organizational activities to campaign against prostitution and vice began in New York City in 1876 when a group of moralists met in the home of Abby Hopper Gibbons and organized the New York Committee for the Prevention of the State Regulation of Vice (NYCPSRV). In 1886, this society began to publish a journal, *The Philanthropist,* "for the Promotion of Social Purity, the Better Protection of the Youth, and Suppression of Vice, and the Prevention of its Regulation by the State."

Gibbons was the key figure in the NYCPSRV, but after her death in 1893, Aaron M. Powell and his wife, Anna, were the leaders of the group. In 1895, the NYCPSRV was reorganized as the American Purity Alliance (APA). Similar local societies developed in other cities throughout the country. In 1906, these groups merged to form the National Vigilance Committee (NVC). The founding meeting of the NVC took place in the New York City home of Grace Hoadley Dodge, the founder of the National League of Associations of Working Women's Clubs,* in 1897, and of the National Board of the Young Women's Christian Association of the United States of America* (YWCA), in late 1906. Others helping to found the NVC included Charles W. Eliot, the president of Harvard University, Dr. Prince Albert Morrow, a prominent physician in New York City who was active in social hygiene circles and who had organized the American Society of Sanitary and Moral Prophylaxis (ASSMP) in 1905, Seth Low, the reform mayor of New York City, James Cardinal Gibbons of Baltimore, and James B. Reynolds, a lawyer and a settlement house worker. This organization, the NVC, enjoyed influence at the highest level of American government and society. Reynolds, for example, served as the tie between the NVC and its supporters and President Theodore Roosevelt. In 1912, the APA and the NVC merged to form the new American Vigilance Association (AVA). The AVA represented the so-called moralists as opposed to the so-called sanitarians.

The sanitary point of view was represented in Morrow's ASSMP, which was organized in New York City in February 1905. At its first meeting, held at the New York Academy of Medicine, the ASSMP had 125 charter members, ninety-three of them physicians. The founder and first president of this group was Dr. Morrow, called the real founder of the social hygiene movement by Isidore Dublin, a well-known statistician in the health field, in 1936. Other leaders of the ASSMP included the first vice-president, Dr. Stephen Smith, a long-time activist in medical social services and reform in New York City and active in the American Public Health Association,* and its treasurer, Dr. Smith E. Jelliffe, who later became an eminent psychiatrist. From the social work community came Homer Folks, the head of the State Charities Aid Association* of New York, and Edward T. Devine, the general director of The Charity Organization Society of the City of New York,* and Dr. Luther Gulick, of the Russell Sage Foundation,* who was active in a number of social service agencies and who was the chief founder of the Camp Fire Girls of America* in 1911. With this link to the social work community, by 1908, the ASSMP was discussing at its sessions such topics as gonorrheal arthritis in children and ophthalmia neonatorum, the same issue that prompted the establishment of what later became the National Society for the Prevention of Blindness.*

A few years later, the ASSMP was developing constructive measures, such as recreation and wholesome amusements, to deal with the problem of prostitution. By 1907, Morrow recognized the need for a national organization and for a journal to serve the needs of all the social hygiene societies. Morrow's calls for a national organization were finally realized on June 6, 1910, when in St. Louis, the American Federation for Sex Hygiene (AFSH) was organized. Eliot became the honorary president, and Dr. Morrow was its president. One of the four vice-presidents was Professor Charles R. Henderson, a prominent social reformer at the University of Chicago. The AFSH moved closer to the social reform community, replacing physicians with social reformers and philanthropists in leadership posts. Charles W. Birtwell, the head of the Boston Children's Aid Society, for instance, became the executive officer of the AFSH. The first year and a half focused on financial matters, but the chief AFSH concern was education, particularly about the damages of venereal disease. The retirement and death of Morrow in March 1913 helped to open the way toward a more unified social hygiene movement. Proposals were made to merge the AVA and the AFSH. There was opposition and dissent within both the AVA and the AFSH, but in October 1913 in Buffalo, New York, representatives from the two organizations met and agreed to consolidate as one new American Social Hygiene Association (ASHA).

With sound finances from the beginning—entirely from voluntary contributions, chiefly from John D. Rockefeller, Jr.—the new ASHA opened its national headquarters in midtown Manhattan, solidified its structure, and began its ambitious programs to suppress vice, an aim that had precedence in these early years over reducing the incidence of venereal disease, (although it was also an organizational concern). In March 1914, the ASHA was incorporated according to the laws of the state of New York. The early structure included as honorary president, Charles W. Eliot, a president, four active vice-presidents, one of whom was David Starr Jordan, four honorary vice-presidents, including Jane Addams of Hull-House,* Cardinal Gibbons, and R. Fulton Cutting, a prominent New Yorker, as treasurer, and a secretary. The executive duties were shared by Reynolds and Dr. William Snow, a professor of public health and hygiene at Stanford University and the secretary of the California State Board of Health.

Reynolds handled legal and legislative matters as well as supervision of the department of investigations, and Dr. Snow supervised medical, educational, and statistical phases of the ASHA's activities. The membership, which numbered 480 in 1916, annually elected the officers as well as one-third of the twenty-one-member board of directors, each of whom served for three-year terms. The board chose from its own membership a seven-member executive committee, which supervised the agency's activities. The ASHA maintained a western division office in San Francisco and a central states division office in Chicago as part of its field services. The agency provided many exhibits of its work, including a large one at the Panama-Pacific International Exposition held in San Francisco in 1915. At this meeting, it won a gold medal. The ASHA lent one of its traveling exhibits to the International Committee of the YMCA, and another was used largely by the General Federation of Women's Clubs (see *Fraternal Organizations*).

In this early period, the ASHA developed and publicized its plans to deal with venereal disease as a community and a public health problem. It helped to influence discussion of this subject at the meetings of the American Medical Association, the APHA, the American Hospital Association (AHA), and the Pan-American Scientific Conference, in late 1915 and early 1916. With the APHA and the AHA, the ASHA planned to obtain data on venereal disease from dispensaries and hospitals throughout the country. The ASHA helped to develop and to promote social hygiene legislation in states. An important aspect of its work was conducting or cooperating with local groups to prepare vice investigations in cities and in states throughout the country. The ASHA also studied the general effectiveness of the so-called abatement and injunction laws, first adopted in Iowa in 1909. These laws generally allowed officials to condemn lewd facilities, such as saloons, as public nuisances. Special investigations by the ASHA included the one of vice in San Francisco in relation to the convening of a major exposition there in 1915. The ASHA also helped to prove the effectiveness of abatement and injunction laws enacted in California for the exposition before the Supreme Court of the United States. To organize a local committee, the ASHA typically conducted a survey of conditions in a city, but only by invitation. Its representatives then conferred with local citizens interested in social hygiene or with leaders of appropriate public or private agencies. The ASHA then helped to form a separate committee with ties to its national office.

On the eve of American entry into World War I, the ASHA had begun successfully to stimulate an awareness of the problems of prostitution and to promote local committees throughout the country. The largest ASHA activity during these early years, however, was the distribution of literature on a wide range of subjects. The agency opened its library at its offices in New York City, and by 1917, over 350,000 pamphlets, reprints, and the like had been distributed throughout the United States.

During World War I, the ASHA moved to the forefront nationally in the fight against venereal disease. Immediately after the United States became embroiled in the so-called Mexican border dispute incident in 1916, ASHA leaders Dr. Snow and Raymond Fosdick sent a four-point program to combat venereal disease to United States secretary of war, Newton Baker, a former reform mayor of Cleveland who had supported vice reformers there. Like Baker, Secretary of the Navy Josephus Daniels accepted the plan by which the entire ASHA professional staff was commissioned as army or navy officers. The ASHA recruited other workers to implement its wartime program. These activities placed the ASHA in the vanguard of efforts to reduce venereal diseases and prostitution in and around military camps. The agency received widespread press coverage, and the ASHA produced a film depicting the tragedy of syphilis affecting two young people, *The End of the Road*, starring Richard Bennet and shown throughout the United States and Canada.

During the war, with the assistance of the United States Public Health Service (USPHS) and with some support from the public, the ASHA helped to close down about two hundred so-called red light districts in American cities and towns. In early 1918, the ASHA helped to influence the Chamberlain-Kahn Act, which provided federal funds for a division of venereal disease in the USPHS and established the Interdepartmental Social Hygiene Board. The ASHA urged local and state authorities to use such federal funds to establish venereal disease controls. In 1919, the organization drafted a model vice repression act, which was subsequently enacted in nineteen states. These laws, however, generally lacked enforcement by public opinion. This general apathy continued through the 1930s, when no significant antiprostitution laws were enacted. Beginning in 1920, the ASHA launched a new nationwide effort to stimulate public opinion and action. In the 1920s, the ASHA conducted studies of the prevalence of syphilis, evaluated programs in local communities, successfully urged the adoption of the first premarital examination laws, and published digests of laws affecting prostitution and vice.

The public education program was a long process that did not begin to be effective until about the mid-1930s. Meanwhile, the ASHA was active by helping to establish, beginning in 1935, a venereal disease control program in New York City, one of the most complete in the nation. Finally, in 1936, the conspiracy of silence that the ASHA had been attacking for over twenty years was broken. First *The Chicago Tribune* and soon after *The New York Daily News* ran feature stories about venereal disease and social hygiene using information the ASHA had supplied.

In 1937, the ASHA began to sponsor its annual Social Hygiene Day, which was celebrated nationally. At that time, the agency perceived public opinion to be highly favorable, and it began efforts to renew federal funds for venereal disease control programs. The legal staff drafted a bill, introduced by Senator Robert La Follette of Wisconsin and in the House of Representatives by Alfred Bulwinkle of North Carolina. The bill passed without opposition and authorized $3 million for 1938.

The ASHA was regaining some of its strength. In 1938, the agency's western division office was reopened, and a local group to control venereal diseases in San Francisco surrendered its charter and merged with the national organization. In the late 1930s and early 1940s, the ASHA continued to supplement the federal program and kept social hygiene work active in states and local communities. The ASHA conducted this nationwide effort with a national headquarters, a liaison office in Washington, D.C., divisional, or regional offices in Atlanta, Chicago, Dallas, and San Francisco, and temporary offices elsewhere. The national campaign included local affiliates involved in social hygiene and in anti-prostitution campaigns, the continued cooperation of such national organizations as the GFWC, the National Congress of Parents and Teachers, and the National Council of Women. Federal agencies, the press, radio, and the motion picture industry also cooperated with the ASHA. Conferences and meetings held throughout the country brought the ASHA in contact with the public. The ASHA field staff provided help wherever needed, and the organization distributed books, pamphlets, films, exhibits, and its publications, including *The Journal of Social Hygiene,* begun in December 1914.

In this period, the program was divided into medical and public health, legal and protective measures, education and conservation of the family, public information and community services, and special efforts and youth service. In 1939, the ASHA established a joint committee with the American Pharmaceutical Association to continue its work against quackery. Dr. Snow served as general director until his retirement in 1938, when he was replaced by C. Walter Clarke.

As American entry into World War II became imminent, the ASHA developed a plan to serve the armed forces once again. By the early 1940s, it had developed an "8 point program in 48 fronts." It included helping industry to reduce venereal disease, helping communities to provide wholesome recreation, studying national and local conditions and programs and keeping the country informed, and helping teachers, parents, and religious leaders to provide sex education. In the early 1940s, the ASHA provided data about the rates and sources of venereal disease to the federal Division of Social Protection, which was established in 1941 as part of the Intergovernmental Venereal Disease Control Committee (IVDCC), which included representatives from the armed forces, the USPHS, the Veterans Administration, and the ASHA. Until shortly after World War II, the ASHA's legal division was responsible for surveys of prostitution. Between 1939 and 1949, the agency conducted 7,745 such surveys in nearly 1,500 communities, including those with a population of over 100,000. On May 11, 1948, a unanimous resolution by the IVDCC gave the ASHA the responsibilities of the former Division of Social Protection.

As the nation prepared for war in Korea, the ASHA participated in efforts to reduce venereal disease and prostitution in and around military camps and in defense communities. Studies in 1948 showed that the worst conditions in the country were found in and near military camps. In 1950, the ASHA became part of the United Defense Fund (UDF), a federated drive. It also became part of the

United Community Defense Services* (UCDS). In 1948, at the request of the IVDCC, the ASHA began operations directly related to the health and welfare of the armed forces. It provided movies, lectures, and printed information and held four institutes, one for each of the armed forces. Educational work continued to be implemented through the ASHA's numerous publications. In the period between 1948 and 1953, the ASHA conducted nearly two thousand fact-finding investigations in almost seven hundred communities, with funds from the UDF for two-thirds of this period. In the early 1950s, the ASHA conducted special training institutes for representatives of social agencies in New Mexico. The ASHA did this in response to requests from the local agencies. At the request of the United States Air Force, Executive Director Conrad Van Hyning conducted a ten-week study of conditions in American air bases and neighboring communities in the Far East.

In the period after the Korean War, the ASHA began to expand significantly. In 1953, it had 168 affiliates, and in the next year, there were 199. When the UDF ended in 1955, the ASHA declined to affiliate with the United Service Organizations,* as did some members of the UDF. In the mid-1950s, the ASHA adjusted its program to continue its traditional concerns with prostitution and venereal disease but expanded to include what it now called family life education. The agency also began some programs to prepare high school boys for the psychological and social strains of military service. An annual grant from the Nancy Reynold Bagley Foundation, beginning in 1953, helped to finance these educational activities. In the summer of 1956, the ASHA ran workshops for teachers at colleges and universities throughout the country. The agency began services to the international community, for example, through the World Health Organization (WHO) and the United Nations Economic and Social Council. During this period, the ASHA also helped states, beginning with California, to enact legislation requiring reporting venereal disease to health authorities. The ASHA lost an important activity in early 1954 when local officials dissolved the New York City Bureau of Social Hygiene, ending a ten-year-old clinic for preventing and treating venereal disease. In 1953, the ASHA initiated an annual project of compiling information on the extent of venereal disease and prostitution in states and cities all over America. The Association of State and Territorial Health Officers and the American Venereal Disease Association cosponsored this annual activity with the ASHA.

Evidence of its national leadership in the field was demonstrated in the early 1950s when the ASHA helped to develop a social hygiene committee in the National Association of Venereology. The ASHA led the drive against venereal disease in Mexico, sending a *Newsletter* to about four hundred key leaders throughout Latin America. In 1954, to inaugurate family life education in the public schools, the ASHA sponsored three regional programs, including teacher-training institutes, a survey of about 250 public schools to determine what was being done in sex education, and a national conference on education, which about 600 leaders attended. In the mid-1950s, the ASHA not only continued to conduct surveys of conditions at the request of the military but also promoted the work of the armed forces character guidance councils. In 1956, the ASHA received foundation grants for a two-year study of teenage venereal disease. In late 1956, the organization established a national committee to direct and guide this project, which began in 1957. Showing its concern with a broad range of social problems, in 1957, the ASHA created a task force to study cities where prostitution was less of a problem than were unregulated bars and other facilities constituting moral hazards for youths. During this period, the ASHA's international division served as the regional office for the Americas of the International Union Against Venereal Diseases and Treponematoses, and at the first international symposium on venereal disease and treponematoses held in Washington, D.C., in 1956, the ASHA hosted delegates from eighteen Latin American countries at an informal gathering. In the late 1950s, the ASHA conducted three pilot projects studying adolescent behavior, centered at the University of California at Los Angeles, Harvard University, and Washington University in St. Louis. Also during this period, at the request of the USPHS, the agency conducted an intensive study of the youths coming to venereal disease clinics in New York City. At the request of the World Health Organization in 1958, the ASHA identified and reported on a group of problem areas in international health. Also in 1958, the ASHA organized a two-day conference on family life education, attended by executives and key personnel from fifty-six national organizations. It conducted local institutes, including a three-day one in the Virgin Islands, an eight-day consultation tour of cities in New England, a five-day workshop for teachers, held in Plymouth, New Hampshire, and conferences with educational personnel in Washington, D.C. In 1959, the agency decided to sharpen its emphasis on family life education and to change its name.

Renamed the American Social Health Association (ASHA) in 1960, the agency continued its traditional programs, surveying incidences of venereal diseases and prostitution, publicizing the problem, and promoting family life education. The ASHA also began to work in the field of narcotic control in the early 1960s. With matching funds from the NCPT, in 1960, the ASHA mobilized its staff and volunteers to initiate and develop family life education programs in twenty-three states and the District of Columbia. It guided or participated in twenty-six pilot projects in the ten states and participated in nine workshops in five states. In 1962, when the ASHA completed a ten-year demonstration project of family life education, the agency reoriented its family life program from the project approach to filling numerous requests for consultation services. The ASHA continued to cooperate with the military, and in 1960, it worked vigorously on studying conditions in the St. Lawrence Seaway area, developing materials for the proposed seaway conference. In the early 1960s, the ASHS conducted a national study of venereal disease incidence. In cooperation with the AMA, the National Medical Association, and the American Osteopathic Association, the ASHA collected data from private physicians showing that the actual rate of venereal disease was three to four times larger than that reported to officials. In 1963, the agency began to increase its attention to venereal disease, conducting a national press conference on problems in the field in 1964. The regional staff and program specialists continued to provide field services, for example, conducting nearly five hundred visits in 250 cities in practically every state.

In late 1961, the ASHA began a formal exploration of the narcotic addiction problem, and before the end of 1962, the agency was swamped with requests for information. In 1962, the ASHA published the helpful *Facilities for the Treatment and Rehabilitation of Narcotic Addicts* and, in late 1962, issued *The Narcotic Addiction Problem* as the first step in its public information program. The ASHA also created its national information center on narcotic addiction and prepared a complete bibliography of all the materials on the problem since 1928. The ASHA also established a national advisory committee, which consulted with community projects, and the staff participated in several meetings, including the White House Conference on Narcotic Addiction and Drug Abuse. In 1964, the ASHA initiated action in the field, conducting a research project to rehabilitate addicts, done in cooperation with the School of Criminology of the University of California. During this period, the agency served as the clearinghouse for narcotics and drug information of the National Institute of Mental Health (see *Government Agencies*).

Basic activities continued in the mid-1960s, a period highlighted by an evaluation of the agency. During this time, *The Narcotic Addiction Problem* by Dr. Charles Winick became one of the classic pamphlets in this field. The agency also published and distributed over fifty thousand copies of *The Glue Sniffing Problem*. In 1966, the ASHA began work on a publication reviewing LSD and other hallucinogens. It issued a documented study of its long-time project, *Family Life Education—A Case for Action*. In November 1965, the board of directors authorized a study of the ASHA by an objective, outside study committee. The study was financed and conducted in 1966, and in January 1967, the board of directors accepted its findings. These findings showed that the ASHA was not adequately meeting its objectives in its areas of interest. The study called for the agency to double its staff within five years and to obtain five times its current level of financial support. The study group noted that the ASHA's vigorous leadership in family life education in the 1950s gave the agency a great opportunity to stimulate further programs. The evaluation also called on the ASHA to expand its drug abuse, field service, and international programs. The ASHA admitted that the analysis was helpful. In early 1967, both the president and the executive committee made clear commitments to implement the study.

In the late 1960s and 1970s, the ASHA did not seem to fulfill precisely the study committee's evaluations and recommendations, but it was quite active. In late 1967, for instance, it published a full report of a conference on controlling drug abuse held in New York City. The agency repeated its 1962 nationwide study of all doctors in private practice to determine the extent of the venereal disease problem. In the spring of 1968, the agency began to sponsor a one-act satire of the drug scene, *The Underground Bird*. Prepared by the Family Service Association of America's* Plays for Living, it was performed over fifty times throughout the country. In October 1968, the agency held a conference of experts for community leaders. In 1969, the ASHA produced two twenty-seven-minute color documentaries, *Drug Abuse: A Call to Action* and *Venereal Disease: A Call to Action*. These were cosponsored with a commercial publisher. In mid-May 1969, the ASHA held a meeting in Chicago of representatives from twenty-three medical and health organizations to determine which agencies in the health field had programs relating to venereal diseases. The ASHA continued serving as the research arm for the Drug Abuse Task Force-West. A major contribution to the field in 1969 was the play about family life education, *Ring Around the Family*. In the late 1960s, the ASHA cooperated with the Kiwanis International's (see *Fraternal Organizations*) Operation Drug Alert, and the ASHA's national information center for studies continued to focus on drug dependency and drug abuse. In 1969, the ASHA held a conference that influenced the establishment in 1971 of the federal National Commission on Venereal Disease (NCVD), the first body of its kind. The ASHA president served as the NCVD's chairman. In 1971, the ASHA developed its united drug abuse councils (UDAC), a new agency program division cosponsored and funded by the American Association Against Addiction. The UDAC concept was utilized in four pilot projects, for which the ASHA's Drug Abuse Task Force-West provided specialized technical assistance. In the early 1970s, the ASHA sponsored a massive venereal disease awareness program. A project with labor and management to deal with drug abuse, begun with the American Federation of Labor-Congress of Industrial Organizations Community Services Department,* received a grant from the federal National Institute on Drug Abuse. In 1973, the ASHA began a pilot project of venereal disease action councils. With the Pfizer Laboratories, the ASHA cosponsored the third International Venereal Disease Symposium, in New Orleans, in 1973, and the agency's regional directors helped to organize state venereal disease task forces. In 1975, the ASHA changed its *Social Health News,* which until 1960 had been the *Social Hygiene News,* to *VD News*. In 1976, the agency moved its headquarters from the so-called health building at 1740 Broadway in New York City to Palo Alto, California.

The primary sources for studying the ASHA's history are diverse. Published *Annual Reports,* appearing in different formats, are helpful materials, as are such agency publications as *Social Hygiene News* and the *American Social Hygiene Association, 1914-1916* (1916). Articles in such contemporary journals as *The Survey* also yield information about the ASHA and its antecedent agencies. The files of the organization are deposited at the Social Welfare History Archives Center at the University of Minnesota, Minneapolis, but minutes of meetings are in the office files at the agency's national headquarters.

James Gardner, Jr., used these files and others for his "Microbes and Morality: The Social Hygiene Crusade in New York City, 1892–1917" (Ph.D. dissertation, Indiana University, 1974), a helpful and detailed study. There are many scholarly studies dealing with the ASHA's early history. These include David J. Pivar, *Purity Crusade* (1973), and John C. Burnham, "The Progressive Era Revolution in American Attitudes toward Sex," *The Journal of American History* 59 (March 1973): 885–908. Less scholarly but nevertheless helpful studies include the section on the ASHA in Harold M. Cavins, *National Health Agencies* (1945), and Charles Winick and Paul M. Kinsie, *The Lively Commerce* (1971). There does appear to be a full-length, scholarly history of this veteran agency.

AMERICAN SOCIAL HYGIENE ASSOCIATION: see AMERICAN SOCIAL HEALTH ASSOCIATION.

AMERICAN SOCIETY FOR THE CONTROL OF CANCER: see AMERICAN CANCER SOCIETY, INC.

ARMY RELIEF SOCIETY (ARS). At the end of the Spanish-American War in 1898, a group of women with ties to the United States Army and other women interested in the plight of Cuban orphans met in New York City to discuss plans to aid these unfortunate children. The women were also concerned about the dependent children of men who served in the Regular Army of the United States. In the fall of 1898, the women met again at the home of Mrs. Daniel S. Lamont, a prominent New Yorker, and established the Cuban Orphan Society (COS). The COS provided a wide range of social services for children and mothers in Cuba and for Cubans in America. On March 26, 1900, a group of twenty-two women gathered again at Mrs. Lamont's home to discuss the COS's upcoming Easter festival. At this meeting, the women decided to establish an organization to aid the dependents of deceased men from the Regular Army. The group promptly appointed a six-member committee to organize a society. This committee met again on March 30, 1900, to adopt the plan of organization of the new Army Relief Society (ARS) to elect officers and to announce the establishment of the first branch, the New York City group. On July 23, 1900, the elected board of managers drafted articles of incorporation, submitted a constitution, which was adopted, and appointed committees to conduct the ARS work. On December 11, 1900, ARS was incorporated according to the laws of the state of New York.

The ARS developed gradually. At the end of one year of operation, it had completed plans to set up branches comprised of sections with a minimum of ten members, each headed by a section president. At the first annual meeting in April 1901—and held subsequently on the last Wednesday in April—six committees were established, including the two important ones of relief and education. The relief committee began immediately to send money and clothing to widows and other dependents of army men. The relief committee sold some articles made by the widows and even helped find jobs for some of them. The committee learned of needy cases largely through the members of the three initial branches in New York, Washington, and West Point. The education committee initiated its work energetically. It sent letters to the presidents of the leading colleges and universities asking for scholarships for the children of deceased soldiers. The clothing committee, which sent such items as shoes, blankets, and clothing to families, also began its work in this early period.

Immediately after the second annual meeting in April 1902, the six-member board of managers, which conducted the affairs of the society, appointed four other committees, including the important organization committee. In 1903, the ARS received the first of a series of gifts of about $9,000 from the proceeds of the annual army-navy football game. The ARS was deservedly proud that it inspired the organization in 1904 of a similar group, the Navy Relief Society.*

The ARS quickly developed a basic pattern for its activities and policies. The education committee, for example, instituted in 1905 its policy of not sending students to private boarding schools, relying instead on the public school systems. In this period, it also began sponsoring and guiding students who attended such universities as Pennsylvania, Johns Hopkins, and, of course, the United States Military Academy. In 1918, the ARS took a major step in organizing auxiliary relief committees in eight large cities near army headquarters and posts. Working closely with the military commanders in their area, these committees discovered needy cases, reported them to the national society, and recommended action in each case. Although not a large national organization, ARS worked with the American National Red Cross,* the International Committee of the Young Men's Christian Association,* and the American Legion. The Needlework Guild of America* contributed garments to ARS's clothing committee. ARS cooperated closely with social workers in such places as New York, Florida, San Antonio, and California.

By the late 1930s, the Great Depression and a decline in donations had forced ARS to question recipients on how they spent their allocations. Partly because ARS lacked adequate funds to disperse, criticism of ARS, focusing on its alleged failure to help people, developed within the army. In rebuttal, ARS stressed repeatedly that it was not a charity but rather a self-help organization. It was true that some beneficiaries remained on the rolls for years, fully reliant on the grants. On the other hand, women not infrequently returned checks, and students whom ARS helped often repaid with sizable donations.

The ARS relied totally on donations and certain fund-raising projects, but, unlike many other national agencies, it never conducted a public financing campaign and never received local funds from community chests or war funds. Aside from the proceeds of the army-navy game, the ARS gained revenue from an annual ball in New York and similar events. Not until 1939 did the ARS have any salaried personnel, a part-time secretary. Volunteer women, particularly in the

New York area, staffed the national headquarters, which had to be in New York.

Although the ARS administration was centered in New York, branches existed all over the country and in some insular territories, such as Hawaii. Beginning in the late 1920s, the organization committee pressed for reorganization of the branches to conform to the army's corps area system. The board of managers rejected this plan in June 1929, arguing that the ARS was functioning well enough. The ARS structure, however, remained confusing. The constitution allowed sections to affiliate with any branch of its choice. The Washington, D.C. section, for instance, was part of the New York City branch. This situation led the board to approve the organization of ARS according to the army corps area system in 1932. Branches existed in most of the nine corps areas, but in 1951, the ARS established its Interstate Branch, administered at the national headquarters, to serve sections in corps areas without branches. In 1942, ARS reached an agreement with the Department of War's newly formed Army Emergency Relief, Inc. (AER). This agreement called essentially for a sharing of funds and for ARS's turning over some of its activities to the AER. By 1943, much of the clothing formerly sent to ARS was going to AER's Bundles for America project.

From the 1940s through the 1970s, ARS continued its basic activities. In 1943, for instance, ARS established a committee to urge Congress and the Veterans Administration to reform the pension plans for servicemen's widows. In December 1942, the board authorized a pension committee, which worked steadfastly through the years. In the late 1940s, this committee counseled the advisory committee on servicemen's pay, a group representing the secretary of defense's office. In the fall of 1947, ARS's pension committee reported on pensions to the Joint Pay Committee of the Armed Service. In the late 1940s, the board of managers created a five-member board of trustees to concentrate the ARS's work in a small group. By 1959, the increased volume of work led to the hiring of a second part-time worker. The public relations committee, established in 1959, conducted publicity and fund-raising campaigns, largely in service journals. This committee also published the *"Blue Books,"* the annual ARS reports. In 1968, ARS moved its headquarters to the Federal Building in Lower Manhattan. In July, first vice-president, then later president, Mrs. John M. Willem, Jr., testified before the Special Subcommittee on Survivor Benefits of the House Armed Services Committee. Supporters of the army, such as Mamie Eisenhower and General Creighton Abrams, served ARS as honorary presidents and honorary vice-presidents. In 1976, ARS was absorbed by the AER. It closed its headquarters, ending its seventy-six year history of service to the Regular Army.

The major primary source for studying ARS's history is its difficulty-to-locate published *Annual Reports*. I found these only in the agency's headquarters in New York City in the summer of 1974. I was unable to determine their location in late 1976 after the headquarters had closed. There are a few articles about ARS in service journals, such as in *Recruiting News* (March 1938): 10–11. The *New York Times* occasionally covered ARS activities. There does not appear to be a scholarly history of ARS.

ASSOCIATION FOR IMPROVING THE CONDITION OF THE POOR OF NEW YORK: see NEW YORK ASSOCIATION FOR IMPROVING THE CONDITION OF THE POOR.

ASSOCIATION FOR THE ADVANCEMENT OF RESEARCH IN MULTIPLE SCLEROSIS: see NATIONAL MULTIPLE SCLEROSIS SOCIETY.

ASSOCIATION FOR THE AID OF CRIPPLED CHILDREN: see FOUNDATION FOR CHILD DEVELOPMENT.

ASSOCIATION FOR VOLUNTARY STERILIZATION (AVS). While doing social service work in Philadelphia in 1927, Marian Norton (later Olden) was struck by her clients' misery and poverty due to unwanted children. These impressions stimulated her interest in birth control. Several years later, she was asked to chair the social hygiene committee of the Princeton League of Women Voters. The committee chose eugenic aspects of social hygiene for its topic. After having reached an impasse in her efforts to persuade the League of Women Voters to more actively support passage of a selective sterilization bill for New Jersey, she asked Eduard Lindeman, the noted philosopher, social reformer, scholar, and teacher at the New York School of Social Work, to assist her in forming a New Jersey group to promote social improvement through selective sterilization. Consequently, the Association for Voluntary Sterilization (AVS) was established on March 20, 1937, as the Sterilization League of New Jersey (SLNJ). The first president was Judge Thomas L. Zimmerman of the Bergen County Juvenile Court. Norton was elected secretary. The organization began as a small, often divided group of dedicated individuals working for an unpopular and misunderstood cause. It went through several changes in name and conception of purpose; by 1976, AVS was a well-known and influential voluntary agency in the sterilization movement. The initial purpose of the SLNJ, however, was to secure passage of a state eugenics sterilization bill.

The committee writing the bill was chaired by Norton and consisted of Dr. Wright MacMillan, a Montclair ear, nose, and throat specialist, Dr. S. Emelen Stokes, the assemblyman for Burlington County, New Jersey, Mabel Boyden, a eugenics professor at Rutgers University, and Harry Young, a Newark attorney. Raymond Berry, also a Newark attorney, put the bill into final form. The bill, introduced on March 9, 1942, as Assembly #170, was entitled "An Act to Create a State Eugenics Commission and to define the powers and duties thereof, so as to promote the general welfare and aid the afflicted by providing for the sexual sterilization of persons unfit for parenthood and to provide for the enforcement and operation of this act and to make an appropriation to carry out the provisions thereof.''

Although SLNJ members lobbied for passage of the bill, it died in the legislature because of organized Catholic opposition and public confusion of sterilization with castration. Failure of the bill led to the realization that a national organization devoted to promoting sterilization was needed. The Sterilization League for Human Betterment (SLHB) was formed on January 7, 1943.

Because of objections to the use of the term "human betterment" by Mrs. William Castle, daughter of Ezra S. Gosney, founder of the Human Betterment Foundation (HBF) of California, the organization incorporated according to the laws of New Jersey on April 15, 1943, under the name Birthright, Inc. (BINC). The new name was taken from the "Child's Bill of Rights," a statement issued by the White House Conference on Child Health and Protection in 1930, which said, "there should be no child in America that has not the complete birthright of a sound mind in a sound body and that has not been born under proper conditions."

In September of 1944, BINC defined its fundamental objectives to be the education of human service professionals and the public. It emphasized in its publications that medical sterilization is not castration and has no deleterious effects on the mental, physical, or sexual characteristics of an individual; that it is protective of those with hereditary defects, of their potential children, and of the taxpayer who would otherwise have to support the defective children of defectives; and that sterilization as a negative eugenic measure contributes to the improvement of the biological stock of the human race.

Between 1944 and 1946, with the financial support of Dr. Clarence Gamble, Birthright sponsored large-scale projects in North Carolina and Iowa. The projects were to demonstrate how best to educate professionals and the public to the benefits of sterilization, to demonstrate how sterilization might be made more readily available to those who could benefit from it, and to help find a more publicly acceptable term than "sterilization." Gamble, long active in the birth control movement, had begun these projects independently and had brought them into Birthright under the control of a semiautonomous fieldwork committee, which he chaired. In 1946, when Birthright's executive committee sought to exert control over the fieldwork projects, Gamble refused to give up his autonomy, and he was expelled from the organization. In September 1949, Gamble founded the Human Betterment Federation (HBF), an organization devoted to biological improvement. Composed of state Betterment Leagues in seven southern and midwestern states, the HBF continued until 1957.

In 1945, H. Curtis Wood, Jr., a Philadelphia obstetrician and gynecologist and former president of Pennsylvania Planned Parenthood, became president of BINC. Plagued by low membership, insufficient funds, and an inability to secure foundation support, the BINC under Wood's leadership sought ways to make its objectives more appealing to the general public. It deemphasized compulsory sterilization for eugenic reasons and emphasized sterilization as a form of birth control suited to particular circumstances. It also determined that BINC should no longer associate itself with the bitter anti-Catholicism evoked by militant Catholic opposition to birth control.

Until 1948, when she was separated from the organization, Olden had virtually been BINC. The organization, its purpose, and its goals had been hers. She had carried out the day-to-day activities, had written many of the educational pamphlets, and had become a recognized authority on sterilization. But her uncompromising anti-Catholicism and her advocacy of compulsory sterilization were no longer compatible with the new, outward-looking national organization. The executive committee found it necessary first to curtail and eventually end BINC's association with Olden, then executive director of the organization.

On July 28, 1950, hoping to capitalize on the prestige of the Human Betterment Foundation, the organization once again changed its name, this time from BINC to the Human Betterment Association of America (HBAA). The change in name came after gaining the approval of Mrs. Castle who now felt the organization worthy of "human betterment," the term her father used to describe social improvement through eugenics.

H. Curtis Wood, Jr., president of BINC from 1945 until 1961 and medical consultant from 1961 until 1973, was most responsible for coordinating the association's change from a small, unsophisticated organization to the present day, international Association for Voluntary Sterilization (AVS). Under his leadership, with the counsel and support of Dr. Robert Latou Dickinson, a noted gynecologist, educator, and author who chaired the HBAA's medical and scientific committee, the AVS expanded its education, research, and service efforts. It undertook fact-finding studies in the medical, legal, eugenic, psychological, and socioeconomic aspects of sterilization; dissemination of information to doctors, social welfare and medical professionals, and the public; the development of a list of doctors to whom individuals inquiring about sterilization could be referred; and the administration of a $10,000 per year assistance fund, made possible by a matching grant from Graham French, a Philadelphia lawyer. The fund assisted those who wanted but could not afford a vasectomy or salpingectomy. Under this program, the agency had assisted hundreds of people seeking sterilization.

At its annual meeting on November 1, 1962, the association changed its name to the Human Betterment Association for Voluntary Sterilization, Inc. (HBAVS). Two years later, on January 7, 1965, "Human Betterment" was dropped and it became the AVS. These final name changes reflected both the growing acceptance by the public of sterilization as a form of birth control and an increasing awareness by the agency that it must dissociate itself from compulsory sterilization. Since 1964, the association's primary objectives have been educating the public to the value of sterilization for limiting family size and for bringing an exploding world population under control. AVS, however, has retained its concern for reducing the number of "mental deficients." In 1966, H. Curtis

Wood, Jr., wrote, "We are still interested in qualitative and quantitative population problems here and around the world and the relationship between birth control and public health, welfare and increased living standards." Working with the American Association on Mental Deficiency,* the association assisted in teaching the mentally handicapped and their parents about the special problems sexuality and reproduction pose for the handicapped and about the advantages of voluntary sterilization.

In 1964, HBAVS received $25,000 from Jesse Hartman, a wealthy New York businessman. The money was to be used for a demonstration project in the Appalachian region of Kentucky. It had been linked intentionally to President Lyndon B. Johnson's administration's War on Poverty. Through it, HBAVS hoped to demonstrate that the people of Appalachia wished information about sterilization—information habitually denied to the lower classes by public health and welfare agencies. HBAVS also wished to demonstrate that sterilization, as well as other forms of birth control, could be employed to help families achieve a standard of living higher than that of families not practicing family limitation. In 1975, AVS began a $100,000 project in Appalachia, which provided training in sterilization techniques for doctors and which taught health and social workers about the advantages and limitations of all forms of birth control.

Since 1966, the aims of the association have been stable. Increased social openness toward human sexuality and birth control, together with AVS's educational programs and research projects, has resulted in a dramatic increase in the number of sterilizations performed in the United States—from an estimated 100,000 in 1964 to an estimated one million in 1975. The AVS budget has similarly increased from approximately $150,000 in 1964 to $1,469,000 in 1975. Included in the last figure is a $1,243,299 grant from the federal Agency for International Development.

In the past few years, while maintaining its domestic programs, AVS has been increasingly active in international programs to promote professional and scientific recognition of surgical contraception as a method of birth control. In 1975, AVS leadership was instrumental in the establishment of the World Federation of Associations for Voluntary Sterilization.

The primary sources for studying the AVS are the records and publications of the association, which are deposited with the Social Welfare History Archives Center at the University of Minnesota. Marian Olden's three-volume history, *Human Betterment Was Our Goal, Sterilization League of New Jersey, 1937–1942*, and *From Birthright, Inc. to Voluntary Sterilization, 1943–1963* (1970), and her single-volume condensation, *History of the Development of the First National Organization for Sterilization* (1974), provide an insider's account of the organization and its shift in emphasis from compulsory to voluntary sterilization. Current publications of the association can be obtained from the association at its offices on 708 Third Avenue, New York, New York 10017.

A University of Minnesota doctoral dissertation, "A History of the Association for Voluntary Sterilization, 1935–1960," is being written by William R. VanEssendelft. The history traces the founding, growth, relations with other social welfare agencies, and ideology of the association. The thesis focuses on the interrelationship of organizational change, ideology, and changing public attitudes toward sterilization.

William R. VanEssendelft

ASSOCIATION OF BLACK SOCIAL WORKERS (ABSW). In the fall of 1966, a group of black social work students at Columbia University's School of Social Work in New York City began to meet and to discuss issues of common concern. Such issues as the supposed failure of schools of social work to play important roles in the Negro protest movement, the charge that such schools had quotas on the number of black students admitted, black social workers' feelings of racism in the field, and most importantly, the need to deal with problems in the ghetto, such as narcotics addiction, all helped to prompt the creation of the ABSW. Stimulated by these discussions and issues, a group of black social workers established the ABSW in late June 1967. The first president of the ABSW apparently was George Silcott, the executive director of the Forest Neighborhood Settlement House in the South Bronx, in New York City. Another founder was Stephen DuBois, the director of social services in the New York State Department of Mental Hygiene. Within a few months of its founding, the ABSW had over four hundred members, and the organization developed ambitious plans to establish its own service agencies in ghetto areas. The ABSW also planned to act as a consultant to existing agencies dealing with blacks.

In the late 1960s, the ABSW stressed issues of primary concern to blacks and helped to elevate the stature of blacks in the profession of social work, as some founders had hoped it would. In late April 1968, the group showed its dissension at a social action workshop in Washington, D.C., on the urban crisis, sponsored by the National Association of Social Workers* (NASW). Groups of black social workers organized in such cities as Chicago, Detroit, Los Angeles, Philadelphia, and Pittsburgh, and black social workers, inspired by the ABSW, were becoming increasingly dissident. In May 1968, at the National Conference on Social Welfare* (NCSW) in San Francisco, the group attacked social work as racist. At these meetings, the ABSW members began efforts to make their organization truly national. The ABSW charged that the NCSW was ignorant of blacks' needs. The ABSW also identified white racism as the major welfare problem in America, urged repeal of Public Law 90-248, the Social Security Amendments of 1967, and voiced support of the National Welfare Rights Organization* (NWRO), an organization of basically welfare recipients.

These grievances, coupled with the general unresponsiveness of the NCSW, led to more meetings, sponsored by the Association of Black Catalysts, which had grown out of the urban crisis conference in Washington, D.C., sponsored by the NASW in April 1968. The first annual conference of the ABSW was held in late February 1969. It was sponsored and hosted by the Philadelphia Alliance of Black Social Workers. The proposed plan to hold the annual conferences on these dates in late February signaled the ABSW's adoption of Malcolm X's views on black oppression and black organization. The theme of the conference in 1969 was "The Black Family: Basic Unit of Survival Toward a Theory of Liberation." At the conference, noting that the ABSW was loosely organized, President Silcott called for a reorientation of the organization to control community social service agencies and to foster black community economic development, as opposed to so-called black capitalism, which the ABSW denounced as a plan for blacks to exploit blacks. The conference also passed a resolution condemning the plan of President Richard M. Nixon to make Head Start, a federal project, the primary thrust of the national antipoverty program. The organization held that this was an attempt to steer the black poor away from their blackness. The ABSW gained nationwide publicity in May 1969 at the NCSW when it asked the executive committee of the NCSW to accede to a number of militant demands, including one that would include 50 percent representation by blacks at all levels of the NCSW and that the NCSW develop a lobbyist for black local and national welfare organizations. The NCSW agreed to each demand, except the one calling for 50 percent representation. The two groups established a joint ABSW-NCSW committee to work on these issues in 1969 and 1970.

The ABSW continued its basic activities in the early 1970s. By mid-1970 there were chapters of the organization in twenty states and in the District of Columbia. All chapters were represented on the national steering committee of the ABSW. By this time, the ABSW had an education program providing black expertise by black professionals on social welfare concerns and technical assistance to other black groups on organizing. "Intrinsic achievements," according to one student, Professor Charles Saunders of New York University, included stimulating the sensitivity of social workers generally to the problems of blacks, encouraging closer attention to be paid to the role of black social workers in black communities, and enhancing the black social worker's understanding of his blackness. In 1972, the ABSW issued a controversial statement condemning transracial adoptions. The ABSW had an Adoptions Task Force, which worked on this statement. In 1973, the ABSW held its annual conference in New York City. More than five thousand people, the largest group ever, participated in the four-day meetings.

The sources for studying the ABSW's history include the files of *The New York Times,* and Charles Saunders, "Growth of the Association of Black Social Workers," *Social Casework* 51 (May 1970): 277–284. There does not appear to be a scholarly history of the ABSW.

ASSOCIATION OF VOLUNTEER BUREAUS, INC. (AVB). In the 1930s, social service agencies once again began to pay special attention to volunteers. Taking the leadership in clarifying the volunteer's role in the early 1930s were the National Organization for Public Health Nursing* (NOPHN), the Family Welfare Association of America* (FWAA), the National League for Nursing, and the Association of Junior Leagues, Inc. In 1933, these agencies helped to establish the National Committee on Volunteers in Social Work (NCVSW) as part of the National Conference of Social Work* (NCSW). The development of community welfare councils in the 1930s also helped to promote volunteerism; about fifty of the larger American cities had volunteer bureaus by the early 1940s. These volunteer bureaus helped to train volunteers and to place them in appropriate social service agencies. During World War II, virtually all of these local volunteer bureaus cooperated with the war effort supervised by the federal Office of Civilian Defense (OCD).

During the war, there were about eleven million volunteers in a variety of services, representing a broad spectrum of the population, not just the elite as in earlier periods. In 1943, the OCD took over the activities of the NCVSW. In 1944, when the federal agency disbanded, the representatives of the former NCVSW became the nucleus of the Community Chests and Councils, Inc.'s* (CCC) advisory committee on volunteer services. In 1945, this committee changed its name to the advisory committee on citizen participation (ACCP), and it began to be sponsored jointly by the CCC and the National Social Welfare Assembly* (NSWA). In the late 1940s, the CCC began to sponsor efforts to unite the local volunteer bureaus. Consequently, in 1951, the Association of Volunteer Bureaus (AVB) was established as the National Association of Volunteer Bureaus (NAVB) to coordinate existing programs and bureaus and to develop new volunteer bureaus.

In the first few years, the NAVB seemed to cooperate closely with the ACCP. Nevertheless, in the early 1950s, when the agency apparently changed its name to the Association of Volunteer Bureaus of America (AVBA), it drafted its bylaws and adopted a national symbol and an awards plan. Apparently the AVBA and the ACCP jointly published a handbook for volunteers and the *Volunteer Viewpoint* to keep constituents abreast of development affecting volunteers. In 1954, the now-named Association of Volunteer Bureaus (AVB) had a membership of eighty-four. Throughout the 1950s, the organization conducted workshops at the annual forum of the NCSW. These sessions focused on different aspects of volunteerism, helping to develop greater communications between professionals and volunteers in social service work.

In the 1960s, a vital decade for social work in general, the organization became increasingly important. In the early 1960s, when many different sources questioned the basic importance of voluntary social service organizations, the now-named Association of Volunteer Bureaus of America (AVBA) worked with the two leaders in the field, the United Community Funds and Councils of America, Inc.* (UCFCA) and the NSWA to promote public understanding of the functions and meaning of voluntary agencies. The AVBA also helped to develop programs to attract volunteers to national agencies and to train volunteer workers in social service. In the early 1960s, the AVBA established a national committee of training and curriculum to work with leading national voluntary agencies and universities to develop curriculum and training programs in the administration of volunteers in social service. In 1965, AVBA became international when local bureaus from Mexico and Canada joined, making a total of 110 constituent agencies. In 1966, the national organization refined its membership accrediting standards and revised the earlier *Volunteer Bureau Handbook*. The expansion of social services nationally as part of the War on Poverty prompted further growth of AVBA. In 1967, local bureaus, for instance, began contracts with such federal programs as Volunteers in Service to America (VISTA) (see *Government Agencies*), Head Start, and Jobs Corps. At the end of the annual meeting in 1968, the AVBA established a new organizational structure: four regions for the United States and one for Canada. Soon thereafter, regional conferences were held more frequently than before. The national organization continued to provide services for its constituents, developing by the early 1970s an insurance plan for volunteers in social service.

In the 1970s, national trends and developments, especially the establishment and operation of the National Center for Voluntary Action (NCVA) (see *Political and Civic Organizations*) affected the AVBA. Since 1969, many local affiliates of AVBA had become associated with the NCVA, often changing their names to include "voluntary action center." This situation prompted the AVBA in 1970 to endorse the concept of NCVA and to approve the principle of AVBA affiliates' changing their names to fit their new roles as action centers. Also, in 1970, the AVBA opened its membership to individuals as well as groups. The organization established a new department for public relations and publications, as well as Volunteerism International, to promote the interests of professionals and volunteers. In response to the expansion of voluntary action generally and an increased number of members, the AVBA explained its structure from five to eight regions. In 1971, the organization published an *Annotated Bibliography and Library Manual* of materials available from local affiliates and in the same year, *Volunteer World,* its own newsletter.

Increasingly feeling its organizational independence and growth, the AVBA decided in the early 1970s to break its formal but not restrictive ties with its parent agency, now called the United Way of America. Apparently in 1973, the AVBA incorporated according to the laws of the state of Missouri as the AVB. The new AVB updated its loan folders on subjects relating to voluntary service, changed its newsletter to *AVB Notebook,* which became a bimonthly publication emphasizing practical advice programs for affiliates, and began to cooperate with the UWA to develop new standards for central community voluntary services. In 1973, AVB membership rose to 250.

Articles on volunteers in social service in various issues of the *Social Work Year Book* contain information about the AVB. The AVB's three-page mimeographed "History of the Association of Volunteer Bureaus, Inc., 1950–1973," is helpful. Copies of the AVB's newsletters, such as the *Volunteer Viewpoint* and the *AVB Notebook,* could not be located. There does not seem to be a scholarly history of the AVB.

_B_

BAPTIST CHURCHES IN THE U.S.A., AMERICAN, DIVISION OF SOCIAL MINISTRIES OF (DSM). The so-called social gospel movement of the late nineteenth century stirred the social conscience of American churches. Baptists such as Reverend Walter Rauschenbusch, whose *Christianity and the Social Crisis* (1870), according to historian Robert Bremner, "was the most influential exposition of the social gospel," and Reverend Samuel Z. Batten were active and influential in this reform movement. In 1896, both Rauschenbusch and Batten helped to organize in Philadelphia a group of Baptist clergymen and interested lay representatives to form the Brotherhood of the Kingdom (BK) to promote the social work of the Northern Baptist Church (NBC) (see *Religious Institutions*). Historian Charles H. Hopkins suggested that the BK was perhaps the most important "social-gospel society" of the period. Efforts to make the BK an official church agency were delayed until the Northern Baptist Convention was founded in 1908. Meeting for the first regular session in Oklahoma City in May 1908, the convention resolved to create a Social Service Commission and appointed a committee of seven members to study Baptist social work and to report their findings in both the denominational press and to the 1909 convention. In 1912, the convention made the group a department, increasing its size to fifteen members. The Northern Baptist Convention in Des Moines, Iowa, in May 1912 recommended that the American Baptist Publication Society (ABPS) (see *Religious Institutions*), another church agency, incorporate this work. On September 26, 1912, the ABPS board of directors established the Division of Social Ministries (DSM) of the American Baptist Churches in the U.S.A. (ABC) as the Department of Social Service and Brotherhood (DSSB) of the NBC. At this meeting, Professor Samuel Z. Batten, then teaching at Des Moines College, was elected secretary of the new DSSB. The Commission of Social Service and Brotherhood and its successors were the advisory group of the DSSB, which conducted the actual work and activities.

The work of the DSSB developed slowly. In its first years, it created similar state social service commissions, submitted and won approval from the convention of its social service program, and, working with another Baptist agency, developed a comprehensive social studies program for Sunday schools, brotherhoods, and other such Baptist study groups. During these early years, the DSSB published a social services series of monographs on particular social issues. Authors included leaders such as Owen R. Lovejoy, "the children's statesman" and later head of both the National Child Labor Committee* and The Children's Aid Society* (CAS) of New York. By 1916, the following departments of the DSSB suggested its activities and interests: prison reform, revival commissions, immigration and foreign-speaking people, temperance and social hygiene, social education, industrial problems, home and the child, international peace and national security, and Lord's day. Batten continued as the chairman of the organization until his death in 1925.

After Batten's death and with the ensuing depression in the country, the agency developed positions and statements on particular issues rather than working actively with needy or troubled people. For instance, in 1928, the now-named Committee on Social Service (CSS) deplored the antiprohibition movement, and it urged greater labor-management cooperation, peace, and creative recreation in light of increasing leisure time. In the early 1930s, the CSS helped to revise the "Social Ideals" statement of the Federal Council of the Churches of Christ in America (FCC) (see *Religious Institutions*). The CSS was represented officially at the conference on permanent preventives of unemployment in early 1931. In the late 1930s, as government-paid workers from the National Youth Administration and Works Projects Administration helped denominational social welfare agencies, the CSS became concerned about and published pamphlets on church-state relations. As World War II approached, the CSS dealt increasingly with issues of peace and conscientious objectors. Lacking a paid executive officer, the CSS conducted its work through volunteer members. At the convention of the church in May 1941, the newly established Council for Christian Social Progress (CCSP) took over the work of the former CSS.

The new CCSP, comprised of representatives from each of the fourteen major Baptist agencies in addition to three members elected at large, began its work by surveying the church's social work. Limited by lack of funds and thus unable to hire a full-time executive secretary, the CCSP also prepared a study kit about conscientious objectors and voiced concern over vice near military encampments. In the early 1940s, prohibition, racism, and war-related issues, such as conscientious objectors and the relocation of Japanese-Americans, occupied the members' energies. On December 1, 1943, Reverend Donald B. Cloward became the first executive secretary. The CCSP moved its offices from Franklin College in Indiana to New York City, where it continued its basic interests but grew increasingly committed to the postwar world community, particularly the United Nations (UN), whose programs became a major activity.

Like other church social service agencies, the CCSP sponsored church participation in the Washington, D.C., and UN seminars, and the CCSP developed its own study seminars as well. In 1948, the growth of local Baptist social action committees prompted the hiring of an associate secretary for fieldwork, but financial problems forced his release the next year. The CCSP also obtained the voluntary services of a representative in Washington, D.C., whose various publications kept Baptists informed of relevant legislation. Dr. Cloward died in September 1956, and a year later, Reverend John W. Thomas became the executive secretary.

In 1960, Reverend Elizabeth Miller began working as the educational secretary. She initiated a newssheet, *Concerns for Christian Citizens,* and she worked with local and state groups. Another important administrative change occurred in 1961 when the American Baptist Convention of the now-named American Baptist Churches in the U.S.A. (ABC) (see *Religious Institutions*) dissolved the CCSP and made it a division of the convention, separating the agency from the American Baptist Publication Society. The new Division of Christian Social Concern (DCSC) moved its headquarters to Valley Forge, Pennsylvania, in late 1961. Thomas resigned in May 1964 and, after serving briefly as acting executive director, Elizabeth Miller became the executive director. Under the reorganization of the early 1960s, the Baptist Joint Committee on Public Affairs, which was concerned with such issues as church-state relations, especially in education, became part of the DCSC. More importantly, in 1963, the DCSC created its department of international affairs, which focused primarily on continuing Baptist activity at the UN. In 1965, the staff addition of Reverend Louis Mitchell involved the DCSC more heavily than before in the civil rights, poor peoples', and the United Farm Workers movements. In the late 1960s, the DCSC participated in the Baptist Crisis in the Nation Team, dealing with civil disorders and racial confrontations. It also participated in some antiwar movements, for instance, observing the moratoriums in October and December 1969 at Valley Forge headquarters. In the 1970s, the DCSC participated with other denominations in the ecology and peace movements. In 1970, it published *Retreat to Tokenism,* which documented the deteriorating status of women on the executive staff of the ABC.

Further organizational changes occurred in the 1970s. On January 1, 1973, the DCSC merged with the ABC's Division of Social Action to form the new Division of Social Ministries (DSM), administratively under the Board of National Ministries. Reverend Miller headed the new DSM. The staff seemed occupied with adapting at first to the expanded structure, but program activities continued. In 1973, for instance, the DSM had an alternative life-styles project involving the aged. In the late summer of 1973, in response to migrant labor tensions, the DSM conducted an extensive field investigation of the situation in the grape industry in Kern County, California. The office of world affairs continued its predecessor's activities at the UN. Adapting to major currents in social work, the DSM also had a well-developed neighborhood action program in the 1970s.

The primary sources for reconstructing the DSM's history include the detailed agency reports in the Northern Baptist Convention, *Annual Containing Proceed-*

ings, and the reports in the ABC's *Year Books.* Some agency reports are to be found in church periodicals, such as in *The Watchman-Examiner* (1935), 566–576. The American Baptist Historical Society in Rochester, New York, has the papers of Samuel Zane Batten.

Charles H. Hopkins, *The Rise of the Social Gospel in American Protestantism, 1865–1915* (1940), discusses briefly both the BK and the early DSM history, but there does not appear to be a scholarly history of the DSM.

BARUCH COMMITTEE ON PHYSICAL MEDICINE AND REHABILI-TATION (BCPMR). Bernard Baruch, a well-known, twentieth-century industrialist and public servant, had a firm belief in medicine as a means of improving the quality of life. This belief was apparently influenced by his father, Dr. Simon Baruch, a pioneer in urban public health in the nineteenth century and the founder of the American Association for Hygiene and Baths* in the early twentieth century. During World War II, the plight of wounded soldiers interested the younger Baruch. Consequently, in October 1943, he appointed a survey committee to study the condition of services in physical rehabilitation. Dr. Ray Lyman Wilbur, a prominent physician and public servant who had served as secretary of the interior under President Herbert Hoover, chaired the committee. The committee's survey began on November 1, 1943, and in April 1944, the committee presented its findings, calling for better services to meet increasing patient needs. Baruch accepted the survey and its recommendations. On April 27, 1944, in New York City, Baruch immediately established the Baruch Committee on Physical Medicine and Rehabilitation (BCPMR) as the Baruch Committee on Physical Medicine (BCPM), donating about $1.1 million to improve the state of medical care for the physically handicapped. The BCPM's planned program included granting funds to medical institutions so they could improve their facilities and services and develop training programs for physicians.

Known simply as the Baruch Committee, the BCPM began its work energetically. It opened a central office in New York City, and Dr. Frank H. Krusen, who headed the Mayo Clinic in Minnesota, became its director. Dr. Wilbur became the chairman of the group, whose early staff also included an educational director, an executive secretary, and office personnel. A three-member administrative board, including Dr. Wilbur, conducted the BCPM business, and a nine-member scientific advisory committee, chaired by Dr. Krusen, reviewed fellowship requests. The main purpose of the BCPM was to provide grants to institutions and to individual research fellows, although its *Bulletin on War and Postwar Physical Rehabilitation and Reconditions* also brought the generally unknown problems of war injuries and rehabilitation work to light. In the first year of operation, the BCPM gave an especially large grant to Columbia University and sizable funds to New York University and to the Medical College of Virginia.

In the next few years, the BCPM worked to promote the establishment of physical rehabilitation medicine as a recognized specialty and to coordinate the activities of the institutions that received grants. In September 1945, the BCPM held a conference in New York City in conjunction with the meetings of the American Congress of Physical Medicine, a professional medical group. At least two representatives from each center or program receiving BCPM funds attended the conference to discuss their work and common problems. The BCPM sponsored similar medical conferences and seminars throughout the late 1940s. In 1947, the BCPM central office conducted a comparative study of physical medicine in medical colleges. The results were published in the February 1948 issue of *Occupational Therapy and Rehabilitation,* a journal oriented toward social service in the rehabilitation field. When the American Board of Physical Medicine and Rehabilitation was established in 1942 as a professional scientific organization to certify specialists, one of the BCPM's major goals was fulfilled.

Promoting the medical aspects of rehabilitation remained the BCPM's major purpose, but it also became involved in social service developments in general. In 1945, for instance, it established two subcommittees to deal with the social aspects of rehabilitation: one on physical fitness and the other on civilian rehabilitation centers. In 1945, the latter distributed ten thousand copies of a helpful report, *A Community Rehabilitation Service and Center.* And the BCPM had an exhibit at a variety of conferences, including those relating to social service in the field of rehabilitation.

Within a few years, the BCPM awakened interest in the importance of physical rehabilitation. It influenced the development of physical rehabilitation services in the federal Veterans Administration (see *Government Agencies*). One of its major goals, the establishment of a permanent section on physical medicine and rehabilitation of the American Medical Association, was fulfilled in June 1949. That year, the BCPM moved its offices to Chicago to be closer to the medical groups in the field, and with a major objective fulfilled, it began to consolidate its activities. In 1949, the agency changed its name and became the BCPMR, and Executive Director Krusen became chairman, replacing the late Dr. Wilbur. BCPMR-sponsored research continued to be published. By 1951, the agency had helped to rehabilitate more civilians than veterans, had promoted many professional developments in the field, and had stimulated the development of community rehabilitation centers throughout the country. As Dr. Krusen said to his colleagues on May 26, 1951, when he announced the disbanding of the agency, the BCPMR "has brought into being a new medical specialty which has already demonstrated its ability to bring relief to many thousands of sick and disabled persons and to restore other thousands of handicapped people to useful citizens."

The primary sources for studying the history of the BCPMR include the hard-to-find published *Annual Reports* and the Papers of Bernard Baruch at Princeton University, which contain unpublished materials of all kinds. The Raymond Lyman Wilbur Papers at the Lane Medical Library at the Stanford Medical Center in Palo Alto, California, contain a vast array of unpublished materials relating to the BCPMR. *The New York Times* reported some of the BCPMR's activities.

There is no scholarly study of the BCPMR, but its contributions to the field are mentioned in several specialized medical publications, such as Dr. Howard Rusk, "The Growth and Development of Rehabilitation Medicine," *Archives of Physical Medicine* 50 (1961): 463–66.

BIG BROTHER AND BIG SISTER FEDERATION, INC. (BBBSF). Early in the twentieth century, men in both Cincinnati and New York City began to serve as so-called volunteer big brothers, or friends and advisers to fatherless boys in their respective communities. In 1909, Ernest K. Coulter, the clerk of the juvenile court in New York City, established the first big brother organization, the Big Brother Movement, Inc., of New York. Local groups patterened after the parent agency in New York, including similar organizations for big sister programs, developed throughout the country. In late May 1917, at the first annual conference of big brother and big sister societies in Grand Rapids, Michigan, the Big Brother and Big Sister Federation (BBBSF) was established as the International Advisory Council of the Big Brother and Big Sister Societies (IAC). Like other national federations of the period, the IAC was established to promote the development of new agencies in the United States and Canada, to provide advice to existing organizations, to publish materials of interest to the field, and to sponsor conferences, training courses, and seminars for workers in the movement and for interested laymen. The major overriding concern of the IAC was, like its affiliates, to prevent juvenile delinquency.

Especially in the early years, the chief activity of the organization was holding the annual conference of affiliates and members. At the third annual conference in 1919 at Cincinnati, Ohio, the group drew up a constitution for a League of Big Brother and Big Sister Federations in America, which was apparently ratified at the annual conference in 1920 at Toronto, Canada. In 1919, the structure of the organization included as president, Ernest K. Coulter, the founder of the Big Brother Movement, Inc., of New York and the superintendent of the New York Society for the Prevention of Cruelty to Children* (NYSPCC), three vice-presidents, including C. J. Atkinson, who had been active with boys in Toronto, Canada, and who served as the first executive director of the Federated Boys' Clubs,* and Dr. H. W. Dingman, president of Big Brothers of Grand Rapids, Michigan. The board of directors included these four officers in addition to the secretary-treasurer and the presidents of each member agency. Beginning in 1920, the executive secretary of the organization was Rowland C. Sheldon, a social worker who was the general secretary of the Big Brother Movement, Inc., of New York. On November 1, 1921, the organization was incorporated as the Big Brother and Big Sister Federation, Inc. (BBBSF). Among the incorporators were Ernest Coulter and Mrs. Sidney Borg, who was active in other charities. The organization gained some national recognition in October 1921, when it made President and Mrs. Warren G. Harding honorary vice-presidents. Ceremonies at the White House marked the occasion. In 1925, the board of directors issued a notice forbidding the use of photographs or the names of the children assisted. The board also took steps in 1925 to improve the big brother and big sister movements and to increase the leadership of the BBBSF in the field. It began to evaluate local agencies, and it required that each member agency have a body of leaders that met regularly and that each organization file an annual report, including data on finances, to the national headquarters in New York City.

In the late 1920s, the organization was helping over ten thousand children through nearly nine hundred agencies. It sponsored annual conferences that, like the one in New York City in November 1931, focused on juvenile delinquency. At the 1931 conference the chairman of the executive committee, Grover A. Whalen, the former police commissioner of New York City, spoke about the activities of a recently established special bureau in the New York City Police Department to deal with juvenile delinquents. The conference also heard the results of a survey by the BBBSF of problem children in medium-sized cities. The structure of the early 1930s included its president, George MacDonald, a prominent lawyer, six vice-presidents, including Mrs. Borg, and Theodore Roosevelt, Jr., a secretary, a treasurer, and the board of directors. An organizational highlight occurred in early 1932, when Senator David Aiken Reed of Pennsylvania introduced a bill in Congress to charter the BBBSF. The group of leaders from the organization working for this charter were President MacDonald, Whalen, Mrs. Borg, and Dr. Lewis H. Mann of Chicago.

In the 1930s, annual conferences tended to feature important individuals in the field of juvenile delinquency prevention. For example, in 1935, meeting again in New York, the conference featured Dr. Lawson Lowrey, a founder of the field of orthopsychiatry. Officers chosen at the annual meeting in 1935 included as president, Dr. Sheldon Glueck, professor of criminology at the Harvard Law School, and, as chairman of the executive committee, Leonard Mayo, an important figure in the national social work community. In 1936, the BBBSF sponsored a study of problem children among about twenty-six thousand schoolchildren in upstate New York. In 1937, however, the agency dissolved, leaving a void in the field of big brother and big sister work. In 1940, representatives from local groups tried, unsuccessfully, to form another national organization. In the late 1940s, a group from Philadelphia, Pennsylvania, did establish the Big Brothers of America.*

The most important sources for the BBBSF are the files of *The New York Times*. Scattered references to the organization can also be found in such contemporary publications as *The Juvenile Court Record* and the published *Annual Reports* of the Big Brother Movement, Inc., of New York City.

Pamela J. Matson includes a brief mention of the BBBSF in "Big Brothers of America, Inc.," *Descriptive Inventories of Collections in the Social Welfare*

History Archives Center (1970), 14–16, but there does not appear to be a scholarly history of the organization.

BIG BROTHERS OF AMERICA, INC. (BBA). Moved by watching a young boy scrounging for food in a garbage can in 1903, a young businessman in Cincinnati, Irvin F. Westheimer, discussed the incident with some of his friends. Westheimer and his colleagues agreed to meet with and to counsel local boys who had no fathers. This development led eventually to the first big brother group in Cincinnati in 1903. Independent of the Cincinnati program, the clerk of the children's Court of New York City, Ernest K. Coulter, spoke about the problems of fatherless boys to the men's club of a local church, which promptly resolved to have its members develop personal relations with individual boys. In 1909, some of these men joined Coulter to incorporate the Big Brother Movement, Inc., of New York as the first formal organization in the field. Local groups, all patterned after the parent agency in New York, including similar organizations for big sister programs, developed throughout the country. In 1917, representatives from these local societies formed the Big Brother and Big Sister Federation,* a national organization that dissolved in 1937. In the absence of a national office, correspondence in the late 1930s was routed to the parent agency in New York, which Joseph McCoy headed. At the annual meeting of the National Conference of Social Work* (NCSW) in both 1939 and 1940, representatives from local organizations discussed the possibilities of a national organization and developed a questionnaire on the subject to poll all local groups. In 1940, workers in local agencies created a national study and planning committee, which was chaired by McCoy and Kenneth Rogers, general secretary of the Big Brother Movement of Toronto, Canada. This group studied the feasibility of and outlined plans for a national organization, but plans materialized only when an energetic group from the Philadelphia organization joined the efforts. In October 1945, promoters of the national organization, chiefly Roger McCoy and Charles Berwind and George Casey, both from the Big Brothers Association of Philadelphia, established the temporary big brother national committee. This committee conducted a study of fifteen existing agencies and proposed plans for a national organization. The next step occurred when the Philadelphia agency hosted a conference of delegates from nine existing local big brother agencies to discuss a national organization. These negotiations took place at Camp Wyomissing in Stroudsburg, Pennsylvania, in late June 1946. Organizational efforts continued, and on December 24, 1946, Big Brothers of America (BBA) was incorporated in Philadelphia according to the laws of Pennsylvania.

The early activities of the BBA centered on developing its administrative structure and establishing the national organization. In February 1947, the BBA opened national headquarters in Philadelphia, where they have remained. Berwind and other members of the Philadelphia organization, especially G. Ruhland Rebmann, channeled funds to the BBA, which also received funds from the local affiliates. The founders established a council of delegates, comprised of two representatives from each local. In 1947, the council elected the board of directors, a group of thirty to a hundred men who had been chosen by either the president, the nominating committee, or local agencies. The board included prominent men in business and civic affairs as directors-at-large or honorary directors. Associate Justice of the United States Supreme Court Thomas C. Clark and Senator Thomas C. Jennings of Missouri have served in this capacity. In 1949, the council of delegates authorized the board to establish an executive committee. The BBA elected traditional officers, headed by a president. Charles Berwind served as the only BBA president until 1972, when he died. An executive director headed the staff at headquarters. In 1948, illustrator Norman Rockwell developed the BBA emblem.

With its structure established, the BBA entered the 1950s committed to publicizing, expanding, and improving big brother work throughout the country. In January 1950, with the help of the Advertising Council, the BBA sponsored the first national Big Brother Week. In 1950, President Berwind appointed a technical planning committee to suggest improvements, to prepare statistical report forms for locals, to prepare a manual of big brother procedures, and to promote the movement generally. Joseph McCoy of the parent New York group chaired the committee, which conducted important work. In 1958, it became the technical advisory committee, composed of executives of locals. The new committee determined to formalize many activities that it had been conducting, such as facilitating communications between locals, the BBA, and the council of delegates. In 1958, the committee also planned to promote wider use of casework principles, to coordinate papers at NCSW, and to professionalize and improve services further. The committee also recommended establishing committees to publicize the big brother movement and to recruit volunteers.

Although the BBA relied so heavily on volunteers, it developed strong professional strengths. The technical advisory committee, composed of executives of local agencies, especially promoted this professional development. In 1958, for the first time, the BBA received foundation grants for research and new projects. As further signs of professional development, various sources, such as the NCSW and the National Educational Association, invited the staff to present papers. The editors of a magazine volume on the use of volunteers in social service asked the BBA to prepare an article. Paving the way for a later organizational development, in 1958, the technical advisory committee held three regional meetings for the first time. The BBA published the papers from these conferences as a manual on casework. In 1959, the BBA received a foundation grant to formulate a research design, and in June 1959, it hired a trained research director. Later in the year, the research director helped to develop the BBA research advisory committee, composed largely of professional staff people from the East Coast.

The structure of the BBA also expanded in the 1950s. In 1959, the organization created a group of national associates, nationally prominent men to help raise funds for the organization. By 1959, the member agencies had grown to a total of fifty. Also, in 1959, the organization established a women's committee, centered in Philadelphia, which decided to raise funds for the BBA. The growth in the number of affiliates led in 1959 to a proposal to divide the United States and Canada into seven regions. But, most significantly, in 1958, the Eighty-fifth Congress of the United States passed a special act giving the BBA a federal charter. President Dwight Eisenhower signed the act, helping to create greater national awareness and prestige for the movement and the BBA as well.

In the 1950s, the BBA also developed some important activities and projects. In 1958, for instance, the staff began work on a series of television films on the big brother program. In 1959, President Dwight Eisenhower's participation helped to make a successful Big Brother of the Year award ceremonies. After discussions with the Child Welfare League of America* (CWLA) and some American Indian groups, the BBA developed a demonstration project on an Indian reservation. Also in 1959, the organization designed a pilot program in low-rent public housing projects.

In the early 1960s, the BBA developed further the patterns it had established earlier, starting new and creative programs, expanding its organization, and becoming increasingly active in the national professional social service community. In May 1961, for instance, the BBA reinstated a training and orientation program for new executive directors. In 1960, to aid affiliates in recruiting volunteers, the BBA published a new brochure, *One Man—One Boy*. An important professional development occurred in 1961 when the BBA established an ad hoc committee of the National Social Welfare Assembly* to explore its relations with other national agencies dealing with boys. In 1961, an article in *The Saturday Evening Post* publicized the BBA further. In the same year, the organization received a grant from the National Institute of Mental Health to measure and to increase the effectiveness of its services among fatherless boys. In 1962, professionals from the BBA met for the first time as the professional staff conference committee. In 1962, to raise funds, the BBA created the position of program development director. Most importantly, a 1962 survey of the BBA influenced it to begin a three-year growth program. To guide this activity, the BBA created a growth national steering committee, which influenced the regional vice-presidents to establish regional growth committees. In 1964, the BBA created a national membership committee to study new affiliates' applications, which increased steadily. In the mid-1960s, the BBA hired its first full-time director of public relations, and in 1964, began to republish *The Big Brother Bulletin,* which it had discontinued in 1960.

In the mid-1960s, the BBA showed clear signs of organizational growth and maturation. In 1966, there were 103 affiliates, prompting President Berwind to predict over 200 such agencies in six years. In 1966, the *Bulletin* had a circulation of sixteen thousand. In October 1965, the Laymen's National Committee gave the BBA its top award. In the mid-1960s, the organization established the Big Brother of America Foundation to finance BBA work. For the first time, the BBA became associated with the International Conference of Social Workers. Another sign of its acceptance in the social service community developed in the mid-1960s when the western regional conference of the CWLA conducted a panel on big brother work. Like other national social service agencies, the BBA developed uniform standards of accounting, which it implemented on January 1, 1967. In April 1968, through funds from the Charles Stewart Mott Foundation, the BBA held an executive training institute on management and administration for over twenty newer executive directors. At the beginning of 1968, the BBA employed as consultants a fund-raising and advertising firm, which drafted fund-raising plans.

Further growth in the number of affiliated member agencies, organizational and administrative changes, and strengthened professionalization of social work activities characterized the BBA in the 1970s. In 1968, there were 128 affiliated agencies in 115 communities; in 1974, there were over 275, helping to make the BBA the fastest growing national children's agency in the mid-1970s. The death of the only BBA president, Charles Berwind, in November 1972, ended an era in the agency's history. In 1973, organizational changes began. The national staff was reorganized, and in 1974, the BBA adopted a new constitution and bylaws, providing for a reorganization of the board of directors and for greater involvement of the board through active committees. But more importantly, the constitution called for a decentralized structure based on regional officers who were now elected. The Charles Stewart Mott Foundation provided continued funding for the central regional office in Flint, Michigan, which served over fifty agencies in the Midwest. In 1973, a three-year grant from the Kellogg Foundation developed in-service training institutes for the professional staff from member agencies, and in 1974, representatives from the national professional field staff conducted over six hundred visits and consultations with member agencies and participated in regional professional workshops. Funds from the Lilly Endowment helped the BBA to administer the Big Sister International program, and the BBA refined its service community concept of extending activities throughout a specified area, a crucial aspect of a truly national movement.

The sources for studying the BBA's history are diverse. *Pony Express,* the publication of the Big Brother Movement, Inc., of New York for the years 1945–1951, covered the BBA. The *Proceedings* of the annual meetings contain reports of the agency's activities, as do the brief but helpful published *Annual Reports,* which apparently began in the 1970s. The papers of the BBA are on file at the Social Welfare History Archives Center at the University of Minnesota in Minneapolis. Pamela J. Matson, "Big Brothers of America, Inc." in *Descriptive Inventories of Collections in the Social Welfare History Archives Center,* (1970), 14–16, is a brief history of the agency. Apparently there is no scholarly history of the BBA.

BOY SCOUTS OF AMERICA (BSA). At the beginning of the twentieth century in the United States, there developed some youth organizations that stressed the American heritage of Indians and nature. In 1902, Ernest Thompson Seton, a naturalist, illustrator, and author, began calling a group of young boys he had organized the Tribe of Woodcraft Indians (TWI) (see *Fraternal Organizations*), known popular as Seton's Indians. In 1901, Seton produced a handbook for his organization, *The Birch Bark Roll*. He gave a copy to a Lord Roberts, who in 1904, gave it to his fellow Englishman, Robert S. S. Baden-Powell, the military hero who had founded the Boy Scouts in England in 1908. Another important youth group in the United States in the early twentieth century was the Society of the Sons of Daniel Boone (SSDB) (see *Fraternal Organizations*). The founder and leader of the SSDB was Daniel Carter Beard, the editor of *Recreation*, the journal of the Playground Association of America* (PAA). Founded in June 1905, the SSDB developed groups of boys—appropriate to the group's pioneer heritage, called forts—throughout the country. Beard promoted his SSDB through the pages of *Recreation*, which he continued to edit, and through a voluminous correspondence. In the period roughly between 1908 and 1910, a number of other scouting organizations sprang up throughout the country. *Association Men,* the journal of the International Committee of the Young Men's Christian Associations* (YMCA), especially promoted these groups. Not unexpectedly, some of the earliest scouting organizations began in areas near active YMCAs—in Springfield, Massachusetts, Utica, New York, and Paterson, New Jersey, for instance. Major YMCAs, such as in Chicago and at the West Side Branch in New York City, held training courses in scouting during this early period. Ernest Seton conducted the training course in New York. Also during this period, a number of Englishmen living or traveling in the United States organized scout groups.

Despite the development of these organizations, other events were more responsible for the origins of the Boy Scouts of America (BSA). During the first decade of the twentieth century, many American travelers in Europe noticed boy scouts. One foggy night in London, England, in 1909, Chicago publisher William D. Boyce was assisted by one of these scouts, who explained that he was doing his good turn for the day. The scout also described his organization and its leader Baden-Powell to Boyce. This unknown British boy scout, later honored by the American organization, introduced Boyce to Baden-Powell. After many meetings with Baden-Powell, Boyce returned home to the United States, laden with literature about the scouting movement. He then began efforts to establish a similar organization in America. Boyce's friend, Colin H. Livingstone, a former journalist and banker and descendant of the British missionary and explorer, helped to prepare the formal organization. Consequently, on February 8, 1910, in Washington, D.C., the BSA was incorporated according to the laws of the District of Columbia.

The YMCA became involved in the early BSA. In February 1910, after seeing an item in a Chicago newspaper on Boyce's having established the BSA, J. A. Van Dis, the boys' work secretary of the state YMCA of Michigan who had been developing groups of scouts in various local YMCAs, urged Edgar M. Robinson, a well-known youth worker from the YMCA, to meet with Boyce about their organization's participation in the BSA movement. On May 3, 1910, Van Dis, Robinson, and Dr. L. L. Doggett, the president of International YMCA College in Springfield, Massachusetts, called on Boyce in his office in Chicago and pledged the cooperation of the YMCA. Boyce agreed to support the movement with $1,000 per month. Robinson promptly enlisted two British YMCA workers, Charles E. Heald and W. B. Wakefield. On May 9, 1910, late in the evening, in response to a telegram from Boyce, Heald, Wakefield, Robinson, and Seton, rushed to Washington, D.C., and, on May 10, 1910, they appeared with Boyce before a congressional committee on education to favor a bill granting the BSA a national charter. In early May 1910, however, the BSA faced a challenge from a new organization when publisher William Randolph Hearst, at a news conference at the Waldorf-Astoria Hotel in New York City, announced the establishment of his American Boy Scouts (see *Fraternal Organizations*). Robinson was at this conference, and he pointed out that the BSA had already been organized. Hearst persisted in his plans, incorporating the group according to the laws of New York State on June 24, 1910. Hearst's group later became known as the United States Boy Scouts (USBS). Also during this period, the National Highway Protection Association (see *Political and Civic Organizations*) developed its Boy Scouts of the United States with Colonel Peter S. Bomus as the chief scout. By November 1910, except for Hearst's ABS, all of the other scouting programs and their leaders, especially Beard and Seton, were affiliated with and were absorbed by the BSA.

During 1910 and early 1911, the BAS continued to develop its structure and to solidify its organization. In June 1910, Robinson convened a meeting in the board room of the YMCA headquarters in New York City to promote the movement. Twenty-five men, including, of course, Seton and Beard, attended. The list of others at this meeting resembles a contemporary who's who in youth and social work: Dr. Luther Gulick of The Russell Sage Foundation,* an important youth worker, Lee F. Hanmer, also from the fund, Ernest P. Bicknell, a social worker and the director of the American National Red Cross* (ANRC), Charles F. Paulison, the general secretary of the Child Welfare Committee, Ernest H. Abbott of *The Outlook,* Ernest K. Coulter, the founder of the Big Brother Movement, Inc., of New York and the head of the New York Society for the Prevention of Cruelty to Children,* and well-known Progressive reformers Lincoln Steffens and Jacob Riis, whose name was synonymous with child welfare and social reform in the late nineteenth and early twentieth centuries. The meeting chose the BSA's initial officers—a chairman, a secretary, and a treasurer. Seton, Hanmer, and George D. Pratt of the Pratt Institute in Brooklyn, respectively, filled these posts. The chairman appointed an eight-member committee on organization, which included these three officers and Luther Gulick, Robinson, Riis, Beard, and Livingstone, the only incorporator at this meeting. The BSA hired its first field secretary, Preston F. Orwig, a former YMCA worker, on a month-to-month basis. Approved as the BSA's first managing secretary was John L. Alexander, a YMCA worker.

Alexander spent most of his time in this first year of operation, 1910–1911, contacting other scouting and other groups and solidifying the BSA. Seton was especially active and helpful in this first year. Following Baden-Powell's model, the BSA leaders held an experimental summer camp late in the summer of 1910 at Silver Bay, New York. This camp was really a demonstration project of Seton and his Tribe of Woodcraft Indians' skills, sponsored by the committee on organization. Baden-Powell himself traveled to America in 1910. His visit featured a dinner in late September 1910 in New York City, giving considerable impetus to the American movement. In September–October 1910, the committee on organization was establishing a national council. Sixty-two names were suggested, and, as the BSA's historian argued, the effectiveness of the BSA was reflected in the quality and respectability of the men joining the first council. Among the initial members were Colonel Leonard Wood, the military leader, Elmer E. Brown, the federal commissioner of education, and philanthropist Mortimer Schiff. President William Howard Taft accepted the position of honorary president of the national council. By February 1911, the national council had grown to seventy-five members, including prominent physician Dr. Richard C. Cabot of Boston, a pioneer in medical social services, Homer Folks, the former commissioner of public charities for New York City and executive secretary of the State Charities Aid Association of New York, the author Hamlin Garland, leading juvenile court judge and reformer Benjamin Lindsey, and Progressive reformers Gifford Pinchot and Oscar S. Straus, a philanthropist identified with the movement to improve the quality of milk for urban children. Meanwhile, on October 25, 1910, the three incorporators, including Boyce and Livingstone, met in Washington, D.C., organized themselves, and elected the first board of managers, each of whom was active in the movement before. The board soon adopted a constitution, which provided for the officers—a president, three vice-presidents, an executive secretary, a treasurer, and a chief scout. The annual meeting was to be held in Washington, D.C., on the second Tuesday of each year.

On October 27, 1910, the committee on organization gave its records and responsibilities to the BSA. The board of managers accepted the materials. Leading social workers in New York and Washington, D.C., urged the appointment of a young lawyer concerned with child welfare, James E. West, as a permanent executive secretary. Himself an orphan, West was especially interested in child welfare work in the Progressive era. He was active in the YMCA of the District of Columbia and in the Washington Playground Association, and he helped to convene the first White House Conference on the Care of Dependent

Children in 1909 through his friend, President Theodore Roosevelt. West and the executive committee agreed to a temporary six-month period of his services, but, as West related the story, the six-month period never ended. In late 1910, the board of managers became the executive board, and Livingstone was elected as the first president of the BSA. On January 2, 1911, West opened the first office in New York City with a staff of seven people.

Under West's skillful executive leadership, the BSA grew and prospered. The field service begin in 1910, and within two years, there were scouts in every state. The first annual meeting in February 1911 was held at the White House, at the invitation of President Taft, the honorary president of the BSA. In 1913, the two major journals, *Scouting* and *Boy's Life,* began to appear. Before 1915, the BSA had concentrated its fund raising on individual solicitations. Philanthropists such as Mortimer Schiff supported the BSA during these early years. In 1911, the BSA initiated its supply service for the official BSA equipment. In 1912, Baden-Powell again toured the United States, noting that the BSA needed at least four field workers to serve the growing nationwide organization effectively. In 1913, the BSA began to push for a federal charter. Through the support of Senator Hoke Smith of Georgia, the BSA obtained a federal charter on June 15, 1916. To conform to the charter, the BSA adopted a new constitution on February 9, 1917, and in the next few weeks, it modified the structure slightly. In 1911, the BSA leaders developed and crystallized the BSA oath, and they established the principle of individual scouts' performing a daily good turn. This last feature established the basis for the BSA's involvement in social services and civic improvement. During this early period, scouts assisted victims of floods in Ohio and Indiana in the spring of 1913, cooperated with the ANRC, and assisted at the inauguration of President Woodrow Wilson in Washington in March 1913. These efforts apparently influenced the Congress and the president to act favorably on the organization's request for a federal charter.

After the enactment of the federal charter in 1916, the BSA continually expanded its programs for boys and crystallized its adult leadership activities. In 1922, the Order of the Arrow for scouts and leaders with superior skills became an official program experiment, and in 1926, the national executive board authorized development of a program for younger boys—the Cub Scouts, launched formally in 1930. The first college course in scouting, held at Teachers College in New York City in 1916, was the first of an incredible array of leadership programs.

BSA social services and civic improvement activities became widely known in the World War I period. Like the Camp Fire Girls* (CFG), the BSA placed its resources at the service of the federal government and its war effort. The BSA operated under the slogan "Help Win the War." It participated vigorously in liberty loan drives, visiting over ten million homes, and it cooperated generally with the ANRC. The BSA also developed food and fuel conservation projects, as well as so-called war gardens. In 1918, after the armistice, the BSA provided nationwide services during the devastating influenza epidemic. Following the death of Chief Scout Citizen Theodore Roosevelt on January 6, 1919, scouts began the practice of planting Roosevelt memorial trees and of making pilgrimages to his home and grave in Oyster Bay, New York. In 1919, the United States Department of Labor invited the BSA to assist in its Americanization program. This activity, coupled with the BSA reverence for the militant Colonel Roosevelt, the enthusiastic support of the war effort, the nationalistic uniforms, ideals, and slogans, and other patriotic activities prompted a number of people in the first decade of the BSA's history to view the organization as a militaristic, nationalistic agency, not necessarily characteristic of the leading social service agencies and of social justice reformers during the Progressive era. For instance, an article in *The Survey,* the leading social work journal and a voice for social justice, argued that millions of Americans saw the BSA as a "training school for the militia."

In the 1920s and 1930s, BSA social services were chiefly responses to disasters. Despite its air of militarism and dedication to the tough outdoor life, the BSA also demonstrated some sensitivity to the underprivileged and handicapped. Almost from the beginning, physically handicapped scouts were part of the program. In 1924, the first achievement badges were earned by such boy scouts. In 1934, in response to a request by President Franklin Delano Roosevelt in a radio address on February 10, the BSA performed a nationwide good turn, collecting nearly two million items of clothing, foodstuffs, supplies, and such for the troubled and the needy. More characteristic of the BSA social services were the assistance rendered after the roof fell in at the Knickerbocker Theater in Washington, D.C., and the aid during floods at Pueblo, Colorado, and San Antonio, Texas, in 1921. In 1925, scouts assisted in such disasters as the tornado in Illinois, an earthquake in California, and a major fire in Louisiana. In 1927, they helped victims of floods along the Mississippi River. In 1930, Chief Scout Executive West served as chairman of the committee on youth outside the home and school for the White House Conference on Child Health and Protection. In 1934, the BSA especially emphasized its health program for boys. In 1936, the American Children's Fund granted the BSA $100,000 in recognition of its health and safety programs.

The BSA enthusiastically assisted the American war effort in the 1940s. As early as 1940, it adopted a program for helping in national emergency and military defense programs. The BSA also established its emergency service corps in 1940. Activities in 1941 included the distribution of defense bonds and stamp posters, the collection of aluminum and wastepaper, surveys of defense housing, victory gardens, the distribution of air-raid posters, cooperation with the ANRC, and by joint agreement with the federal Office of Civil and Defense Mobilization, BSA services in three areas: delivering messages, assisting emergency medical units, and, in recognition of BSA outdoor skills, watching for fires. In 1942, the BSA conducted a concentrated drive for salvage, based on the government-issued pamphlet, *Scrap and How Scouts Collect It.* Scouts also worked on farms and harvest camps to aid the war effort. In 1946, boy scouts carried out three national postwar service projects requested by the government. In the mid-1940s, highlights included the development of a formal conservation program. In 1945, for instance, scouts distributed circulars on conservation projects, and the BSA inaugurated its Green Thumb program. In 1945, 20,000 scouts earned the General Douglas MacArthur Medal for growing food. In 1949, the BSA adopted new procedures for handicapped boys, whereby local councils would determine the requirements for their advancement—a policy that allowed for more flexibility in the requirements.

In the period from 1950 to the 1960s, a generally conservative era in the United States, the BSA continued its characteristic social services and civic improvements as programs implementing the good turn principle. Conservation programs expanded in the early 1950s. Consistent with the nationwide concern for civil defense, the BSA conducted activities in this area. In 1951, the BSA collected two million pounds of clothing for domestic and foreign relief. In 1952, scouts cooperated nationwide in securing blood donors' pledges. In 1954, the national office moved from New York City to a new building in North Brunswick, New Jersey. The organization participated regularly in nonpartisan, get-out-the-vote campaigns. Characteristic of this era in American life, the national Safety Good Turn and the Onward for God and My Country programs were outstanding successes. In 1968, the BSA adopted BOYPOWER '76, an eight-year program to increase the number of scouts.

Some of the social issues of the 1970s provided the substance for BSA activities. In 1970, for example, the BSA mobilized for Save Our American Resources (Project SOAR). In the fall of 1971, Operation Reach against drug abuse was begun nationwide. Also in 1971, the BSA inaugurated a new paraprofessional plan. The BSA also participated regularly in Keep American Beautiful days and programs in the 1970s.

The sources for studying the BSA's history are voluminous. The published *Annual Reports* are detailed. The BSA archives are located at the national headquarters in North Brunswick, New Jersey. The archives are open to properly qualified students. The various serial publications, such as *Scouting,* provide information about the organization, as do a host of contemporary agency pamphlets and journal articles.

A detailed historical study by an active participant is *The History of the Boy Scouts of America* (1937) by William D. Murray. Fulton Ousler, *The Boy Scout Story* (1953), is a popular history. The BSA gave me a year-by-year account of the highlights, an obviously helpful document. Roy Lubove's sketch of James West in *The Dictionary of American Biography,* Supplement 4 (1974), 871–873, is an informative and interesting piece. Surprisingly, there does not appear to be scholarly historical studies of the BSA.

For details of BSA merit badges, jamborees, training courses, campsites, handclasps, expeditions, national conferences, and such, see the entry for the BSA in *Fraternal Organizations.*

BOYS' CLUBS OF AMERICA, INC. (BCA). In 1860, a group of civic-minded women in Hartford, Connecticut, established the first boys' club. The Dashaway Club, as it was called, was reorganized in 1880 as the Good Will Boys' Club, but the first organization to use the term ''boys' club'' was the one on the Lower East Side in New York City. Edward Henry Harrison, an industrial leader and railroad magnate, organized this group after a young boy hit him with a rock thrown through a window at the Wilson Industrial School for Girls, a Lower East Side religious and charitable institution. Harrison's motives helped to establish the long-standing boys' club work in preventing juvenile delinquency. In the late nineteenth century, boys' clubs developed throughout other cities in the East and Northeast. Various boys' clubs leaders made plans in the late nineteenth and early twentieth centuries to establish a national organization, a federation of existing clubs. Only in 1906, however, did such efforts succeed, partly because of the dedication of such leaders as Thomas Chew, who headed the club in Fall River, Massachusetts, David Armstrong, who was the director of the club in Worcester, Massachusetts, and C. J. Atkinson, who had been active in work with boys in Toronto, Canada, for many years. Finally, at a meeting of club leaders to discuss common problems and plans to establish a national organization, on May 18, 1906, in Boston, Massachusetts, the Boys' Clubs of America (BCA) was established as the Federated Boys' Clubs (FBC).

The group of founders worked to establish a structure and to develop a respectable national organization. The group elected as its first president Jacob Riis, whose name was synonymous with the troubled plight of urban children in the nineteenth and early twentieth centuries. A police reporter, author of the classic *How the Other Half Lives* (1885), active in the housing, playground, and other urban Progressive reform movements, Riis became the first in a succession of prominent American men who were associated with the organization. The group also elected other traditional officers—vice-president, treasurer, and secretary—and chose a seven-member executive committee, which included Chew and William R. George, the founder and head of the George Junior Republic, a unique experiment in a rural setting in upstate New York in dealing with troublesome boys from the city. Such prominent social workers as Ernest K. Coulter, who founded the Children's Court in New York City in 1902 and who later headed the New York Society for the Prevention of Cruelty to Children,* Benjamin Lindsey, the pioneer juvenile court judge from Denver, and Rabbi Stephen Wise, who participated in a host of social reform agencies and movements, joined the first, twelve-member board of directors. Until 1914, the organization lacked a permanent executive director, but local club workers, especially some founders, worked to keep the struggling national organization alive. Some important organizational developments occurred within a few years. In 1914, when C. J. Atkinson became the first executive director, he moved the headquarters from Boston to New York City, where they have remained. In 1915, the agency became the Boys' Clubs Federation (BCF). In 1916, the former treasurer, government servant, and corporation lawyer, William Edwin Hall, became the president of the organization. In 1929, the organization changed its name to become the Boys' Club Federation of America (BCFA).

Hall's long presidency—he retired in 1954—laid the basis for the agency to become a leading, successful national group. Hall determined that the board of directors needed to attract even more well-known national leaders than Rabbi Wise and Judge Lindsey. The organization lacked both a national public relations department and a formal field service, but President Hall and Executive Director Atkinson themselves toured the country to publicize the BCF, to strengthen affiliates, and to develop new ones. To promote development in the South, the BCF held its annual convention in 1928 in Birmingham, Alabama. In 1930, the organization established regional committees to bring club executives and workers closer together.

More important developments occurred in the 1930s, strengthening significantly the structure and national reputation of the organization. At the 1931 annual meeting, the members changed the name of the agency to the Boys' Clubs of America, Inc. (BCA), which became official at the beginning of 1932. The organization lost a dedicated and important worker when Executive Director Atkinson—known affectionately as "CJ"—resigned. The BCA continued to grow nevertheless. A trip to New England in the early 1930s convinced President Hall of the need for closer relations between the local affiliates and the national organization. Beginning in the mid-1930s, the field staff paid numerous visits to affiliates, providing advice and guidance in a variety of ways. In the fall of 1935, the BCA approved a "national-mile-post-plan" for five years beginning in 1936 to raise funds. In 1936, former United States President Herbert Hoover joined the BCA as the chairman of the national board of directors. Hoover became especially interested in the agency, and he attended all but one of its board meetings. When he joined the BCA, he brought with him as executive director Sanford Bates, a former president of the American Prison Association* and the former head of the federal Bureau of Prisons, who served the BCA from 1936 to 1940. Another major event occurred on December 9, 1935, when the BCA held its thirtieth anniversary dinner in Boston. The paid registrants numbered over three times what the planners had expected, suggesting the increased popularity and enthusiasm for both the boys' club movement and its chief promoter, the BCA. Reflecting again both the commitment to the movement and to the BCA and the success of national organizing strengths, not one local boys' club terminated its activities or its affiliation with the BCA during the depression of the 1930s.

In the 1940s, the organization began to attract businessmen and conservatives rather than, as earlier, social activitists and progressives. Indeed, since about the late 1930s, the BCA—clearly an important youth-serving agency—seemed to cooperate more with officials from judicial and law enforcement agencies than with colleagues from child care organizations like the Child Welfare League of America* and the United States Children's Bureau. National board members have tended to be businessmen, including some from large corporations, rather than social activists. This trend was likely the result of the influence of President Hall and Herbert Hoover, a self-made man himself, who throughout his career generally felt comfortable with these kinds of leaders. In the early 1940s, the organization established the national associates of the BCA, composed of prominent local leaders who used their influence to attract contributions and other forms of support. The BCA sent letters, signed by Herbert Hoover in 1941, to such leaders to add enthusiasm for these campaigns. In 1941, the former commissioner of public welfare in Massachusetts, BCA founder David W. Armstrong, began to serve as national director, a position he held until 1956. Under him, the organization gained national attention. To resolve some organizational problems, particularly those relating to local fund raising, in late 1941, the BCA hired its first field representative in finance. During World War II, Armstrong initiated the concept of victory volunteers, using boys' clubs to raise food, collect salvage, prepare games for the wounded, expand clubs' swimming and life-saving programs, and participate in war bond drives. Armstrong strengthened the organizational structure of the BCA, establishing regional offices and developing a service to recruit, train, and place boys' club workers. He also developed both a pension plan for the staff and a formal public relations program. Suggesting its shift away from its earlier ties to the social justice movement, the BCA, led by Armstrong, ridded itself of settlement house boys' clubs and other such organizations considered not truly boys' clubs by the BCA leaders. These efforts culminated in the adoption at the annual convention in 1944 of a new constitution, dropping 150 such local affiliates.

By 1950, largely a result of the efforts of such leaders as Armstrong and Hoover, the BCA was a well-established national agency. In 1954, Hall retired as president, convincing his friend, Albert L. Cole, a writer and publisher, to fill the office. On August 6, 1956, the BCA received a federal charter from the United States Congress, incorporated according to the laws of the District of Columbia, and began to provide, as stipulated in the charter, annual reports and financial statements to both the speaker of the House of Representatives and the vice-president of the United States in his capacity as president of the Senate. Indeed, 1956 proved to be an important year for the BCA. The field service added thirty-six new clubs and coordinated the activities of seven regional offices. The Center for Community Study and Field Service of New York University began a study of the effectiveness of boys' clubs services in reducing juvenile delinquency, a major nationwide concern in the 1950s. And the United States Department of Defense designated the BCA as an educational activity of special interest, making it eligible to receive government surpluses. Through the years, these gifts have been important to boys' club work. Continuing its involvement in preparing trained personnel for local clubs, in 1956, the BCA received a grant of over $60,000 from the Lilly Endowment for scholarships to students interested in boys' club work, an ongoing program. Later in the decade, in 1958, with the cooperation of the National Dairy Council, the BCA initiated a pilot study to determine the most effective way to use health educational materials to influence the boys. Continuing to serve the field, the BCA conducted institutes and seminars, and in 1958, it began a major research project, supported by funds from the Grant Foundation Inc., to determine the needs and interests of boys' club members aged seven to eighteen years old. An organizational highlight occurred in 1958, when, for the first time in its history, the BCA's Boy of the Year met the president of the United States. The BCA acquired a building on First Avenue in New York City, opposite the United Nations, for its new national headquarters, which it called, appropriately, The Herbert Hoover Building.

During the 1960s, although the BCA continued to court corporate support, it also participated in the expansion of social services so central to those years. In 1960, the agency dedicated its new building in New York. Continuing another service to the field, in 1962, it began its management training program to serve affiliates. The death of Herbert Hoover in 1964 signaled the end of an era of the BCA. In that year, the BCA initiated the Herbert Hoover Memorial Fund, headed by James F. Farley, the former postmaster general of the United States. Also in this period, the BCA appointed two committees to work with the staffs of the field service and the finance service respectively: the national committee for the expansion of boys' clubs and the national committee for the corporate support of the BCA. A ten-year plan, adopted in 1964, sought to add one thousand clubs, and in the next three years, the active and energetic field service and its volunteer advisers added clubs at the rate of one per week. Operation lift-up, a project of the 1960s, encouraged boys to stay in school.

Volunteers continued important activities in the BCA. For instance, prominent men on the national board worked with the staff to develop services in areas not yet reached by the BCA and the boys' club movement. Responding to the urban riots of the late 1960s, in the fall of 1967, the BCA held a conference on how local clubs, particularly those located in inner city neighborhoods, could be effective in times of social unrest. During the riots of 1967, not a single BCA affiliate was damaged. Many clubs' services and programs qualified for and received federal funds for the disadvantaged. In the late 1960s, for example, an affiliate in San Francisco conducted a project funded by the federal Office of Economic Opportunity to develop indigenous leadership in a depressed area of the city. To provide ties with federal funding programs, in 1969, the BCA established its department of special services. This department, for instance, coordinated federal assistance for local boys' clubs programs in depressed areas, which provided lunches and dinners for the boys, an activity the BCA had initiated even before federal funds became available. Such services and programs prompted the associate director of the United Community Funds and Council of America, Inc.,* Charles X. Sampson, to argue in 1967 that boys' clubs were in the right place at the right time, "serving the inner core areas of the large urban communities." Sampson further described boys' clubs as providing "such vital services." A set of goals adopted in 1969 established guidelines for the BCA in the 1970s: to develop new personnel, to develop programs to motivate boys, to provide more services to local affiliates, to focus on the problems of the inner cities, and to raise more money in the next five years.

In the 1970s, while maintaining its interest in character building and in instilling fundamental American values as well as continuing its ties to the business community, the BCA continued to develop some important social services! It continued to provide leadership in the boys' club field. With support from the J. Edgar Hoover Fund, the BCA in 1971 launched Operation Respect to promote citizen education. Social services of the BCA in the 1970s addressed some of the basic needs of urban youths. In the early 1970s, the BCA founded its urban services to help the organization become more sensitive than before to such issues as population mobility and community organization. In 1973, with funds totaling $500,000, the BCA began its urban fellowship training program for local staffs and boards. Located in Chicago, the training center had the former mayor of Cleveland, Carl Stokes, as a consultant. A grant from the United States Department of Labor in 1972 helped to initiate a demonstration project in career exploration and work training experience for older boys. One of the most significant projects in the BCA's history was the Robert Wood Johnson Foundation health survey. It showed the need for health care services for disadvantaged youth, stressing boys' clubs' central locations as the core of the delivery of these services. In 1975, the BCA founded its national task force on delinquency prevention, which included figures from the judicial and academic communities as well as boys' club professionals. Throughout the 1970s, National Director William R. Bricker, a boys' club professional and an authority on juvenile delinquency, served in a number of advisory capacities, and he became chairman of the National Collaboration for Youth, an alliance of leading youth-serving agencies. The BCA also worked in 1975 with the Law Enforcement Assistance Administration in writing the guidelines for implementing the Juvenile Justice and Delinquency Prevention Act of 1974. Consistent with the ideals and activities of the founders of the boys' club movement and of the BCA, the BCA worked to prevent juvenile delinquency by providing some basic and innovative social services for young boys, especially in inner cities.

The primary sources for the history of the BCA include the Papers of Herbert Hoover and oral history transcripts of BCA leaders at the Herbert Hoover Presidential Library in West Branch, Iowa, and the files of the BCA, stored in the headquarters in New York City. These records are closed to the public and are available only to qualified scholars. More accessible but nevertheless difficult to locate, are the published *Annual Reports* of the agency, which apparently began to appear in the 1930s. William Edwin Hall, the long-time president of the BCA, wrote a self-serving but still helpful history, *100 Years and Millions of Boys: The Dynamic Story of the Boys' Clubs of America* (1961). There apparently is no scholarly history of the BCA.

BRETHREN SERVICE COMMISSION (BSC).   After World War I, there had been organized a Brethren committee for relief and rehabilitation activities, but unlike the contemporary American Friends Service Committee* (AFSC) and the Mennonite Central Committee* (MCC), the Brethren group dissolved quickly. During the Spanish Civil War in the 1930s, the Church of the Brethren (see *Religious Institutions*) conducted relief work. Beginning in 1937, for example, the Brethrens cooperated with the AFSC and the MCC, especially to help children. These developments prompted interest in a permanent relief organization. Consequently, in November 1939, the Brethrens established the Brethren Service Committee (BSC) as a joint executive committee serving two boards of the Church of the Brethren, the Board of Christian Education, and the General Mission Board for relief and peace work. Two important principles prompted and continued to inspire the BSC: that brotherhood should be practiced and that war is contrary to God's will.

The BSC's early structure featured a five-member executive committee, with two representatives from each board and one person from outside the two boards. In December 1940, a special meeting in Chicago dealing with the military draft appointed a subcommittee to study the BSC. The subcommittee's report to the church's annual conference in 1941 at La Verne, California, reconstituted the BSC as a permanent and major board of the church. The new structure included five members at large, approved by the annual conference for five-year periods, and one each from the four other church boards appointed ex officio to serve for one-year terms. The BSC received its charter in 1941. The BSC office was established at the church headquarters in Elgin, Illinois, a Chicago surburb.

The earliest years of the BSC's activities, 1941–1945, concentrated on work for the Civilian Public Service, (CPS), a project conducted by the so-called peace churches—the Brethrens, Quakers, and Mennonites—to provide alternative activities to the military for conscientious objectors. The BSC's CPS camps were generally located in former camps of the Civilian Conservation Corps of the 1930s, with the largest number of Brethren groups in forest service. The BSC participated in soil conservation programs and in public health projects, especially in Florida to eliminate hookworm, and as experimental subjects in a human starvation study at the University of Minnesota. The important findings of these projects helped to shape postwar relief and rehabilitation activities. Many men on the CPS program, however, refused to do emergency farm labor because they feared the food would be used for military purposes. By 1943, a number of participants felt their work was not socially important, so the BSC began to establish service units in mental hospitals and in training schools for the mentally deficient. Shocked by the conditions and treatment in the institutions, the BSC, with the AFSC and the MCC—both of which did similar work in mental facilities—formed the National Mental Health Foundation* in 1946. Beginning in 1946, BSC workers served as "seagoing cowboys," attending the cattle and horses shipped overseas by the United Nations Relief and Rehabilitation Administration (UNRRA). During the war, the BSC was barred from service in afflicted areas, but the agency did begin medical, public health, and community services in Puerto Rico during this period.

After the end of the war in 1945, the BSC began to focus on relief and rehabilitation abroad. During the years of postwar reconstruction, the largest proportion of BSC funds was spent on overseas relief and rehabilitation, principally in Europe. Beginning in 1940 and through 1948, the BSC participated with the National Council of the Young Men's Christian Association of the United States of America* (YMCA) in a project aiding German war prisoners in England. This program, to which the BSC contributed personnel and which the YMCA directed, was also conducted in Belgium and Germany. In Carrarra, Italy, the BSC formed a children's club, and under the auspices of the World Council of Churches and many denominations, the BSC participated in agricultural rehabilitation in Greece. Germany, the country where the Brethrens were founded, was the major area of activities, beginning in 1946. The BSC sent all types of supplies there, and it became a charter member of the Council of Relief Agencies Licensed to Operate in Germany. Activities in Germany expanded by 1948; the BSC coordinated a youth rehabilitation project that established a well-publicized village for homeless teenage boys. The BSC also expended considerable efforts in Austria, establishing a diverse program that featured the distribution of all types of materials, a nursery and a kindergarten for refugee children, and a vocational school for refugee boys. The BSC helped to establish a hospital for tubercular refugees and conducted a general public health program in refugee camps in Austria. Asian and African services were limited. In 1947, with the UNRRA, the BSC began to teach Chinese farmers how to use tractors, a disappointing effort. The job of reeducating these farmers was too enormous a task. In Africa, in late 1950, the BSC provided staff members at the Asaba Rural Training Center in Nigeria, a project with the Brethren's Foreign Mission Commission and many other Protestant agencies. In Latin America, efforts continued in Puerto Rico. With the AFSC, the BSC developed a project in the mountain village of Huitzilac, Mexico. This project, which closed in 1946, provided first aid and simple medical treatments. In the early 1940s, in the capital city of Quito, Ecuador, the BSC established a boys' club. Terminated in 1947, this project fulfilled a basic BSC tenet that indigenous groups assume responsibility for projects.

During its first decade, the BSC also conducted an impressive program of relief and rehabilitation in the United States. In 1942, the group decided to implement what became the famous Heifer for Relief project, which sent animals to Puerto Rico and to Mexico and to sharecroppers in Arkansas, beginning in 1944. Also in 1944, the BSC obtained the property of the former Blue Ridge College in New Windsor, Maryland. The BSC developed this as a center for collection, distribution, training, conferences, and the heifer projects, and as a reception center for refugees and displaced persons, which the BSC helped to settle in the United States. This facility, which other denominations utilized, became the symbol of Protestant overseas aid in the late 1940s. The BSC had other, smaller centers, including one at Nappanee, Indiana, which featured a soap factory. In 1944, the BSC initiated its appeal for relief abroad. During the war, the BSC aided Japanese in the United States who were forced to relocate from the West Coast, establishing hostels in Chicago and Brooklyn, New York, as temporary shelters. A project to help Spanish-speaking people of Mexican origin in Falfurrias, Texas, began in 1946. An important organizational development was the formation of the Brethren Volunteer Service (BVS), initiated by youths at the church's annual conference in Colorado Springs, Colorado, in 1948.

This BVS conducted a number of worthwhile projects, for instance, rehabilitating two depressed communities in California and serving at a federal women's reformatory. A similar program for domestic social action was the series of summer work camps for youths. Their efforts included community organization in South Modesto, California, aiding black migrants in Fresno, California, and a pilot project in Baltimore, Maryland, in cooperation with the city's Housing Bureau to demonstrate how deteriorated housing could be rehabilitated. In 1946, the annual conference of the church transferred peace activities from the Board of Christian Education to the BSC. The BSC added two staff positions in peace at its national headquarters and sponsored peace conferences and institutes in the late 1940s. At a session in Salina, Kansas, in 1947, a group of youths decided to conduct peace caravans. For the next three years, the young people traveled throughout the United States, visiting churches and promoting the idea of peace.

A reorganization of the BSC occurred in the mid-1940s. In 1946–1947, the church reshaped itself into one governing body, the General Brotherhood Board, with five subdivisions, one of which was the BSC. Renamed the Brethren Service Commission (BSC) in 1947, the agency was now responsible to the General Brotherhood Board rather than, as earlier, to the annual conference. Budget cuts in 1949 reduced the BSC's staff and program.

In the 1950s and 1960s, under the leadership of Dr. W. Harold Row, the BSC continued its basic programs of overseas aid and peace work, but it branched out to include domestic activities. BSC peace work, for instance, cooperated especially in programs with Eastern and Russian Orthodox church groups. During this period, the BSC renewed and continued an agricultural exchange program with Poland. Through major activities by the staff, the BSC worked in the field of race relations. This activity featured Reverend Ralph E. Smeltzer's efforts in Selma, Alabama, in the mid-1960s. The BSC expanded its Brethren Service Center in New Windsor, Maryland, to include material aid collection centers on behalf of Church World Service* and other denominational agencies. Through the activities of Dr. Row, the BSC participated in the beginnings of International Voluntary Services, an agency headquartered in Washington, D.C., which helped to influence the development of the federal Peace Corps. The BSC ended its existence as a separate agency in 1968, when during a reorganization of the church structure, it was incorporated with the foreign mission program under a World Ministries Commission. Many of the traditional activities continued under this new structure.

The primary sources for studying the BSC's history include the reports of the agency in the conference reports of the Church of the Brethren. An agency publication, Lorell Weiss, *Ten Years of Brethren Service, 1951–1951* (n.d.), is helpful. The files of the agency are deposited at the Historical Library at Elgin, Illinois.

Roger E. Sappington, *Brethren Social Policy, 1908–1958* (1961), has a few references to the BSC. There does not appear to be a scholarly history of the BSC.

BUREAU OF JEWISH SOCIAL RESEARCH (BJSR). In 1914, in an effort to understand the diverse nature of organizational life in the American Jewish community, the American Jewish Committee (AJC) (see *Political and Civic Organizations*) organized its bureau of statistics and research to gather data from all types of Jewish organizations. In 1916, the National Conference of Jewish Charities* (NCJC) founded its field bureau to visit Jewish communities and to advise their leaders about communal and philanthropic problems. The third predecessor agency of the Bureau of Jewish Social Research (BJSR) was the Bureau of Philanthropic Research of New York City, founded in 1916 by the New York Kehillah, an Old World community structure, to study Jewish social work in New York City. The leaders of these three agencies gradually saw the similarity of their work, and they decided to consolidate their efforts. Consequently, in New York City in 1919, the BJSR was established generally to promote Jewish social and communal services in the United States.

To fulfill the activities of its predecessors, the BJSR established, early in its history, its department of surveys, which carried on the work of the former field bureau of the NCJC. Its division of investigations conducted brief studies for local federations, for organizations, and even for individuals. In 1922, it conducted and then published the results of a study of the general condition and care of dependent Jewish children in New York City, a continuing social problem for the community. In 1920, the BJSR created its department of information and research, which conducted work similar to that of the AJC group. This department, for example, cooperated with the United States Bureau of the Census in its census of religious bodies, issued in 1926.

Increasingly in the late 1920s, however, the BJSR wanted to focus on Jewish social work, so on January 1, 1928, the work of the department of information and research was transferred back to the AJC. Community surveys remained the heart of the BJSR's work. Beginning in early 1923, the BJSR organized local citizens' groups to cooperate with surveys. Such surveys included, for instance, one of Greater New York, and of particular problems, such as ones on child care in Philadelphia, New York, and Chicago. In the 1920s, the BJSR also conducted an analysis of medical services in Passaic, New Jersey, and one on delinquency in Cincinnati, Pittsburgh, and New York. With the famous Milford Conference of social caseworkers, founded in 1922, the BJSR conducted a special study of the social problems in Erie, Pennsylvania. It also analyzed and reported on national organizations for the National Appeals Information Service, created in 1926 to provide data about national Jewish agencies for local communities to use in determining their donations. In the 1920s, all requests to The Charity Organization Society of the City of New York* (COS) about Jewish agencies were forwarded to the BJSR, which had a similar arrangement with the National Information Bureau, with the New York State Board of Charities, and occasionally, with the State Department of Institutions and Agencies in New Jersey, the public welfare department. Many studies resulted in the formation of local federations of Jewish social service and other appropriate agencies. In a midwestern community, for instance, a BJSR survey prompted the establishment of a Jewish hospital. To a large degree, the BJSR, although nationwide in its scope, was a research agent for the New York Federation for the Support of Jewish Philanthropic Societies. The list of BJSR studies on specific issues in New York City is impressive. Its project included a survey of the Jewish blind in New York, an analysis of the casework of the Jewish Board of Guardians* (JBG), and a feasibility study of a possible combined federation between New York and Brooklyn in delinquency, child care, hospitals, and relief.

The steady expansion of the BJSR's activities in the 1920s prompted further organizational growth. For the surveys, the agency utilized experts in appropriate fields, adding them temporarily to the staff. In September 1928, the BJSR established its field service, adding to the staff a director of field service. In his first seven months of work, he visited thirty-eight cities in nine states, contacting Jewish social workers, community chest officials, and family welfare agency executives. In October 1928, the statistical department established a reporting system that encouraged agencies and hospitals to send monthly statements of their work. There was a moderately sized professional staff in 1929, and the organizational structure included a twenty-member board of trustees from throughout the country. The four traditional officers of president, vice-president, treasurer, and secretary sat on the board, along with sixteen others, including, from Philadelphia, Cyrus Adler, a prominent educator and communal figure, William J. Shroder, a civic leader from Cincinnati who was the first president of the National Council of Jewish Federations and Welfare Funds* (NCJFWF), and Mrs. Sidney Borg of New York, who was active in a host of charities, such as the JBG and the Big Brother and Big Sister Federation.* There was an eight-member executive committee, including Lee K. Frankel, the former manager of the United Hebrew Charities of the City of New York* and a leading Jewish social worker.

Although headquartered in New York City, where many of its surveys and activities took place, the BJSR continued to provide nationwide services in the 1930s. In 1930, for instance, it was collecting monthly statistics from Jewish agencies operating in five major fields of welfare, such as child care and homes for the aged. The agency also conducted special studies on the effect of the depression on local Jewish federations and another one on the cost of child care agencies. Partly because of the influence of Associate Director George Rabinoff, an important figure in Jewish social work, the BJSR became the service agency of the National Committee on Transients of the now named National Conference of Jewish Social Service* (NCJSS). In March 1930, the BJSR became the central office for collecting information about transients in sixty cities. Providing an important service to the field of Jewish social work, the BJSR built up a library of case records, which it offered to the professors and students at the Training School for Jewish Social Work. Also in 1930, the BJSR established its personnel committee to deal with the problem of job placement for Jewish social workers. Demonstrating the value of its services to both national and local social service agencies, in 1930, for example, the BJSR completed a study of the National Desertion Bureau* (NDB) and another of the proposal for a tuberculosis sanitarium in Asheville, North Carolina. The BJSR also participated actively in the work of the National Council of Jewish Institutions to improve relations between national and local agencies. The structure of the BJSR in the early 1930s included an honorary president, Adolph Lewisohn, a prominent merchant and philanthropist who was active in other social agencies, a president, two vice-presidents, a treasurer, and a secretary. The newly named board of directors numbered fourteen members in 1930, including Cyrus Sulzberger, a leader of the Jewish Social Service Association* (JSSA) of New York, Cyrus Adler, and Mrs. Borg. Among the staff were thirteen consultants for surveys of special studies. Three of these in 1930 were Dr. Haven Emerson, the former New York City commissioner of health, associate editor of *The Survey,* and a professor of public health at Columbia University, Frances Taussig, an important Jewish social worker and executive director of the JSSA, and Jacob Kepecs, another prominent figure who specialized in child welfare.

During the early 1930s, before it merged with the NCJFWF in 1935, the BJSR was especially active. At the height of public concern and debate about the issue, in early 1933, the organization completed and issued a report on homeless boys and young men in New York City. In January 1931, because of the effects of the depression, the BJSR organized the Continuing Committee of Jewish Family Welfare Executives to discuss the social problems related to the depression. During this period the BJSR, with the cooperation of the Research Bureau of the New York State Department of Welfare, collected materials on the problems of Jewish dependency in the state. At the request of a committee of social agencies, the BJSR began to study ways of dealing with husbands charged with not supporting their children. In mid-1933, the BJSR prepared a report on the status of the Jewish social worker for a committee of the NCJSS dealing with this subject. In late June, the BJSR began a study of the Cleveland Welfare Association for Jewish Children. The BJSR obtained Ethel Taylor of the New York School of Social Work as a consultant for this project. Continuing its interest in transients and the homeless, a concern probably resulting from Rabinoff's influence, the BJSR participated in a variety of programs and agencies dealing with this problem. In late 1933, as Jewish organizations began to deal with the ominous events in Adolf Hitler's Germany, the BJSR obtained information about placing German-Jewish children in the United States, and it prepared materials to help coordinate national Jewish agencies and services. The BJSR also completed some studies and considerably helped the NCJFWF to prepare for its general assembly in Chicago in early January 1934. In the mid-1930s, the BJSR continued its basic activities, moving steadily closer to the NCJFWF, which it joined in 1935. This action ended the BJSR's brief but important sixteen-year history.

The sources for studying the history of the BJSR include its published *Annual Reports* for the later period. Also helpful is the National Appeals Information Service, *Bureau of Jewish Social Research* (May 1929). There are items relating to the BJSR in the Papers of Harry Lurie at the Social Welfare History Archives Center at the University of Minnesota, Minneapolis, and in the George Rabinoff Papers at the American Jewish Historical Society at Waltham, Massachusetts.

Harry Lurie mentions the BJSR briefly in *A Heritage Affirmed: The Jewish Federation Movement in America* (1961), but there does not appear to be a scholarly history of the organization.

C

CYO FEDERATION, NATIONAL (NCYOF). During the early stages of the Great Depression, Auxiliary Bishop of Chicago Bernard J. Sheil served as a prison chaplain. During this experience, Bishop Sheil realized the beneficial effects on prisoners of an athletic program. Bishop Sheil consequently became interested in a recreational program for youth, and the boxing program he started in Chicago developed into the nationwide Golden Gloves program. George Cardinal Mundelein of Chicago directed Sheil to organize a Catholic Youth Organization (CYO) in Chicago for the spiritual, mental, and physical development of Catholic youngsters. Established in 1930, the Chicago organization became the first diocesanwide CYO. In 1932, the dioceses of Chicago established a CYO center. Catholic youth work was still in its infancy in the early 1930s, but in July 1935, the National Council of Catholic Women (NCCW) (see *Fraternal Organizations*) held the first institute for youth workers at the National Catholic School of Social Work in Washington, D.C. There was another, similar institute in 1936, when the NCCW began to sponsor other training programs for youth leaders. During this period, the NCCW added to its staff a field representative to organize diocesan youth programs throughout the country. Further development occurred in February 1937, when the bishops of the United States, represented on the administrative board of the National Catholic Welfare Conference (NCWC), authorized the establishment of a youth bureau. Consequently founded as part of the NCWC structure in Washington, D.C., the Youth Bureau served as a centralized information center for the growing number of local youth programs, some of which were called the CYO.

In 1940, Cardinal Pizzardo of the Central Office of Catholic Action expressed the need for a national Catholic youth council. In 1940, the Youth Bureau was raised to the status of a NCWC department. It had two sections, one for diocesan work like the CYOs and the other for college and university activities, such as Newman Clubs. In 1940, the newly created youth department began holding its national conferences of diocesan youth directors. Short leadership courses held in local dioceses began in 1941 by the youth department of the NCWC. On August 25, 1941, Reverend Amelto Giovanni Cicognani wrote his famous letter to diocesan youth directors explaining the theoretical and practical aspects of a proposed national youth council, and he urged its establishment. Consequently, in late 1941, the National Catholic Youth Council (NCYC) was created as part of the youth department of the NCWC. In 1941, the first professional publication appeared, *Diocesan Director's Bulletin*. World War II and the Korean War delayed further significant organizational developments on both the local and national levels. Finally, at the third national conference of Catholic youth work in November 1951, in Cincinnati, Ohio, the National CYO Federation (NCYOF) was established as the National Federation of Diocesan Catholic Youth Councils (NFDCYC). This completed the structure of the now called National Council of Catholic Youth (NCCY) of the NCWC.

Local Catholic youth organizations had been developing and growing in the decades before 1951. Basically parish based, these youth agencies provided recreational activities, camps, social events, and retreats. The local organizations were known by three different names: Catholic Youth Council, Catholic Youth Association, and, most commonly, CYO. In 1963, the national advisory board to the director of the NCWC's youth department recommended that "CYO" be used uniformly throughout the country. Local organizations voluntarily complied. As one student of the CYO wrote, the CYO was "national in scope, diocesan in authority, and parochial in function."

The national organization of the CYOs, the NFDCYC adopted a revised constitution in November 1953, changing the name of its parent body to the NCCY. The NFDCYC continued as a service agency, providing ideas for local affiliates, helping to develop new ones, and the like. In 1967, the group adopted a new constitution, calling for, among other things, a change of name to the National CYO Federation (NCYOF). The headquarters of the NYCOF were to be located in Washington, D.C., at the youth activities desk of the department of education of the newly named United States Catholic Conference, the former NCWC. The NCYOF director was to be the representative for youth activities of the USCC. The national director, in turn, appointed the full-time, paid executive director, who administered the program. The program still consisted of coordinating activities, providing resources and ideas for programs, helping to start new CYOs, sponsoring biennial conferences, and such. In the early 1970s, the focus of CYO programs shifted from basically recreational activities to address the broader concerns of youths and communities. The CYOs, for instance, conducted programs such as IMPACT and SEARCH, retreats for youngsters that featured leadership training, group dynamics, and other activities to deepen the participant's commitment to Christian religious morality. In the mid-1970s, the NCYOF sponsored Project SPERO to develop adult leadership. In 1975–1976, the NYCOF sponsored Operation SIGN (Service in God's Name). Through this project, youths volunteered for a variety of civic activities and social services, such as reading to the blind and assisting in centers for the aged.

The sources for studying the NCYOF's history are limited and difficult to locate. Marguerite T. Boylan, *Social Welfare in the Catholic Church* (1941), refers briefly to Catholic youth work. There are agency publications describing some CYO projects, such as SPERO. There is, unfortunately, very little information about the NCYOF in the *New Catholic Encyclopedia* (1967). Two in-house mimeographed brief histories provided some information, but at certain points they contradict each other: Reverend Edward Hajduk, "A History of CYO," and the more helpful Ben Debinski, "The History and Tradition of the CYO." There does not appear to be a scholarly history of the NCYOF.

CAMP FIRE GIRLS, INC. (CFG). Activities at girls' camps and other incidents in the summer of 1910 led eventually to the creation of the CFG. The most important of these activities was held at Camp Sebago, near South Casco, Maine. It was founded and led by Dr. Luther Halsey Gulick and his wife, Charlotte Vetter Gulick. Dr. Gulick was a prime mover in the creation of and the first president of the Playground Association of America* (PAA) and beginning in November 1910, the head of the department of child hygiene of the Russell Sage Foundation* (RSF). Beginning in 1909, with their children, the Gulicks conducted this camp in Maine. Influenced by discussions with Ernest Thompson Seton, naturalist, illustrator, and author who founded and led the Tribe of Woodcraft Indians, a predecessor of the Boy Scouts of America* (BSA), the Gulicks decided to weave Indian lore and ceremonial dress into the camp's program. In this ritual each child adopted an Indian name, a practice that developed as an important CFG tradition. Dr. Gulick became known as Timanous and his wife as Hiteni. The other important development in the creation of the CFG occurred in Thetford, Vermont, where, in the summer of 1910, a group of young girls watched eagerly as a group of boy scouts prepared for a pageant. William Chauncy Langdon, the consultant on pageantry at Gulick's department at the foundation, assured the girls they would have a similar organization. Another development that converged to form the CFG was the idea of Lina Beard, the sister of Dan Beard, the founder of the Society of the Sons of Daniel Boone in 1905, another predecessor of the BSA, and the editor of *Recreation,* the journal of the PAA. In the fall of 1910 and the winter of 1910–1911, the camp experiences and the idea of a girls' organization were constantly discussed at the offices of the RSF and at the nearby offices of the BSA, headed by James West, an important child care worker in the Progressive era.

All of these events led a group of educators, group workers, physicians, and social workers to meet on March 22, 1911, at the Horace Mann School at Teachers College of Columbia University in New York City to establish the Camp Fire Girls of America (CFGA). Among those present at the founding meeting were Dr. Gulick, the chairman, West, Howard S. Braucher, the secretary of the PAA, and Dr. Anna L. Brown, the health education director of the National Board of the Young Women's Christian Associations of the United States of America* (YWCA). Gulick stressed that he did not want the organization simply to copy the BSA. The group agreed to try to implement its ideas further and to appoint a committee on organization, composed only of women but authorized to appoint a men's advisory group. The women's committee held its second meeting in New York City on April 7, 1911, and agreed to the Thetford girls' request that they be the first to enroll in the CFGA.

The newly established CFGA began to flounder in the next few months. In the spring of 1911, for health reasons, Dr. Gulick took a leave of absence from the Russell Sage Foundation and left the CFGA temporarily. His and his wife's absence certainly prompted the CFGA's decline. In May 1911, the organization issued its *Bulletin of Suggestions for the Formation of Groups Leading to a National Organization.* Many agreed that this document was too masculine and that it read like a diluted boy scout manual. During this period, two groups rivaling the CFGA were established. In Des Moines, Iowa, a newspaperwoman founded the Girls Scouts, and in Spokane, Washington, the Reverend David Ferry established Girl Guides. In early June 1911, with Gulick still away, West chaired a meeting with these two rivals. The meeting worked out a plan of amalgamation, forming a new group, the Girl Pioneers of America (GPA). Because there was no effective merger of either programs or personalities, the GPA venture failed. The leaders, including Mrs. Gulick—named in absentia—resigned, and by the autumn of 1911, the amalgamation was abandoned.

Only Dr. Gulick's return to New York revived the CFGA. On September 27, 1911, he chaired a meeting of the women's committee on organization, which agreed to accept men. Gulick became its chairman. This committee had prominent workers and philanthropists from New York, and its newly formed council attracted key national leaders, such as Jane Addams of Hull-House* in Chicago, Grace H. Dodge, the national president of the YWCA, and Mary Richmond, a prominent social worker. Late in 1911, office space was lent by the northeastern territorial committee of the YWCA, and the YWCA's national board lent the CFGA a stenographer. Doctors Gulick and Brown of the YWCA focused on raising funds, funds that soon allowed the CFGA to rent an office at 118 East

28th Street and to hire an executive secretary as an assistant to Gulick. In February and March 1912, the CFGA held a five-week training course for women leaders of girls' groups. The leader was called the guardian of the fire, and each group had between six and twenty teenaged girls. On March 15, 1912, Mrs. Gulick and two Washington, D.C., residents incorporated the organization according to the laws of the District of Columbia. The incorporation papers called the organization the CFG, leaving out "America," reportedly in the hopes of establishing groups in other countries. In the spring and summer of 1912, Dr. Gulick traveled widely, speaking and writing about the CFG and the movement. He emphasized both the ceremonial aspects as a means of relieving the monotony of daily activities and the need to strip away the by-products of industrialism to reveal what he and CFG manuals called the beauty of life. So close himself to the child hygiene movement and to the promotion of physical education, Gulick stressed healthful habits and living for the girls.

In March 1912 the first manual appeared; it was a 100-page book prepared by Mrs. Gulick. It contained the "wood gatherer's desire," the central tenets of the organization and later called its "law." The "desire" was a list of goals, beginning with "seek beauty" and "give service." In 1942, "worship God," implicit in the earlier "desire," became the first point of the CFG's "law." There was an array of honors that the girls could win. The health craft required girls, among other things, to sleep out of doors or with wide open windows for two consecutive months between October and April, and they could not miss work or school because of ill health or a headache for three consecutive months. The "home craft" called for volunteer service in "homes, hospitals and settlements" for the sick. One of the requirements for "business craft" called for a girl to earn three dollars and to donate the money to a "worthy cause." Gulick called the CFG not a social work agency but one that kept girls living properly. An article in the leading social welfare journal of the Progressive era, *The Survey,* argued that social workers welcomed the CFG movement but that many people viewed it, like the BSA, as a "training school for the militia."

In these early years, further crystallization of the organization took place. By July 1912, there were groups in forty-two states and in Hawaii and Canada. In 1912, the CFG signed a contract with a private company to produce uniforms. The CFG initially received 2 percent and later 5 percent of the sales. The CFG's attorney, Thomas G. Frost of New York City, drafted the constitution and bylaws and set up the administrative structure. At the incorporator's meeting in Washington, D.C., on June 3, 1913, the committee on organization disbanded, and the CFG established an elected board of managers, with a maximum of eighteen members, to conduct the CFG's business and to implement its policies. A twenty-four-member board of selectors was formed to choose the board of managers. The board of managers had two units—a seven-member executive committee and a five-member business committee. The CFG had the traditional four officers; Gulick was president. In late December 1912, Gulick quit his position at the Russell Sage Foundation and became the paid executive leader of the CFG. In July 1913, the first issue of a journal appeared, *WoHeLo,* adopted from the first two letters of the three basic tenets, work, health, and love. Initially prepared in a corner of Hiteni's dining room in her home, the journal moved with the organization to new headquarters in the fall of 1914. In July 1913, the CFG created the Blue Birds for younger girls. It had its own but similar rituals. Gulick and other founders and leaders wanted to make the CFG self-supporting. In this early period about one-sixth of the girls were from YWCAs or settlements and were not expected to pay dues. In April 1913, then, the agency began its burden badge plan, whereby girls who paid more than the minimal dues received special citations. The obvious drawbacks of this scheme forced its abolition in August 1913.

On January 18, 1914, the CFG took out new incorporation papers in New York State. All active guardians became part of the board of electors, with the right to vote on issues at the annual meeting, held in New York City. Because it became virtually impossible to have a one-third quorum at these meetings, the board of managers became largely self-perpetuating, dominated by New York area residents. Many leaders resigned over the decision to charge membership fees, and more dissension developed from complaints that the Gulicks profited financially from their positions in the CFG. These charges prompted an investigation by certified accountants, clearing the founders. A group of thirty-eight of the six hundred guardians resigned nevertheless, as did some staff members.

After the investigation, the CFG began to experience solid growth. In the late spring of 1914, the organization acquired larger headquarters in New York City. In late 1915, the CFG finally got its first full-time field secretary, ''Alaska'' Edith Kempthorne, known to the headquarters staff because of her lively letters describing her CFG activities in Alaska. Kempthorne served the CFG for thirty-four years, and before 1923, she was the only field staff member, traveling all over the country. Gulick announced that the highlight of 1915 was that the CFG had supported itself from dues, sales, and contributions. In November 1916, the CFG hired as national secretary—still really an assistant to Gulick—Lester F. Scott, a former resident of a settlement house in New York City who became active in boys' club, boy scout, and community work.

More so than with other social agencies, training leaders was an early important CFG function. In early 1912, the organization trained about one hundred women in the New York area. Seizing a unique opportunity to reach leaders outside the New York area, the CFG held a training institute in the summer of 1914 at the Rural Life Conference at the Iowa State College of Agriculture and Mechanical Arts in Ames, Iowa, and followed that with another course at Lake Okoboji, Iowa. The CFG was given Camp Shawnhequa, near the Delaware Water Gap on the New Jersey-Pennsylvania border, which became a model training camp and a famous training institute. The name Camp Shawnhequa was used for similar training institutes all over the country. Institutes were held at camps and, often, in connection with summer schools of physical education. Gulick's influence and later that of Dr. Jay B. Nash, the director of physical education at New York University and active in the CFG, established and strengthened these ties.

The World War I years and after tested the agency's resiliency. On April 17, 1919, two days after the United States' declaration of war, Gulick presented to President Woodrow Wilson the CFG's war program designed to conserve food, to cooperate with the American National Red Cross,* and to generally toughen up. Dr. Gulick revealed much about the CFG when he said, "Our country has but little use at this time for girls who have headaches, tender feet, nerves, indigestion, or who are lazy and eat candy." Gulick's commitment to the war effort led him in November 1917 to take a three-month leave of absence without pay from the CFG to work for the war council of the International Committee of the Young Men's Christian Associations* (YMCA). At the CFG, there had been continuing conflicts between Gulick and his assistant, Scott, and in August 1918, Gulick resigned as president for reasons that, according to an official history, remain unclear. Scott then became head of the organization, but friction continued. Another setback occurred on August 13, 1918, when Timanous, "the guiding spirit," died.

Following Gulick's death and faced with the lack of aggressive leadership and a nationwide depression, the CFG floundered. In July 1920, *WoHeLo* became *Everygirl's* magazine, featuring such topics as child labor, the American Indian, migratory birds, and conservation. Local councils were irresponsible in not reporting accurate enrollments and, like other national organizations, in not forwarding dues to the national office. An important organizational development occurred in 1928 when the CFG established its national council, composed of representatives from local councils. At its first meeting, the national council divided the United States into nine districts for administrative purposes. In 1946, the scheme was changed to have ten regions. In 1933, *Everygirl's* ceased publication. In the field of training, however, the national organization maintained its services. In September 1920, at the Russell Sage Foundation Building, the CFG held a national convention of the chairmen of guardian associations and local executives. This became known as the organization's first annual conference. In June 1922, the CFG sponsored a major training camp at Camp Shawnee near Grandview, Missouri. Because not all volunteer leaders could come to summer-long institutes, in 1930, the CFG initiated two-day weekend institutes, which were held for four days after 1933. Called "shutankas," these courses were given by the national headquarters staff. In 1930, Dr. Nash helped to establish a CFG professional training program in connection with New York University's summer training for physical education. This was terminated in 1948. During this period, the CFG had no endowments or investments and lacked a sound financial basis.

The CFG began to flourish again in the 1940s under new leadership. Scott retired on April 1, 1943, and was replaced as national director by social worker Martha F. Allen, the former assistant national director, who had come to the CFG in late 1941 from the Cincinnati Metropolitan Housing Authority. In the fall of 1942, the board of directors sent a top staff member on an extended field trip to the major councils to try to end the carelessness in dues and registration. Local-national relations were a major problem. The national council had no authority except at the annual meeting. There was a feeling, discernible in other national agencies, that the New York people were out of touch with the rest of the nationwide organization. But, in 1946, the national council was reorganized to give local volunteers greater authority. These actions also limited the board of directors to an advisory group directing operations at national headquarters in accordance with policies of the national council. The CFG participated in the National Budget Committee from its inception in 1946, submitting its budget for approval for funds from community chests and united funds in local communities. During World War II, many war bonds were bought for the CFG, and in 1946, the organization cashed them in, using the money to expand the field staff and to hire a public relations staff. In September 1946, the CFG hired a trained group worker as national associate director. In 1947, the CFG bought its own building in New York City, and in June 1953, the CFG acquired the private outfitting company and began operating it as the supply division of the CFG. In 1944, the CFG began a research project attempting to make its programs more relevant than before. To direct this project, the CFG hired Dr. Rosemary Lippitt, a specialist in child psychology from the Research Centre for Group Dynamics at the Massachusetts Institute of Technology. The study featured an advisory committee of prominent educators, group workers, and the like, such as Dr. Nash and Professor Nathan Cohen of the New York School of Social Work, as well as consultants, statisticians, and the national staff. This study showed that the most popular activities were those when the girls were physically active and that the most unpopular programs were those in which the girls were least active. It also revealed that CFG activities were more attractive to younger than to older girls. These results prompted a revision of the seven crafts and the ending of unpopular activities, such as keeping a health chart, something founder Gulick favored. In the mid-1940s, the CFG made the ceremonial gown optional, suggesting a series of actions to make the program more relevant to modern girls. This trend was accelerated in the 1950s.

The changes in the 1950s were stimulated largely by the findings of research studies. In 1952, for example, the CFG national staff began to study new patterns of development in local councils, leading to a new manual on organization in the spring of 1954. In 1952, when a study showed that volunteers were very vague about the CFG's purposes, the principles were revised and then circulated. In 1955, the CFG amended its articles of incorporation to include these changes. The relation between the board of directors and the national council was refined in the late 1950s when the CFG changed its structure, consolidating six departments and one division into four major divisions: program services, field services, public relations, and business administration. The heads of these divisions, along with the national director, constituted a new staff executive committee. In 1957, the agency adopted higher standards for its professional workers, inaugurated a scholarship plan to help train future leaders, and in 1958, began to train its volunteer organizers, who served as an extension of the paid field staff. In 1957, the CFG hired the Audience Research of Princeton, New Jersey, to conduct a nationwide study of group leaders and to do an in-depth study of the program in one community. Influenced by this study, the CFG decided to conduct a pilot action-research project, resulting in an activity for the agency's golden jubilee in 1960. Beginning in September 1959, the girls could chose either a tree census and tree planting project or a survey of outdoor recreational resources. About four thousand communities participated, and, by 1961, more than a million trees had been planted. The golden jubilee celebration in New York in early November 1960 featured the issuance of a postage stamp honoring the CFG, which, on January 24, 1961, staged a Thank Your Community Day throughout the country.

Although founded by people like the Gulicks and James West, who were in the core of the national social welfare community, the CFG did not see itself as a social work agency. The CFG had limited but successful programs in underprivileged areas and with physically and socially handicapped girls, and in 1952, the program department published a booklet on services with and for handicapped children. In 1957, a study showed that nearly 80 percent of the CFG's groups had a majority of middle-class girls and that only 2 percent had a majority from lower-income groups. CFG spokesmen were not ashamed to argue in the early 1960s that training the middle class for leadership was a needed social service. The CFG did, however, perceive of itself as part of the constellation of social service and youth organizations, and National Director Allen had helped to organize in the mid-1940s the renamed National Social Welfare Assembly,* to which the CFG still belonged in 1976.

In the 1960s and 1970s, the leaders of the CFG realized that the organization and the movement had to adapt to the new needs of girls in a rapidly changing and complex society. After two years of experiments, in 1962, the CFG program was revised and enriched. In June 1966, Dr. Hester Turner, an educator, replaced the retiring Martha Allen as the national director. In 1967, the CFG completed its metropolitan critical areas study, a three-year project funded jointly by the CFG and the United States Children's Bureau. This project was an attempt to serve girls living in poverty areas. During this period, a number of councils provided special programs to reach girls from low-income families. In conjunction with these programs, the CFG conducted three seminars for leaders. A report of the seminars was published as *Creative Adaptation to Change,* which was distributed to schools of social work, education, and home economics and to national social service and youth-serving agencies. Federal Jobs Corps personnel also used this book, as did local youth employment counselors. During the mid-1960s, with funds from the federal Office of Juvenile Delinquency and Youth Development, the CFG conducted a complementary project to develop materials to train indigenous leaders for work with culturally and economically deprived girls. CFG also participated in programs of the federal Office of Economic Opportunity. In the early 1970s, as with the BSA, conservation was reaffirmed as a major issue. In this period, CFG also sponsored the Horizon Club Conference Aware for high school–aged girls. Conducted on three college campuses and attended by about twelve hundred participants, both boys and girls, these conferences focused on such issues as drinking, drugs, changing morals, family relations, and, consistent with CFG's traditional emphases, conservation and ecology.

The sources for studying the CFG's history include the files of the agency at its headquarters in New York City, agency publications, especially *WoHeLo* magazine, and contemporary articles in *The Survey* and other journals. All of these sources were used in *Wo-He-Low: The Story of Camp Fire Girls* (1961), researched, compiled, and edited by Helen Buckler, Mary Felder, and Martha F. Allen. This is a highly informative official history. Corrinne Moller is preparing a continuation of CFG's history for the period from 1960 to 1977, and she kindly assisted me with materials for the recent history of CFG. The CFG has apparently not been studied by professional historians. There is considerable room for studies of various aspects of the CFG, especially by social historians.

CATHOLIC CHARITIES OF THE ARCHDIOCESE OF NEW YORK, THE (CCANY). Beginning in 1817, when Saint Elizabeth Seton opened the first Catholic home for orphaned children in New York City. Catholic churches, orders, and volunteer lay organizations provided a wide range of charities and social services in New York City. The Catholic Church in New York especially bore the burdens of an overwhelmingly immigrant and generally poor group of people. Throughout the nineteenth and early twentieth centuries, Catholic social services in New York City, as indeed in dioceses and archdioceses throughout the United States, remained essentially at the parish level. By the early twentieth century, in the archdiocese of New York, there were some two hundred health and welfare organizations, including child care institutions and hospitals such as St. Vincent's Hospital in Manhattan and the New York Foundling Hospital, as well as the Society of St. Vincent de Paul* (SSVDP), a lay organization.

The first major step toward organizing and coordinating these diverse and far-ranging charities occurred in 1902, when Monsignor D. J. McMahon, the director of Catholic charities in New York, called a meeting to develop women's auxiliaries of the SSVDP in the parishes. Monsignor McMahon felt that this new group, the Association of Catholic Charities of New York (ACCNY), could develop such projects as committees in hospitals, children's institutions, and day nurseries. The ACCNY had a broad, citywide vision, rather than a parochial view of parish-level charities, the dominant form. Members of the ACCNY acted as volunteer probation officers in the children's courts, visited prisoners, and conducted English, civics, and religious studies classes for immigrants. In 1912, the ACCNY became affiliated with the Ladies of Charity in Paris. In 1919, at McMahon's suggestion the ACCNY changed its name to the Ladies of Charity of the Catholic Charities of the Archdiocese of New York, Inc. For many years, the women had been wanting to honor the agency's founder. In 1920, their goal was realized with the opening of the McMahon Memorial Shelter for Children. Another important step toward coordination of charities occurred in the fall of 1913 when John Cardinal Farley established the United Catholic Works.

American entry into World War I ended attempts to achieve unity and coordination. Soon after he became head of the archdiocese in June 1919, Archbishop Patrick Hayes admitted that even he was not fully aware of the multifaceted welfare programs of the archdiocese of New York. Subsequently, on September 1, 1919, Archbishop Hayes directed that a study of the social service agencies and institutions in the archdiocese be conducted. About four hundred people involved in Catholic charities participated in the survey, for which the group solicited opinions of public officials as well. The year-long project resulted in a massive study, which included six complete reports on divisions of activities, such as health and hospitals. A two-hundred-page general report compiled by the directors of the study supplemented the division reports. Archbishop Hayes received the study on February 15, 1920, and he consequently called for the establishment of the Archbishop's Committee of the Laity to raise funds and otherwise aid in the archdiocese's charitable works. With gradually increasing support for this venture, Hayes appointed his secretary for charity, Right Reverend Monsignor Robert F. Keegan, to organize a central committee. These efforts led to the creation of the CCANY, which was incorporated in May 1920 according to the laws of the state of New York. The CCANY's purpose was to organize, improve, and extend the charitable works in the Archdiocese of New York. The New York State Board of Charities called the creation of the CCANY "the most significant and important event of the year in the field of charitable work."

The new CCANY, which spent its first few months organizing itself, quickly became a leader in the field of private welfare agencies and served as the model for a number of other Catholic dioceses and archdioceses. The early structure included Archbishop Hayes as president and treasurer, a vice-president, and a secretary. These three officers, in addition to six other men, comprised the nine-member board of directors. Hayes appointed his secretary for charities, Reverend Keegan, as the first executive director. The organizational arrangement featured six divisions—on families, children, health, protective care, social action, and finance—each headed by a director. Financing quickly became an important aspect of the CCANY's activities. The CCANY was aided by the Cardinal's Committee of the Laity and, beginning in 1920, an annual Catholic charities appeal in churches throughout the archdiocese. The first appeal, attracted nearly $1 million for the new CCANY. Such enthusiastic, regular support allowed the agency to weather the depression of the late 1920s and 1930s.

The agency began to function in September 1920. Its initial headquarters were at the Grand Central Palace in New York City. With such a large structure of about two hundred agencies and institutions, there was obviously a lot of activity, but the recognized highlight of the early years was the establishment in March 1922 of the Guidance Institute. Operating initially in a small, crowded office in the out-patient department of St. Vincent's Hospital in Manhattan, the institute examined and treated difficult and problem children. Within a few years, it had become a family clinic. In the early 1920s, the division of families conducted a special study of homeless men and began successful negotiations with the Holy Name Mission to extend work with and for such men. Conceived initially as a supervisory and supplementary relief-giving auxiliary of parish-based welfare services, the division of family service had begun gradually to apply modern casework techniques in the 1920s. The division of families also maintained twenty-four day nurseries, four of which were established by the CCANY itself. In a number of these nurseries, the CCANY provided standard medical services and clinics for mothers and children. Conducting an activity for which the CCANY was organized, the division of health held a conference of hospital superintendents and established a central bureau of information and service, which helped the clergy to place the sick with whom they had contact. The division of protective care maintained two full-time staff workers at the city's Court of Domestic Relations, and the division of social action supervised and organized boys' and girls' clubs, settlement houses, and recreational and social activities of the archdiocese. As a leading student of Catholic social work pointed out, the CCANY in the 1920s was one of the few diocesan and archdiocesan agencies that gave special attention to recreation and character-building youth programs, such as big sisters, Catholic boys' brigades, and girl scouts. Although it did not develop the first Catholic Youth Organization (CYO)—that distinction went to the archdiocese of Chicago in 1930—the CCANY initiated its diocesan-wide CYO program in 1936 under Cardinal Hayes.

The substantial funds generated by annual appeals and other efforts helped the CCANY to weather the difficult times of the depression of the 1930s. In 1933, under the leadership of former New York governor and Democratic Party presidential candidate Alfred E. Smith, the fund-raising capacity was expanded with the establishment of the special gifts committee of the Cardinal's Committee of the Laity. In its very first year, the seventy-four-member special gifts committee raised about $144,000. (By 1968, for instance, the approximately one thousand members raised $1.7 million.) From 1931 through 1936, the CCANY participated in the community fund raising efforts by the Citizens Family Welfare Committees, which also benefited ten other major family service agencies in the greater New York area. The CCANY also participated in the united hospital campaigns to help its volunteer hospitals, and the CCANY participated in the first Greater New York Fund, which began in May 1938. The financial success and program activities of the CCANY in the 1920s and 1930s helped to earn for its leader, Cardinal Hayes, the popular title of the Cardinal of Charity. The CCANY assisted in the development of public social services. For example, the agency loaned its experienced social worker, Mary Gibbons, to the city as the first director of home relief, a service established in 1931. On behalf of the city's Emergency Work Bureau, the division of health and hospitals initiated work opportunities for the unemployed. With the implementation of the New York State Old Age Pension Act of 1931, the division of family service began to focus on guiding disintegrating families and to helping unwed mothers, the aged, and the jobless, for instance. During the 1920s, the division absorbed the responsibilities of parish-based relief activities. During the 1920s and 1930s, the number of such parish-based youth centers grew rapidly. Also in the early 1930s, the CCANY inaugurated a traveling clinic exclusively for child care homes and institutions. Cardinal Hayes's death in September 1938 ended an era of the CCANY.

Under Hayes's successor as head of the archdiocese and as CCANY president, Francis Cardinal Spellman, the CCANY experienced remarkable growth and consolidation of charities, fulfilling an initial goal of the agency. In 1939, it opened a day-time shelter for homeless men, continuing its efforts in behalf of a group neglected and forgotten by the New Deal social service programs and agencies. In the early 1940s, the structure featured five major divisions—family welfare, children, health care, social action, and finance—each with a full-time director and assistants. Perhaps the most innovative division, the division of family welfare, provided special casework services. Home economists from the division gave information on budgeting to families, an activity also conducted by such progressive and important agencies as the Community Service Society.* The division served as the liaison between homes for the aged in the archdiocese and the state Department of Welfare's Division of Old Age Security. The division of family welfare took over the functions of the former division of protective care, providing a full-time caseworker in the Domestic Relations Court. The Catholic Protective Society, under the division, supervised girls and women committed by the Magistrates' and Children's Courts to Westfield State Farm and to other facilities. It also helped to train students from two New York City schools for social workers and from the School of Social Work at the Catholic University of America in Washington, D.C.

In the early 1940s, the division of children conducted and coordinated fifteen child care institutions, the Catholic Home Bureau, the Guidance Institute, twenty-five day nurseries, the McMahon Memorial Shelter, and the Catholic Big Brothers and Catholic Big Sisters. In 1942, the CCANY reaffirmed the right for summer vacations for all children, inaugurating "integration not segregation" as a motto for its youth activities. That summer, it sponsored the first interracial

CYO summer camps. The division of health care had twenty-six hospitals and four convalescence homes, and the division of social action supervised youth activities, such as CYO, boy scouts, and the like, as well as nine Catholic settlement houses. During World War II, the CCANY hospitals provided blood banks, increased its programs for training nurses, and participated in the federal maternity and infant care plan for servicemen's dependents. During the war and its aftermath, family services featured vocational counseling for veterans and focused on readjustment problems of families and behavior problems in children.

The death of Executive Director Keegan in 1947, who had served in this position since the CCANY's inauguration in 1920, signaled the end of another chapter in the agency's history. Cardinal Spellman called Keegan "the soul and inspiration of Catholic charities." Indeed, under Keegan, the CCANY had become perhaps the largest private charity in the country. Its vast network of over two hundred health and welfare agencies dealt obviously with large numbers of clients. In the period of Spellman's leadership, 1939–1967, the CCANY spent over $125 million. Highlights of these years included the establishment of two new homes for the aged and substantial additions to seven others, six new child care agencies, a free employment and vocational guidance bureau, fifteen parish day centers for the aging, four new psychiatric clinics for children, and the modernization and expansion of nearly all the archdiocesan hospitals. Two annual, special events, the Cardinal's Christmas Party and the Alfred E. Smith Memorial Dinner, helped to finance the modernization of The New York Foundling Hospital in the late 1950s and the expansion of St. Vincent's Hospital into a medical center. The CCANY was sensitive to the changing composition of New York City after World War II, providing bilingual social workers, for instance, in Spanish-speaking areas. The child care department increased its staff of mental health specialists, educators, psychiatric social workers, and recreational workers. It also converted the institutions from a congregate type into more homelike facilities.

During the next phase of the CCANY's history in the late 1960s and 1970s, under the leadership of Terence Cardinal Cooke, the agency developed innovative and interesting social services. It established a number of community-based psychiatric treatment centers. In 1968, it opened a day camp in Yonkers, New York, as a tribute to the late Dr. Martin Luther King, Jr. In the South Bronx, a very troubled area of New York City, a staff member helped the community to organize and to get funding for a much-needed Head Start program. It established a day treatment center for disturbed children unable to attend school daily, and it funded a comprehensive treatment program for predelinquent and drug-prone girls. In the early 1970s, the CCANY had thousands of young people active in AMEN, mobilized to end narcotics. The CCANY also had special training programs that increased staff awareness of and skills in identifying symptoms of drug use. The CCANY had a vocational service and a neighborhood youth corps to help youngsters find jobs. The New York Foundling Hospital extended its famous child abuse prevention program to the community in East Harlem. Severe reductions in public funds and the general economic slowdown forced the CCANY to curtail and even to close some services in the mid-1970s, but this large social service agency continued its diverse and far-reaching program.

The primary sources for studying the CCANY's rich history are the especially detailed published *Annual Reports*. The archives of the archdiocese of New York at St. Joseph's Seminary in Yonkers, New York, unfortunately, have very little unpublished material relating to the CCANY.

An agency publication, *Fifty Years of Service* (1970), is helpful. There is information about the CCANY in Marguerite T. Boylan, *Social Welfare in the Catholic Church: Organization and Planning Through Diocesan Bureaus* (1941), and in Reverend James A. Reynold's entry for the archdiocese of New York in the *New Catholic Encyclopedia* (1967), 10: 404–406. There does not appear to be a scholarly history of the CCANY.

CATHOLIC RELIEF SERVICES–UNITED STATES CATHOLIC CONFERENCE (CRS). In the mid-1930s, at the request of the Catholic Hierarchy in Germany, the American bishops began to aid refugees from the Nazi regime. In 1936, the American bishops established the Catholic Committee for Refugees and Refugee Children within the structure of the National Catholic Welfare Conference (NCWC). After World War II began, Catholics in America founded a number of other relief agencies, and in 1940, to coordinate these efforts, the leaders created the Bishops' War Emergency and Relief Committee. To raise funds to help refugees in about fifteen countries, in 1941, the committee held the first so-called Laetre Sunday collection in parishes through the United States. On January 15, 1943, Catholic Relief Services-United States Catholic Conference (CRS) was established as the War Relief Service of the NCWC (WRS-NCWC) by the administrative board of bishops, an agency of the American Catholic church. The bishops organized the WRS-NCWC as a temporary agency to coordinate official war-related Catholic social services and to participate in and to receive funds from the National War Fund (NWF), which was established to coordinate and to centralize fund raising in the United States during World War II. To organize the WRS-NCWC, the bishops appointed Monsignor Bryan J. McEntegart of The Catholic Charities of the Archdiocese of New York* (CCANY) and long active in charitable work in New York. On April 28, 1943, the WRS-NCWC was incorporated according to the laws of the District of Columbia.

Operating from an office in New York City, which opened in August 1943, McEntegart helped to lay the groundwork for what became one of the largest charitable agencies in the United States. The early structure of the WRS-NCWC included a board of trustees, comprised of the members of the administrative board of the NCWC, in addition to the military vicar and his military delegate. Five members of the board constituted the governing committee, and there was an eleven-member advisory committee. Reverend McEntegart assembled a staff, leased a warehouse, and coordinated the work of training the new staff. At the end of the first year, the WRS-NCWC had relief programs in England, Malta, China, Albania, and Tunisia. During the war, the WRS-NCWC assisted German and Polish refugees, homeless people in Spain and Portugal, and the needy in Allied countries. In Nationalist China, it provided medical stations and day nurseries for civilians and for war orphans, and it aided refugees in Switzerland. By early 1944, the WRS-NCWC had offices in Lisbon, Portugal, and in Madrid, Spain. The WRS-NCWC also aided seamen, sending portable libraries to clubs throughout the world serving them. During the last stages of the war, the WRS-NCWC aided civilians in Malta, and WRS-NCWC supplies were among the first American relief packages to Italy; by May 1944, seventy-two archdioceses and dioceses in the United States had raised over six million pounds of shoes and clothing. In 1946, the WRS-NCWC mobilized the largest donations of food and clothing by a voluntary agency in American history to that point. In 1945, the annual thanksgiving clothing collection began, and in 1949, WRS-NCWC leaders decided to appeal to all Catholics in one unified drive.

The period after the end of World War II witnessed the real expansion of the WRS-NCWC as it faced the enormous problems of relief and rehabilitation for people in war-torn countries abroad. In 1945, the agency established 245 welfare centers throughout the world for refugees from Poland, and it also assisted some Jewish refugees. Soon after the Allies liberated areas from the Axis, the WRS-NCWC began to assist inmates of concentration camps, using a fleet of trucks shipped abroad from the United States. During this period, the WRS-NCWC had eight representatives in Europe to develop services for displaced persons. To deal with one of the most pressing issues during this period, the WRS-NCWC urged the creation of local diocesan refugee committees in the United States. Through these groups, the WRS-NCWC helped to admit about one-third of the refugees to the United States. The agency's activities were directed first by Monsignor Patrick A. O'Boyle, the former administrator of the Mission of the Immaculate Virgin at Mt. Loretto, Staten Island, New York, one of the largest Catholic children's homes in America. O'Boyle became executive director on June 28, 1943, when McEntegart became the bishop of Ogdensburg, New York. O'Boyle chose as his assistant, Monsignor Edward Swanstrom, who became executive director on August 1, 1947. On July 28, 1945, an airplane crashed into the headquarters of the WRS-NCWC in the Empire State Building, killing seventeen staff members and destroying three-fourths of the office.

Swanstrom shaped the agency into a leader in relief abroad. Support from the NWF ended in December 1946 when that organization terminated its activities. In 1947, the board of trustees developed a plan to settle refugees in the United States. This project led to the creation of the National Catholic Resettlement Council, under the administration of the WRS-NCWC. Through 1958, this agency had helped to settle about 250,000 refugees in the United States. Rehabilitation efforts in Eastern European countries, begun after the war, ended as communists gained control and banned the WRS-NCWC. Nevertheless, the WRS-NCWC worked with and aided the United National Relief and Rehabilitation Administration (UNRRA), providing medicine, clothing, food, and the like to such countries as Greece, India, Korea, and Madagascar. With other American social agencies, the WRS-NCWC aided undernourished children, orphans, the sick, the aged, and the infirm. Indeed, between 1945 and 1950, the WRS-NCWC spent over $85 million on such relief and rehabilitation efforts.

During the 1950s, the WRS-NCWC continued to expand. As early as April 1950, the WRS-NCWC began to distribute surplus American food as part of its general operation, making it one of the first voluntary agencies to do so. Large amounts of funds donated by American Catholics through programs like the annual thanksgiving clothing collection, which began as an annual event in 1950, and the bishops' relief fund appeal, enabled the agency to participate in the United States escapee program, authorized by federal officials, the international Intergovernmental Committee for European Migration, and the activities of the United Nations High Commissioner for Refugees and to cooperate with local governments and voluntary agencies throughout the world. Cooperative efforts by the Catholic Medical Mission Board and the pharmaceutical industry provided most of the agency's medical and hospital supplies. In 1955, the agency helped to establish the Institute of Rural Education in Chile to train rural leaders in modern agriculture. After they learned the techniques, these leaders returned home and taught others in their communities, an early self-help community development program. In Colombia in the late 1950s, the agency helped to organize CARITAS, a social service organization. Realizing that the WRS-NCWC was no longer the temporary agency the bishops had envisioned in 1943, on April 20, 1955, the agency changed its name to the Catholic Relief Services-NCWC (CRS). In March 1957, the CRS instituted its first formal Laetare Sunday appeal. In the mid-1950s, Reverend Swanstrom himself participated in a survey of conditions and needs in Central and South America and in Africa, leading to projects and activities by the CRS. Most importantly, however, the CRS effectively utilized Public Law 480 of 1954, which allowed American voluntary agencies to obtain government surplus agricultural products at minimal rates and to distribute them abroad.

Enthusiastic support for and participation in this commodities supplies program marked the CRS's activities in the 1960s. During the presidency of John F. Kennedy, Executive Director Swanstrom was active in utilizing Public Law 480, especially developing alliances with and sustenance from liberal congressional Democrats, who consistently supported the federal-voluntary agency cooperative venture. During the first three years of the law, the CRS expanded its feeding programs overseas significantly. By the early 1960s, the CRS feeding program operated in sixty-four countries. By mid-November 1961, the cumulative value of the CRS relief since 1943 passed the $1 billion mark. In 1963, as a student of these activities argues, the CRS began to obtain "impressive financial backing" as well as agricultural surpluses for its school lunch programs throughout the so-called underdeveloped parts of the world. Like progressive voluntary agencies abroad, the CRS began to encourage self-reliance and self-development. One significant result of the CRS was to stimulate the development abroad of organizations similar to the NCWC. The surveys of the mid-1950s helped to develop programs in Africa, Asia, and Latin America. The emphasis in the 1960s was increasingly on technical assistance and self-help, especially for refugees from communism in Vietnam, Korea, and Hong Kong. In the early 1960s, for example, the CRS stimulated housing programs in Hong Kong, Chile, and India. In January 1963, following two years of negotiations, the federal Agency for International Development approved a CRS program to ship 40,500 tons of grain in five years to the Isidore Development Association of Cheju Island, Korea, a self-help corporation headed by a Catholic priest designed to improve the breeding and production of hogs.

During the 1960s, the administrative structure of the CRS—perhaps the largest voluntary organization in the United States—was tightly knit and efficient. The board of trustees still appointed the executive director, and each staff member was directly responsible to the executive director. In September 1961, Executive Director Swanstrom issued to all professionals on the staff a *Manual of Personnel Policies,* a detailed brochure. Each new employee had an intensive orientation at national headquarters in New York City. Internal publications, such as the "Field News Letter," kept the staff posted on the latest activities and developments, as did weekly staff meetings and the use of a teamwork approach of cooperation between department heads and project supervisors. Reverend Robert Charlebois, who had worked in the office, suggested in 1963 that because the staff was almost all Catholic, there was an increased commitment to this charitable organization by its workers.

Basic programs of long-range, self-help activities, as well as emergency relief, characterized the CRS in the 1970s. In 1969 and 1970, it led a joint effort by American churches to aid the victims of the Biafran civil war. Swanstrom was chosen its president, and a member of the CRS staff became its executive director. Other typical programs included the relief efforts for Pakistani refugees and drought relief and rehabilitation in African Sahel. Special collections in local parishes helped to support the latter program. The CRS maintained a special disaster response reserve unit close to John F. Kennedy International Airport in New York, allowing the quick mobilization of relief. At its New York headquarters, the CRS maintained a liaison section with Catholic women who contributed garments and layettes for infants. A major organizational event occurred in 1976 when Bishop Swanstrom retired as executive director. Bishop Edwin B. Broderick, the former bishop of Albany, New York, replaced Swanstrom as head of the CRS.

The history of the CRS can be followed in an agency publication, *The Story of*

Catholic Relief Services, United States Catholic Conference (1976), and in Reverend Robert L. Charlebois, "Catholic Relief Services—N.C.W.C.: a Study of the Official Agency of The Catholic Church in America for International Relief" (Master's thesis, Catholic University of America, 1963), a helpful work which indicates that a huge mass of primary, unpublished materials is available. There are annual reports, but they are confidential and circulated only among the American bishops.

Robert Sullivan, "The Politics of Altruism" (Ph.D. dissertation, Johns Hopkins University, 1968), discusses the CRS's aggressive role in the surplus food program. There does not appear to be a scholarly history of the CRS.

CATHOLIC YOUTH ORGANIZATION FEDERATION, NATIONAL: see CYO FEDERATION, NATIONAL.

CHARITY ORGANIZATION SOCIETY OF THE CITY OF NEW YORK, THE (COS). In New York City in the late 1870s, Josephine Shaw Lowell was one of the most perceptive students of charities, including their excesses and their general ineffectiveness. In 1876, she was appointed to the New York State Board of Charities, a position from which she viewed and studied closely the New York City charities. In October 1881, Lowell presented what became a famous report on the condition of these charities to the state board. Organizing the other state commissioners from New York City as a core group, she asked representatives from other major city charities to constitute an organizing committee to create a new society like other charity organization societies that had developed recently in other cities. Shortly after the state board meeting in October 1881, the organizing committee met, drew up a constitution, and then reported its work to the New York state commissioners, who in turn asked the committee to serve as a central council. The commissioners also called a meeting on February 8, 1882, at which the officers were appointed. Lowell and a friend, Gertrude Rice, who, with Lowell, had helped to found the State Charities Aid Association* (SCAA) of New York in 1872, began to visit the charity organizations in the city to ask their cooperation in this new venture. The women primarily wanted to coordinate activities and hoped to reduce waste and ineffectiveness. The organization meanwhile hired its first executive Charles D. Kellogg, who held a similar position at the Philadelphia Society for Organizing Charity. On April 15, 1882, Kellogg opened the central office in lower Manhattan in the room of a club that offered the new COS desk space. The COS was incorporated on May 10, 1882, according to the laws of the state of New York. Following the incorporation, a special meeting on June 5, 1882, which adopted the constitution, set the COS in motion.

As the COS began to cooperate with other charity societies and set up its own offices, it also developed its basic structure and method of operation. The governing body was the central council, which had an executive committee and standing committees, such as membership, finance, district work, and cooperation. The committee on district work governed the central feature of the COS: the district committee activities. The central council initially appointed each of the district committees, which had then become self-perpetuating bodies. An elected delegate from each district represented his or her group on the central council. The chairman of most standing committees also served on the central council. The system provided considerable autonomy for each of the districts, which hired their own agents or friendly visitors and which conducted their own programs, such as lectures and other neighborhood activities. Partly because the paid agents were overwhelmingly women, within five years a central auxiliary committee of women was organized. This committee, in turn, prompted some districts to develop ladies' auxiliary committees, which raised funds and increasingly sponsored and conducted their own neighborhood social action activities.

At the central office at 67 Madison Street, the COS established its registration bureau for all applicants for relief in the city. In the first year, 138 agencies used this service. The COS began a file of fraudulent cases, initiating a service that reflected a consistent theme in the history of social service: trying to eliminate welfare fraud. The central district committee cared for families outside the districts, the number of which was expanded, for instance, in March 1895, when the COS opened an office for and in the Bronx. The COS and the New York Association for Improving the Condition of the Poor* (AICP) established the committee that was responsible for the construction and opening of the United Charities Building in New York City on March 6, 1893. Cooperation with the AICP developed in other activities, such as in the Joint Application Bureau and in dealing with the homeless in New York City.

In addition to cooperating with other agencies, and coordinating charity relief in New York City, the COS developed its own activities and programs, some of which were in the vanguard of local and national movements. In 1891, it established its journal, *The Charities Review,* which was the forerunner of the most respected national social service journal, *The Survey,* which the COS also helped to organize. In 1884, the COS established its wood yard to encourage the unemployed to work, an activity that persisted into the twentieth century. In 1903, the COS began to issue its *Confidential Bulletin,* which contained the names and photographs of alleged impostors soliciting funds. More importantly, in December 1898, the COS founded its tenement house committee, which Lawrence Veiller, the leading figure in national housing reform, served as secretary. This committee and its secretary had long and distinguished careers in this important social reform. The tenement house committee was the central factor in the creation of the National Housing Association* in 1910. Similarly, in May 1902, the COS appointed its committee on the prevention of tuberculosis, which had an influence on the national movement.

While the COS played a central role in the national Progressive movement, it also stimulated and developed important local programs, many of which had national significance. On September 15, 1893, it convened the leading New York agencies to deal with what the COS foresaw correctly as a major depression. In November of the same year, it opened its wayfarer's lodge to serve temporarily until the establishment of the municipal lodging house. The COS played a significant role in the movement to deal with transients. In the next year, the COS initiated its cooperation with Columbia University, an alliance that not only produced important studies in the field of social service but led also to the establishment of the first and most important professional social work school, The New York School of Philanthropy. This school had its roots in the COS training school established in the summer of 1898. Also in 1898, the organization appointed its special committee on dependent children with representatives from other leading New York agencies. The committee helped to shape state and local policies in the care of such children.

One of the outstanding features of the COS's history was its ability to attract the most important philanthropists in New York and the nation and some of the most important and distinguished workers in social service. Robert de Forest, who was important in a number of other agencies and movements, was COS president from the late 1880s through the early 1930s. Lawrence Veiller, the most significant individual in the nationwide housing reform movement of the Progressive era, served the COS. Edward T. Devine, the long-time general secretary, like his colleague at the COS, Paul Kellogg, was active in many Progressive movements. In the late 1930s, such COS workers as Joanna C. Colcord and General Secretary Stanley P. Davies continued the agency's tradition of having widely respected national figures in social service on its staff.

In the first decade of the twentieth century, the COS continued to develop creative Progressive social service programs. On April 29, 1903, for example, it sponsored a conference on family desertion, which led to the creation of a committee to press for enactment of reform legislation. Well ahead of the national concern for the physically handicapped, the COS established a special employment bureau for the handicapped in 1906. This bureau closed on June 30, 1912, when the COS-inspired training school for crippled adults opened. At the suggestion of Vice-President Jacob Schiff, the prominent banker and philanthropist, the COS established, in May 1909, the national employment exchange, which operated into the 1930s. In 1909, the COS initiated, through the city's Department of Health, weekly conferences in the districts between teams of doctors and nurses and neighborhood mothers with their babies. This program helped to give New York City the top rating in the reduction of infant mortality within a few years. During the Progressive era, the COS prompted similar local-level reforms, for instance, creating, through its various district committees, several local associations for general neighborhood improvement.

On October 1, 1912, the COS implemented a reorganizational plan that came about largely because General Secretary Devine left to head the COS-affiliated New York School of Philanthropy. The COS did not replace him but vested executive functions in three individuals: the directors of the COS departments of general work and of the improvement of social conditions and the director of the school, Devine. Not until 1933 was there again a single executive officer. The loss of Devine did not prevent the COS from contributing importantly to developments in the field. Still aware of the need for professional development and sound studies in the field, the COS began in 1914 to supply data from its case records to various private and public agencies, for instance, to the committee on woman's work of the Russell Sage Foundation's* study of wage losses due to sickness, a timely and informative study. In the forefront of the professionalization of social service agencies, in 1916, the COS appointed, for its central office staff, professional consultants for the volunteer district visitors and specialists to deal with desertion cases and with home economics. In 1917, the COS trained social workers for the New York work of the home service bureau of the American National Red Cross.* The COS initiated "junior month," whereby college students were invited to analyze and therefore understand the workings of the agency. The COS also capitalized on its own and other volunteers, realizing their value. In 1913, it began a successful campaign to enlist more volunteers to serve the district committees. In 1917, the COS sponsored an intercity conference on volunteers, one of the first programs of its kind in the country. In November 1923, the COS conducted a course for volunteers, the Art of Helping, which enrolled nearly four hundred people. When the course ended in 1924, the participants organized the Association of Volunteers in Social Service and themselves offered a similar course.

In the post–World War I years, the COS continued to focus on professional developments and, aware of the health problems surfacing during the war, on nutrition and public health. In June 1919, for instance, the home economics committee conducted a month-long institute for home economics teachers. In 1920, the home economics committee influenced the establishment of the New York Nutritional Council. With students from Teachers College of Columbia University, the committee operated the Morningside Nutrition and Homemaking Center as a demonstration project. In February 1922, the COS established, with a full-time secretary, its research bureau, whose studies led to the publication of a pamphlet in 1925, *The Social Workers' Approach to the Problems of Venereal Disease,* which was circulated widely. Continuing its trend toward professionalization, the COS organized its extension bureau to develop public relations and in 1929, published another timely account, *Some Aspects of Relief in Family Casework.*

These professional concerns did not diminish the sensitivity of this important social service agency to the problems of unemployment and the Great Depression. In October 1929, its consultant on industrial problems began a nearly two-year study of unemployment, which described current problems. Cooperating with the local Riverside Church, in January 1931, the COS established an employment service for the New York State Employment Service. In 1932, the

COS helped establish the public Home Relief Bureau and, for transients, the central registration bureau of the homeless. The development of programs by the private Welfare Council of New York City and by a host of public agencies diminished the significance of the COS, but in 1937, its home economist helped many agencies, public and private, to develop family budgets for their clients. In 1938, when it both opened the Queens Family Service as a district office and helped to certify applicants for National Youth Administration positions, the COS began a study of homeless men, one of the groups neglected by New Deal and other public programs. Despite these activities, on April 12, 1939, the COS disbanded when it joined with the AICP to form the new Community Service Society* (CSS) of New York.

The sources for the COS's history are diverse. The detailed published *Annual Reports* are an important source, and many of the agency publications describe the agency's activities. The archives of the Community Service Society* contain the COS files. References to its activities can also be found in such contemporary publications as *The Survey* and its predecessors.

Historians have paid considerable attention to the COS. Dorothy Becker's several publications, such as "Early Adventures in Social Casework: The Charity Agent, 1880–1910," *Social Casework* 44 (May 1963): 255–261, deal informatively with the agency. Lilian Brandt, *Growth and Development of the AICP and COS,* (1942), is a helpful summary by a long-time staff worker. Social work theses, such as Ruth Scannell, "A History of the COS, 1882–1935" (Master's thesis, New York School of Social Work, 1937), also deal with this agency. Standard histories in social welfare, such as Robert H. Bremner, *From the Depths* (1956), treat the COS, as do such specialized studies as Roy Lubove, *The Progressives and the Slums* (1963), and Paul T. Ringenbach, *Tramps and Reformers* (1973).

CHILD HEALTH ORGANIZATION: see CHILD HEALTH ORGANIZATION OF AMERICA.

CHILD HEALTH ORGANIZATION OF AMERICA (CHOA). In 1917, physicians, nutritionists, social workers, and others became increasingly aware of malnutrition in children, a problem dramatized by the numbers of young men rejected during the wartime draft. Around the country, agencies and individuals began to work to improve conditions. One such organization was the People's Institute, a general civic-philanthropic community agency in New York City. In May 1917, the institute hired as its community health worker Sally Lucas Jean, who had worked previously in medical social work in Baltimore. Jean directed a program at Public School (PS) 40 in New York to improve health habits of schoolchildren and to combat malnutrition, a phenomenon that another New York agency, the New York Association for Improving the Condition of the Poor* (AICP), had been studying. These activities apparently influenced a discussion in December 1917 by the section on pediatrics of the New York Academy of Medicine (NYAM), featuring a paper by a prominent New York pediatrician, Dr. Henry Dwight Chapin, on the dangers facing children during the war, such as food shortages and malnutrition. Chapin's paper prompted a lively discussion among the assembled pediatricians, the most prominent in New York and perhaps in the nation. At the December meeting, the section on pediatrics of the NYAM established a committee on wartime problems of childhood (CWTPC), which asked social welfare and health agencies in New York what doctors could do to help children. Meanwhile, three women from the People's Institute pursued their concerns with malnourished children, traveling to Washington, D.C., in late January 1918 to urge a host of federal officials, such as from the United States Bureau of Education (USBE) and the Food Administration, to help promote nutrition programs for the children of New York. Interior Secretary Franklin K. Lane suggested the New York women publicize their work and the information being learned about nutrition; the women in turn asked the pediatricians' CWTPC to prepare the medical information. Impressed with the success of programs for malnourished children in New York, United States commissioner of education, Philander P. Claxton, called a conference in Atlantic City, New Jersey, in February 1918, to discuss health education programs for schoolchildren.

Secretary Lane grew interested in these activities, and at the conference in Atlantic City, he met with the New York group and suggested that they establish a national organization to promote the kind of work being done at PS 40 in New York. The CWTPC agreed, offering the leadership on March 15, 1918, to one of their members, Dr. L. Emmett Holt, a distinguished pediatrician. Responding to Dr. Holt's letter urging them to participate in the new agency, the group of founders met in New York City in late March 1918 to establish the Child Health Organization of America (CHOA) as the Child Health Organization (CHO). Because the National Child Labor Committee (NCLC) had been concerned with the health of children who worked, the pediatricians invited NCLC leaders Dr. Samuel Lindsay of Columbia University, Alexander McKelway, and Owen Lovejoy, who gained a reputation as the children's statesman, to participate in the founding meeting. Other founders included Sally Jean, Dr. Thomas Wood of Columbia University, a national authority on child health, Mrs. John Collier, the wife of a leader of the People's Institute, and Mrs. Frederick Peterson, the wife of a pediatrician member of the CWTPC who herself became important in the CHO. With the enthusiastic support of the NCLC leaders—Lovejoy became the first secretary of the CHO—the new organization affiliated with the NCLC, moving into its offices in New York and using its equipment in an effort by the CHO to save expenses and to prevent duplicating activities in the field.

In its first months, the CHO retained a simple organizational structure—as it did throughout its brief but important history—and pursued its activities vigorously. Dr. Holt became and remained chairman and, there were a treasurer and a secretary; Jean, the only paid staff member, became the director of fieldwork. Beginning in early May 1918, the CHO conducted a broad publicity campaign about malnutrition in schoolchildren, and the organization began describing programs, such as those at PS 40 in New York and others, to deal with problem. In the spring of 1918, following a suggestion made by the three New York women on their visit to federal officials in January 1918, Jean became a consultant to the USBE, which agreed to publish and to distribute much of the CHO literature. At the New York City Food Conservation Show in June 1918, the CHO displayed an exhibition and weighed and measured over three thousand children; it found two-thirds of them underweight and malnourished. The CHO published height-weight charts for school officials to use, as well as a teachers' service booklet. Pursuing the CHO goal of spreading child hygiene in the schools of the country, Field Director Jean spoke to the annual meeting of the National Education Association (NEA) in early July 1918, promoting further interest and inquiries. Continuing its initial concern for the children of New York, the CHO worked with other agencies to conduct all-day summer health and play schools for malnourished children in the summer of 1918. Working even more closely with the war effort, the CHO cooperated with the American National Red Cross* to supervise the health of servicemen's children in New York City. The CHO also worked in these early months to create a Bureau of School Lunches in the New York City Department of Education. Suggesting the growing national influence of this new, energetic organization, in 1918, the governor of Rhode Island asked the CHO to study the health conditions of women and children in his state. An experienced public health doctor who did similar work in other parts of the country, Dr. Lydia DeVilbliss, conducted the study. The CHO gained further national recognition in late 1918 when it agreed to have one of its workers, Lucy Oppen, prepare articles on child health during the war in *The Good Housekeeping Magazine*. The CHO helped to influence New York Governor Alfred Smith to include a pediatrician on the Reconstruction Committee to promote constructive postwar activities. Governor Smith appropriately appointed founder Dr. Henry Dwight Chapin to the Committee.

In the 1920s, the CHO continued its unique and energetic program to promote child hygiene, which, because of its own work, was developing nationwide as an issue of considerable concern. In December 1919, the CHO had cooperated with the NEA to convene a meeting for teachers of health education at the Russell Sage Foundation* Building in New York City. This initial gathering led to a series of health education conferences, which, under the apparent auspices of the CHO, developed its first project, to award fellowships in health education. These conferences led to another, nationally prominent one, at Lake Mohonk, New York, in June 1922, sponsored by the recently named CHOA and the USBE. That conference stressed a consistent theme of the CHOA: the need for adequate training for health education teachers. In the early 1920s, the CHOA developed characters, such as the health clown Cho-Cho and a health fairy, to demonstrate healthy eating. These characters participated in plays for children and in parades, such as the one in New York City which prompted the leading social service journal, *The Survey,* to note how enlivening the technique was for the children, who seemed to enjoy this method of learning about food.

The CHOA staff traveled throughout the country, holding institutes and training courses for health education teachers and for others. In the summer of 1922, with the Chautauqua Institute, the CHOA offered a course taught by staff member Mabel Bragg on the health education of children. Seventy teachers took the course. At the request of the New York State Department of Health, a staff member spent one week in each of three state normal schools.

CHOA influence extended nationwide. In 1922, for example, a representative from the staff worked with the Tuberculosis Association of San Francisco, California, to introduce health education into many schools in California, and Director Jean visited the city in February 1922 to survey existing health education activities. The CHOA also worked with the Commission for Relief in Belgium Educational Foundation, releasing Jean for six weeks to study Belgium's health problems. Through her efforts, fifteen Belgian teachers were given one-year health education scholarships in the United States. A Healthland exhibit proved popular; it was shown at twenty-four national, state, and local organizations. So impressive was the CHOA's record that in June 1922, the Commonwealth Fund,* a leader in the health field, proposed to fund a five-year child health demonstration project in each of three cities. The fund chose the CHOA and the American Child Hygiene Association* (ACHA) to conduct the project. Dr. Holt continued to participate fully in the CHOA, which was not quite the "one-man organization" that his biographers suggested. By 1922, Holt could not find a suitable young successor, so he began to promote the idea of a merger with the ACHA. Consequently, on January 1, 1923, the CHOA amalgamated with the ACHA to form the American Child Health Association.* As the CHOA itself suggested in 1922, its history revealed the value of demonstration and promotion in dealing with an important social issue, the health of children.

The sources for studying the brief CHOA history are diverse. The Papers of the People's Institute at the Manuscript Division of the New York Public Library and the archives of the New York Academy of Medicine both contain materials on its origins. The files of *The New York Times* are valuable, as is one hard-to-obtain published *Annual Report* for 1922. Agency leaders published reports and addresses, such as those of Sally Jean and Lucy Oppen, and Dr. Holt's article in *The New York Times,* June 30, 1918, is helpful. There is considerable material relating to the CHOA in both the Papers of the United States Children's Bureau and the Papers of the United States Bureau of Education, both at the National Archives in Washington, D.C.

There is no secondary study of the CHOA, but Robert Luther Duffus and Luther E. Holt, Jr., *L. Emmett Holt: Pioneer of a Children's Century* (1940), does have an account of the organization. Some of the interpretive statements in the text derive from Peter Romanofsky's research on the national and Missouri child hygiene campaigns immediately after World War I.

CHILD WELFARE LEAGUE OF AMERICA, INC. (CWLA). In the early twentieth century, both the increasing concern for child welfare services and the development of issue-oriented national social service agencies in the Progressive era influenced social and child care workers to consider forming a national agency for child welfare. They began to discuss the need for such a national organization at the famous White House Conference on the Care of Dependent Children in 1909, where the delegates, convened by President Theodore Roosevelt, resolved in favor of such a group. Following important child welfare worker Carl Christian Carsten's influential paper at the National Conference of Charities and Correction* (NCCC) in 1915 on the need for developing standards in child welfare work, eighteen representatives from fourteen child welfare organizations established the Bureau for the Exchange of Information among Child Helping Agencies (BEI) on May 17, 1915, in Baltimore at the NCCC.

The BEI engaged as its secretary C. Spencer Richardson, the associate director of the child-helping department of the Russell Sage Foundation.* The BEI met annually between 1916 and 1920. At the second annual meeting, in June 1917, the members decided to become a separate agency. Richardson conducted the BEI's activities until he left to serve in World War I in the summer of 1918. With secretarial services by the New York School of Social Work and clerical services by the State Charities Aid Association* (SCAA) of New York, the group of agencies continued minimal service. Designation of 1918–1919 as the Children's Year, the postwar problems affecting children, such as malnutrition and dependency, and other issues in the field, such as child labor and mothers' pensions, led the members of the BEI to press more vigorously for the establishment of a national organization similar to the American Association for Organizing Family Social Work* (AAOFSW).

In December 1919, at the children's Christmas conference, an annual gathering of leaders of the children's agencies, the group determined to establish a strong national organization. The child care workers decided to apply for foundation grants to support their plans. Their applications had not been decided on by the time of the BEI's annual meeting in April 1920, but an important stimulus to develop a national organization as the spokesman in the field occurred in 1920 when the National Children's Home and Welfare Association* (NCHWA) asked to affiliate with the proposed new group. Unexpectedly, on June 26, 1920, the Commonwealth Fund* agreed to provide at least $25,000 per year for four years. On August 4, 1920, the BEI's executive committee accepted the grant and its terms, with the understanding that they develop a new national organization. The executive committee then agreed to organize the sixty-five member agencies of the BEI into a new national agency to raise standards in and to stimulate the development and distribution of literature in the field of child welfare. The members of the BEI elected Carstens as director of the new agency on September 8, 1920, to begin in January 1921. On December 30, 1920, at the Christmas conference in New York City, the BEI's members adopted the first article of a proposed constitution, calling the new agency the Child Welfare League of America (CWLA). At the annual meeting of the National Conference of Social Work* (NCSW) in 1921, the CWLA completed organizational details, adopting the rest of the constitution, and electing traditional officers, a secretary, a treasurer, a vice-president, and, as president, Ida Curry, a leading child care worker, from the SCAA. The group also chose an eighteen-member executive committee. The CWLA, which began operations on January 2, 1921, established headquarters in New York City in the Russell Sage Fund Building.

Carstens shaped the early CWLA into the most important national child welfare agency in the United States. Throughout its history, CWLA standards on the full range of child welfare services have helped to improve the field nationwide. The early CWLA included sixty-five charter organizations as members, with a wide range of principles and practices among them. The debate over institutionalization or placing out dependent children had been raging among child welfare organizations and asylums since the late nineteenth century. One of the most important contributions of the CWLA was to influence a standardized national child welfare program, stressing temporary rather than permanent institutional care for dependent children and preserving the natural family home in cases threatening to make a child dependent. In March 1925, as a result of this concern, the CWLA adopted standards for foster care placements. Realizing that children's institutions were part of the total child care system, the CWLA also included institutions in its activities. This led to a series of surveys of child care facilities, which contributed to the improvement of standards and practices in the institutional field in the 1920s. In 1924, for example, the CWLA analyzed Protestant children's institutions and child-placing agencies, initiating the long-time association of Howard Kopkirk, an important worker specializing in church-related agencies. Hopkirk and these surveys provided the basis of CWLA services to these groups. With the Federal Council of the Churches of Christ in America (FCC), the CWLA sponsored the conference on church work for dependent and neglected children held in New York City in April 1927. Other surveys included one in 1926 of the Children's Home Society of Virginia and, at the request of the local community chest, several agencies and the juvenile court in Houston, Texas, in 1926. Other typical studies were those of all the children's agencies in a single locality, such as the one begun in 1926 in Richmond, Virginia. Contributing even further to the standardization and improvement of child welfare services, the CWLA developed a department of children's case work in 1924, conducted important regional conferences for workers in the field, and, beginning in the late 1920s, held training institutes for executives and experienced staff workers.

In the early years of the CWLA, the organization also participated actively in national social work developments and solidified its own organizational structure. Demonstrating its early national leadership in child welfare, the CWLA helped the American Legion (see *Fraternal Organizations*) to establish its child welfare agency in the early 1920s, acquainting its organizers with recognized child welfare principles and standards. During the 1920s, the NCHWA operated under the CWLA's auspices. In 1923, cooperating with the National Tuberculosis Association* and the National Association of Travelers Aid Societies,* the CWLA developed a new national transportation agreement relating to migrants and transients. In 1923, CWLA Director Carstens served as chairman of the Committee on Transportation of Allied National Agencies,* cementing the CWLA's position in the national social work community. At the 1924 CWLA meeting, the agency established a membership fee and, in an effort to broaden its base, expanded its executive committee to twenty-one members, including at least seven of whom were not to be from the staff of a constituent agency. Pressing financial problems in 1927 led to the use of quota contributions from constituent agencies as a method of financing the CWLA. In 1928 the CWLA completed efforts it had begun in the mid-1920s to incorporate according to the laws of New York State.

The legal incorporation of the CWLA in 1920 produced some organizational changes and heralded an expanding role for the agency. Chiefly through the personal activities of Executive Director Carstens, the CWLA participated in the White House Conference on Child Health and Protection in 1930. In 1931, the executive committee appointed a special group to supervise the CWLA incorporation of the Inter-City Conference on Illegitimacy,* one of several agencies to merge into the CWLA. In the early 1930s, the CWLA continued some of its basic activities, for example, publishing the *Manual for Cottage Mothers in Institutions* and completing a study of Presbyterian services for dependent children. Initiating an early CWLA contribution of the problems created by the depression, the board of directors in early 1933 discussed the national and dramatic issue of transient youths and then endorsed the plans and work of the Committee on Care of Transient and Homeless* (CCTH). Other CWLA leaders participated in developing programs, and The Children's Aid Society* of New York lent its secretary, Owen Lovejoy, to become, beginning in March 1933, the CWLA representative in Washington, D.C. In late 1933, the board influenced President Franklin D. Roosevelt to hold a conference under the auspices of the United States Children's Bureau (USCB) on dependent and neglected children. Locally the CWLA sponsored and led the Crusade for Children in New York City. In November 1935, the CWLA began a nationwide campaign, chaired by Major General James G. Harbord of New York, chairman of the board of the Radio Corporation of America, to focus attention on the country's half-million dependent, neglected, and delinquent children. Responding to the increasingly grim problems of children overseas, in 1937, the CWLA urged its constituents to help find foster homes for refugee German children. In the late 1930s, responding to the continued problems in adoption in America, the CWLA developed a campaign to publicize minimum safeguards and standards in adoption. A national radio broadcast in the spring of 1938 by a long-time adoption activist, novelist Dorothy Canfield Fisher, highlighted this CWLA effort.

While the CWLA leaped into the national limelight, some important organizational developments occurred in the decade after incorporation in 1928. By 1929, a shift away from primarily foundation support—suggested by the end of the grant from the Commonwealth Fund in February—to a greater reliance on members' contributions was evident. In the early 1930s, the publicity and extension work, organizing new and strengthening existing agencies, developed full time, strengthened by an additional staff member in 1933. In 1934, noted child welfare agent, C. W. Areson, began to share executive duties with Carstens, who was busy with national developments. In 1934, following a reclassification of membership categories, the CWLA eliminated public as opposed to private agencies from its constituency. A four-year grant, beginning in 1937, from the Commonwealth fund, allowed the CWLA to develop a pediatric advisory and consultation service for its constituent agencies. Dr. Florence A. Browne conducted this activity until September 1939, when she joined the staff of the USCB. A much more important loss was the death of Carstens on July 17, 1939, ending a phase in the history of the CWLA.

C. W. Areson and Alfred Whitman of the Boston Children's Aid Society piloted the CWLA through the unstable period following Carstens's death. Although Sybil Foster had replaced Carstens as acting executive director, she resigned in November 1939, having served only a few months. In 1940, led by a subcommittee of the committee on reorganization, the CWLA reevaluated its activities and drafted a new program. Discussions centered on becoming either a limited agency dealing with casework in foster home care or developing as a broader organization to promote benefits for disadvantaged children. In September 1940, Howard W. Hopkirk became executive secretary. Beginning to cooperate more with the USCB, the CWLA quickly showed that it was a broad agency serving all children. In December 1940, in an unusual development, the CWLA summoned executives from ten leading national social welfare agencies, presented its program, and asked their support for it. The group agreed that the CWLA should continue its field service to children's agencies around the country and that it should expand into new areas, such as services for black and migrant children. Continuing its services to professionals in the field, in late 1941, the CWLA held the first of a series of seminars for supervisors.

Events related to World War II ushered in new activities for the CWLA. Although it had begun to absorb the work and concerns of the National Association of Day Nurseries* (NADN) in the late 1930s, in 1941, the CWLA began cooperating with the USCB to promote day care for children of working mothers. Field visits to and consultations with public child welfare facilities, services, and staffs expanded. Day care continued as a major CWLA activity for about two years. In late 1942, the CWLA absorbed completely the now defunct NADN, expanding CWLA's interest in day care. As historian Howard Dratch has shown, however, the CWLA had, in light of the massive needs, a limited program in day care. Although in early 1940 Alice Dashiell joined the staff as a day care specialist and the CWLA organized a committee on day care, the agency did not establish a separate department to deal with this pressing social problem. Rather, it felt that its existing departments could deal with this important and specialized social service. Although the CWLA did sponsor a conference in June 1945 on day care needs after the war, the agency did not make day care a major activity. Other wartime activities included the establishment in 1943, with five other agencies, of the American War-Community Services, special studies of facilities for dependent and neglected children and studies of the care of children under two years old. In 1945, noting the increased importance of organized labor in social services, the CWLA initiated efforts to develop closer ties with both the American Federation of Labor and the Congress of Industrial Organizations (CIO). Alice Dashiell, who had joined the staff to conduct day care work, supervised this new CWLA activity, and the CWLA supplied a staff worker to cooperate with the CIO National War Relief-Community Services Committee, which was planning a conference with labor and social workers.

In the postwar period, the CWLA expanded a little but continued its basic program. In late 1946, the agency added the position of assistant executive director, and in early 1947, as an expanding service, it began to offer outside consultants to constituent agencies. In the late 1940s, as the sentiment to contribute local funds to national agencies grew, the CWLA began to receive funds from local community chests. In 1950, with a grant from the Field Foundation of New York and following requests from constituents, the CWLA began a major activity, a study of residential treatment centers for emotionally disturbed children. Interest in day care seemed to pick up a bit. In late 1950, for instance, the day care committee, established in the mid-1940s, urged state and federal funding for day care for defense workers' children, and some of the CWLA's materials on day care were used during the Midcentury White House Conference on Children and Youth in 1950. In late 1951, a grant from the United Community Defense Services* allowed the addition of two staff consultants on day care.

In the 1950s, the CWLA grew as a national social service agency and emphasized the importance of both old and new issues in child welfare. Beginning in 1951, the CWLA cooperated with the National Committee for Homemaker Service* to increase the use of homemaker services to prevent institutionalizing children. The CWLA's study of adoptions culminated with an adoption conference in 1955. In the mid-1950s, the CWLA once again promoted placing out children, citing recent studies indicating higher incidences of mental illness among institutionalized children. The CWLA urged paying foster parents more money to increase the number of foster homes available. A review of a decade of research led the CWLA to reaffirm in 1957 its policy of not accrediting agencies that institutionalized young children. The adoption of American Indian children developed in the late 1950s as an agency project. In 1958, the CWLA assigned a full-time staff worker to interest member agencies in finding adoptive homes for Indian children. These and other projects gave the public the impression that the CWLA dealt only in adoptions, but other issues attracted major efforts. Day care again emerged as an agency concern in the late 1950s. In November 1958, the board of directors recognized the need to give this activity high priority, and in 1959, the CWLA received a grant of $100,000 from the Ford Foundation to do a nationwide study of day care. The CWLA remained as the leading national agency in the field of child welfare, developing a program in the late 1950s to provide field services to nonmember agencies. Grants from the Bronfman Foundation supported this project.

In the 1960s, when federal government programs began to dominate social services in the United States, the CWLA developed as a model voluntary agency, constructively criticizing public programs, pioneering in the development of new projects and programs, and conducting research on a number of subjects. The board of directors discussed the widespread attacks on the federal Aid to Dependent Children (ADC) program, and the CWLA provided information for a widely circulated article in *The Saturday Evening Post* dealing with ADC. In 1960, the CWLA called for an investigation by the federal Department of Health, Education, and Welfare of an episode in Louisiana whereby the state removed about 23,000 children, mostly black, from the federal ADC program. In 1961, the CWLA hired two sociologists to study the incident. Later in the decade, in 1968, with the National Council of the Churches of Christ in the U.S.A., the CWLA filed an amicus curiae to the United States Supreme Court to uphold the rights of children in the ADC. To deal further with public welfare, in 1960, the CWLA had established a committee, chaired by Ellen Winston, the commissioner of public welfare in North Carolina, to determine how the organization could best improve public child care agencies.

Adoption and foster care continued to be major agency concerns. In 1962, the CWLA began a study, supported by the USCB, of the nationwide decline in adoptions. In late 1964, the CWLA received $1.25 million from the USCB for a five-year study of foster care, and in 1965, the CWLA established a foster care project. Also in the mid-1960s, the CWLA established a national adoption resource exchange. In the late 1960s, the adoption exchange became the Adoption Resource Exchange of North America, an independent agency sponsored by the CWLA. In an area related to adoption, in 1964, the CWLA agreed to sponsor, with the Family Service Association of America* (FSAA), the National Association on Services to Unmarried Parents.* Always concerned with the care of children in institutions, in 1960, the CWLA began a series of conferences, institutes, and training sessions to improve the quality of institutional child care workers. In late 1963, the board of directors established the research department, which became a major agency activity.

In the 1970s, when research grew in importance as an agency activity, the CWLA also developed close ties with other national social service agencies. In 1973, the research center began to evaluate a neighborhood program in Brooklyn, New York, that attempted to divert families and children from courts and institutions. In the same year, the CWLA received a grant from the federal Office of Child Development to conduct a four-year study of child rearing by young, white mothers. As other specialized child welfare groups developed and grew in influence in the 1970s, the CWLA moved to retain its leadership in the field. In early 1972, it invited representatives of other agencies to help develop its national program for comprehensive child welfare services. Also in 1972, the joint committee of the FSAA, the Florence Crittenton Association of America* (FCAA), and the CWLA met to discuss amalgamation. This was the result of earlier discussion between the CWLA and the FSAA on joint efforts. In early 1976, CWLA absorbed the FCAA, but the FSAA remained an independent organization. Two programs tried to improve the continuing problem of children's institutions. In 1973, the CWLA began a national project to assess the strengths and weaknesses of institutions, and the agency received a grant from the National Institute of Mental Health for a two-year project to improve staff development in institutions. Dr. Martin Wolins of the University of California School of Social Welfare designed and directed the project. Characteristically in the vanguard of child welfare, the CWLA not only played an important role in the federal legislation adopted in February 1974 to deal with child abuse and neglect but also launched a nationwide campaign to develop and maintain effective child protection services throughout the country.

The primary sources for studying the CWLA's history include the papers of the agency on microfilm at the Social Welfare History Archives Center, University of Minnesota, Minneapolis. The CWLA's library in New York City retained some of these files, such as minutes of meetings. The issues of the CWLA *Bulletin,* which became *Child Welfare* in 1948, provide a little information on the agency, as do *The President's Letter,* 1956–1969, and the more recent *Newsletter. The New York Times* also covered major events of the CWLA.

Aside from Howard Dratch's mention of the CWLA in his "The Politics of Child Care in the 1940s," *Science and Society* 28 (Summer 1974): 167–204, there does not seem to be any other scholarly study of this leading national social service agency.

CHILDREN'S AID SOCIETY, THE (CAS). In New York City in the midnineteenth century, a number of missionaries, social reformers, and officials became concerned with the general conditions of neglected, delinquent children. In 1848, A. D. F. Randolph of the Carmine Street Presbyterian Church began to meet with boys hoping that religious inspiration would reshape their broken lives. The 1849 semiannual report of the New York City police captain dramatized the increase in crimes by young boys. The report and the publicity surrounding it prompted other clergymen, including William C. Russell, Benjamin

Howland, and Charles Loring Brace, to act. Brace had been to European cities in 1850, and he had seen the way vagrant youths contributed to revolutionary activity and violence abroad. When he returned from Europe in 1851, Brace joined another missionary with a reform program in the Five Points section of New York, the most dangerous and degrading area of the city. Brace also resumed his visits to the New York City Almshouse on Blackwell's Island, exposing him further to poverty and degrading conditions in the city. In 1853, Russell, Howland, Brace, and others began to meet with and to work to reform groups of vagrant boys, realizing increasingly that they needed a greater effort to produce changes in the boys' lives. They promptly organized their efforts as The Mission. On January 9, 1853, the missionaries offered Brace the leadership of this enterprise to deal with vagrant and delinquent children. In February, the organization became The Children's Aid Society (CAS) of New York.

As soon as he became the head of the new group, Brace developed and activated the program of the CAS. In February 1853, the group organized itself, featuring a board of trustees comprising fifteen leaders from various Protestant denominations. The CAS decided to continue boys' meetings and to initiate similar one for girls. A group of church women associated with the CAS opened an industrial school for vagrant youths in February 1853, but the principal early industrial school of the organization developed later in 1853 in the basement of the Mariners' Chapel, suggesting further the religious underpinnings of the CAS. The CAS opened its first office in the New Bible House in 1853. A workshop to conduct shoe pegging opened in the first year, evidence of early and continuing CAS interest and activities in industrial education for wayward children in New York City.

The most important CAS program was the so-called placing-out system. It developed early and stemmed directly from Secretary Brace's experiences and ideas. In its first year, the CAS issued a circular expressing Brace's ideas. In it, Brace announced his plan to train vagrants in industrial schools and then to send them to live and to work with farm families. Dangerously close to the virtually defunct indenture system, the plan attempted to reform delinquent boys in an atmosphere that Brace and many of his generation believed best for children: rural family homes. The CAS took children from the streets and even from what it thought were degrading parents and sent the children to rural areas around New York, and then, increasingly, to the Midwest. Typically an agent representing the CAS, generally a minister, would accompany a trainload of children, each carrying the Bible, to a rural town away from New York. The local press cooperated widely, announcing the availability and arrival time of the children. The children gathered at the railroad station or, more often, in a local church. Farm families came and picked up children about whom they had corresponded with either the agent or the New York office. In many cases, farmers simply chose a young boy or girl on sight. The CAS did try generally to place children with families it considered respectable, a standard that remained difficult to define precisely and even more troublesome to determine and to maintain, especially when the New York–based agency lacked a fully developed, trained network of social workers to investigate and to follow up on the placed-out children.

Not surprisingly, the placing-out system became a controversial but nevertheless important development in the care of dependent and delinquent children. Throughout the late nineteenth century, social workers criticized the CAS for its failure to provide professional caseworkers to conduct the home finding and follow-up work. Local communities in rural America charged that the CAS dumped troubled and troublesome New York City youngsters in their peaceful environments. New York Catholic leaders protested, probably correctly, that Brace's organization took Catholic children and then sent them to Protestant family homes. Because they either missed the life and excitement of the city or because their foster families overworked or otherwise mistreated them, many children ran away from their new families. Despite the shortcomings of the placing-out system, it did help to shape many homeless and troublesome children into respectable and even leading citizens, a phenomenon that founder Brace repeated proudly and constantly in his wide-ranging speeches and writings. Most importantly, this pioneering home-finding venture spearheaded the national movement in the late nineteenth century to place out children rather than to institutionalize them in orphanages, houses of refuge, and other asylums. In the late nineteenth century, the CAS of New York developed as the model agency for similar societies in other cities, such as in Philadelphia and Boston, both of which developed programs to promote social services for poor, homeless, and troubled children.

The CAS also developed important services for the children of New York City. By 1863, the CAS was conducting eight industrial schools, providing over sixteen hundred children with basic skills in the rapidly developing industrial economy. By the 1870s, Brace was urging half-day industrial schools for children too poor to attend school all day long, and the CAS industrial schools helped throughout the late nineteenth century to keep many troubled children in school. In the early 1870s, Brace and the CAS influenced the enactment of the first compulsory education law in New York City, and three years later, the CAS founded the first kindergarten; both activities were important educational reforms in the city.

Following a tradition of medical charities and early public health measures, which urban missionaries influenced in the early nineteenth century and anticipating later visiting nurse services, in 1873, with funds donated by readers of the *New York Times,* the CAS established its sick children's mission. The mission supplied food, nutrition education, and general medical care to needy parents and their children in New York. Also in 1873, with the contribution of one of the many philanthropists who enthusiastically supported the activities of the organization—in this case, Anson Phelps Stokes—the CAS established the first fresh air camp on Staten Island. The sick children's mission and the fresh air work both helped in the 1870s to reduce the infant mortality rate in the city. Anticipating the day nursery movement of the Progressive era, the CAS opened in 1881 the first crèche in New York to care for the babies of working mothers, a socially important activity that continued to operate until 1928. The death of founder and leader Charles Loring Brace in 1890 ended an era in the agency's history. Carrying on a long family affiliation with the CAS, Charles Loring Brace, Jr., replaced his father as head of the organization. In 1893, the CAS opened the Brace Memorial Farm School at Valhalla, New York, to give boys being placed out a taste of both rural life and appropriate training in farm work. A philanthropist provided funds for this venture, honoring Brace, who remained, despite the criticism and controversies, a major reformer in the history of American social services for needy children.

Under its new leader, the CAS developed in the early twentieth century as a modern, multipurpose child care agency. By the early twentieth century, when the industrial schools were part of the public school system but remained financed by the private sources of the CAS, experiment and reform in the CAS schools developed more fully than before. In 1902, for instance, the CAS provided the first free classes in the city to mentally defective children, whose special problems the organization had begun to realize. Years before the public schools in New York had school nurses, each CAS school had one by 1909. With its school nurses and other affiliated medical personnel, in 1906, the CAS initiated an educational campaign against tuberculosis, paralleling and supplementing the efforts of social reformers and public health activists in dealing with this predominantly urban disease. Pioneering an idea that others developed later in New York, the CAS converted the roof of its West Side School as an open air playground in 1909. It also opened its sanitarium for convalescing and anemic children in Chappaqua, New York. Other similar CAS facilities and services developed in Progressive-era New York, including the first open air class for anemic children in 1915.

In the 1920s, when the spirit of the Progressive movement waned even among some other social work and social reform organizations, the CAS continued to improve the lives of New York children. After the end of World War I, the CAS began activities in the spontaneous but apparently unorganized movement nationally to improve child hygiene, developing a comprehensive nutrition campaign under its own medical director. Providing a new service to troubled families and children, in 1924, the CAS organized its new department of boarding homes to board children temporarily while their parents resolved health, unemployment, marital, and other problems. Increasingly, hospitals and social agencies throughout the New York area sent children to the CAS medical bureau, which had been established in 1915. The children then went to a variety of CAS convalescent homes, including the one at Chappaqua, New York, later called the Elizabeth Milbank Anderson Home after the philanthropist. In December 1927, when the second Brace retired, the CAS hired a child welfare reformer as secretary who had been especially active in the long fight against child labor, Owen Lovejoy. Winding up the decade under Lovejoy, the CAS in 1929 ended its controversial but influential placing-out system.

Under Lovejoy's leadership in the late 1920s and early 1930s, the CAS developed important new programs and services, despite the Great Depression. Lovejoy led the CAS to develop services for Negro children, a neglected but needy group in New York City. In the late 1920s, for instance, the CAS opened its Harlem Colored Children's Center. In the early 1930s, it provided special summer camps for black children at its facility at Valhalla, New York. The agency hoped this effort would stimulate others to provide similar programs for blacks. The CAS also maintained a facility for black girls at its Goodhue Home on Staten Island. So respected were the CAS activities for blacks that in 1932 the New York City Department of Welfare asked the agency to care for a group of older black boys, generally neglected by black child care institutions, which seemed to prefer children between two and twelve years old. The CAS responded to the severe conditions in mid-1933 in Harlem by inaugurating a feeding program for a hundred of the most undernourished children at its children's center in Harlem. Owen Lovejoy paid special attention to the needs of Negro children; his *The Negro Children of New York* (1933) was a timely and detailed study.

After a study in 1929 showed that nearly 70 percent of the boys in Manhattan were not reached by boys' work programs, the CAS expanded its boys' club work, renovating four health centers to serve as clubs. The CAS continued to be virtually the only agency providing convalescent care for older boys, at the facility in Valhalla, New York. Largely because of the efforts of an advisory committee chaired by Dr. Henry W. Thurston of the New York School of Social Work, the family home department increased its services in the late 1920s, participating in the trend of keeping children together with their families rather than placing them in foster homes or in institutions. In 1933, to strengthen this work, the CAS cooperated with the New York Junior League to establish a housekeeper service so children could remain with their own families during family crises. In early 1931 the CAS reorganized its placement work, combining its free home and boarding programs into one department of foster home care. This new department had separate headquarters (on East Forty-fifth Street), and a committee of laymen and social workers, chaired by Thurston, advised this enterprise. In the early 1930s, the CAS began to assume special responsibility for boys aged sixteen to twenty-one, providing educational opportunities and work for about four thousand of them. Some of the boys lived and worked at the Bowdoin Memorial Farm School at New Hamburg, New York. President Franklin D. Roosevelt visited the school in August 1933. When the federal Civilian Conservation Corps began in 1933, the CAS closed this facility. Also during the period of the depression, the CAS increased public interest in the plight of transient boys, chiefly through radio broadcasts by prominent individuals.

Under the leadership of Arthur Huck, the former comptroller and assistant treasurer who replaced Lovejoy as executive director in 1930, the CAS continued its creative and important role in the city and the nation. In the mid-1930s, it established its counseling and guidance service, as well as a department of personal relationships. In 1935, the CAS conducted a six-month study of the factors that tended to produce problems in children. A psychiatrist from the famous Payne-Whitney psychiatric facility supervised this project. Its findings stimulated the CAS to expand its department of personal relationship services in the agency's boys' club work. The counseling and employment service continued to help older boys in the 1930s. In 1933, the CAS organized the popular Yankee Sandlot Baseball League, which played some games in Yankee Stadium, provided by the generosity of Colonel Jacob Ruppert, the owner of the New York Yankees. When the federal Transient Service (see *Government Agencies*) was dissolved in late 1935, the CAS again assumed the major responsibility for transient older boys in New York City. During this period, the CAS initiated a program of foster day care for children whose parents worked. In late 1937, the CAS assumed full responsibility for the housekeeping service and organized a new committee to stimulate greater interest in this program. Among the demonstration projects, in 1937, the CAS attempted to return to normal life in their community a group of delinquent black boys who were cared for in foster homes.

During the period before American entry into World War II, the organization still cared for black boys twelve to seventeen years old who were public charges and for whom no other agency would assume responsibility. In the summer of 1937, the CAS abandoned its practice of dividing campers according to their neighborhoods, a decision that eventually led to racial integration at the camps. Late in the decade, a group of prominent citizens asked the CAS to administer an extensive foster placement service for dependent and neglected black children. With funds from several foundations and individuals, the CAS opened this special bureau in May 1939. At the CAS's request, the founders of this plan acted as a special committee to aid this work generally, which the CAS planned as a five-year demonstration project that the municipal Department of Welfare would eventually incorporate.

World War II affected the programs and services of the CAS. The Brace Memorial Lodging House sheltered soldiers on furloughs and new recruits awaiting assignments. In the early 1940s, the CAS trained a volunteer group of canteen and nutrition workers to staff kitchens in case of emergencies. In this project, it cooperated with the federal Office of Civilian Defense, the American Women's Voluntary Services, and the American National Red Cross* (ANRC). The CAS's boys' and girls' clubs, as well as its playgrounds and centers, served so-called war work orphans. Both the housekeeper service and the foster care programs expanded to handle the increased loads caused by the wartime social dislocations. During this period, the CAS administered locally the program of the United States Committee for the Care of European Children* (USCCEC). In

1943, the CAS began an experiment in placing in family homes young delinquent children who had not reached the stage of serious delinquency. In that same year, the organization integrated its service bureau for black children with its regular foster home department on East Forty-fifth Street. A gift from the Rotary Club of New York allowed the CAS to expand its dental services at its boys' clubs, and the CAS opened a new health clinic for the increasing number of babies cared for by the foster home department.

In the late 1940s and 1950s, the CAS, which celebrated its centennial anniversary in 1953, continued to adapt to the rapidly changing conditions that affected children in New York City. As the population of blacks and Puerto Ricans increased in the city, the CAS began to develop new foster homes farther from the city in Dutchess, Ulster, and Suffolk counties. It began to experiment with the use of intensive psychiatric services for troubled children, a psychiatrist began to meet weekly with all the workers, and the counseling and employment service increased its services for teenagers. In the late 1940s, each of its seven children's centers were located in marginal and troubled neighborhoods, plagued by low-income and poor health facilities and housing. Each center offered boys' and girls' clubs, supervised playgrounds, summer camp programs, medical and dental examinations and clinics, nutritious lunches, convalescent care and services in foster home and homemaker, delinquent prevention, and counseling and employment services. As neighborhoods changed in the early 1950s, the CAS closed, shifted, and opened childrens' centers. In 1954, the CAS opened a new center in Harlem. By the mid-1950s, the municipal Department of Welfare provided foster care services, but it often called on the CAS, especially to care for emotionally disturbed children. In 1956, the CAS opened Wagon Road Camp in Chappaqua, New York, for handicapped children. In the late 1950s, the CAS established a teenage council, with representatives from the centers, each of which cooperated with the mayor's summer delinquency prevention program.

During the creative years of the 1960s, the CAS participated in mainstream social services, developing new programs and expanding old ones. In 1960, for instance, the homemaker service began a demonstration project to provide twenty-four-hour service to families from which children would otherwise have to be placed in shelters. On May 10, 1965, the Child Care and Adoption Service, Inc., formerly affiliated with the State Communities Aid Association* (SCAA) of New York, and the CAS foster home department merged to form under the CAS a statewide program of counseling and services to natural parents, children, and adoptive families. The various convalescent facilities were consolidated into one enlarged facility at Chappaqua. In the mid-1960s, the CAS added to its staff people from group work and education disciplines. Increasingly the CAS was involved in remedial reading, tutoring, and help with homework. Five centers participated in the federal Head Start program for very young children. In 1964, the board of directors authorized a new position of assistant executive director to help lead and coordinate a multitude of programs. In the summer of 1965, the

CAS began to sponsor an experiment in reading for boys and girls about to enter high school, Take a Giant Step (TAGS). During this period, the agency both hired two professional fund raisers to work closely with volunteer committees to raise more money and installed a computer system to process direct mail appeals. In 1967, in light of new drugs and a changing philosophy in pediatrics, the CAS closed its Elizabeth Milbank Anderson Convalescent Home for Children at Chappaqua, which had operated for fifty-eight years. The CAS used the facility, however, for winter camping for children from the centers in the city. In the late 1960s, all the programs—medical services, foster care, Head Start, camping, counseling and employment, and so on—were expanded.

In the 1970s, the CAS had eleven physical plants but it still spent over 80 percent of its funds on its direct services to improve child life in New York City. In the late 1960s and early 1970s, the CAS experimented with substituting intensive work with small groups of children for the older mass recreation programs. Because of what the CAS felt was widespread malnutrition, it continued the free breakfast program in the early 1970s. The CAS naturally developed community organization activities. For example, the agency helped parents to participate in public school affairs during and after the well-publicized decentralization in the city. The CAS also began a special activity to examine ways of breaking down misunderstanding and mistrust in ethnic neighborhoods. A special pilot program in East Harlem, Neighbors in Training toward Action (NTTA), developed to help people improve their environment: members became experts in institutions, social services, and housing. With the Margaret Sanger Bureau, the CAS began a pilot project in sex education for teenage girls. Another pilot program at a children's center showed that having a psychotherapist at the facility every day as just another staff worker almost eliminated the stigma of his help among the children. In 1973, five of the CAS's centers were licensed by the New York State Department of Mental Hygiene to conduct mental health programs, which provided immediate psychiatric help. The CAS developed a learning center on the Lower East Side of Manhattan, a bright, open classroom with one teacher for every five children. The foster care program moved more actively into crisis prevention, and in the mid-1970s, the CAS was chosen as one of seven agencies for a state-funded demonstration project attempting to show to what degree intensive services could prevent the need for foster placement or ensure the return of a child to his own family. The homemaker service, which expanded steadily, played an important role in this project.

The sources for studying the CAS's history are extensive. The best and most readily available primary source is the published and detailed *Annual Reports*. *The New York Times* covered the CAS extensively. The CAS published a helpful, brief history, *The Crusade for Children* (1928). Other contemporary agency publications indicate its history as well. The CAS has many of its files, including minutes of meetings and the like, but the use of these records is restricted.

A number of historians have studied the CAS, especially its early period.

Miriam Z. Langsam, *Children West: A History of the Placing-Out System of the New York Children's Aid Society, 1853-1890* (1964), is an informative study that generally depicts favorably the CAS's controversial system. There is a helpful section of the CAS's history in Henry W. Thurston, *The Dependent Child* (1930). Much has been written by historians about founder Charles Loring Brace. See, for instance, Thomas Bender, *Toward an Urban Vision* (1975). Standard works in the history of social welfare in the nineteenth century, such as Robert Bremner, *From the Depths* (1956), and Joseph M. Hawes, *Children in Urban Society* (1971), deal with the CAS. Carroll Smith Rosenberg, *Religion and the Rise of the American City* (1971), stress the CAS's religious origins, Interestingly, historians of twentieth-century social welfare history have generally not paid much attention to the CAS. For example, Robert Bremner, editor, *Children and Youth in America: A Documentary History* (1970-1974), has numerous references to the CAS for the years before 1910 but not for after. There is thus room for further studies of this important and interesting agency, particularly in the twentieth century.

CHURCH MISSION OF HELP: see EPISCOPAL SERVICE FOR YOUTH.

CHURCH WORLD SERVICE (CWS). During and after World War II, a number of church-related relief agencies focusing on people abroad were established. By early 1946, representatives of some church agencies decided to form a united, coordinated effort by American Protestant and Orthodox churches. Discussions to found such an agency began in March 1946 by an eleven-member committee, chaired by Wynn C. Fairfield of the Congregational Christian Mission Board and who later served as the executive director of CWS. As a result of these discussions, in early May 1946, representatives from the Federal Council of the Churches of Christ in America (FCC), the Foreign Missions Conference of North America, and the American Committee of the World Council of Churches met and established CWS to coordinate the numerous church relief efforts. Three predecessor church relief agencies joined together in May 1946 to form CWS: the Church Committee on Overseas Relief and Reconstruction, the Commission for the World Church Service, and the Committee for Relief in Asia.

The new CWS invited the denominations to appoint representatives to its governing board. At the beginning, seventeen denominations became part of CWS, which did not intend to pool resources but rather hoped to serve as a forum for church relief agencies to discuss the total relief program. The establishment of the agency was significant, according to Professor Merle Curti's *American Philanthropy Abroad* (1963), because it was the "first fully unifying and coordinating instrument for overseas relief and reconstruction in the history of American Protestant and Orthodox churches." The first officers included a president, Harper Sibley, a Rochester, New York businessman, a treasurer, and an executive vice-president, A. L. Warnshuis, the former secretary of the International Missionary Council. Warnshuis had also been the first American to visit Europe after D-Day on June 6, 1944. There were also two executive associates, each of whom had experience in missionary work abroad.

In its earliest years and in its first activities, CWS tried to avoid proselytizing abroad, but relief efforts inevitably aided churches, pastors, youth groups, and the like. In 1946, CSW assumed responsibility for eight material aid centers in the United States, which had belonged to the Church Committee on Overseas Relief and Reconstruction, one of CWS's predecessors. In the first few months of 1947, its first full year of operation, CWS resettled nearly fifteen hundred refugees in thirty-two cities and 124 other communities throughout the United States. This work predated the establishment of the United States Displaced Persons Commission (USDPC) (see *Government Agencies*), which was created in 1948. Thirty-six CWS workers in immigrant and general welfare helped displaced persons in refugee camps, aided war prisoners, and set up summer camps in Europe, feeding about forty-one thousand children. In 1947, CWS also helped to bring European theological students to America. More importantly, in 1947, with the Lutheran World Relief* (LWR) and the National Catholic Rural Life Conference, CWS organized the creative Christian Rural Overseas Program (CROP), through which American farmers donated commodities. In the first year, the farmers gave 1.4 million pounds of commodities.

In its second year of operation, 1948, CWS conducted activities that were typical of its work: resettling displaced persons in the United States and elsewhere, organizing homes for the aged abroad, providing supplies and services for people in refugee camps, aiding orphans and orphanages in Germany, Hungary, Austria, and Holland, helping to provide food, milk powder, vitamins, and medicine to refugees in Lebanon, Syria, Jordan, and Jewish Palestine, and serving in soup kitchens and milk centers in Jerusalem.

The organizational developments in 1948, however, were not typical. A reduced budget forced CWS to close warehouses in Boston and Dayton, Ohio. Dr. Warnshuis retired, and he was replaced for six months by Cannon Almon P. Pepper, an experienced administrator who then was serving as the director of the Department of Christian Social Relations* of the Protestant Episcopal church (PEC). Pepper headed the church policy division, and Dr. Herbert C. Lytle, Jr., a Methodist minister who had served as an executive assistant to Dr. Warnshuis, headed the church administration work. Nationwide radio appeals by the presiding bishop of the PEC helped CWS, increasing its contributed supplies and generally promoting its prestige. In 1949, the resettlement of displaced persons was the major activity, as the agency served as a direct line to and provided much of the budget of the department of interchurch aid and service to refugees of the World Council of Churches (WCC). Also in 1949, CWS initiated its first Great Hour of Sharing, a radio network broadcast to raise funds and donations.

During the 1950s, CWS continued its relief and refugee programs, developed new services, and even became involved in some controversial incidents. In 1950, a reduction in donations forced some curtailments, but CWS slashed its promotional activities rather than cut into relief services. Remarkably, CWS brought over nineteen thousand displaced persons to the United States in 1950. In the early 1950s, the agency operated centers for displaced persons in New Windsor, Maryland, St. Louis, Oakland, and Seattle. In 1952, when the USDPC dissolved, CWS also ended its resettlement program in the United States, but it immediately began immigrant services. In a well-publicized case in 1956, CWS prevented a little girl born in America from being taken back to the U.S.S.R. by her father. Relief abroad continued in 1950 when workers in Korea helped children and the aged to evacuate war-torn areas. On February 29, 1952, CROP severed ties with the two other agencies and became affiliated solely with CWS. In the early 1950s, CWS—which dealt in large quantities rather than in individual relief packages—clarified its relations with Cooperative for American Remittances to Everywhere* (CARE) and other agencies. From 1953 on, CWS was able to meet disasters quickly because it had stockpiles located in disaster-prone areas throughout the world. CWS provided a variety of services in the Far East, but in 1957, the largest amount of aid went to the Middle East. In 1958, with LWS, CWS began a successful five-year program in Yugoslavia to promote the establishment of kitchens and serving of better food in schools. In December 1949, immediately after President Dwight Eisenhower's press conference arguing that people abroad who wanted birth control information should go to private agencies, not to United States government agencies, the CWS director, R. Norris Wilson, called a press conference to denounce the president's position. Wilson announced, for the first time publicly, that CWS had been giving birth control information in about twelve countries. On January 1, 1951, the previously independent and temporary CWS had become a permanent department of the new National Council of the Churches of Christ in the U.S.A. (NCC) (see *Religious Institutions*), but this change did not affect its activities.

In the 1960s, CWS continued its basic services, including birth control programs, and reacted to new situations. For example, in response to developments in Cuba, the agency's immigration service director, James MacCracken, organized Flights for Freedom, a cooperative venture with other organizations. An effort to settle Cubans in areas other than Miami, the flights, and a creative use of planes for charity enhanced CWS's national image. CWS helped to train national leaders abroad, and it had a policy of having nationals work in CWS offices abroad. In 1964, the agency coordinated food-for-work projects, as well as land reclamation projects abroad. In line with this, the agency phased out a family feeding program in Taiwan, strengthening the peoples' abilities to help themselves. Operation Doctor, which flew volunteers to Africa to provide food, self-help projects, and medicine, aided people in many countries. In 1964, CWS began projects to improve the quality of life, such as developing a solar distillation project off the Greek island of Symi. In 1964, the agency became administratively part of the division of overseas ministries of the NCC.

In the late 1960s and 1970s, CWS maintained its relief work, but it stressed its self-help projects throughout the world. In 1966, in cooperation with LWR, it established Vietnam Christian Service (VCS), which featured a wide range of rehabilitation, self-help, and agricultural projects. To serve war-torn people better, in the early 1970s, VCS expanded its physical therapy and training programs. In India and Indonesia, for instance, CWS cooperated with indigenous church agencies and church councils to provide material assistance and self-help. CWS provided emergency shipments of food and supplies to Niger in the Sahel in the mid-1970s. CWS aided refugees in Ethiopia, provided material assistance to people in areas in Africa that had become independent, and sponsored water development and public health projects in the Malagasy Republic. Its goal of promoting indigenous leadership was partly realized in east Asia in 1963 when, for the first time since CWS programs began there in 1946, not one Christian service agency was directed by an American. In the Middle East and Europe, similar services for refugees and the needy were provided. In the early 1970s, CWS maintained mother-child care centers in India, Brazil, Ghana, and Indonesia, for example, and it continued its planned parenthood programs throughout the world. In 1973, CWS also provided emergency relief after floods, tornadoes, and fires in thirteen communities in the United States, including Wounded Knee, South Dakota. The One Great Hour of Sharing remained an annual event. About thirty denominations and related agencies worked through CWS in 1974.

Throughout its history, CWS conducted its activities in the best tradition of charity and of ecumenism. Although some denominations were skeptical of and even opposed the agency—the Southern Baptist Convention, for instance, joined CWS at its inception but then dropped out—many churchmen praised CWS.

The sources for studying CWS's history include reports of its activities in the published reports of the FCC and the NCC. For the recent years, there are separately published *Annual Reports,* which contain considerable details. *The New York Times* covered some of its activities. Some of CWS's files are in its headquarters in New York City, and others are at the Presbyterian Historial Society in Philadelphia, Pennsylvania.

Harold Fey, *Cooperation in Compassion* (1966), is a favorable year-by-year account of CWS's activities. Merle Curti, *American Philanthropy Abroad* (1963), describes CWS. Robert R. Sullivan, "The Politics of Altruism" (Ph.D. diss., The Johns Hopkins University, 1968), used the files relating to CWS's material resources division and surplus commodities activities. There does not appear to be a scholarly history of CWS.

COMMISSION ON CHRISTIAN SOCIAL ACTION OF THE EVANGELICAL AND REFORMED CHURCH: see EVANGELICAL AND REFORMED CHURCH, COMMISSION ON CHRISTIAN SOCIAL ACTION OF THE.

COMMISSION ON THE CHURCH AND SOCIAL SERVICE OF THE FEDERAL COUNCIL OF THE CHURCHES OF CHRIST IN AMERICA: see NATIONAL COUNCIL OF THE CHURCHES OF CHRIST IN THE U.S.A., DIVISION OF CHURCH AND SOCIETY OF THE.

COMMITTEE ON CARE OF TRANSIENT AND HOMELESS: see COUNCIL ON INTERSTATE MIGRATION, INC.

COMMITTEE ON TRANSPORTATION OF ALLIED NATIONAL AGENCIES (CTANA). Starting in the late nineteenth century, social workers became aware of and concerned with the interrelated problems of transiency, homelessness, joblessness, and vagrancy. During this period, social service agencies and charities, such as The Charity Organization Society of the City of New York* (COS) developed a number of responses to and programs for people suffering under these conditions; for instance, it advocated and developed work relief projects for men. In 1891, the National Conference of Charities and Correction* (NCCC), the leading forum for social workers, expanded its committee on immigration to include "immigration between the states." In 1900, responding to the problems of cities that indiscriminately passed on hard-core welfare cases to other cities, the National Conference of Jewish Charities* (NCJC) developed its pioneering transportation agreement in 1900. The NCJC's agreement quickly gained a number of enthusiasts in the national social work community. In 1902, at the annual meeting of the NCCC, a session on needy families in their homes prompted the establishment of a four-member Committee on Transportation of Dependents (CTD), an affiliate of the NCCC. The chairman of this committee was Charles F. Weller, the general secretary of the Associated Charities of Washington, D.C. Max Senior, who worked for the Jewish Charities of Cincinnati and was active in the development of the NCJC agreement of 1900, also served the CTD. The agency circulated rules for social service agencies for comments. The CTD apparently published these regulations in January 1904 as the *Handbook Concerning the Issuance of Free Transportation and Charity Rates,* which held that ending free transportation would eliminate problems causing poverty. By the time of the publication of the third edition of this *Handbook* in 1910, 338 agencies had signed the transportation agreement promoted by the CTD.

The next committee of the NCCC, established at the annual meeting in 1910, became a permanent program, and its members were appointed annually. The idea for this type of structure stemmed from Francis H. McLean, who helped to establish the National Association of Societies for Organizing Charity* in 1911. This new Committee on Transportation (CT), chaired by Jeffrey Brackett, a key figure in social services for migrants and director of the Boston School of Social Work, included two other members in addition to Alexander Johnson, the president of the NCCC who served ex officio. The CT received help from the Russell Sage Foundation* (RSF), whose charity organization department was appointed the agent for the new group. Initially Margaret F. Byington and, after 1911, Fred S. Hall, both from the RSF staff, supervised the CT. In 1911, the CT published *Passing On as a Method of Charitable Relief*. Most important for the future of the CT, between 1910 and 1920, national agencies strengthened their activities with and concerns for migrants. It was thus appropriate that the national social service agencies, rather than the National Conference of Social Work* (NCSW), organize the next committee in 1921.

The Committee on Transportation of Allied National Agencies (CTANA) was established in 1921 by representatives from four national social service agencies, each of which had services for and experiences with migrants: the American Association for Organizing Family Social Work* (AAOFSW), the Child Welfare League of America* (CWLA), the National Association of Travelers Aid Societies* (NATAS), and the National Tuberculosis Association* (NTA). The CTANA had direct ties with the previous committees of the NCCC and the NCSW.

Supported by many national agencies, the CTANA played a useful role in the national social welfare community. In 1925, the National Council of the Church Mission of Help* joined the CTANA. Each of the member agencies appointed one representative to the CTANA; this group, in turn, chose the members at large. Jeffrey Brackett, Fred Hall, Carl Christian Carstens, a leader in child welfare and the head of the CWLA, and Bertha McCall, long interested in the problems of migrants and general director of the NATAS, for instance, represented their respective agencies. In 1923, the CTANA decided that agency signatories to the transportation agreement be renewed each year. By 1927, 685 local agencies had signed the agreement; in 1930, about 1,100 agencies did. The CTANA had a decisions committee to consider disputed cases involving the transportation of clients. Unlike the Jewish committee, it always refused to consider cases before the actual transportation had occurred. Most disputed cases dealt with whether clients were a "proper charge" on the services of the receiving city. Increasingly during the CTANA's history, it emphasized the spirit rather than the letter of the agreement. The CTANA cooperated consistently with the Jewish committee. In 1928, the two groups appointed a joint committee to consider their relationship and to consider joining together. The American National Red Cross,* largely because of its organizational form, never joined the CTANA, but it conformed to the principles of the group through the home service program.

Even though two important national agencies—the Salvation Army* in 1931, and the American Public Welfare Association* in 1932—joined the CTANA, its significance declined in the 1930s. During the depression, especially public agencies accepted the standards of the agreement, influencing the CTANA not to ask local agencies to sign the agreement every year. Its existence and interest, however, did help to influence the founding of the Federal Transient Service in 1933. Five of its members, including Bertha McCall, helped to form the Committee on Care of Transient and Homeless* in late 1932. As the APWA suggested in the early 1930s, the CTANA had helped to reduce the cases of passing on clients indiscriminately. Despite its eclipse by the federal service and the newer organization, in the true spirit of voluntary agencies the CTANA kept intact in the mid-1930s and was ready to reenter the field if no other public or private agency did. But apparently in 1934, the CTANA terminated its existence.

The sources for studying the history of the CTANA are difficult to locate, but information about it can be found in Jeffrey Brackett, *The Transportation Problem in American Social Work* (1936), and in such contemporary publications as Ruth Hill, "Goals for Wanderers," National Conference of Social Work, *Proceedings, 1925, 264–271.*

None of the standard histories in the field of social welfare history, such as Clarke Chambers, *Seedtime for Reform* (1963), mentions the organization, and there is no scholarly history of the CTANA.

COMMON COUNCIL FOR AMERICAN UNITY (CCAU). In November 1939, when the Foreign Language Information Service (FLIS)* disbanded, the decision had already been made that a new organization with a new name would have to come into existence to do a larger job. Incorporated in New York, it took the name Common Council for American Unity (CCAU), which indicated an ideal or goal, not a method. The CCAU defined its mission to deal not only with European immigrants but also with other ethnic and racial groups in the United States, as well as second-generation Americans.

It was organized (1) "to help create among the American people the unity and mutual understanding resulting from a common citizenship . . . and the acceptance of all citizens, whatever their national or racial origins, as equal partners in American society," (2) "to further an appreciation of what each group has contributed to America . . . and to encourage the growth of an American culture truly representative of all the elements that make up the American people," (3) "to overcome intolerance and discrimination because of foreign birth or descent, race or nationality," and (4) "to help the foreign born and their children solve their special problems of adjustment, know and value their particular heritage, and share fully and constructively in American Life."

In addition to a twenty-four-member board of directors and a forty-member committee of sponsors, carried over from the FLIS, the CCAU added a large national committee consisting of representatives from different sections of the country and from different ethnic and racial groups. Prominent people serving on this committee included Eleanor Roosevelt, Albert Einstein, Edward Corsi, Norman Thomas, and Paul Kellogg. The purpose of this new committee was to review and guide the work of the CCAU and consider its program in relation to the conditions and needs existing in the United States.

The CCAU continued to serve as an information center about American nationality groups and to work with these various organizations and the foreign-language press, sending weekly press releases in twenty-two languages to some 850 foreign-language newspapers. The council's service to the foreign-language press was unique and influential, particularly since the releases helped these newspapers make up for a lack of staff. Without such a service, the people who relied primarily on the foreign-language press would have had little reliable information about the United States.

The financial problems that plagued its predecessor, the FLIS, began to diminish with the new organization's growth. The CCAU initiated new activities, such as the publication between 1940 and 1950 of *Common Ground,* a radio service, and the American Common, which the CCAU established at its headquarters in New York City in 1943. In colonial days, every town had its "common" or "village square"; in providing a center called the American Common, the CCAU had in mind a meeting place where all Americans, regardless of national origin, race, creed, or color, could assemble to become better acquainted, discuss common problems, and hold meetings, programs, and conferences. It was designed to further the general aims of the CCAU.

Work with the government continued, as in the case of alien registration, which began in 1940. The council handled foreign-language publicity for the Department of Justice and advised aliens on the registration program. Similar requests came from other government departments involved in the war effort, but one of the most intimate relationships developed with the federal Immigration and Naturalization Service (INS) (see *Government Agencies*). The CCAU conducted investigations for the INS, advised it on the development of new procedures, and worked with it in making recommendations to Congress for legislation. When interviewed in 1946, INS officials expressed a feeling that it was "essential to keep in touch with groups like the Council in order to know what the problems are." They considered the CCAU a spokesman for other groups. The CCAU had a Washington representative who followed the day-to-day action in Congress. The CCAU continued its public stands in support of or in opposition to legislation affecting the foreign born. It played a major role in 1946 in the defeat of the Gossett bill, which proposed cutting immigration quotas. It followed the daily developments in Congress and issued a series of *Legislative Bulletins* to keep interested organizations and individuals informed on pending legislation dealing with immigration and naturalization.

The CCAU continued to publish *Interpreter Releases,* supplying them to social work agencies, government officials, libraries, foreign-language organizations, lawyers, and others. Aware of the impact of radio, the council in 1943 began issuing weekly bulletins to some 550 radio braodcasters and program directors of stations broadcasting in foreign languages. These bulletins treated topics in American history, writings of prominent Americans, questions and answers on immigration and naturalization, and miscellaneous features, such as music and art. It played a very active role in helping to organize the Citizens Committee on Displaced Persons (CCDP) in 1946. One of the principal objectives of the CCDP was to secure a liberalization of United States immigration laws in order to facilitate the entry of such displaced persons into this country. Read Lewis, the director of the Common Council, was also the CCDP executive director.

Another major project undertaken by the CCAU in 1950 and lasting until 1965 was the Letters from America campaign. Its purpose was to encourage first- and second-generation Americans to use the millions of letters sent to relatives and friends abroad each year to present a true picture of America and to promote goodwill.

Before the 1952 election, the CCAU participated in the national Register and Vote Campaign to stimulate a wider interest in active citizenship on the part of American nationality groups. A sponsoring committee of nationality organizations was formed, and it was through these organizations that the CCAU advertised the campaign. The CCAU prepared a "Voter's ABC," which explained eligibility requirements for voting, the literacy test, the poll tax, and voting machines—all problems a voter, especially a new one, could encounter.

The CCAU aided hundreds of immigrants each month by helping to unite families, untangling discriminations in employment, and answering questions about citizenship, deportation, taxes, and other problems the newcomer might encounter. It also provided social agencies with weekly articles and reports giving the latest technical information needed in working with refugees, the foreign born, and minority groups. The CCAU worked closely with other organizations. The American National Red Cross* sent the council periodic articles for translation and distribution to the foreign-language press. The Anti-Defamation League of B'nai B'rith (see *Fraternal Organizations*) and the CCAU established a joint operation, the Tolerance Project, to combat anti-Semitism and other forms of prejudice and to promote better intergroup understanding. The CCAU edited and translated two articles per month into sixteen languages for distribution to the foreign-language press. These all dealt with ways to overcome prejudice and discrimination. When various individuals and ethnic organizations reported instances of discrimination to the CCAU, it looked into them. Even the veteran International Institutes sometimes called on the council for advice in immigration and naturalization matters.

Throughout the years, the CCAU published and reprinted several handbooks and pamphlets. Among these were *How to Become a Citizen of the United States* (1940); *Life in America* (1955), translated into several languages, primarily for those expected to immigrate to the United States to prepare for life in this new country and also for the newly arrived not yet familiar with this country's ways and customs; *What Should I Know When I Travel Abroad?* (1955), a booklet to help Americans traveling overseas to serve as unofficial ambassadors; and a study, *European Beliefs Regarding the United States* (1949). Two other publications—*The Admission and Resettlement of Displaced Persons in the United States: A Handbook for Local Use* (1949) and *The Immigration and*

Nationality Act (1952) (a summary of the principal provisions of the McCarran-Walter Act of 1952)—both provided as simply and concisely as possible the legal and technical information needed by local agencies and others in dealing with these important matters. Between 1940 and 1950, *Common Ground* was the leading periodical in the United States devoted to intercultural and interracial problems. In the early 1940s, *Common Ground* paid particular attention to doing articles on the background, culture, and contributions of the Japanese, Germans, and Italians to help in fighting discrimination brought about by the war. Contributors of articles to *Common Ground* included Louis Adamic, Eleanor Roosevelt, and Langston Hughes.

The idea of a merger between the CCAU and the American Federation of International Institutes* (AFII) had been suggested many years before. In 1957, with some financial problems facing both organizations, serious discussions of the possibility of a merger began. Finally, with the approval of the national budget committee of the United Community Funds and Councils of America, Inc.,* the AFII and the CCAU effected a merger on January 1, 1959. The combined organization is now known as the American Council for Nationalities Service* (ACNS).

Sources used in preparing this article were the Papers of the ACNS, deposited in the archives of the Immigration History Research Center (IHRC) at the University of Minnesota, Minneapolis. These papers consist of 175 linear feet of correspondence, minutes, reports, and publications of the ACNS, as well as its predecessor organizations. In addition, see *Common Council for American Unity* (1940) and *The Work of the Common Council for American Unity in 1942* (1943).

Lynn Ann Schweitzer

COMMONWEALTH FUND, THE (CF). "To do something for the welfare of mankind," the Commonwealth Fund (CF) was incorporated in New York City on October 17, 1918. A group of five incorporators organized the agency with the nearly $10 million grant from Mrs. Stephen V. Harkness, a philanthropist. The first meeting of the incorporators took place in New York on October 23, 1918. Yale University history professor Max Farrand was one of the incorporators, as was Edward Harkness, Mrs. Harkness's son, a business leader and philanthropist who was elected the CF's first president. The group established offices immediately in New York. On February 4, 1919, the CF elected Professor Farrand as general director, a position that became full time in September 1919. In 1919, Mrs. Harkness gave the CF a second large contribution to help it in its charitable work.

The CF's initial activities related to relief efforts during World War I. In 1919, the two largest grants were awarded to the United War Work Campaign and the American Committee on Armenian and Syrian Relief, one of the many such relief agencies. During the second year of the CF's existence, more than 80 percent of its appropriations went to the American Relief Administration* (ARA), initially a government-sponsored charitable agency headed by Herbert Hoover. These funds to the ARA included $750,000 for the European Children's Fund. In 1920–1921, the largest portion of CF grants continued to go to the ARA. Although it emphasized child welfare in these early years, in its third year (1920–1921), the CF awarded grants to both the Association for the Prevention and Relief of Heart Disease, which later became the American Heart Association,* and to the American Society for the Control of Cancer,* which later became the American Cancer Society,* to expand their general services and to develop their field departments.

During the 1920s and 1930s, programs in child welfare brought the CF close to the social work community. The CF pioneered in the field of orthopsychiatry. Its first major project in social work and health was a program to prevent juvenile delinquency. In the vanguard in the use of psychiatry in social work, this CF project emphasized mental hygiene and cooperated with other agencies to develop specific activities. With the New York School of Social Work, the National Committee for Mental Hygiene* (NCMH), and the National Committee on Visiting Teachers of the Public Education Association of New York (PEA), the CF established in 1922 the Joint Committee on Methods of Preventing Juvenile Delinquency (JCMPD) to act as the coordinating unit for the juvenile delinquency program. Its first executive director was social worker Arthur W. Towne, the former superintendent of the Brooklyn Society for the Prevention of Cruelty to Children, who was succeeded in 1922 by Graham Taylor, Jr., the son of the famous settlement house worker, Graham Taylor, of the Chicago Commons. The program emphasized the establishment of child guidance clinics in cities.

Working with the division of prevention of delinquency of the NCMH, the CF sponsored a series of demonstration clinics in such cities as St. Louis, Los Angeles, Cleveland, and Philadelphia. This program led to the founding of the famous Institute for Child Guidance in New York City in July 1927. Dr. Lawson Lowrey, who helped to found the American Orthopsychiatric Association* (AOA), became the director of the institute, which was conducted in cooperation with the NCMH, the New York School of Social Work, and the Smith College of Social Work. The Institute for Child Guidance closed in 1933. Through the New York School of Social Work, the CF sponsored fifteen annual fellowships to promote the training of psychiatric social workers, visiting teachers, and probation officers. With the cooperation of the New York City Board of Education, the CF established a bureau of children's guidance to serve the public schools. Then, in the early 1920s, with the help of the PEA, the CF established the National Committee on Visiting Teachers, which worked to place social workers in schools, established demonstration centers, and placed visiting teachers in each of the five New York City public schools served by the bureau of child guidance. The CF's program to prevent juvenile delinquency ended in 1927, after influencing the establishment of other child guidance clinics and after awakening the social work field to orthopsychiatry. In 1927, the JCMPD became the CF's division of publications, with Graham Taylor, Jr., as its own director.

During the 1920s and 1930s, another program in child welfare brought the CF to the fore of social welfare activities. During the later period of World War I and its immediate aftermath, many local and national social service and health agencies focused on the problems of child hygiene, especially in rural America. CF-sponsored child health demonstrations in rural and semirural localities contributed meaningfully to this nationwide child hygiene movement. On June 7, 1922, the board of directors adopted child hygiene as an agency activity. The CF then established its child health demonstration committee, which at first entrusted the work in selected counties to the recently formed American Child Health Association* (ACHA), presided by Herbert Hoover. The director of the ACHA, Courtney Dinwiddie, acted as the director of demonstrations for the CF. By 1926, the CF was sponsoring full-time demonstrations in two small cities (Fargo, North Dakota, and Athens, Georgia) and in two rural counties (Rutherford in Tennessee and Marion in Oregon). It became clear that this CF program demanded more active administration, so in 1926, the child health demonstration committee assumed complete administrative authority for the projects. Dinwiddie, a widely repsected worker in child welfare, left his post at the ACHA and became full-time director of child health demonstrations for the CF. In both Marion and Rutherford counties, the demonstration projects functioned as the county health departments. In the two cities, the demonstrations became integral parts of the local health departments. Fulfilling its goal, the projects did influence better community medical facilities and services in these and other communities.

Between 1923 and 1929, the CF program included a health education and preventive medicine project for children in Vienna, Austria, an activity that continued the CF's wartime concern for children in war-torn countries. In Rutherford County, Tennessee, the project revealed the need for a hospital to serve the entire community, and it became the first of many rural hospitals helped through the CF's division of rural hospitals, established in 1926. On December 31, 1929, the child health demonstration committee dissolved, giving way to a stronger public health program through the CF's new division of public health, created on January 1, 1930.

The establishment of the CF's division of public health in 1930 ushered in an emphasis on community health that has remained important to the foundation. The division's initial purposes in 1930 were to function as a consultant for the former demonstration areas and to coordinate efforts to improve rural hygiene. A further commitment to the public health field became clear in April 1931 when the CF established its division of health studies. Publishing became a vital aspect of all CF health programs, and in 1944, this division merged into the division of public health. During the 1940s, the CF subsidized the departments of preventive medicine and public health at both Tulane and Vanderbilt universities' medical schools. In the late 1940s, the CF moved increasingly toward a comprehensive approach to medicine rather than through the divisional system it had maintained. For two weeks in July 1948, in one of its last activities, the division of public health, working with the California State Department of Health, held an institute on mental health in public health at Berkeley. When the director of the division, Dr. Clarence L. Scamman, retired in 1948, the division was dissolved. Similarly, the division of rural hospitals ended with the retirement of its director in 1949. Another era for the CF closed in September 1947 when the general director, Barry Smith, retired after serving for twenty-six years.

The CF began the 1950s by moving its headquarters to the former Harkness family residence at Fifth Avenue and Seventy-fifth Street in New York in February 1952. Grants for medical research was never a coordinated program, but in 1952 and 1953, the agency tried to define its priorities. The most notable development during the 1950s was the series of grants for a consultant service, for planning, for comprehensive community health activities, for a countywide inventory, and for the building that became the Hunterdon (County) Medical Center in New Jersey. These grants were made through a program in experimental health services, which also helped Montefiore Hospital in New York City to establish a home care plan, to the Richmond, Virginia, Department of Public Health to provide medical care for poor people, and to the Tennessee Medical Foundation to improve services in medically underprivileged areas.

In the 1960s, the CF withdrew from its extensive support of medical research, claiming that the voluntary health agencies could well finance research. Early in the decade, it began to concentrate on medical education broadly defined and on international fellowships that had begun in 1925 to sponsor students and doctors from other English-speaking countries to come to the United States. Initially benefiting only the British, the program eventually brought students from New Zealand and Australia to the United States. In the mid-1960s, the CF completed a review of its programs and reached two major conclusions: to continue its focus on improving health and to strengthen its efforts to increase international understanding, especially through the Harkness Fellowships. The CF decided to increase the number of fellowships by about one-third (to sixty-five) by 1966. A group of medical colleges received major grants for such things as revising curricula and for developing community health projects. The CF also provided funds to help publish some reports of the National Commission on Community Health Services, a joint project of the National Health Council* and the American Public Health Association.* Later in the decade, the CF decided to allocate a greater percentage of its funds to strengthen medical education and to improve systems for delivering health care in the United States. Noting the need to deal with the problems of medical care in this country, the CF decided also to reduce the Harkness Fellowship program. While medical issues clearly dominated the CF's interests and grants, the foundation retained some interest in projects more related to the social work than to the medical community, supporting organizations such as the International Planned Parenthood Federation, which worked on population control abroad.

In the 1970s, the overwhelming interest of the CF was promoting medical education and other medical programs, as opposed to social services programs and institutions. But since it never really lost its ties to the social service community to which it was so close earlier in its history, it granted funds to the Maternity Center Association* of New York to begin a national program to expand the training and the use of nurse midwives and to the University of Colorado Medical Center for a project on child abuse and neglect.

The primary sources for studying the history of the CF consist of its published and detailed *Annual Reports*. The organization itself published a helpful history, *The Commonwealth Fund: Historical Sketch, 1918–1962* (1963). There does not appear to be a scholarly history of the CF.

COMMUNITY CHESTS AND COUNCILS, INC.: see UNITED WAY OF AMERICA.

COMMUNITY CHESTS AND COUNCILS OF AMERICA, INC.: see UNITED WAY OF AMERICA.

COMMUNITY SERVICE SOCIETY (CSS). As public welfare became an increasingly important part of social services in the 1930s, private agencies began to reduce and reshape their programs. In New York City, two of the oldest and most influential social service agencies in the United States—the Charity Organization Society of the City of New York* (COS), established in 1882, and the New York Association for Improving the Condition of the Poor* (AICP), founded in 1843—had been conducting similar work. These situations prompted the leaders of the two veteran agencies to discuss a merger. Consequently, on April 12, 1939, in New York City, the Community Service Society (CSS) was established when the COS and the AICP merged.

The staff and volunteer leaders of each predecessor agency were blended into the complex structure of the new CSS. The initial structure included a president, a secretary, two assistant secretaries—each of the former executive officers of the COS and the AICP—and thirteen honorary presidents. The eighty-two-member board of trustees included its chairman, a prominent public servant and philanthropist, Walter S. Gifford. Reflecting the two agencies' traditions of power and influence in New York City, seven ex officio members of the initial board were the mayor of New York and appropriate city commissioners, such as welfare, hospitals, health, and housing and buildings. The chairman of the executive council was Bailey Burritt, the former AICP executive. The CSS's first executive director and director of general services was Stanley P. Davies, the respected former head of the COS. William Mathews from the AICP, became the CSS's third highest staff executive, director of special services.

Despite the problems created by World War II, the CSS, accustomed to crises through its predecessor agencies, conducted useful and important programs and services during the period. Because many social workers left for service in the war, the CSS staff was reduced, but CSS nurses, for instance, nevertheless helped to mobilize nurses throughout the country for service in hospitals and defense plants and for both civilians and the armed forces. Continuing a health and welfare service especially associated with the AICP, the military bureau helped mothers and their families in New York to adjust to the rationing and scarcities caused by the war. Basic services to families remained, and the CSS played an active part in the creation of the Veterans Service Center in New York City, which helped the men and their families in a variety of ways. For its contributions to the war work at home, the CSS was awarded the Certificate of Commendation by the commanding general of the Second Service Commission.

Even during the war, the CSS maintained its interest in promoting improved public and private school services. In 1944, for example, its study of the children's court of New York City prompted the enlargement of the probation service. In 1945, CSS's studies of state aid to crippled children led to the program's removal from the New York City Children's Court to, more properly, the city's Department of Health. During this period, as later, part of the CSS work was conducted by volunteers who served on special committees, such as the famous one on housing. Trained staff workers collaborated with these citizens to produce studies and recommendations. The creation of the Institute for Welfare Research (IWR) provided another basic aspect of the CSS's total program. The IWR quickly gained a reputation for producing excellent studies in the field of social welfare and social planning.

In the postwar period, the CSS was among the first groups to recognize a new set of urban problems, thus following the tradition of social service agencies' being attuned to people's and society's problems. In early 1946, to help families and especially temporarily troubled families, the CSS began its homemaker service. The CSS also began to deal more fully than before with the aged, pioneering in this new field of specialization in social work. In the late 1940s, the CSS conducted a pilot project on caring for the aged, and the CSS staff consultant on services for the aged, Ollie Randall, served as the program consultant for the first national conference on the aging, called by President Harry S. Truman in 1950 and sponsored by the Federal Security Administration. Symbolizing the significance of the CSS at this conference, Randall was cited for twenty-five years of pioneering in the field.

At the other end of its spectrum of clients as a family welfare agency, the CSS established its youth bureau in 1950 to provide unified services for older children. In this period, the CSS contracted with the Youth Board of New York City to have older children from neighborhoods with high delinquency rates participate in CSS's family services. One of the chief CSS aims was promoting the development of trained professional social workers. Its predecessor organization, the COS, had founded and sponsored what became the New York School of Social Work. In 1950, in the tradition of promoting the eventual independence of its ventures—this principle had, for instance, led the COS to help organize the National Housing Association* in 1910—the CSS agreed to have the school become a separate entity. CSS's interest in promoting better health was evidenced in its family health maintenance demonstration, a cooperative effort with the Montefiore Hospital and the College of Physicians and Surgeons of Columbia University.

In the 1950s, when there was some streamlining of the organizational structure, the CSS seemed to focus especially on improving housing, the care of the aged, the problem of juvenile delinquency, and, as usual, the effectiveness of casework dealing with group therapy. Following plans developed during the one hundredth anniversary evaluation, the CSS, in January 1952, combined three departments to form the new division of family services. The committee on housing worked for a long time, and finally, with other groups in the city, helped to develop a city multiple dwelling code in the mid-1950s. During this period of so-called urban renewal, some neighborhoods were destroyed and the residents, usually minorities and the poor, had trouble finding new homes. Sensitive to these problems, the CSS became a leader in relocating such people, and in 1958, it published *Not Without Hope,* to guide agencies and others in dealing with this difficult problem. Throughout the 1950s, its housing activities consisted of testifying at a number of legislative hearings, including those on enforcing the code that the CSS helped to draft.

In caring for the aged, the CSS developed an impressive array of projects, services, and research studies. In the early 1950s, the agency created its central services for the aging, and it quickly began an analysis of services to the aged in residences maintained by the CSS. These were a home at Ward Manor in upstate New York, the Tompkins Square House on the Lower East Side of Manhattan, a residence for the aged, and Sunset Lodge, a camp on the grounds of Ward Manor. In the mid-1950s, with money from the Rockefeller Brothers Fund, the CSS conducted a study of the problems connected with aging. Casework services increased at the residence homes, and in June 1959, the agency began an important study of the rehabilitation of older, chronically ill, and disabled patients discharged from Goldwater Memorial Hospital on Welfare Island in New York City. Done in cooperation with such other groups as the department of physical medicine and rehabilitation at New York University-Bellevue Medical Center, this project was funded partly by the federal Office of Vocational Rehabilitation.

In the early 1950s, the CSS began to provide group therapy sessions for children, and it conducted a study of the problems of children in institutions. The CSS studied the complex juvenile and family courts, and in the mid-1950s, to try to improve the system, published *Justice for Youth* and *A Pattern for Family Justice.* In the spring of 1955, participating in a new trend in family social welfare, the use of plays, the CSS produced *The Maze,* depicting the problems of the courts. It premiered before the women's council of the CSS in April 1955. The youth bureau committee of the CSS conducted an important study of the resources of the city for neglected and deserted boys and girls aged sixteen to twenty. This study showed severe shortages in services. By the late 1950s, the

CSS had ten groups using therapy for eight-to fourteen-year-old children. So respected was the CSS that Governor Nelson Rockefeller asked for its views on juvenile crime in New York.

The CSS followed its predecessors—the COS's—concern for providing effective casework and services. Through its IWR, the agency conducted a study showing how to predict the length of service a particular client would need. In 1954, with a grant from the Greater New York Fund, the CSS began a project to test the effectiveness of long-term homemaker services, a service previously used for only brief periods of time. The IWR also developed a means of measuring a client's progress, as well as the factors responsible for it. In the spring of 1956, the CSS began a project to identify the traits and problems of court-referred clients and to determine casework principles to deal with them. While not related to sophisticated research, a highlight of 1956 was a play on the use of family casework, *Broken Circle,* acted by The American Theatre Wing Community Players. Other important activities of the 1950s included the continuance of the family health maintenance demonstration project and a series of three luncheons for businessmen in the spring of 1959, called "New York Close Up," which focused on the most critical problems of the city. An important organizational event occurred in July 1956 when Stanley P. Davies, a long-time worker with the CSS and the COS, retired as general director.

In the early 1960s, even before the onslaught of federal welfare projects and programs, the CSS continued its pioneering as well as its traditional services, some of which were nationally significant. Opening the decade, the CSS, along with other organizations, criticized forcefully the so-called Newburgh, New York, philosophy of abolishing welfare. In its comments, the CSS added material showing the need to strengthen public assistance programs. Beginning in October 1959, the CSS initiated an important demonstration project in community organization and community action. Directed at the request of the New York City Youth Board, this Community Action Program (CAP) tried to determine if group workers could mobilize the community, the St. Mary's Park area of the South Bronx, to reduce high juvenile delinquency rates and other types of social problems. In the early 1960s, the CSS also initiated, with the New York City Board of Education, a demonstration project to bring the techniques of casework to the schools in New York. In East Harlem, the CSS conducted a three-pronged demonstration project: the school project, with funds from the National Institute of Mental Health (NIMH); the family rehabilitation project, with support from the Welfare Administration of the federal Department of Health, Education, and Welfare (DHEW); and a neighborhood conservation project. Such activities made the CSS one of the few family welfare agencies in the country involved in community action. Further studies of the effectiveness and the application of social casework, publication of these studies, and the opening in 1961 of the Center of Casework Research—all were important contributions nationally. At the fiftieth meeting of the Family Service Association of America,* the CSS pointed out, correctly, that combating the breakdown of the family and its concomitant problems would be one of the major social battles in the years ahead. Services for and further studies of the aged and the process of aging continued creatively, but in August 1963, the CSS disposed of the last ninety acres of Ward Manor, leasing back, however, one building for the fourteen remaining aged tenants.

In 1965, the president of the CSS, Mrs. Garret J. Garretson, II, argued that the best tradition of voluntary social service agencies was their flexibility in adapting to new situations. As expected, the CSS adhered to that tradition, retaining and even strengthening its creativity in this period of significant programs sponsored by the federal government. Dealing with a personnel problem facing social agencies throughout the country, the CSS began to utilize volunteers more creatively and effectively. Volunteers had, of course, played important roles in each of the CSS's predecessor agencies. The CSS developed New Worlds for Children, a program through which volunteers took children to places outside their ghetto neighborhoods, such as zoos, museums, and theatres. In Chinatown, the Each-One-Teach-One program had volunteers teaching English. The most significant program using volunteers was the Serve and Enrich Retirement by Volunteer Experience (SERVE), a nationally recognized project. Beginning in January 1967 in the area of New York most like other American communities, Staten Island, SERVE recruited older people to serve, for instance, at the Willowbrook State School for the mentally deficient, at hospitals, and at other community facilities. Money for SERVE came initially from the Administration on Aging of the DHEW, with matching funds from individuals, foundations, and the CSS. In February 1969, the CSS terminated its Adopt-a-Family program, begun in 1932 by philanthropist Mrs. August Belmont to provide for families temporarily in need.

In the field of community organization and social action, in the mid-1960s, the CSS began a four-year demonstration project in the South Bronx to determine ways to defer the emotional, social and physical deterioration of older people. The CSS worked closely with the Mobilization for Youth, an antipoverty program on the Lower East Side of Manhattan. The CSS opened offices in East Harlem and Queens. The CSS center in South Ozone Park, Queens, helped a local day camp by providing a volunteer worker, a case aide, and two summer social work students. In 1965, it began a pilot project for young families in the South Bronx, trying to teach mothers—some of whom were as young as thirteen years old—the essentials of prenatal care. During this period, the CSS conducted a project in the largest low-rent public housing project in the city, Claremont Village, to determine if group discussions could help tenants adjust to this lifestyle. The agency began to pay increased attention to the problems of child abuse and neglect, and it also worked to rehabilitate released prisoners and juvenile delinquents. Continuing efforts to improve casework, the IWR developed the CSS Movement Scale to measure a client's progress during treatment. During this period, the CSS completed a four-year casework methods project to test the effectiveness of different patterns of casework. This study was published as *Brief and Extended Casework* (1969). Another CSS study, *Dynamic Approaches to Serving Families* (1970), was received favorably, reminding social workers of "the values in serving people in multiple ways."

Following a study in 1970 of urban problems and what the CSS could do to help—a traditional analysis that the CSS conducted every ten years—the agency continued its basic programs, emphasizing the creative use of volunteers and caring for the aged. Because of the success of SERVE on Staten Island, the CSS was asked to and did coordinate the effort to establish similar volunteer programs throughout the state by the New York State Office for the Aging. In the early 1970s, blind and handicapped people began to participate in SERVE. The CSS also created its Retired Senior Volunteer Program (RSVP), through which volunteers served in social agencies; it was adapted by communities through the country.

Volunteers participated in virtually every CSS project in the early 1970s. In October 1972, the CSS initiated a demonstration project for the elderly in Jamaica, Queens, which *Family Circle* magazine called perhaps America's "most innovative self-help program" for the aging. In 1973, with the cooperation of the local community chest, the CSS began its community agency for senior citizens (CASC) to promote expanded and new services for the aged on Staten Island and featuring an outreach program. For the elderly, the CSS established a storefront service center in the East Village in Manhattan in late 1973.

In the field of community organization and social action, in the early 1970s, the CSS helped to prepare a profile of existing services and institutions, as well as the needs in the community for Central Harlem's new James Varick Community Center. In August 1973, in cooperation with Beekman Downtown Hospital, the CSS began to provide comprehensive health care in its outpatient clinic in Chinatown. Community Association United in Service for Everyone (CAUSE) in the Chelsea section of Manhattan pioneered in reaching out to find the needy and the troubled. This project also integrated the public and private agencies and resources in the area, thus creating a model for delivering social services. In 1973, the CSS initiated its Aid to Communities Concerning Entitled Support Services (ACCESS) to help people eligible for but denied public assistance. The CSS continued in the 1970s to stimulate concern in such areas as drug and child abuse and maintained its tradition of speaking out on legislation. The agency, for instance, consistently fought to restore cuts in federal programs. In the mid-1970s, the CSS led the opposition to a federal proposal to require each community to assume the total cost of RSVP programs after four years.

The primary sources for studying the CSS's history include the detailed and published *Annual Reports, The New York Times,* and contemporary publications and journals, such as *Social Casework.*

There is a brief account of the early CSS in CSS, *Frontiers in Human Welfare*

(1948). There does not appear to be any scholarly study of the history of this important agency.

CONFERENCE OF BOARDS OF PUBLIC CHARITIES: see NATIONAL CONFERENCE ON SOCIAL WELFARE.

CONFERENCE OF SOUTHERN MOUNTAIN WORKERS: see COUNCIL OF THE SOUTHERN MOUNTAINS.

CONGREGATIONAL CHRISTIAN CHURCHES, COUNCIL FOR SOCIAL ACTION OF THE (CSA). The social gospel movement of the late nineteenth century stirred the social conscience of American churches. Representatives of the Congregational Christian Churches (CCC) (see *Religious Institutions*) played important roles in this reform movement. In 1892, the national council of the CCC appointed a temporary Committee on Capital and Labor, chaired by Washington Gladden, a recognized leader of the national social gospel movement. The institutional precedent of the CSA, however, related more properly to the Labor Committee, appointed by the national council in 1901. This group became the Industrial Committee in 1904, and in 1907, Graham Taylor, an important national social worker and founder of the pioneering settlement house, the Chicago Commons, became chairman. The committee, which continued to change names, was given permanent status in 1910 when it hired its first paid secretary. In 1913, the Industrial Committee merged with another church group, the Congregational Brotherhood, to become the Commission on Social Service. In October 1916, the commission became the adviser to the Department of Social Service of the Congregational Education Society (CES), another church agency.

Welfare work for the armed forces occupied the commission during World War I, and in the 1920s, it focused on industry, race, international relations, and rural problems. In 1927, it became the Commission on Social Relations and its head, Reverend Herbert C. Herring, Jr., began in 1928 to publish the four-page *Church and Society*. Seminars, discussions, and retreats led ultimately to Herring's suggestion that the agency become a major part of the denominational structure. The administrative committee of the CES approved the suggestion in 1934, and an eighteen-member committee drew up plans. Supporters brought the plan before the annual meeting at Oberlin College. On June 25, 1934, at Oberlin, the Council for Social Action (CSA) was established by a formal resolution that linked the new agency to the Commission on Missions of the church. The general council of the church elected the members of the new CSA; nine of them were from the committee that designed the CSA. The general council provided funds for it to begin work on January 1, 1935.

The members of the CSA met in September 1934 to develop their agency. A series of seminars before January 1935 discussed the controversial "profit motive resolution," calling for the abolition of the profit system. The incident caused some local Congregational churches to insist that their funds not be allocated to the new agency. In March 1935, the general council called it an "unauthoritative minority report," but the incident helped to give the CSA its reputation as a radical group within the denomination. Meanwhile, the CSA elected Herring as director and Katherine Terrill as associate secretary for information and literature. In October 1934, the executive committee met, elected Graham Taylor honorary chairman for life and created a department of international relations. The CSA gradually added some part-time and full-time staff. The department of international relations became the most active in this formative era of the CSA. It conducted, for example, a peace plebiscite within the church on November 3, 1935. In September 1938, Herring resigned as director of the CSA, but he remained for seven more months as both international relations secretary and as director of publications.

The only other program within the CSA to have its own secretary in January 1935 was the department of industrial relations. Established in September 1934, this department held a four-day study conference in the summer of 1935. Its secretary, Frank W. McCulloch, worked in Chicago, separated from the New York staff of the CSA. McCulloch helped to organize the Brotherhood of Sleeping Car Porters, tried to organize the unemployed, and worked to improve Negro housing in the city. McCulloch's full range of activities and his separation from national headquarters meant that the New York staff conducted much of the official work of the department of industrial relations. The New York staff contributed articles to *Social Action,* the CSA's monthly publication. A similar situation developed with the CSA department on agricultural relations. Created in September 1934 as the department of rural life, it had many names, including in the late 1940s, the agricultural relations comittee. Its first secretary, Reverend Ferry L. Platt, began his work at the Merom, Indiana, Institute, which the CSA and other denominations conducted as a rural life center. The institute promoted cooperatives in the area and developed as a popular conference center and library for rural ministers. In the late 1940s, through its secretary, the department conducted discussion groups on agricultural life throughout the country.

Despite being involved in controversy, the CSA continued its traditional activities in the 1950s. In the early 1950s, it seemed to be coming into its full stature with a seven-member staff. But at the general council meeting in Claremont, California, in 1952, resistance to the CSA developed within the still-conservative denomination. The general council reaffirmed the right of CSA to voice its opinions, but an investigation that followed prompted a reduction of the staff to less than one-half of its earlier strength. CSA programs were curtailed, and its Washington, D.C., office was closed. The church's conservative reaction to its CSA resulted largely from the improved national economy, the disillusionment with world events following American frustrations in Korea, and the general conservatism of the 1950s. Despite this jolt, the CSA expanded its international relations activities, which, like other denominational agencies, focused on the United Nations and travel seminars abroad. The town and country conference at

Oberlin College in September 1959 reinvigorated the CSA's efforts in rural America. Within an hour after the closing of the first general synod of the new United Church of Christ (UCC) in Cleveland, Ohio, in June 1957, the CSA joined with the Commission on Christian Social Action* (CSSA) of the Evangelical and Reformed Church (ERC) to form the new Council for Christian Social Action* of the UCC. The CCSA and the CSA, however, continued to maintain separate staffs, councils, and budgets until the formal merger of the ERC and CCC. Finally in late 1961, after the ERC and the CCC had merged officially to form the new UCC, the CSA disbanded.

The primary sources for studying the CSA's history include the agency's reports in the *Minutes of the General Council* of the CCC and the issues of *Social Action*.

Cyrus R. Pangborn, "Free Churches and Social Action: A Critical Study of the Council for Social Action of the Congregational Christian Churches of the United States" (Ph.D. diss., Columbia University, 1951), is a sound historical study.

COOPERATIVE FOR AMERICAN RELIEF EVERYWHERE (CARE). During the final stages of World War II, American relief agencies grew increasingly interested in programs to provide food for war-torn countries abroad. Anticipating the need for food in postwar Europe, Arthur Ringland of the President's War Relief Control Board (PWRCB) recalled the brilliant successes of Herbert Hoover and the American Relief Administration* after World War I and urged the members of the recently established American Council of Voluntary Agencies for Foreign Service* (ACVA) to act in a similarly humanitarian fashion. ACVA itself had been created in 1943 to coordinate all types of relief abroad. The ACVA responded positively to Ringland's suggestion particularly because the PWRCB in October 1945 had declared that large stockpiles of United States Army "ten-in-one" ration packages were in surplus and thus were available for use by private relief agencies. The opportunity was too inviting to pass up. Consequently, on November 27, 1945, in New York City, Cooperative for American Relief Everywhere (CARE) was established as Cooperative for American Remittances to Europe (CARE) by the representatives of twenty-two member agencies of ACVA. The army ration kits were the original CARE packages and thus achieved an almost-legendary fame. The first shipload reached Le Havre, France, on May 11, 1946, and on that day CARE began its actual operations.

The operational history of CARE can be divided into four phases covering the last thirty years. The first phase lasted from 1946 to 1950, roughly the period of the Marshall Plan, and it was no doubt the heroic phase. The CARE operation was simple. For fifteen dollars, an American donor could order a CARE package and have it delivered to a relative, friend, or other needy recipient in Europe. Within ninety days, the donor would receive a receipt signed by the recipient or the donor's money would be refunded. When the original army surplus was exhausted, CARE began making up its own packages. It delivered tens of millions of packages in this period, and very quickly the CARE package attained the stature of a symbol for American generosity on both sides of the Atlantic.

The second phase of CARE's history lasted roughly from 1950 to 1955, and these are no doubt the most troubling years in the organization's history. The political environment in which CARE operated changed greatly. With the outbreak of the Korean War, the Truman administration ended the Marshall Plan and began placing its heaviest emphasis on military aid. In the popular mind, Europe had recovered, and the focal point of the cold war had shifted to Asia. CARE thus lost much of its popular impetus in the United States, and under the leadership of the irascible Paul Comly French, CARE's second executive director, the agency moved forcefully toward replacing its popular base with a partnership with the United States government. The government used CARE in its efforts to bolster Marshall Tito's Yugoslavia in its conflict with Joseph Stalin, CARE quickly moved into South Korea when hostilities ceased, and French even sounded out the Central Intelligence Agency on the possibilities of cooperation. These initiatives of CARE disenchanted several of its sponsoring agencies in the ACVA, and more than a few stopped backing CARE. The second period of CARE's history is mean and lean, and it provides a striking contrast to the happy, heroic quality of the first period.

CARE's salvation came in 1954 with the passage by Congress of Public Law 480, a complex piece of legislation that aimed at a rational disposal overseas of the burgeoning American agricultural surplus. Title III was a reenactment of Section 416 of the Agricultural Act of 1949. It provided that voluntary agencies could use the surplus in their overseas feeding programs. In 1956, Congress amended PL 480 by authorizing the government to pay the ocean freight on the commodities. This cleared the way for a massive expansion of CARE.

Operations overseas now shifted radically. CARE phased out European operations and replaced them with operations in Asia, the Middle East, and Latin America. The remittance program quickly took second place to large-scale feeding programs, and for a while in the late 1950s and early 1960s, it seemed there was no limitation to CARE's expanding partnership with the government. CARE fed millions of children in school lunch programs, it distributed food to preschool children and lactating mothers at health centers, and beginning in the Kennedy administration, the government extended its cooperation with CARE to new endeavors. The government and CARE linked food to aid in the Food for Work program, CARE established a close liaison with the Peace Corps, and in 1962 President John F. Kennedy chose CARE's executive director, Richard Reuter, to replace George McGovern as the head of the White House Food for Peace program. CARE also extended itself in an entirely unexpected direction in these years by taking over the administration of Dr. Tom Dooley's MEDICO organization. This work involved CARE in providing medical education to physicians and nurses in less developed countries.

This third phase of CARE's operations lasted until the mid-1960s. The coming of the Vietnam War, like the Korean War fifteen years earlier, changed the tone of United States government policy. The Johnson administration deemphasized economic aid and stepped up military aid, and this trend was intensified with the sudden development of food shortages throughout the world and the consequent reduction of the American farm surplus. The partnership with the American government was contracting, forcing another painful adaptation upon CARE.

The end of the 1960s to the present marked the fourth phase of CARE's history. This period has brought with it some remarkable changes, not the least of which have been internal. Like many other social service agencies, CARE has professionalized its fund-raising activities under the leadership of Frank Goffio, its present executive director. Its operation has been computerized, and a constant effort is made to expand CARE's basic mailing list of a million contributors. As a result, CARE between 1972 and 1975 nearly doubled its financial contribution from the American and the Canadian public. CARE also adopted a five-year planning concept, enabling it to act more systematically and requiring it to tighten up its internal organization considerably. It has done so without losing any of its top executives.

CARE has also radically changed its overseas operations since 1971. It has moved away from the comparatively simple mass feeding programs of the mid-1960s in the direction of programs aimed at fostering greater self-sufficiency for the recipient country. First, CARE now engages in Partnership Development Programs (PDP): the host national government assigns engineering talent and construction materials, the local community contributes labor, and CARE provides management, food, and some building materials in a team effort aimed at completing a project that will make a significant and permanent change in the face of the local community. CARE now focuses its energies on the development of water resources through drilling wells and building dams, and it constructs houses in large numbers (fifteen thousand in Bangladesh alone), as well as schools. As a second new initiative, CARE now engages in Partnership Nutrition Programs (PNP), which aim to upgrade the local food supply and ensure balanced diets. CARE has added several nutrition experts to its overseas staff, and it has begun to attempt some far-reaching nutrition changes in Madhya Pradesh in Indian and in Ceylon. CARE is also upgrading the quality of its MEDICO training programs and working to improve its disaster relief techniques.

The primary sources for studying CARE's history consist largely of its files located at CARE headquarters in New York City. In these files, there is a helpful unpublished manuscript by Charles Bloom, "History of CARE" (1952).

Secondary studies include Stanford O. Cazier, "CARE: A Study in Cooperative Voluntary Relief" (Ph.D. diss., University of Wisconsin, 1964), John Hutchison and Philip W. Foster, *Foreign Donations of American Agricultural Abundance by Voluntary Agencies, 1950–1964* (1966), and Robert R. Sullivan, "The Politics of Altruism" (Ph.D. diss., The Johns Hopkins University, 1968), which deals with the surplus food program.

Robert Sullivan

COOPERATIVE FOR AMERICAN REMITTANCES TO EUROPE: see **COOPERATIVE FOR AMERICAN RELIEF EVERYWHERE.**

COOPERATIVE FOR AMERICAN REMITTANCES TO EVERYWHERE: see **COOPERATIVE FOR AMERICAN RELIEF EVERYWHERE.**

COUNCIL FOR CHRISTIAN SOCIAL ACTION OF THE UNITED CHURCH OF CHRIST: see **UNITED CHURCH OF CHRIST, OFFICE FOR CHURCH IN SOCIETY OF.**

COUNCIL OF JEWISH FEDERATIONS AND WELFARE FUNDS, INC. (CJFWF). In the late nineteenth and early twentieth centuries, a nationwide network of local Jewish charities began to develop, and national agencies arose to coordinate their activities. Established in 1899, the National Conference of Jewish Charities* (NCJC) promoted the development of Jewish social work generally. Its field service provided advice about philanthropic issues to local communities. That service ended in 1918. Another national agency was the National Appeals Information Service (NAIS), which was organized in 1927 to gain an understanding of the diverse Jewish national and overseas agencies, headquartered generally in New York City. The most important national agency, however, was the Bureau of Jewish Social Research* (BJSR), which was established in 1919 and which conducted surveys of Jewish communities, studied particular problems, such as the care of dependent children in New York City, and promoted the specialization of Jewish social work. The most direct and immediate influence on the establishment of the new National Council of Jewish Federations and Welfare Funds (NCJFWF), however, was the creation in 1931 of the Coordinating Committee of Federation Secretaries to discuss common interests and problems relating to agency finances during the early years of the Great Depression. In May 1932, an organizing committee met in Philadelphia to discuss forming a national organization of local federations and welfare funds. The chairman of this organizing committee was William J. Shroder, an attorney and civic leader from Cincinnati who retired in 1921 to serve social and civic movements. These discussions led directly to the founding of the CJFWF as the NCJFWF in Cleveland, Ohio, on October 30, 1932. Representatives from fifteen local Jewish federations formed the NCJFWF to promote the federation movement and to coordinate and improve services to local communities.

The early structure of the NCJFWF included as president, William Shroder, and as executive director, George Rabinoff, an important figure in Jewish social work. Financial support for the new agency came from the New York Foundation, the Hofheimer Foundation, the Rosenwald Fund, and the Warburg Foundation. At its first meeting, the NCJFWF established a committee to deal with four areas of major concern: the financing of Jewish federations and their relation to community chests; the relation between voluntary and federal government agencies to meet the needs of the unemployed; the relation of federations to Jewish culture and education; and the issue of local responsibility for financing national and international Jewish agencies, which developed as a major concern of the organization. Responding to the appeals for aid to Jews overseas, in 1934, at the general assembly—an annual forum that the agency continues to hold—the NCJFWF initiated its mobilization for Jewish needs. The campaign stimulated the development of local committees to support the national overseas agencies. In 1935, an important organizational development occurred when the BJSR merged with the organization, which now became the CJFWF. At that time, Harry Lurie, a major figure in Jewish social work, became the executive director.

With the addition of both the resources and the staff of the BJSR, the CJFWF began more energetically to provide services to local Jewish social service agencies, focusing largely on the problems of fund raising and budgeting. With fund raising reduced considerably during the depression years of the early and mid-1930s, the CJFWF established a committee, chaired by Dr. Ben Selekman, the executive of the famous and pioneering Boston federation, to examine critically the roles of local federations. In late 1936, CJFWF demonstrated a service that became central to its work: it helped to resolve the competitive fund raising of two overseas relief agencies, the American Jewish Joint Distribution Committee* (JDC) and the United Palestine Appeal (UPA). In 1938, in light of the problems of Jews overseas, the CJFWF helped to organize the General Council for Jewish Rights. By 1939, 152 organizations in 135 cities in the United States and Canada belonged to the CJFWF.

During World War II, from 1939 to 1945, the CJFWF continued to play a leadership role in the national Jewish social work community. The organization helped to establish the United Jewish Appeal (UJA) in the late 1930s. The field staff of the CJFWF helped to develop regional organizations of Jewish federations. In May 1940, the board set up a committee to deal with a controversial national advisory budgeting proposal, which called for a service to review national agencies' budgets. In 1941, delegates to the general assembly approved the establishment of such a group, but because of a very close referendum within the CJFWF, the board decided not to implement it. The proposal was defeated at the general assembly in 1946, but the delegates adopted resolutions that prompted the expansion of the CJFWF's budget and research department to supply independent, objective analyses and reports on national and international Jewish agencies. Beginning in the early 1940s, the CJFWF worked for about a decade to promote coordination among such overseas agencies as the United Service for New Americans* (USNA) and the Hebrew Sheltering and Immigrant Aid Society.* In the late 1940s, a CJFWF analysis of the USNA and its recommendations prompted the creation of the New York Association for New Americans. In 1944, the CJFWF founded the independent National Community Relations Advisory Council. Demonstrating its leadership, the CJFWF helped to mediate a conflict between the UJA and the JDC. With the aid of the President's War Relief Control Board, the CJFWF prompted the reconstituting of the UJA in June 1945.

In the postwar period, when the Jewish refugee issue, the establishment of the state of Israel in 1949, and the increase of federations in the expanding number of American suburbs all meant changes for inner-city federations, the CJFWF dealt well with the new issues and problems. In 1945, for instance, after surveying existing services and needs in Essex County, New Jersey, and after assessing its population shifts, the CJFWF organized the countrywide Jewish Community Council of Essex County, the first of its kind. The CJFWF founded its institute for overseas studies in 1947. It informed Americans about the economic and welfare needs of Palestine and then of Israel. Through its committee on national-local relations, the CJFWF often solved financial and other problems between local federations and national agencies. In 1948, when the activities of the overseas agencies became more widely known than before, the CJFWF began to function as the secretariat for the Large City Budgeting Committee (LCBC), composed of large-city federations, to develop their responsibility for the national and overseas agencies. The LCBC developed into a permanent project, and the CJFWF established its campaign and interpretation department to help federations with fund raising and to develop literature in the field. The CJFWF offered further services to local communities when it established, in 1950, its advisory committee on social planning, which was concerned with central planning, the care of the aged, the relation between hospitals and federations in financing and planning, the problems of emotionally disturbed children, and the development of facilities to meet these children's needs. The committee also promoted generally the notion and practice of central planning by local federations. The CJFWF helped to establish the Training Bureau of Jewish Communal Service, headed by George Rabinoff, the CJFWF's first executive director.

In the 1950s, the CJFWF continued its basic services, focusing on some of the central issues in Jewish social service. In 1951, it began to deal with the issue of uniform accounting practices through the institute of comptrollers of Jewish communal agencies. In 1954, along with other leading national social service agencies, the CJFWF adopted a statement on standards in accounting. More importantly, in the early 1950s, Robert Morris of the CJFWF conducted a study of Jewish social agencies in Springfield, Massachusetts. His report showed that although Jewish social services there lacked a clearly defined purpose, the community wanted a separate Jewish agency. Responding to the question of sustaining separate Jewish social agencies, in 1951, the recently established CJFWF's family services planning committee began a three-year study to define the scope and function of a Jewish family welfare agency. A number of leading voices in Jewish social work participated in discussing this issue, and in 1954, the CJFWF issued its famous statement, "The Value of Jewish Family Services to the Client, the Social Worker and the Community: A Rationale for the Jewish Family Agency." In 1958, the CJFWF created its committee on leadership development to recruit trained professionals in social service, and in 1959 and 1960, the CJFWF worked with fifty-four federations to establish the National Scholarship Fund to encourage professionally trained Jewish social workers. Beginning at the general assembly in 1942, the CJFWF had awarded yearly the best fund-raising campaigns, and in the 1950s, it established two awards: in 1953, the William J. Shroder Award, honoring community achievement in services, and in 1956, the Edwin Rosenberg Award for community leadership and national cooperation.

Like the earlier BJSR, the CJFWF served the larger Jewish community. Its 1958 comprehensive survey of Jewish cultural activities led to the establishment in 1960 of the National Foundation for Jewish Culture. In the late 1950s and early 1960s, under its health planning committee, the CJFWF sponsored an intensive study of the care of the aged and of the chronically ill. Funds from the United States Public Health Service supported this project. Its findings and recommendations influenced the national field of social services for these groups of people.

In the early 1960s, improving services for the aged, community organization, and, of course, fund raising were the CJFWF's priorities. With other national social agencies, in 1963 the organization testified before Congress about tax proposals that threatened contributions to charities. The CJFWF began a program to increase an understanding of Israel. It continued serving its constituents, for instance, by holding institutes for executives from medium-sized cities. Late in 1963, the board of directors authorized the establishment of a legacies and endowment fund. Continuing its interest in the aged, in 1964, the CJFWF began a three-year study of the mental impairment of old people. Later in the decade, it participated in the War on Poverty and developed programs affecting the American Jewish community. During this period, the CJFWF conducted its major study of the American Jewish community. This study led to the establishment of a task force on Jewish identity in the early 1970s and to other activities and programs to strengthen Jewish life in America, such as the Institute for Jewish Life, founded in 1972. The CJFWF's public welfare committee coordinated the CJFWF's role in antipoverty programs, providing advice to its affiliates. In the mid-1960s, the CJFWF dealt with the problem of personnel shortages in Jewish social services, working with schools to place students in local Jewish federations and welfare agencies. A scholarship program bolstered this effort. In the late 1960s, an ad hoc committee on board composition discussed whether non-Jews should serve on the boards of Jewish agencies, especially Jewish hospitals. A new social planning and research committee helped communities deal with planning concerns, such as the rationale for sectarian agencies and how to use effectively the growing number of services that cut across agency lines.

In the 1970s, the CJFWF continued its leadership role in Jewish social services and dealt with issues concerning American Jews, such as the status of Jews in the Soviet Union and the Middle East. In September 1970, a CJFWF meeting confirmed support for Israel's great needs. In the early 1970s, CJFWF efforts resulted in an increased number of locals' developing endowment fund programs. In the fall of 1972, the CJFWF began a new program to recruit and educate Jewish executives. CJFWF workshops and seminars focused on public relations, suggesting ways for affiliates to publicize Soviet Jewry and to counteract "hostile propagandist advertising" on the situation in the Middle East. In April 1973, the CJFWF testified before the House of Representatives Ways and Means Committee on tax proposals that threatened charitable giving. Programs for the aged continued. In the mid-1970s, the CJFWF reexamined its own general assembly, especially the voting procedures of this annual event. Concern for fund raising and accounting procedures continued to be emphasized throughout the period. Again demonstrating its leadership in the field of Jewish social service, the CJFWF established an office in Washington, D.C., which effectively aided local affiliates in obtaining federal grants in a variety of areas.

The primary sources for studying the CJFWF's history are diverse and difficult to locate in libraries. For the early years, the *Proceedings of the General Assembly* proved helpful, and for the other years, publications such as *Jewish Community* and *Board Highlights* provide accounts of the agency's activities. Most of these items can be found in the library at the CJFWF's New York City headquarters. The CJFWF has deposited some of its materials at the American Jewish Historical Society in Waltham, Massachusetts. The Harry Lurie Papers at the Social Welfare History Archives Center at the University of Minnesota, Minneapolis, contain references to the CJFWF.

An agency publication, *The Council's First Quarter Century* (1956), is detailed and helpful. Harry Lurie, *A Heritage Affirmed* (1961), is somewhat helpful. There is no scholarly history of the CJFWF.

COUNCIL OF SOUTHERN MOUNTAIN WORKERS: see COUNCIL OF THE SOUTHERN MOUNTAINS.

COUNCIL OF THE SOUTHERN MOUNTAINS (CSM). In the early twentieth century, John Charles Campbell and his wife, Olive Dame Campbell, were educational workers in the mountain areas of Alabama, Tennessee, and Georgia. From 1901 through 1907, Campbell served as dean and president of Piedmont College in Demorest, Georgia. Beginning in the fall of 1908, the Russell Sage Foundation* (RSF) supported the Campbells' plans to do a field study of the physical, social, and educational characteristics of the southern highlands, during which they would consult physicians, educators, home missionaries, social workers, nurses, and others. John Campbell's travels convinced him to consider a united and coordinated effort to deliver and to improve existing social services in the region. Consequently, he issued the call for a meeting, which convened in Atlanta, Georgia, on April 24, 1913. At this conference, about thirty-five representatives from the home missionaries of the major Protestant denominations and representatives from the southern highland division of the RSF discussed their work. Impressed by the proceedings, the group decided to establish the Council of the Southern Mountains (CSM) as the Conference of Southern Mountain Workers (CSMW).

The conference either undertook or allied itself with the major social service movements in the southern mountain region. At the 1926 conference, for example, the group not only established its public health section to promote much-needed maternal, child, school, and community hygiene, but also sponsored Professor Lewis C. Gray's socioeconomic study of the region. In 1930, it founded the Southern Mountain Handicraft Guild to help preserve and promote the folk traditions of the mountain people. In that same year, it began its association with both the Golden Rule Foundation (see *Foundations and Research Associations*) and the soon to be organized Save the Children Fund* (SCF) to promote child welfare in the region. Chiefly through Orin Keener, editor of *Mountain Life and Work,* the CSMW supported the movement in the mid-1930s to establish the Southern Conference for Human Welfare (see *Political and Civic Organizations*), a progressive force in the modern South.

Headquartered at Berea College in Berea, Kentucky, the CSMW met annually. Its staff, members, and committees advocated, supported, and participated in health, welfare, educational, and other such movements in the region. Berea College sponsored the publication of the CSMW's journal, *Mountain Life and Work,* which became a major reform organ. In 1928, the journal grew closer to the conference with the appointment of its editor, Helen H. Dingman, as the executive secretary of the agency. By 1938, the staff was increased to six, reflecting the growing activities of the conference.

Throughout the 1940s, the CSMW continued its normal activities, promoting recreational, adult, and cooperative educational work and sponsoring both folk festivals and the annual Christmas party for children from Berea, Kentucky. At the annual meeting in March 1944, the CSMW changed its name to the Council of Southern Mountain Workers (CSMW). Two important decisions, influenced by the lack of funds, highlighted the 1944 meeting: the style and content of *Mountain Life and Work* were curtailed significantly, and the organization moved its headquarters to the offices in Asheville, North Carolina, of the Southern Highland Handicraft Guild. The head of the guild, Florence Goodell, now also directed the CSMW. In August 1951, when she retired from both positions, the CSMW returned to Berea. In 1954, the CSMW changed its name to the CSM. In the fall of 1955, it moved into larger, four-room headquarters. By 1956, its expanded structure included a twenty-one-member board of directors and an advisory board of eight representatives from institutional members. The following committees functioned in 1956: executive, finance, nominations, publications, conference, education, health, economic development, recreation, spiritual life, and youth. In 1958, the first of many southern colleges developed student units of the CSM. In the early 1960s, always sensitive to the region's peculiar problems, the CSM sponsored annual workshops on the urban adjustment of southern Appalachian migrants.

The doctrinal orientation of the CSM changed radically in the late 1960s. Significant developments erupted in 1960, particularly at the annual conference held at Fontana Dam, North Carolina. Increasingly concerned with social issues, the liberalism of the CSM led almost naturally to the democratization of the group. For example, all participants, including nonmembers, were allowed to vote at the Fontana meeting. A striking shift to the left resulted as the council resolved against the Vietnam War and the draft. The entire structure of the CSM was altered, with twelve commissions operating independently becoming the real governing body. Militant blacks, youths, and poor people, each of which had a new commission, seemed to dominate the CSM. Following Fontana, the board of directors disbanded in favor of the new board of commissioners, which quickly endorsed such resolutions as CSM opposition to strip mining and support of the National Welfare Rights Organization's* guaranteed annual income plan of $5,500 for a family of four. More conservative forces feared that the CSM would lose its foundations support and described Fontana as a "takeover." Aggravated by the failure of the new board of commissioners to respond satisfactorily to the crises at the headquarters, Loyal Jones resigned as executive director in May 1970.

When Warren Wright replaced Jones as executive director in 1970, the transformation and reorientation of the CSM were virtually completed. In late 1970, the organization began efforts to develop consumer health advocacy in Appalachia. Further egalitarianism became evident, after Wright resigned in mid-1971 when the board of directors abolished the position of executive director and created the post of staff coordinator. The staff voted to equalize all salaries and to implement Office of Economic Opportunity guidelines for salaries for poverty workers. Reflecting its part in the welfare rights movement, in November 1971, the CSM sponsored its March for Survival Against Unfulfilled Promises, an event in Washington, D.C., that criticized bureaucratic insensitivities and that resulted in pickets at relevant government agencies. By mid-1972, the commission system was not working as envisioned; consequently the CSM revised its bylaws to allow representatives of particular interest groups rather than commission members to join the board of directors. The organization also restricted institutional membership to indigenous organizations "working for a democratic and economically secure future for Appalachia and our people." Institutional membership was previously open to a wide range of civic and liberal organizations. In the summer of 1972, the CSM donated its files to the Berea College Library, packed its office furniture, and moved its headquarters to rural Clintwood, Virginia, an area plagued by strip mining.

The most useful primary source for studying the CSM is *Mountain Life and Work*. The Hutchins Library of Berea College has the manuscript files of the agency, but they were not available to researchers in early 1975. The Dr. Alva Taylor Papers at the Disciples of Christ Historical Society in Nashville, Tennessee, shed light on the history of the organization.

Surprisingly, secondary accounts—even of modern southern liberalism—rarely mention the CSM. John M. Glenn et al., *Russell Sage Foundation, 1907–*

1946 (1947), however, describes the Campbells' organizing activities. Davis E. Whisnant, "Controversy in God's Grand Design: The Council of the Southern Mountains," *Appalachian Journal* 2 (Autumn 1974): 7–45, is an interesting interpretation of the CSM's history but it exaggerates the conservatism of the agency's early history.

COUNCIL ON CHRISTIAN SOCIAL ACTION OF THE CONGREGA- TIONAL CHRISTIAN CHURCHES: see CONGREGATIONAL CHRIS- TIAN CHRUCHES, COUNCIL FOR SOCIAL ACTION OF.

COUNCIL ON INTERSTATE MIGRATION, INC. (CIM). Welfare agencies had been aware of the problems of transients for a long time, but by 1929, as the economic depression worsened, organizations such as the National Association of Travelers' Aid Societies* (NATAS), local family welfare agencies, city missions, lodging houses, The Salvation Army,* and other agencies saw a striking increase in the number of transient and homeless people. By the early 1930s, the enormous depression-caused burdens on local agencies forced some cities to begin registering outsiders, demonstrating the fear of indigent outsiders, a consistent theme in American social history. The federal government refused to become involved in these matters, even though the transients' problems were interstate in nature.

Studies begun in the early 1930s by the Family Welfare Association of America* (FWAA), the NATAS, and the Bureau of Jewish Social Research* (BJSR) focused increasing attention in social work circles on these problems. At the National Conference of Social Work* in May 1932, representatives of the FWAA's committee on homeless men and the NATAS's planning committee began efforts to coordinate the activities of national agencies involved in the care of transients. A United States Children's Bureau (USCB) study by Professor A. Wayne McMillen of the University of Chicago, released in August 1932, and testimony before Congress depicting boys on the loose in the Southwest dramatized the issue. More directly related to the establishment of the Council on Interstate Migration (CIM) as the Committee on Care of Transient and Homeless (CCTH), however, was the public sympathy generated by the famous Bonus Expeditionary Forces' (BEF) march to obtain veterans' benefits immediately. The well-publicized activities of the episode in Washington, D.C., resulted in a conference, convened by the Pennsylvania secretary of welfare, Alice F. Liveright, in Harrisburg, Pennsylvania, on August 11, 1932. The conference focused its discussions on the BEF's relation to the general national problem of unemployed migrants and then appointed a committee to draft recommendations quickly. This committee included Josephine Brown of the FWAA, Bertha McCall, the general director of the NATAS, J. Prentice Murphy, the head of the Pennsylvania Children's Aid Society, and, most importantly, Dr. Ellen Culver Potter, the medical director of the New Jersey Department of Institutions and

Agencies. Dr. Potter became, as the long-time chairman of the CCTH, the national spokesman in the private social work community on transiency.

The committee's recommendations, coupled with the earlier efforts of the FWAA and the NATAS, led to the founding of the CCTH in New York City in early October 1932. Representatives of fifteen national agencies formed the initial CCTH. The most important founders included Bertha McCall, Dr. Potter, J. P. Murphy, George Rabinoff of the BJSR, Professor McMillen, and Carl Christian Carstens, the widely respected child welfare leader and the director of the Child Welfare League of America.* Later in October 1932, at the request of the CCTH, the group became affiliated with the National Social Work Council* (NSWC). At a meeting on October 31, 1932, the CCTH decided that its chairman would be Bradley Buell of the American Community Chests and Councils, Inc.* (ACCC) and who later became the executive editor of *The Survey,* the leading social work journal. The CCTH also decided that its secretary be Ella Weinfurther of the staff of the NATAS, and that fourteen other individuals, including the head of the NSWC, David Holbrook, as ex officio, constitute the organization. The NATAS gave the new CCTH office space in its national headquarters in New York City and contributed some basic services. Most of the early CCTH funds, which were placed with the NSWC, came from the Tracy McGregor Fund of Detroit, whose founder, leader, and namesake was long interested in the plight of homeless men and who was another founder of the CCTH.

The CCTH began immediately to work to bring about progressive developments in the field. The CCTH influenced the first delegate conference of the American Association of Social Workers* in 1933 to join the effort to separate the problem of transiency from other relief issues and to thereby enlighten public officials. The CCTH's first major activity was to have its representatives tour the country to gather data about the homeless and transient, asking local agencies to cooperate with the census they planned for early 1933. On two separate days, one in January and one in March 1933, the CCTH implemented its censuses, giving the organization data that it subsequently presented as testimony in support of relief services for transients in the proposed bills by United States Senators Bronson Cutting, Robert F. Wagner, and Philip LaFollette. Although these bills did not pass, the CCTH presented further evidence in 1933, influencing section 4C of the Relief Act of 1933, which established the Federal Emergency Relief Administration (FERA).

This successful legislation initiated a period of CCTH influence on government social services. In July 1933, FERA administrator Harry Hopkins consulted with CCTH members in formulating the federal transient program. In August 1933, the FERA established its Transient Division, which provided funds for state programs, services, and facilities for the homeless. In 1933, Dr. Potter replaced Buell as the chairman of the CCTH, a position she held until the demise of the organization and its successor in 1939. In the summer of 1933, Dr. Potter temporarily left her position in the New Jersey Department of Institutions and Agencies to help establish the Federal Transient Program, better known as the Federal Transient Service (FTS).

The first director of the FTS was Morris Lewis, one of the two men the CCTH had employed in early 1933 to help with the censuses. He served until March 15, 1934. The next director of the federal agency, William J. Plunkert, had been a field director for the CCTH, which continued to influence the policies and programs of the FTS. The federal agency grew rapidly and had programs in all the states except Vermont by October 1934. In 1934, it began to evaluate the federal program. CCTH members, as well as staff workers from social agencies throughout the country, investigated sixty-two treatment centers, ninety-four shelters, and twenty-five camps in twenty-two states. The CCTH published the results in 1934 as *An Evaluative Survey of the Federal Transient Program* by Dr. Ellery F. Reed.

While focusing on implementing the federal program, the CCTH also strengthened its activities in private social work. Some organizational changes helped this development. In 1934, Abel J. Gregg of the boys' work division of the National Council of the Young Men's Christian Associations of the United States of America* (YMCA) began to serve as part-time executive secretary, but he had full-time clerical help. Dr. Potter provided an important link to the social work community. The CCTH began to develop more structures, appointing in September 1934 a subcommittee on the local homeless, which conducted hearings on transiency in New York City. Representatives from various New York institutions and agencies, along with transients, testified at these sessions, giving CCTH members firsthand information about the conditions affecting these people during the depression. The CCTH successfully encouraged committees in other localities to conduct similar hearings in late 1934.

In early 1935, the CCTH focused on strengthening federal programs in the field. Chairman Potter urged both the decentralization of the federal program with emphasis on state services for transients and the hiring of transients on local projects of the Public Works Administration. She even suggested in a letter in January 1935 to Louis Howe, President Franklin D. Roosevelt's secretary, a series of special projects for the Civilian Conservation Corps to serve the homeless. In the spring of 1935, a meeting of the CCTH focused on the recent field experiences of its members. Also in the spring of 1935, the organization urged FERA administrator Hopkins to maintain provisions for the homeless in the pending social security program. A few weeks later, on May 14, the CCTH sent its recommendations to Hopkins and to Aubrey Williams, the deputy administrator of the Works Progress Administration. When calls for retrenchment and right-wing criticisms of New Deal programs led to the closing of all federal transient intake offices in September 1935, the CCTH protested strongly. With the NATAS, it began a nationwide campaign to continue the FTS by wiring influential people throughout the country to pressure President Franklin

Roosevelt and by organizing regional conferences to support the federal program.

Despite setbacks, particularly the elimination of the FTS in late 1935, the CCTH persevered in promoting the interests of its constituents. It helped to keep the social work community aware of the problems, cosponsoring, with the newly named National Association for Travelers Aid and Transient Service (NATATS), a panel on transients at the New York State Conference on Social Work in Buffalo in 1935. In 1936, with MacEnnis Moore of the NATATS as its executive secretary, the CCTH issued *Clearings*, a mimeographed publication dealing with developments in the field. Working with the Florida Transient Coordinating Committee, the CCTH informed senators and congressmen about bills dealing with transients, and in the summer of 1936, in Washington, D.C., it convened representatives from the federal agencies dealing with transients.

In late 1936, an important organizational development occurred when Philip E. Ryan succeeded Moore as executive secretary. Ryan had more than three years' experience with the New York Temporary Emergency Relief Administration's Transient Division. Under his leadership, the CCTH sponsored, with the Florida group, United States Senate Resolution #298, introduced by Senator James P. Pope of Florida, which called for a Labor Department report on transients' conditions. In late 1937, the CCTH presented data on the transient problem to the Special Senate Committee to Investigate Unemployment and Relief. In 1936 and 1937, the CCTH helped plan regional conferences on transiency, cooperated with states, especially Florida, to develop their own programs, and continued to focus public opinion on the problem. On June 24, 1937, the CCTH held a conference in Washington, D.C., with representatives from national voluntary organizations and federal agencies to develop a comprehensive plan for transients.

In the late 1930s, the CCTH still struggled against conservatism and retrenchment, but its demise was imminent. Its representatives appeared before the Special Senate Committee again in March 1938, proposing both that under the Social Security Act of 1935 the United States Public Health Service (USPHS) grant funds to state departments of health to care for transients and that public assistance be granted to nonresidents, an important point in American social welfare principles. Suggesting the effectiveness of the CCTH in keeping the transiency issue alive, the federal Interdepartmental Committee to Coordinate Health and Welfare Activities appointed the Technical Sub-Committee on Migration Problems, apparently in early 1939. In the spirit of social justice photojournalism of the earlier Progressive era, the CCTH, along with the National Child Labor Committee* and the Council of Women for Home Missions, helped *Life Magazine* in photographing migrants. Also in 1938, the CCTH helped to prepare the *Survey of the Present Status of the Problem of the Transient and State Settlement Laws*, by the Council of State Governments, and it brought to the attention of the proper agencies the high incidence of tuberculosis among homeless men in New York City. Despite the lack of funds and the increasing lack of interest in transient as opposed to migrant families—popularized in the late 1930s by John Steinbeck's *The Grapes of Wrath*—the CCTH began an ambitious program to develop coordinated federal services, to stimulate social service agencies to create yet another agency, and to continue to promote conferences and planning sessions. To pursue these objectives, the CCTH executive committee incorporated itself in New York State on June 11, 1938, as the new Council on Interstate Migration (CIM). The CCTH continued to exist, and it met often with the CIM.

By late 1938, the futures of the CIM and the CCTH did not appear bright, but a core of activists and reformers persisted in their efforts in behalf of the truly forgotten men of the New Deal, the transients. The new CIM hoped to influence people interested in this issue to join it as associate members. The recently renamed Travelers Aid Association of America (TAAA) was not confident that the CIM's ideals would be implemented, but it nevertheless voted to remain part of the group. The important people in the CIM included Bertha McCall, Rabinoff, Potter, Russell Kurtz, who had worked considerably for the CCTH, and Margaret Rich of the FWAA. Philip Ryan became the executive director of this small but energetic group, committed to acting as a clearinghouse facilitating joint planning and representing transients' interests. The CIM kept the issues alive, helping to develop a panel at a meeting of the American Public Welfare Association* in December 1938. The CIM, however, failed to obtain suitable funds, forcing it to suspend operations in mid-1939. On October 15, 1939, the CIM turned over its files to the TAAA. This ended about six and one-half years of an excellent cooperative venture of national social service agencies, itself an important legacy. Key people from the CIM and the CCTH continued their efforts for transients, working through a committee of the TAAA. But, as the historian of the FTS concluded, the CIM's demise was a real blow to reform.

The sources for studying the CCTH are diverse. Essential are the minutes of its meetings for the period from 1932 through late 1938. They can be found in a bound volume at the headquarters of the National Travelers Aid–International Social Service of America in New York City. Other papers can be found in the collection of the National Social Welfare Assembly at the Social Welfare History Archives Center at the University of Minnesota, Minneapolis. Some correspondence is in the Papers of the Federal Emergency Relief Administration at the National Archives in Washington, D.C., and a few minutes, memorandums, and the like are in the YMCA library in New York City. *The Transient,* a TAAA publication, which appeared first in early 1934, carried several items about the CCTH. Other social work journals, such as *The Survey* and *The Family,* reported on the activities of the CCTH. The CCTH publication with the greatest historical value is *After Five Years: The Unsolved Problem of the Transient Unemployed, 1932–1937* (1937).

Standard histories of the 1930s generally neglect not merely the CCTH but also the topic of transiency and homelessness. Helen Hawkins, "A New Deal for the Newcomer: The Federal Transient Service" (Ph.D. diss., University of California-San Diego, 1975), however, does deal with the CCTH.

COUNCIL ON SOCIAL WORK EDUCATION, THE (CSWE). In the national social work community during the 1940s, there were disputes about the nature of social work education. These differences were expressed by two organizations dealing with education in the field of social service: the American Association of Schools of Social Work (AASSW), a membership organization of graduate social work education programs, and the National Association of Schools of Social Administration (NASSA), an organization of schools that provided a general undergraduate social work–social science education plus a fifth year of specialized training. Both the AASSW and the NASSA set standards independently. Conflicts between the two became untenable in the period after World War II when the need for professionally trained social workers was acute. This situation prompted representatives from the NASSA and the AASSW to establish the National Council on Social Work Education (NCSWE) for the purpose of coordinating the programs of the two social work education organizations.

The NCSWE commissioned a study of social work education, which led to the founding of the Council on Social Work Education (CSWE). The product of this study was *Social Work Education in the United States* (1951), by Ernest V. Hollis, the chief of college administration in the Office of Education of the Federal Security Administration (FSA), and Alice L. Taylor, a training consultant from the FSA's Bureau of Public Assistance. The book became both a catalyst for immediate action and a touchstone for continuous evaluation. Commissioned to help solve the issue of accreditation, the study recognized that since social work education was directly related to social work practice, it was necessary to establish what constituted social work. Thus, the study became a major review of past and present social work practices and programs, as well as a thorough description of all aspects of social work education. The insights and proposal that Hollis and Taylor presented led both the AASSW and the NASSA to disband in favor of a new organization. Consequently, in New York City on July 1, 1952, the Council on Social Work Education (CSWE) was established. Its major concern was with standards and the accreditation of graduate schools of social work.

The CSWE established its headquarters in New York City. Helen Russell Wright, professor and dean of the School of Social Service Administration of the University of Chicago, was elected the first president. For the next twenty years, women usually held this position. Jane M. Hoey, Grace Coyle, and Ruth Smalley were others who were president in the early years of the organization. The first executive director was Ernest Witte. Katherine A. Kendall occupied the office for a short time (1964 and 1965); she was followed by James R.

Dumpson, dean of the Fordham University Graduate School of Social Service. The executive in 1976 was Richard Lodge. Complex categories of membership to the new organization were established, which included both individuals and institutions involved in social work practice and education. A category of membership for general citizens was also established. A special and powerful group within the CSWE was the deans and chairpersons of the schools. The constitution of the organization, adopted in 1952, put the administrative responsibilities in the hands of an elected board of directors, and the legislative duties were given to an elected house of delegates, made up of representatives from all of the membership categories. Several committees were established. The most central one was the commission on accreditation; like the council itself, it had members from social work practice and education.

The problem faced by Hollis and Taylor of defining social work and its professional needs became an ongoing issue of the CSWE as it struggled with its major task of accreditation. A related task was recruitment, a topic that included everything from concern for salaries and the status of the profession to how to recruit more minority students and faculty in the late 1960s. The curriculum, the administration, the teaching staff, and the teaching methodology in graduate schools of social work were all considered in the accrediting process. Concerned with the negative aspects of the concept of standardization, the CSWE focused on broad principles of education and social work practice and the relationship of the two. Standards were set for administration and curriculum; but a degree of flexibility in how these were met in any particular program and a process of assisting schools in both short- and long-range planning for improvement mediated the onus of standardization. In 1974, after ten years of discussion and experimentation, the CSWE also took on the task of accreditation of undergraduate programs of social work.

Workshops, short courses, and seminars for social work teachers and practitioners, consultation, production of teaching materials, and improved communication were other responses to the educational needs of the profession. The CSWE also brought educators and practitioners together for discussions of the needs of social work practice as related to education. The programs of the annual meeting, held in February or March, consisted mainly of papers about issues of practice and education in relationship to each other. Each of these was seen as part of the single process of delivery of social services. Education informed the profession, and the profession informed the educational process in one continuous relationship.

The CSWE also enhanced the close relationship between social work education and the federal government. The relationship grew naturally from the educational relationship to practice. By the time the CSWE was founded in 1952, the federal government was providing, either through local and state programs or its own direct programs, the resources for a large proportion of social work in the United States. Social workers in local, state, and federal agencies became members of the CSWE in the same way that members of private agencies did. In addition, as federal programs and funding of social work increased, the need for trained workers increased. Concern for the quality of programs funded led to concern by federal agencies about the recruitment and education of personnel. As part of this concern, federal funds for social work education and student stipends or grants to programs were given only to accredited schools. By 1953, the federal Office of Education and the National Commission on Accrediting (see *Educational Organizations*), an association of colleges and universities concerned with standards in higher education, recognized the CSWE as the sole agency accrediting social work schools and programs.

By 1957, membership in the CSWE included 500 individuals, 59 graduate schools (7 Canadian), 92 undergraduate departments, and 148 private and public agencies. Private agencies were members through their national offices, and public ones were members through local, state, and federal offices. In this year of the council's fifth anniversary, the major areas of the CSWE's responsibility were named: accreditation, assistance with improving educational programs, recruitment, and coordination of information about social work education. A small staff carried out these responsibilities through facilitation, stimulation, and coordination. As Executive Director Ernest Witte said, the real work of the CSWE was carried out by volunteers, meaning social work practitioners and educators.

From 1958 to 1968, the CSWE established itself as the leader in social work education by expansion as well as by putting its roots down deeper. It began a program of assistance to social work schools in India and later added those other countries. These projects eventually led to the founding of the International Association of Social Work Education. It also commissioned and published in 1959 a three-year, thirteen-volume curriculum study, which was considered a milestone in social work education. This study, as well as consultations and discussions, led to one of the most important developments in social work education. CSWE accreditation would no longer evaluate specialized programs. So-called generic programs or core curriculum would, from 1960 on, be the basis of accreditation, although specializations were expected to continue in both curriculum and practice. Actually CSWE often provided seminars and consultation on some specializations in the years after 1960.

The low status of the profession was an often-expressed concern during these years because it was seen as one of the major blocks to recruiting qualified students, especially men. The CSWE hired a consultant on recruitment in 1959, and by 1962, there was rejoicing over the increased enrollment of 53 percent in graduate schools from 1954, when enrollment in general was at a low. But the CSWE was still asking, "What is social work?" The executive director of CSWE pointed out that until the nature of social work practice could be defined with clarity and precision, the educational program was resting on a very insecure basis. Werner Boehm, in volume 1 of the CSWE curriculum study, *Objec-*

tives of Social Work Curriculum of the Future (1959), had concluded that only a definition so broad as to be meaningless was possible. His study, therefore, focused on the values, goals, function, and method of social work. He wrote, "The knowledge needed for social work practice is determined by its goals and function and the problems it seeks to solve." An examination in 1973 of the same question, put in the form of the effectiveness of social work, also failed to find a successful answer.

The greatest change in the function of CSWE and in the structure of social work education and practice took place in 1974 when the CSWE's commission on accreditation took on the task of expanding accreditation to include undergraduate programs. There was serious disagreement about this action, especially by some of the graduate school educators. The vote in the house of delegates in 1970 to begin to work toward baccalaureate accrediting by establishing a committee on standards for undergraduate programs had been carried by representatives from agencies, undergraduate programs, and the federal government, which had been advocating an expansion of the social work baccalaureate since 1965. By September 1975, 209 undergraduate programs had been acted upon by the CSWE's committee.

In 1964, as pressures were increased to produce more trained social workers to staff programs funded by the federal government, an interagency committee was organized to promote further expansion of federal assistance for training social work personnel. Representatives from CSWE, the National Association of Social Workers* (NASW), the American Public Welfare Association,* the National Social Welfare Assembly,* and the National Association of Statewide Health and Welfare Conferences and Planning Organizations were included. A committee of deans from CSWE also met with federal officials to assist in plans for expanded federal aid.

Strong relationships and cooperation between the government welfare bureaucracy and social work education were not new in the mid-1960s. Personnel from the Department of Health, Education, and Welfare (DHEW) had long participated on CSWE committees and at annual meetings. CSWE, however, nurtured the relationship and gave it some direction. As early as 1955, at the CSWE's annual meeting, Joy L. Roney of the federal Bureau of Public Assistance was expressing concern about the inadequate numbers of trained social workers. Jane Hoey, president of CSWE, responding to information from Roney that the Congress had some interest in providing scholarships for social workers, said that any funding should include money for the schools of social work so that they could handle the influx of new students.

CSWE also benefited directly from federal funding in the 1960s. A seven-year grant of $240,000 was made in 1967 to CSWE by the National Institute of Mental Health (NIMH) to recruit, prepare, and induct new faculty into social work education. In 1967, amendments to the Social Security Act authorized $5 million to be appropriated for fiscal 1968 and in the following three years to be used as grants to colleges and universities with accredited graduate schools of social work and to develop and expand undergraduate social work programs. The bill specified that half of the money was to go to the latter. The bill illustrated a two-way cooperation between the CSWE and the government. The money went only to accredited graduate schools that only CSWE could accredit, and half of the money was given to encourage undergraduate social work education to produce more of the social work baccalaureate graduates that the government had proposed in 1965. In 1969, the CSWE received money to strengthen its consultation role to undergraduate social work education, including standardizing programs, recruiting minorities, and identifying jobs for which the baccalaureate degree could be the basic social work degree. Fifty undergraduate schools received grants at the same time, and two graduate schools received money to get involved with undergraduate programs. This development was a long distance from earlier principles stated at the CSWE first annual meeting when Helen Wright from the University of Chicago said that social work educators did not favor two types of education, one for workers and one for leaders and decision makers.

As President Richard Nixon's budget-cutting policies in Washington began to take hold in 1969, CSWE leaders and the deans of schools of social work began to spend more time in Washington with DHEW personnel and with elected representatives to get information from the former and to encourage the latter to maintain funding of social work programs and education. By 1969, there were seventy-five schools of social work in the United States and a constant increase of new students. No one in social work wanted to see the gains that had been made since the mid-1960s loss. In 1970, more than fifty deans out of seventy-five gathered in Washington in response to a call from CSWE to review federal programs and to lobby at DHEW and with Congress for an increase in its appropriations to social work education and social services. In 1973, the CSWE expanded its public affairs program and lobbying efforts in the bureaucracy and Congress. The deans and directors of schools of social work, as members of the CSWE, became more and more involved in the lobbying process, along with NASW and other social work organizations. Three staff personnel were assigned from CSWE to work on national legislation and administration policy as the house of delegates of CSWE gave highest budget and staff priority to action for reversing the federal government cutbacks in social service and training of social workers. This work was difficult because former social work–trained allies who headed many bureaus had been replaced by nonsocial workers, and the reorganization had destroyed former lines of communication and power. In 1974, CSWE and other social welfare organizations brought suit against the Nixon administration to obtain funds voted by Congress in 1973 for mental health traineeships. The Supreme Court ordered the release of those funds.

Some of those funds and other funds came directly to the CSWE in 1974 and 1975. For example, NIMH provided a three-year grant to CSWE to study, discover, and disseminate information about the best programs in community mental health at all levels of social work education. Also, a special grant to encourage more ethnic representation in student bodies was received, and a DHEW grant went to the CSWE to develop curriculum in the teaching of administration and management. Another grant was awarded the CSWE for an eighteen-month planning project on regional needs for mental health workers. In general, however, the financial situation in social work education and programs worsened. By January 1976, through its committee on national legislation and administration policy, organized in 1974, CSWE marshalled all of its resources to recruit educators, students, advisory boards, and practitioners to lobby for an increase in social work education grants for the programs on alcohol and drug treatment, child abuse and other maternal and child care, gerontology, and juvenile delinquency control.

The CSWE house of delegates in 1976 reaffirmed the role of social work education and the CSWE as related to social work practices. It said that social work education and practice had the same concern to improve and advance social service delivery but that each had a different function in working for the goal. Therefore, although the CSWE worked primarily for the betterment of education, it ultimately worked for better service for people. The future tasks were defined as strengthening the ties of agencies to the educational system via teachers, training, and fieldwork and reviewing the core program necessary in social work education. This was also the basic task when the CSWE was founded, and since its inception, it has not changed, in spite of tremendous growth in both education and practice as a result of federal funding.

The Hollis and Taylor study and the thirteen-volume Boehm study of social work curriculum are basic resources for studying the CSWE. Numerous other books discuss social work education, but these are not central to the history of the CSWE. Primary sources are available in many libraries. These are the various proceedings and published papers of the council. In addition, the CSWE has two serial publications that are valuable resources, *The Social Work Education Reporter* and *The Journal of Social Work Education*. An important government study on manpower is *Closing the Gap in Social Work Manpower* (1965).

There does not appear to be a scholarly history of the CSWE.

Marilyn A. Domer

___ *D* ___

DAY CARE AND CHILD DEVELOPMENT COUNCIL OF AMERICA, INC., THE (DCCDCA). During World War II, when women in large numbers worked in defense and other industrial plants, there were complaints by women and social and child care workers that not enough funds were spent for the day care of children and that there were simply not enough day care facilities and services. At this time there was no single nationwide interest group committed to day care. The Child Welfare League of America* (CWLA) had absorbed the former National Association of Day Nurseries* (NADN) in 1942, but, as historian Howard Dratch suggests, the CWLA was not an especially strong advocate in this postward period. During those years, part of the struggle for public funds for day care centered in New York City.

In April 1948, the New York City Day Care Council was organized. After ten years of struggle to have the New York State legislature appropriate funds for day care, the leaders of a New York group recognized that if federal funds were available, the state would be induced more readily to support public day care facilities. At the National Conference on Social Welfare* (NCSW) in Philadelphia in 1957, the New York group posted a notice convening people interested in day care. Sixteen people participated and agreed to establish an informal group. In 1958, the group adopted an appropriate name, the Intercity Committee on the Day Care of Children (ICDCC). It set up an office in the headquarters of the New York City Day Care Council. This was the origins of The Day Care and Child Development Council of America, Inc. (DCCDCA). In 1959, after conferring with representatives of other national educational and child welfare agencies— including both the CWLA and the Family Service Association of America* (FSAA)—the ICDCC decided to expand its energies in promoting the idea of day care and to establish its own national office. The ICDCC helped to influence the convening of a session on day care at the annual conference of the CWLA, and the ICDCC helped to plan the day care aspects of the White House Conference on Children and Youth in 1960. In the late 1950s, the ICDCC convinced the United States Department of Health, Education and Welfare (DHEW) to give $35,000 to the federal Bureau of Labor Statistics to produce and disseminate accurate information about day care.

The ICDCC's concern with the socioeconomic importance of day care became the theme of an early major organizational highlight. With the United States Women's Bureau, the NCDCC sponsored the first national conference on day care, in Washington, D.C., on November 17–18, 1960. Another important development in 1960 occurred when the ICDCC became incorporated as the National Committee for the Day Care of Children, Inc. (NCDCC). Grants from three foundations enabled it to move to its own national offices in New York City. Despite its incorporation and national standing, the NCDCC retained its rather simple organizational structure.

The volunteer and unpaid leaders of the agency, particularly the chairman, Elinor Guggenheimer, and cochairman, Sadie Ginsburg, played significant roles in this early stage of the history of the organization. For instance, Guggenheimer led a delegation of NCDCC representatives in brief discussions on August 3, 1961, with the secretaries of the DHEW and the Department of Labor and their staffs. This meeting apparently convinced DHEW Secretary Abraham Ribicoff to include federal day care funding in the Social Security amendments of 1961.

Federal funding for day care facilities, however limited, and the NCDCC's activities helped to popularize the concept of day care nationally. In 1960 and early 1961, for example, Guggenheimer and other leaders traveled to cities throughout the country, advising and encouraging local groups to organize day care facilities and campaigns. On August 1, 1961, the agency's first executive secretary, Mariana Jessen, assumed these duties, in addition to preparing the group's *Newsletter*. Cooperating with a local group, the NCDCC held the first Massachusetts Day Care Day celebration on October 21, 1963. In the early 1960s, the NCDCC gathered relevant case records that the Council on Social Work Education* helped to adapt for professional training. This activity and others helped to bring the NCDCC closer to the social work community.

As federal funding for social welfare expanded dramatically in the mid-1960s, the functions and activities of the relatively new NCDCC paralleled those of the best and most established national social welfare agencies. It influenced federal legislation, stimulated public opinion, conducted both research and demonstration projects, and provided interpretative materials on particular issues. In 1964, for example, the organization influenced the formation of the National Day Care Advisory Committee; conferred frequently with representatives of leading private and public child care agencies—particularly the CWLA and the United States Children's Bureau (USCB) (see *Government Agencies*)—to shape developments in the day care field; enlarged its own publications and information services; and sent specific proposals for day care programs in the federal War on Poverty to Sargent Shriver, a presidential adviser. In 1965, the organization cosponsored the second national day care conference and felt duly proud in early 1965 when Executive Director Jessen was asked to serve as a consultant on day care to the community action program of the federal Office of Economic Opportunity (OEO). Simultaneously, other NCDCC representatives helped the United States Office of Education to prepare materials for preschool children in day care centers.

With day care seemingly accepted as an issue of recognized importance, the NCDCC began in the mid-1960s to broaden its interests and activities in the field of child welfare. Special issues of the *Newsletter,* other NCDCC publications and conferences, and some activities dealt with the welfare of migrant children. In May 1967, the agency helped to sponsor in New York City a one-day conference, "The Child and the City." Senator Robert F. Kennedy was the keynote speaker, and Whitney Young, executive director of the National Urban League,* addressed the conference. The legislative committee of the NCDCC followed several congressional bills, and members testified on HR 5710 to amend the Social Security Act in 1967. Largely because many board members felt the expanding activities of the agency necessitated a name change, the NCDCC became the DCCDCA in 1967. Therese Lansburgh, a recognized leader in the day care movement, became president in 1967 when the organization moved its headquarters from New York City to Washington, D.C.

The DCCDCA grew, in the words of a founder of the organization, from a "small, almost amateur operation, to a large and well recognized national agency." In the late 1960s and early 1970s, the DCCDCA campaigned militantly not only for universal publicly funded day care but also for other pressing social issues, such as minority rights. With these increased activities and the flush days of the mid-1960s, the agency expanded its staff and service. Ted Taylor became the executive director in June 1971. In the winter of 1970–1971, however, lack of funds almost forced the agency to close and led to delayed mailings and other hardships. But new membership categories, other rund-raising and budgetary devices, and the contributions of some supporters helped it to reemerge within a few months as an advocate agency with a clear purpose.

Back on its feet and with a new, aggressive executive director, Ted Taylor, the DCCDCA expanded its activities once again. In the fall of 1971, for example, the agency initiated a new field service, a mobile field team, consisting of husband and wife professionals who toured the country, conducting workshops and seminars and recruiting new members. In 1971, the organization, cooperating with the Colorado Migrants Service, began a special educational project for migrant children. With a year grant from the federal OEO, the DCCDA began to provide information on day care to a broader spectrum of the public through a series of *Child Care Bulletins*. In late 1971, the DCCDCA issued a widely publicized, point-by-point rebuttal of President Richard M. Nixon's veto statement of the Comprehensive Child Development Act of 1971.

As suggested in its denunciation of the veto, the DCCDCA participated increasingly and actively in the contemporary progressive social welfare movements. An aggressive plan adopted in late 1972, calling for an honorary chairperson to campaign for an expanded child care program, led in late November 1972 to the resignation of the honorary chairman, Mrs. Richard M. Nixon. The board of directors increasingly included more minority representatives, and the DCCDCA plan called for a women and minority affairs plan, under a new associate director, to involve these groups in the struggle for universal child care. By May 1973, the DCCDCA formulated its bicentennial plans, Child Care '76, initiated formally on Labor Day 1973. The DCCDCA also helped in the successful campaign in 1973 to defeat the enactment of more restrictive federal social service regulations. Continuing its services in the child welfare field, the agency contracted in 1973 with the Appalachian Child Care Project to plan and to implement a development program in rural Georgia. By the mid-1970s, the DCCDCA's increasing activism and aggressiveness and the move to Washington, D.C., had disassociated the New York group of founders and early leaders from the agency.

Organizational developments paralleled agency activities. The DCCDCA created a new associate director for public relations in late 1972, when the board of directors also decided to implement a four-year plan of expansion. In early 1973, the region VII Child Care Advisory Conference became a midwestern affiliate of the DCCDCA. In late March 1973, the DCCDCA launched the first of a series of fund-raising benefits. To preserve its tax-exempt status, the board decided to establish a new organization to engage actively in politics. Later in the year, the first regional office opened in Atlanta, and in January 1974, representatives of the Connecticut Social Welfare Conference became another DCCDCA affiliate. In the summer of 1974, the DCCDCA hired at its Washington, D.C., national headquarters, five young workers, reaffirming its commitment to the Washington Youth Corps. The annual meeting in St. Louis in October 1974 featured a downtown parade demonstrating enthusiasm for Child Care '76.

The primary sources for studying the DCCDCA's history are its variously named *Newsletter* and the helpful *Annual Reports,* published since the early 1970s. Honorary Elinor Guggenheimer, "Origins of the Council," *Voice for Children* (October 1974): 7–8, is a helpful account. The *Voice* was one name for the agency's newsletter.

Histories of the day care movement, such as Margaret O'Brien Steinfels, *Who's Minding the Children?* (1973), do not mention the organization, and there is apparently no scholarly history of the DCCDCA. Historian Howard Dratch's point appeared in his "The Politics of Child Care in the 1940s," *Science and Society* 38 (Summer 1974): 167–204.

DEPARTMENT OF CHRISTIAN SOCIAL RELATIONS OF THE PROTESTANT EPISCOPAL CHURCH: see EPISCOPAL CHURCH, DEPARTMENT OF CHRISTIAN SOCIAL RELATIONS OF THE PROTESTANT.

DISCIPLES OF CHRIST, CHURCH IN SOCIETY OF THE (CS). The social gospel movement of the late nineteenth and early twentieth centuries did not have as profound an impact on the leaders of the Disciples of Christ (DC) (see *Religious Institutions*), also known, especially later, as the Christian churches, as it did on spokesmen from other denominations. One of the leading progressives from the DC, Dr. Alva Wilmot Taylor of the Bible College of Missouri, however, led the movement to establish a social service agency in his church similar to the ones created by the other denominations. Taylor apparently organized a petitioning committee, and he became its secretary. At the International Convention of the DC in Louisville, Kentucky, in 1912, the petitioning committee influenced the denomination to establish Church in Society (CS) as the Committee on Social Service (CSS). The convention simply designed the petitioning group as the CSS, responsible administratively not to the convention itself but to an organization of the church, The American Christian Missionary Society (ACMS). Dr. Taylor became the first executive officer. In 1913, the CSS was renamed the Commission on Social Service and the Rural Church (CSSRC) at the convention in Toronto, Canada. In 1920, it merged with another DC organization, the American Temperance Board (ATB), to form the Board of Temperance and Social Welfare (BTSW), administratively still under the ACMS. In 1920, Dr. Taylor went to the ACMS's headquarters in Indianapolis, where he and the former acting secretary of the ATB, Milo J. Smith, administered the new BTSW jointly.

Taylor, who became an important figure in national social work, particularly in the rural South, influenced profoundly the direction of the agency. By his participation in the investigations in 1920 of conditions in the Pittsburgh steel industry and in his role in writing the *Report on the Steel Strike of 1919* (1920), which denounced industrialists and sided generally with the strikers, he helped to give the BTSW its radical reputation within the church. Taylor's lecturing throughout the country to both college and church groups and his commitment to the peace crusade left a lasting imprint on the BTSW and on his successor, Reverend James A. Crain. In 1927–1928, Taylor studied Negro housing conditions in Indianapolis, and in February 1928, he began to publish a journal, *Social Trends*. Taylor joined the faculty of Vanderbilt University in September 1928, and Crain became general secretary on January 1, 1929.

Crain continued Taylor's basic activities, but he became more energetically involved than Taylor had been in the temperance movement. Between 1929 and 1932, Crain's almost exclusive preoccupation was to save the Eighteenth Amendment. In December 1933, he even left the BTSW temporarily to head the National Prohibition Emergency Committee. His absorption with temperance, coupled with the financial troubles of the early to mid-1930s, left little time or money for other social services. On July 1, 1935, structural changes in the church abolished the BTSW and created the new Department of Temperance and Social Welfare (DTSW), which became part of the new United Christian Missionary Service (UCMS), another DC organization. Both BTSW and DTSW leaders opposed its integration into the new structure, fearing that the merger might mean the restriction of its previous controversial stands.

Contrary to such expectations, in the period after 1935, Crain was able to expand the activities of the agency, even into controversial areas. Under his leadership, the DTSW and the independent, more militant Disciples of Peace Fellowship (DPF) developed a close relations. In 1936, the DTSW sponsored the DC convention resolution dissociating DC from war and the war system. During World War II, through funds raised by the DPF, the DTSW paid the living expenses of Disciples conscientious objectors in the Civilian Public Service (CPS), an agency established and run by the so-called peace churches, such as the Church of the Brethren. Beginning in June 1943, the DTSW administered the Disciples Commission on World Order, developing a nationwide series of workshops on international order, and the United Nations seminars, both of which became continuing DTSW functions.

In March 1947, Ruther Milner became national director of church and community service. She administered the aid and refugee program of the Disciples, sending contributions abroad and sponsoring the settlement of refugee families in the United States. Beginning in 1943, she also directed the program in which Disciples worked in migrant labor camps. In the early 1950s, the DTSW influenced the international convention of the church to improve significantly its treatment of Negroes.

The DTSW was responsible for weaving social action education into the Disciples program. Earlier Taylor had tried, but failed, to establish state committees engaged in meaningful social work. By 1947, however, when the DTSW published its manual of local activities, the agency was clearly promoting Disciple social conscience. Taylor's *Social Trends,* Crain's "Social Trends" page in *The World Call* and in *Front Rank,* and the *Social Action News Letter* gradually influenced the brotherhood of Disciples. Regional groups of Disciples churches, as well as individual churches, established welfare agencies. Reverend Barton Hunter became the executive secretary on June 30, 1954, when Crain retired. On July 1, 1960, the agency became the Department of Christian Action and Community Service (DCACS) under the Division of Church Life and Work, still part of the UCMS in Indianapolis.

Under Barton's leadership in the 1950s and 1960s, the agency continued its activities in the fields of international understanding and relief and of peace, and it expanded to include two new important areas: civil rights and the care of the aging. Sensitive to the problems of blacks, the DCACS sponsored a host of seminars and discussion groups in the 1950s, such as the annual Disciples conference on desegregation, held initially in Cleveland in June 1955. The department's commitment to improving race relations featured a reconciliation counseling project to sensitize ministers to race relations; ministries to racially troubled areas in the late 1950s; voter registration work among southern Negroes in the early 1960s; a grant from the Field Foundation in 1958 to extend the race-related work of a special minister-at-large; a pilot city project in Indianapolis in the early 1960s and a major one in Detroit in the mid-1960s; campaigning for the Civil Rights Act of 1964; and, beginning in the mid-1960s, a program to collect and distribute food to impoverished Mississippi Delta blacks. Programs for the aging included a special ministry to the aging and the publication in November 1959 of *Housing Needs of Older People.* As part of its peace activities, the DCACS supported the nuclear test ban in the early 1960s and participated in both the vigil at the Pentagon in May 1965 and the Negotiate Now! movement. In 1969, the DCACS became Church in Society (CS), still administratively under the Division of Church Life and Work of the UCMS in Indianapolis. In the late 1960s, the agency provided draft counseling services and continued to support two pilot projects: the Change through Involvement Program, which recruited over six hundred volunteers for community work in inner cities, and one that established an Appalachian resettlement house in cities to assist rural newcomers in adjusting to the city. The CS also continued to aid refugees and the aging.

In the 1970s, CS continued the basic agency activities in civil rights, poverty, social justice, and peace and reconciliation. Early in the decade, it initiated a major shift emphasizing local church groups' participation in the legislative process. CS had a full-time staff worker assigned to pilot projects in community organizations and on the criminal justice system. With the African Methodist Episcopal church, CS began low-rent housing programs in Louisiana, Mississippi, and Georgia. It participated in the anti-Vietnam War movement. It also cooperated with the interfaith Crusade Against Hunger and lobbied for the full and fair implementation of the federal school lunch act. A successful effort to change the bail system for certain misdemeanors and crimes in Missouri reflected CS's efforts to effect a more humane criminal justice system. By 1973, the Change through Involvement Program had paid staff workers in twenty-four cities. In this period, CS incorporated the Mt. Beulah Development Corporation in Mississippi to help blacks. In the 1970s, CS persisted in its support of the equal rights amendment, opposition to the Vietnam War, and, consistent with its concern for social justice, the United Farm Workers' Union and its boycotts, strikes, and programs.

The annual reports of the agency, which appear in the Disciples of Christ *Year Books,* describe its activities and developments. Other primary sources for studying the history of the agency are the personal papers of leaders Dr. Alva Taylor and Reverend James Crain at the Disciples of Christ Historical Society in Nashville, Tennessee, which also has the official records of the agency for most of its years. The agency's *Social Action News Letter,* which is on microfilm, is another good primary source. Contemporary articles describing the agency appear in DC journals, such as *The Christian Standard.*

Secondary sources include the helpful James A. Crain, *The Development of Social Ideas Among the Disciples of Christ* (1969), and various short biographies of Dr. Taylor. There does not appear to be a scholarly history of the CS.

E

EPISCOPAL CHURCH, DEPARTMENT OF CHRISTIAN SOCIAL RE-LATIONS (DCSR) OF THE PROTESTANT. The social gospel movement of the late nineteenth century awakened the social conscience of American churches. A number of members and leaders of the Protestant Episcopal church (PEC) were active and important in this general reform movement. To institutionalize the PEC's efforts to achieve social justice, the general convention of the PEC appointed a Commission on the Relationship of Capital and Labor

(CRCL) in 1901. Distinguished social gospellers, such as Bishop Henry Codman Potter, the Episcopal bishop of New York, and other reformers, such as Jacob Riis and Seth Low, worked for the commission. In 1910, the CRCL became the Joint Commission on Social Service (JCSS). In 1913, the JCSS became a permanent church agency, and in 1919, it was enlarged to form the Department of Christian Social Service (DCSS). Unlike the more radical Church League for Industrial Democracy, the DCSS was the official social service agency of the PEC, reporting to the annual general convention.

The department began its work energetically, thrusting itself into the mainstream of American social welfare work. Reverend Charles N. Lathrop, who authored and coauthored some important handbooks on social welfare in the early 1920s, became the first executive secretary, serving in the post until 1929. Like other church welfare organizations, the DCSS coordinated and supervised local Episcopalian-related social work and institutions throughout the country. Particularly through its publication, *The Social Opportunity of the Churchman* (1921), the DCSS developed local discussion groups to sensitize Episcopalians to the need for Christian social service. To help supervise and strengthen local social work, the DCSS sponsored, in Milwaukee in June 1921, the first annual Conference of Social Service Workers of the Episcopal Church. At the conference, the delegates founded a Council on Advice, an informal organization of church people interested in social service who wanted to promote such work in the parishes. The council met first in December 1921.

In the 1920s, like other national social service agencies, the DCSS remained committed to Progressive principles. For example, it supported the Sheppard-Towner Bill for maternal and child care, urged restrictions of dangerous narcotics, called for equal distribution of coal during the strikes of the early 1920s, and promoted more liberal immigration laws and peace, particularly in its widely distributed publication, "The Church and the Warless World." In 1924, the DCSS created its division of rural work, which dealt with rural problems. Beginning in 1924, this division sponsored annual conferences for rural ministers at the University of Wisconsin. In 1926, to help sensitize ministers to social problems and social service, the department sponsored an institute for pastors at the New York School of Social Work. During early 1926, Executive Secretary Lathrop helped the Child Welfare League of America* (CWLA) survey the child-caring institutions of Houston, Texas, and he taught a course in social problems at Wellesley College Summer School. Although industrial strife had initiated its predecessor agencies, only in 1927, when the Church Association for the Advancement of Labor (CAAL) transferred its work to the DCSS did the National Council create a division of industry. Spencer Miller, Jr., who joined the division as a temporary agent, became a full-time secretary for industry on January 1, 1929. In the late 1920s, another secretary, for institutions, worked closely with other national agencies, particularly the CWLA, and in the mid-1920s, the department sent the seventy or so managers of Episcopal-related children's institutions complimentary copies of *Institutions for Children*. In 1929, the department established diocesan family relations institutes, discussion groups, and counseling aimed at preserving the family. While the department participated actively and creatively in many phases of social service, prison work seemed to be its primary focus in the 1920s.

As Professor Robert Miller suggests in his *American Protestantism and the Social Issues* (1958), the DCSS responded to the depression and the ensuing New Deal as middle-class liberals critical of the exploits of capitalism but, unlike some other church welfare groups, it did not advocate the demise of the economic system. Continuing its projects in rural sociology, in family relations, and in surveying diocesan welfare institutions, the DCSS, particularly through its division of industrial relations, expanded its activities. In 1933, for example, Spencer Miller not only established conferences on ''The Present Industrial Crisis and the Christian Way Out'' for clergymen in the eastern United States but also held conferences on social and industrial problems in large industrial centers throughout the country. In 1937, the DCSS prepared a syllabus on social security and sponsored a two-day conference on the church and slum clearance, which was attended by representatives from Jewish and Catholic organizations and from the Protestant Federal Council of the Churches of Christ in America (FCC). In 1937, the highlight of the PEC's general convention was the mass meeting of the DCSS, featuring B. Seebohm Rowntree's address on Christianity and industrial relations.

The financial problems of the depression years affected the structure of the DCSS. The unprecedented financial crisis of the general convention in 1934 forced a significant reduction in its allocation to the DCSS, which reduced its staff to the full-time executive secretary, C. Rankin Barnes, and a part-time consultant on industrial relations, Spencer Miller. The DCSS had to reduce the number of commissions of the FCC with which it cooperated. In 1939, the DCSS was renamed the Department of Christian Social Relations (DCSR). In October 1942, the DCSR became part of the newly created division of home department, but continued its function to develop the PEC social service program.

In the World War II and postwar years, the DCSR continued some of its activities, and it expanded and diversified to meet the challenge of new problems. It continued to serve local Episcopalian institutions and local church social work. It still conducted surveys, developing such new services as the regular bulletin, *Christian Social Relations,* beginning in October 1947, for those interested in social service work. In September 1948, the DCSR sponsored an exploratory conference on the church in urban America. This proved to be the first in a series of events culminating in the joint urban program of the 1960s. In 1949, the department organized the Episcopal church welfare conference for child care workers, and in December 1949, the PEC's National Council authorized it to establish a committee and later a division of health and welfare services to advise and fund, for example, local Episcopalian institutions and agencies, such as Episcopal Service for Youth* (ESY). The DCSR diversified its labor program, still holding conferences on the relations between capital and labor but also organizing new urban workers' fellowships and participating more fully in national labor conventions, such as those of the American Federation of Labor and the Congress of Industrial Organizations. The DCSR responded to the problems of war, sponsoring the Bishops Fund for World Relief, urging general amnesty for conscientious objectors, advocating more liberal immigration and naturalization laws, and protecting the civil rights of Japanese-Americans.

Basic DCSR activities continued in the 1950s and 1960s. In May 1951, for example, a study conference on social action led to the establishment of the division of Christian citizenship. In 1953, to strengthen the DCSR's program in training for alcoholic rehabilitation work, the agency established a joint committee on alcoholism. In December of that year, the DCSR gained official observer status at the United Nations, inaugurating such program activities as UN-related seminars, a popular area for American church social service agencies. To improve its programs in this area, the DCSR established its division of world relief and interchurch aid in 1960. The development of a program for the aging was strengthened by a consultation on the church and the aging in May 1958. The DCSR launched its antipoverty work with a diocesan Christian social relations executive conference on poverty in the spring of 1964. An ad hoc committee on poverty's open letter to the church's house of bishops at the general convention in 1964 led to the bishops' position statement on poverty. These events triggered further activities, such as the establishment of a voluntary group, Episcopalian Action Group on Poverty, to focus on the inequities of public welfare, especially in the federal Aid to Families with Dependent Children program. In the mid-1960s, the DCSR was encouraging local Episcopalian churches and agencies to develop programs for children, especially day care services. It was also promoting expanded homemaker services, particularly for the ill and the elderly. The agency began to mobilize for activities dealing with poverty in native American communities. A mandate from the PEC general council prompted greater involvement in race relations in the mid- and late 1960s. Despite these activities, the DCSR was weakening. At no time in the early and mid-1960s were all the staff positions filled, and in October 1965, the agency had five staff vacancies, a substantial percentage of the total program. By 1966, the skillful and experienced administrator, Reverend Almon Pepper, was no longer directing the agency. The last issue of the *CSR Bulletin* appeared in March 1968, and the DCSR disbanded shortly after.

The primary sources for studying the DCSR's history include the generally detailed published annual reports, which appeared in the *Annual Reports* of the National Council of the PEC. Contemporary agency publications, such as Charles N. Lathrop, *The Department of Christian Social Service* (1922), and *Main Street and the New Jerusalem: The Aims and Projects of the Department of Christian Social Relations* (1924?), are generally available. For the recent years,

Christian Social Relations and the *CSR Bulletin* proved helpful. The minutes and other records of the DCSR are in the Archives and Historical Collection of the Episcopal church in Austin, Texas.

A number of secondary studies, such as Robert Moats Miller, *American Protestantism and the Social Issues* (1958), and James Thayer Addison, *The Episcopal Church in the United States* (1951), discuss the DCSR and its predecessors briefly. There is apparently no scholarly history of this agency.

EPISCOPAL SERVICE FOR YOUTH (ESY). During the late nineteenth century, the social gospel movement prompted reform-minded clergymen, such as Episcopalian Reverend James O. S. Huntington, to become involved in reform movements and in social services. In the late nineteenth century, Reverend Huntington was active in the single-taxer Henry George's campaign for mayor of New York City in 1886 and in the group that became the Church Association for the Advancement of the Interests of Labor, an important Progressive body. A mediator in labor-management disputes, Reverend Huntington began to strengthen his concern for wayward girls when, in the early twentieth century, he worked at the Holy Cross Mission on the poverty-ridden Lower East Side of New York City. He became even more familiar with the problems of illegitimacy during his work at St. Faith's House, a home for unwed mothers, in Tarrytown, New York. To establish a society to aid troubled young women, Huntington approached Reverend William T. Manning, then the rector of Trinity Church in New York and a skillful organizer. Reverend Manning brought together three other interested Episcopalians, Jacob Riis, the noted urban reformer, John Glenn, a lawyer active in a host of social welfare movements and agencies, and Mary Wilcox Glenn, a social worker and activist. This group of five well-known Episcopalians met in the library of Trinity Church in November 1909 and formed a charitable society to help wayward young women. Reverend Huntington, the leader of the group, chose its name, the Church Mission of Help (CMH).

The CMH began its work modestly. An early effort resulted in generous financial support, allowing the CMH in April 1910 to hire a young social worker, Emma L. Adams, to conduct a study of rescue work in the church. The study appeared later as *The Wayward Girl and the Church's Responsibility*. In January 1911, Reverend Huntington presented an "Outline for the Work to be Done by the Church Mission of Help," stressing new casework principles and featuring the need for follow-up work, a relatively new objective in the field of illegitimacy casework.

The first president of the CMH was Dr. Manning, who later became the bishop of New York during the 1920s. The honorary president in 1910–1911 was the bishop of New York, and the CMH had three honorary vice-presidents, including Huntington. Adams became the first executive secretary, a position then responsible directly for the work with the girls. By 1912, the organization had a trained visitor and a sex instructor for education and preventive programs. In 1913, at the general convention of the Episcopal church, held in New York, the CMH sponsored a mass meeting, which Reverend Huntington addressed. In 1915, when a shift in emphasis to include more work in the courts occurred, Adams resigned. The CMH continued its efforts for young women in the courts, and the organization helped to influence better parole and probation departments in both the city and the state. Activities for and with unmarried mothers also increased before 1920 as the work became well known and respected. In 1915, the Philadelphia CMH was established, and in 1918, the dioceses of Long Island and of Newark founded groups, as did the diocese of New Jersey in 1920.

In January 1919, Dr. Manning convened representatives from Philadelphia, Long Island, and Newark to discuss coordinating their work with the New York society. Other New York members wanted to establish a national agency so the work would be eligible for funds from the national budget of the church. On June 13, 1919, these representatives met again in New York and voted to establish the National Council of the CMH (NCCMH). At another meeting, in February 1920, the NCCMH asked the officers of the New York CMH to serve the national agency. In May 1920, the NCCMH adopted bylaws and then elected its first officers, including Mary Glenn as president, two vice-presidents, and a treasurer. The executive secretary of the CMH had especially hoped for a national agency, and she became the temporary organizing secretary to represent the NCCMH at the church's general convention. Funds for the new NCCMH came initially from the Newark society, from money given by the war commission of the church in October 1917 to the New York group, and from both the presiding bishop and the national council of the church. A church stipulation called for the NCCMH to act generally under the auspices of the Joint Commission on Social Service,* the official church welfare agency. The relation between the two agencies remained ill defined for about thirty years.

The national agency, the NCCMH, developed its program and established ties with local diocesan groups in the 1920s. In 1920, the new organizing secretary began her work with a study of existing societies. By the end of the year, the societies from the dioceses of Maine and Southern Ohio had joined the NCCMH. In the early 1920s, the NCCMH established the first of many scholarship funds to train students for work with wayward girls and unwed mothers. In January 1921, immediately after its meeting, the NCCMH held a three-day institute on the work. In 1923, when Christine Boyleston became the new organizing secretary, the agency began to improve its relations with other Episcopalian organizations, holding summer school programs in eight different localities, sponsoring a three-day institute in New Haven, Connecticut, and convening an all-day conference in New York City, attended by representatives from many other organizations in the church. Boyleston strengthened NCCMH ties with its affiliates, securing a total of fourteen societies by early 1926. An important organizational event occurred in 1927 when the widely respected Church Home Society of the diocese of Massachusetts affiliated with the NCCMH, adding its prestigious social workers to the network. In 1925, the Newark organization asked the NCCMH to conduct a field study and evaluation of it. This inaugurated a service the national office repeated often. A typed newsletter kept affiliates informed of programs and personnel. In 1923, *The Messenger,* issued three times a year, appeared. The NCCMH published it until 1933 when it was hampered by a lack of funds. The NCCMH cooperated with other national social service agencies, for instance, signing the Transportation Agreement not to pass along indiscriminately welfare cases to other communities. In the late 1920s, especially through the McLean Farm Conferences of 1927 and 1929, the NCCMH showed interest in defining the spiritual aspects of casework. Located in upstate New York, in 1925, the McLean Farm was given to the CMH, which used it as a vacation home for girls and young mothers.

The years of the Great Depression brought consolidation, improvement, and some organizational changes to the NCCMH. The decade began with the resignation in February 1930 of Boyleston, who was replaced by a new executive secretary in June 1930. In November 1930, some members felt the NCCMH was overorganized and too expensive, and in February 1931, its committees were reorganized. A more important change occurred in the mid-1930s, when the organization decided to elect a board of directors rather than have a council of locally appointed representatives. The new board held its first meeting in October 1935.

In the early 1930s, the NCCMH began to publicize and interpret its work. Articles about the agency appeared in such social work journals as *The Family* and in such church journals as *The Spirit of Missions.* In 1933, a long-time supporter of social work for unwed mothers and illegitimate babies, novelist Dorothy Canfield Fisher, wrote *The Church Mission of Help: Lessons It Teaches, Needs It Stresses,* a publication for laymen that stressed society's responsibility for the wayward.

As with other social work agencies, financial problems proved taxing. Two affiliates closed, and the NCCMH ended its scholarship program in the early 1930s. The two top staff workers took voluntary pay reductions, and the national council of the church cut its annual appropriations by 50 percent. Faced with such financial straits, the NCCMH decided to replace the executive secretary and her assistant with a half-time director and a full-time general secretary. The plan failed, and both executives resigned. The end of an era came to the NCCMH in the mid-1930s. On June 29, 1935, founder Reverend Huntington died. In 1936, Mary Glenn, another founder, declined further election as president, but she continued to serve the organization until her death in 1940.

Problems continued to plague the NCCMH in the late 1930s. Finally, in late 1935, the NCCMH found the ideal executive secretary, Reverend Almon R. Pepper, who assumed the post in January 1936. But in 1936, the national council of the church decided that Reverend Pepper should also serve part-time as the executive secretary of the Department of Social Service,* the official Episcopalian welfare agency. In 1937, Reverend Pepper became the department's full-time executive, serving the NCCMH only as secretary pro tem until the fall of 1939, when an ad interim committee of the board of directors took over his duties. Respect for Reverend Huntington, who had apparently wanted to retain the organization's original name, had prevented a much-desired name change, but in 1937, the board resolved to recommend that affiliates conduct activities as the Youth Consultation Service of the CMH; the national agency, however, did not change its name. A lengthy period of reorganization and evaluation climaxed in 1939 with a report by Francis McLean, the widely respected former general secretary of the Family Welfare Association of America.* The report, which called for improved personnel practices in the affiliates, drew heavy criticism from local executives. The report also called ominously for closer relations with the Department of Christian Social Relations.

The NCCMH began the 1940s with a new executive secretary, Edith F. Balmford, who became an important worker in the field of illegitimacy casework. Fortunes seemed to improve in 1940. The organization established a personnel committee, which proved to be one of the most productive committees, and, at the general convention in October, the church increased its appropriation. Convention participants showed keen interest in the NCCMH exhibit booth. The agency grew closer to the Department of Christian Social Relations, cooperating with it on a study of church child care agencies and institutions. Conflict within the NCCMH occurred when the pioneering New York society resigned from the NCCMH for a variety of reported reasons. This prompted founder John Glenn to resign from the New York society as an honorary adviser. The expansion of the staff forced the NCCMH to move to a separate headquarters in New York. On May 8, 1946, the organization changed its name to the Episcopal Service for Youth (ESY).

Beginning in 1950, the ESY became more involved in the national social work community and, ironically, increasingly lost its identity in the Episcopal church structure. During the 1950s, the ESY hired professionals for special projects. A major publicity and interpretation technique coincided with a new trend in social welfare. The play *Thursday's Child,* first performed at the general convention of the church in 1952, dramatized ESY work. In 1957, the ESY published a *Handbook for Public Relations* for affiliates. Many affiliates developed preventive vocational and educational guidance programs, a project for which the ESY hired a special consultant. The ESY participated in the White House conferences on children and youth in both 1950 and 1960. Following its traditional concern for unwed mothers, ESY was a member agency of the National Association on Services to Unmarried Parents.* Responding to a resolution at the general convention in 1958, which seemed to threaten ESY funds, the group established a special committee to study the future of the agency. The existence of the Division of Health and Welfare Services of the Department of Christian Social Relations,* established in April 1950, continually threatened the independence of the ESY.

The year 1960 signaled both the absorption of the ESY into the Division of Health and Welfare Services and the eventual demise of ESY. In 1960, changes in the bylaws and constitution reduced significantly the number of ESY standing committees as ESY board members were assigned to equivalent committees of the division. Also, the ESY closed its office, and its executive secretary became the ESY secretary pro tem. In light of these and other similar developments, the ESY began to discuss its possible dissolution. In September 1961, the creation of the position of associate secretary for services to children and youth in the division spelled the end of ESY. In January 1964, at its final membership meeting, the group approved bylaws changing the ESY to a membership corporation of five individuals appointed by the national council of the church. For years, the only agency utilizing casework principles, the ESY and its predecessor agency both sensitized the church to constructive social work and infused religious values in professional social workers and their casework.

The primary sources for studying the ESY's history consist of minutes and records of the agency in the Archives and Historical Collections of the Episcopal church in Austin, Texas. Published primary materials include pamphlets not widely available and articles in both church and social work journals describing its work and philosophy.

A very detailed and helpful historical account of the agency, compiled by agency officials using the unpublished files of the group, is a pamphlet, *Episcopal Service for Youth: The Development of Social Casework in the Church* (n.d.).

EVANGELICAL AND REFORMED CHURCH, COMMISSION ON CHRISTIAN SOCIAL ACTION (CCSA) OF THE. In the mid-1930s, when the Reformed church (RC) (see *Religious Institutions*) and the Evangelical church (EC) (see *Religious Institutions*) planned to merge, the leaders of their respective social service agencies, the RC's Commission on Social Service (CSS), and the EC's Commission on Christianity and Social Problems (CCSP), decided to combine their efforts before their parent bodies joined. Consequently, in January 1935, in Lancaster, Pennsylvania, representatives from the two social service agencies met and formed the Commission on Christian Social Action (CCSA) as the Joint Commission on Christian Social Action (JCCSA). This merger came well before the parent bodies joined in 1936. At the initial JCCSA meeting in January 1935, the group elected its chairman, Reverend C. E. Schaeffer, of Philadelphia, the general secretary of the Board of Home Missions, and its secretary, Professor Elmer J. F. Arndt, of the Eden Theological Seminary in Webster Groves, Missouri. The agency held its second organizational meeting at Webster Groves in the fall of 1935, awaiting its formal establishment at the first general synod of the new denomination, the Evangelical and Reformed church (ERC) (see *Religious Institutions*). Meeting in June 1936 in Fort Wayne, Indiana, the general synod of the ERC endorsed the JCCSA and gave it a broad mandate in the field of social service.

In its early history, a period roughly from its inception until American entry into World War II in December 1941, the JCCSA did very little without a full-time executive officer. Its most ambitious enterprise in 1935 was publishing and distributing a thirty-two-page pamphlet, *Facing Our Social Responsibility,* a statement of the JCCSA's aims. The new JCCSA also distributed to its constituency several publications of the Federal Council of the Churches of Christ in America (FCC), notably *Churches in Social Action* by James Myers. At the general synod of the new ERC in 1936, the JCCSA appealed unsuccessfully for more funding. Following the general synod in the early summer of 1936, the JCCSA contacted local committees on Christian social action, urging them to adhere to the "Objectives" of the JCCSA. In response to a general synod mandate of 1936, the JCSSA studied the profit system and distributed to its constituency a pamphlet on this issue by H. Paul Douglass, which he had prepared for the Council for Social Action* (CSA) of the Congregational Christian Churches (CCC). But the JCCSA delayed this type of educational work within the denominations until the issue of its freedom was resolved. Such issues as whether the executive committee or its supervising committee on Christian Social Action would review each JCCSA statement and if the denominational press would publish its pronouncements were resolved only partly by the enactment of the JCCSA's constitution and bylaws in 1940. Also in 1940, Professor Elmer Arndt became chairman, a position he held until 1957.

In this early period, still without an executive secretary, the JCCSA, which became the Commission on Christian Social Action (CCSA) in 1938, conducted limited programs, mostly educational. The agency sold and distributed pamphlets, its members wrote on social issues in the denominational press, and the agency published a *Bulletin,* initially a quarterly sent to a limited audience. Secretary Reverend Charles D. Spotts edited the publication, whose list of readership expanded gradually. In the early 1940s, the CCSA began to prepare, as directed by the general synod, a "Statement on Marriage and Divorce" and to revise its earlier "Objectives for Christian Social Action." In this period, the CCSA's major activity was initiating, raising, and then administering the Fund for Assistance to Evangelical and Reformed Young Men in Civilian Public Service to aid conscientious objectors who did public service as an alternative to the military. Increasingly involved in antiwar activities, the CCSA prepared in the early 1940s a study packet, "A Just and Durable Peace." In 1944, the general synod allowed the CCSA to hire Reverend Huber F. Klemme as executive secretary.

The activities of Reverend Klemme as the first full-time worker and the opening on February 1, 1945, of a headquarters—a cooperative venture with the Commission on Evangelism of the denomination in the Central Publishing House in Cleveland—inaugurated a new era in the history of the CCSA. From early December 1944 through late September 1945, at the request of the National Service Board for Religious Objectors, the CCSA conducted a unit at the state hospital in Independence, Iowa. Through a grant from the ERC's World Service

Commission, the CCSA financially assisted some conscientious objectors' dependents. In 1946, the CCSA published and distributed *Shall Conscription Be Permanent?* and in December 1947, *Should the United States Adopt Military Training?* which included CCSA testimony before the United States Congress. The CCSA developed its *Christian Social Action Bulletin* as a more frequently appearing and more widely distributed publication. Under Reverend Klemme, the CCSA began extending its fieldwork; members lectured and conducted study courses, and the agency conducted a social action conference at the general synod in the mid-1940s. The CCSA answered questions and supplied information, such as the *Christian Social Action Handbook,* to local and regional groups. It also sent *The Social Action Committee in the Local Congregation* to all pastors, the heads of women's guilds, and over five hundred lay church members and synodical leaders. In the mid-1940s, the agency also studied, through questionnaires, the labor standards in church-related institutions, such as orphanages and hospitals. Beginning in the mid-1940s, the CCSA worked with the Congregationalists' CSA, antedating the proposed merger between the two denominations, the ERC and the CCC. In 1947, the CCSA expanded its activities further, hiring a secretary for racial and cultural relations.

In the late 1940s, the CCSA developed a program in race relations, hiring in September 1947 a full-time secretary to work in this field. The CCSA shared this position jointly with the Board of National Missions of the ERC. Under Executive Secretary Klemme, the CCSA also expanded its field services. Members of the agency lectured and conducted study courses around the country, and the CCSA conducted a social action conference at the general synod in 1947. The CCSA answered questions and supplied information, such as the *Christian Social Action Handbook,* to local and regional groups. Beginning in 1947, the agency cooperated with the city church committee of the ECR's Board of National Missions to conduct an annual workshop on the city church, which sensitized pastors to urban problems. In July 1947, the CCSA published *Social Problems of the Evangelical and Reformed Church,* a handbook for workers and others in the field. Under Executive Secretary Klemme, the CCSA expanded its publication, *Christian Social Action Bulletin,* which in January 1949 combined with a similar publication of the Congregational CSA to form *Christian Community,* which Reverend Klemme edited. The cooperative publishing venture reflected not only a growing cooperation with the FCC but also, and more importantly, unification with the Congregationalist social agency.

In the 1950s, following a mandate of the general synod in 1950, the CCSA expanded its services to the field and in race relations, reduced its work against militarism and with conscientious objectors, and developed an entirely new activity, international relations. Negotiations with the general synod led in the early 1950s to the addition of one and then another field worker. In September 1952 in Dunkirk, New York, the CCSA held its first regional conference on synodical social action. Agency publications continued to serve the field. The

CCSA sponsored conferences and institutes, such as Churchman's Washington Seminars and United Nations World Order Seminars, which reflected its recent involvement in international relations. The CCSA issued statements on public issues; in January 1954, it opposed the so-called Bricker amendment, which was designed to prevent American participation in broad international agreements concerning human rights that might offend one or more states. In the mid-1950s, the CCSA issued another statement on the problems in the Middle East. The CCSA worked even more closely with the similar agency of the CCC. In June 1957, the CCSA merged with the CSA to form the Council for Christian Social Action* (CCSA) of the new United Church of Christ (UCC) (see *Religious Institutions*). Between June 1957 and 1961, according to the "structural resolution" of the unifying meeting, the ERC's CCSA maintained the structure it had adopted in the mid-1930s; however, the two staffs were pooled, and the two agencies issued joint statements. The CCSA looked forward to being the newly created, truly unified agency under the United Church of Christ, which was accomplished with the establishment of the Council for Christian Social Action of the UCC on June 27, 1957.

The primary sources for studying the CCSA's history include the agency's annual reports in the ERC's *Acts and Proceedings of the General Synod*. The CCSA's minutes are in the Archives of the Historical Society of the Evangelical and Reformed Church in Lancaster, Pennsylvania.

David Dunn et al., *A History of the Evangelical and Reformed Church* (1961), contains a brief outline of the agency's history. There does not appear to be a scholarly history of the CCSA.

F

FAMILY LOCATION SERVICE, INC. (FLS). The effects of emigration and immigration, coupled with the widespread poverty in the Jewish sections of the Lower East Side of New York City, helped to make immigrant Jewish family life somewhat unstable in the late nineteenth and early twentieth centuries. Jewish social workers, particularly those from the United Hebrew Charities of the City of New York* (UHC), had been concerned with the problem of desertion among Jews and had been calling for nationwide cooperation to find deserters and to return them to, or force them to support, their families. In 1900, for instance, the UHC manager, Lee K. Frankel, asked Morris D. Waldman, a UHC agent, to study 250 Jewish families made dependent because of the desertion of the wage earner. In 1904, Solomon Lowenstein, a rabbi and a social service executive, delivered a paper at the National Conference of Jewish Charities* (NCJC), which argued that desertion was one of the major problems causing dependency of Jews.

Waldman's study and report influenced the UHC and other major New York City social service agencies, particularly the New York Association for Improving the Condition of the Poor* (AICP) and The Charity Organization Society of the City of New York* (COS), to develop projects in this field. In October 1905, for instance, the UHC established its special bureau on desertion. Waldman's report also led to the enactment of state legislation in 1905 that made child abandonment by deserting husbands and fathers an extradictable crime. Despite the laws, the UHC had continual problems locating deserters. At the NCJC in 1906, Frankel proposed a nationwide organization to register deserters. In 1908, when Waldman became UHC manager, he placed two energetic and resourceful men, both lawyers, in charge of this work. Monroe W. Goldstein and Charles Zunser developed an idea to publish a picture "gallery" of deserters in the *Jewish Daily Forward*, the leading Yiddish newspaper in the country. The photographs became such a popular section of the paper that publisher Abraham Cahan had to resist competitors' efforts to publish and to expand the gallery. Waldman and the UHC continued to study desertion. At the NCJC in 1910, Waldman presented a paper on the subject, resulting in the appointment of a six-member NCJC committee on desertion. Goldstein was secretary and Waldman chairman of this committee. The NCJC executive committee agreed with Frankel's plans for a national organization, and its president, Professor Jacob Hollander of Baltimore, influenced the New York Foundation to grant $5,000 for the establishment and operation of an agency through 1912. Particularly through Goldstein, the committee prepared the organizational structure and activities based primarily on the ten years' experiences of the UHC. At the NCJC in 1911, the executive committee established the Family Location Service, Inc. (FLS) as the National Desertion Bureau (NDB) of the NCJC.

The early activities and history of the NDB related primarily to the UHC, in whose building in New York by 1912 it opened its first office. Because New York remained the national center of the American Jewish community, much of the NDB's work was done there. In 1912, the board of trustees of the UHC gave the NDB $1,000 for the following year if it raised $10,000, which the group did because of its increasingly successful activities. Over 150 Jewish organizations cooperated with the NDB, and Jewish newspapers throughout the country published the gallery of deserters and cooperated in other ways, gaining nationwide support for the agency. In New York City, the NDB helped to reduce the number of Jewish dependents, as public officials, such as the comptroller of New York City, noted. In 1914, the UHC reported a reduction by one-half of desertion cases. Other local and national agencies and social workers, such as Francis H. McLean, the general secretary of the American Association of Societies for Organizing Charity,* in 1913, praised and wanted to duplicate the exemplary services of the NDB.

The agency continued to grow. Convinced that it was not an administrative body and therefore could not continue to conduct the NDB, the executive committee of the NCJC asked the organizers to develop an independent agency. Incorporated separately in New York State as the NDB, Inc., in September 1914, the agency asserted national and local leadership. In 1914, a serious issue developed: orthodox rabbis, particularly in New York, had been granting rabbinical divorces, or *ghets,* to those not divorced legally. Representatives of the NDB, especially Goldstein, worked with distinguished national leaders, such as Louis Marshall, the president of the American Jewish Committee, and Dr. Jodah L. Magnes, the head of the New York Kehillah, to explain the issue to the rabbis, who agreed to stop the practice. In 1915, the NDB's organizational structure included the traditional officers (president, vice-president, treasurer) and a thirteen-member board of directors, which included David Bressler, the manager of the Industrial Removal Office,* Minnie Low, a Chicago social worker, and Professor Felix Frankfurter of the Harvard University School of Law. NDB President Walter H. Liebmann of New York chaired the seven-member executive committee.

The NDB's influence was established quickly beyond the Jewish community. In 1914, for instance, it helped two local but nationally important agencies, the COS and the AICP, to establish their own similar agencies. The independent NDB began a continuing activity of influencing legislation and local agencies. In 1922, NDB efforts eliminated Canada as a refuge for deserters. The agency influenced an agreement providing that Canada deport deserters even though there was no reciprocal American agreement. In 1922, the NDB assisted the development of a United States-Canadian treaty extradicting fathers who abandoned their children. By the early 1920s, the NDB had developed a nationwide and international network of cooperating agencies. It worked especially with the National Council of Jewish Women and with the international Hebrew Sheltering and Immigrant Aid Society* to locate deserters. The NDB also allied with other national social service agencies, such as the National Probation Association* in 1918 to urge the establishment of a family court in New York.

In the post–World War II period, the organization faced major economies and reductions, but it nevertheless continued to pioneer and to play a unique role in the social work field. The NDB grew increasingly closer to the national social work community. In 1946, with its largest staff ever, the NDB affiliated with the National Association of Legal Aid Organizations* (NALAO), a major national reform agency. The NDB influenced the review in the late 1940s of social security laws stipulating that state plans for the Aid to Dependent Children (ADC) program report individual desertions to law officials. In December 1946, an experienced public social worker in New York City, Mrs. Jacob T. Zuckerman, joined the NDB as its new assistant to the executive director, relieving Zunser of much of his routine. In 1948, when the increased caseload hit the agency, Zuckerman became executive director, and chief counsel, and Zunser became a consultant. Zunser remained as secretary to the fourteen-member board of trustees. The administrative change, however, did not in itself dissolve the problems of the NDB, which turned away nearly six hundred applicants in 1948, as it skimped and saved in a variety of ways. The financial problems led the board to appoint a two-member financial committee, which discussed and then rejected a fee system. The committee also recommended, and board member Philip Sokol worked out, an agreement for the NDB to conduct services for the New York City Department of Welfare, which agreed to supply staff and to support various administrative functions.

Some of the financial problems of the overburdened agency remained, but the NDB prospered and grew in the 1950s, when it developed some important programs. The city gave the NDB a social investigator and a typist in December 1949, and the program utilizing NDB experience in desertions saved the city nearly $52,000 in the first 130 location cases in 1950. The caseload increased significantly in the next few years because of the requirement that ADC cases report desertions. The program for the city, called the New York City Unit, continued to run smoothly; but still pressed for funds, the NDB tried unsuccessfully to obtain further support from the city. In 1953, the agency instituted a new statistical system and codified many procedures. Still trying to deal with its financial problems, the NDB instituted a fee system for clients in February 1954.

In the early 1950s, the NDB grew closer to the social work community. NDB caseworkers increasingly conducted casework rather than administering simple legal procedures. The agency stressed professional staff development, sponsoring training courses and encouraging other professional activities for its workers. By the mid-1950s, the NDB was helping other localities to develop desertion programs, and NDB staff was conducting training sessions and institutes, such as Zunser's institute sponsored by the California Department of Social Welfare for local welfare officials and district attorneys. In 1954, the NDB clarified its relations with both the Family Service Association of America* (FSAA) and the National Travelers Aid Association.* Many state and other public and private agencies reprinted NDB materials. Still faced with financial problems, the NDB pointed out that although it was happy to provide these services in the field, it would like to be reimbursed for its staff time.

From the mid-1950s on, the organization changed. Celebrating its fiftieth anniversary in 1955, the NDB became the Family Location Service, Inc. (FLS). It continued increasingly to stress professional casework principles. Still pressed for funds, it terminated its work for the city unit in 1956, but, continuing the practice of influencing public developments, the FLS helped to establish a unit for the New York City Department of Welfare. Introducing further new developments in the field, the executive staff worked in the late 1950s, to bring the legal and social work fields closer together on the sociological issue of desertion. Executive Director Zuckerman worked on committees for both the American Bar Association and the National Legal Aid and Defender Association (NLADA).* Other staff personnel represented the FLS at the White House Conference for Children and Youth in 1960.

Its importance as an influential agency blossomed in the 1960s. Board member Philip Sokol served as deputy commissioner for the New York City Department of Welfare, and Zuckerman helped to develop NLADA pilot projects in interagency cooperation and worked closely with an FSAA committee. She also helped to arrange in 1960 the New York State Conference of Social Welfare session on confidentiality in social work records. The NDB was rightfully proud in 1961 when the United States Department of Health, Education, and Welfare (DHEW) administrative decisions embodied some sociolegal points the FLS had been making for years. The FLS continued to train students from the New York School of Social Work, and in 1961, it helped to establish the desertion registration and location service of the New York State Department of Social Welfare. The FLS helped to establish the National Conference of Lawyers and Social Workers in 1962, when its much-pressured New York family court service developed statewide services. Not everything the FLS did succeeded. It cooperated with the Community Council of Greater New York to sponsor a conference on desertion in New York City, but as the FLS itself pointed out, the conference failed to arouse other agencies to consider the multifaceted problems of desertion more seriously.

Despite its nationwide activity, the FLS continued and even expanded its services to the Jewish community of New York. In 1960, it developed the Jewish federation family court unit to provide consultation and other services to Jewish families in the Domestic Relations Court of the City of New York. In the early 1960s, no longer cooperating with the New York City Department of Welfare, it worked more frequently with caseworkers in New York Jewish social service agencies, particularly with those from agencies in the Federation of Jewish Philanthropies of New York. On January 1, 1963, the FLS expanded its federation unit to the Brooklyn Family Court. In the summer of 1967, the FLS was absorbed by the organization that founded it in the early twentieth century—now called the Jewish Family Service* (JFS)—and became the JFS's family location and legal services. Continuing its basic services in social work and legal aid, the group maintained and strengthened its ties with Jewish social workers in the Bronx, Brooklyn, and Staten Island.

The primary sources for studying the FLS's history are diverse. The published *Annual Reports,* available generally for the early period and for the years after 1946, are extremely helpful. Contemporary articles about its work, such as Charles Zunser, "The National Desertion Bureau," National Conference of Jewish Social Service, *Proceedings, 1923,* 386–404, and reprinted elsewhere, are similarly helpful. Morris Waldman's autobiography, *Nor by Power* (1953), contains a discussion of the NDB. Several other social welfare and Jewish publications, such as the *Annual Reports* of the UHC, deal with the FLS and its activities. The YIVO Institute for Jewish Social Research in New York City has around twenty-five thousand FLS case records, but they were unavailable for research in the summer of 1976. There is apparently no scholarly history of the FLS.

FAMILY SERVICE ASSOCIATION OF AMERICA (FSAA). In the late nineteenth century, charity workers and reformers began to discuss the need for a nationwide organization of the charitable societies that functioned in various cities. In 1879, for instance, at the National Conference of Charities* (NCC), such discussions took place. Several committees and proposals in the late nineteenth and early twentieth centuries led finally to the establishment in 1905 of a Field Department with an Exchange Branch of *Charities,* the leading social work journal at the time. The main purpose of the Exchange Branch was for the major local family welfare agencies to exchange ideas, reports, and other publications and to promote, chiefly through correspondence, the founding of new societies and the strengthening of existing ones. The originator of the idea, Francis H. McLean of the Brooklyn Bureau of Charities, became an associate editor of the journal in charge of this correspondence. The Field Department of the journal continued to develop and to study local agencies. In 1909, it became the charity organization department of the Russell Sage Foundation* (RSF). At the now named National Conference of Charities and Correction* (NCCC) in 1907, the Exchange Branch became a separate activity with its own executive committee. Discussions conducted within the independent Exchange Branch led in 1910 to its establishing an organizing committee. The work of this committee led to the establishment of the Family Service Association of America (FSAA) as the National Association of Societies for Organizing Charity (NASOC) on June 8, 1911, in Boston at the annual NCCC. The constitution of the new NASOC provided for the full participation and representation of the member agencies. A meeting on June 14, 1911, completed the formal organization, electing an executive committee, which approved a $10,000 budget and appointed a finance committee. At a meeting in July 1911, the executive committee unanimously elected McLean as the general secretary.

Aided significantly by the RSF, the new organization solidified its structure and functions. Initially the NASOC shared the offices of the RSF in the Charities Building in New York City. When the RSF moved to its own new building in 1913, so did the organization, known since July 1912 as the American Association of Societies for Organizing Charity (AASOC). RSF staff, particularly Fred Hall and Mary Richmond, advised and generally helped the agency. Although it initially had a limited staff of two, the AASOC developed a field service that provided help to local family welfare societies throughout the country. In the spring of 1919, this time named the American Association for Organizing Charity (AAOC), the organization began to publish the monthly *The Family,* which became *Social Casework* in 1946, an important journal in the social service field.

Even as it was shaping its organizational structure, the organization emerged early as a proponent of vanguard issues in American social welfare. In 1912, the AASOC appointed a committee on the homeless, which changed its name frequently and which became part of the independent Committee on Care of Transient and Homeless* in 1932. Foreseeing the future importance of public welfare, AAOC recommended in 1918 that its affiliates work to develop strong local public welfare departments. As early as 1922, even before Senator Robert Wagner recognized the threat of large-scale unemployment, the organization had appointed a committee on industrial problems to deal with this increasingly significant social issue. In the winter of 1927–1928, the organization described the hardships of unemployment. It encouraged its affiliates to combine with other groups in their communities to deal effectively with this major national problem. In some cities, affiliates helped develop community councils. In the 1930s, the recently re-named Family Welfare Association of America (FWAA) promoted efforts to deal with the social problems of the depression, such as sponsoring discussions among caseworkers and local community councils and supporting what became the Social Security Act of 1935. The FWAA also focused on the problems of families under duress. In 1934, it held a conference in New York City on family life and national recovery, and in 1936, it established a committee on family and marriage counseling, formally initiating a major agency activity. Even before the United States entered World War II, the FWAA provided guidelines for local activities of the national defense program. When the country declared war, the FWAA president appointed a committee on family welfare programs in the war and postwar period.

In the postwar period, the agency, which became the Family Service Association of America (FSAA) in 1946, stayed in the mainstream of social service, expanding its staff and services and involving itself more heavily in psychiatry, family counseling, and casework with the aged and with children, especially after the report of its review committee in May 1955. The FSAA committee on psychiatric consultation, established in 1953, urged affiliates to make greater use of this new service in family counseling. In the mid-1950s, the organization began producing multimedia projects seeking to popularize the family welfare field and FSAA services. Such projects included the 1955 film, *A Family Affair,* the Museum of Modern Art poster exhibit encouraging people to use local affiliates, and the establishment and expansion of Plays-for-Living, which dramatized FSAA's aims and services. In 1957, when the FSAA initiated its campaign to raise $300,000 to help expand family counseling services and to improve the professional standards of its staff, the leading publication in social work, *The Social Service Review,* hailed the plan as an important stimulant for the family counseling field.

FSAA participated fully in the experimentation and new projects in social services in the creative years of the 1960s. In 1965, for instance, with a grant of $796,000 from the federal Office of Economic Opportunity (OEO) and with the cooperation of the Child Study Association of America (CSAA) and the National Urban League* (NUL), FSAA began a joint demonstration project to help eliminate the causes of poverty. Operating in fifty-nine communities, the program was entitled Education and Neighborhood Action for Better Living Environment (ENABLE). It trained both professionals and the indigenous population in community organization and showed the feasibility of neighborhood coalitions in the War on Poverty. In July 1965, the FSAA board of directors established the new department on services for the aging, and the organization received a grant from the Ford Foundation for this work. In 1966, FSAA published *Casework with the Aging*. Another project, developed jointly with the CSAA, trained family caseworkers to lead family life education seminars for interested parents.

As public welfare expanded dramatically in the postwar period, the FSAA became a model for private agencies, studying and criticizing constructively the public programs. An important resolution in June 1956 of the FSAA committee on public issues, for example, urged adequate funding, abolishing categories in the federal welfare system, expanding old age, survivor, and other insurances, and improving public hospital care. In the late 1960s, FSAA took strong public stands on such issues as opposing the Vietnam War and extending the OEO.

The FSAA also expanded its services to its local affiliates, which numbered 302 in 1961. A grant in 1962 allowed the organization to strengthen its field services as well as its public relations and publication program. In February 1966, the FSAA established a department of statistic systems and statistics to implement long-time objectives, analyzing local programs and advising affiliates on their management information systems. In the late 1960s and early 1970s, the FSAA sponsored the independent IMPAC Systems, Inc. (which provided improved information systems for local agencies), operated a mini computer at New York headquarters, and provided a host of library services, each giving affiliates highly developed specialized tools in the field of social service. In 1967, it employed a management consultant firm to study the future program and structure of the agency. The firm's recommendations in 1968 led to the formation of eight regional councils under a new division of regional services at national headquarters. Another result of this study, the FSAA established an office of specialized agency services in 1968 to coordinate special services to member agencies. This office, for instance, quickly established a training course for new executives. Other staff development programs conducted in the late 1960s and 1970s strengthened affiliates, as did a program in the early 1970s to advise member agencies about services for the aging.

The FSAA cooperated with other national agencies. Since the 1950s, the FSAA had worked closely with the National Committee on the Aging* and its successor, the National Council on the Aging.* In the early 1960s, cooperating with the Child Welfare League of America* (CWLA), it established the National Association on Services to Unmarried Parents,* and the general director of the FSAA helped to establish the National Council on Homemaker Services.* Beginning in July 1962, the FSAA and the CWLA initiated a joint dues program. Cooperation between the two agencies continued, and in the early 1970s, the Florence Crittenton Association of America* joined them in serious and extended discussions to merge the three organizations. In 1974, the FSAA approved the amalgamation, which was abandoned suddenly. In June 1974, the FSAA president, George O. Nickel, had suggested that the merger discussions, which involved close self-evaluation, prompted the significant changes of the recent years: family advocacy, minority concerns, regional and generally more democratic structures, and the like. But these changes related more directly to the militancy and changes in the field of social service in the late 1960s.

The FSAA's biennial conference in 1969 proved to be an important turning point in the history of the organization. The black caucus disrupted the meeting, changing a planned "Day of Challenge" to a "Day of Black Challenge." At the conference, a hastily established FSAA negotiating committee responded positively to such demands as at least 50 percent minority representation on the board and the payment of black board members' expenses; cease studying blacks as social problems; special funds for the black caucus of FSAA; and reserving a percentage of the FSAA budget for blacks.

These ideological commitments became evident in the early 1970s when the board adopted statements affirming the principle of equal employment opportunities. In early 1970, cooperating with the NUL and the National Association for Retarded Children,* the FSAA developed a program to reach and to involve low-income families in working with mentally retarded members. FSAA supported and supplied free to member agencies the minority resource council facilities, which identified minority personnel with special skills in the field of social service. This group was sponsored by the black caucus, which merged with the Spanish-speaking caucus, established in 1971, to form the minority caucus in March 1973. In 1972, the board resolved to appoint a task force for migrant workers, and in July 1972, voiced its support of the United Farm Workers' Union, urging affiliates to develop services for migrant workers. Since the early 1970s, the FSAA had been encouraging affiliates to develop family advocacy, and with the Unitarian Universalist Association it sponsored the first institute on advocacy in Boston in May 1973. In 1974, the FSAA opposed reductions in the federal food stamp program. The appointment of a minority woman in 1973 as regional representative-at-large demonstrated further FSAA affirmation of its expressed ideals.

The most helpful primary sources for studying the history of the FSAA are its published and variously named *Annual Reports,* its *News Letter,* and *Family Service Highlights,* which also went through many name changes, the last of which was *Highlights of FSAA News.* Since its inception, the organization has been centrally involved in the social work community. Manuscripts relating to its history, therefore, appear in different collections, such as those of the National Social Welfare Assembly* at the Social Welfare History Archives Center at the University of Minnesota, Minneapolis. FSAA headquarters in New York City have their organizational files, which are generally closed to researchers but are available to properly qualified scholars.

The secondary literature is not as rich as the primary sources. Margret Rich, *A Belief in People: A History of Family Social Work* (1956), is helpful, but a more detailed and scholarly study of the FSAA is needed. Like Rich, the author of another volume of historical interest, Ralph Ormsby, *A Man of Vision: Francis H. McLean, 1869–1945* (1969), was affiliated with the agency. The standard historical scholarship in social welfare history pays, at best, brief attention to this important agency.

FAMILY WELFARE ASSOCIATION OF AMERICA: see FAMILY SERVICE ASSOCIATION OF AMERICA.

FEDERAL COUNCIL OF THE CHURCHES OF CHRIST IN AMERICA, COMMISSION ON THE CHURCH AND SOCIAL SERVICE: see NATIONAL COUNCIL OF THE CHURCHES OF CHRIST IN THE U.S.A., DIVISION OF CHURCH AND SOCIETY OF THE.

FEDERATED BOYS' CLUBS: see BOYS' CLUBS OF AMERICA, INC.

FLORENCE CRITTENTON ASSOCIATION OF AMERICA, INC. (FCAA). In October 1882, Charles N. Crittenton, a prominent, self-made New York City businessman, apparently had a religious conversion following the death of his four-year-old daughter, Florence. Crittenton subsequently began to attend religious services at the Grand Street Church in Lower Manhattan. With a local missionary, Smith Allen, Crittenton began to tour the nearby area, which teamed with vice and prostitution. After talking with two sympathetic prostitutes about his dead daughter, Crittenton resolved to help this group of women. Some local missionaries helped him to open on April 19, 1883, the Florence Night Mission on Bleecker Street in New York, the so-called mother mission of the organization. Vigorously pursuing local missionary work among degraded women and conducting sidewalk sermons, by 1889 Crittenton was ordered by doctors to curtail his work, to rest, and to travel.

Crittenton persisted in his missionary and rescue work with women. On a trip to San Francisco in 1892, he developed the idea for a national organization. Rescue missions had been opening in California, and one in San Francisco caught his attention. He began to finance it, changing its name to the Florence Mission. In 1892, a home in San Jose, California, became affiliated with his work, and in that same year, Crittenton, who had run for Mayor of New York City on the Prohibition party ticket in 1883, met Frances Willard, a famous prohibition worker, at the conference of the Women's Christian Temperance Union (WCTU) in Denver, Colorado. Crittenton pledged $5,000 to the WCTU's department of rescue work, allowing it to choose the site for five new homes. All of these homes eventually became part of his organization. More importantly, in the 1890s, Crittenton corresponded with an Episcopalian minister's wife, Dr. Kate Waller Barrett of Atlanta. This correspondence led to the establishment of another such home in that city. Crittenton finally met Dr. Barrett at the Christian Workers convention in Atlanta in 1893.

Long interested in rescue work for prostitutes, Dr. Barrett helped Crittenton to found the Florence Crittenton Association of America, Inc. (FCAA) as the National Florence Crittenton Mission (NFCM) in Washington, D.C., in 1895. The group chose Crittenton as president, Dr. Barrett as vice-president, and as secretary, Charles S. Morton, an evangelist who had been associated with Crittenton. F. B. Waterman became the first treasurer. Dr. Barrett, who also became general superintendent, established national headquarters at a former WCTU home in Washington, D.C., which had recently become affiliated with the Crittenton group. Dr. Barrett, whose husband served as the general missioner of the Protestant Episcopal church (PEC) in Washington, D.C., traveled around the country, helping to establish other homes. By July 1897, when the NFCM held its first national conference, there were fifty-one affiliated homes. On April 9, 1908, through the cooperation of United States Senator James McMillan of Michigan and Charles Moore, the secretary of the Senate Committee of the District of Columbia, the NFCM received a federal charter, one of the first of its kind for a philanthropic organization. In the late 1890s, local Florence Crittenton Circles, composed largely of church-affiliated women, were organized. The women raised funds through bazaars and other social functions to aid local Crittenton homes. General Superintendent Barrett and President Crittenton continued to travel throughout the country, organizing local homes and condemning public hostility to unwed mothers. The strong religious and humanitarian elements in this late-nineteenth-century agency suggested the important contributions of the social gospel movement to the later social justice Progressive movement.

In the early twentieth century, the NFCM crystallized its structure and continued to expand. On February 11, 1903, a special act of Congress amended the charter and reorganized the NFCM, giving it a five-member board of trustees. The organization attracted nationwide attention when, in 1904, acting on rumors, it campaigned to bar prostitutes from that year's World's Fair in St. Louis. Following the death of Crittenton in December 1909, General Superintendent Barrett became also the president of the NFCM. Another organizational highlight occurred in February 1914; the so-called Kenyon red light bill proposed to eliminate the prostitutes' district in the District of Columbia, but President Woodrow Wilson refused to sign it until provisions for the women had been made. The NFCM stepped in and agreed to care for the women. Following resolutions at the annual meeting in 1919, the national organization moved to create an extension committee to maintain better contacts with the generally autonomous local homes.

Further organizational changes occurred in the 1920s. From its inception in 1903, the board of trustees selected its own members, allowing no real voice representing the affiliated homes. The expansion of the board first to six members in 1925 and then to nine in the 1930s provided greater participation by the affiliates. The NCFM leaders had hoped to broaden involvement of affiliates in the national organization through the creation of the central extension committee in 1925. Initially composed of fifteen representatives from the local homes but enlarged to nineteen members in 1933, this committee did not succeed fully in assisting the national officers. Inactivity by the members generally caused this disappointment. The central extension committee was also responsible for the national conferences of the NCFM, a responsibility that it fulfilled more successfully.

In the 1920s, by which time Dr. Barrett and the NCFM had helped to shape more lenient public attitudes toward illegitimacy, the agency improved its services and associated increasingly with professional social workers in the field of illegitimacy and child care work. Many homes modernized their facilities in the 1920s, when the NFCM also helped to construct new homes. Especially in Boston, local Florence Crittenton superintendents and workers developed ties with social workers, instituting follow-up and other such services for clients. The attitude of the NCFM, reiterated soundly during the 1920s by President Barrett, coincided with the trend among specialists: both strove to keep unwed mothers and their babies together, and both denounced the practice of having illegitimate babies placed in adoptive family homes. In the late 1920s, the NFCM began providing professional training for its workers, a continuing organizational activity. Affiliates strove to meet the standards of state welfare agencies. When Dr. Barrett died in 1925, her son Robert Smith Barrett became president, and her daughter, Reba B. Smith, became general secretary.

The next twenty years of the NFCM's history were generally uneventful. The NFCM matured gradually as a national social service agency, but it still remained outside the mainstream of the field. For example, it did not participate in the National Conference of Social Work* (NCSW) and did not cooperate with other national agencies. In the late 1920s, under President Robert Barrett, the NCFM hired its first permanent field secretary to assist local homes. Mrs. J. E. Collier of Nashville, Tennessee, became the first such national extension director, and was replaced, apparently in the 1930s, by Hester Brown, who became executive secretary in 1940. In the early 1930s, the NFCM developed its regional conferences, and in the mid-1930s, it revived its training school for Crittenton workers.

In the 1930s, some affiliates began to participate in their local community chest fund-raising campaigns, but they remained generally indifferent to involvement in the activities of their national organization, the NFCM. In 1945, President Barrett seemed frustrated with some modern trends. In a pamphlet commemorating his twenty years as president, he argued that national and state regulations made NFCM activities more difficult; that community chest leaders sometimes interfered in affiliates' work; that professional social workers did not seem interested in the NFCM's religious work; and that some friends and even agency workers violated the long-standing NFCM policy of keeping unwed mothers and their illegitimate babies together. This NFCM policy opposed adoption, an increasingly popular social service in the mid-1940s.

During the World War II era, services were curtailed as many local workers became active in the American National Red Cross* (ANRC) and other war-related social services. But in 1946, many homes returned to capacity and resumed their services. The NFCM had not participated in the meetings of the NCSW because it feared the more aggressive workers of The Salvation Army* (SA) would dominate the field and because little at these professional conferences appealed to NFCM's interests. In 1946, however, the agency held its meeting concurrently with the NCSW, at which the NFCM even had an exhibit. The NFCM entered increasingly into the social work field, participating in 1947 again at the NCSW and, in the same year, establishing a committee to study national agencies similar to the NFCM. In the late 1940s, the agency began to cooperate with the SA on the Committee on Service to Unmarried Parents (CSUP) of the NCSW. The CSUP presented sessions at the NCSW, such as at the one in 1948.

In 1947, an incident reaffirmed NFCM's heritage. The extension committee had urged the organization to change its name, but President Barrett explained that because it and the ANRC were the only welfare agencies with federal charters, this change might cause complications, as well as reduce the NFCM's prestige. In the mid-1940s, both President Barrett and General Superintendent Smith had announced plans to retire around the early 1950s, and so did National Executive Director Hester Brown, who had held the position since 1940. These plans prompted organizational activities to shape the future of the NFCM. A joint committee representing the board of trustees and the central extension committee, working with Barrett and assisted by Community Surveys, Inc., on June 11, 1949, reported plans to establish a new organization. These proposals, which called for forty affiliates to ratify a new organization of Florence Crittenton homes, dominated the activities of the NFCM in 1949.

Culminating years of reorganizational work, the Florence Crittenton Homes Association (FCHA) was founded formally in Atlantic City, New Jersey, on April 25, 1950, when delegates approved the plans. Of the fifty-five homes, fifty-three agreed to join the new FCHA, which then elected nineteen directors. By agreement, the NFCM, which remained a separate agency, appointed two directors. The initial ones named were President Barrett and his son, Rear Admiral John P. B. Barrett. This new twenty-one-member board of directors of the FCHA held its first meeting on April 25, 1950, and elected a new president, three vice-presidents, a secretary, and a treasurer. All of these initial officers were from the six-member organizing committee. The FCHA established headquarters in Chicago, a more central location than Alexandria, where the NFCM remained. The FCHA was incorporated according to the laws of Illinois on July 20, 1950. In 1951, it hired Virgil Payne as executive director. In 1950, Robert Barrett retired as president of the NCFM, but he served as chairman of the board of trustees until his death in 1959. His son succeeded him as president of the NFCM, a position he still retained in 1973. Since 1950, the NCMF has chiefly provided grants to local Florence Crittenton agencies. The new FCHA conducted the traditional activities, supervising the homes, establishing new ones, and providing a range of services to affiliates.

In the 1950s, the FCHA served largely as a clearinghouse for the affiliated homes. By 1956, the organization had special services, such as the Florence Crittenton League (FCL), which provided casework to women and was a licensed adoption agency. The FCHA also administered both Iakota Farms in Virginia, which had been established by the NCFM in the early twentieth century, and the Barrett House of the FCL in New York, a residential treatment center for young women. By the late 1950s, the old matrons of the earlier days had been generally replaced in local homes by professionally trained social workers. In 1960, the delegate assembly of the FCHA changed the name of the agency to the Florence Crittenton Association of America (FCAA).

In the 1960s, FCAA, which still received some funds from the NFCM, functioned as a truly national social service agency, cooperating with others, providing services to its affiliates and to the field, and conducting demonstration projects. The agency nevertheless retained some of its long-standing principles. In 1963, for instance, it prepared material for some national publications and issued a recording for women's discussion groups, "The Case for Chastity." Throughout the 1960s, FCAA continued to hold annual regional conferences and to conduct institutes for boards and staffs. More importantly, FCAA participated with the National Social Welfare Assembly* (NSWA) to obtain better legislation for unmarried mothers. To serve the field, FCAA published *Unwed Mothers,* a report of a two-year project to develop a reporting system concerning the characteristics of and services to individual unwed mothers. Also in 1963, with the National Conference of Catholic Charities* and the SA, FCAA received a grant from the United States Children's Bureau (USCB) to develop a major research project on data collection in agencies serving unwed mothers. In the early 1960s, the FCAA conducted a pilot project that led to the development in 1966 of the Crittenton Comprehensive Care Center (CCCC) in Chicago, sponsored by the Chicago Board of Health but administered by the FCAA. The CCCC served teenagers attending school at the Chicago Board of Education's Family Living Center. The CCCC was the first project of a national voluntary agency working with local, state, and national public agencies to serve unwed mothers. In the mid-1960s, FCAA adopted the standards of uniform accounting and reporting services, and it began to help its affiliates to develop this important plan in the social service field. In 1966, FCAA began a self-study through its range and scope committee. Throughout the 1960s, local affiliates had been moving away from residential home treatment into communities, providing outpatient services in inner cities and developing group, as opposed to individual, casework. In 1969, the delegate assembly endorsed this trend, adopting a policy of having affiliates call themselves "services" rather than "homes." In the late 1960s, FCAA provided consultation services to nonmember communities seeking new programs. In 1969, the agency developed a proposal for unmarried parents' programs in the Chicago model cities project, a Great Society social program sponsored by the federal government.

In the early 1970s, as affiliates moved increasingly into community services, FCAA, which had been providing medical, educational, and other services, began to discuss working with the Child Welfare League of America* (CWLA), and the Family Service Association of America* (FSAA) to form a new national organization. The FCAA continued its conference and discussion meetings for its affiliates and in 1973, to maintain the concern for unmarried parents, distributed to social work schools, social service agencies, and others, *The Vulnerable— Crittenton's Concern*. But, it was clear that the FCAA would cease as an independent agency. Negotiations with the FSAA and the CWLA continued, and in 1974, FCAA left its national headquarters in Chicago and moved into the CWLA offices in New York. In early 1976, with FSAA having dropped out of the merger plans, FCAA merged officially with the CWLA and became the Florence Crittenton division of the CWLA.

The primary sources for studying FCAA's history include its separately published *Annual Reports* and annual reports that appeared in NFCM's *The Florence Crittenton Bulletin*. The very recent *Field Reporter* is also helpful. The papers of the agency are filed at the Social Welfare History Archives Center at the University of Minnesota, Minneapolis.

Two agency publications are helpful: Otto Wilson, in collaboration with Robert S. Barrett, *Fifty Years Work with Girls, 1883–1933* (1933), and Robert S. Barrett, *Twenty Years as President of the National Florence Crittenton Mission, 1925–1945* (n.d.). Peter Romanofsky, "The Early History of Adoption Practices, 1870–1930" (Ph.D. diss., University of Missouri, Columbia, 1969), describes the agency's principles, policies, and practices. A brief but helpful history by Pamela J. Matson appears in "An Inventory of the Papers of the National Florence Crittenton Mission," *Descriptive Inventories of Collections in the Social Welfare History Archives Center* (1970), 482–483. There does not appear to be a scholarly history of this veteran agency.

FOREIGN LANGUAGE INFORMATION SERVICE (FLIS). On the entry of the United States into World War I, the government felt the necessity of getting its wartime message across to its thousands of residents who did not speak English. Therefore, in 1918, the United States Committee on Public Information added sixteen foreign-language bureaus whose purpose was to furnish the nearly one thousand foreign-language newspapers with material, written in their own tongue, relating to the United States war effort, liberty bonds, and thrift stamps. It was called the Division of Work with the Foreign Born. When the war ended in November 1918, so did the appropriation for this service. Since valuable and strong contacts had been made with the foreign-language newspapers, efforts were made to continue the relationship under private auspices. Consequently, the name of the division changed to Foreign Language Information Service (FLIS), and under the directorship of Josephine Roche, was affiliated for brief periods with the Carnegie Corporation, Community Service, Inc., and the American National Red Cross* (ANRC). Prior to this, Roche had done a study of foreign-born girls in industry for the Russell Sage Foundation* (RSF). In Denver, she had been the chief probation officer and director of girls' work for the Juvenile Court. Finally in May 1921, the FLIS became an independent organization. At the beginning, it was supported by grants from the Laura Spelman Rockefeller Memorial and the Commonwealth Fund* until general public support could be built up.

In October 1922, Josephine Roche appointed Read Lewis, who had been with the organization for several months, to take her place as the FLIS director. Previously he had worked at the American embassy in Moscow and earlier with The Charity Organization Society of the City of New York.* Roche also appointed the FLIS's first advisory board consisting of eight members, including herself, Allen T. Burns, the head of the American Association for Community Organization,* and Julia Lathrop, the first chief of the United States Children's Bureau. This advisory board soon evolved into the first board of trustees. The next few years continued to bring alterations and modifications to the FLIS organization as it attempted to broaden its base of support and increase its authority. In 1925, the FLIS decided it was time to organize a system of local affiliates. Chicago, Cleveland, and Detroit were chosen as the cities for experiment. But the locals did not generate the prominence or support that had been anticipated, and maintaining them became a burden on the national office. By the end of 1928, the local committees had been eliminated.

In the fall of 1921 the federal commissioner of immigration granted the FLIS permission to station a representative on Ellis Island. His function was "to gather technical and legal information relating to immigration procedures for release to the foreign language press, organizations, and for the benefits of individual immigrants and foreign-born residents of America."

At the beginning, the FLIS derived much of its character from opposition "to the current hysteria about immigrants and 'foreigners,' which had been strengthened by the war and the economic difficulties of the immediate post-war years." Education was the FLIS's primary purpose: "to interpret America to the immigrant and the immigrant to America." Its aim was Americanization, but did not ask the immigrant to shed his Old World traditions and customs upon landing in the United States. To the hundreds of foreign-language newspapers being published in this country, the FLIS sent out articles covering such topics as employment and economic problems. American government and history, educational opportunities for both the immigrant and his children, public libraries, and health, all of which were translated into more than twenty languages. Materials about the foreign born, their life in America, obstacles they faced, their problems and contributions were also sent to the English-language press, schools, and libraries in the hope that an understanding of immigrant groups and their cultures would help eliminate intolerance and discrimination.

Service to immigrant organizations was another major aspect of the FLIS's work. By sponsoring conferences for the leaders of such groups, the service aided in planning educational work and establishing contacts with American agencies. The conference on the alien in America held on May 2, 1936, in Washington, D.C., was one such example. Sessions treated such problems as "Is the alien entitled to an equal chance in getting a job?" "Is the alien entitled to Relief?" "Are the foreign born responsible for our crime?" and "The second generation in relation to crime and delinquency." Direct service to individuals eased the adjustment to life in America for thousands of immigrants with problems ranging from income taxes to legal advice. If a local organization working with the foreign born could handle a problem, the individual was referred to it; otherwise the FLIS's staff provided the necessary personal help.

The FLIS published *Interpreter Releases* on a weekly basis. They were sent to organizations working with immigrants and contained pertinent information about immigration, quota laws, naturalization, and other relevant matters. The *Bulletin* began publication in 1922; a year later, the title changed to *The Interpreter*. Published monthly, it was sent to schools, libraries, and the English-language press. Its purpose was to describe the work of the FLIS and present the foreign born with their problems, achievements, and ideals. It existed until 1930. *Fraternity,* begun in 1929 and sent to officers of national foreign-language organizations, emphasized educational work, closer contacts with American agencies, juvenile activities, better understanding between immigrant parents and their children, and group contributions to American life. Two items published by the FLIS were revised and reprinted many times: *Handbook for Immigrants,* edited and compiled by Marian Schisby, and *How to Become a Citizen of the United States.*

Over the years the FLIS began expanding its services. One new service was in the area of adult education, which also included musical recitals and the presentation of plays, as well as vocational training. In January 1928, Read Lewis hired Thomas Cotton, who had been with the National Council of the Young Men's Christian Associations of the United States of America,* to head the new service. Cotton and his staff became known as a resource for advice on educational programs, parent-child relationships, and contacts with American agencies.

Upon receiving two grants in 1929, Cotton's division, known as the division of foreign-language organizations, established an adult education advisory committee to "offer suggestions and make criticisms." In addition, a lecture bureau was created, drawing on a manpower pool of forty-five individuals, primarily university people in the New York City area with competency in ten foreign languages. But by the end of 1929, the FLIS was again in financial difficulties, and thus the lecture bureau operated as a fee-charging activity.

By 1930, the FLIS was faced not only with financial problems but also a declining public image. Lewis felt some sort of revamping was necessary, including a new name to describe more properly the work of the FLIS. Although it went through a reorganization, basically nothing was changed, and the economic situation remained bleak for the next few years.

One of the highlights of this time period was the development in July 1931 of the folk festival council under the auspices of Thomas Cotton's division of foreign language information. It was composed of various ethnic, educational, and social groups in New York City. Although designed to be an independent, self-supporting activity, in practice, it was always part of the FLIS. Its purpose was to give the people of New York a chance to enjoy the folk arts of foreign-born groups and to promote these arts by providing the foreign born with "opportunities for artistic expression."

In January 1932, the council presented the Folk Festival of the Homelands. It was so successful that more festivals were planned for February and May. In March, the Council began publishing *Folk-News,* a newsletter providing information concerning dates of activities of the council and affiliated organizations, as well as articles on immigrant contributions to American life. The council cooperated with the New School for Social Research and used its facilities. In October 1932 courses on folk singing and dancing were begun.

Louis Adamic joined the board of trustees of the FLIS in 1934, and it was he who raised an issue that had been discussed before but that had been largely ignored: the "priority of the second generation problem to that of the Service's other major concerns." He stressed the need to encourage the second generation to appreciate their cultural background, to promote loyalty to America, and to eliminate inferiority feelings. But little was done for the second generation at this time.

The FLIS's legislative programs during the 1930s demonstrated its commitment to make "immigration legislation humane and eliminate discrimination against the alien." Along with other groups, the FLIS became a member of the Joint Conference on Alien Legislation. Read Lewis testified before the Congress on several occasions on bills that dealt with immigration or naturalization problems. In 1937, he was particularly active in support of the Dies deportation bill. He was chairman of the bill's proponents and arranged the appearances of individuals to testify before the House of Representatives and for its companion bill in the Senate.

During its existence, the FLIS had many well-known people affiliated with it, some on the board of trustees, others serving on various committees. Among these were such notable individuals as Paul U. Kellogg, editor of *The Survey,* William Hodson, commissioner of public welfare in New York City, Jacob Riis, and Graham R. Taylor, a noted settlement worker.

Throughout the 1930s, the FLIS was plagued by problems, particularly financial ones. The language bureaus were eliminated in 1934, and in addition, only seven nationality groups continued to receive the FLIS's press releases. Lewis was still convinced of the FLIS's purpose but was even more aware of the necessity to make it more attractive to the public. By 1939, it was obvious the FLIS had reached the end of its life. With conditions so different and with the decline in immigration since 1924, it had outlived its usefulness. A new agency was born, and Louis Adamic's suggestion, Common Council for American Unity (CCAU), was the name chosen for it. The FLIS disbanded on November 13, 1939.

Sources used in preparing this article on the FLIS were the papers of the American Council for Nationalities Service* (ACNS), which include the papers of the FLIS, deposited at the archives of the Immigration History Research Center at the University of Minnesota, Minneapolis. These papers consist of 175 linear feet of correspondence, minutes, reports, and publications of the ACNS, as well as its predecessor organizations. Also helpful were the following FLIS publications: *The Work of the Foreign Language Information Service* (1921), *Five Years' Work with the Foreign Born* (1922), and *A Job of Understanding* (1924).

In addition, see Daniel E. Weinberg, "The Foreign Language Information Service and the Foreign Born, 1919–1939: A Case Study of Cultural Assimilation Viewed as a Problem in Social Technology" (Ph.D. diss., Department of History, University of Minnesota-Minneapolis, 1973).

Lynn Ann Schweitzer

FORTUNE SOCIETY, THE (FS). In New York City in 1967, an off-Broadway play, *Fortune and Men's Eyes,* dealt with prison conditions; it was written by John Herbert, a former convict. The young producer of this play and a theatrical publicist was David Rothenberg. Rothenberg and one member of the cast were especially concerned about prison conditions, and they decided to hold discussions with the audiences following the performances on Tuesday nights. Rothenberg moderated these forums, which became increasingly popular. Ex-convicts began to identify themselves during these discussions, and some of them even joined Rothenberg and the actors in leading the sessions. Interested citizens began to contact Rothenberg to arrange similar discussions about conditions in prisons and jails with student, civic, church, and other organizations. For several months, Rothenberg and a group of former prisoners traveled throughout the New York area speaking in the evenings and on weekends about prison-related topics. In November 1967, thirty-seven people at a forum decided to establish an organization. They left their names and addresses and soon received a mimeographed, one-page newsletter. The group decided to use part of the title of the play as its name, The Fortune Society (FS). The purpose of the FS was to encourage prison reform and to aid former prisoners.

The early FS developed gradually as "a kind of social worker organization," according to *The New York Times.* The first president of the FS was Isidore

Zimmerman, a fifty-year-old private investigator who had himself been imprisoned. Rothenberg became the first and the only executive secretary in the FS's brief history. In March 1968, some FS members and leaders appeared on "The David Susskind" television discussion program. As a result of the show, many ex-convicts came to Rothenberg's tiny theatrical office, which was serving as the FS's headquarters, seeking jobs, housing, and conversation. The group of regulars and early members realized that they needed to establish an agency to help their fellow ex-prisoners.

The FS was basically a lobby to publicize conditions and the problems of rehabilitating prisoners, but in New York City, the FS also fed and clothed men and helped them to find jobs. For about one year in the late 1960s, the FS helped to secure jobs for about two hundred ex-convicts, even though the agency did not focus on this activity. It also assisted prisoners' wives, helping to get babysitters and such. Early offices were established in two cluttered rooms on the Upper West Side of Manhattan. During this period, the FS had only one paid staff worker, but there were numerous volunteers. In August 1969, the agency established its Fortune Store in Sheridan Square in Manhattan. Staffed by former convicts, the store sold jewelry, pottery, and paintings. Executive Secretary Rothenberg proved to be an inordinately effective organizer. By 1969, about sixty-five hundred people in forty-three states received the monthly newsletter (which was banned from prisons in New York State). Rothenberg made several speeches and radio appearances, and he and other members of the FS continued to travel throughout the New York area speaking to all kinds of groups. During the late 1960s, the FS became a member of the advisory panel of the National Council on Crime and Delinquency* (NCCD). Indeed, in the late 1960s, the FS was one of the most widely discussed agencies in the field of prison reform.

Chiefly through Executive Secretary Rothenberg, the FS seemed to be in the vanguard of efforts to reform conditions in prisons in the early 1970s. In 1970, for instance, it commented on conditions in the House of Detention in New York City. In 1971, representatives of the FS told students at the New York Police Academy that prison reform was essential, a theme explicated often by the agency. Later in 1971, FS leaders denounced plans to build a new maximum-minimum security prison. The FS was, of course, involved in the disturbances at the Attica State Prison in New York State; some of its representatives were among the group who met and negotiated with the prisoners. In 1972, Rothenberg condemned the indictments against Attica prisoners, criticizing justice in New York State.

Rothenberg was one of the first national figures to speak out about conditions at the New Jersey State Prison at Trenton, which he urged officials to close. The owner of the building housing the Fortune Store broke the lease in 1971, apparently ending this constructive activity. In 1971, however, the FS worked with Volunteers in Service to America (VISTA) to place some ex-convicts in jobs. The FS's concerns and interests extended beyond the boundaries of prison reform. In 1973, for instance, it denounced Governor Nelson Rockefeller's plans, which it considered harsh, to fight the use and sale of narcotics. FS ideals of self-help and individual rehabilitation affected wrongdoers other than prisoners. In March 1973, a prostitute announced that the FS had influenced her to try to stop being a prostitute. By the mid-1970s, the FS had lost some of the glamor and publicity that characterized its earlier years.

The primary sources for studying the FS's brief history include the files of *The New York Times* and the agency's difficult-to-locate *Fortune News,* a monthly publication issued eleven times a year. There does not appear to be a scholarly history of the FS.

FOSTER PARENTS PLAN INTERNATIONAL, INC. (FPPI). In 1937, a British war correspondent in Santander, Spain, John Langdon-Davies, was moved by the sight of a homeless boy wandering in the streets. Appalled by the plight of this and other children made homeless by the tragedies of the civil war raging in Spain, Langdon-Davies worked with both Eric Muggeridge, a British travel agent, and Edna Blue to found the English Foster Parents Plan for Children in Spain. Blue became the chief promoter of this British organization. In 1937, Blue, Muggeridge, and Langdon-Davies came to the United States, solicited American support, and helped to establish the Foster Parents Plan International, Inc. (FPPI) as the Foster Parents Plan for Children in Spain (FPPCS). A host of prominent American social workers and reformers helped to found the new society. They included Eleanor Roosevelt, the wife of the president and herself active in other social service agencies; Helen Keller of the American Foundation for the Blind* and a well-known humanitarian; economist and social activist Paul Douglas of Illinois; and former President Herbert Hoover, who remained active in other national child welfare agencies, such as the American Child Health Association* and The Big Brothers of America.*

With initial headquarters in New York City and supervised by Eric Muggeridge, the FPPCS began its work of helping Spanish children affected by the civil war. The FPPCS solicited contributions from the American public. By the end of 1939, the agency was caring for about twelve hundred Spanish refugee children in France and England. Throughout the course of the Spanish civil war, ten facilities of the agency in France cared for about a thousand homeless children.

As the conflict spread throughout Europe and as Adolf Hitler's ravagings began to endanger other European children, the FPPCS opened its shelters in England to children from all countries. The only relief agency created to aid victims of the civil war in Spain that continued to function after that war, the agency was incorporated and broadened its name, appropriately to the Foster Parents Plan for War Children, Inc. (FPPWC), in September 1939. In 1939, Muggeridge became the executive secretary, and in December 1939, Blue was appointed the vice-chairman. In 1940, she became the executive chairman of the agency. In 1940, when Hitler's armies invaded France, the Spanish refugee children who had been living there fled once again, this time to England. With thousands of children made homeless, the headquarters in New York intensified its efforts to find individual sponsors of children who were now being sent all over Europe—to Malta, Holland, and Czechoslovakia, for instance—to escape the plight of war.

In the postwar era, the FPPWC, like other American social service agencies, participated in rehabilitating war-ravaged countries and children. Initially the agency maintained offices in France, Holland, Belgium, Czechoslovakia, China, Poland, Italy, Greece, West Germany, and, of course, England; the ones in Poland, Czechoslovakia, and China were closed when the communists gained control in these countries. The FFPWC quickly developed its practice of providing basic supplies, community centers, and the like, hoping to rehabilitate children as well as their families. In 1953, when war broke out in Korea, following its initial purpose to aid children endangered by war, the FPPWC began its activities there. Reflecting its increasingly broadened role, the agency changed its name to Foster Parents' Plan, Inc. (FPP) in 1956, when it incorporated itself legally according to the laws of New York State. By 1957, the agency had helped 76,000 children of twenty-six nationalities and had prompted over 600,000 so-called foster parents to contribute money either as individuals or as part of a group. About 1,200 schools, colleges, and fraternal and employee groups sponsored foster children abroad. In the late 1950s, the FPP was sponsoring about fourteen thousand children annually, even though in the late 1950s and early 1960s, as the European economy was recovering, the FPP phased out most of its European programs.

Consistent with its ideal of helping needy children for whatever reasons and in any place, the FPP expanded its activities into new areas. In the early 1960s, for instance, it established a rudimentary program in Ecuador, Peru, Brazil, and Bolivia, the most poverty-stricken South American countries. In 1962, the FPP initiated a more formal program, sending a field director to Bogotá, Colombia, to implement it. The FPP maintained a special service fund to help pay for children's medical operations, and the agency maintained health services plans, which included preventive and community medicine in most countries in which it operated. In 1964, Dr. Keith R. Turner, an important staff worker in the FPP, arranged with Sears, Roebuck, and Company to conduct Operation Santa Claus, through which foster children selected Christmas gifts paid for by foster parents. The tremendous growth of the activities of the FPP necessitated the agency's installing a new computerized data-processing system in its headquarters in 1968. In response to suggestions advocating a possible domestic program for American children, in 1968, the board of directors discussed and then rejected this idea, claiming it would be too expensive and that the FPP's purpose was to function in countries that were unable to deal with their own problems. In 1969, the FPP produced and distributed an award-winning film, *Child of Darkness, Child of Light*.

In the 1970s, the organization expanded its program and developed as a well-known American social service agency. In 1969 and 1970, it held its first annual art show of children's art, featured in a FPP publication and displayed at the Donnell Branch of the New York Public Library, directly across the street from the Museum of Modern Art. In 1970, after a survey by Executive Director Gloria L. Mathews and with a grant from the Edna McConnell Clark Foundation, the FPP opened offices and a program in Australia. Economic progress in Hong Kong and Greece led the FPP to phase out its programs there. Activities abroad included medical and dental clinics, vocational training, work to improve literacy rates, and instruction in hygiene, budgeting, and family planning.

By 1974, the FPP was helping over fifty-two thousand children and their families. Famous individuals and organizations, such as Julie Andrews, Mr. and Mrs. Steve Allen, Burt Bacharach, Senator John Towers, the Boston Symphony Orchestra, and Kiwanis International supported foster children. Sponsors received a case history and photographs of their foster children and exchanged monthly letters with them. The FPP had a well-structured organization, including a ten-member board of directors. The international executive director, Gloria Mathews, headed the staff, which included her deputy, an international director of field services, a controller, and a national director, Keith Turner. After moving from New York City in the early 1970s, the headquarters of the recently renamed FPPI were located in Warwick, Rhode Island.

The sources for studying the FPPI's history are not substantial. For the early years, *The New York Times* contains helpful information. An agency publication, *Facts About Foster Parents Plan* (1974), contains a brief outline of the agency's history. For the 1960s and 1970s, the difficult-to-locate quarterly *Foster Parents Plan Reports* provides information. Inquiries to determine the availability of agency files proved unsuccessful.

Merle Curti, *American Philanthropy Abroad* (1963), mentions the agency briefly. There does not appear to be any scholarly work on the history of the well-known FPPI.

FOUNDATION FOR CHILD DEVELOPMENT (FCD). In the late 1890s, Mabel Irving Jones was inspired by a lecture by a pioneer woman pediatrician who cited the need for schools for handicapped children. In the fall of 1899, Jones convinced The Children's Aid Society* (CAS) of New York to cooperate in providing a school for crippled children. The sponsor of numerous schools for underprivileged children, the CAS agreed to provide a classroom, chairs, desks, books, and a teacher if Jones arranged for transporting the children. Consequently, under the auspices of the CAS, a class for crippled children opened at a local CAS school in February 1900. Within one year the venture was educating forty-two children from the East Side of Manhattan. The staff at the school— which challenged the prevailing view that crippled children should be segregated and be treated in institutions and homes—consisted initially of a teacher, a nurse, and a volunteer sewing teacher. The CAS enterprise was supervised by an auxiliary board of managers; Jones was president. Other officers included a vice-president, a secretary, and a treasurer. There was also a clothes committee, which indicated clearly the charitable aspects of the program.

The work of the CAS program grew gradually. By 1902, the staff included a total of eleven nurses and teachers. The original classroom proved too small, and within a few years, the group provided services for some children at another school. The program also established a trade department for girls, who were paid to make such items as lamp shades and do embroidery. In 1903, a series of mothers' meetings—a useful activity in many agencies' child welfare programs—began, as did annual summer outings in which the program cooperated with other New York agencies that conducted country and/or seashore homes.

Jones had apparently always conceived of the classes as preparing children for public schools. Fortunately, in 1904, the district superintendent of the New York City Board of Education visited the class and was impressed, leading Jones to argue for the opening of public schools to crippled children with the president of the Board of Education and with Superintendent William H. Maxwell. Jones prevailed; in 1906, the first public school class for crippled children opened at Public School 104 on the East Side of Manhattan.

With some of the program's purposes being fulfilled, the members of the auxiliary board of managers decided in 1907 to establish an independent organization to pursue the work. Consequently, the group established the Foundation for Child Development (FCD) as the Association for the Aid of Crippled Children (AACC) in 1908. The goals of the new AACC continued to be to provide classes and transportation as well as medical and social services to crippled children and their families. Catherine A. Bliss became the first president of the AACC, and Jones became chairman of its educational committee. The organization also had a relief committee and five nurses in addition to the supervising nurse. The AACC established offices at 5 Livingston Place in Manhattan. In 1908, the Guild for Crippled Children of the Poor of New York City, presided over by Lyman Beecher Stowe and which conducted a class for handicapped children, joined the AACC. Seven guild members became part of the AACC board of directors, which numbered fifteen in 1908.

The AACC's early activities were similar to those of the CAS's enterprises. Reaching handicapped children who needed attention continued to be a chief problem. AACC surveys in 1913, 1914, and 1916 showed that agencies had failed to serve these children and, in 1915, the AACC urged child welfare agencies to refer crippled children to it. Attacking the problem further, the AACC nurses began to visit public health and milk stations to locate handicapped children. In 1915, the six nurses handled 1,436 cases, conferring with families and referring children who needed other services to other social welfare agencies. Initially the AACC limited its services to children aged six to sixteen; but because its survey in 1913 showed that large numbers of younger children did not get proper services, the AACC began to serve preschool handicapped children.

The Board of Education began to conduct the kindergarten in 1910 and initiated its transportation service in 1913. In 1915, to serve communities better, the AACC opened its first nurses' district office. And, in 1919, the AACC distributed milk to the special classes, another service that the Board of Education took over in 1920.

Epidemics in the second decade of the twentieth century led to expanded services by the AACC. Despite already burdened services and finances, the AACC responded to the infantile paralysis epidemic of 1916 by taking four hundred stricken children and by increasing its nursing staff to ten. In 1917, the agency cared for nearly fifteen hundred cases from the New York Committee on After Care of Infantile Paralysis Cases, adding five more nurses and a masseuse to the staff. The epidemic in 1917 also prompted the AACC to open an office in the Bronx, to which the five new nurses were assigned. Because of the expanding services, the board of directors was enlarged to twenty-four members in 1921.

The 1920s and the depression years of the 1930s were generally quiet ones for the AACC. New services, however, began in the late 1930s. In 1936, for instance, the agency began its clinic service through which nurses attended clinics at cooperating hospitals with orthopedic clinics. Occupational therapy began in Queens in 1937, when the AACC initiated home treatments as a regular service in Queens. Also in 1937, the agency began to train nurses to teach relaxation techniques, muscle education, and massages to patients unable to get to clinics. To meet ever-improving standards of care, in 1935, the AACC started a program to keep the staff abreast of new developments, educating them in such subjects as nutrition, mental hygiene, and social conditions. In 1935, the agency also began a series of radio talks on infantile paralysis, services available in New York, and other such issues.

In the early 1940s, the AACC dealt increasingly with children—and adults—afflicted with cerebral palsy and infantile paralysis and emphasized more than before preventive activities in the field. Interest in prevention led quickly to the establishment of an advisory service in 1943, which cooperated with the Bureau of Nursing of the city's Department of Health and the Visiting Nurse Service of New York (VNSNY). Responding to the serious infantile paralysis epidemic in 1944, the AACC cooperated with a Department of Health plan, as the nurses visited all reported cases, coordinating their special services with other agencies. During the epidemic, the AACC also helped adults. The scope of the AACC work increased considerably in the next year when the AACC raised the age limit of children it helped to twenty-one. Most importantly, in 1944, the agency received $11 million from the will of the late Milo M. Belding, an event that affected the very nature of the AACC.

The large size of the Belding grant initially prompted some organizational changes to adapt to the new wealth. To make the executive committee more flexible and efficient, the AACC reduced its size. The finance committee began to emphasize investments and to determine the financial policies, and a new business and budget committee was established to handle the details formerly done by the finance committee. The AACC rewrote its bylaws to incorporate these changes. The bequest also prompted the organization to sense a broader social responsibility than before. For instance, during the World War II years, despite program disruptions in other social service agencies, the AACC increased its orthopedic services and its home nursing for crippled children. The study division as well as a committee of the board of directors discussed the agency's future, and in late 1947 and early 1948, they determined new objectives: to conduct a grant program to promote research, demonstration projects, and education and to continue to be a direct service agency for crippled children.

To implement its new program, the AACC reorganized its structure in 1949 and 1950. It developed a council with thirty-two members, reduced the board of directors to fifteen members, and established these officers: a president emeritus, a president, two vice-presidents, a treasurer, a secretary, an assistant secretary, and the chairman of the council. The director was Leonard W. Mayo, an important child welfare worker. There were seven committees, including the medical advisory committee to the nursing service, composed of seven physicians. The executive staff included such positions as an educational director, a statistician, and three consultants, one each in public health nursing, medical social work, and mental hygiene.

The AACC began its new program energetically. In December 1949, it made a grant to help organize and to conduct the International Conference on the Care and Education of Crippled Children, held under the joint auspices of the United Nations and the International Union for Child Welfare. In 1950, the AACC awarded its first grant, on a contingent basis, to the New York City Department of Health and to the Board of Education to establish an experimental demonstration of an educational and therapy unit for cerebral palsied children in Public School 118 in Queens. The goal was to influence the city to take over this program in three years, but it did so after only two years. In 1950, the AACC joined with the New York University-Bellevue Medical Center to establish a children's division in the Institute of Physical Medicine and Rehabilitation, a pioneer program in the field. AACC council members often volunteered to help in the in-patient department. In the fall of 1950, the board of directors approved a long-range plan, through the cooperation of health and welfare agencies in Queens, to develop a comprehensive rehabilitation program. The board viewed this as another demonstration project. To promote better cooperation in research, the AACC invited thirty distinguished scientists to confer in June 1951, and the agency initiated steps to cooperate with small foundations interested in handicapped children. A few months later, the AACC awarded, through the National Education Association, a grant to the United States Office of Education for a nationwide study of the qualifications of teachers of the handicapped and of teacher-training curriculums.

During the middle and late 1950s, the agency continued its program of helping to develop demonstration projects, to promote research, and to develop educational programs and materials. In December 1953, the AACC transferred its orthopedic nursing service to the VNSNY, marking the final step in phasing out its direct service functions. Similar services in Manhattan and the Bronx had been transferred in April 1951. The cooperative project in Queens resulted in the establishment in November 1953 of a diagnostic and evaluation program at the Queens Hospital Center. In June 1954, the AACC held its second meeting for scientists, and the annual meeting in 1954 focused on "Rehabilitation '64," as two radio networks carried special programs discussing the AACC and its activities. In 1952, the group held its first scientific conference; the proceedings were published in 1954. In 1953, the agency helped to establish programs for dependent and disabled children in Korea. In the mid-1950s, the division of publications and health education broadened its publishing functions to include working with other agencies in the National Health Council* to distribute information about the handicapped. The demonstration projects in both the children's division of the Institute of Physical Medicine and Rehabilitation and in Queens continued. From the 1950s through the 1970s, the bulk of the grant funds supported research in genetically based disorders and in abnormalities of fetal development.

In the 1960s and 1970s, the grant program continued, but major organizational changes occurred. In March 1965, long-time Director Leonard Mayo retired. In April 1967, the bylaws were amended to establish the position of chairman of the board, the policy-making and planning post, and the president was redefined as the chief executive officer with overall responsibility for administration. During the 1960s, the AACC continued its Belding scholarship and research programs and developed a project to identify new patients for research. By the early 1970s, the agency called itself a private foundation. The council met annually to receive officers' reports and to elect a board of directors, which met regularly to determine policy and to approve programs and expenditures. In the early 1970s, the agency redefined its purpose to emphasize the coordination and delivery of services for preschoolers. Prompted by the failure of federal programs, the AACC began in the early 1970s to focus efforts on improving communications between community-initiated programs for children and professional agencies. In line with its new emphases and grants program, the AACC became the Foundation for Child Development (FCD) in 1972, ending the history of a unique and influential social service agency.

The primary sources for studying the agency's history include the unpublished minutes of the executive committee meetings, 1904–1933, on microfilm at the Social Welfare History Archives Center at the University of Minnesota, Minneapolis. The published *Annual Reports,* which are not widely available, provide fairly detailed reports of the FCD's activities. The Papers of Leonard W. Mayo, also at the Social Welfare History Archives Center, relate to the history of the organization. Memoirs of agency leaders, deposited at the Oral History Project at

Columbia University, discuss the FCD's shift from a service agency to a foundation.

Apparently, there is no scholarly history of the FCD, but the agency's *Growth, 1900–1945* (1945) contains a helpful history.

FRESH AIR FUND, THE (FAF). In the late nineteenth century, the sordid plight of children in American cities concerned a host of reformers and citizens. Imbued with a dual sense of charity and a more favorable view of rural than urban life, reformers began to think of giving city children the advantages of a rural environment. Reformers and nonreformers alike believed generally that rural towns provided more healthful and more wholesome conditions and, of course, more fresh air than did cities. Partly in response to these two major themes—charity and ruralism—The Fresh Air Fund (FAF) was established in 1877. It began with a Sunday morning sermon at the Scott Presbyterian Church in Sherman, Pennsylvania, on June 3, 1877, by Reverend Willard Parsons. Reverend Parsons, who had worked previously in a mission in the congested districts on the Lower East Side of Manhattan, reflected on how city children could benefit from experience in rural towns such as Sherman. He apparently stressed the charitable theme of "Inasmuch as ye have done it unto the least of these, ye have done it unto me." Parishioners responded immediately, pledging to have children from New York City visit their homes for a summer vacation. Parsons quickly arranged for children from New York City to come to Sherman that very summer. Through his efforts, the children received one-half fare on the railroads transporting them from the city to the country, and Parsons himself persuaded the railroads to give him a pass so he could accompany each group of children. In the late 1870s, Parson's Fresh Air Work (FAW) was only one of many similar agencies and projects, but his gradually became the most well-known such enterprise in the United States.

The simple activities of the organization grew quickly as word of Reverend Parsons's work spread among people in the country. News of his activities also reached mission, charity, settlement workers, and the like in New York City, who recommended specific children to the organization. In the first summer, 1877, sixty children were served by Parsons's fledgling FAW. Beginning in 1878, because of Parsons's efforts, a well-known New York City newspaper, *The New York Evening Post,* began to sponsor the organization. The work grew steadily, and by 1881, Parsons influenced Whitelaw Reid, the editor of *The New York Tribune,* to administer the work. Reid and four of his friends, each a wealthy and prominent New Yorker, organized The Tribune Fresh Air Fund Society (TFAFS) in 1881. The four other founders were the wealthy and prominent Cornelius Vanderbilt, Morris K. Jessup, a banker who was active in a number of charities, philanthropist Cleveland E. Dodge, and Darius O. Mills, a banker, financier, and philanthropist.

The TFAFS was entirely independent of the newspaper, but it enjoyed its support and name. In 1888, the TFAFS was incorporated in the state of New York to provide children living in New York City "the benefit and enjoyment of fresh air in the country." By the late 1880s, people in rural areas around New York City were so anxious to have children visit them in the summer that some even built bed bunks and converted barns into sleeping quarters. In Deposit, New York, a local hospital was turned over to the enterprise. Local communities began to develop so-called fresh air homes, giving them such names as "Holiday House" and "Happy Land." At the peak of this type of venture, there were fifteen such homes. In some cases, local communities funded and operated the homes, which the organization in New York City otherwise maintained. By the late 1880s, settlements, community centers, churches, hospitals, and both private and public welfare agencies in New York were affiliated with the TFAFS. Parsons remained the executive head of the organization until his death in the summer of 1906.

Parsons built the TFAFS into a nationally known agency and the model of its kind. Representatives from American and Canadian cities visited New York to study its methods, and others obtained information by mail. Among other things, the TFAFS set the example in the fresh air field of keeping systematic records. Unlike other similar societies, the TFAFS did not pay for boarding the children in family homes. The TFAFS not only paid for transporting youngsters to its homes but also provided transportation expenses for children sent by other societies and individuals. In 1895, however, it almost abolished the latter activity because *The Tribune* provided less funds for this work. In 1895, the agency had twelve fresh air homes of its own and sent over three thousand city children to country vacations in the summer.

Parsons continued to visit cooperating towns and villages and others to solicit new family homes and support. He typically called on local clergymen and held public meetings. The TFAFS was aware of and sensitive to questions of children's and hosts' nationalities and religions. In 1905, the TFAFS established the first of its numerous summer camps, Shepherd Knapp Camp, at Litchfield, Connecticut. During the first phase of the society's history, from 1877 to 1906, nearly 238,000 children from the city were sent on vacations in the country for two weeks, and the organization provided over 429,000 all-day outdoor excursions up the Hudson River for mothers and their children. In 1912, at ceremonies unveiling a plaque in Parson's honor, a speaker appropriately called him "the Apostle of Fresh Air—the Sunshine Philanthropist—the Bishop of the Child-World."

After Parson's death, the organization continued to grow. Replacing him as chief administrator and executive officer in 1907 was Reverend John Bancroft Davis, like Parsons, a Presbyterian. A journalist for *The New York Tribune,* Davis had the understanding of a social worker, having been a foundling who grew up in an orphanage. Under his short administration, which ended when he died in 1911, the TFAFS began camping with its own facilities, first at The Life

Camp, in Ridgefield, Connecticut, where Parsons had earlier supplied a staff. Leslie Marsland Conly, who had extensive experience in camping, replaced Davis. In 1919, Conly created the "vacations in perpetuity" program, whereby a donor provided an endowment, and the TFAFS utilized its interest to finance children's vacations. By 1957, vacations in perpetuity provided seventy-three vacations for children each summer. Conly also coined the phrase "friendly town" in the early 1920s to distinguish between towns that invited city children as opposed to communities where there were camps run by either the society or local townspeople. In 1928, the TFAFS was given what became the Marks Memorial Camp near Lafayetteville, New York, in northern Dutchess County, New York. The Fresh Air Association of Ridgefield, Connecticut, provided Camp Hidden Valley, a coeducational facility serving about one hundred children, both handicapped and able-bodied. This camp's professional staff featured a year-round medical social worker, provided by the National Foundation for Infantile Paralysis* (NFIP), who worked with hospitals and clinics in selecting handicapped children and following up on their activities. The medical social worker also advised Hidden Valley's staff during the summer. In 1940, the agency received a gift of land near Putnam Valley, New York, from Bird S. Coler, a former city official who had served as commissioner of the Department of Public Welfare in the late teens and the early 1920s. This tract became the society's Camp Coler for boys between eight and ten years old. The end of another era in the agency's history occurred in 1946 when Leslie Conly retired as manager.

After 1946, the society continued to expand and to prosper. In the late 1940s, the organization received from Dr. and Mrs. William Sharpe a vast tract of land on the Sharpe Reservation in East Fishkill, New York. On this land, the organization opened Camp Pioneer for teenage boys in the summer of 1948. In 1948, the now renamed Herald-Tribune Fresh Air Fund (HTFAF) established its Community Trust-Fresh Air Chorus of thirty children. In 1953, this group began being supported by the Musical Arts Fund and the Clara Lewisohn Rossin Fund of the New York Community Trust Fund. In 1954–1955, on the Sharpe land also, the HTFAF constructed its Ernest Bliss-Little Mothers' Aid Association Camp with funds donated by the late Anita Bliss. After the sponsoring *New York Herald-Tribune* ceased publication in 1966, the agency soon became The Fresh Air Fund (FAF). In 1976, having purchased a total of two thousand acres adjacent to the Sharpe property by 1976, the FAF's acreage formed the site of seven camps run by the FAF. In the mid-1970s, this veteran agency had a year-round staff of thirteen, and representatives from the most prestigious New York families, such as Mrs. John Hay Whitney, Franklin D. Roosevelt, Jr., and Arthur Ochs Sulzberger of *The New York Times,* served on its nineteen-member board of directors.

The sources for studying the FAF's history are diverse and extensive but somewhat difficult to locate in libraries. The published *Annual Reports,* which are not available widely, record the agency's development. Journals such as *Sunday Afternoon* and *Scribner's Magazine* published nearly contemporary accounts of the early agency. The Papers of Helen Reid at the Library of Congress in Washington, D.C., contain materials relating to the agency's history, as do some materials at its headquarters in New York City. Fortunately the New York press covered the society. The morgue of the defunct *New York Herald-Tribune* at the Queensboro Public Library in Jamaica, New York, has agency materials, and *The New York Times Index* and files are available widely.

Historians, even specialists in child welfare history, seem to have neglected studying the FAF.

— G

GIRL SCOUTS OF THE UNITED STATES OF AMERICA (GSUSA). In England, a group of girls influenced by Robert Baden-Powell's recently established Boy Scouts formed the Girl Guides in 1910. Juliette Gordon Low, from a well-established family in Savannah, Georgia, but who was suffering from a recently broken marriage, traveled to England frequently. Through mutual friends and a mutual interest in sculpturing, Low and Baden-Powell became close. Impressed with the British girls organizing their groups and influenced by Baden-Powell himself, Low began and led groups of so-called Girl Guides in rural England and in an impoverished section of London. In early 1912, Low decided to form a similar organization for girls in the United States. Consequently, on March 12, 1912, she established the Girl Scouts of the United States of America (GSUSA) as the Girl Guides (GG).

Low assembled eighteen young women in Savannah and constituted them as the first members of a troop. She registered her niece, Daisy Gordon, as the first member of this group even though Daisy was not at the March 12 meeting in Savannah. Low threw himself almost completely into the GG regimen of knot tying and nature lore. Following the example of the recently established Boy Scouts of America* (BSA), in July 1912, she purchased "Lowland" in Georgia as a campsite for the Savannah Girl Guides. Indeed throughout the early history of the GSUSA, Low personally provided much of the funds for operations and salaries for personnel. Low seemed to place an emphasis on the attractiveness of the uniform that the girls and their adult leaders wore.

With her organization established, Low set about expanding the program and solidifying the structure. In 1913, the agency's name was changed from GG to the Girl Scouts (GS). In June 1913, the organization established its first national headquarters in Washington, D.C. At the same time, the GS hired its first national secretary, Edith D. Johnston. Also in 1913, the first Girl Scout handbook, *How Girls Can Help Their Country,* was adapted from the British GG handbook by Agnes Baden-Powell and Robert Baden-Powell himself. By 1914, there were over one thousand members of the fast-growing GS. Low was striving for national recognition of her organization, and on June 10, 1915, the GS was incorporated according to the laws of the District of Columbia as Girl Scouts, Inc. (GS). Immediately following this event, the GS held a meeting of its first national council. The constitution and bylaws were adopted, and, as expected, Juliette Low was elected president. In October 1915, the GS instituted national membership dues at twenty-five cents a year. By the end of 1915, there were about five thousand members. The GS joined other youth-serving agencies such as the BSA and the Camp Fire Girls* (CFG) by moving its headquarters to New York City in April 1916. In 1916, Low rewrote the handbook, and, for the first time, uniforms became available from the national GS organization in New York. An important organizational development occurred in May 1917 when the first local council, composed of the troops in a given city or other locale, was authorized in Toledo, Ohio. In the early summer of 1917, the GS, like other national youth agencies, held a national training school, its first, at Miss Winsor's School in Boston, Massachusetts. In October 1917, the GS inaugurated its tradition of having the First Lady as honorary president. Mrs. Woodrow Wilson was the first woman to hold this position. Also in October 1917, the GS began to publish its monthly magazine for girls and their leaders, *The Rally.* The first troop of physically handicapped girls in the United States was organized in 1917 at the School for Crippled Children, Public School 75, in New York City.

Like the BSA and the CFG, the GS participated enthusiastically in the American war effort during World War I. In recognition of the GS's bond sales, the United States Treasury Department created a bronze Girl Scout liberty loan medal. In 1919, the first nationwide celebration of GS week was held in November.

In the 1920s and 1930s, the GS continued to grow, adding new facilities and establishing new programs. In June 1920, *The Rally* became *The American Magazine,* a publication for all girls, issued by the GS. In 1922, the GS received Camp Andre Clark in Briarcliff Manor, New York. It was donated by Senator and Mrs. William A. Clark in memory of their daughter. The camp functioned as a national campsite until 1941, when it was leased to the Girl Scout Council of Greater New York. In 1924, the national council developed a regional structure, dividing the United States into twelve regions. Also in 1924, the headquarters moved to its own building in New York. In 1926, the GS opened Camp Edith Macy, also at Briarcliff Manor, as a national training center. The first all-Indian troop, at the Indian Boarding School in Pawnee, Oklahoma, was recorded in 1930. In 1932, the GS designated March 12 as its official birthday. New handbooks were issued constantly during these years.

In January 1935, the first analysis of the GS program began. A group of social scientists, educators, and GS professional and volunteer leaders formed an advisory study group. In 1936, the GS initiated its famous, nationally franchised cookie sale. Another national campsite, in Rockwood, in Potomac, Maryland, was acquired in 1938. During this period, the GS developed ties with the national social work community as it became an early member of the National Association for the Study of Group Work (NASGW). Agnes Leahy of the GS served as the NAGSW's secretary from 1938 to 1941.

Similar developments occurred until the 1940s and 1950s. Not until the 1960s, did the GSA become involved in traditional social services and social action and in the national social work community. In 1940, however, the GS registered the first troops from institutions for mentally and socially handicapped people. As in World War I, the organization pledged its services to the American war effort in the early 1940s. In May 1943, the GS introduced its first services aide program with the publication of *Senior Girl Scouting in Wartime*. By 1944, there were over a million members. The GS was an original member of the reorganized National Social Welfare Assembly* (NSWA). In 1947, the name of the national organization was changed from GS to Girl Scouts of the United States of America (GSUSA). In November 1948, after two years of field work, the field committee began a major effort to establish effective councils throughout the United States. On March 16, 1950, GSUSA was reincorporated by a congressional charter.

After the end of World War II, a series of international activities developed, including leadership training and encampments. Typical of such activities was the exchange of people, beginning in 1958, with The Experiment in International Living under the auspices of the Juliette Low World Friendship Fund (JLWFF). In 1955, the Survey Research Center of the University of Michigan began a two-year study of adolescent girls. In 1957, when the study was completed, the GSUSA also moved its national headquarters to a new building built for the GSUSA at 830 Third Avenue in New York City, the site of the national headquarters in 1976. In 1959, the GSUSA participated with girls from six Latin American countries under the auspices of the JLWFF in an international service project, a camp for children in Puerto Rico.

Only in the late 1960s and 1970s did the GSUSA develop programs that brought it to the center of the national social work community. In 1967, for instance, with the CFG, the GSUSA cosponsored an experimental project for administrative trainees in community service agencies to help train older women in six cities. Funds from the United States Department of Labor supported the project. Also in 1967, the GSUSA held a national conference for senior Girl Scouts on the inner city. Called "Girl Scouting Makes the Difference," this conference was held at Marion College in Indianapolis, Indiana, in August 1967. In 1968, the national board of directors established the Girl Scout National Center West on about fifteen thousand acres in Ten Sleep, Wyoming. A reorganization in 1968 consolidated the national branch officers from the previous twelve to six. Also in 1968, the GSUSA held senior Girl Scout "Speak Out" conferences throughout the country to discuss how to break down prejudice and misunderstanding between social and minority groups. Delegates at the thirty-eighth national council meeting in October 1969 launched Action '70, a nation-wide effort to overcome prejudice and to build relations among persons of all ages, religions, and races. In 1970, the GSUSA held a conference in Atlanta on scouting for black girls. Also in 1970, it held a national antidrug abuse workshop in Washington, D.C., and began Eco-actions, a nationwide environmental education and improvement program. The so-called urban crisis was explored by adult leaders at a special meeting at national headquarters in March 1971. In 1973, with funding from the federal Bureau of Indian Affairs, the GSUSA extended its program to American Indian girls in eight western states. More to the core of the national social service community, in June 1973, the GSUSA began a three-year federally funded national project, Education for Parenthood, to help teenagers learn about child development and human interactions. Other national social service agencies, such as The Salvation Army,* also participated in this program. In July 1974, with federal funds, the GSUSA began a two-year program, Hand-in-Hand: Cross-age Interactions, which involved young people and the elderly poor. A few months later, in September 1974, with a generous grant from the Irwin-Sweeney-Miller Foundation, the GSUSA began a three-year pilot program to link councils with migrant families. As part of its bicentennial project, the GSUSA began efforts in 1975 to discover "hidden heroines" and commitments to service projects. In 1976, the GSUSA presented the names of over six hundred "hidden heroines" to Queen Elizabeth II of England on her visit to Philadelphia to help celebrate America's bicentennial in the summer of 1976.

The sources for studying the GSUSA's history are diverse. The Low Family Papers at the Georgia Historical Society in Savannah and at the Southern Historical Collection at the University of North Carolina shed light on the origins and early history of the organization and on the activities of its founder. The GSUSA archives at its national headquarters in New York City has about 2,500 linear feet of materials on all aspects of the agency's history. Various pamphlets describe agency programs and activities. Since 1950, there are detailed published *Annual Reports*.

There are a number of biographies of Juliette Low, invariably dealing with the GSUSA. The best of these is Gladys Denny Schultz and Daisy Gordon Lawrence, *Lady from Savannah* (1958), which is based on Low's family archives and other manuscript sources. Unfortunately, there are no citations in this otherwise rich source. A convenient summary of Low's life can be found in *Notable American Women 1607–1950* (1971), 2: 432–434, by Kenneth Coleman. An agency publication, "GSUSA, Highlights of the First 65 Years" (1976), is helpful. Professor Mary Rothchild of Arizona State University is working on the GSUSA's early history. For a more extended treatment of the folklore, camping, and other such aspects of the GSUSA, see the entry in *Fraternal Organizations* in this series.

GIRLS AND BOYS SERVICE LEAGUE (GBSL). The GBSL was established largely as a result of the interests and efforts of Maude Miner in the first decade of the twentieth century. After she graduated in 1901 from Smith College, a training ground for many women in social service in the Progressive era, Miner became a probation officer in the women's night court in New York City in 1906. Her concern for hardened women on probation without families or places to go led her to found Waverley House in February 1908. Located at 165 West Tenth Street in New York City, Waverley House was a group home for such women. Miner received funds for personnel and facilities from the Russell Sage Foundation* (RSF), a leading Progressive agency in New York and the nation. The RSF was encouraged to provide the funds by two important philanthropists—Gertrude Stevens Rice, a benefactor of the State Charities Aid Association* (SCAA) of New York, and John M. Glenn, who had been important in the charity organization movement. Encouraged by this early and prestigious support, Miner wrote leading people in the field asking for their support as well. Philanthropists Andrew Carnegie and Mrs. Russell Sage were included in the prominent group that supported the early work. Others interested in the agency, such as Homer Folks, a nationally prominent social welfare leader and the executive secretary of the SCAA, and Mary Simkhovitch of Greenwich House, a leading settlement, helped to form a board of directors. The board met initially on April 28, 1908. Led by Miner, the group was organized formally as the New York Probation Association (NYPA) on May 19, 1908.

In its early phase, the organization developed and strengthened its activities and solidified its organizational structure. The agency encouraged judges and probation officers from women's night courts and other courts to send women on probation to Waverley House, which became the NYPA's major facility. To help prevent young, single, working-class women from becoming criminals and social deviants, some churches in New York City helped the NYPA to organize clubs for them. These clubs worked with the NYPA and Waverley House to establish, in 1909, an employment bureau to help such women find jobs. This activity paralleled the efforts of social Progressives in Chicago, who had organized the Immigrants Protective League* in 1908 to prevent single immigrant girls from being enticed into prostitution or other disreputable activities.

As in Chicago, the most important prominent Progressives supported the NYPA. The forty people who incorporated the NYPA according to the laws of New York State on January 25, 1909, included John Glenn of the RSF; Edward T. Devine, the founding editor of the most important national social work journal, *The Survey;* Louisa Lee Schuyler, who had established the SCAA in 1872 and who remained active in a host of social welfare agencies and movements; Homer Folks; and Mary Simkhovitch. The first group of officers included New

York State Govenor Charles S. Whitman as president, two vice-presidents, one of whom was Devine, a treasurer, and Maude Miner as secretary. There was also a fifteen-member board of directors, which included Folks, Simkhovitch, Glenn, and, suggestive of the agency's broad sectarian base, Milton I. D. Einstein, a leading figure in New York Jewish charities. With this strong structure, the NYPA expanded its services, establishing its first summer vacation home for women on probation at Mardean, New Jersey, in the summer of 1909.

The NYPA's early activities reflected and even spearheaded other Progressive trends in social service and social reform. Maude Miner's article on night courts in *The Survey* in 1909 helped to stimulate new programs in girls' courts throughout the country. As illustrated by Miner's *Probation Work in the Magistrate's Court,* published in late 1909, the NYPA also began to emphasize preventive and protective activities, an emphasis consistent with Progressive reform trends stressing prevention. In 1911, the self-supporting neighborhood clubs of working women in New York established the Girls Protective League (GPL), which adopted the slogan "Girls for Girls." Similar groups developed around the country, particularly in cities. Executive Secretary Miner helped to outline a policy for women offenders in Kansas City, Missouri, and worked also on reports of vice in Chicago and Minneapolis. The NYPA supported the movement to hire female probation officers in Albany, New York.

Reflecting the broadening of activities, the organization changed its name in 1912 to the New York Probation and Protective Association (NYPPA). In that year, Miner studied a thousand cases to determine the causes of prostitution, and in 1913, the NYPPA joined others in blaming social deviance on mental weakness. The agency instituted psychological examinations of women and added Dr. Anne T. Bingham as the staff physician. In the next few years, the NYPPA moved its offices to the RSF Building, where it joined other local and national social service agencies. It also opened Hillcrest Farms in Salisbury, Connecticut, as a summer vacation home for working women and campaigned successfully to have policewomen in New York City.

When the United States began to mobilize for World War I, the organization lent Executive Secretary Miner to the government, appropriately, as the chairman of the Committee on Protective Work for Girls of the Commission on Training Camp Activities, an organization to instill in both men and women sound social and hygienic behavior in and around military camps. In 1918, the NYPPA joined the already-established campaign for better legislation protecting women workers, and in 1924, Miner conducted a course on protective work for girls at the New York School of Social Work.

In the decade following World War I, the NYPPA, like other social service and social reform agencies, lost some of its crusading fervor. Organizational development and an emphasis on individuals rather than societal problems characterized the NYPPA. In 1920, for example, with a grant from The Commonwealth Fund,* the NYPPA established its mental hygiene clinic, signaling the agency's emphasis on mental disorders to explain social deviance. In 1923, the organization became the Girls Service League of America (GSLA), and in the late 1920s, it became concerned with establishing both special and permanent funds, especially the Twentieth Anniversary Fund. That fund of over $250,000 allowed the expansion of agency facilities. In 1930, the GSLA opened two new residences for single women, one in New York City and one on an estate in Roslyn, Long Island.

The Great Depresssion created extra demands on the GSLA, bringing it partly back to its earlier concern with social issues. This renewed concern was foreshadowed in the late 1920s when the GSLA created a new vocational job assistance program. In the early 1930s, the GSLA's cooperation with the President's Emergency Committee for Employment won the commendation of President Herbert Hoover. In 1936, taking another step toward the social work community that had participated so actively in its founding, the GSLA provided fieldwork placements and training for social work students. In 1937, the agency noted in its published *Annual Report,* that such social conditions as broken homes and home environments leading to adjustment problems in school and poor health prompted young women to seek the GSLA's services. The organization determined that it should thus stress vocational guidance and employment, as well as industrial maladjustment problems. Vocational training in domestic service, begun in 1933, became increasingly popular, influencing other agencies in the country to conduct similar courses. A vocational conference, sponsored jointly by the GSLA and the New York League of Business and Professional Women, offered young women career advice and helped them find jobs.

As World War II approached, the GSLA geared itself for defense-related activities. Members and alumnae of the residences developed classes in first aid, Red Cross knitting, home nursing, motor mechanics, and the like. The young women also donated blood, collected salvage and books, and entertained soldiers and sailors, legitimately. In 1943, the GSLA modified its policies to include work with girls as young as fourteen.

The postwar years brought more sophisticated casework techniques, and the GSLA began some new activities. In 1947, for instance, it established a scholarship committee to help girls further their education; in 1950, it extended its nonresident program; and in 1951, it initiated a major new service, a group psychotherapy project for adolescents, with an initial group of sixty-four boys, under the auspices of the New York City Youth Board. This group therapy project was expanded in 1955, when it was transferred from the auspices of the Youth Board to the Community Mental Health Board. Three years earlier the New York State Department of Mental Hygiene had licensed the GSLA as a psychiatric clinic. Thus one of its pioneering objectives, set up three decades earlier, was realized. In 1957, with the cooperation of the New York City Board of Education, the GSLA began its group therapy program in Washington Irving High School for girls. The GSLA ended the 1950s with its fiftieth-anniversary celebrations, which included a drive to raise funds to help it strengthen its programs and services and to modernize its facilities. A phase of the agency's history ended in 1960, when, largely because of spiraling costs, the GSLA closed Preston Hall, its remaining residential center.

In 1962, Cecile Schwartzman, previously the director of casework services, became the first executive director, replacing the former administrative director as the agency's leader, and the organization became the Girls and Boys Service League (GBSL) in 1963. In the 1960s, the agency developed its services still further, establishing individual and group therapy programs in local schools, especially in vocational and special schools. The agency's individual treatment department for girls began in 1960, and individual services for boys began in 1963. In 1964, the GBSL, cooperating with The Children's Aid Society* (CAS) of New York, provided group therapy programs for children in the CAS's foster home division. A few years later, the GBSL trained a CAS staff worker to conduct group therapy sessions. Contributing further to the development of psychiatric services for adolescents, beginning in 1966, the GBSL and the Hunter College School of Social Work cosponsored a course on the dynamics of adolescence. This course, which the GBSL later gave independently, was included in the training program for guidance counselors in the New York City public schools. The GBSL also developed mothers' group discussions, which proved popular, and in 1969, trained a caseworker to lead a group of unwed mothers whose children were under the auspices of the Spence-Chapin Adoption Service in New York.

In the 1970s, the GBSL continued to develop psychiatric and other services for adolescents and children. In 1971, with a grant from the local Federation of Protestant Welfare, it conducted a workshop for teachers at a vocational high school. Working with the Brooklyn Bureau of Community Service, it also developed therapeutic services for extremely deprived adolescent boys. With the dissolution of the Manhattan Trade School Fund in 1972, the GBSL obtained $300,000, which it used to develop a vocational guidance program for adolescents. Thus, the agency moved more into community education programs. With grants from the Glazier Foundation, workshops for guidance counselors have continued, and the GBSL has also conducted an increasing number of Rap Room programs for adolescents.

The published but not widely available *Annual Reports* of the GBSL are the basic primary source for studying its history. The agency's headquarters in New York has unpublished materials, such as minutes of meetings.

Apparently there is no scholarly history of the agency, nor is it mentioned in the standard literature in the field.

GIRLS CLUBS OF AMERICA, INC. (GCA). In the mid-nineteenth century, clubs to protect working women were established, especially in New England industrial towns and cities. Predating a number of twentieth-century social service agencies to protect single working women, one of the earliest girls' clubs was opened in 1864 in Waterbury, Connecticut, to provide a social center for single girls who worked in the textile mills. Like other nineteenth-century girls' clubs in New England, this organization, which later became the Waterbury Girls Club, also provided social services for poor workers' children, neglected youths who roamed the streets of the mill and other working-class districts. This early activity involved the girls' clubs in preventing juvenile delinquency.

In 1936, in Worcester, Massachusetts, the president of the local girls' club, Mrs. J. Herbert Johnson, and others began to see the need for discussing common problems, particularly those related to their new emphasis on young girls rather than on older working women. The executive director of the Worcester Girls Club, Dora Dodge, knew that others felt similarly, and she contacted them, but only two other clubs showed interest. Nevertheless, on March 29, 1937, seven representatives met to discuss, "The Need, Aim, and Scope of Club Work for Little Girls." Those at the meeting then planned what became the first annual conference of girls' clubs, held in September 1937. The group of founders, led by Mrs. Johnson, were especially delighted that the Waterbury club, the first in the country, joined the group. Attendance at such annual conferences increased steadily, and with both board and staff members attending consistently, the group held separate, specialized meetings for each interest group. In 1941, the representatives of the participating clubs, now representing a broader geographical area and realizing the need for funds and for publicity, began a mimeographed news bulletin, which was put together by the Worcester group. The annual conference had developed working committees, and when two of them, conference and public relations, met jointly in June 1942, they decided to adopt the name the Eastern Association of Girls Clubs (EAGC) for the group. Beginning in 1942, the EAGC initiated a dues collection program, a step toward greater organization. Finally, after years of efforts, especially by Johnson, the group met on May 19, 1945, in Springfield, Massachusetts, to form the Girls Club of America (GCA). A month later, on June 29, 1945, representatives met in Worcester to adopt the bylaws of the new GCA, which was incorporated in the commonwealth of Massachusetts on July 5, 1945.

The new group moved quickly and with dedication to solidify its organizational structure. At the founding meeting in May 1945, delegates had elected the board of directors and the traditional officers, including Johnson as president. Composed of the seven officers and ten directors, the board of directors met monthly for about a year to give the organization early focus and commitment. Indicating Johnson's personal enthusiasm, the first headquarters of the GCA was established in a room in her home in Worcester. In March 1946, the GCA hired its first worker, a part-time secretary, and later in the year, it began to print (instead of mimeograph) its monthly bulletins.

Concerned both with expanding the national organization and with maintaining standards, within months of its founding, the GCA developed a standards committee and decided to open memberships to any girl-serving agency that joined before the 1947 annual meeting. The GCA received an early boost in 1946 in an article about it in *Youth Leaders' Digest*. In 1947, when the agency moved to headquarters in Springfield, Massachusetts, it also hired its first executive director, Henrietta Aull of Northampton, Massachusetts. In September of that same year, the GCA published its initial handbooks; the first one was *The Formation and Administration of Girls Clubs*. Other important organizational events followed. In December 1947, the GCA was admitted to membership in the National Social Welfare Assembly* (NSWA), the leading coalition of national social service agencies, and a few months later, the National Information Bureau certified the GCA as a legitimate fund-raising organization. Demonstrating even further concerns for professional social work, the education committee of the GCA began to discuss the need for better-trained executives and staffs for local affiliates.

In the 1950s, the GCA expanded its structure and began to provide services to its affiliates, which numbered thirty-seven in 1952. In May 1950, the GCA hired its first field secretary, Adelaide St. Jacques, to help new affiliates and to provide consultation services to members. In 1951, the GCA held its first regional institute in Johnson City, Tennessee, for girls' clubs workers. In May 1952, the agency hired its first public relations director; and later in the year, at national headquarters in Springfield, it held its first public relations forum for representatives of affiliates. Another boost to the GCA and the girls' club movement came in 1952, when the General Federation of Women's Clubs, a nationwide organization, established forming new clubs as an important state or community project for its members.

The tenth anniversary fund drive, with a goal of $250,000, began in 1953, when Mamie Eisenhower, the president's wife, became honorary chairman of the GCA. Also in 1953, the GCA held its apparently first institute for club workers at Boston University. The GCA received a grant of $10,000 from Stanley Home Products, Inc., to conduct such training programs. In 1954, when the GCA became international with the joining of a Canadian club, the organization received a sizable tract of land for a summer camp, Iron Rail, in Wenham, Massachusetts. The donor, who had been conducting a vacation home for working girls, was influenced by former President Herbert Hoover—himself an important figure in many child welfare agencies, including the Boys' Clubs of America* (BCA)—who urged that she donate the land to the GCA. The fortunes of the organization continued in the late 1950s, when it received grants from philanthropic foundations headquartered generally in New York City. This trend, coupled with the steadily increasing nationwide memberships of the GCA, influenced its leaders to decide, reluctantly, to move national headquarters to New York, which it did in January 1960. Another important organizational event had occurred in 1957 when the GCA established nine geographical regions for its structure.

With its national headquarters in New York, in the 1960s, the GCA continued its basic activities of services to affiliates, developed some organizational changes, and grew a little closer to the national social welfare community, but it never really participated in the innovative and general excitement of the social service field in the 1960s. In April 1960, the GCA established its professional association for staff workers, and the agency began its continuing association with *Reader's Digest* magazine, initiating the first *Reader's Digest* career key awards for girls who belonged to affiliated clubs, which numbered 110 in 1965. Suggesting the nationwide growth of the GCA and of the girls' club movement, the organization founded its first regional headquarters in Los Angeles in 1964. A series of successful fund-raising drives and a sizable donation helped the GCA, in 1967 and early 1968, to purchase and to move to its present national headquarters in a nineteenth-century townhouse on the Upper East Side of Manhattan. Also in 1967, while other national agencies were initiating innovative projects to deal with poverty, housing, and child care, the GCA began with beauty instructor Bonnie Prudden its Fit for Life Institutes for girls.

The GCA did participate in some nationwide trends in social services. In 1967, it formed a federal projects' committee to coordinate local clubs' activities with some federal programs. A survey in the fall of 1968 showed that nearly forty clubs were conducting projects that related to the so-called urban crisis. But, the national organization, the GCA, did few such projects itself. More typical of its activities, in 1968, it developed a Board Van Guard program to strengthen local boards and prepared and then distributed to all member clubs a manual on uniform accounting procedures, a subject that the National Health Council* and the NSWA, the spokesmen in their respective field, had focused on in the 1960s.

Some basic organizational goals and activities were changed in the 1970s, although the GCA continued its general activities. In 1970, for instance, the organization increased services in two areas: field service and, with the appointment of a division of programs and training, leadership training. Funds from the DeWitt Wallace GCA Fund supported a four-day leadership training institute in September 1970, a conference that led to another gathering in April 1971 to restudy the basic purposes and policies of the girls' club movement and of the GCA. At the meeting, the national council formally adopted a new purpose, stressing the development of young girls' confidence. Extensive membership programs and the use of mobile units to reach more girls from low-income families had succeeded, as the membership increased by 15,600 girls in 1971. In the early 1970s, the GCA also appointed a Washington, D.C., representative to develop ties between the agency and the federal government. In the mid-1970s, the GCA stressed physical fitness, a program assisted by Bonnie Prudden. In 1974, the national board and the national council adopted five new goals, launching the GCA into the girls' rights movement. The GCA worked closely with the interagency Collaboration of Youth Serving Agencies and with the women's concerns committee of the National Assembly of National Voluntary Health and

Social Welfare Organizations.* In 1974, the GCA inaugurated a three-year financial development program, featuring a pilot regional fund-raising program in the western region. The agency also developed new national programs in youth leadership, sports, alternative education, and, activities close to the earliest working girls' clubs, career development and delinquency prevention.

The sources for studying the GCA's history are difficult to locate in libraries. At the national headquarters in New York City, however, there are a number of helpful items, including Mrs. J. Herbert Johnson, "History of Girls Clubs of America" (1965), a four-page history by the founder. The agency also has other unpublished histories. For the recent period, there are helpful published *Annual Reports*. Rachel Harris Johnson and Dora Estelle Dodge, *Thirty Years of Girls' Club Experience: A Handbook for Girls' Work Agencies* (1945), has some data on the working women's clubs. There does not appear to be a scholarly history of the GCA.

GOODWILL INDUSTRIES OF AMERICA, INC. (GIA). In the late nineteenth century, Reverend Henry Morgan developed charities at the South End Boston Church. When he died, he left a building for these charitable activities, and he stipulated that a Methodist minister must be in charge. In 1896, Reverend Edgar J. Helms assumed the position of the leader of the now called Morgan Chapel in the South End of Boston, one of the worst slums in the country. In the late 1890s, Reverend Helms began to receive spare clothing from the wealthier people in the church. Donating these and other household items to the poor and to immigrants, Helms grew concerned about the distribution system: some poor people received too much, and others got none. To remedy this situation, Helms decided that the poor should work to renovate the clothing and household items, gaining credit toward the items through their work. Thus began a basic Goodwill activity. In April 1902, the renovated clothing that was not distributed to the workers was sold to other Bostonians, and Helms then divided up the small amount of money earned among the workers. This incident prompted the development of the Goodwill Industries of America, Inc. (GIA), as the Morgan Memorial Cooperative Industries and Stores, Inc. (MMCIS), on August 29, 1905.

Helms's project developed steadily in the early years of the twentieth century. One of the early problems was to maintain the flow of used clothing and household items so the workers could keep active. An associate of Reverend Helms's, Fred Moore, a local coffee and tea merchant, suggested that Helms place discarded coffee bags in the homes of donors, who would then bring them to the Morgan Chapel when full. A representative of a Boston-based coffee firm, Chase and Sanborn Company, donated thousands of such bags, which grew increasingly attractive and became the national symbol of the work of the agency. In 1905, Helms secured a charter for his growing work.

Because of its location in the slums of Boston, the Helms enterprises developed a range of charitable activities. The children's settlement, for example, grew from the work of the organization with poor and even dependent and homeless children. The MMCIS also developed day nurseries for the children of working mothers and families. In Boston, the organization maintained the Eliza A. Henry Home for women and students and a rescue mission, the Fred H. Seavey Seminary Settlement. In South Athol, Massachusetts, the MMCIS maintained a complex that included a fresh air farm for city children and an industrial plantation similar to those of some charity agency colonies.

The work of the MMCIS developed slowly, and the administrative structure of the agency emerged gradually after 1905. Reverend Helms, who was active in the work of the Methodist Federation for Social Service,* helped to charter in 1910, again in Massachusetts, the National Cooperative Industrial Relief Association, Inc. (NCIRA), to stimulate similar church-related programs for the poor in other cities. In 1915, when a group of businessmen from Brooklyn, New York, proposed a program, the name Goodwill Industries began to gain wider use. A total of seven such local agencies were organized by 1918 when the work became affiliated more closely with the Methodist Episcopal church (MEC) structure. In November 1918, the department of city work of the Board of Home Missions and Church Extensions of the MEC organized its Bureau of Goodwill Industries (BGI), but the NCIRA continued as a separate lay agency.

The enterprise, composed of two separate national structures, grew rapidly after affiliating with the MEC. Seeing the potential for the development of such industries in other cities, the Methodist Centenary Fund donated money to organize new self-help programs. This prompted the development of twenty-four new ones by 1924. Each of the local Goodwill Industries remained autonomous from the beginning, each secured a state charter, and each was operated by a local volunteer board. Businessmen, philanthropists, civic, and other leaders generally served on the local boards.

Important changes occurred in the mid-1930s as programs shifted emphases and as structures crystallized. Prompted by large-scale government programs dealing with the poor during the depression and the increased but temporarily limited activities of private relief agencies, the NCIRA moved increasingly to deal with the special groups of the handicapped and the aged. The agency, however, still retained its Christian missionary and charitable enterprises, such as settlements, rescue missions, fresh air farms, housing projects, and the like. An important administrative development occurred in 1933 when the MEC solidified its sponsorship of the BGI, which helped to establish another distinct agency involved in Goodwill work, The National Association of Goodwill Industries, Inc. (NAGI), a nonsectarian organization of local Goodwill Industries, some of which were initiated by local community chests, by civic leaders, and by other nonsectarian sources. The two agencies, each of which had separate administrative boards, shared an executive secretary, founder Edgar Helms. The NAGI assisted the development of new industries, developed and implemented standards for local constituents, accredited them, recruited and trained executive leaders, publicized the work nationally, and the like. The NAGI had a thirty-member lay board of directors, elected annually by the delegate assembly, which represented the constituent groups. An executive committee of the board of directors supervised the work. The organizational structure also included a number of departments that reflected both old and new activities: sales and purchase, fresh air camps, publicity and promotion, and religious and cultural work. Helms was the first national executive, the leading staff position. He retired in June 1939, but he continued to direct the national leadership programs that he had originated, a major organizational activity in the 1930s. In 1939, the national headquarters moved to Milwaukee, Wisconsin, to the offices of the new executive secretary of the local affiliate. In 1940, following the merger of three Methodist church bodies, the BGI became the Department of Goodwill Industries (DGI) of the Board of Home Missions and Church Extension of the new Methodist Church (MC).

Although founded to deal primarily with the poor, in the late 1930s and 1940s, the agency shifted its attention to the physically and mentally handicapped. The general developments that influenced gradually this adaptation were the relief programs of the New Deal and the proliferation of private welfare organizations, which began to duplicate the GIA's efforts for the poor and the advances in physical medicine and rehabilitation work, particularly the federal expansion of vocational rehabilitation through Public Law 565.

The period of World War II helped to crystallize activities for the handicapped as the agency moved further away from serving the aged and the poor. The national wartime slogan, "Salvage for Victory," had special meaning to the Goodwill Industries. The agency increasingly developed workshops for the hand-icapped that produced useful materials from scrap. In 1941, the national institute, a conference that grew from the regional and other training programs of the NAGI, voted to use the *Blue Book of Purpose and Policies,* adopted in 1936, as the guide to providing standards for and accrediting local affiliates. Revised in April 1944, this statement continued to provide guidelines for affiliates. The death of founder Helms on December 23, 1942, ended an era in the history of the movement and the organization. Increasingly, in the early 1940s, local affiliates held contracts in defense-related industries, and in 1944, the Wage and Hour Division of the United States Department of Labor (DL) recognized affiliates meeting the NAGI's standards as sheltered workshops. In the summer of 1943, the NAGI sponsored an institute to develop postwar plans.

The organization expanded in the postwar years. Plans to have both a full-time executive secretary and a staff materialized in 1946, when the NAGI became Goodwill Industries of America, Inc. (GIA). The organization developed new programs to provide work for the handicapped, such as the industries develop-ment committee clinics in 1946 for small industries and the national rehabilita-tion and personnel management conference in Detroit. An aggressive campaign in the late 1940s to develop new affiliates, aided partly by the Methodist church, helped to raise the number to 101 at the end of the decade. GIA gained national prestige when the federal Office of Vocational Rehabilitation distributed a publicity packet—prepared in connection with GIA sponsorship in 1947 of the Employ the Handicapped Week—to every state and local rehabilitation officer. The golden anniversary year, 1952, brought further national publicity. Feature articles in leading popular magazines such as *Time* and *Look,* a major celebration in Lake Geneva, Wisconsin, billboards and car cards on buses and the other displays, a Goodwill float in the Tournament of Roses parade, the film *Salute to Courage,* and a fifteen-minute nationally broadcast radio show starring Kate Smith all focused on Goodwill Industries. In 1957, GIA began to function as part of the federal-state vocational research and demonstration program.

In the 1960s, the GIA developed organizational facilities that established the basis for its national leadership in the expanding field of rehabilitation. Increasingly providing a full range of services for the handicapped, including counseling and guidance, in 1961, the GIA adopted an accreditation plan for the entire network. Early in the decade, the Advertising Council recognized National Goodwill Week, the first week in May. This provided the GIA and its affiliates with considerable publicity. In the early 1960s, the GIA developed its council of executives, which advised the board of directors on vocational training, employment, and other such issues. In mid-1966, an important organizational change occurred when Robert Watkins replaced the retiring Percy J. Trevethan as executive vice-president, the chief administrative officer. This initiated what President Eugene Caldwell heralded as modern administrative practices of rotating both officers and the board.

Beginning in the mid-1960s, the expansion of GIA more clearly than before paralleled the expansion of federal social service programs, especially in the rehabilitation field. In 1966, for example, the GIA received an increase in federal grants. In the next year, with a grant from the Rehabilitation Services Administration (RSA) of the Department of Health, Education, and Welfare (DHEW), the GIA developed its supervisory training program to improve foreman-worker relations in the workshops. Another grant from the RSA in 1967 designed to improve the accounting practices of GIA initiated a series of programs that made the organization a leader in promoting improved accounting systems for other voluntary health and welfare agencies. Continuing this trend, later in the decade, the GIA installed a modern computer center in its national headquarters in Washington, D.C.

The expansion in 1970 of the computer services into a USERS (Uniform Socio-Economic Reporting System) for other agencies, supported by a grant from the Social and Rehabilitation Service (SRS) of the DHEW, suggested the leadership role the GIA played in the 1970s. In 1972, the GIA's department of rehabilitation began to provide complete vocational evaluation and work training guidance to its affiliates, and the education and training department received a large three-year grant from the W. K. Kellogg Foundation to expand its training course for local executives and department heads. By 1972, 115 of the 148 affiliates had joined the GIA standard accounting and comparative financial reporting services. In the early 1970s, the GIA influenced amendments to the Wagner-O'Day Act, expanding the federal purchase of products made in sheltered workshops. Demonstrating its leadership within the Goodwill movement, GIA then helped affiliates to benefit from the legislation. To aid affiliates further, in 1973, GIA established an office of grants administration to help them prepare proposals. In 1974, the GIA developed a national leadership training program with support from the Lilly Endowment, Inc. Beginning in 1974, the department of project development advised affiliates on programs available through the Comprehensive Employment and Training Act of 1973.

In the 1970s, the GIA provided leadership not only for its affiliates but also in the field of rehabilitation generally. In 1972, for instance, it contracted with a leading data processing company to install its USERS in voluntary agencies throughout the country. Its *The State of the Act of Volunteering in Rehabilitation Facilities* helped the entire field. Determining in 1973 to become active in securing a range of rights and benefits for the handicapped, GIA began in 1973 to develop, with the federal Department of Housing and Urban Development, a 292-unit of specialized housing for the handicapped in Houston, Texas. In 1974, with a grant from the DHEW, GIA began a feasibility study for a national center for the handicapped in Washington, D.C., to provide a full range of services.

The primary source for studying the GIA's history is its published but difficult to locate *Annual Reports*. Some of the entries in *The Goodwill Industry: A Manual* (1935), by Helms and others are helpful.

Horace W. Kimbrell, *This Is Goodwill Industries* (1962), and Percy J. Trevethan, "Goodwill Industries" in Nolan B. Harmon, ed., *The Encyclopedia of World Methodism* (1974) 1: 1021–1022, are brief histories by GIA leaders. There does not appear to be a scholarly history of this veteran agency.

_H

HEBREW SHELTERING AND IMMIGRANT AID SOCIETY (HIAS). As immigrant Jews entered the United States in the late nineteenth century, a number of immigrant aid organizations were established. Most relief agencies were established by generally assimilated German Jews rather than Eastern European Jews. One of the first aid organizations founded by Eastern European Jews was the Hebrew Sheltering Society (HSS), or the Hevra Hachnosas Orchim. Established in New York City on November 23, 1889, the

HSS's purpose was to feed, clothe, and lodge immigrants and to help them find jobs. The HSS provided lodgings at 210 Madison Street in New York, which became so busy during the 1890s that expansion seemed inevitable. As Jewish immigration increased, so did the organizations. In 1902, in New York City, the Hebrew Immigrant Aid Society (HIAS) was established as a typical *landsman-shaften* organization, a self-help society of people from the same locale in the old country. HIAS's original purpose was to help provide a traditional burial for immigrants who died on Ellis Island, the point of entrance. But it broadened its activities gradually to aid immigrants generally. With the volume of Jewish immigration increasing dramatically in the first decade of the twentieth century, these two groups agreed to combine their efforts to provide better services. Consequently, in New York City, on March 16, 1909, the Hebrew Sheltering and Immigrant Aid Society (HIAS) was established. Unlike most of the other turn-of-the-century Jewish charities, HIAS began and developed as a group for and led by Eastern European Jews, themselves recent immigrants. Uptown, more assimilated, philanthropic German Jews, however, supported the new organization.

In the first few years, the merger worked smoothly. The forty-member board of directors had twenty people from each predecessor organization, and a similar mix filled the important offices. The president, Judge Leon Sanders, for example, had served the HSS. One of the two vice-presidents was Leon Kamaiky, a publisher of Yiddish newspapers, an Orthodox leader, and, for many years, the Hebrew Immigrant Aid Society representative at Ellis Island. The general manager was Samuel Mason from the same predecessor organization. A fifteen-member advisory board included such important leaders in the American Jewish community as Jacob Schiff, Louis Marshall, Oscar Straus, Cyrus Sulzberger, Stephen Wise, all from New York, and Simon Wolf of Washington, D.C.

In this pre–World War I phase, which represented the period of greatest Jewish immigration, HIAS expanded its services and facilities to meet the needs that arose. In August 1911, it developed a national board of directors with representatives throughout the United States. Directors' reports included data on immigrant adjustment in their areas. By 1913, there were 918 national directors working with HIAS, and branches were established in Boston, Philadelphia, and Baltimore. Throughout the period, the Ellis Island bureau, which the HSS had opened in 1892, helped numerous immigrants, battling officials to permit their entry, finding them both jobs and their relatives, and lodging them temporarily in the organization's shelter in New York.

Between its inception in 1909 and August 1914, when World War I began, HIAS marked its first phase of development as an outstanding immigrant aid organization. Its employment bureau cooperated with other groups, such as the United Hebrew Charities of the City of New York* (UHC) and the Industrial Removal Office* (IRO), to find jobs. Like the later Kehillah experiment—to impose a formal community structure in New York City—HIAS often mediated conflicts between workers and their employers. HIAS's department of education organized English classes and helped immigrants attain citizenship. In 1911, HIAS established an Oriental department to help Sephardic Jews. Discovering that some immigrants who refused to eat nonkosher food became weak and malnourished and were deported, the Ellis Island bureau established a kosher kitchen for the immigrants in 1911. Simon Wolf in Washington, D.C., worked closely with the law committee in New York to argue cases for particular immigrants, and Wolf became the counsel when HIAS opened a permanent Washington office in 1913. Between 1912 and 1920, the organization published the *Jewish Information Bulletin* in both Yiddish and English.

HIAS expanded its activities further in the war and postwar periods, developing facilities abroad to help oppressed Jews. By 1922, for instance, the organization had established offices in Poland, Rumania, Latvia, Lithuania, Danzig, Turkey, and France. When restrictive American immigration laws in the mid-1920s limited settlement in the United States, HIAS strove to help oppressed Jews settle in Mexico, Canada, and Cuba. This activity established a HIAS pattern of finding countries for emigrating Jews. In the famous "St. Louis Affair" in 1939, HIAS worked to have France, England, and Belgium each take about three hundred German Jews who had traveled to Cuba only to be rejected there. In 1936, the agency effected a reduction in Russian passport fees to $40; they had ranged between $550 and $1,100. HIAS cooperated with other international agencies, particularly the Jewish Colonization Society (ICA) and the Emig-direkt, which HIAS had helped to establish in 1921. When World War II began and ICA could not spend funds outside the British sterling area, HIAS doubled its commitment to its Eastern European transportation fund to help get Jews out of these increasingly oppressive countries. With the ICA, HIAS helped 14,145 emigrants to reach Palestine between 1933 and 1939.

HIAS continued to work energetically throughout the trying period of World War II. The joint HIAS-ICA office was forced out of Marseilles, France, but agency leaders moved the office to New York. Between 1941 and 1945, the two organizations worked to open Latin America further for Jewish refugees. In 1944, HIAS helped to establish the American Council of Voluntary Agencies for Foreign Service,* and HIAS issued a pamphlet, *Free Ports for Refugees,* urging the United States to accept refugees. Throughout the war period, the employment bureau placed immigrants in war-related industries.

With other agencies in the American social welfare community, HIAS participated actively in the humanitarian efforts in behalf of refugees and other oppressed people in the postwar period. But, because of the unique condition of Jews abroad, HIAS's efforts had special importance. With European headquarters established in Paris, HIAS had representatives in the displaced persons camps. Cooperating with the American Jewish Joint Distribution Committee* (JDC), HIAS established the displaced person coordinating committee, which functioned through late 1951, when the immigration of displaced persons to

America virtually ended. Following Allied troops to liberated areas, HIAS established offices to help refugees. In early 1944, HIAS organized at the New School for Social Research in New York a course to prepare social workers to deal with refugees. HIAS established alien registration bureaus throughout the country to comply with the Internal Security Act of 1950, and it campaigned actively for the repeal of the McCarran-Walter Act, which severely restricted immigration to the United States. After launching a sheltering program for refugees in Israel in July 1951, HIAS was designated by Cooperative for American Remittances to Europe* (CARE) as the official American agency to accept CARE relief for Israel.

To avoid duplication and to make refugee and displaced persons work more effective, United States Service for Americans,* the migration services of the JDC, and HIAS signed an agreement to merge on December 23, 1953. Lengthy discussions finally produced compromises, particularly HIAS's insistence on preserving its name, methods, and fund raising. Nevertheless, on August 30, 1954, HIAS's thirty-member board of directors—with some internal opposition—voted to join with the others to establish the new United HIAS Service.*

The primary sources for studying the HIAS's history are voluminous. In 1976, the YIVO institute for Jewish Research in New York City had about two million microfilm frames and about 2,400 linear feet of materials deposited by the agency, which continues to send its materials to YIVO. There is an index to this huge collection; it is in Yiddish. *The New York Times* reported agency activities. The published *Annual Reports* contain helpful details.

Students interested in HIAS's history should begin with Mark Wischnitzer, *Visas to Freedom: The History of HIAS* (1956), a gripping story of refugees, displaced persons, and other problems and calamities. Many other publications in American Jewish history, such as Moses Rischin, *The Promised City: New York's Jews, 1870–1914* (1962), mention the agency, and the brief entry for HIAS in the *Encyclopedia Judaica* (1971), 15: 1539–1540, is a convenient, helpful, short sketch.

HENRY STREET SETTLEMENT URBAN LIFE CENTER (HSSULC). Between 1889 and 1910, four hundred settlement houses opened in cities across the country, including New York City's Neighborhood Guild, College Settlement, and Henry Street Settlement (HSS), Chicago's Hull-House,* and Boston's South End House. The idea of settlement by social reformers in poverty-stricken neighborhoods was developed by an Anglican clergyman, Canon Samuel Barnett, who in 1884 had founded Toynbee Hall in Whitechapel, London. The settlement idea appealed to some youthful, eager Americans, many of whom were educated and middle class and sensitive to the consequences of nineteenth-century industrialization and urbanization. The nation of yeoman farmers envisioned by Thomas Jefferson was rapidly being transformed, and although America remained primarily rural and small town in 1890, the significance of the city and factory loomed large in the national consciousness. Rural Americans who had moved to urban areas seeking work and new immigrants, with languages and customs understood by few, were crowded together in dirty tenements marked by inhumane sanitation and health conditions. Individuals took up residence in settlement houses and neighborhood centers in order to do something about the second nation, urban and industrial, growing up around them.

Henry Street Settlement Urban Life Center (HSSULC) was established on the Lower East Side of New York City in July 1893 by two nurses, Lillian D. Wald and Mary M. Brewster. Both founders were enrolled at the Women's Medical College in Philadelphia but were deflected from their plans to become doctors through visits to the indigent sick of the East Side. Moved by the unhealthy conditions of the community populated by Jews, Italians, and Irish, the two nurses proposed "to move into the neighborhood; to carry on volunteer nursing, and contribute our citizenship to what seemed an alien group in a so-called democratic community."

In September 1893, Wald and Brewster located Nurses' Settlement (NS), as it was initially named, in a rented top floor of a tenement house. Fortified with Board of Health badges, they explored neighboring tenement houses and provided medical care. Shortly after their work began, Brewster resigned because of illness, but Wald continued to offer private home nursing service. She interested philanthropic New Yorkers such as Mrs. Solomon Loeb and her banker son-in-law, Jacob Schiff, in aiding her financially and, within two years, calls for nursing services multiplied so rapidly that the house at 265 Henry Street was purchased to provide accommodations for more nurses. Furthermore, the pattern was set for the support of settlement activities primarily through financial gifts from the wealthy. In the 1960s, this pattern was eventually supplemented and then supplanted through grants from public funds.

NS offered a nonsectarian private home nursing service that the family could pay for according to its means, thus eliminating the stigma attached to the free nursing services of charity clinics and various religious groups. Wald soon realized that providing medical care alone was not enough; the settlement nurses expanded their program to include preventive medical care through education in hygiene. This program, however, was insignificant in view of the intense poverty of their patients, who lacked the means to battle the unsanitary conditions of the slums.

Under Wald's leadership, the HSS was incorporated on March 27, 1903, and began to press the city government for needed reforms and to offer more varied services to the community. Settlement leaders learned that it was impossible to transform the neighborhood slum without also changing urban society. Genuine change in areas such as child labor, working conditions, housing, sanitation, and education could not be effected on the neighborhood level alone. All of these matters involved public policy, which was decided in city halls and state houses. Recognizing the importance of influencing this policy, Wald and other settlement leaders were soon involved in lobbying for legislation, promoting political candidates, and serving on advisory committees and on public boards.

Social research through investigations and surveys was a significant tool of the settlement leaders. During its early history, HSS conducted numerous social research projects, including investigations of dispossessed tenants (1897), the licensing of midwives (1907), unemployment (1908), child labor (1908), and working conditions for girls in department stores, factories, and canneries (1909).

In addition to social research programs designed to influence public policy, the settlement residents strove to improve local health conditions. In 1893, realizing the danger to the community from those suffering from tuberculosis, Wald's nurses sought out the afflicted, visited them, provided disinfectants and other necessities, and instructed the patients on proper hygiene. In 1905, the city's Department of Health, convinced of the program's usefulness, systematically took over the tuberculosis work of the HSS nurses.

HSS cooperated in a campaign for public recreation facilities. In 1895, the settlement created one of the first playgrounds in the city after Wald noticed the great numbers of injuries incurred by children who played in the streets. The settlement was also instrumental in securing Seward Park and Corlears Hook Park as recreational areas for the Lower East Side neighborhoods. In addition to providing areas for recreation, the settlement organized and supervised play, sports, folk dancing, theatricals, parties, clubs, and courses in arts and applied crafts.

The first residents of the settlement knew that poor health and hunger contributed to a high level of truancy among neighborhood children. HSS succeeded in establishing medical inspection in the public schools, bringing to the attention of the Department of Health children suffering from diphtheria, scarlet fever, and pneumonia. The inspection system proved inadequate, however, because the ill children were suspended from school and tended not to return. The settlement proposed in 1902 to demonstrate to city health and education officials the value of a public school nursing service to supplement the medical inspectors. Through the efforts of these first public school nurses, whose salaries were paid by HSS, the health of students improved, and truancy resulting from illness subsided. The city soon thereafter adopted the model program.

The public school nursing system coincided with the settlement's concern for the adequate care of the sick in their homes, which was the primary mover in the settlement's establishment. The nursing staff increased from two in 1893 to fifteen in 1900 to forty-seven by 1909 and to ninety-two nurses by 1913. By then, the nurses were visiting more than 200,000 patients annually. The settlement established a citywide system of visiting nurses and provided first-aid stations, convalescent homes, a staff for the care of contagious diseases, and a milk and baby hygiene clinic. In establishing this extensive nursing service, in 1896, HSS created a branch on the Upper East Side, Uptown Nurses' Settlement, a branch in the Bronx in 1906, and Stillman Branch for Colored People in 1906 on the West Side of New York City.

The HSS worked continuously for an improved educational system. The residents campaigned in the first decade of 1900 for more and better schools, study rooms for students living in small tenement apartments, and school lunches. The settlement provided space for public school kindergartens, encouraged adult education, and sponsored a number of scholarships for talented students to enable them to pursue their education in high schools, colleges, and trade, technical, and art schools.

In 1900, HSS pioneered in the establishment of experimental ungraded classes for mentally deficient children. The HSS staff provided special equipment, medical treatment, and lunches and made visits to the children's homes. In 1906, the city established this program as a special department in the public school system.

HSS was dependent solely on voluntary contributions and was always in need of funds, so its twentieth-anniversary celebration in 1913 provided an opportunity for an endowment campaign, which proved successful. Wald's ability to express her enthusiasm for the settlement's programs made her a talented fund raiser. As one friend observed, "It costs five thousand dollars to sit next to her at dinner." Although Wald's settlement aims were generally supported by her wealthy supporters, many patrons quickly withdrew their financial support for HSS because of Wald's unyielding pacifism during World War I. Others withdrew their support in protest against her aid to the Progressive party and a cloakmakers' strike and her involvement with the Women's Trade Union League.

Despite these financial setbacks, HSS expanded its services in many areas between 1913 and 1918. The number of settlement nurses doubled in this period and provided invaluable service during the influenza epidemic of 1918.

Another area of expansion was in the dramatic arts. In 1904, three young women gifted in the arts, Alice and Irene Lewisohn and Rita Wallach Morganthau, became volunteers at HSS. Beginning with their informal dance and drama lessons, the women found enough enthusiasm and creativity that the end result was the establishment of the famous Neighborhood Playhouse in 1915, one of the most important arenas of the little theater movement. The affiliation of HSS with the Neighborhood Playhouse lasted until 1927 when the Lewisohns and Morganthau moved uptown to open a new school for drama and dance. The theater on Grand Street was renamed the Henry Street Playhouse and continued to provide excellent productions.

The Henry Street Music School also came into being in 1927 and was attached to the playhouse. Besides lessons, the school had numerous groups that supplied music for all occasions. The music school and playhouse were licensed by the New York State Board of Regents following World War II. The HSS Dance

School, directed by Alwin Nikolais, was then created, and together with Murray Louis and Betty Young, the HSS Playhouse again became a center for serious and important artistic endeavors.

HSS created one of the first vocational counseling services in the country in 1920 to aid young people in finding suitable employment. This counseling formed the basis for the Vocational Advisory Service, which later worked in cooperation with the New York State Employment Service.

Wald's health began to worsen by the mid-1920s. She weakened further through her attempts to aid those affected by the Great Depression, and in 1933, shortly after its fortieth anniversary, she resigned as head worker at HSS. She had actually relinquished effective control of HSS two years earlier, leaving Karl Hesley in charge of settlement programs and Margaret Wales the nursing service.

The board of directors in 1933 asked Helen Hall to succeed Wald as head worker of HSS, a position she held from 1933 to 1967. Former head worker at Philadelphia's University Settlement and president of the National Federation of Settlements,* Hall was among the second generation of settlement workers; like Wald, she was committed to social action and justice.

Following her involvement in a nationwide study of unemployment conditions in settlement neighborhoods during the Great Depression, Hall created a community studies department at HSS. Investigations of neighborhood conditions had always been a primary function of the settlement, but Hall created the department in order to conduct systematic and continuous studies of economic and social conditions on the East Side. The department investigated the problem of single homeless men in the area (1933), unemployment (1933), milk consumption in relation to family income (1934), housing conditions (1935), medical care in families on relief (1935), industrial survey of wartime wages and expenditures (1944), and numerous other surveys and investigations. While these could not all be called objective reports, they did serve to stimulate legislative activity.

When Helen Hall arrived at HSS, settlement work and the nursing service were technically under one administration. The visiting nurses had grown to include 265 nurses working in three boroughs. A social worker and not a nurse, Hall separated the two services administratively in 1937, and seven years later two separate corporations were formed, with the nursing service becoming the Visiting Nurse Service of New York.

With the advent of public housing in the 1930s, the settlement was faced with changing its strategy for providing services. No longer could the staff easily reach their neighbors, who were now hidden in large low-income housing projects. With the cooperation of the New York Housing Authority, HSS was provided with space in Vladeck Houses to provide such services as the home planning workshops, craft classes, and the whole range of settlement programs.

In 1946, HSS established the first neighborhood mental health clinic, which served as a model throughout the nation. The clinic was founded to make psychiatric help available to the poor as a preventive tool rather than just a service for advanced emotional problems.

Throughout the post–World War II period, the ethnic population of the Lower East Side changed rapidly. Up to this time, the neighborhood had been composed mainly of Russian Jews, with some Italian and Irish representation, and those who were able to move away from the slums were replaced by blacks, Puerto Ricans, and some Chinese. The changing nature of the populace resulted in many problems, especially among the young. Juvenile delinquency was the most blatant manifestation of the hostility between old and new neighbors. In the late 1950s, HSS initiated many programs within the community to combat juvenile delinquency, including a predelinquent project in 1956. A year earlier, the Lower East Side Neighborhood Association was founded at HSS; it included representatives from all the ethnic groups, religious leaders, social workers, businessmen, union leaders, and policemen. In 1957, a demonstration program, Mobilization for Youth (MY), which originated at HSS, went into effect to stem the near-epidemic proportions of juvenile delinquency.

Improved health care for the people of the area, especially in the form of a new hospital to replace the old Gouverneur Hospital, which was built in 1880, was also a settlement goal in this era. After forty years of battle, a new Gouverneur Hospital was completed in 1973.

The meaning of the settlement idea changed irrevocably during the 1960s. No longer could settlements claim to be the sole articulate representative of the dispossessed, as many community-based organizations proliferated throughout the nation's ghettos. The idea that individual settlements and leaders belonged to a historical movement dedicated to long-range goals with widespread implications for areas outside a particular neighborhood was replaced with ideas that are more parochial and presentist in nature and that are related more closely to providing services for a community. These changes undoubtedly have numerous causes, not least of which is the notion that community problems are best dealt with by members of the community itself.

The implications of self-determination led to many changes in settlement leadership, and HSS was not immune to change. In 1967, Helen Hall retired, partly because of her advanced age (seventy-five) and partly because of a movement away from the model of settlement leaders as social activists. A new breed of leaders—such as Bertram Beck, who viewed himself as a resource person interested in service-oriented programs—increasingly served and led settlements.

To replace Hall, the board of directors asked Bertram Beck to become executive director of the settlement. Former director of MY and associate director of the National Association of Social Workers,* Beck agreed with the shift in settlement roles: "I am personally less certain as to what are the paths in life that people should follow than some early settlement people were. Our focus is on people defining for themselves where they want to go in life."

Another significant change in settlement houses was in the method of funding programs. HSS had depended almost entirely on private donations for its existence for about seventy years. In 1975, however, government funding accounted for two-thirds of the HSS annual budget of $4.5 million. Many of the staff of five hundred were involved in programs contracted with government units as ways of providing services that otherwise would be left to large, centralized bureaucracies. The program included day care, remedial education, housing for families who would otherwise live in welfare hotels, a junior high school for troubled children excluded from the public school system, and a work release program for teenagers in trouble with the courts. The settlement also continued to offer programs for preschoolers, schoolchildren, adults, and the elderly. The new Arts for Living Center building provided more space for the performing and visual arts. To accentuate the new settlement role, HSS in the early 1970s was renamed the HSSULC.

The primary source for studying the HSSULC consists largely of the settlement's papers deposited at the Social Welfare History Archives, University of Minnesota, Minneapolis. Also on deposit at the archives are the Papers of Helen Hall and the Lower East Side Neighborhood Association. For the settlement's early history, the Lillian Wald Papers at the New York Public Library and at Columbia University should be consulted. Also helpful are Lillian Wald's two books, *The House on Henry Street* (1915) and *Windows on Henry Street* (1934), and Helen Hall's autobiography, *Unfinished Business* (1971). Although there is no scholarly study of the history of HSS, there is a historical study of its music school by a former director of the school, Robert F. Egan, "The History of the Music School of the Henry Street Settlement" (Ph.D. diss., New York University, 1967).

William Wallach

HULL-HOUSE: see HULL-HOUSE ASSOCIATION.

HULL-HOUSE ASSOCIATION (HHA). The origins of Hull-House (HH), the most famous settlement in the United States, related to the personal experiences of its cofounder and long-time leader, Jane Addams, whose name became synonymous with the concept of social welfare and reform in the United States in the early twentieth century. Miss Addams, as she was called by residents and others throughout her years at HH, grew up in a modestly wealthy family from rural Illinois, traveled to Europe, attended college and even, for a while, the famous Women's Medical College in Philadelphia, suffered from apparently psychosomatic illnesses, and, right before she helped to establish HH, was moved by spiritual and religious factors. She was baptized at the Presbyterian church in Cedarville, Illinois, in late 1888, and about a year later, she became a member in full standing. In Chicago in 1889, she and Ellen Gates Starr, a former classmate at Rockford College, took classes in industrial arts and volunteered to teach a class at a training school, which soon became the Moody Bible Institute.

As Jane Addams's biographer, historian Allen F. Davis, wrote, "her commitment to live in a working class neighborhood [was] essentially a religious act." In late January 1889, she and Starr rented an apartment in Chicago and began to search for support for their venture to work and teach in an inner-city neighborhood. Speaking to such groups as the Chicago Women's Club, a local and influential civic action group, the local Women's Christian Temperance Union, and as expected, church groups, the young women attracted surprising numbers of supporters. Jane Addams was the most important figure in the establishment of HH, but Starr was especially important in translating Miss Addams's ideas into social action.

HH was not the first such social settlement in the United States. Influenced by the experiences of one in England, Toynbee Hall, for instance, the Neighborhood Guild was established, chiefly by Stanton Coit, in New York City in 1886. In 1887, some Smith College graduates established the College Settlement Association, but Miss Addams and her cofounder were unaware of these precedents when they began their venture in September 1889. On September 18, 1889, the two young women moved into a deteriorating old mansion on Halsted Street in Chicago. The house had been built in 1856 for an early real estate man and philanthropist in Chicago, Charles J. Hull.

The activities at HH—the founders experimented with other names, but they settled quickly on HH—began slowly, reflecting the interests of the two young women. The institution soon became a place of enormous energy and activity. Reflecting their earlier experiences in teaching at the Moody Bible Institute, the young women began teaching, lecturing, and explaining their art objects to the people of the neighborhood. The early emphasis on art was due especially to Ellen Starr, who saw art as a way to relieve the pervasive drabness of their urban neighborhood. The activities at HH quickly attracted other women interested in such work. In the first year, for example, Julia Lathrop, a graduate of Rockford College in Illinois and beginning in 1912, the first chief of the new United States Children's Bureau, joined the group and became one of its most important residents. Another early resident was Aliza Stevens, a former labor leader, who, with Florence Kelley—who became a resident in late December 1891 and head of the National Consumers' League* (NCL) in 1899—helped involve HH in labor organizing and activities. Another influential figure in this early period was Mary Kenny, a labor organizer who, with the help of Miss Addams and others, established in 1891 the Jane Club for working young women.

Reflecting the founders' interests, the Butler Art Gallery was added to the HH building in 1891. In 1893, HH founded its music school. In this period, the residents also began a kindergarten, hoping to interest the neighborhood mothers in their activities. HH also organized homemaker clubs and conducted other social activities. Labor unions often met in HH during this period. Because they lived close to impoverished and struggling people and because of their sensitivity to social injustices, the HH residents became early students of urban life, or sociology. Leading others of their generation—historian Robert Bremner called it the "statistical generation"—the HH residents analyzed conditions, for instance, those of children. Data from firsthand studies by Kelley and Aliza Stevens resulted in "Wage Earning Children," which appeared in *Hull-House Maps and Papers* (1885), an influential publication. In 1895, the Children's Building, often called the Smith Building after its benefactors, was completed. In 1896, the organization began to publish *Hull-House Bulletin,* which appeared monthly except during the summer. In 1902, it became a semiannual publication, and in 1906, it became the *Hull-House Year Book,* an annual report of activities.

During the later years of the Progressive era, HH was a center of intellectual ferment and social reform in Chicago and the nation. Two local agencies of national significance, the Juvenile Protective Association of Chicago* (JPA) and the Immigrants Protective League* (IPL) were both housed in HH. In 1901, the HH staff helped to organize the first major survey of housing conditions in Chicago. A resident, Robert Hunter, directed the study. During the early years of the twentieth century, HH residents investigated the licensing and practices of midwives in the city. In 1903, the citywide attempt to get municipal ownership of the street railways was based at HH. On the national level, HH residents helped to organize the National Women's Trade Union League and the National Child Labor Committee* (NCLC) in 1904. Classes at HH in English and American government helped to Americanize their immigrant neighbors. Indeed, as Allen F. Davis and Mary McCree argued, an HH graduate or resident was involved in virtually every reform campaign in the social justice Progressive movement. HH and its leaders, especially Miss Addams, bore the brunt of attacks charging that HH harbored and aided radicals and socialists.

In the period from the beginning of World War I through 1935, when Jane Addams died, HH lost some of the vitality it had displayed during the Progressive era. The financial situation of HH suffered as donors withdrew their support because of Miss Addams's controversial pacifism and opposition to the war. HH, however, vigorously supported the war. Its band went overseas to entertain the troops, and there was a Selective Service recruiting station at HH, which also participated patriotically in conservation efforts. Residents conducted special campaigns to finance war relief. Despite these contributions, superpatriots viewed HH as an unpatriotic, communistic place in the 1920s. Leading contributors of the earlier period were dying, and potential other supporters feared HH's reputed radicalism. Miss Addams refused also to join the local community chest, a stance that contributed to declining income. Only her personal efforts to raise funds kept HH solvent during this period. There was also a problem in the 1920s of attracting bright, young reformers. Young people entering the field seemed to choose social work as a profession rather than as a crusade.

HH was really not a vital institution in the 1920s, but it still conducted social services for neighborhood residents. During the early years of the Great Depression, HH raised emergency funds for people who could not qualify for regular charity, and it lent rent money to people faced with eviction. The agency also provided free milk for infants and lunch money for schoolchildren. In January–February 1932, over 100,000 families appealed to HH for food. Beginning in 1933, several residents of HH cooperated with and worked for New Deal social service agencies. HH's diversity was revealed in the mid-1930s: some gangland figures participated in plays and art classes, promoting rumors that HH harbored them also. Miss Addams's death in May 1935 truly marked the end of an era of this "remarkable institution." Indeed the personification of HH, Jane Addams had headed the board of trustees and was the head resident. Consequently, her death precipitated a series of organizational crises in the years ahead.

Because HH lacked strong leadership, confusion generally characterized the period between the mid-1930s and the early 1940s. Long-time supporter Louise DeKoven Bowen assumed the leadership when she became president of the board of trustees. She urged that the new head resident be Adena Miller Rich, who had been an HH resident for fifteen years. Rich took the position with the conditions that she receive no salary and that she serve only half-time so she could continue as director of the IPL, also a half-time post. Rich continued the traditional HH programs. Her interests also led to the creation of a new department of naturalization and citizenship, as well as a new housing and sanitation committee to improve such conditions in the neighborhood. Headed by Professor Wayne McMillen of the University of Chicago, a respected figure in the national social work community, this committee helped to influence officials to build the Jane Addams Homes, a public housing project in the HH neighborhood.

A financial crisis in the mid-1930s prompted Bowen to lead in the establishment of the Jane Addams Memorial Fund. In late 1935, HH hired Kennicott Brenton, a social worker with experience in fund raising, to raise money. The continuing depression in the country, the absence of Jane Addams, and the development of other charities in Chicago made funds increasingly difficult to obtain. Finally, the HH leaders decided to seek support from the community fund, a path Miss Addams had resisted. An eight-year power struggle between President Bowen and Head Resident Rich developed largely because of the unclear definition of power, a new situation because under Miss Addams, there had been only one source of power; the president and the head resident were the same person. Bowen and the board of trustees usually won the conflicts because they controlled the funds. At any rate, in April 1937, Rich resigned, partly because the Chicago Community Fund demanded a full-time, salaried head resident. Bowen influenced the board to hire Charlotte Carr, the director of the New York City Emergency Relief Bureau, as the new head resident.

Under Carr as head resident in the late 1930s and early 1940s, HH was reorganized, and it expanded its activities in what was becoming known as community organization. HH had had a generally informal administrative structure, but Carr tightened it up. She consolidated departments and committees, eliminated others, and created two new sections. The new community service department formally organized HH's work in behalf of different nationalities. This department also organized community clubs to improve the neighborhood, an early bit of community organization. The new workers' education department was closer to Carr's heart than other HH activities. It was formed basically from the naturalization and citizenship department that Rich had developed. An organizational highlight during this period was the fiftieth birthday party, held May 17–26, 1940. HH's significance as a pioneering urban social service was reflected in the participation of not only Mayor Edward Kelly of Chicago but also of Mayor Fiorello La Guardia of New York. More at ease in talking in saloons about labor problems than discussing settlement house work with residents, Carr left HH in late 1942. At this point, HH was closer to its demise as a settlement than ever before in its history. The end of federal social programs hurt, especially the Works Project Administration, which supported many HH projects. The war was creating problems, such as the need to have day care for the children of working mothers, but funds were difficult to attract. Many residents, staff, and volunteers left either because of Carr's departure or to join the war effort. For a period, there was no head resident or directory, and the finances, staff, and activities became disorganized.

During the next era of HH's history, from 1943 to the mid-1960s, social services and community organization continued, but some significant changes occurred. In 1943, for the first time and over the initial protests of Bowen, a man became the head resident. An experienced social worker and administrator, Russell Ward Ballard had special expertise in youth work. Among other things the former director of the Illinois State Training School for Boys at St. Charles, Ballard tried to make youth work a major activity once again. His talents were especially valuable in dealing with the problems of juvenile delinquency, which he saw as related to bad housing. HH's heritage of community organization and housing reform combined to promote citizen participation in redevelopment planning affecting the HH neighborhood.

During this period, lack of funds continued to reduce programs. Bowen was no longer active on the board, which was more businesslike than earlier boards and which seemed to lack the HH tradition of social activism. Head Resident Ballard, however, did not have problems with the president, as had his two predecessors, Rich and Carr. HH activities with the community led to the establishment of the Near West Side Planning Board in 1949. A study in 1957–1958 showed that many people using HH were not from the immediate neighborhood but traveled there from different parts of the city. In light of this situation, the board developed plans in the late 1950s and early 1960s to decentralize HH. Meanwhile, during this period, HH was notified that the University of Illinois was buying its site and its environs to create a new urban campus. The community groups that HH fostered were justifiably angered, and they appealed to the board for help. The board, however, refused to fight city officials. A symposium on the future of the settlement, held in June 1961 at the Bowen Country Club after the loss of the site to the university, seemed to confirm the idea of decentralization. By November 1962, HH had three new settlement facilities throughout the city. On March 5, 1963, the board accepted $875,000 from the city of Chicago for the buildings. During this period, with the actual physical destruction of HH, the group became known as Hull-House Association (HHA).

An obviously new era for HH began in February 1962 when Ballard retired and was replaced by Paul Jans, who came from the Lighthouse, a settlement in Philadelphia. Jans brought the idea of Meals on Wheels for the aged and an enthusiasm for music, theater, and the arts. The HHA was bolstered by the federal welfare programs of the mid-1960s. By 1968, for instance, HHA was administering about $1 million per year through the federal poverty programs. HHA had a training center for Volunteers in Service to America (VISTA), as well as Head Start and neighborhood leadership programs. From 1962 to 1969, the staff grew from thirty or forty people to over three hundred. The budget expanded accordingly: from well under $1 million to $2 million in 1969. The demise of the federal poverty program during the Nixon administration brought financial problems to the agency once again. In March-April 1969, budget cuts affected especially the arts head resident Jans had promoted, and in early April 1969, he resigned as head resident.

In the early 1970s, with its decentralization plan implemented, the HHA provided a full array of social services. In the mid-1970s, it had neighborhood centers in about twenty locations throughout the Chicago area; seven of these were settlement houses. Reminiscent of Jane Addams's and Ellen Starr's earliest activities and interests, the HHA had a large-scale day-care program, to which the agency allocated about half its funds. The HHA program also included such services as drug and job counseling and home-delivered meals for the elderly.

More than any other American settlement, HH has been studied by historians. Students should begin first with the publications of historian Allen F. Davis, such as *Spearheads for Reform: The Social Settlements and the Progressive Movement, 1890–1914* (1967), which conveys the significance of HH in promoting reform, and *American Heroine: The Life and Legend of Jane Addams* (1973). With Mary Lynn McCree, Davis edited *Eighty Years at Hull-House* (1969), which is more a history of the institution itself than his other two publications. It contains documents relating to HH's history through the 1960s, and its well-informed introductions give the reader information about its history. A host of standard publications in the field, such as Clarke Chambers, *Seedtime for Reform* (1963), deal with HH, but there is, despite the considerable attention to it by historians, no detailed and scholarly history of this important agency.

As the sample of primary sources in Davis and McCree, *Eighty Years,* suggests, the contemporary publications about HH were diverse and voluminous. Standard guides to the literature, as well as a careful study of the sources

Davis has used, provide materials for further study of this important institution. The Jane Addams Papers at numerous places, but especially at the Swarthmore College Peace Collection and at the University of Illinois-Chicago Circle, are essential sources. Other collections at the Manuscript Division of the University of Illinois-Chicago Circle contain primary sources about HH as do a host of archives around the country, such as the Social Welfare History Archives Center at the University of Minnesota, Minneapolis, the Wisconsin State Historical Society in Madison, and the Arthur and Elizabeth Schlesinger Library at Radcliffe College in Cambridge, Massachusetts. These are just a sample of the primary sources. A fuller account of the relevant sources can be found in Davis's publications, essential studies for the serious student of HH.

___ *I* _____

IMMIGRANTS' PROTECTIVE LEAGUE OF CHICAGO: see IMMIGRANTS' SERVICE LEAGUE, THE.

IMMIGRANTS' SERVICE LEAGUE, THE (ISL). In the late nineteenth and early twentieth centuries, social workers and reformers became concerned about the plight of single, foreign-born, recently arrived women in America's large cities, where they seemed likely targets for exploitation. In response to these concerns, the Women's Trade Union League (WTUL) (see *Labor Unions*) of Chicago, which was close to the social work and social reform communities, established an immigration committee to assist such women. By 1908, the WTUL concluded that its protective work with alien women should be extended to all newcomers and supported by a separate association. Consequently, in Chicago, on April 9, 1908, the Immigrants' Service League (ISL) was founded as the Immigrants' Protective League (IPL). Although a local organization, the IPL epitomized similar efforts in other major urban immigrant centers to help the frequently bewildered newcomers, mostly Southern and Eastern Europeans. Furthermore, many of the league's founders and supporters, who were leading Chicago social workers and philanthropists, also had national reputations and envisioned their local programs as examples for broader state and national efforts.

The IPL's leading ideologues were Jane Addams of Hull-House* (HH) and her protégé, Grace Abbott, the league's director from 1908 until 1921, when she became head of the federal Children's Bureau. Other major supporters of the organization, all of whom were closely associated with Miss Addams in a multitude of projects, were Sophonisba P. Breckinridge, a distinguished authority on child welfare and labor legislation and prominent in the research department of the Chicago School of Civics and Philanthropy; Julia Lathrop, active at HH and first director of the federal Children's Bureau beginning in 1912; Mary E. McDowell, head resident of the University of Chicago Settlement; Sabina Marshall, Agnes Nestor, and Margaret Dreier Robins, all of the Chicago WTUL and the latter on the staff of Graham Taylor's famous settlement, Chicago Commons; and Julius Rosenwald, one of the city's leading philanthropists and humanitarians, who contributed nearly 10 percent of the IPL's annual budget from 1912 through 1916.

Reflecting the values of many social reformers in the early twentieth century, Abbott and the IPL rejected the increasingly influential and racially based movement for immigration restriction and asserted that the newcomers would make significant economic and cultural contributions to the United States if they were protected from exploitation, acquainted with the nation's ideals, and assisted in adjusting to a new life. This the league attempted to accomplish in its early years with a staff of between ten and fifteen foreign-language-speaking caseworkers and a yearly budget averaging $12,000. Believing that the newcomers' first experiences in Chicago were crucial, the IPL tried to supervise the arrival of all immigrants at the city's rail terminals in order to keep them out of the clutches of unscrupulous baggagemen and cabbies. The IPL was especially concerned that female aliens might be led astray. Consequently, using a list provided by the Ellis Island authorities in New York, a league worker attempted to meet each female immigrant at the train station in Chicago and to visit her in her home within one year of her arrival to offer personal assistance. The IPL, however, provided social services to both male and female immigrants. It traced lost baggage, located relatives, secured employment, provided food and clothing, aided those maimed in industrial accidents, and gave legal help to those fleeced by crooked employment bureaus, bankers, policemen, and steamship ticket agents.

Typical of social agencies during the Progressive period, the league's casework was only part of a broader plan—to study the immigrants' problems scientifically and to devise effective, ameliorative programs for which government at all levels was to assume responsibility. Few of the league's suggestions in this regard, however, were followed. The federal government's immigrant receiving station in Chicago never opened its doors; legislation for state and city regulation of immigrant banks, steamship agents, and midwives was not enacted; the courts did not provide free interpreters and public defenders; laws regulating private labor agents were rarely enforced, and although, at the IPL's urging, Illinois improved the service rendered by the State Employment Bureau, a comprehensive, nationwide labor exchange run by state and federal governments was never organized. The Chicago public schools expanded their programs to immigrants, but they were not sufficiently numerous or flexible to meet the newcomers' needs.

The IPL did convince the state of Illinois to establish a Commission of Immigration in 1919 with Grace Abbott as its executive secretary to take over the league's programs. But the expectation that the IPL would be able to close its doors was disappointed when the commission's already inadequate funding was totally eliminated in 1921. Consequently, the IPL was reactivated, though on a severely reduced budget. After Abbott's departure in 1921 for Washington, the organization was led by Marian Schibsy between 1921 and 1925 and by Iris L. Wood from 1925 to 1926. The IPL, however, now confronted a new set of problems. The restrictive quota laws of 1921 and 1924 ended mass immigration and erected a legal jungle that was made constantly more dense by subsequent legislation and administrative rulings, through which each entrant had to journey. Though never abandoning counseling and friendly visiting, the IPL spent most of its time providing legal and technical services—filling out affidavits, giving legal aid in deportation proceedings, assisting in naturalization matters, and, especially important from the league's point of view, attempting to reunite families divided by immigration statutes.

In 1926, the IPL acquired a new director, Mrs. Kenneth Rich, and expanded its services with funds provided by the Chicago Community Trust and the local Young Men's Christian Association. To the technicalities of the immigration laws were added lives disrupted by depression, World War II, and the cold war. As unemployment rose after 1929, many aliens needed help in returning to Europe, others in taking out naturalization papers to be able to take advantage of New Deal job programs. The conflagration in Europe brought requests for the league to find relatives lost in the upheaval. The War Brides Act of 1946, the Displaced Persons Act of 1948, the McCarran-Walter Act of 1952, and the Refugee Relief Act in 1953 all created special classes of immigrants, which in turn necessitated more bewildering paperwork.

By 1956, under the leadership of Ione DuVal, who replaced the retiring Rich in 1954, the league's yearly budget had reached more than $60,000. Reflecting both the changing sources of immigration and the needs of the agency's clientele, more than half of the new cases in 1956 involved efforts to secure the admission of relatives; 30 percent of the new cases were of Greek nationality. The IPL's name was changed to the Immigrants' Service League (ISL) in 1958, and in 1967, in order to achieve both greater efficiency and financial stability, it merged with the Travelers Aid Society of Metropolitan Chicago, keeping, however, its separate identity within the larger organization. By 1975, the league's staff had nearly tripled to include the director, a full-time attorney, three supervisors, and thirteen immigration consultants, most of whom were foreign-language-speaking paraprofessionals. Its budget, representing slightly more than half of the Travelers Aid Society's total funding, had reached nearly $429,000, 50 percent of which was provided by the Chicago Community Fund and the rest by individual donors and nationality committees. During the same years, because of the Castro revolution in Cuba and the Johnson Immigration Act of 1965, among other factors, the ethnic origin of league-assisted aliens changed dramatically from primarily European to West Indian and especially Central and South American. In 1974, for example, 94 percent of the persons served were Spanish-speaking; 75 percent were Mexican, for whom a satellite office had been opened in their neighborhood. The number of Peruvians assisted rose 150 percent, Colombians 100 percent, and Guatemalans 80 percent.

Despite this ethnic change (and in 1975 the league was aiding South Vietnamese refugees) and the continuing trend toward providing legal and technical assistance rather than social services (in 1974 the league rendered legal and technical aid to 4,720 individuals but social services to only twenty-two), the objective still remained the same: to ease the immigrants' adjustment to ensure that they became productive American citizens.

The records of the ISL are in the manuscript division of the University of Illinois Library at Chicago Circle, Chicago, Illinois. The history of the league is recounted in Grace Abbott's *The Immigrant and the Community* (1917) and in two recent scholarly studies—Robert L. Buroker, "From Voluntary Association to Welfare State: The Illinois Immigrants' Protective League, 1908–1926," *Journal of American History* 58 (December 1971): 643–660, and Henry B. Leonard, "The Immigrants' Protective League of Chicago, 1908–1921," *Journal of the Illinois State Historical Society* 67 (Autumn 1973): 271–284.

Henry B. Leonard

INDUSTRIAL REMOVAL OFFICE (IRO). Throughout the late nineteenth century, the United Hebrew Charities of the City of New York* (UHC) tried to conduct programs for the resident poor of New York, but the burden of impoverished and unskilled Jewish immigrants, especially from Eastern and Southern Europe, frustrated the agency's plans. Consequently, throughout the late nineteenth century, the UHC developed plans to move immigrants to areas in Connecticut, New Jersey, and upstate New York, away from New York City and the increasingly congested Lower East Side, the Jewish district of Manhattan. The economic depressions of the period, especially in the 1890s, almost forced the UHC, still burdened by caring for indigent newcomers, to disband. UHC leaders were forced to pay attention to fund raising and other such matters. Little wonder, then, that when the UHC leaders learned of anti-Semitic activities in Rumania and the concomitant emigration of Rumanian Jews, they took action to develop a sounder plan than before to distribute immigrants to places away from New York City. Meeting in July of 1900, the leaders of the UHC, particularly Cyrus Sulzberger and Nathan Bijur, two important figures in the New York Jewish community, agreed to have their agency and the Roumanian Aid Society, a local group, cooperate with the nationwide B'nai B'rith (BB) to find jobs outside New York for the newcomers.

Because the BB was not prepared to conduct this professional social work, the leaders gave the distribution work to the one-year-old Jewish Agricultural and Industrial Aid Society* (JAS). Consequently, on January 24, 1901, in New York City, the Industrial Removal Office (IRO) was created at a meeting of the JAS's executive board. The IRO's removal (or distribution) work began in February 1901 as a branch of the JAS. In 1903, UHC leaders Sulzberger, Bijur, and others formed the removal committee of JAS. The Roumanian Aid Society was dissolved, and its funds were transferred to the committee. David Bressler, a former BB officer and the manager of the Roumanian Aid Society removal work, became the general manager of the IRO, a position he held until 1916.

Despite the initial reluctance of the interior communities to take the Eastern European immigrants, the IRO developed a nationwide program. In 1902, the IRO began to pay communities to hire agents to find jobs for the newcomers. Communities such as Detroit and Milwaukee, both of which began full cooperation in 1902, organized local committees to help in the effort. Increasingly such communities as St. Louis, Kansas City, and Cincinnati developed fully cooperating local agencies; gradually, interior cities began to welcome the immigrants as additions to their growing Jewish populations. In areas that did not have local committees, IRO field agents and correspondence from Bressler in the New York headquarters worked to find jobs in small factories, shops, and hotels.

Although many immigrants found satisfactory jobs and adjusted well in interior communities, other newcomers and their spokesmen criticized the program. Radicals and socialists, for example, denounced the IRO as an exploitative employment agency, supplying manufacturers with cheap, unorganized labor. Others argued it was unfair to uproot immigrants from their friends and institutions and *landsmanshaften*, or mutual aid societies of people from the same old country locale, in New York City, where the diverse Jewish community structure had many attractions for immigrants of all religious and political persuasions.

In 1907, the IRO separated from the JAS. Leaders in the New York City community, such as Nathan Bijur, and increasingly, leaders from other areas, such as Max Senior of Cincinnati, became members of the board of directors, which had nine members in 1913. The board chose the officers—a chairman, a vice-chairman, and a secretary—from among themselves. Money for the IRO came not only from the Baron de Hirsch Fund but also from such philanthropists as Jacob Schiff, who financed the so-called Galveston plan. Between 1907 and 1914, the plan, allied with the IRO, diverted immigrants to the entry port in Galveston, Texas, from which they were distributed to interior communities.

The 1904–1914 period of heavy Jewish immigration, which virtually ended with the outbreak of war in 1914, were the IRO's peak years. By 1917, when the war significantly curtailed Jewish immigration, the IRO had placed nearly seventy-four thousand people in seventeen hundred different localities. Adjusting to the changed situation, the IRO created its bureau of information and advice in 1921, counseling potential investors about possible ventures in interior communities. The virtual end of large-scale immigration caused the IRO to disband in 1922.

The IRO never fulfilled its founders' vision of diverting the mass of Jewish immigrants away from New York, but the magnet theory of a few Jews settled in an area attracting others had worked reasonably well. The official statistics do not indicate the uncounted newcomers who did not settle in New York because they had friends or relatives whom the IRO placed in other communities. Praised widely, the IRO served as a model for other distribution efforts, such as those for Italian immigrants.

The primary materials for studying the IRO are in the voluminous Baron de Hirsch Papers at the American Jewish Historical Society in Waltham, Massachusetts. The New York Jewish press and the *Annual Reports* of the IRO and the JAS contain relevant information. The *Annual Reports* of the UHC are helpful in understanding the origins of the IRO.

There is a thesis completed at the old Graduate School of Jewish Social Work by Rose Margolis, "A History of the IRO," but I have not been able to locate it. Many other secondary studies mention the IRO briefly. The standard Jewish encyclopedias contain short but helpful sketches of the IRO, and many of the Jewish community studies, such as Louis Swichkow and Lloyd Gartner, *The History of the Jews of Milwaukee* (1963), treat the impact of the IRO on local Jewish populations. For the origins of the IRO, stressing the importance of the Jewish charities, see Peter Romanofsky, "'. . . To Rid Ourselves of the Burden. . .': New York Jewish Charities and the Origins of the Industrial Removal Office, 1890–1901," *American Jewish Historical Quarterly* 64 (June 1975): 331–343.

INTER-CITY CONFERENCE ON ILLEGITIMACY: see NATIONAL COUNCIL ON ILLEGITIMACY.

INTERNATIONAL COMMITTEE OF THE YOUNG MEN'S CHRISTIAN ASSOCIATION: see YOUNG MEN'S CHRISTIAN ASSOCIATIONS OF THE UNITED STATES OF AMERICA, NATIONAL COUNCIL OF THE.

INTERNATIONAL MIGRATION SERVICES: see INTERNATIONAL SOCIAL SERVICE—AMERICAN BRANCH, THE.

INTERNATIONAL RELIEF ASSOCIATION (IRA). In the early 1930s, reports of Nazi oppression under Adolf Hitler in Germany reached concerned individuals in America. Subsequently, agencies to aid those affected, particularly Jews, developed in the United States. In 1933, the American branch of the International Relief Association (IRA) was established as the International Relief Committee (IRC) at the request of internationally renowned physicist and humanitarian, Albert Einstein, by a group of clergymen, journalists, and others concerned about Hitler's atrocities. The leaders of the group, which had little funds and which developed no major plans at the beginning, were noted educator John Dewey, reformer Amos Pinchot, well-known theologian Reinhold Niebuhr, and Paul Brissenden, a labor expert from Columbia University. The secretary of the group was Sheba Strunsky, who later became the executive secretary of the International Rescue and Relief Committee* (IRRC). The small IRC had its first headquarters, appropriately, in an office in one of the buildings of Trinity Church in Lower Manhattan in New York City. The simple but yet difficult to implement goals of the IRC were to provide financial assistance to families victimized by the Nazis, to resettle anti-Nazis who escaped, and to help so-called democratic leaders to escape oppression in Europe. The agency gradually compiled a list of individuals to be aided, and the first contacts the IRC made with Europeans were through Albert Einstein and Kathe Kollwitz, the first woman elected to the Berlin Academy but subsequently expelled by the Nazis in 1933 because she was Jewish.

During the 1930s, the organization, now called the International Relief Association (IRA), remained an antifascist relief agency. By 1933, when Amos Pinchot headed the IRA, it had its headquarters in midtown Manhattan, apparently in the office of *The Nation,* a liberal journal. In 1936, the IRA held a mass meeting to honor Carl van Ossietsky, a German pacifist and editor recently released from a Nazi concentration camp and who received the Nobel Prize for peace in 1936. Mayor Fiorello La Guardia, John Dewey, and others spoke at this meeting. In 1938, consistent with its antifascism, the IRA issued a study, "Youth Betrayed," prepared by an economic analyst from the National Youth Administration. It dealt with the militarization of youth and with the persecution of Protestant, Catholic, and radical youth organizations. The IRA continued to issue reports and statements, and in early 1942, it merged with the similar Emergency Rescue Committee to form the new IRRC.

The sources for studying the IRA's history include the files of *The New York Times* and such agency publications as International Rescue Committee,* *They Chose Freedom: Thirty Years of the IRC, 1933–1963* (1963). There does not appear to be a scholarly history of the IRA.

INTERNATIONAL RESCUE AND RELIEF COMMITTEE: see INTERNATIONAL RESCUE COMMITTEE, INC.

INTERNATIONAL RESCUE COMMITTEE, INC. (IRC). For a number of years in the 1930s, Americans were concerned about the plight of democracy in Europe struggling against nazism. Reacting to the Nazi takeover of France, in 1940, a group of prominent American liberals decided to take action, and they established the Emergency Rescue Committee (ERC) in the summer of 1940. The initial leadership body of the ERC, its national committee, had eleven members, including radio commentator Raymond Gram Swing and Robert M. Hutchins, president of the University of Chicago. The ERC's spokesman and leader seemed to be Dr. Frank Kingdon, the president of the University of Newark in New Jersey. The ERC immediately dispatched a representative to Europe who quickly established contacts with several European cultural leaders. In its brief history, the ERC tended to focus on assisting professionals and intellectual and cultural figures. The ERC also arranged in 1940 for many South American countries to take refugees because restrictive American immigration quotas prevented them from coming to the United States as a refuge.

The activities of the ERC paralleled those of the American committee of the International Relief Association* (IRA). Some individuals, such as Dr. Kingdon, were active in both. The leaders of the ERC and the IRA discussed a merger, and in early 1942, the two groups amalgamated to found the International Rescue Committee, Inc. (IRC) as the International Rescue and Relief Committee (IRRC). Dr. Kingdon announced the establishment of the new IRRC on February 5, 1942. The IRRC set up its headquarters in New York City, where it has remained. The purpose of the new IRRC was to continue its predecessors' work of aiding refugees from Europe. Columnist Dorothy Thompson, the wife of novelist Sinclair Lewis, and other American intellectuals actively supported and worked with the IRRC, whose ideology seemed clearly antifascist and anti-Nazi, as well as anti-communist.

The new IRRC faced an obviously formidable task, and it began immediately to develop its characteristic activities of rescuing and aiding refugees. In a daring venture, the agency sent journalist Varian Fry to Europe as an undercover agent to help antifascist intellectuals. He conducted most of his work in France, and he was helped by Franz van Hildenbrand, a young Catholic from Austria. By 1943, such activity in France, now occupied by the Nazis, became most difficult. When France was liberated in the summer of 1944, the IRRC reopened its headquarters in Paris to resume the work. As the war ended, other branches were reestablished in Belgium, Holland, Italy, Austria, and Germany. During the war, begnning in 1943, the IRRC received the bulk of its funds from the National War Fund, to which it belonged, and in 1943, the IRRC was a charter member of the American Council of Voluntary Agencies for Foreign Service* (ACVA). Also, during the war, the IRRC was licensed to operate by the President's War Relief Control Board. Immediately after the war, the IRRC was one of the first voluntary agencies to reach American personnel in Germany and Austria.

The IRRC participated in the postwar rehabilitation abroad. It was authorized by the federal government to serve as a guarantee agent for displaced persons from camps, and it helped to resettle Sudeten Germans who had been loyal to the Allied forces. The IRRC also aided Spanish Republicans in France and helped others of them in Mexico through employment and retraining. The IRRC continued to repatriate political refugees from France, Switzerland, and Sweden, where it cooperated with labor unions to provide vocational retraining. For the stateless and for refugees, the IRRC provided clothing, food, medicine, and funds.

During the immediate postwar period, the IRRC became one of the leading agents for disbursing reparation funds to over a thousand proven antifascists in Austria and to non-Jewish Germans. The structure of the IRRC in 1946 included historian Charles A. Beard as honorary chairman, a chairman, a treasurer, and, as executive secretary, Sheba Strunsky, who began her work with the IRRC through one of its predecessor agencies, the IRA. The national committee of thirty-one members included a host of prominent Americans, such as Roger Baldwin, the founder and leader of the American Civil Liberties Union, educator John Dewey, and political activist Oswald Garrison Villard, editor of *The Nation,* a liberal weekly.

As European countries became communist in the period of the late 1940s and 1950s, the IRRC, which was renamed the International Rescue Committee (IRC) in 1950, became more involved in escapes than before and increasingly active and anticommunist. In May 1949, for instance, the IRRC began Project Berlin, sending large amounts of supplies, especially powdered milk and butter, to the embattled city. In 1953, the project sponsored the tour of Mayor Ernst Reuter in the United States to raise funds. Also in 1949, the agency initiated its iron curtain refugee program to create a favorable public opinion in the United States to support escape and rescue operations generally and the United States Escapee Program (USEP).

The Hungarian revolution of the mid-1950s prompted characteristic activities by the IRC. In 1955, when news of the events in Hungary first broke, the organization established its emergency commission, chaired and led by war hero and lawyer General William J. Donovan. In February 1956, Donovan organized and directed the Soviet redefection campaign, which studied communist methods and practices from countries bordering the iron curtain. For Hungarian and other anticommunist refugees, the IRC conducted mental health programs and vocational training in Austria and Germany. With funds from the USEP and from the United Nations High Commissioner for Refugees, the agency also developed housing and supplied vocational tools, funds, and clothing for the refugees. Following a nationwide television discussion of the situation in Hungary by IRC Chairman Leo Cherne, the IRC raised about $2.5 million in sixty days, and the agency administered about $200,000 worth of medical supplies donated by the Charles Pfizer Company. The IRC characteristically assisted intellectuals, students, and professionals. By agreement with other agencies, in the Hungarian situation, the IRC dealt with students and professionals, establishing a university in exile, the University of Soprow, near Salzburg, Austria. The IRC also provided library services in camps for Hungarian refugees, and it helped to establish a seventy-member symphony orchestra, the Hungarica Philharmonica, in Baden, outside Vienna, Austria. For refugee youths, the IRC also maintained children's homes and a rest facility. Between December 1956 and September 1958, the IRC alone dispensed $2 million in projects for Hungarian refugees and shipped them about $463,000 worth of food, clothing, and medicine.

Turning to another area threatened by communists, as early as 1954, the IRC began work in Vietnam to assess the relief needs. The services in South Vietnam characteristically centered initially on education. One major activity provided relief to refugee students and teachers as well as intellectuals from North Vietnam, and another dealt with a variety of educational programs. In February 1955, the IRC worked with the United States Chamber of Commerce to drum up support for Operation Brotherhood to provide emergency medical, sanitary, and general aid to people in South Vietnam. The IRC also sponsored Dr. Thomas A. Dooley's clinic in Laos, and beginning in February 1958, the IRC developed Medical International Cooperation (MEDICO), which later became a service of Cooperative for American Relief Everywhere* (CARE).

In the early 1960s, with aid from the American Council for Judaism Philanthropic Fund (AJCPF), the IRC assisted Jewish refugees from Egypt. During this period, more important activities began in Hong Kong for refugees from the People's Republic of China. In May 1962, the IRC president, William J. vanden Heuvel of New York, arrived in Hong Kong to assess the situation. The IRC then arranged, through CARE, to distribute food and clothing. It also found jobs and provided vocational training. With the cooperation of Hong Kong's Social Welfare Department, it opened a day nursery in 1963. Cuban refugees, of course, became beneficiaries of the IRC during this period. The agency operated the only clothing center in the Miami, Florida, area for these refugees during the mid-1960s. The IRC also rendered a unique service by helping Cuban physicians to practice in the United States; special grants from foundations aided this project. As of the mid-1960s, the IRC maintained fifteen offices overseas. The IRC was fully prepared to deal with and in fact was dealing worldwide with refugees from totalitarian oppression and from war.

Characteristically focusing on refugees from communism, in the late 1960s and 1970s, the IRC developed broad programs in the Far East, especially in South Vietnam, where it conducted day care centers and medical dispensaries, as well as medical and public health projects. The agency also maintained a reception center and convalescent center for children undergoing reconstructive surgery. The IRC resettled refugees from North Vietnam and provided training and community development projects, all of which stressed self-sufficiency. In the early 1970s, in the vicinity of Da Nang, IRC development specialists assisted refugees and child care institutions through agricultural, animal/poultry production, and electrification and irrigation projects. Beginning in 1972, the IRC developed a program to train war widows to supervise home day care units for from four to eight children. In April 1973, a special mission of IRC volunteer leaders conducted an on-the-spot survey of refugee and children's programs throughout Vietnam. The group's report to the board of directors urged an expanded program, especially for children and war orphans. Consequently, in June 1973, anticipating federal government actions two years later, the IRC initiated its special programs for Vietnamese children.

When refugees from South Vietnam began pouring into the United States in 1975 in the greatest sudden influx of refugees in American history, the IRC assisted. It provided staff personnel in each of the four government-built reception centers in California, Pennsylvania, Florida, and Arkansas. IRC workers remained in beleaguered South Vietnam until asked to leave by the insurgents in 1975. The IRC also assisted Cambodian refugees. In late 1975, IRC representatives studied the refugee situation in Thailand, and their recommendations prompted the agency to send a medical team there by February 1976. The IRC also helped to resettle some refugees from Thailand in the United States. In Hong Kong, the IRC found jobs for refugees from China and supported an organization and facilities to promote self-support. The IRC maintained five day care centers in Hong Kong, where staff workers visited homes to determine needs. The IRC also conducted several programs in Bangladesh, including social rehabilitation and job training for women and community health services. The IRC provided funds for training doctors at nine medical schools and for nurses at two hospitals. In April 1973, the IRC initiated a one-year program in Bangladesh to rehabilitate the wounded and disabled.

While the IRC focused on assisting refugees in Asia, it maintained its traditional pattern of aid in Western Europe for refugees from Eastern Europe, who came especially to Sweden, Germany, Austria, and Italy. The IRC office in Paris, with significant aid from the ACJPF, assisted Jews from Morocco, Tunisia, Egypt, and, of course, the Soviet Union. The IRC also aided refugees from the Greek junta and refugees from Cuba in Spain, especially children. By the early 1970s, services for Cuban refugees in the Miami area were reduced, but in the twelve years of the IRC program there since 1960, it had provided counseling and other services to about one-fourth of all Cuban refugees in the United States. In the mid-1970s, consistent with its ideology of aiding people oppressed by totalitarianism, the IRC helped some noncommunist Chilean refugees. In 1975, the IRC's sixty-eight-member board of directors included such American liberals as author Irving Howe, United States Senators Jacob Javits of New York and Claiborne Pell of Rhode Island, rehabilitation pioneer Dr. Howard Rusk, and Albert Shanker, the leader of the United Federation of Teachers.

The sources for studying the IRC's history include its published *Annual Reports* and some agency publications, such as the helpful *They Chose Freedom: Thirty Years of the IRC, 1933–1963 (1963) and the IRC, Fourteen Years, IRC, 1933–1947* [1947]. The files of the agency have apparently not been retained.

There do not appear to be any scholarly historical studies of the IRC.

INTERNATIONAL SOCIAL SERVICE—AMERICAN BRANCH, THE (ISS-AB). In 1914, at the meeting of the World's Young Women's Christian Association (YWCA) in Stockholm, delegates from seventeen nations discussed the need for an international social service agency to provide casework services to individuals and families whose problems demanded coordinated efforts in two or more countries. The outbreak of World War I delayed action on establishing such an agency until 1920, when Mary Hurlbutt, migration secretary of the World's YWCA, conducted a survey of the conditions of refugees, migrants, travelers, and displaced persons. In 1921, the World's YWCA sponsored experimental service programs in France, Belgium, Czechoslovakia, Greece, Poland, Turkey, and the United States. The overwhelming need for international casework led, in 1924, to the establishment of the International Migration Service (IMS) as an independent organization with headquarters in Geneva, Switzerland, and national branches in Europe and the United States. Viscountess Gladston of Great Britain served as the first international president. On April 7, 1924, the International Social Service-American Branch (ISS-AB) was established as an affiliated bureau of the International Migration Service (IMS) under the leadership of Mary Hurlbutt and with the assistance of the American Committee of IMS, whose members represented numerous social agencies in the United States and abroad. On November 11, 1926, after obtaining official branch office status, the IMS-American Branch (IMS-AB) was incorporated by the State of New York.

The incorporation of IMS-AB in 1926 resulted from a five-year organizing effort by the New York City–based American Committee of the IMS under the leadership of Ruth Larned, who succeeded Hurlbutt as migration secretary of the World's YWCA; Elinor Prudden of the foreign-born department of the World's YWCA; and Margaret Curtis, formerly of the American National Red Cross* (ANRC) in Europe and financial chairman of the Family Welfare Society of Boston. Representatives from the ANRC, the Institute of International Education, the migration bureau of the National Board of the YWCA of the United States of America,* and various other charities and social welfare organizations contributed to the design and organization of the American Branch (AB). Hurlbutt served as its director until its incorporation in 1926, when Ruth Larned became general director.

The administrative structure of the AB in 1964 closely resembled that of the original organization. In 1964, a board of directors elected for a three-year term supervised the overall operations of the agency; a ten-member executive committee in conjunction with the president, two vice-presidents, and other executive officers served as the principal administrators. The general director assumed the direct responsibility of implementing the policies and programs of the agency.

As a private, nonsectarian organization, the AB sought private funds to support its operations and to contribute to the international headquarters. In its early years, the AB received much of its funding from private foundations, especially the Laura Spelman Rockefeller Memorial. Private contributions, however, were the major source of funding. With headquarters in New York City, IMS-AB, especially after World War II, built a nationwide fund-raising network.

The purpose of the IMS and its national branches was to provide specialized casework services to clients referred to them by local, national, and international social agencies. IMS's greatest asset was its network of trained social caseworkers to investigate, evaluate, and facilitate the resolution of social, legal, and personal problems that demanded action simultaneously in two or more countries. The casework techniques of IMS-AB in its early years reflected the transition in casework practice in the decade following World War I from focusing on the family as the appropriate unit of diagnosis and treatment to an emphasis on the centrality of the individual and a more psychological orientation. Throughout its history, the AB maintained this focus and instructed caseworkers from various countries in the methodology and techniques of individualized treatment as advanced by Virginia Robinson in her publication, *A Changing Psychology in Social-Case Work* (1930).

In the AB's early years, much of its work involved the transference of funds from American clients to their European relatives. The IMS-AB also addressed problems arising from the separation of families across national borders; desertion and child support; child custody; paternity claims; legal questions concerning deportation, repatriation and immigration; and, most importantly in recent years, intercountry adoption. As this brief listing of the concerns of ISS-AB suggests, the majority of cases involved the welfare of children. In addition to these casework services, IMS-AB sought to modify conditions in various countries that gave rise to sociolegal difficulties. In the first decade of its existence, the AB lobbied for a more professional consular system and established a liaison with the Passport and Visa Division of the United States Department of State. As a nonlegislative, fact-finding organization, the AB developed statistical studies on international legal aid, desertion, and deportation. Throughout its history, IMS-AB maintained its commitment to "study conditions of an international character, calling for social service work, and to bring these conditions to the attention of the organizations and individuals who can appropriately handle them."

The worldwide economic depression of the 1930s and the rise of Nazi Germany strained the resources and threatened the survival of IMS. The AB responded vigorously to this dual crisis. It provided casework service to aliens residing in the United States who faced compulsory or voluntary deportation and repatriation. Mary Hurlbutt and George L. Warren, general director of the AB from 1928 to 1940, served as the United States delegation to the League of Nations Committee of Experts on Assistance to Indigent Aliens. The AB also sought to modify New Deal legislation to permit aliens to be employed in both state and national work projects, to strengthen the enforcement of child-support legislation, and to provide governmental funds to aid Americans stranded abroad.

As war approached in Europe, the AB began a campaign to provide services to refugees and displaced persons. In 1934, it cooperated with other national organizations in the National Coordinating Committee for Aid to Refugees and Emigrants Coming from Germany.* In recognition of the expertise of IMS in international social work, President Franklin D. Roosevelt in 1938 appointed

George L. Warren secretary of the President's Advisory Committee on Political Refugees (PACR). By 1939, the AB had organized a special children's project to provide homes for refugee children and to coordinate temporary shelter with American families for British children threatened by German bombing. The AB vigorously supported the Wagner-Rogers children's bill of 1939 to expand existing immigration quota regulations. The twin focus of IMS activities during the war years was providing services to the American armed forces overseas and harkening to the needs of the hundreds of thousands of refugees and displaced persons in Europe, the Middle East, and the Americas.

In 1940, Patrick Murphy Malin, former vice-chairman of the American Friends Service Committee* and chairman of the Economics Department of Swarthmore College in Pennsylvania, replaced George L. Warren as general director of IMS-AB. In the first year of his directorship, the AB was instrumental in settling over one hundred thousand German and Eastern European refugees in the Sosua area of the Dominican Republic. In 1944, before the cessation of hostilities, IMS, under the sponsorship of the British and American Intergovernmental Committee and the United Nations Rehabilitation and Relief Agency, conducted a survey of refugee camps in Switzerland, the Middle East, and Mexico. This study provided statistical information on thousands of refugees. In that same year, the AB concluded a demonstration project among displaced persons transferred from an Italian refugee camp to one in Fort Ontario, New York. The results of the survey indicated that detailed information on the residents of refugee camps facilitated their resettlement. The following year, the AB initiated a war emergency project to concentrate on the resettlement of nonrepatriable refugees in Germany and Western Europe.

The AB maintained its commitment to aiding refugees in the postwar era. During the Korean conflict of the early 1950s and in the aftermath of the Hungarian revolution of 1956, the AB demonstrated its nonsectarian, nonpolitical principles of serving all those in need. In 1958, it participated actively in the resettlement of unattached Hungarian youths by influencing the United States government to issue special nonquota visas to youths with American relatives. In the next two decades, crises in Southeast Asia and Latin America elicited a similar marshalling of the resources and influence of the AB.

The immediate postwar years were ones of redefinition and rebuilding. In 1946, in recognition of the true scope of the organization, the name was changed to International Social Service (ISS). In conformity to a directive from the international executive committee, the AB became the International Social Service-American Branch (ISS-AB). During the next two decades, the ISS-AB supplied the funds to rebuild the war-shattered organization. Only four branches—in France, Italy, Switzerland, and the United States—survived the war years; but by 1959, thirteen national branches and numerous national delegations, affiliated bureaus, and correspondents around the world joined in the mandate of the International Social Service.

In 1951, William T. Kirk became executive director of the ISS-AB, and in ten years before his resignation in 1961 to become the executive head of the Motion Picture Relief Fund, the AB expanded its programs and gained the financial recognition of numerous community chests. Financial pressure had led in 1949 to consideration of affiliation with the National Travelers Aid Association* (NTAA). Community chests' support and the establishment in 1954 of the World Adoption International Fund (WAIF) as the fund-raising arm of the AB's children's division, however, relieved the more acute funding difficulties. By 1959, WAIF had chapters in seven cities and over five hundred active members. It contributed the largest single source of income for the AB, approximately one-third. WAIF sponsored charity balls, lectures, and performances by some of the most popular entertainers in America. Broadway and film actress Helen Hayes served as chairperson of the New York City chapter.

The importance of this source of funding reflected the major activity of the American Branch in the quarter century following World War II. ISS-AB maintained its traditional services, but the focus during these years was on intercountry adoption. For the most part, these adoptions involved placing a foreign-born child in an American home. The AB cooperated with a number of national and international organizations in providing services to adoptive parents and children. The cooperating agencies included the Church World Service,* Hebrew Sheltering and Immigrant Aid Society,* the Child Welfare League of America,* and Family Service Association of America.*

ISS-AB was especially concerned that proper preadoption investigation and casework services be observed strictly by both foreign and American agencies. Throughout the 1950s, the AB opposed the practice of proxy adoption, arguing that the interests of the child and the prospective family could be served only by careful and professional investigation and guidance. In 1959, the charter of the AB was amended to allow that agency to assume custody of children and to provide certain adoptive services. In that year, intercountry adoption accounted for over 70 percent of the caseload of the AB.

Of vital importance to the intercountry adoption program of the AB was the passage of a permanent immigration law with special provisions for "eligible orphans." In 1962, President John F. Kennedy signed the Walter-Keating immigration bill, which provided for such cases. In that year the new general director of the AB, Paul Cherney, celebrated the arrival of the ten thousandth orphan placed through its agency. The following year the American Branch, in recognition of the importance of intercountry adoption in its total program of service, reorganized its administrative structure into two service units, one for intercountry adoption and the other for all other casework services. This internal reorganization was completed in 1964 with the integration of the administration of WAIF through cross-representation on both governing boards.

Although intercountry adoption constituted the bulk of AB activities since the 1950s, other aspects of international social service were not ignored. In 1963, the AB cooperated with the United States Department of State and the United States Children's Bureau in the recruitment and training of international caseworkers.

Throughout the 1960s, the AB expanded its traditional services by adding a medical social work unit to answer inquiries, to investigate the benefit of overseas care, and to make arrangements for travel and treatment. The influx of immigrants from the Caribbean, West Indies, and Mexico presented ISS-AB with serious problems of exploitation and mistreatment by employment and contract labor agent. In addition to providing services to the new immigrants, the AB was actively involved in a number of United Nations committees, including the Population Commission, the Sub-Commission on Prevention of Discrimination and Protection of Minorities, and the Human Rights Commission.

United States involvement in Vietnam in the 1960s led to an expansion of ISS services in that part of the world. The AB sponsoring of an office in Saigon in 1965 resulted in a heated debate between the AB and the ISS international executive committee. The international executive committee felt that the American Branch was ill advised to sponsor such an office without the consent of the international headquarters. The committee argued that the political nature of American involvement in South Vietnam compromised the operations of that office as a nonpolitical, nonsectarian agency. In 1966, the AB transferred the responsibility of the Saigon agency to the international headquarters. The AB maintained an active interest in providing social services to the Vietnamese and American armed forces. In 1971, it sponsored the Washington Conference on the Special Needs of Vietnamese Children, which focused on the American responsibility for children fathered by Americans. In that year, Congress appropriated funds for child welfare services in Vietnam and for United States-Vietnam Children's Agency.

The ISS-AB has responded intelligently and expertly throughout its history to the demands and needs of all those requiring its services. In the mid-1970s, these have included helping a growing number of transient American youth without financial support throughout the world. As the character and problems of their clients have changed, the AB adapted to each new need. In recognition of this changing clientele, the AB affiliated with the Travelers Aid Association of America* in 1972 after two years of negotiations. The purpose of the consolidation was to "broaden and strengthen service for those people whose problems derive from, or are compounded by, geographical movement or separation, on either the national or international level." The combined organization was known in 1976 as Travelers Aid-International Social Service of America (TA-ISS) and had its headquarters in New York City. TA-ISS maintains the basic ISS program of international casework and a continuing relationship with the international structure of ISS.

The Papers of the ISS-AB are deposited at the Social Welfare History Archives, University of Minnesota, Minneapolis. These papers span the life of the organization (1926–1972) and include two microfilm reels of the meetings of the board of directors and the executive committee. Pamphlets, reports, financial records, correspondence, and a newsletter (1961–1972) are also contained in the collection. In 1958, Ruth Larned prepared an unpublished, forty-three-page sketch of the history and structure of the ISS. A copy is available at the Social Welfare History Archives Center.

Much has been written about the plight of refugees and displaced persons during World War II; unfortunately no single work details the ISS-AB's activities. The work of IMS-AB and particularly of George L. Warren as secretary of the PACPR is mentioned briefly in David S. Wyman's *Paper Walls: America and the Refugee Crisis, 1938–1941* (1968). Henry L. Feingold in *The Politics of Rescue: The Roosevelt Administration and the Holocaust, 1938–1945* (1970) details the work of the PACPR and Warren's service as a delegate to the Bermuda Conference of 1943, at which the Allied governments considered plans for rescuing refugees under German control. Saul S. Friedman in *No Haven for the Oppressed: United States Policy Toward Jewish Refugees, 1938–1945* (1973) discusses the background of the Wagner-Rogers children's bill of 1939 and the service of Patrick Murphy Malin as vice-director of the Intergovernmental Committee on Refugees.

In addition to the deposited records of ISS-AB, the following publications provide information on the intercountry adoption program: Margaret Kornitzer, *Child Adoption in the Modern World* (1952); Eugenie Hochfeld and Margaret A. Valk, *Experiences in Intercountry Adoptions* (1953); and Eugenie Hochfeld, "Across National Boundaries: Problems in the Handling of International Adoptions, Dependency, and Custody Cases," *Juvenile Court Judges Journal* 14 (October 1963): 3–7. These works detail the ISS-AB program of intercountry adoption, emphasizing the benefits of careful preadoption casework services.

A broad range of topics concerning international social service is presented in the various volumes of *International Social Service Review*, published jointly by the United Nations Department of Economic and Social Affairs, the United States Department of Health, Education, and Welfare, the United States Social Security Administration, and the United States Bureau of Public assistance.

Mary L. Ostling

INTERNATIONAL SOCIETY FOR CRIPPLED CHILDREN: see NATIONAL EASTER SEAL SOCIETY FOR CRIPPLED CHILDREN AND ADULTS, THE.

__ J

JEWISH AGRICULTURAL SOCIETY, INC., THE (JAS). In 1887, Baron Maurice de Hirsch of Bavaria, a financier and railroad builder who devoted his fortune to the welfare of East European Jews, became convinced that secular education could ameliorate the lot of his oppressed brethren; and he offered the Russian government fifty million francs to establish schools in the Pale of Settlement. Yet, with the failure of these negotiations and the worsening position of Jews in Russia, mass emigration became a stark necessity. Hopes for regenerating East European Jewry into a new class of farmers and craftsmen were thus combined with resettlement in the New World.

On the advice of Oscar S. Straus, a leader of the American Jewish community, Baron de Hirsch initially allocated the proceeds of a $2 million fund toward agricultural colonies and trade schools for immigrants in the United States. After further consultation with the Paris-based Alliance Israelite Universelle, as well as American Jewish notables such as Jacob Schiff, the Baron de Hirsch Fund (BHF) (see *Foundations and Research Associations*) was incorporated in New York in 1891. Its officers included Judge Myer S. Issacs as president, Schiff as vice-president, and Straus, Mayer Sulzberger, and William Hackenburg among the trustees. The rural colony of Woodbine was soon established in southern New Jersey; it later included an agricultural school. In New York, the Baron de Hirsch Trade School continued to serve a generation of immigrants. In addition, the BHF supported legal aid, classes in English, and a variety of Americanization services.

Thus, a pragmatic philanthropy was guided by successful businessmen aimed at helping the immigrants to become self-sustaining American citizens. Training in the useful trades, including agriculture, was intended to divert the newcomers from such scorned occupations as peddling. Trained workers, moreover, could be moved away from the congested city slums to a more healthful environment.

Painfully aware of age-old, anti-Jewish stereotypes and biases in Western society, the philanthropists hoped to deflect such hostilities through educational and acculturation programs. Not only the newer forms of anti-Semitic racism, but a rising tide of varied anti-immigrant sentiment in America on the eve of the twentieth century presented major societal challenges to freedom of entry. With the frontier era ending, many Americans grew fearful that the new immigrants (including Orientals, as well as diverse European nationalities) were unassimilable, and the melting pot could not stand the strain of such varied races, religions, and language. Consequently, to cope with the growing tide of Eastern European Jewish immigrants, especially the challenge of training them, in Baron de Hirsch's words, "as free farmers on their own soil . . . to show that Jews have not lost the agricultural abilities which their forefathers possessed," the Jewish Agricultural Society, Inc. (JAS) was established as The Jewish Agricultural and Industrial Aid Society (JAIAS) in New York City on February 12, 1900, when the state of New York chartered the new organization. As a subsidiary of the older BHF, the JAIAS intensified support to Jewish agricultural activities, with industry as a means of supplementing farm income. Its Industrial Removal Office,* autonomous after 1907, relocated thousands of immigrant workers from eastern urban centers to job opportunities throughout the United States. From the JAIAS's outset, Baron de Hirsch determined the organizational goals as well as the financing.

Massive immigration was by no means encouraged and even was regarded as a source of embarrassment, with the vast majority of immigrants having to fend for themselves as individuals and families. Yet, at least a significant minority among the almost 3 million European Jewish immigrants to America since the 1880s were aided in some way by the self-help programs of the BHF and the JAIAS.

Among the JAIAS's major initial functions was the extension of loans on generous terms to cooperatives, as well as to individual farmers. It offered a placement service and advice to potential farm operators. While its extension specialists described new developments in the field, the bureau of educational activities stimulated cultural life, especially in the older rural communities of southern New Jersey and Connecticut.

A shift from group colonization to individual farm enterprise was evident even in the first decade of JAIAS operations. These operations continued to assist Jewish farmers in New Jersey, New York, New England, and California, including refugees from Hitler's Germany in the 1930s and displaced persons in the post–World War II era.

Initially the JAIAS focused on the related goals of training artisans as well as farmers, attempting to establish a balance between industry and agriculture in the rural communities. The society extended loans for land or equipment at a rate of only 4 percent interest, repayable in installments. Most of these loans were on a second mortgage, some on a third or fourth; they came at a time when no other credit was avilable to the colonists and when American farmers generally complained of excessive interest charges and tight credit. It was not until 1916 that the Federal Farm Loan Act provided more adequate credit facilities for the nation's farmers and then at interest rates averaging about 6 percent.

Emphasis on repayment of loans and sound business practices was considered part of the Americanization process—an effort to create a sound middle class tied to the soil. Such goals were influenced by the sensitivities of first- and second-generation Jewish philanthropists—usually of the older German immigration—oriented toward private enterprise and assimilation. Among these were the founding directors of the JAIAS: Eugene S. Benjamin (1900–1941), Henry Budge (to 1902), Julius Goldman (to 1903), William B. Hackenburg (to 1902), Morris Loeb (to 1912), Sigmund Neustadt (to 1902), Marx Ottinger (to 1901), and Fred M. Stein (to 1904). Soon, the list of directors read like a *Who's Who* of American Jewry; Cyrus L. Sulzberger (1902–1932), Percy S. Straus (1902–1932), Eugene Meyer (1902–1909), Henry Morgenthau, Jr. (1925–1934), as well as (later) Arthur Ochs Sulzberger, Orvil Dryfoos, and Lewis L. Strauss. Among the few directors of East European background and outside of business or banking was Jacob G. Lipman (1914–1939), who had grown up on a farm in Woodbine, New

Jersey, and had achieved prominence as an agronomist and dean of Rutgers University's Agricultural College.

At times, friction developed between newly settled farmers and their benefactors over such issues as terms of repayment, individual rather than group obligations, or an admixture of industry with farming. Yet, despite its general policy of favoring privately owned individual farms, the society continued for many years to offer assistance to communities in southern New Jersey, including Alliance and Woodbine, as well as subsidizing such short-lived agrarian experiments as Arpin Colony in Wisconsin. Financial aid and guidance were provided to poultry and egg cooperatives, especially in the interwar years, as well as cooperative creameries, storage, and marketing facilities. As early as 1909, the JAIAS helped to establish the Federation of Jewish Farmers (FJF) (see *Fraternal Organizations*) on a national basis.

Agriculturists from the society visited the farm communities periodically to lecture on new developments and to give individual assistance. Starting in 1908, a Yiddish monthly, the *Jewish Farmer,* offered a means of communication for the immigrant on the land, and its timely articles on vegetable crops, dairying, poultry, and other topics were doubly welcome because they were written in the people's language. Its columns devoted to letters from the readers helped to relieve the cultural monotony of country life. Later, a page in English was added for children.

Americanization services, as well as instruction in gardening and hygiene, were provided by the society's bureau of educational activities, represented in the southern New Jersey communities by resident director Louis Mounier (1901–1917). Not only the practical arts but also aesthetic, intellectual, and cultural activities were fostered; these were attuned to the recommendations of President Theodore Roosevelt's Country Life Commission of 1909 and earned the praise of the United States Immigration Commission's report, "Hebrews in Agriculture" (1911). Aside from the activities of the JAIAS's farm labor bureau in tracking down jobs throughout the country, more talented farm youth were offered scholarships to agricultural colleges. Though beneficial, the latter also became counterproductive to agrarian goals because young people were attracted away from farming into related scientific areas such as microbiology. A desire for education, even on the high school level, soon proved a deterrent to staying on the farm.

By 1910, there were five thousand widely dispersed Jewish farm families and twice that number by the early 1920s when some postwar immigration from Eastern Europe resumed briefly. With the practical guidance and loans from the JAIAS, individual farming often seemed to thrive where group colonization had failed. The shift was eased by a significant economic breakthrough during the prosperous World War I years; increasingly, it was recognized that poultry farming could support a newcomer and his family without requiring such costly expedients as subsidized manufacturing to supplement income from crops. In

New Jersey, there were pioneering Jewish poultry farmers in Vineland, as well as some newly dispersed in Toms River, Lakewood, and Farmingdale.

Still, the departure from group colonization brought a mixed bag of blessings. Jewish farmers had become more professional and self-reliant; their cooperative purchasing bureaus, credit unions, and fire insurance companies from Sullivan County, New York, and the Vineland-Woodbine axis to the Midwest fulfilled specific economic needs. The FJF grew from thirteen branches to sixty-three, even in its first five years, 1909-1914. Yet, the new-style individual farmer, often isolated on his homestead, generally suffered from a meager cultural environment as compared to that of the city or the old Jewish rural colonies of South Jersey.

Annual conventions of the FJF, usually held at the Educational Alliance in New York, presented one opportunity to meet fellow Jews, both farmers and nonfarmers. Distinguished speakers addressed them: Louis Marshall, president of the American Jewish Committee, Jacob H. Schiff, and the Honorable Marcus M. Marks, president of the borough of Manhattan. But when the farmers went home, they dropped back into the old ways with little else in Jewish cultural activity or social ties.

The onset of World War I resulted in cutting off immigration entirely, interrupting the work of the JAIAS. This period, however, marked a notable step forward in the availability of farm credit when the Federal Land Bank system began to grant farm mortgages on easier terms than could be obtained commercially. This was in part a recognition of the work being done by the JAIAS. The society's experience helped to shape the federal legislation; Leonard Robinson, general manager of the JAIAS from 1908, collaborated in drafting the bill.

With the end of World War I, Jewish immigration to the United States from Eastern Europe resumed, though it was soon reduced drastically by the Immigration Act of 1924. This influx, like previous ones, brought increased activity. In 1920, a peak of $417,000 in loans granted was reached, and two years later a new record was set. To meet these postwar responsibilities, the society underwent a reorganization, its work allocated among the following departments: loan, settlement, farm employment, rural sanitation, and extension. In 1922, the JAIAS changed its name to the JAS.

The settlement department was an outgrowth of the farm finding service established in 1913. The society recognized that in large part success or failure in farming was attributable to the kind of farm the newcomers originally settled on. Therefore, the JAS turned its attention to determining whether farms were worth the price asked to save buyers from being exploited by unscrupulous real estate agents.

The rural sanitation department was established because so many farmers in Ulster and Sullivan counties in New York had gone into the boarding business; although their sanitation practices were no different from those of most other nearby farmers at that time, they were not adequate for rooming houses. Soon the society's sanitation department functioned not only in New York but also in neighboring states, working in conjunction with municipal, state, and federal authorities. The United States Public Health Service later praised this work as "a record of remarkable progress under exceedingly interesting conditions . . . not only of local importance but of state-wide and national importance from a demonstration standpoint." As sanitary standards improved, the work of this department declined, and it was finally eliminated in 1950. But in the course of its existence, about one-quarter million people had been reached by its activities.

In the Midwest, the JAS's office in Chicago worked chiefly with farmers in the Benton Harbor area of southwestern Michigan who specialized in producing fruits and vegetables and with the grape growers in the area around Geneva, Ohio, in the northeastern part of that state. This office functioned also as an information center for the many Jews interested in farming, conducting well-attended classes in agriculture at the Jewish People's Institute in Chicago until its termination in 1952.

The most important long-range development, however, was the decision to expand poultry farming. In an age when American agriculture generally was in decline, poultry farming presented important advantages. Most notably, its modest land requirements made it feasible in relatively well-settled areas of high-priced land that offered adequate public services, including transportation to city markets and contacts with fellow Jews as businessmen or consumers. At least some income return was available almost immediately, even if the poultry farming was done on only a part-time basis at the start—a significant factor for families with small savings. Nor were the natural hazards such as drought or storm as dangerous as in other types of farming; undoubtedly, neither was the physical labor as tiring as that for "real dirt farmers." With aid from JAS, Jewish poultry farming flourished between the wars and beyond, from Toms River, Vineland, Farmingdale, and Freehold in New Jersey, the Ulster-Sullivan county area in New York and Colchester in Connecticut, to Petaluma north of San Francisco, California.

This transformation proved particularly urgent with the coming of the Great Depression of the 1930s. By then, the JAS had advanced nearly eleven thousand loans totaling over $6 million. Moreover, even before the New Deal's program of subsistence homesteads, the JAS developed a plan for unemployed urban workers in the form of agroindustrial settlements. Located within commuting distance of urban industrial centers, these would permit workers to tend their farms in their spare time and slack seasons along with the help of family members. The concept was implemented at Bound Brook, New Jersey, about twenty miles southwest of Newark, where forty families by 1929 lived on developed farms ranging from four to fifteen acres.

The impact of the Great Depression hit the Jewish farm movement and the JAS as hard as it did the other segments of agriculture. One result was that people who had lost jobs or business in the city flocked to the society's offices because they hoped to be able to make a living on farms. Thus, the number of new applicants in 1932 was one of the highest on record; at the same time, established farmers were in great distress. On top of this, with repayments dropping, the JAS's capacity to make loans was at a low ebb. Moreover, new resources were soon required to cope with the consequences of Nazi terror, both before and after World War II. Though all too few found haven from the holocaust, farm loan applications from refugees increased from 600 in 1938 to 741 in 1940; a training program for such applicants was established by JAS. Following World War II, thousands of new farm families were aided by JAS loans and guidance. Especially in the Ocean and Monmouth County areas of New Jersey, but also in Connecticut and California, rural communities flourished. New synagogues appeared in the countryside, as in the budding East European Jewish community of Dorothy, New Jersey. And experienced American Jewish farmers, including some served by the Los Angeles office of the JAS, helped to guide the poultry industry in Israel.

By the mid-1970s, however, the massive secular decline of American family farming proved irreversible. As agribusiness triumphed, fewer than 4 percent of the population remained farmers. A succession of natural calamities, as well as economic conditions, forced the new Jewish farmers out of business too. JAS ceased its operation by the mid-1970s. Former operations of the society have been phased out under the aegis of the surviving BHF. Yet, the JAS's historic record remains as a vital bridge to the New World for many thousands of immigrants.

Samuel Joseph's *History of the Baron de Hirsch Fund* (1935) is still the most authoritative secondary work, including lengthy sections on the JAS, with documents and extensive original citations. Gabriel Davidson, long-time general manager of JAS, is the author of *Our Jewish Farmers: The Jewish Agricultural Society* (1943), a useful account. More recent, by a JAS farm extension worker, is Abraham Dobin's *Fertile Fields: Recollections and Reflections* (1975). See also Joseph Brandes, *Immigrants to Freedom: Jewish Communities in Rural New Jersey Since 1882* (1971). Original source materials include the documents and published *Annual Reports* of The Jewish Agricultural Society, Inc. (New York), as well as the papers of the BHF in the archives of the American Jewish Historical Society in Waltham, Massachusetts.

Joseph Brandes

JEWISH BOARD OF GUARDIANS (JBG). In the late nineteenth and early twentieth centuries, the strains of immigration, congestion on the Lower East Side of Manhattan, and poverty began to affect the social behavior of the Jewish community in New York City. The reportedly high incidence and public disapproval of juvenile delinquency among Jews in New York prompted philanthropists and community leaders to establish the Jewish Protectory and Aid Society (JPAS) in 1902. This early concern with juvenile delinquency by a predecessor agency continued as a focus of the later Jewish Board of Guardians

(JBG). In 1906, the JPAS established Hawthorne School for Boys in Hawthorne in Westchester County, New York. Another predecessor agency of the JBG was the Jewish Big Brothers Association (JBBA), established in New York City in 1907 to serve boys referred by the Children's Court of New York City. The JBBA also served as parole officers for boys discharged from the Hawthorne institution. In 1911, a group of philanthropic women, led by Mrs. Sidney Borg, an important figure in Jewish charities, founded the Jewish Big Sisters (JBS) to conduct similar work for delinquent girls. In 1912, the JBS established Cedar Knolls School of Girls, on the same grounds as the Hawthorne School for Boys. Another institution dealing with delinquent young women, which helped also to form the JBG, was the Lakeview Home for Unmarried Mothers on Staten Island, New York; it was founded in 1905. The earliest predecessor agency was the Jewish Prisoners Aid Society (JPAS), which was organized in 1893 to serve Jewish prisoners and their families. And in 1919, the Central Committee for Friendly Aid to Jewish Girls, another predecessor agency, was formed.

The overlapping and duplication of work conducted by these agencies and institutions prompted their leaders to begin to think of amalgamating these activities into one unified agency. Consequently, on April 23, 1921, the JBG was incorporated by the New York State legislature as the result of a merger between these precedessor agencies. The founders of the JBG included community leader Louis Marshall, Mrs. Borg, and social worker Alice D. Menken.

In the JBG's first decade, the 1920s, psychiatry became an important tool for social service agencies, and the JBG was one of the pioneering agencies in the United States applying psychiatry to delinquent behavior in children, practicing what became known as orthopsychiatry. As early as 1922, for instance, the JBG founded its first mental hygiene clinic for children. An important development occurred in 1921 when the organization hired its first paid professional staff member. In 1925, the JBG created three demonstration guidance bureaus in New York City public schools: in Seward Park, Hunt's Point, and Crotona Park. These projects were the predecessors of the Bureau of Child Guidance of the New York City Board of Education. In 1926, the JBG established its guidance department to promote psychiatry in the treatment of children. Despite the use of psychiatry and the concomitant professionalism of the JBG, the agency remained influenced most heavily by volunteers.

In the 1930s, when services continued to be informal and volunteer oriented, the JBG focused on developing and perfecting its psychiatric services for children and transforming its institutions into residential treatment centers. In the early 1930s, Mary Froelich, a long-time volunteer who served as JBG president from 1968 to 1972, and another young volunteer colleague became the first group-therapy leaders. They were trained and supervised by Samuel R. Slavson, perhaps the Father of Group Therapy. By 1934, the JBG had a group therapy department. In 1935, when the Hawthorne and Cedar Knolls facilities were coeducational in some aspects, the JBG established a psychiatric clinic at the

Hawthorne school. Educational services were always important at these institutions in Westchester County, and in 1939, a special act by the New York State Legislature created the Union Free School District in Mt. Pleasant for the schools. During the 1930s, the JBG staff and John Slawson, a well-known social worker, published studies in such publications as *The Journal of Orthopsychiatry* and *The Jewish Social Service Quarterly*. Suggesting also the importance the JBG placed on its volunteers, in 1937, it began to publish a journal, *Volunteer Worker*, one of the few such publications nationally to focus on this group of practitioners.

Influenced by developments at home during World War II, the JBG began in the mid-1930s to focus on community and neighborhood mental health centers, stressing, of course, services for mentally disturbed children. JBG caseworkers assisted community centers throughout the city. To fulfill community needs, the JBG opened an office in Brownsville in Brooklyn and one in Coney Island, also in Brooklyn. With the Lieutenant Lester N. Hofheimer Estate and the New York Section of the National Council of Jewish Women, the JBG established in New York City the Council Child Development Center for preschool children. In the autumn of 1943, the JBG established working relations with the Juvenile Aid Bureau of the New York City Police Department, and it continued to serve in the children's and adolescents' court of New York City. In 1946, the JBG reorganized its structure, developing three divisions. The division of community services included the adult welfare department, which carried on the early services for Jewish prisoners and their families, the unmarried mothers' service, the court and police work, and the community relations committee. The division of institutional services supervised the schools in Westchester County and the Union Free School District in Mt. Pleasant, New York, the Lakeview Home, and the agency's summer camps for children. The other division was the child guidance institute.

This emphasis on community-based services led to the proliferation of JBG services in the 1950s and 1960s. In 1951, for instance, on St. Mark's Place in Lower Manhattan, the JBG founded its Stuyvesant Residence Club for older boys, and in 1953, it opened the Henry Ittleson Center for Child Research, named after a prominent philanthropist in the mental health field. In 1955, to honor a long-time and important volunteer and benefactor, the JBG renamed the Child Guidance Institute in honor of Madeline Borg. Also in 1955, the Hawthorne and Cedar Knoll schools began to share the same campus in Westchester County. In 1964, the JBG established its Coney Island mental health service for children and youth, the agency's first community-based mental health project. In the next year, the JBG founded Phoenix House in Manhattan, a pioneering day treatment and educational program for emotionally disturbed adolescent boys. In 1968, in collaboration with The Roosevelt Hospital, the JBG opened its West Side mental health services for children and youth as the first unit in a proposed comprehensive community mental health center on the West Side of Manhattan.

From the 1960s on, the JBG emphasized day care as an agency priority, establishing in 1970, the Carey Garden Day Care Center in Coney Island as part of its services there. This day care center featured a therapeutic nursery for emotionally troubled youngsters.

In the 1970s, under Froelich's presidency, the JBG expanded its services dramatically, despite the cutbacks in federal and state funds for social services. In so doing, it exemplified the best tradition of voluntary social service agencies. In 1970, the JBG opened an infant care unit at the de Hostos Towers, a low-income housing project in upper Manhattan. This unit served high-risk babies aged two months to three years old. It also provided counseling and crisis intervention services for the mothers. In 1972, the JBG established a day care center at the Great Northern Hotel in Manhattan where victims of fire, condemnations, and such were temporarily relocated. In August 1971, the new committee on public interest and social concern publicly supported the elimination of the present system of juvenile detention centers. Carrying out the spirit of this principle, in late 1971, the JBG established its important Geller House as an alternative to juvenile detention. This short-term intensive treatment and diagnostic residential facility for disturbed youths remanded by the family courts of New York City provided a homelike environment with individual rooms. There was a ratio of one and one-half staff member to one youth at this facility. The Geller House featured an open door policy, and the JBG was proud that in the first six months of operation, only two youths tried to run away; both returned voluntarily. The Phoenix School and similar day facilities also showed a commitment to reforming the system by providing model programs. The Hawthorne Cedar Knolls School, often cited as a model facility, was now one of the very few in the nation to deal with older, emotionally disturbed juvenile delinquents.

In the 1970s, research and professionalism were important aspects of the JBG's program. In 1970, the agency founded its own professional journal, *Psychosocial Process—Issues in Child Mental Health,* and in 1971, to honor a former staff member, the JBG established its Peter Blos Biennial Lecture on Adolescence. The first one, held in December 1971 at the New York Academy of Medicine, attracted over eleven hundred people and featured the well-known Professor Erik H. Erikson, a long-time friend of Blos. The best-known JBG research was the study at the Henry Ittleson Center into the multiple causes and complex treatment of childhood schizophrenia. In this period, the JBG established its educational institutes to teach and to train mental health workers. It received a provisional charter from the regents of the State University of New York. The professional staff continued in the 1970s to publish widely in the field of mental health for children.

The sources for studying the JBG's history include the published *Annual Reports. The New York Times* covers the activities of the organization. Some agency publications, such as *The Story of the Jewish Board of Guardians* (n.d., 1946?), provide helpful information, as does Herschel Alt, *Forging Tools for*

Mental Health (1955). Some of the agency's unpublished materials, such as minutes of meetings and correspondence, are on file at the agency's central headquarters in New York City. These materials are generally closed to researchers but can be made available to properly qualified scholars.

There does not appear to be a scholarly history of the JBG.

JEWISH FAMILY SERVICE (JFS). In New York City in the early 1870s, leaders in the American Jewish community began to criticize the apparently indiscriminate alms giving by Jewish organizations and individuals. The *Jewish Messenger,* edited by Myer S. Isaacs, especially spoke out against this situation. In April 1873, Isaacs introduced a resolution to deal with this problem at the annual meeting of the Hebrew Benevolent and Orphan Society (HBOS), the leading Jewish charity in the city. His work led to the creation of a special fifteen-member committee to study the relief practices of the HBOS. Isaacs's efforts were part of a campaign in the spring and summer of 1873 to form a union of the Jewish charities in New York. The report of the committee became the plan of union of a new agency. These existing agencies approved the plan in early 1874: the Hebrew Benevolent Fuel Association, the Ladies' Benevolent Society of the Congregation of the Gates of Prayer, and the Hebrew Relief Society. On April 24, 1874, when the most important of the five predecessor agencies, the HBOS, signed the plan, the Jewish Family Service (JFS) was established as the United Hebrew Charities of the City of New York (UHC). Shortly after the HBOS approved the merger, a fifth organization, the Yorkville Ladies' Benevolent Society, joined the plan of union, which became the charter of the new UHC.

The plan called for each of the constituent agencies to contribute at least $500 to help solidify Isaacs's point that the new UHC have the most funds of any Jewish agency in the city. For every $2,000 it gave, each of the founding groups had one of its members on the governing body, the board of relief; thus each organization could have more than one board member. The representatives from the HBOS outnumbered the others, and they dominated the new organization. The establishment of the UHC, designed to stem the tide of indiscriminate giving, related to the so-called scientific philanthropy, propounded in forward-looking social service circles in the late nineteenth century.

The structure of the new UHC reflected the nature of Jewish charities in New York City in the late nineteenth century. There were initially six standing committees: on employment, loan and deposits, supplies, medical and sanitary relief, finance, and emigration (from New York to other Jewish communities in the United States). The efforts to move poor Jews out of New York and away from the responsibility of the UHC was one of the major—and controversial—activities in the nineteenth century. The officers, technically the board of relief, included the president, a vice-president, a treasurer, and a secretary. In 1875, the UHC chose Henry Rice, a prominent dry goods merchant, as its president. He served in that position until 1908 and influenced the history of the UHC for almost a generation of agency leaders. A feature of the structure was the division of the city into seventeen districts, each with a five-member visiting committee to investigate conditions and to appeal for donations and then to report recommendations to the board of relief. The board granted most of the benefactions, but each district chairman could and did give people a fixed five-dollar emergency relief payment. The new UHC opened the first of its many headquarters at 59 West Fourth Street in October 1874.

With new headquarters, its structure established, and a dedicated leadership, the UHC began its work in New York City. From its inception, the UHC helped individuals and families to leave the city. Although the UHC rhetoric argued that there was more opportunity away from the city, the efforts to get people out of New York resulted from self-interest and even from self-preservation. Indeed, because New York was the major port of entry for immigrant Jews, most of them settled there rather than in communities in the interior. Often unskilled and without jobs, the immigrants frequently taxed the UHC resources. Not surprisingly, the UHC developed many programs to transport clients out of New York. Another activity, begun immediately in the 1870s, was the program to develop self-support among the Jewish poor. Consistent with the principles of scientific philanthropy, the UHC loaned funds and supplies to heads of families. Funds were used to purchase such items as tools or a pushcart, a step toward self-support.

The UHC also dispensed traditional charities. In its first year of operation, for instance, volunteers distributed garments prepared by the Ladies' Sewing Society to the poor. In the 1870s, President Rice appealed successfully for volunteer women to visit the homes of the poor to teach them ventilation and nutrition, for example. The UHC was incorporated according to the laws of the state of New York in 1877. The first years of activity resulted in a profit for the new organization, but the immigration of the 1880s changed this situation drastically.

The dominant theme of the UHC's history in the 1880s—and even for the late nineteenth century—was the agency's financial crisis generated by the mass immigration of impoverished Jews beginning in the early 1880s. The financial problems led to continuing efforts by the UHC to remove Jewish immigrants from New York. As early as 1881, "to prevent many immigrants from becoming a burden on the [UHC]," board of relief member and honorary secretary Isaac Isaacs proposed that a UHC committee be stationed at Ellis Island to divert immigrants away from New York City to communities in the West and the South. His proposal led eventually to the founding of the Hebrew Emigration Aid Society, which conducted early removals. In the mid-1880s, with funds from the Baron de Hirsch Fund (BHF), the UHC's committee on general relief supervised a project to find work outside New York for immigrants. The UHC established industrial classes, chiefly in the needle trades, provided supplies, tools, and jobs outside New York, and sought out job opportunities in the interior. This effort was implemented by the UHC's employment bureau, which had been established in the mid-1880s. The removal efforts by the UHC resulted in a conference of Jewish charities from other cities in 1885. In the spirit of scientific philanthropy, the conference agreed not to send the poor from city to city indiscriminately; the receiving city should not be simply a dumping ground. These issues, expressed at the conference in 1885, were important themes in late nineteenth-century removal work by the UHC. Despite some opposition from interior Jewish communities to New York charities sending poor immigrants to their communities, the UHC's board of relief resolved in October 1886 that relieving immigrants should not block other activities of the society, and the board reiterated its support for rural settlements. Financial problems continued unabated. "We have burdens enough," cried President Rice in 1888. During that year, with its large indebtedness, the UHC nearly exhausted an emergency fund established by a donor. To help relieve this highly unfavorable situation in the 1880s, the UHC also tried, unsuccessfully, to encourage the growth of industrial communities in upstate New York, New Jersey, and Connecticut. In 1887, the society even suggested that Jews in Russia develop trade schools and the like at home to prepare them for jobs in America and to keep them off the UHC charity rolls.

The financial problems intensified in the depression-ridden 1890s. A combination of increased immigration, greater unemployment and poverty among the settled Jewish community, and reduced contributions from the community prompted stronger efforts by the UHC to resettle immigrants outside New York. In 1890, with the help of a large grant from the BHF, the UHC developed another removal plan, arguing that other Jewish communities should cooperate because the problems of poor Jewish immigrants should concern all American Jews. The UHC complained repeatedly that the mass immigration and its concomitant problems frustrated agency plans to develop a program for the settled Jewish poor of New York City. In February 1897, the UHC even considered disbanding. It tried desperately to raise funds, establishing special committees and prompting, unsuccessfully, the federation of Jewish charities in New York to lessen the competition for funds from newer charities. In the absence of widespread community support, the burden fell most heavily on the UHC leaders, who participated in six times more emergency meetings to discuss finances between 1896 and 1900 than between 1879 and 1885. Little wonder, then, that the leaders of the UHC—Cyrus Sulzberger, Nathan Bijur, and General Manager Lee K. Frankel, a prominent social worker—helped to initiate the Industrial Removal Office* (IRO) in 1900 to divert Rumanian Jewish immigrants and others away from New York City.

Despite the financial problems of the 1880s and 1890s, the UHC developed a program to deal with the impoverished Jews of New York, especially the sick, the aged, and the dependent. The agency also developed truly needed services for the community. For example, in the early 1880s, as the Hebrew Free Burial Society was disbanding, the UHC founded its committee on free burials to deal with the chaotic situation. In its first year, the UHC established a committee on medical and sanitary relief, headed by Dr. Simeon Leo, a civic- and reform-minded physician and surgeon. This committee attracted other physicians who saw the relation between poverty and environmental conditions. In 1883, the committee conducted a survey of six hundred tenements in the Lower East Side of Manhattan where the bulk of Jews lived. The study prompted Dr. Leo to argue for a revision of the city's sanitary code.

To help train immigrant youths, the UHC opened an industrial school for girls in 1880, and in May 1884, it founded the Hebrew Technical Institute for boys. As early as 1883, when the Ladies' Hebrew Lying-in Relief Society became a constituent member of the UHC, the UHC began to help deliver babies in women's homes. In 1884, the UHC helped to establish the Montefiore Home for Chronic Invalids, a group of clients with which the UHC was concerned. Changes in the disbursement of relief developed in the 1880s. The volunteers on the district visiting committees were often out of town, so assistant clerks, who were paid, often conducted investigations. By 1887, the UHC employed such visitors, and the volunteers began to conduct other duties.

In the 1890s, despite the financial problems, the UHC continued to provide services for the community and emerged as an important and efficient social service agency. In November 1890, the UHC became affiliated with the local Federation of Sisterhoods, providing the UHC with offices throughout the city. In 1891, the UHC began to publish one of the earliest charity journals in the country, *Charity Record*, which lasted only a few years.

With the hiring of Nathaniel S. Rosenau in 1893, the UHC moved closer to national social service circles. Rosenau had served previously as the secretary of the Buffalo Charity Organization Society. At the UHC, he established five bureaus, which corresponded to the activities of the society: registration, relief, medical, employment, and of course, immigration. He also initiated a new system of recording case histories. In 1899, Lee K. Frankel became the manager, a position he filled until 1908. Also in 1899, the new UHC building at Twenty-first Street and Second Avenue, was completed.

Although continuing immigration and a nationwide economic slump caused financial problems for the UHC in the first decade of the twentieth century, the agency developed some new and innovative services and continued to fill community needs. In 1902, the UHC launched a new publication, *Charity Work,* which quickly became *Jewish Charity,* the official publication of the National Conference of Jewish Charities (NCJC).* Suggesting the UHC's ties to the national work community, in 1906, *Jewish Charity* became part of *Charities and the Commons,* the leading and Progressive social work publication. Continuing a nineteenth-century theme, in 1900, through the support of banker and philanthropist Jacob Schiff, the UHC initiated a self-support fund to help clients establish small businesses. Schiff's continuing contributions, as well as other such funds, led to the development of the self-support department of the UHC in the 1920s.

Reacting to a situation in New York whereby Jewish dependent children were placed in Gentile institutions, UHC leaders, including General Director Lee Frankel, initiated the nationwide Joint Committee on Dependent Children in 1903. Efforts to place Jewish dependent children in Jewish family homes succeeded, as the New York City Department of Welfare hired a special agent to handle this particular work. To deal with a nagging social problem, in 1905, the UHC established its pioneering committee on desertions. In 1910, the committee began to cooperate with the Jewish press to publish photographs of men who deserted their wives.

Reacting to the charges that the uptown leaders of the UHC slighted the Lower East Side community, beginning in 1904 and lasting until 1908, the UHC developed a project to divide the Lower East Side into branches. Each branch had at least one paid visitor, but an indigenous board of directors supervised the work. The UHC returned two-thirds of the funds it raised in that area to each branch. In the midst of a nationwide financial crisis, the chief source of funds for the UHC, the Hebrew Orphan Asylum Society, closed, forcing the UHC to stop its work in December 1907. After three days, however, with help from the local Council of Jewish Communal Institutions, the UHC reopened. Continuing financial problems forced the UHC in 1908 to curtail pensions to widows—a long-time activity—and to place some of their children in institutions. This emergency prompted the founding of the Widowed Mothers Fund Association in 1908. Important organizational changes occurred in 1908 when Rice became honorary president and in 1910 when Morris D. Waldman, who had served as the assistant manager of the IRO, became the new executive officer.

By about 1910, the caseload of the UHC was reduced by the proliferation in the immigrant Jewish community of *landsmanshaften,* or mutual aid societies of people from the same locale in the old country, and such other factors as the resettlements by the IRO and the natural dispersion of the New York Jewish community to Brooklyn and the Bronx. This lightened load allowed the UHC after 1910 to realize more fully than before the carefully planned services its leaders had envisioned earlier. Fulfilling a long-time need, in 1911, the UHC hired a nurse to supervise the immediate care of Jewish tuberculars. In 1912, with the Social Service Department of the Free Synagogue, a local congregation, the UHC established the Joint Tuberculosis Committee. The committee developed a model garment factory in the Bronx in 1915 when the committee became independent. In 1915, the UHC became one of the first family welfare agencies in the country to develop a vocational guidance department to guide youngsters about to leave school into suitable occupations. Reflecting again its leadership role in the community, the UHC surveyed the relief work on the sisterhoods and the UHC. This study was done at the request of the New York Foundation and of the Bureau of Municipal Research. In 1919, Frances Taussig became the general manager, inaugurating a new era for the agency.

After the establishment of the local Federation for the Support of Jewish

Philanthropic Societies (FSJPS) in 1917, the UHC received less funds from the FSJPS than it spent for relief. To improve this situation, the board of trustees decided to use the reserve funds for agency operations. The reserve funds lasted from 1919 to late 1923, when the UHC developed a new structure. The first step in the reorganization occurred when the UHC dissolved its working relation with the sisterhoods. It then opened five new district offices—in Harlem, in Yorkville, and three on the Lower East Side. Each district had an indigenous advisory committee. In 1925, the agency amended its bylaws to make all chairmen of such advisory committees members of the board of trustees, bringing the policy-making body closer to local communities. Under Taussig, the staff became more professionalized than before.

Throughout the 1920s, the organization strove to develop its nonrelief functions. While the material aid of the poor remained its primary task, the agency also initiated programs in the areas of mental hygiene, services to transients, and home economics. In 1921, for instance, the UHC became one of the first agencies to hire a psychiatric social worker, and in 1924, it added a psychiatrist to its mental hygiene department. The UHC trained its workers at the New York School of Social Work, developing the Stuyvesant District as a UHC training area in 1924. Grants from both the Hofheimer and New York foundations helped to support this project. Consistent with the new functions of the UHC—the service in the 1920s became less of an emergency nature—the staff asked the board of trustees in 1922 to change the name of the organization. Finally, in early 1926, the agency became the Jewish Social Service Association (JSSA). The JSSA maintained such functions as the self-support and vocational guidance departments. The home economics department, founded at the end of World War I, conducted a study of food and living expenses, dealt with the problem of nutrition, and in 1920, began an experiment of sending undernourished children to a summer camp, Camp Rainbow, which became a permanent part of the agency's program. At the same time that it was working to perfect its financial assistance activities, the JSSA saw its developing professional role increasingly in terms of nonmonetary personal casework. The Great Depression reversed this trend toward nonrelief service. In the face of tremendous economic hardship, the JSSA was forced to concentrate most of its money and resources in meeting the needs of the Jewish unemployed. Both the number of applicants for relief and the sheer volume of material expenditures pushed the agency almost beyond the limits of its helping potential.

JSSA, like other Jewish agencies, responded to the crisis of the depression in two ways. First, it resolved to maintain its high standards of relief despite the monetary and material shortage. While non-Jewish agencies across the country limited their assistance at this time to basic food relief, often in kind, JSSA and other Jewish relief groups held to their policy of aiding a family according to a full relief budget, including food, clothing, rent, and other necessary items. No matter how severe the economic crisis, professional standards had to be honored.

Second, JSSA joined with Jewish and non-Jewish social work organizations in calling for a greater government role in relief. Frances Taussig, among other leaders of the Jewish agencies, consistently supported and advocated programs of public assistance that would reduce the unmanageable caseloads of private social work bureaus. This would have the dual effect of increasing the role of government in basic income maintenance and allowing the private social work organizations to resume their concentration of the nonmonetary aspects of social service, which had begun to become their primary focus in the 1920s.

As JSSA emerged from its relief-oriented depression experience, the field of professional social work was engaged in an often bitter dispute between the adherents of functional social work, who followed the theory of will psychology developed by Otto Rank, and the proponents of diagnostic casework, who advocated Sigmund Freud's theories of personality. The functional approach, developed at the University of Pennsylvania School of Social Work under the direction of Jessie Taft and Virginia P. Robinson, postulates the existence of a will, or central organizing force in the personality, and views the function of the social work agency as helping the client to release his innate capacity to organize his own personality. The diagnostic school, on the other hand, believes in no central organizing force in the personality equivalent to the functional concept of will, but rather sees the personality as the product of many conflicting forces that relate to each other and to the environment in complex ways. The social workers' task, according to this theory, is to understand these various interacting forces and to develop a treatment program geared to the diagnosed inner and social needs of each client.

JSSA, under the leadership of Dr. M. Robert Gombert and Frances Beatman, who received at least part of their social work educations at the University of Pennsylvania, became indentified as a functional agency, although it always claimed to be somewhat eclectic in its approach to social casework. Indeed, so prominent was this agency among functional social work organizations that when the Family Service Association of America* published its *A Comparison of Diagnostic and Functional Casework Concepts* in 1950, three of the six members of the study's functional group, Celia Brody, Regina Elkes, and Gombert, came from its staff. Further, in 1950, the New York School of Social Work of Columbia University, a leading proponent of the diagnostic school, threatened to sever its student training program at the agency because of the difference in casework orientation. This threat was never carried out.

In 1946, JSSA merged with the Jewish Family Welfare Society of Brooklyn and assumed its present name of Jewish Family Service (JFS). Two years later, Dr. M. Robert Gombert became executive director of JFS. Frances Beatman served as associate executive director and succeeded Gombert as executive director when the latter died in 1958. Sanford N. Sherman was assistant and then associate executive director during these years; he became executive director in 1974.

In the early 1940s, JFS pioneered in the introduction of fee payments for its casework program. This practice was later followed by other agencies and quickly became standard casework procedure. The agency believed that clients who paid fees would be more likely than free-service applicants to take counseling seriously and less prone to view the service in terms of relief only. Studies conducted by the agency in these years confirmed that fee-paying clients more often utilized the counseling services of JFS and stayed with the agency longer than nonpaying applicants did. The same investigations also revealed that long-term cases constituted a minority of the caseload and that most applicants dropped out of service before the second interview.

Another development in the 1940s that helped JFS concentrate on its counseling function was the referral of refugees from war-torn Europe to the United Service for New Americans* (USNA). Jewish agencies in other American cities accepted the refugees as part of their caseloads and therefore continued to provide relief and material service for a significant portion of their clientele. But after a brief period in which JFS took on refugee cases in the middle and late 1940s, it transferred all of its refugee caseload to USNA, freeing itself to focus on improving its counseling activities for a basically native clientele.

In seeking new ways to help its clients, JFS in the 1950 explored the field of family therapy. In 1956, it founded the family mental health clinic, with Dr. Nathan Ackerman as its supervising and research psychiatrist. Through this clinic, JFS strove to combine social and psychiatric means of helping individuals and families. It also carried out research on the family that later became the basis for further treatment.

JFS also conducted research on its entire caseload as part of its normal functioning. Its research department produced two major monographs based on the JFS clientele, *A Study of Short Term Cases* (1951) and *A Study of the Return Interview* (1956). Ackerman, Beatman, and Sherman edited and published two significant symposia on family therapy, *Exploring the Base of Family Therapy* (1961) and *Expanding Theory and Practice in Family Therapy* (1967). JFS has also opened its material for use by outside researchers. In 1967, for example, Hope Leichter and William Mitchell published *Kinship and Casework,* a volume based on cases served by JFS. In addition, JFS has explored the use of films of family interviews for case study and evaluation.

In the 1960s and 1970s, JFS continued to expand the scope of its work to keep up with new developments in its field. A sex therapy and counseling clinic, a family life education department, and group therapy sessions have been added. Older agency functions have also been continued in the family location and legal services and the community homemaker service.

The primary sources for studying the JFS's history include the published *Annual Reports,* which contain helpful descriptions of the agency's activities. The local Jewish press also provided information about the JFS. Board meeting minutes, statistical files, and selected case records are located at the JFS's headquarters in New York City. These materials are being utilized by Gary E. Rubin for a forthcoming dissertation at Columbia University on Catholic and Jewish social work. The agency published *Fifty Years of Social Service: The History of the UHC of the City of New York* [1926], which is detailed and helpful. Two articles by Peter Romanofsky deal with the activities of the UHC: " 'To Save . . . Their Souls': The Care of Dependent Jewish Children in New York City, 1900–1905," *Jewish Social Studies* 36 (July–August 1974): 253–261, and " '. . . To Rid Ourselves of the Burden . . .'. New York Jewish Charities and the Origins of the Industrial Removal Office, 1890–1901," *The American Jewish Historical Quarterly* 64 (June 1975): 331–342. Harold Silver deals with some conflicts between the United Hebrew Charities and its Eastern European clientele in the 1890–1900 decade in his thesis written in 1934 at the Graduate School for Jewish Social Work, "Some Attitudes of the Eastern European Jewish Immigrants Toward Organized Charity in the United States in the Years 1890–1900." The only known copy of Silver's work is at the New York Public Library. Sections dealing with JSSA and JFS can be found in Herman David Stein, "Jewish Social Work in the United States, 1654–1954" (Ph.D. diss., School of Social Work, Columbia University) (a shortened version of this work appears in the 1956 *American Jewish Year Book,* pp. 1–98); Harry Lurie, *A Heritage Affirmed: The Jewish Federation Movement in America* (1961); and Alfred J. Kutzik, "The Social Basis of American Jewish Philanthropy" (Ph.D. diss., Brandeis University, 1967). There is no scholarly history of the JFS.

Peter Romanofsky and Gary E. Rubin

JEWISH SOCIAL SERVICE ASSOCIATION OF NEW YORK: see JEWISH FAMILY SERVICE.

JEWISH WELFARE BOARD: see NATIONAL JEWISH WELFARE BOARD, THE.

JEWISH WELFARE BOARD, U.S. ARMY AND NAVY: see NATIONAL JEWISH WELFARE BOARD, THE.

JOINT COMMISSION ON SOCIAL SERVICE OF THE PROTESTANT EPISCOPAL CHURCH: see EPISCOPAL CHURCH, DEPARTMENT OF CHRISTIAN SOCIAL RELATIONS OF THE PROTESTANT.

JOINT DISTRIBUTION COMMITTEE OF AMERICAN FUNDS FOR THE RELIEF OF JEWISH WAR SUFFERERS: see AMERICAN JEWISH JOINT DISTRIBUTION COMMITTEE, INC.

JUVENILE PROTECTIVE ASSOCIATION (JPA). Responding to the social disruption of the late nineteenth century, members of the Chicago Woman's Club initiated and supported a broad child welfare movement. The club women were particularly concerned with the plight of dependent and delinquent children, for whose care Illinois lagged behind other industrialized states. In April 1898, after a decade of intermittent activity, the club organized a special committee to provide informal probation for young offenders through the city's police courts. The club women elected Julia C. Lathrop chairman of this committee. Lathrop, a Hull-House* (HH) resident and a state commissioner of public charities, was an authority on child welfare. A staunch advocate of supervised foster placement and probation, she soon drew many of her fellow club members into the emerging Illinois juvenile court movement.

During the winter and spring of 1898–1899, a coalition of club women, charity commissioners, settlement workers, placement officials, and jurists drafted and lobbied for "An Act to regulate the treatment and control of dependent, neglected, and delinquent children." This so-called Juvenile Court Act passed the forty-first Illinois General Assembly on April 14, 1899, and was signed into law one week later. The legislation established in Chicago the world's first juvenile court system, the Cook County Juvenile Court, but made no appropriation for its personnel. Lathrop and her peers were not concerned, however; they feared the exploitation of a public probation department for political patronage unless it was protected by civil service regulation. At its first session on July 3, 1899, Lathrop's committee began to support the salaried probation officers of the Cook County Juvenile Court.

The probation committee of the Chicago Woman's Club performed an important function; it required commensurate stability. On April 28, 1900, Lucy L. Flower, the committee's principal patron, became its chairman. An experienced child welfare reformer, Flower believed that philanthropic agencies started by the Woman's Club should separate from it as soon as possible, so before moving from Chicago, she supervised the founding of an independent Juvenile Court Committee under Julia Lathrop on September 30, 1902. Shortly thereafter, on January 16, 1903, the Juvenile Court Committee adopted a constitution, reelected Julia Lathrop chairman, and elected Louise de Koven Bowen—society matron, social feminist, and treasurer of the Hull House Association* (HHA)—vice-chairman. To free Julia Lathrop for other reform activity and to facilitate fund raising, Lathrop and Bowen exchanged offices on November 23, 1903, just after the committee had agreed to supervise the juvenile court's detention home. On March 26, 1904, the Juvenile Court Committee incorporated. Bowen became president and mentor of its nine-member board of directors. Julia Lathrop served as vice-president for three more years, acquiring administrative experience that served her well when she became the first chief of the United States Children's Bureau in 1912.

The establishment of the Cook County Juvenile Court did not end child welfare reform in Chicago. On the contrary, Progressive men and women turned their attention to the practices and conditions that seemed to cause so much family misery. On April 13, 1906, a juvenile court judge, Julian W. Mack, who presided that year over the National Conference of Jewish Charities* and six years later over the National Conference of Charities and Correction,* joined with members of the Juvenile Court Committee and other Chicago reformers to found the Juvenile Protective League (JPL) district branches. This federation was designed to organize communities, advocate reform, and visit families. The league would be a friend of the juvenile court, an agent of civic reconstruction, a public conscience, and a defender of children threatened by a lapse of parental or communal responsibility, in short, a volunteer child welfare bureaucracy.

A period of reorganization began in 1907. Under the form (if not the substance) of civil service, Cook County assumed the complete maintenance and control of the juvenile court's probation staff and detention home, ending the support and supervision of the Juvenile Court Committee. At the same time, however, the JPL proved incapable of effective organization. Upon the recommendation of Judge Mack, the Juvenile Court Committee took over the functions of the JPL on November 22, 1907. Establishing its base at HH, the Juvenile Court Committee formally changed its name to the Juvenile Protective Association (JPA) on June 4, 1909, to reflect its ambitious new program.

The history of the JPA lends itself to a three-part periodization. From its founding through World War I, it was a federation of district leagues concerned with general and particular hazards to children. Louise Bowen and an expanded board of twenty-seven directors lobbied for prohibitory and regulatory legislation, advised the juvenile court, and supported parental education programs. They also participated in the establishment of Chicago's socialized courts from 1911 to 1916, and the passage of the first state mothers' pension law in 1911, and the founding of the world's first child guidance clinic, the Juvenile Psychopathic Institute, in 1909. From the association's office at HH, special field workers investigated practices and conditions harmful to children, such as the cocaine traffic and the baby farm industry, and produced a number of studies in amateur descriptive sociology. In 1913, Bowen wrote the first survey of "The Colored People of Chicago." With varying success, the district leagues monitored neighborhoods, mobilized residents, and sponsored recreation. Salaried "protective officers" advised the leagues and visited troubled families. Through friendly visitation, the JPA hoped to improve family relationships and to prevent family fragmentation. Even abusing and neglecting parents, who traditionally had been either upbraided or prosecuted, experienced the moral suasion of the protective officers. When this counseling failed, when public officials flouted their duties, or when commercial interests pandered to youth, the association's attorney resorted to legal redress. Still, the JPA emphasized voluntary effort. Even the protective officers were determined not only to inform, but also to arouse, a progressive public.

From the armistice to the middle of the Great Depression, the JPA consolidated and refined its activities. The board of directors encouraged the vigorous enforcement of existing child welfare statutes, as well as the scrupulous efficiency of public officials. Board members with academic connections supervised special research projects, two of which, Nels Anderson's *The Hobo* (1923) and Paul G. Cressey's *The Taxi Dance Hall* (1932), became classics of the so-called Chicago school of sociology. The district leagues expired, ending community organization, if not the monitoring of dangerous practices and conditions. The most significant change was a new emphasis on social casework. Increasingly the family itself became a unit of treatment for troubled children and children in trouble.

Hull-House stalwart Jessie F. Binford served as executive director of the JPA throughout this period. She had begun her colorful career in 1906 as an investigator for the Juvenile Court Committee. Rising through the ranks, she assumed the post of executive director after special service on the United States War Department's Commission on Training Camp Activities and on the United States Interdepartmental Social Hygiene Board, and held that position until June 30, 1952. Binford personified the JPA's settlement heritage. She prized the qualities, not necessarily the qualifications, of its staff. Operating from HH, Binford and the dedicated but rudely trained protective officers contacted, assisted, persuaded, and sometimes coerced the most demoralized and disorganized families in the city, clients whom other agencies shunned. Since no national organization of child or family welfare agencies examined protective casework in detail, there were no effective standards of service. During this period the JPA was centralized and self-assured. Binford and the salaried staff had their vocation. They persevered despite the relative impassivity of the public and indifference of their peers.

The Great Depression tested Chicago's private social welfare agencies. Traditionally the JPA and other agencies had defined their ends and means with only casual regard for each other. Shrinking contributions forced their realignment into a comprehensive system. Even before the Wall Street crash, the Milford Conferences of national social welfare leaders in the 1920s had promoted social work as a discipline with generic skills, many of which were rooted in psychoanalytic theory. This professional surge further stimulated self-examination. In the early 1930s, committees of the Chicago Council of Social Agencies, the interwar sponsor of organized welfare, undertook to make social work cooperative and accountable. Though the JPA had attacked the problems of children on a variety of fronts, it became apparent by the middle of the decade that fame and good intentions were not enough. Academic sociologists had tapped foundtion grants. Less often did they require the assistance of private welfare organizations or settlements. Newer agencies had elected to develop group work with juvenile delinquents. The association's monitoring of practices and conditions and its enforcement of particular statutes had, moreover, become haphazard. The future of the JPA clearly rested in a specialized social service.

In the late 1930s, the Chicago Council of Social Agencies, through its own deliberations and its reflection upon the principles avowed by the Child Welfare League of America* (CWLA) and the Family Welfare Association of America,* began to allocate casework responsibilities among the city's private agencies. The duty to intervene in instances of child abuse and neglect fell to the JPA by default. Wealthier and better-staffed agencies were unwilling to take up this discouraging work. Though disagreeable and often hopeless, it had to be done. With misgiving, Jessie Binford and her staff began a shift from eclectic child welfare to the specialized field of child abuse and neglect. They were as willing as ever to reach out to children in need of protection but were ill prepared to adopt even the preliminary professional standards for protective agencies developed by the CWLA in 1936. With little guidance and no assistance, the JPA entered its professional period.

The professionalization of the JPA, like that of other social welfare agencies, was delayed by World War II and the subsequent demobilization. Yet the need for therapeutic skills remained, especially in the field of child protection. In 1949, the renovated children's division of the American Humane Association* promulgated its professional standards for protective agencies. Two years later, at the urging of the Welfare Council of Metropolitan Chicago, successor to the Chicago Council of Social Agencies, the board of directors of the JPA hired a new executive director. G. Lewis Penner, who had been a county director and state coordinator for the Kansas Social Welfare Department and a field consultant for the American National Red Cross,* came to the JPA to institute a staff development program. Penner recruited certified social workers and implemented casework supervision, providing the expertise to complement the specialization already begun by Jessie Binford. In fact, the JPA was one of the first agencies in the nation to integrate "reaching out" with extended-term casework. Research, moreover, supplanted unguided monitoring. In 1965, just two years after the demolition of its beloved Hull-House, the JPA founded the Bowen Center, the nation's first comprehensive treatment facility for abused or neglected children and their families.

In 1964, Illinois took an active role in the protection of children by establishing its department of children and family services. The JPA encouraged and aided this public commitment. It provided internships for masters of social work candidates from nearby professional schools. In 1971, after six years as a federally funded demonstration project, the Bowen Center became the nation's first professional training institute for child protective services. For five years, it prepared caseworkers for the department of children and family services. In 1976, the JPA itself assumed this function.

Through eight decades, the JPA has played several roles in relation to the development of public social welfare. It has alternately lobbied for public services, trained the public personnel, criticized the shortcomings of the public sector and provided complementary services. It is one of the few agencies in the nation, public or private, willing to provide extended-term treatment to neglected children and their parents, clients who are all too often forgotten by society in its zeal to counter the battered child syndrome of child abuse.

G. Lewis Penner directed the JPA until his retirement in 1976. Pairing child advocacy with protective service of the highest standards, he preserved the agency's renown. The innovations and contributions of the JPA substantiate the position that the competence and the integrity of private associations, not their longevity of wealth, determine their importance to the development of a just and compassionate society.

This entry is based upon the author's research for his dissertation, "The Good to be Done: A Study of the Juvenile Protective Association of Chicago," which will be submitted to the department of history of the University of Chicago. The principal collection of primary sources for this study is the JPA Papers at the Manuscript Collection, University of Illinois at Chicago Circle Library, Chicago, Illinois. This collection consists of minutes, reports, bulletins, published materials and *Annual Reports,* correspondence, and memorabilia from the founding of the association through 1951. More recent material is retained by the JPA itself. Other important collections are the Chicago Woman's Club Records and the Welfare Council of Metropolitan Chicago Papers at the Chicago Historical Society, Chicago, Illinois; and the Survey Associates Papers at the Social Welfare History Archives Center of the University of Minnesota, Minneapolis. There is not yet a scholarly history of the JPA, but researchers may wish to consult Jessie F. Binford's *Fifty Years of Pioneering* (1961). This twenty-two-page pamphlet contains a chronology of activities, a listing of publications, and a paean to the founders of the JPA. Several historians have referred to the association with regard to its role in the establishment and development of the Cook County Juvenile Court, but none has yet examined its contributions to the suasive, and then therapeutic, treatment of child abuse and neglect.

Paul Gerard Anderson

_L_

LEGAL AID, see: NATIONAL LEGAL AID AND DEFENDER ASSOCIATION.

LUTHERAN COUNCIL IN THE UNITED STATES OF AMERICA, DIVISION OF MISSION AND MINISTRY (DMM). During the era of the social gospel in the late nineteenth and early twentieth centuries, Lutheran charities and social work became institutionalized in so-called inner mission groups. In 1929, these local societies formed the National Lutheran Inner Mission Conference (NLIMC). Beginning in the early 1930s, two groups of Lutheran workers in church-related welfare projects appealed to the National Lutheran Council (NLC) (see *Religious Institutions*) to help develop standards of Lutheran social work and to coordinate the diverse welfare work being done by Lutherans. These two groups were the NLIMC and the Commission on Inner Missions (CIM) of the American Lutheran Conference (ALC) (see *Religious Organizations*), another body of Lutherans. In the 1930s, the NCL was the major body of American Lutheranism. It agreed with the social workers who wanted it to appoint a committee to survey existing Lutheran social services and institutions and to study the opportunities to develop Lutheran service in prisons and jails. The five-member committee completed its detailed report in 1935. The NLIMC officially approved of the committee's work, and in 1938, the NLIMC asked the NLC to create a new organization. Consequently, at the annual meeting of the NCL in late January 1938, in Detroit, Michigan, the NLC established the Division of Mission and Ministry (DMM) as the Department of National Lutheran Welfare (DNLW). This group was founded to supervise and to coordinate inner missions, or Lutheran welfare activities, to standardize Lutheran social work, and to assist local agencies and institutions. The establishment of the DNLW was an important development in the NLC, representing the first major breakthrough in programs and structure for the NLC.

Within six months, the agency—which became the Department of Welfare (DW) in 1939—began to function in a manner similar to that of other church welfare departments. The Reverend Clarence E. Krumbohlz left his post as executive secretary of the United Lutheran Church Board of Social Missions and became the executive secretary of the agency. Like other church welfare agencies, the DW began to coordinate the diverse local, church-related welfare institutions, such as orphanages, hospitals, and old-age homes. In the early 1940s, the DW took over some of the work of the NLIMC, planning both the biennial national and various local welfare conferences, collecting dues, and editing proceedings of conferences. The DW helped local Lutheran agencies to evaluate their methods and to determine policies and practices. Fieldwork visits by the national staff and a publicity program helped to strengthen local Lutheran social work. The DW developed a placement service, recruiting and training students for Lutheran social service. The placement service also published a pamphlet to encourage students, *Thinking About Social Work?* Within months after its founding, the agency initiated its long series of immigrant-related work.

The refugee-immigrant service became one of its important activities. During the period of World War II, cooperating with the Lutheran World Action Appeal for War Emergency Work, the recently renamed Divison of Welfare (DW) helped to settle some eighteen hundred refugees in America by 1946. The DW aided the refugees in finding jobs and adjusting generally to American life. The postwar work brought more activity. In 1948, for example, the DW added a new program to its work of helping European Lutherans settle in America: the Lutheran Resettlement Service (LRS). It aided refugees under the Displaced Persons Act of 1948, which expired in 1953. Cooperating significantly with the Lutheran Church-Missouri Synod (LC-MS), the DW created the Lutheran Refugee Service (LRS) in 1953. Eventually becoming the jointly sponsored Lutheran Immigration Service (LIS) in 1960, the organization continued to work through the Lutheran World Federation. It assisted Hungarian refugees in the 1950s, for instance. In the early 1960s, the LIS helped more than sixteen hundred non-Lutheran Cubans to settle in the Miami, Florida, area, distributing food and clothing and providing job counseling.

Along with the refugee activities, the DW developed a strong chaplaincy program in church-related and Veterans Administration hospitals and in prisons and jails. In 1962, the Division of Welfare secured a full-time secretary to work with theological seminaries in developing a clinical pastoral education program that encouraged young ministers to devote themselves to, or to become more aware of, the social service of the church. This area of the work of the DW developed as an ongoing activity.

Other activities and programs strengthened the social work of American Lutheranism. Career Days and a steady flow of publications helped attract more and better-trained social workers and field students. DW-sponsored consultants continued to strengthen existing programs and to develop new local ones. In the 1960s, the division began preparing the annual *Lutheran Health and Welfare Directory* and cosponsoring *Lutheran Social Welfare,* a quarterly journal, which became *Lutheran Social Concern* in 1972. Some of the DW's activities helped create new activities for other agencies of the NLC. For example, in the 1940s, Reverend Krumbohlz supervised surveys of the needs of war-related defense industries communities and of neglected American Indian groups, an activity that became part of the work of the Commission on American Missions, another NLC branch.

Expanding and solidifying its work, the DW reorganized. In the mid-1940s, its own separate executive committee was established to help the executive secretary determine policy. After fifteen years as executive secretary, Reverend Krumbohlz resigned in 1954 and was replaced by Reverend Henry J. Whitting, whom Reverend C. S. Thompson succeeded in 1963. Cooperating increasingly with the similar organization of the LS-MS, the DW helped to create unity in American Lutheranism. When the merger of the major Lutheran groups creating the Lutheran Council of the United States of America (LCUSA) occurred in November 1966, the social welfare agency became the Division of Welfare Services (DWS). The DWS continued to strengthen Lutheran social work generally, for instance, by establishing the social welfare scholarship fund in 1967 to encourage students to enter the profession and by sponsoring regularly the biennial conference of Lutheran social workers.

By the mid-1960s, the division was involved in some of the major social welfare issues of the decade. The race riots of 1967 led to conferences on the subject of discrimination and a movement to advocate open housing. In 1968, the executive committee adopted "An Affirmation on Racial and Ethnic Relations." This statement was drafted initially by the staff of the office of social research of the DWS, which also served the "continuing forum," a yearly conference to discuss issues of contemporary social concern. The DWS still continued such established functions as the institutional chaplaincy in prisons and the refugee service programs.

In the 1970s, agency development paralleled national trends in the field of social welfare. Like other national agencies, the DWS developed the uniform accounting and reporting system, and it introduced planning and programming in budget systems to make administration more efficient and to help local regional groups. A program initiated in 1970 to train volunteers in social service added to the nationwide movement to broaden the base of the delivery of social services. In its role as coordinator of and spokesman for Lutheran social service programs, the DWS in the 1970s analyzed the relationship of Lutheran hospitals to official church bodies, Lutheran residential child care programs and official church publications on sex, marriage, and the family. Other program highlights included participation in the national farm worker ministry to aid migrant laborers and the planning of the use of volunteers in disaster relief work, a practice the DWS discussed with representatives of such agencies as the Mennonite Central Committee,* Brethren Service Commission,* and Church World Service.*

Some important administrative changes occurred in the 1970s. At the end of 1970, Dr. Harold Haas replaced Reverend Thompson as executive secretary of the increasingly joint staffs of the DWS and the LC's Division of Mission Services, whose two executive committees already met jointly. In March 1973, the two agencies merged formally to establish the new Division of Mission and Ministry (DMM), which continued to function as the social service agency of the LCUSA.

The primary sources for studying the history of the agency are quite adequate. Informative annual reports of its activities are found in published records of the *Annual Meetings* of the various national church bodies, such as the NLC and the LCUSA. The library at the national headquarters of the LCUSA in New York City has bound mimeographed *Minutes* of the agency since 1940. The agency's manuscripts, also in the library, are extensive and are filed chronologically and by subject, facilitating research considerably.

There is no complete, detailed history of the agency, but standard publications in the history of American Lutheranism, particularly Frederick K. Wentz, *Lutherans in Concert: The Story of the National Lutheran Council, 1918–1966* (1968), are helpful. There are other studies, primarily unpublished theses, dealing with specific issues in the history of Lutheran social work, but apparently none deals fully with the history of the DMM.

LUTHERAN WORLD RELIEF (LWR). In the aftermath of World War II, a group of American Lutherans from the National Lutheran Council (NLC) decided to provide material assistance and relief to war-torn countries in Europe with heavy Lutheran populations. The executive secretary of the NLC, Dr. Ralph Long, organized some of his colleagues in New York City to conduct this work. In October 1945, he and four others founded Lutheran World Relief (LWR), which was not officially part of the NLC's structure. In late 1945, the five founders incorporated LWR according to the laws of the state of New York. The group held elections and chose Reverend Dr. Clark Fry as the president, a post he held for about twenty years. The early structure of LWR included a president, a secretary, and a treasurer. These three officers, along with the two other people, comprised the initial board of directors. The new agency soon opened administrative offices in New York City, and it registered with the President's War Relief Control Board to receive permission to provide material relief in Europe. The group soon convinced Reverend Clarence Krumbohlz, the executive secretary of the Department of Welfare* of the NLC, to become the agency's first executive leader.

LWR began its work slowly, but it expanded gradually as the years passed. At the beginning, it had difficulty obtaining a warehouse to store the clothing it collected, so it contracted with a private company to provide this service. Soon after it was organized in late 1945, LWR sent a representative in Europe to supervise the arrival and distribution of goods shipped under LWR auspices. LWR became a member of the Council of Relief Agencies Licensed to Operate in Germany (CRALOG), sending representatives to aid its efforts. It also became a member of the American Council of Voluntary Agencies for Foreign Service* (ACVA). In 1946, LWR began shipping supplies to Japan, a venture that terminated in 1952 when it decided that Japan had recovered sufficiently from the war damages. In the fall of 1947, an LWR representative, Reverend Carl Schaffnit, visited textile manufacturers in the South, obtaining agreements from over twenty of them to help with material aid in these early relief projects. Almost since its inception, LWR received aid from German-American fraternal organizations, especially from the Plattdeutsche Volkfest-Verein of New York. In August 1947, an agreement with Church World Service* (CWS) to appeal for wheat and other crops led to the establishment of the Christian Rural Overseas Program (CROP), which the Catholic Rural Life Conference joined on June 1, 1948, to become CROP's third sponsoring organization. LWR had its main warehouse in Easton, Pennsylvania, and in this early period, it had receiving stations in Los Angeles, San Francisco, and Nappanee, Indiana. In New York and in San Francisco, LWR used CWS warehouses. During these years, LWR received some large special donations; for example, the H. J. Heinz Company of Pittsburgh, Pennsylvania, donated baby food in 1948. In 1949, LWR bought a million surplus army rubber half-soles from a manufacturing company in St. Louis, Missouri. And, in April 1949, it entered into an agreement with the Medical and Surgical Relief Committee, Inc., of New York City, to receive medical supplies solicited by that organization. During this early period, and through its later history, LWR was assisted by the United States of America Committee for the Lutheran World Federation, another church agency.

The 1950s featured the expansion of LWR's programs and the beginnings of joint efforts with other Lutheran groups. In the early 1950s, LWR began to receive government surplus foodstuffs. Continuing its basic emergency relief services, it sent privately raised wheat to famine-stricken India in 1951. In September 1951, the main warehouse was moved from Easton to Phillipsburg, New Jersey. Also in 1951, CROP was disbanded, but because LWR wanted to continue to provide food, it developed a food program of its own. In the summer of 1952, LWR concluded an agreement with the Yugoslavian Red Cross (YRC) to provide material aid there. As in most countries served by LWR, local agencies, in this case, the YRC, distributed the shipments to the people. In other countries, such as Korea, churches or religious groups (in this case, the Korean Church World Service) received LWR shipments and then distributed them. In the early 1950s, the largest portion of LWR aid went to Germany, where it was distributed through the Evangelical Hilfswerk, a church organization. During the period, LWR was one of the first American organizations to protest the so-called security requirement of the Mutual Security Act of 1952, which provided government reimbursements for shipments deemed to be in the security interests of the United States. Its efforts, helped to bring about new legislation, which tied reimbursements to the more charitable objectives of the Economic Cooperation Act.

An important event occurred in 1953 when LWR began to cooperate formally with the Board of World Relief (BWR) of the Lutheran Church-Missouri Synod (LC-MS) (see *Religious Organizations*). Congregations of the LC-MS contributed clothing, layettes, and such to LWR campaigns, and representatives from the BWR participated on a consultative basis with LWR's board of directors. A year earlier, in 1952, the BWR and LWR had begun to cosponsor the all-Lutheran food appeal. The enactment of legislation in the early 1950s, including Public Law 480 in 1954, which allowed voluntary agencies to obtain and to disburse government surpluses of basic food commodities, obviously strengthened LWR's relief program considerably. In the 1950s, LWR envisioned its services as supportive of indigenous churches or missions overseas. During this period, Executive Director Bernard A. Confer, who had begun work with LWR in 1946 and who remained its executive director in 1976, traveled abroad, occasionally with the executive director of the BWR, Reverend Werner Kuntz, to survey conditions and needs in various countries.

During the 1950s, with other church relief organizations, LWR provided various types of assistance to over 100,000 refugees in Taiwan and to refugees and other needy people in Jordan, for instance. Another important program was the joint breakfast feeding project with CWS for over a million schoolchildren in Yugoslavia, which after just a few years, improved child health markedly. In 1956, when the United States Department of Agriculture announced it would make surplus cereal grains available for shipment by the voluntary agencies, LWR decided to suspend the all-Lutheran food appeal. In April 1958, LWR established its DORCAS project with the BWR, through which women's groups bought precut cloth from LWR and then sewed new garments for schoolchildren in the Holy Lands.

Within the federal government's food surplus program with the voluntary agencies, LWR emphasized its belief that the more commodities and other forms of support the voluntary agencies obtained from the government, the more they would diminish their voluntarism and become increasingly dictated by the government. LWR therefore campaigned against the expansionist efforts to obtain greater government support by such agencies as the Cooperative for American Remittances to Europe* (CARE) and especially the Catholic Relief Services-National Catholic Welfare Conference* (CRS). In the spring of 1950, for example, when the government announced that personnel from voluntary agencies might be eligible for travel funds from the government, LWR questioned the ruling in light of its belief in preserving voluntarism. Similar motives prompted LWR to reverse an earlier decision to use government largesse in Operation Reindeer in 1953 because the project, a government program to give voluntary organizations surplus commodities for distribution abroad, was too heavily involved in politics. By the late 1950s, according to a student of these issues, Robert Sullivan, LWR was in open opposition to the efforts of the CRS to expand government contributions under Public Law 480. In 1964, LWR opposed an amendment to allow voluntary agencies access to surplus foreign currencies generated by Title I of Public Law 480; LWR opposed it on the basis of an increasing tendency of voluntary agencies to rely heavily on government contributions.

In the 1960s, basic LWR programs continued and new projects began. During this period, LWR expanded its services to South American countries. For instance, in Chile, cooperating with CWS, LWR sent supplies that were distributed by the Ayuda Cristiana Evangelica, an organization of Protestant churches in Chile. Emergency relief consisted, for example, of relief in Chile after floods in May 1960 and for refugees in Hong Kong after Typhoon Mary in June 1960. In the early 1960s, LWR worked with other church organizations to establish a special voluntary agency—the Interchurch Medical Assistance, headquartered in New York City—to solicit donations for hospital equipment, medical supplies, and such. In the mid-1960s, LWR paid increased attention to the issues of food production and population problems. And, in 1964, it initiated Project Esther, through which women purchased denim fabrics and then sewed new garments for African children. In 1967, LWR announced a major new policy: to seek blankets, bedding, and children's clothing and to sell excess clothing and use such funds to fulfill needs overseas; the program proved impractical and was quickly disbanded. LWR provided emergency relief to people in Jordan after the war with Israel in 1967. Beginning in 1966, with CWS and the Mennonite Central

Committee,* LWR helped to found and then to participate in Vietnam Christian Service, a project that provided all types of service personnel.

The most important long-term development within LWR in the 1960s and 1970s was the increasing commitment to and the implementation of self-help and community development projects, as opposed to traditional material relief. The first significant involvement in such a development project occurred in 1962 when LWR assisted about a thousand refugee families from North Korea in damming up part of the China Sea to reclaim rice-growing lands for the refugees. Another example of this type of service was helping to form in Brazil the DIACONIA, the local Protestant welfare agency. The DIACONIA used supplies sent by LWR and conducted such community projects as building roads, community centers, homes, and reservoirs, as well as a technical training program. In India in the late 1960s and 1970s, the LWR helped the local Indian Christian Agency for Social Action, using food shipments to compensate the workers who were building much-needed dams. Similar self-help and community development projects continued and were implemented in Hong Kong, Taiwan, Chile, and Bangladesh. Another project begun by CWS in the mid-1970s and assisted financially by LWR aimed at one cause of famine in Niger: saving date palm trees by incubating lady bugs, which killed the dangerous insects. In South Vietnam, LWR helped to train local physical therapists to rehabilitate war victims. Consistently concerned with policies and practices affecting the people they served, in 1974, LWR communicated with the United States delegation to the World Food Conference in Rome, calling for an American policy to encourage increased food production both at home and abroad and to develop an international food supply to meet emergency needs. In the true spirit of Christian humanitarianism—a consistent LWR motive—LWR continued to provide disaster relief, responding charitably, for example, to the earthquake victims in Yugoslavia in late 1969 and in early 1970 and to the victims of Hurricane Fifi in Honduras in 1974.

Early in its history, LWR had pledged its cooperation with other agencies. It fulfilled that commitment primarily through CWS and the Lutheran World Federation's Department of World Service, which has operated large programs in Jordan, Hong Kong, and Tanzania.

There are ample primary sources for studying LWR's history. The annual reports for the years through 1966 are published in the *Annual Meeting* of the NLC. For the period beginning with 1967, the annual reports of LWR bound in the volume of *Minutes* of the agency are filed at the library of the Lutheran Council in the United States of America (LCUSA). For the most recent years, there are separate *Annual Reports*. A series of updates issued by LWR describe the many self-help and community development projects. The archives at the library of the LCUSA also contain the records of the agency. Discussions with Executive Director Bernard A. Confer in New York City in January 1977 provided helpful information about LWR.

Frederick K. Wentz, *Lutherans in Concert: The Story of the National Lutheran Council, 1918–1966* (1968), refers briefly to LWR, and Robert Sullivan, "The Politics of Altruism" (Ph.D. diss., The Johns Hopkins University, 1968), treats its involvement in the government surplus commodity program. There does not appear to be a scholarly history of LWR.

__ *M*

MATERNITY CENTER ASSOCIATION (MCA). In the early twentieth century, in New York City, as in other major cities in the United States, the death rate of babies was especially high. The very high infant mortality rate in New York City prompted Dr. Haven Emerson, the health commissioner of New York City, to appoint in 1915 a committee of three physicians to study obstetric conditions in Manhattan. This committee—which included Dr. Ralph W. Lobenstine, a pediatrician who became a founder and long-time medical chairman and leader of the Maternity Center Association (MCA)—secured the cooperation of the New York Milk Committee (NYMC), which promoted milk stations and general child care in New York. In March 1915, the three-member committee, with the NYMC, conducted a survey. It revealed that very few women had prenatal care and that, despite the number of health and welfare agencies in New York conducting prenatal work, the delivery system lacked uniformity and coordination. The report urged dividing Manhattan into ten zones for maternity care.

A group of doctors, social workers, and general philanthropists began to work to develop interest in a maternity center. In September 1917, the first such center opened. It was funded by the Woman's City Club (WCC), a civic organization that showed considerable interest in the care of children in New York. In January 1918, the NYMC sponsored maternity centers in two other zones. Discussions among a group of interested people to form an organization to conduct the centers resulted in the founding of the MCA as the Maternity Center Association of New York (MCANY) on April 18, 1918, at the home of Mrs. John S. Rogers. The founding group included Dr. Lobenstine and Frances Perkins, a New York social worker who later became the United States secretary of labor under President Franklin D. Roosevelt in 1933. Perkins was appointed the first executive secretary of the new MCANY, which was designed to promote the establishment in Manhattan of health centers to focus on the care of mothers and their young babies.

In its first few years, the MCANY worked to fulfill its initial goal of establishing maternity centers in the city. In its first year of operation, the organization began to coordinate the activities of other agencies attempting to develop a unity in maternity and child care previously lacking in Manhattan. It established a clearinghouse in 1919 to prevent the duplication of efforts. The group also began to strengthen its program of teaching groups of mothers the essentials of child care and related issues. In April 1919, the MCANY became incorporated legally in the state of New York. As early as 1920, the energetic activities of the organization resulted in thirty centers and substations in nine of the ten zones in Manhattan. Also in 1920, the MCANY took over full responsibility for the early centers established by both the WCC and the NYMC. In response to requests, the MCANY developed *Routines,* a booklet describing the agency's method of work. Most importantly, it began in 1920 to develop its model district on the East Side of Manhattan. Headquartered at a branch office shared by three groups—the MCANY, the Henry Street Visiting Nurse Service (HSVNS), and the New York Diet Kitchen Association—the district served as field experience for public health nursing students at Teachers College of Columbia University. at the request of the HSVNS, the MCANY conducted the maternity work in the Morningside health district, an important demonstration project in the early 1920s. In 1921, the Metropolitan Life Insurance Company analyzed the records of over eighty-seven hundred patients of the MCANY; further study by Dr. Louis I. Dublin, a noted statistician in the health field, showed the success of the agency's methods. In 1921, a group of voluntary agencies and the New York City Department of Health (NYCDH) agreed to take over the MCANY's prenatal work, allowing the organization to focus on developing complete maternity services in one small district in the city.

The use of this activity as a model district, which served as field experiences for many students and staff from other agencies, helped to launch the MCANY into nationwide activities in the 1920s. Located on the East Side of Manhattan, the project began with an intensive, house-to-house canvass for pregnant women. In 1924, the agency enlarged the boundaries of its model district to include the Bellevue-Yorkville Health Demonstration, a project funded by the Milbank Fund. The success of the MCANY's model district, as well as other services of the agency, led to its developing in 1925, at the request of the New York State Department of Health, a twenty-four-hour maternity nursing service in Tioga County.

All the requests to train at the MCANY facility could not be met, so in 1929 the agency began to send a nurse to conduct classes in other states and cities. By 1935, the agency had conducted such institutes and classes in thirty-nine states, in the District of Columbia, and in Canada. Ten thousand of the twenty thousand public health nurses in the country attended these sessions. The MCANY began its nationwide activities in 1922, publishing and distributing around ten million copies of a series of educational pamphlets throughout the country. In 1923, it began to supply teaching exhibits to agencies in the United States. Back in New

York, in 1923, it transferred its maternity clearinghouse to another local group, while the Lafayette Guild, a local organization, became an auxiliary of the MCANY, paying the salaries of three nurses and providing supplies for mothers and babies. In 1927, the board of directors saw a need to ensure the services of the MCANY nationwide, and in 1928, it began to create a reserve fund for programs that exceeded allotted budgets.

During the depression years of the early 1930s, the MCANY continued to expand, especially broadening its nationwide activities. In May 1931, the agency initiated its annual Mother's Day campaigns to teach the public about the need for adequate maternity care. As part of this educational effort, the MCANY sent a twelve-page, illustrated pamphlet on maternity care, *If the Public Only Knew,* to about four thousand magazines and around two thousand newspapers. Amid the hard times created by the depression, the agency established its junior auxiliary in 1931 to provide the food needed by mothers with newborn babies.

In 1931, founder Dr. Lobenstine died. Dr. George W. Kosmak, a leading obstetrician, replaced him as chairman of the board of directors. As a testimony to Dr. Lobenstine's efforts, in 1931, the agency established the Lobenstine Midwifery Clinic after Mrs. Marshall Field had raised funds for the first three years of its budget. In 1932, to improve the agency's ability to teach nurses, the MCANY affiliated its field service with the women's clinic of the New York Hospital, and in August 1932, the field center itself moved to the clinic. At this time, the MCANY ended the clinics it had founded in other agencies' offices. An important publication, *The Maternity Handbook,* by Anne Stevens, was issued in 1932. The MCANY enhanced its nationwide reputation in 1933 with an exhibit at the Hall of Science at the Chicago World's Fair. In 1934, the Association for the promotion and Standardization of Midwifery became affiliated with the MCANY. This association had conducted the Lobenstine Midwifery Clinic, which amalgamated with the MCANY in 1934.

An important step occurred in 1935, when the MCANY revised its charter to include the entire United States as its field of work. In the late 1930s, the agency changed its name to the Maternity Center Association (MCA). The flood of requests from nurses for courses in maternity care led the agency to hold the first of a series of regional institutes in 1935 in New York City. Sponsored jointly by the National Organization for Public Health Nursing* (NOPHN), the session was attended by 250 nurses from eleven eastern states. Important activities of the late 1930s included an evaluation of maternity care in the hospitals of the New York metropolitan area at the request of the Hospital Survey of New York; the beginning of classes for expectant fathers; and, at the request of the New York World's Fair Exhibit, the development of an exhibition on safe maternity care, placed in the Hall of Man. Organizational developments included the initiation in December 1936 of *Briefs,* a publication reporting on trends in maternity care; the discontinuance in June 1939 of the nursing service, which was taken over by the Lying-in Hospital; and the disbanding of the clearinghouse in December 1939.

The MCA continued its basic service during World War II. In 1940, an important publication, *The Birth Atlas,* depicting the process of birth, first appeared. Continuing to provide social services in maternity care, the MCA developed services in health centers and in a public housing project in 1941, when, cooperating with the United States Children's Bureau, the Julius Rosenwald Fund, and the Macon County, Alabama, Health Department, the MCA organized a nurse-midwifery school in Tuskegee. In 1944, at the request of the NYCDH, the MCA began to conduct counseling services for wives of men in the armed forces in the New York area who were eligible for care under the federal Emergency Maternity and Care Act of 1943. In 1947, the MCA received an award of mention from the army for these services. Throughout the period, the MCA continued to lead in developing educational programs for nurse-midwives.

During the period after World War II, beginning with the American tour in 1947 of Dr. Grantly Dick Read, author of *Childbirth Without Fear* (1943), the MCA began to shift its emphasis to promoting natural childbirth for individuals, a technique in obstetrics, from its earlier efforts to provide social services for large and disadvantaged population groups. The MCA sponsored workshops in nurse-midwifery, increasingly cooperating with universities. To further these aims, in 1948, the MCA helped the Grace-New Haven (Connecticut) Hospital to begin a study of applying the principles of natural childbirth to a modern hospital.

In the 1950s and 1960s, the MCA continued to promote the idea and practice of natural childbirth. Seminars and workshops, cooperation with university courses, films, pamphlets, and a ten-minute segment for national television in 1954 helped to stimulate interest in natural childbirth, as well as the use of nurse-midwives. One film, first shown in 1959, *From Generation to Generation,* was nominated for an Oscar award by the Academy of Motion Pictures; it received other awards. In 1963, the MCA amended its charter to authorize the agency to establish a school for nurse-midwifes and to certify graduates. Some important organizational developments occurred. After meeting weekly since 1924, the Lafayette Guild disbanded in 1959. In September 1965, Hazel Corbin retired as general director, a position whe had held for forty-two years. In her honor, the agency established a fund with her name to assist the education of nurse-midwives. A gala fiftieth anniversary dinner was held in 1968 at the Waldorf-Astoria Hotel in New York City.

In the late 1960s and 1970s, the MCA continued to emphasize natural birth methods and education, but it once again provided, as it had in its early days, some services and programs for disadvantaged groups. For example, in 1967, the agency initiated an experimental project to determine ways to reach low-income women who generally did not seek adequate maternity care. Aware of the low-level reading ability of these women, the MCA prepared comic books describing maternity care and distributed them to municipal hospital maternity clinics throughout the United States. In 1968, the MCA assigned a staff member to a junior high school on the Lower East Side of Manhattan to aid in a special project, administered by the New York City Board of Education, for thirteen- to seventeen-year-old girls who quit school because they were pregnant. In 1970, the MCA received its largest grant ever, nearly $450,000 from the Commonwealth Fund,* to improve the preparation of and to increase the use of nurse-midwives. In 1973, the board of directors approved a demonstration project to show alternatives to traditional hospital maternity care. This effort resulted in the opening, at its headquarters in 1975, of the MCA's childbearing center, which created a homelike environment for deliveries. A top priority item for the MCA, this project attracted nationwide attention.

The primary sources relating to the history of the MCA are diverse. The published *Annual Reports* are quite helpful. In the Papers of the American Association for Labor Legislation* at Cornell University and on microfilm, there is the correspondence of Irene Osgood Andrews relating to the origins of the MCA. The minutes of various meetings exist at the agency's headquarters in New York City, but they are not part of the library and are not available generally to scholars. In the Papers of the United States Children's Bureau at the National Archives in Washington, D.C., there are many letters relating to the MCA. There is also primary material in the Hazel Corbin and Frances Perkins Oral History Memoirs at Columbia University. The MCA published summaries of its history. The most helpful of these are *Six Years in Review, 1930–1935* (1936) and *Log, 1915–1975* [1976].

There does not appear to be any scholarly history of this interesting and pioneering agency.

MENNONITE CENTRAL COMMITTEE (MCC). In the aftermath of the Russian Revolution and World War I, Mennonites in Russia in 1919–1920 were suffering from terror, plundering, and hunger. In 1920, the Russian Mennonites sent the Studien Kommission of four members to the United States to ask for help. The group traveled throughout the United States and Canada, seeking a place to which their coreligionists could migrate. Meanwhile, some American Mennonites began to promote the need for aid to Russia. On July 13, 1920, at Newton, Kansas, an informal meeting of various Mennonite branches in the Midwest took place. Representatives of the Kommission, however, appealed for a broader, more unified effort, prompting the American group to appoint a committee to help the Russians. This committee, in turn, urged a meeting of all Mennonite relief agencies. Two weeks later, on July 27, 1920, representatives from thirteen Mennonite relief organizations met at the Prairie Street Mennonite Church in Elkhart, Indiana, and established the Mennonite Central Committee (MCC). At this founding meeting, the group elected Dr. H. Bender as its chairman and P. C. Hiebert as its secretary. The group also established a temporary body of three delegates, representing different Mennonite groups, to elect temporary officers and to develop a tentative plan of cooperation. At a later session, Hiebert was elected chairman, and Levi Muman was chosen secretary-treasurer.

Another meeting, held in Chicago, refined the organizational structure to include a three-member executive committee. This venture, the establishment of the MCC, was the first united relief effort by all the American Mennonite groups.

Developed to aid needy people abroad, the MCC began its activities immediately. The actual relief work in Russia, headed by Alvin J. Miller, began in March 1921. Initial MCC aid to Russia consisted of tractors and plows. At the peak of the MCC program in Russia, a few years later, over twenty-five thousand Mennonites received daily food at MCC kitchens. Another major activity was assisting more than fifty-five hundred Russian Mennonites to migrate to lower South America, especially to Paraguay, beginning in 1929. The MCC continued this pioneering rehabilitation program, including road building, through the period of World War II. In its early history, the MCC also worked in orphanages and for refugees in Constantinople. In the 1930s, it aided civilians during the civil war in Spain.

The era of World War II elicited humanitarian responses by the MCC toward people suffering both at home and abroad. In the early 1940s, the Mennonite Central Peace Committee merged with the MCC, which in the 1940s opened its clothing collection and distribution center at Ephrata, Pennsylvania, near the MCC headquarters in Akron, Pennsylvania. Between 1940 and 1942, the MCC fed undernourished schoolchildren in Lyons, France, and it distributed food to adult refugees. Despite restrictions by the Nazi Germans, the MCC coordinated relief projects in Poland. Later, under the auspices of the United Nations Relief and Rehabilitation Administration (UNRRA), the MCC helped to retrain refugees in the Near East. Also during this period, the agency had over thirty-five workers in Puerto Rico in a project to help poverty-stricken people, especially in the delivery of health services.

The most ambitious project was the domestic Civilian Public Service for conscientious objectors. At the peak of the program in 1944, over twenty-five hundred workers, including those in mental hospitals, were supervised by the MCC.

The conditions in these American mental institutions, coupled with the conscientious objectors' reactions to them, prompted the MCC, along with other so-called peace church groups, like the American Friends Service Committee* (AFSC), to focus on the care of the mentally ill. After the end of the war, the MCC decided to establish three small hospitals for such patients, one each in the East, Midwest, and West. The first opened in 1948 in Leitersburg, Maryland, as a twenty-four-bed hospital; it later became Brook Lane Farm. Others opened in Reedly, California, in 1952, and in Newton, Kansas, in 1954, and then in Elkhart, Indiana, in 1963, and in Bakersfield, California, in 1965. The MCC's mental health service committee administered these centers initially, but as the activity grew, the committee incorporated itself independently in Pennsylvania in 1952 as a nonprofit corporation to develop effective church mental health activities. This new Mennonite Mental Health Services (MMHS) apparently reorganized in early 1957. Three representatives of the MCC's executive committee sat on the leadership group of the MMHS, which reported to the MCC.

As suggested by its earlier activities, the MCC participated in the postwar rehabilitation. As early as 1943, it began work with refugees from Poland and from the Balkan states in the Middle East. It was the first American agency to cooperate with the Middle East Relief and Refugee Administration (MERRA), a British organization and, after 1944, with the UNRRA, which assumed MERRA's work. During the famine in Bengal, India, the MCC helped to feed the sufferers, and it administered relief during the independence struggle of the 1940s. In Hungary, it founded two children's feeding programs and, with the AFSC and Swiss and Swedish relief agencies, fed about five thousand university students. In postwar Germany, it fed over 140,000 people in the British and French zones. By the end of 1946, nearly 85 percent of the food received by Evangelisches Hifswerk through the Council of Relief Agencies Licensed to Operate in Germany (CRALOG), an American agency, had come through the MCC. In 1947, the MCC donated one-third of the total relief to Germany, and in 1948, the tiny organization (compared with such major overseas relief agencies as the War Relief Services of the National Catholic Welfare Conference* and the AFSC) ranked fourth among American relief agencies in aiding Germany. Cooperating with Church World Service,* the MCC settled over two hundred families in the United States. It also fed refugees in Korea. In Jordan and elsewhere, it maintained vocational schools for orphans and fed and clothed refugees. From the clothing distribution relief program in Europe developed the agency's inspirational slogan, "In the Name of Christ."

In the 1950s and 1960s, the MCC continued its basic activities, relieving suffering and poverty throughout the world. In this period, the MCC maintained an administrative headquarters for European relief in Frankfurt am Main, Germany. By the late 1950s, the MCC was serving in twenty-two countries, with the bulk of its material aid going to Korea and to Jordan. In 1957, the MCC distributed three million pounds of surplus food. A relief program began in Vietnam in 1956 and featured a medical and other volunteer teams at a leprosarium of the Christian and Missionary Alliance. Summer service units worked in mental institutions, with agricultural migrants, and in camps for crippled children. Some organizational changes, such as the establishment of the material aid advisory committee in 1958, occurred, but the agency remained basically unchanged. In early 1958, meetings between the executive committee and the Mennonite Missionary Board secretary's continuation committee resulted in the further cooperation in relief between the MCC and mission boards of the church. The MCC gained some national recognition in 1958, when *Coronet Magazine* publicized its disaster relief activities in Fremont, Missouri. The MCC began relief programs in both British Honduras and Thailand. Self-help projects became the basic type of MCC service, illustrated by agricultural projects in Algeria and by demonstrations in hygiene, homemaking, and the like in Greece. Attention still focused on the care of impoverished and refugee children abroad; for example, it conducted elementary education classes to fight illiteracy in underdeveloped countries.

MCC's basic activities persisted in the 1970s. At the church's annual meeting in 1973, the MCC apparently influenced the passage of a resolution concerning the world food crisis. A major MCC project in Bangladesh emphasized food production and self-help. MCC was proud that its presence in Bangladesh seemed to make banking institutions and cooperatives more responsive than before to farmers' needs. The MMHS featured assistance to youthful offenders in North America and to the government of Paraguay to deal with its country's mental health problems. In the mid-1970s, in Botswana, the government was promoting a dryland farming tool carrier designed by a former MCC volunteer. Such volunteers still formed the core of MCC's activities. Often acting alone or in pairs, members of the North American services, known as Voluntary Service, continued efforts in the mid-1970s in the seemingly forgotten, poverty-stricken areas of urban America and Appalachia.

The sources for studying the MCC's history are extensive. Helpful primary sources include the published *Reports, Annual Reports,* and the variously named *Bulletin.* The MCC archives is at Goshen College in Goshen, Indiana, but there are also historical materials at the national headquarters in Akron, Pennsylvania.

MCC is strikingly conscious of its history, and consequently a number of agency publications describe it. M. C. Lehman, *The History and Principles of Mennonite Relief Work—An Introduction* (1945), and the much longer *In the Name of Christ: A History of the Mennonite Central Committee and Its Services, 1920–1950* (1952) by John D. Unruh are two examples. There is an extensive bibliography about the MCC in *The Mennonite Quarterly Review* 44 (July 1970), the entire issue of which focuses on the agency's history. Merle Curti, *American Philanthropy Abroad* (1963), mentions the MCC, but only briefly.

METHODIST FEDERATION FOR SOCIAL ACTION, THE (MFSA). The social gospel movement of the late nineteenth and early twentieth centuries prompted the establishment of a number of religious organizations to implement the tenets of social justice and social reform. In the early twentieth century, some prominent leaders of the Methodist Episcopal church spearheaded the movement to found a Methodist reform organization: Frank Mason North, composer of "Where Cross the Crowded Ways of Life"; Worth M. Tippy, pastor of the Epworth Memorial Church in Cleveland, Ohio; Herbert Welch, president of Ohio Wesleyan University; and Harry F. Ward, pastor of the Union Avenue Methodist Church (the "Stockyards Church") in Chicago. Their efforts led to the founding of The Methodist Federation for Social Action (MFSA) as The Methodist Federation for Social Service (MFSS) in December 1907 at an organizational conference called for that purpose in Washington, D.C. The twenty-five delegates who participated in the meeting represented a cross-section of Methodist clergy and laymen of some strength and standing: parish ministers, public officials, businessmen, religious educators, and journalists. Some twenty-eight other prominent churchmen were unable to attend but endorsed the purpose of the conference: the formation of a society to stimulate a wide study of social questions by the church, side by side with practical services, and to bring the church into touch with neglected social groups.

It would be erroneous to conclude that the MFSS sprang full grown out of the consciousness of a little company of Methodist clergy. The organization was more the creation than the creator of the incipient social consciousness arising within the church. Its founding in 1907 marked the social reawakening of the denomination, which coincided with the transition of America from an agrarian to an industrialized culture. The necessity of social action to meet the acute needs fomented by factory and city produced modern, scientific charities, efforts to stamp out preventable diseases and to obtain tenement reform, institutions for dependents, delinquents and defectives, the establishment of public parks, and legislation aimed at curbing sweatshops and child labor. There were also strenuous efforts to control temperance, prostitution, and gambling.

The MFSS was the product of antecedent social forces, and its appearance, like the social service commissions of other contemporary Protestant groups, marked the maturation of the social gospel movement. The members of the group were drawn together, more in the spirit of social justice reformer Jacob Riis than Karl Marx, to rid their society of the encroachments of extreme individualism and the resulting monopoly that was endangering the physical and spiritual welfare of men. The reception of the group by President Theodore Roosevelt following the adjournment of the organizing conference suggests that the group was part of the evangelistic, democratic crusade against the plutocratic concentrations of power that the president symbolized.

From the outset, the MFSS, unique among denominational social service commissions of its day, was not absorbed with promoting itself. Rather, its overall aim was to permeate the church and all its agencies with the social service message, setting forth projects for Epworth leagues, deaconess homes, women's societies, and men's clubs. The MFSS's initial social emphasis was community service, challenging every local church to have a constructive program for serving the social needs of its community, both individually and through the largest possible cooperation with other agencies of social uplift. A natural corollary of this objective was an emphasis on the necessity of cooperation between the local church and organized social work within the community. Usually the associated charities was specified as the agency with which to work. Indeed, the first annual meeting of the MFSS, held in St. Louis in 1908, was characterized by its president, Herbert Welch, as "the first conference of Social Workers of Methodism."

The most popular publication among the leaflets, monographs, and bibliographies put out by the MFSS during this period was a pamphlet, *The Methodist*

Church in Organized Charity, by J. W. Magruder, a member of its executive committee and general secretary of Federated Charities in Baltimore. In this compact but comprehensive study, Magruder revealed the philosophy of social service that characterized the MFSS's approach during this period. Scientific social work demanded "order, economy, and an avoidance of the very appearance of the evil of pauperizing." Organized charity was in reality a threefold process involving emergency relief, adequate relief, and "radical relief." Emergency relief was merely a temporary expedient, "first aid to the injured," pending adequate relief, which required time, thought, and skills and aimed at "the physical, moral, intellectual, social, and spiritual redemption of any individual or family in distress." Magruder used "radical relief" to designate the type of relief that works to root out the causes of distress, such as lawlessness, disease, poor housing, child labor, and any other evil that attacks the life, health, and character of the community. Radical relief would gradually supersede the necessity for either emergency or adequate relief.

The note of optimism and confidence for the future that Magruder prophesied constituted a significant dimension of the MFSS's spirit during its early years. The work of the organization throughout this period was enhanced by the deep conviction that the social movement of which it was a part was steadily moving toward the consummation of the Kingdom of God on earth. While the MFSS's leaders recognized the immediate social imperative of community service and cooperation with scientific social work in the church, they were not satisfied with anything less than the fulfillment of a Christian social order that would grant social justice to all men. A volume of essays, *Social Ministry,* printed by the MFSS in 1910 foretold the significance this conviction would have for the future direction of the group. An essay by Harris F. Rall, an important Methodist theologian, for example, asked how mankind was to secure its rights against every form of vested interest. Rall responded by declaring that the "interest of humanity," not the protection of property or promotion of industry, was the "final right" and that the world was "moving today toward a new democracy, not political alone but industrial and social."

Several decisions within the MFSS in the early part of the second decade of the century set the stage for the drama that characterized the organization's history for decades to come. One was the publication in 1911 of the first issue of its quarterly, *The Social Questions Bulletin,* which opened new areas of service to the MFSS and presented opportunities that were not conceivable under the spasmodic policy of printing leaflets and pamphlets. Among other things, it brought individual members directly in touch with the MFSS as a local agent propagating social service ideas and initiating practical work in behalf of the MFSS.

Still more significantly, in response to an expanding and successful program that was too demanding for volunteers to handle, the MFSS appointed a salaried executive secretary, Harry F. Ward. Ward's thorough scholastic training at

Northwestern and Harvard universities and his experience in settlement and pastoral work in the needy sections of Chicago equipped him admirably for the work ahead. His appointment yielded far-reaching significance. Second only to his appointment was the election of Bishop Francis J. McConnell as president of the MFSS in 1912, when Herbert Welch departed for Europe for a year. Well known for his brilliance in defense of academic freedom and civil liberties in general, McConnell brought rare powers of leadership to the MFSS. The minds and energies of these two men—Ward and McConnell—dominated the drive and direction of the MFSS for several decades.

From 1912 to 1916, the fervor of the MFSS was given to social evangelism missions that took the executive secretary and several field workers engaged for the purpose to all parts of the country at a pace characteristic of current national presidential primary campaigns. During 1912–1913, for example, Ward alone addressed 347 meetings and conducted thirty-six institutes in seventeen states. What made these meetings significant was the attempt in every community visited "to leave behind some practical result," to focus the attention of the group addressed on setting up one practical social service project. Ward and field workers visited mill, timber, and coal camps, as well as churches, civic organizations, and schools. These missions became so successful and so demanding that by 1916 the MFSS decided that its social service advocacy mission had generated such general acceptance at the local community level that consideration should be given to turning over its community service programming to the denomination's Board of Home Missions (BHM).

At its session in 1916, the governing body of Methodism (the quadrennial General Conference) adhered to the MFSS's wishes and committed the promotion of community service to the BHM. The MFSS was thus able to devote more of its time and energy to its basic task: "Christianizing the social order, trying to find out what it means and how it may be realized." Translated into the industrial society of that time, the MFSS's gradual release from community service advocacy permitted more vigorous campaigning in behalf of a shorter workday, a living wage, collective bargaining, and other components of a "complete industrial democracy" that had been part of the MFSS programming from the beginning and thereafter assumed a central place in its program.

While the MFSS discontinued the promotion of social service programming at the national level during this period, at the local level, community service projects stimulated by the MFSS continued to proliferate through the 1930s. *The Social Questions Bulletin* regularly ran stories citing examples of effective social service projects. One of the authors of this sketch remembers as a young boy the leadership his young Methodist pastor gave to community improvement projects during the Great Depression aimed at providing work for the unemployed to help men retain their self-respect. Years later as a doctoral graduate student, he encountered in the course of research an article in *The Social Questions Bulletin* from the 1930s depicting the hometown project in considerable detail as a suggestion for other communities.

The church's 1916 General Conference also accepted, with one or two exceptions, the MFSS's report on the industrial issues related to complete industrial democracy. Typically during those early days, social pronouncements that came out of the General Conferences became the official platform and program of both the MFSS and the denomination in the field of social action. Technically an unofficial agency of Methodism, the MFSS continued to be recognized as the "executive agency to rally the forces of the Church in support of the measures specifically approved."

World War I marked the beginning of differences between the Methodist church and the MFSS. The unanticipated involvement of the nation in the European war deflected the MFSS from its industrial democracy program. Imperialism, nationalism, disarmament, and militarism became prominent issues. The reactionary frenzy of the postwar period, reflected in the persecution of social liberals and radicals, rallied the MFSS to a stubborn defense of civil liberties. Throughout the apparent prosperity of the 1920s, the agency had warned of an impending economic disaster. The 1929 collapse convinced the MFSS that the heart of the problem in realizing the ideal society lay in the economic order. By 1933, it had moved to an all-out attack on capitalism, dedicating itself to the abolition of the profit system and the establishment of a classless society based on mutual service.

The aggressions of Italy, Germany, and Japan evoked a variety of compromising responses within the MFSS, necessitating several policy shifts toward World War II during its duration. The retirement of Harry F. Ward and Francis J. McConnell in 1944 raised the immediate question of the wisdom of continuing the organization. Its periodic financial struggles and the attacks it had endured because of its radical program had taken their toll. Nevertheless, the membership voted emphatically to continue the organization and its program, electing Methodist minister Jack R. McMichael to head the MFSS that same year.

Under McMichael's leadership, the MFSS experienced a mild renaissance in membership and financial strength between 1945 and 1950. Ironically, it was subjected during this same period to intense external and internal pressures, which left the organization virtually crippled by 1953. Following World War II, the MFSS continued its economic attack on capitalism, but it also increasingly stressed racial justice in church and society. These issues, however, were not ultimately as controversial as the MFSS's posture regarding the United States foreign policy and the defense of civil rights of communists. The federation fiercely attacked the cold-war policies of the Truman administration, opposing the Marshall Plan and calling for détente with the Union of Soviet Socialist Republics, the recognition of the People's Republic of China, and the boycott of "fascist" regimes in Greece, Spain, and Argentina. It also made demands for disarmament under United Nations supervision, repeal of the Selective Service Act, and international control of atomic energy. In 1948, the agency was renamed The Methodist Federation for Social Action (MFSA).

Although the MFSA came under extended attack from the Un-American Activities Committee (HUAC) of the House of Representatives, the most effective external attack on it was waged in the press. In December 1947, a series of articles written by Frederick Woltman for the *New York World-Telegram* characterized the MFSS as a "sounding board" for the Communist party. No sooner had the Woltman controversy quieted than these charges were renewed by Stanley High in "Methodism's Pink Fringe," an article written for *The Reader's Digest* (February 1950). Despite the articulate refutation of these charges by the MFSA and leading officials in the Methodist church, High's article received wide attention and was accepted throughout America. A storm of vilification was therefore directed against the MFSA at the General Conference of 1952. The conference demanded that the MFSA vacate its offices in the Methodist building in New York City and that the agency stop using the name "Methodist" (though this matter was not legally within the jurisdiction of the conference). Thus ended the long and fruitful relationship that existed between the MFSA and the Methodist general conference.

Internal dissension within the MFSA was even more damaging. Many prominent liberals in the federation became alienated from Jack R. McMichael. The extent of the defection became evident in 1952 when prominent liberals refused to protect the MFSA from the attacks of the general conference, supporting instead the formation of an "official" Board of Social Concerns. Paradoxically, McMichael voluntarily resigned as executive secretary in 1953, thus bringing to a close the most productive years of MFSA history.

Since 1953, the MFSA has been struggling to maintain its existence. Between 1953 and 1960, the MFSA operated without an executive secretary; Lloyd Worley served as its president and chief executive officer. In 1960, Reverend Lee Ball, an important Methodist theologian who had been professor of theology at the Garrett Bible Institute in Evanston, Illinois, was elected executive secretary and editor of the *Social Questions Bulletin*. Throughout the 1950s, the MFSA cooperated with the Religious Freedom Committee (see *Political and Civic Organizations*), which had been organized to protect radical clergy from conservative attacks and legal prosecution; it also demanded the repeal of the harsh Smith and McCarran Acts, as well as the abolition of the HUAC. It worked for the elimination of racial discrimination within the Methodist church and advocated sit-in's "and related non-violent actions which have for their objective the end of our segregated society." As early as 1962, the MFSA attacked the "undeclared war" in Vietnam and urged President John F. Kennedy "to withdraw our troops from Thailand and recall our navy from Southeast Asia [*sic*] waters, before we get another Korea, or worse."

In recent years, the MFSA has been striving to appeal to younger Methodist radicals. In 1974, Lee Ball passed leadership responsibilities to Reverend George McClain. A new study/action program was instituted; it dealt with socialist theory, economics, "liberation theology," and the building of a Third World coalition.

The sources for studying the MFSA's history are diverse. The Rose Memorial Library at Drew University in Madison, New Jersey, has the papers of the organization through 1930. The *Social Questions Bulletin,* which unfortunately is not widely available, is most helpful, as are agency publications and mimeographed materials. Other collections at Drew, such as the Frank Mason North Papers, also relate to the MFSA. The most recent files of the MFSA since 1953 are in the possession of Reverend Lee Ball, Ardsley, New York.

The MFSA has been widely studied. Milton John Huber, "A History of the Methodist Federation for Social Action" (Ph.D. diss., Boston University, 1949), and William McGuire King, "The Generation of Social Gospel Radicalism in American Methodism" (Ph.D. diss., in progress, Harvard University), are examples of secondary histories. Donald F. Gorrell, "The Methodist Federation for Social Service and the Social Creed," *Methodist History* 13 (January 1975): 4–32, is a recent and detailed piece.

Milton John Huber and William McGuire King

METHODIST FEDERATION FOR SOCIAL SERVICE: see METHODIST FEDERATION FOR SOCIAL ACTION, THE.

MUSCULAR DYSTROPHY ASSOCIATION, INC. (MDA). In the mid-twentieth century, Dr. Ade T. Milhorat of the New York Hospital-Cornell University Medical Center was virtually the only physician working in the field of muscular dystrophy. Perhaps based on the successes of other, recently founded or reorganized national health agencies, such as the Association for the Advancement of Research in Multiple Sclerosis,* which later became the National Multiple Sclerosis Society,* and the American Cancer Society,* a diverse group of housewives, business executives, parents of afflicted children, and some muscular dystrophy patients decided to form an association to promote their and Dr. Milhorat's interest in muscular dystrophy. Consequently, in New York City on June 6, 1950, the Muscular Dystrophy Association, Inc. (MDA) was organized as the Muscular Dystrophy Association (MDA). The group elected as its first president one of its founders, Paul Cohen, a successful businessman from New York and himself a victim of muscular dystrophy. Headquarters was established in New York City, and in the first four months of its operation, the organization raised $19,000 to support the research and work of Dr. Milhorat. The agency also developed a slogan, "Give Hope to the Hopeless." The new MDA changed its name to the Muscular Dystrophy Associations of America, Inc. (MDAA) in 1952. The agency grew quickly, organizing affiliated chapters throughout the country. By 1953, there were 120 such chapters.

The year 1953 was a turning point in the MDAA's history. In August 1953, MDAA President William Mayer and Dr. Milhorat addressed the annual convention of the International Association of Fire Fighters (IAFF), who then voted unanimously to support the efforts of the new health organization. Former President Cohen had laid the groundwork for the IAFF's assistance. Mamie Eisenhower, the wife of the president of the United States, launched the important MDAA fund-raising campaign in 1953, which Paul Cohen directed and which the IAFF aided. On Thanksgiving eve, a two-hour-long radio and television show, conducted by the comedy team of Dean Martin and Jerry Lewis, initiated the highly successful tradition of MDAA telethons. Three hundred and sixty-five radio stations and 133 television stations carried the production, "A Salute to the Letter Carriers of America." This was the largest single network show ever assembled prior to that point. The program helped to net nearly $4 million for the MDAA, as the National Association of Letter Carriers (NACL) joined local volunteers throughout the country in soliciting funds. The IAFF spearheaded the drive in 1954, "marching" similarly and helping to gain nationwide publicity for the MDAA.

Funds from these highly successful early campaigns helped finance MDAA programs. The MDAA's patient service program provided funds to clinics throughout the country to develop diagnostic facilities, physical therapy programs and social services to patients' families, and other such rehabilitation activities. In the summer of 1955, in conjunction with the New York City Board of Higher Education, the MDAA initiated the first class for dystrophic children, and it sponsored its first summer camp for children with muscular dystrophy, a program that grew steadily. The organization, which had established a ten-member medical advisory board in the early 1950s, also expanded its research program, which was distinct from its patient-oriented programs. In 1955, the MDAA began planning to establish its long-dreamed-of Muscle Research Center, adjacent to the New York Hospital-Cornell Medical Center in New York City. The organization also initiated its sponsorship of scientific conferences on muscular dystrophy in 1951.

Still conducting such programs as classes for children with muscular dystrophy, the MDAA expanded significantly beginning in the mid-1950s. The annual campaign drives, held during the Thanksgiving holidays, continually attracted national personalities, such as Mrs. Lou Gehrig. Dean Martin and Jerry Lewis continued to serve as national cochairmen of the campaigns. On June 15, 1956, an important organizational event occurred when the Institute for Muscular Dystrophy, Inc., was chartered in New York State. By March 1957, there were 316 active MDAA chapters, and the so-called march was emerging as a key national event. The organization also developed a new professional medical service, *Muscular Dystrophy Abstracts*. The campaign in 1958 began with an important national planning session held in Atlantic City, New Jersey, and featuring the first appearance of the annual poster child.

In the late 1950s and 1960s, despite some organizational disputes, the MDAA assumed leadership in the field. In the early 1950s, a split occurred when a group of members who opposed a reorganizational plan resigned and established the National Foundation for Muscular Dystrophy, Inc. (NFMD). In the mid-1950s, the MDAA sued the NFMD for, as the courts agreed, causing confusion in the use of its name. Consequently, in the early 1960s, the NFMD changed its name to the National Foundation for Neuromuscular Diseases, Inc., and was known in 1976 as the National Genetics Foundation, Inc. Particularly after the opening in 1960 of the $5 million Institute for Muscle Disease, which became the center of the muscular dystrophy research in the country, the MDAA supported a nationwide research program. Its medical exhibit was displayed initially at the 1962 meeting of the American Medical Association (AMA). As of March 1963, the fifty-member board of directors and the MDAA included Mrs. Fiorello La Guardia, Mrs. Lou Gehrig, and, of course, Jerry Lewis. The fifteen-member executive committee came from the membership of the board of directors. The president was again Paul Cohen, and there were thirteen vice-presidents, including Herman Badillo of New York City. The medical advisory board of seven experts in the neuromuscular field received the cooperation of their colleagues in the field. The fact that in 1964, the MDAA ranked second among the top thirteen national voluntary health agencies in the percentage of income spent for research testified to the agency's commitment to research. In 1965, five new MDAA clinics opened, making a total of sixty-seven; there were about 350 local chapter affiliates. Also in 1965, the MDAA received a grant from the Neurological and Sensory Disease Service of the United States Public Health Service to produce a film on differential diagnosis of muscular dystrophy and related conditions. In 1967, the organization produced two films, including *The Sun Never Sets,* which showed that because MDAA's research program was worldwide in scope, the association's grantees were working literally around the clock. Also in 1967, the labor advisory committee, whose job was to support the Jerry Lewis telethon, was established.

Further expansion and growth characterized the MDAA's activities in the 1970s. In 1971, there were twenty-three summer camps for children—now called Jerry Lewis camps. In January of that year, the organization instituted a similar winter camp for adult patients. Also in 1971, the MDAA held its first national conference of MDAA clinic directors. In 1973, the organization developed a pilot transportation project to help patients obtain education and employment. The Jerry Lewis telethon—now held annually over the Labor Day Weekend— began in the early 1970s to generate about half of the MDAA's income; the other funds came from volunteers' residential campaigns and from special events, such as the summer Carnivals against Dystrophy, which children's radio and television personalities promoted throughout the country.

The expanded structure in 1973 included a president, a secretary, a treasurer, a first vice-president, and forty-five other vice-presidents, including many well-known personalities. There were four special activities chairmen: national teen, women's division, national youth, and Carnivals against Dystrophy. The members of the corporation—from whom came the sixteen-member board of directors—numbered sixty-three and featured George Meany, Mrs. La Guardia, television star Hildegarde, and Jerry Lewis, who was also an honorary board member and MDAA's national chairman.

The enormously successful fund raising led by Jerry Lewis allowed the MDAA to expand its services to patients and its research and scientific programs. Consistent with its commitment to broadening and strengthening research and social services in the field, in April 1972, the organization increased the size of its medical advisory committee from five to nine members who counseled the board of directors. The enlarged committee promptly launched a new three-part program: to fund more clinic fellowships at universities, hospitals, and research centers throughout the country; to sponsor research projects at MDAA clinics themselves; and to purchase new and innovative equipment for MDAA clinics, which numbered 123 in 1973. In early 1973, the scientific leaders of the MDAA decided to reorient MDAA research; the agency would continue its grants to individual researchers, but university-based research centers would be the focus of the program. Among the first of these new research centers was the Jerry Lewis Neuromuscular Disease Center at the Institute of Rehabilitation Medicine at the New York University Medical Center. At its opening in September 1973, Dr. Howard Rusk, a pioneer and leading spokesman in the rehabilitation field, praised Lewis's contributions. In 1974, the MDAA restored its initial name, MDA. The MDA's history reflects the importance of this beneficent volunteer, Jerry Lewis.

The primary sources for studying the MDA's history include the detailed published *Annual Reports* and the files of *The New York Times*. The complete records of the agency, including minutes of meetings and correspondence, are kept in the offices of the MDA in New York City, and under appropriate circumstances, they can be made available to properly qualified and identified scholars.

There is a brief mention of MDA's history in Richard Carter, *The Gentle Legions* (1961), but there does not appear to be any scholarly history of the agency.